Political Philosophy and Taxation

Robert F. van Brederode
Editor

Political Philosophy and Taxation

A History from the Enlightenment to the Present

Springer

Editor
Robert F. van Brederode
BrederodeTax, LLC
Fuquay-Varina, NC, USA

Global Humanistic University
Sint Willibrordus, Curaçao

ISBN 978-981-19-1094-4 ISBN 978-981-19-1092-0 (eBook)
https://doi.org/10.1007/978-981-19-1092-0

This Springer imprint is published by the registered company Springer Nature Singapore Pte Ltd.
The registered company address is: 152 Beach Road, #21-01/04 Gateway East, Singapore 189721, Singapore

Preface

The study of taxation is related to the role of the state and its relationship with its constituents, the concept of private property rights, the concepts of societal fairness and justice, and the battle between the individual and the collective. Students and scholars who want to know how philosophers in the past and present think about taxation, in the context suggested above, and how their thinking has developed through cross-influencing, will find that there exists no comprehensive study providing such an overview. Rather, they are forced to wrestle through all the work of each individual philosopher to discover their insights into the state's power to tax and then analyze these insights and views to find analogies and differences.

This volume's ambition is to fill that gap by offering a treatise on the views of several schools of thought as to the philosophical justification of taxation (qualitative aspect) and the normative qualifications required of tax law to constitute tax that is just and fair (distributive or quantitative aspect). The latter includes evaluation of what type of tax is morally correct or acceptable to realize distributive justice. The period covered is from Enlightenment until the present.

Tax law does not operate in isolation; it is a subset of public law. Also, there exist no separate political philosophy of taxation; rather the philosophical and ethical basis of taxation and tax theory is a derivative of a wider political philosophy. For that reason, we chose as the title of this book Political Philosophy and Taxation.

The authors of this book are a healthy amalgamate of established scholars, namely professors Jennifer and Stefan Bird-Pollan, Walter Block, Robert van Brederode, Tessa Davis, Jane Frecknall-Hughes, Hans Gribnau, Robert McGee, John Prebble, and Darien Shanske, and young, emerging talents, namely Gregory Collins from the USA, Charles Delmotte from Belgium, Daniel Nientiedt from Germany, and Jørgen Pedersen from Norway.

The bibliography and overview of case law are organized separately for each chapter and found directly following each individual chapter. For the benefit of the readers and researchers, we have prepared extensive name and topic indices displayed also at the end of the book.

This volume is current with literature and case law through October 2021.

The authors of these chapters deserve my deepest gratitude not only for their thorough and stimulating work but also for their persistence in continuing this project during the upheaval of the pandemic and its detrimental impact on work schedules and teaching preparation. Most of all, I am grateful for their kindness in response to my queries and for their gracious patience with my insistent prodding and nagging.

Fuquay-Varina, NC, USA Robert F. van Brederode

Contents

Editor and Contributors

About the Editor

Robert F. van Brederode (LLM, Utrecht University, 1985; PhD in tax law, Amsterdam University, 1993) is a university professor at the Global Humanistic University, Curaçao, name partner of a niche tax consultancy firm, and an independent legal scholar. He is a former Big 4 partner, practicing in Europe and the USA, and former in-house tax counsel to a Fortune 100 company. Previously, he served as assistant professor at Maastricht University, School of Law; Professor of Tax Law at the Erasmus University, School of Economics; and adjunct professor at New York University, School of Law, graduate tax program. His research area is public law and tax law both from a legal and economic perspective with concentration on international tax and global indirect taxes and particular interest for comparative studies, tax law interpretation, tax policy, and normative aspects of taxation. Robert published dozens of journal articles and 10 books on tax topics. His most recent books are *Virtues and Fallacies of VAT: An Evaluation after 50 Years* (Kluwer Law International, 2021), *Ethics and Taxation* (Springer, 2020), and both with Richard Krever *Legal Interpretation of Tax Law* (Kluwer Law International, 2nd ed., 2017) and *VAT and Financial Services: Comparative Law and Economic Perspectives* (Springer, 2017).

Contributors

Jennifer Bird-Pollan College of Law, University of Kentucky, Lexington, KY, USA

Stefan Bird-Pollan Department of Philosophy, University of Kentucky, Lexington, KY, USA

Walter E. Block College of Business, Loyola University, New Orleans, LA, USA

Gregory M. Collins Yale University, New Haven, CT, USA

Tessa Davis University of South Carolina School of Law, Columbia, SC, USA

Charles Delmotte College of Law, Michigan State University, East Lansing, MI, USA
School of Law, New York University, New York, NY, USA

Jane Frecknall-Hughes Nottingham University Business School, Nottingham, UK

Hans Gribnau Tilburg University, Tilburg, The Netherlands
Leiden University, Leiden, The Netherlands

Robert W. McGee Broadwell College of Business and Economics, Fayetteville State University, Fayetteville, NC, USA

Daniel Nientiedt Department of Economics, New York University, New York, NY, USA

Jørgen Pedersen Department of Business Administration, Western Norway University of Applied Sciences, Bergen, Norway

Sol Picciotto Lancaster University, Lancaster, UK

John Prebble Victoria University of Wellington, Wellington, New Zealand

Darien Shanske School of Law, University of California, Davis, CA, USA

Robert F. van Brederode BrederodeTax, LLC, Fuquay-Varina, NC, USA
Global Humanistic University, Sint Willibrordus, Curacao

Abbreviations

ADAV	Allgemeiner Deutscher Arbeiterverein (General German Workers' Association)
BCE	Before the Common Era
BEPS	Base Erosion and Profit Shifting
BTA	Board of Tax Appeals
CCA	Court of Criminal Appeals
Cf.	Confer (Latin: compare)
Ch.	Chapter
COPD	Chronic Obstructive Pulmonary Disease
CRS	Common Reporting Standard
d	Pence (past English monetary unit: 1/12 of a shilling)
Div.	Dividend
Ed.	Edition or editor
Eds.	Editors
e.g.	exempli gratia (Latin: for example)
esp.	Especially
Et al	et alia (Latin: and others)
etc.	et cetera (Latin: and so on)
EU	European Union
FATCA	Foreign Account Tax Compliance Act
FDR	Franklin D. Roosevelt
Fed.	Federal
Ff	Folios following (and pages following)
FRA	Financial Reform Association (UK)
GAAR	General Anti-avoidance Rules
GDP	Gross Domestic Product
Gen.	Genesis
Ibid	Ibidem (Latin: in the same place)
i.e.	id est (Latin: that is)
IMF	International Monetary Fund
IRC	Internal Revenue Code (USA)

IWA	International Workingmen's Association
LGBT	Lesbian, Gay, Bisexual and Transsexual
MECW	Marx/Engels Collected Works
n.	Note
NAP	Non-aggression Principle
NATO	North Atlantic Treaty Organization
NGO	Nongovernmental Organization
No.	Number
Nos.	Numbers
NRZ	Neue Rheinische Zeitung
OECD	Organisation of Economic Coordination and Development
OJ	Official Journal
Passim	Latin: in one place or another; here and there
s	Shilling (past English monetary unit: 1/20 of a pound)
SDAP	Socialdemocratische Arbeiterpartei (Austrian Socialdemocratic Workers' Party)
Sec.	Section
SPD	Sozialdemokratische Partei Deutschlands
UK	United Kingdom
UN	United Nations
U.S.	United States
U.S.C.	United States Code
USSR	Union of Soviet Socialist Republics
v.	versus (Latin: against, opposed to)
VAT	Value Added Tax
viz	videlicit (Latin: namely)
WTO	World Trade Organization

List of Tables

Chapter 1
Introduction: The Value of a Political Theory for the Proper Application of Taxation

Robert F. van Brederode

Abstract This chapter is the introduction to the book and provides an overview of the content of each chapter as a context for a broader discussion on the role of taxation. It comments on certain findings and elaborates on other aspects or philosophical positions, which have received less pronunciation in the chapters. In particular, the author elaborates on social contract theory, libertarianism by evaluating Murphy and Nagel's (The myth of ownership. Oxford University Press, Oxford, 2002) critique against it, and egalitarianism including an evaluation of the concept of desert and, within that context, taxation of natural endowments. An ideal society is a metaphysical concept. People have different values, which often conflict with one another. In reality, therefore, choices between non-compatible values and alternative policy options need to be made. That is also true for one's approach to the role of government in society and the function and modalities of taxation. Tax policy should be driven by an underlying political philosophy, otherwise taxation becomes arbitrary and deprived of the moral basis necessary to ensure societal acceptance and compliance.

Keywords Justification of tax · Obligation to pay · Equality · Social contract · Desert · Merit · Natural rights · Property rights · Forced labor · Self-ownership · Liberty

1.1 Introduction

Critiques of liberal individualism point to the negative consequences it may bring forth in terms of selfishness, exploitation, and inequality. But it goes too far to depict individualism as the root of all evil. Moreover, an ideal society can simply not exist

R. F. van Brederode (✉)
BrederodeTax, LLC, Fuquay-Varina, NC, USA

Global Humanistic University, Sint Willibrordus, Curacao

R. F. van Brederode (ed.), *Political Philosophy and Taxation*,
https://doi.org/10.1007/978-981-19-1092-0_1

as it is a metaphysical concept. Liberal individualism means freedom and freedom by consequence is a value that conflicts with other values, such as solidarity or equality. People have different priorities, desires, and goals, and make different choices; it is impossible at the aggregate for all choices to be compatible with one another. 'Some among the Great Goods cannot live together. That is a conceptual truth. We are doomed to choose, and every choice may entail an irreparable loss' (Berlin 1990, 13). If there are alternative solutions for a given problem, the choice for one may eliminate the use of the others. If you choose freedom as the most important value, you may have to accept a degree of inequality. On the other hand, if your policy choice is to take measures to combat inequality, you must accept the consequence of loss in freedom. You cannot arrive at both full freedom and full equality and the balancing act is a political one.

This book is about finding that balance. Contemporary tax literature is often quite technical and seems to ignore the need for philosophical or moral foundation. But without moral compass, the technical research publications are just drifting in the wind like a loose kite. We contribute to the effort of finding balance and moral foundation by presenting the views, approaches, insights, and wisdom of a select number of 'philosophical schools' to provide context to the topic of tax policy and show cross-connections between different schools of thought, and where they build on and borrow from each other, even when they disagree.

It is important, if not imperative, that we consider the ideas from the past when we formulate the policies for today because ignoring our common intellectual heritage when finding moral answers for contemporary challenges compares to building a house without a blueprint. Over the centuries, many ideas have emerged on freedom, equality, fairness, justice and together they form a rich source of inspiration, and none was developed in isolation. Even if we have an intellectual or intuitive preference for a certain political philosophy, we would be fools to ignore the value of those theories we have dismissed or rejected. Research that pursues a narrow alley of investigation within a certain school of thought would benefit enormously if it could keep reference to the insights that reach beyond its narrow scope; otherwise, we are managing a forest based on studying a single tree. The aim of this book is to provide that broader context without pretending to be complete: this book is limited in its historical scope, excluding periods prior to the Enlightenment; is exclusively focused on Western political philosophy of taxation; and size limits forced the chapter authors to prioritize and make choices as to what to include and what to leave out.

Tax law is a subset of public law; theories of taxation are a subset of political theory. As such, taxation gives rise to important and fundamental questions regarding the nature of government, the relation between the state and its citizens/subjects, property rights, the distribution of the tax burden, and the use of tax revenue. There exists a direct link between our understanding of taxation and our conceptual understanding of the state. Theories of taxation cannot and do not operate independently but are developed and applied within the broader political philosophy of which they are part (Brederode 2020, 2). Logically, each chapter in this book examines first the main features and general characteristics of the political school of thought to which it is dedicated, and then investigates the consequences of the general for the particulars of taxation, such as the justification of taxation, incidence distribution, fairness, the object of taxation, and the use of taxation for purposes of distributional and social justice, enhancing equal democratic participation, etc. The authors made efforts to portray the philosophical school dealt with in their respective chapter objectively, i.e., providing an accurate account of its bearings without inserting (too much) personal opinion, support, or opposition. Politics generally tend to polarize, offering a black and white picture of policy choices. This introduction tries to show that different schools of thought have influenced each other, each school highlighting different but equally valuable aspects of social reality, how certain approaches lose favor and then return in mainstream thought; demonstrating that in fact political thought, including thought on the role and use of taxation, consist of a wide spectrum of colorful ideas. This chapter offers a summary of the content of each chapter but in the context of a broader discussion on the role of taxation. The author comments on certain findings and elaborates on other aspects or philosophical positions, which have received less pronunciation in the chapters. The final chapter is not focused on any particular philosophical school but contains a commentary on the current administrative state followed by an effort to provide a prospective view on society, the role of government, and taxation. It is critical of the trend to concentration, of legislative delegation, and of majoritarianism, which are all inherently undemocratic and an obstacle to the exercise of true citizenship. The idea is to combine the private contract structure underlying feudalism with individual autonomy and Nisbetian communitarianism. To enhance democracy and the direct influence of citizens over their own lives, it argues for decentralization of government, and the privatization of functions, allowing individual citizens to attend to most of their interests through private allegiances with others. This would at least vastly reduce the need for regulation by the unelected administrative state, counter illiberal tendencies to forms of absolutism, and restore efficient governance as political fragmentation would disappear. As first step it proposes to democratize taxation by delegating the allocation of tax revenue to the taxpayers. Allocating budgetary authority to taxpayers would enhance public involvement in the decision-making process, reduce dominance, improve the democratic legitimacy of tax law in terms of consent of the governed, reduce wasteful spending and the influence of special interest and lobby groups, improve democratic equality by empowering minority views, and infuse a needed grass-root element in the political decision-making model.

1.2 Enlightenment

Gribnau and Frecknall-Hughes, in Chap. 2, discuss several important political philosophers and writers of the Enlightenment, i.e., Hobbes, Locke, and Hume from Great Britain; Montesquieu and Rousseau from France; Paine, an Englishman who played important roles in both the American and French Revolutions; and the Federalist and Anti-Federalist factions in post-colonial America. The main contributions of the enlightenment period affecting taxation and property rights are social contract theory and the natural rights theory, which have remained influential until the present day. Several contemporary philosophical approaches (egalitarians, such as John Rawls; libertarians, such as Nozick) to property rights and taxation can be traced back – in support or opposition – to either theory. We discuss these two theories in the next sections.

1.2.1 Social Contract

1.2.1.1 Fiction and Function

Although it could be argued that the concept of a social contract was first theorized by Hobbes ([1651] 1991), it was most convincingly promoted a century later by enlightenment philosophers, most notably Jean-Jacques Rousseau ([1762] 1963) and John Locke ([1689] 2008). However, the roots of social contract in Europe as an idea reach further back to the *Declaration of Arbroath* of 1320, a letter written by Scottish nobility to Pope John XXII asking for recognition of Scotland's independence and of Robert de Bruce as its legitimate king, in the following passage:

> Yet if he [Robert de Bruce] should give up what he has begun, seeking to make us or our kingdom subject to the King of England or the English, we should exert ourselves at once to drive him out as our enemy and a subverter of his own right and ours, and make some other man who was well able to defend us our King (Transl. Fergusson 1970, 4–10).[1]

Remarkably for the age of divine right kingship and absolute monarchy, Robert de Bruce added his seal to the document, thus recognizing the right of the Scotts to remove him from the throne if he would act against their interests.

The Celtic-Irish-Scottish ideas of individualism, freedom, and 'consent of the governed' are erroneously often overlooked as foundational for the development of Western political and legal thought (Nagan et al. 2017, 92). It has been argued that the *Arbroath Declaration* is the intellectual foundation of the American Revolution and the Declaration of Independence; and the origin of the concept of the 'consent of the governed' is located not in John Locke but in the medieval Scottish philosopher/theologian John Duns (Klieford and Munro 2004) who, 400 years earlier, radically opined that:

> A king whose power was legitimate was king because his people granted him their consent, and if that consent were to be withdrawn for any reason then the man was king no more… A king was chosen not by God … [but]… was selected by the community around him. As long as he satisfied that community he was entitled to rule, but as soon as he failed them he could be disposed and replaced (Oliver 2009, 126–127).

Gribnau and Frecknall in Chap. 2 examine in more detail the enlightenment period in terms of political theory and its approach to taxation. They discuss and explain

[1] For the origins and background of the Arbroath Declaration, see Cowan (2020).

the differences between the leading philosophers of this period, as well as their influence on post-revolution American constitutional thinking. Their starting point is Thomas Hobbes who argued that the uncertainty of self-preservation in 'the state of nature' convinced people to agree to a covenant between themselves whereby they agree to submit to a mutually recognized public authority. The Sovereign is not a party to the covenant and his authority follows from the transfer of power by the contracting individuals. The obligation to obey is an obligation foremost to these other contracting individuals. Since the sovereign is given authority by covenant to which he is not a party, he cannot forfeit the authority given to him. Hobbes' theory of the state is absolute: all laws, even unfair ones, must be obeyed; the only exception is made for laws that infringe on the unalienable right of self-preservation. Reminiscences of this absolute approach can be found with some present-day egalitarians in regard to property rights and taxation (see Sect. 1.5.2.3 *infra*). For Locke, social contract also serves the purpose of security but not of life – as with Hobbes – but of individual property rights. He does not accept Hobbes' absolute perception of the state demanding unconditional obedience. Legislative power cannot be applied arbitrarily, in Locke's view, but requires consent of the citizenry, either in person or through a representative, and he supports majority rule. Rousseau's political thought is rich but difficult and may seem even contradictory. He is concerned about individual freedom but also social inequality in the sense that no one should be dependent on someone else. He develops a natural history of inequality within the framework of a natural history of civil society, which Gribnau and Frecknall-Hughes describe in their chapter. Liberty is central to Rousseau's conception of a legitimate state with the understanding that equality is indispensable for liberty. Social contract is the device for men to constitute themselves as a people and create the basis of a legitimate civil order. To preserve liberty and enhance self-preservation, Rousseau grounds the individual's duty to submit to an authority in a voluntary act. Rousseau, unlike Hobbes, does not transfer political authority to a sovereign at the loss of individual freedom but instead sovereignty is retained by the people.

This form of association does not involve a loss of liberty, but rather an exchange of natural liberty for civil liberty, the latter being limited by the general will. True liberty is embodied in self-government, i.e., rules we impose on ourselves when an individual becomes both citizen and subject. Paine was one of the most radical thinkers of his time and a fierce opponent of conservative Edmund Burke, discussed in Chap. 4 of this volume. Unlike Burke and also Hume, Paine would not leave things that work alone. He had clear ideas of the role of government in a society where morality dominated economics. Society for him was also a given, a necessity, as nature created humans for social life, and society for Paine was based on natural rights. He strongly believed in the need for reform of government in case of corruption or tyrannical behavior. Paine was a thinker and an activist. Paine's writings were published in polemical context which left little room for extensive theoretical reflection. One needs to collect his thoughts on certain topics as they are scattered throughout his work and then reconstruct an often not fully consistent system of thought (Lounissi 2016, 175). Paine believed in social contract theory as a basis for legitimacy of governmental institutions. All men should participate in government, in his mind, and had that right because they paid tax.

Social contracts arguments, typically, posit that individuals have consented to surrender some of their natural freedoms and submit to the authority of the state in exchange for the protection of their remaining rights. The obligation to pay taxes naturally follows from the necessity to enable the state to perform these duties. Such a contract is, of course, a myth, fiction, or a metaphor as Delmotte and Nientiedt call it in Chap. 5. Nobody is asked to sign a contract when reaching the age of legal adulthood agreeing to the terms of societal participation and the respective roles of the state and citizens, nor does an ancient document exist between a group of free men embodying such a 'contract' (Brederode 2020, 5).[2] The social contract theory has no basis in historical reality: people did not join together under a form of contract and created society; rather anthropological theory suggests that people have always lived in a form of society. Rawls (1971) tries to overcome this problem by presenting a hypothetical contract but, as Dworkin (1973, 501) correctly points out, a hypothetical contract means essentially 'no contract at all'. As a theoretical construct only, its terms cannot be binding. However, it does not follow therefrom that the hypothetical contract has no meaning or is deprived of any function. On the contrary, Rawls uses the hypothetical contract as the basis of a method of reasoning for the purpose of identifying the composites of a just society. By abstracting from our current, real-life situation, we are able to remove our bias caused by our own particular interests and value systems and arrive at an impartial model of societal justice (cf. Wolff 2016, 153–158).

1.2.1.2 Quid Pro Quo: Taxation as Payment for Public Services

Liam Murphy and Thomas Nagel in their impactful book "The Myth of Ownership", published in 2002, argue, within a wider context of egalitarian utopia, that the right of taxation is based on the vital role of the state in society and services rendered by the state to its citizens. It is a *quid pro quo*, a notion that echoes social contract theory as a justification for taxation. This may counter the forced labor objection of libertarians as citizens have 'agreed' to the payment of taxation on a contractual basis, but it would not remove the inconsistency of taxation of earnings with the conception of self-ownership (see *infra* Sect. 1.6 and Chap. 7). Before reaching the conclusion that 'contract' constitutes a reasonable basis for taxation, one should

[2] This is generally correct. However, as Gribnau and Frecknall-Hughes point out in Chap. 2, n. 10, there does exist some evidence of actual contracts between rulers and subjects, notably the Magna Carta between King John and the barons but this was a contract among the elites and did not encompass the whole populace, and the arrangement of the Pilgrim Fathers when establishing the tiny Plymouth Colony in today's Massachusetts. These are exceptions, though, and it remains debatable whether any next generation would be bound by a contract signed by their ancestors. It could be argued that the U.S. Constitution is a form of a social contract between the 13 original states after the war of independence from Great Britain.

consider two things. First, that the social contract is a forced contract – all citizens are bound by it, unless one decides to emigrate.[3] Second, that the state determines the terms of the contract fully, i.e., both the *quid* and the *quo*. Herein lies the moral problem of the social contract theory, going back to the origin of the state and taxation, which is coercive power.[4] The social contract theory justifies taxation as payment for services rendered by the state. To be valid, a contract, generally, requires parties to voluntarily agree to its terms. If I were to buy my neighbor's bicycle as a means for my young son to travel to school and my neighbor accepts my offer of 200, a contract has arisen. My neighbor hands over the bicycle, thus transferring both possession and ownership, and I hand over the money in return. However, if I were to sneak into my neighbor's garage and take the bicycle without her consent, that would constitute theft, even if I would put 200 in an envelope and leave it on a shelf for her to find including a kind note stating that the money is 'for her bike'. The fact that I pay for the bicycle does not remove from my action the classification of theft (cf. Huemer 2017). Likewise, the state cannot extract taxes, claiming this does not constitute an involuntary taking, merely on the argument that it provided services in return for the taxes extracted.

Where social contract theory forms the justification of taxation, the consent-of-the-governed-principle imbedded in the theory must mean that taxation requires such consent also. Logically, taxation loses its justification when consent is or becomes absent. The required consent encompasses all aspects of taxation, the type of taxes, the choice of tax base, rate structure, the degree of fairness, the enforcement of tax law, the distribution of the tax burden, and the purposes for which the revenue is used.

For the *quid pro quo* justification for taxation to have some basis of justification, citizens, at a minimum, would have to approve of the services rendered and role played by the state, and the price to be paid in exchange.[5] A notion that goes back to classical liberalism, discussed further below at Sect. 1.5.1. In other words, the output of the state is a vital constitutive part of the process of assessing whether

---

[3] Emigration does not necessarily fully relieve a person from the control of the exited state. The U.S., for example, tax citizens on their worldwide income regardless of residence. Thus, emigration would require also change of citizenship. The U.S. allow renunciation of citizenship for a fee of $2350 (8 U.S.C. § 1481 (a)(5)) which is basically an exit penalty; and depending on meeting certain income and wealth criteria, so-called 'covered expatriates' are due an exit tax (sec. 877 and 877a of the IRC).

[4] The first forms of warfare were essentially raiding parties on neighboring tribes for material gain, what we would call looting. That was the practice of the North American plain Indians, for example. When institutionalized, raids and loot were replaced with the payment of annual tribute by conquered or weaker tribes or kingdoms to more powerful ones. This was the case after the Scythians defeated Babylonia (Phillips 1972) and the price to be paid by the kingdoms defeated by Alexander the Great on his journey to India, and of peoples defeated by the Romans. Criminal gangs exercise their power over neighborhoods they control in the same manner by demanding and coercing payment of 'protection money.'

[5] Consent can only be considered a given if one adheres to a Hobbesian absolutism, reasoning that the sovereign authority acts on behalf of the citizens as if they write the laws themselves.

paradoxical, which Locke solves by introducing democratic consent as a condition for taxation to be justifiable.

Rousseau argues that the obligation to pay tax follows from the social contract. He transposes the emerging new ideal of equality to taxation which not only is to enable government to protect its citizens, but also to consider their subsistence. Taxes should enhance liberty and equality (distributive justice). Thus, progressive taxation based on the ability to pay is put on the agenda.

Paine has written quite extensively on taxation. He opposed taxes on consumption as these were oppressive to the poor and, instead, proposed a graduated income tax, based on reasoning that contains an early form of application of the benefits principle. Paine argued for a more radical redistribution as taxes should pay for welfare provision, which was part of his proposals for reform, making him an intellectual forerunner of the idea of the welfare state.

1.2.3 Non-social Contract Enlightenment Views on Taxation

Not all Enlightenment philosophers (fully) adhered to social contract theory. For Montesquieu and Hume social contract theory was redundant because living in society is the natural state of affairs, a fact, and searching for the origin of society seemed absurd and absented from rationale. Montesquieu's focus is on the conditions of good governance and the institutions necessary to guarantee political liberty, and he opposed absolutism and concentration of power, leading to the development of his proposition of the separation of legislative, executive, and judicial powers, also known as the *Trias Politica*. Montesquieu also regarded taxes to be a payment to the state in the context of a reciprocal relationship, which makes him a semi-contractualist similarly to Murphy and Nagel (see Sect. 1.2.1.2 *supra*). Montesquieu was the first to recognize the need of a subsistence threshold below which no taxation would be assessed and was an early proponent of a form of progressive taxation.

Hume is critical of social contract theory because of its assumption of consent where most people simply do not have another territorial option. The foundation of government, for Hume, follows from the need to protect public interest as well as the rights to property and justice. A government is needed to maintain the law and therewith peace between citizens. However, government authority must be balanced against the need to maintain liberty. Hume is concerned with the public debt and excessive taxation. He prefers taxation of consumption, especially luxury goods, rather than the necessities of daily life because the purchase of luxury goods is often a matter of choice, whereas buying daily necessities is not. From that perspective, taxes on luxury items carry some measure of voluntarism. He opposed arbitrary taxes, including land taxes, because of their inequality and effective punishment of industry. Although he did not offer a solution, Hume realized the challenge in designing a tax system compatible with the idea of liberty.

1.2.4 Natural Rights

Natural rights theory remains important in regard of property law. The most prominent enlightenment scholars in this regard are Rousseau and Locke. Natural rights theory has had a strong influence on the American Revolution against Britain where the Declaration of Independence speaks of inalienable rights bestowed on all by the Creator. Our contemporary age being far less religious, we might state that these rights derive from our humanity. In any instance, crucial is that these rights are derived from a higher authority, God or humanity, and therefore provide protection even against the ambitions of absolute kings. Natural rights theory is foundational for the emancipation of the common man. For Rousseau the core is the right to self-preservation. Thomas Paine extended the idea of natural rights to include the rights of citizens to education, old-age pensions and other financial benefits. John Locke's rights-based theory of acquisition posits that laborers are entitled to the products of their labor. Consequently, they acquire property rights in items in the common pool by mingling their labor with those items.

> [E]very Man has a Property in his own Person. … The Labour of his Body, and the Work of his Hands, we may say, are properly his. Whatsoever then he removes out of the state that Nature hath provided, and left it in, he hath mixed his Labour with, and joined to it something that is his own, and thereby makes it his Property. … For this Labour being the unquestionable Property of the Labourer, no Man but he can have a right to what that is once joined to, at least where there is enough, and as good left in common for others (Locke 2008 [1689], 287).

The most important aspect of private property rights is that it can be made exclusive, i.e., the owner can preclude others from the use of the property in contrast to property held in common (such as grazing meadows or hunting forests) to which all members of the common have an equal use right.

When it comes to natural capital such as land, Locke limits a person's ability to what can be acquired to his capacity to use or improve it.

> As much Land as a Man Tills, Plants, Improves, Cultivates, and can use the Product of, so much is his Property. Whatever is beyond this, is more than his share, and belongs to others (Locke 2008 [1689], II § 32 and 31).

Given this limitation, wealth taxes could be defended as being Lockean in nature, insofar these taxes would serve only to remove access wealth, i.e., wealth accumulated beyond what can reasonably be conceived as generated by one's own labor or effort. Interestingly, the Lockean limitation of ownership rights to land is shared by native American tribes. In a letter to the U.S. Congress, Cherokee Nation Principal Chief D.W. Bushyhead stated: "… The only difference between your land systems and ours is that the unoccupied surface of the earth is not a chattel to be sold and speculated in by men who do not use it."[7]

[7] D. W. Bushyhead, P. N. Blackstone, and George Sanders, Cherokee Delegation to Congress of the United States (Jan. 17, 1881), in SEN. DOCS., 49th Cong., 1st Sess., Serial 2362, vi; cited in Bobroff (2001, 1571).

Locke's argument, accepted by libertarian philosopher Nozick, that the laborer has a moral right to the fruits of his labor is appealing in the context of created capital, where labor is added to a tangible good, such as a farmer plowing land for cultivation, or a sculptor applying the hammer and chisel to a block of granite, or a carpenter making a kitchen table out of wood. Opponents to that view point out that modern created capital is always an amalgamate of the laborer's efforts and society's vast stores of accumulated social capital, because the sculptor's and carpenter's skills and knowledge are the product of millennia of trial and error by others. If we were to allocate the fruits of the sculptor's or carpenter's labor based on their contributions relative to the contribution of "society's commonwealth, we would probably be able to justify tax rates far in excess of any now generally imposed" (Seto 2016, 20).

I disagree with that reasoning. The agricultural, sculpting and carpentry knowledge acquired over millennia belongs to our common heritage. A society is the aggregate of the people that form it, both presently and historically; an abstract concept that cannot be separated from its constituents. Our common heritage is not owned by society, in other words: collectively, not even in a moral sense, but is held in common, i.e., each individual has an equal right to use it. A common right still remains an individual right. In contrast, a collective right is no longer individualizable; it is held in ownership by the state, at best acting as agent of society. That is exactly what the word 'commonwealth' means: wealth held by all in common; thus, not owned by any individual nor by any societal institution, such as the state. Thus, where Seto claims that society is owed compensation (taxes) for the use of our social capital, our human heritage, our commonwealth, he makes a logical fallacy by allocating property rights to society as if it were a separate or separable entity from its constituents. Interjecting the state to hold ownership rights does not change this conclusion because, given their agency relationship, the state cannot on behalf of its principal exercise rights that the latter does not have. If our common heritage were owned by the state, even if the state acts as agent of society, then it is no longer held in common because individuals would have lost their rights to use it. Instead, individual rights to the common would then be transformed into collective rights, essentially eliminating individual rights. Common rights leave each individual in society with relative equal power to what is held in common, rights vested with the state are in their allocation to individual citizens dependent on the arbitrary powers of the bureaucracy, which is vulnerable to manipulation by the more powerful members or interests in society. Moreover, as demonstrated by Seto's reasoning, the state uses the rights it alleges to hold as representative of the commons as a basis to justify its claims on taxation. Allocating our common heritage to society, or to the state as agent of society, echoes Hobbesian absolutist sentiments, still vibrating today in egalitarian theory of property rights (see Sect. 1.5.2.1 *infra*).

1.3 Utilitarianism and the Benefits Principle

Because utilitarianism has its birthplace in the Enlightenment, there is some overlap between Chaps. 2 and 3 in that the latter chapter discusses several enlightenment thinkers as a steppingstone to utilitarianism. Jennifer and Stefan Bird-Pollan in Chap. 3 take a distinctive approach by investigating utilitarianism from a historical evolutionary perspective, which offers more insight into the relationship between utility and tax.

Utilitarianism has dominated American political theory for most of the last century until the emergence of egalitarian theories of Rawls and Dworkin in the 1970ies. Welfarism is currently the most popular academic implementation of the utilitarianism of Jeremy Bentham, who claimed that property was not a natural right but solely a creation of law and therefore lacked any inherent ethical content, a position that contemporary egalitarians, such as Murphy and Nagel, share (see Sect. 1.5.2 *infra*). In Bentham words: "Natural rights is simple nonsense: natural and imprescriptible rights, rhetorical nonsense, nonsense upon stilts" (Bentham 1973 [1791], 257, 269). Utilitarianism argues that morals and legislation should be guided by the objective of realizing the greatest good for the greatest number. As such, it is consequentialist in its moral perspective. Where the goal is to maximize overall happiness, questions related to rights and duty, justice and fairness are considered to be of secondary order, which places utilitarianism opposite Kantian deontology which focuses precisely on these questions (Solt 2004, 1). Utilitarianism fits well within the pragmatic Western intellectual culture of most of the twentieth century until the renaissance of deontological philosophy with Rawls, Dworkin and also Nozick. Chapter 3 does not treat utilitarianism as a philosophical entry point to the theory of taxation. Rather, it takes a historical approach which offers more insight into the relationship between utility and tax. As the authors explain, the modern usage of the term 'utility' arrives through a complex history of the idea of subjectivity from the reductivist conception of self-preservation in Hobbes, through Hume's and Smith's conception of subjects as ineluctably tied to each other through fellow-feeling, to the theory of liberal autonomy as articulated in Bentham and Mill. This shift in paradigm from the individualistic-political (Hobbes and Locke) to the mediate realm of the social (Hume, Smith) allowed the state to become a function of the social or society with all its nuances rather than merely a collection of rationally consistent actors. Indeed, rather than supposing the individual to be essentially driven by self-interest, Smith's view of human nature is fundamentally the same as Hume's in that he believes humans to be both self-interested and always concerned with the benefits of society. For Smith, the individual is not just the beneficiary of equal security but connected to others through a notion of intersubjectively grounded moral feelings.

Utilitarianism tries to improve welfare at the aggregate level. This objective carries the inherent risk of prioritizing community welfare over individual welfare to the extent that individual rights and preferences are always considered to be subordinate to societal welfare. The connection between individual rights to self-determination and the principle of utility began to strain the theory of utilitarianism proper in Mill. The big issue for utilitarianism is to reconcile individual liberty with general utility. This is a modern dilemma that did not exist under classical utilitarianism. Rawls tries to reconcile utilitarianism with libertarianism by formulating his first principle of liberty in combination with the difference principle which accepts differences in outcome only to the extent these provide benefits for the worst off.

During the period from the seventeenth century to the nineteenth century, from Hobbes to Mill, the justification for taxation gradually shifted from a taxation model of 'payment for benefit' to taxation as 'ability to pay'. Specifically, Chap. 3 shows that it is the enlightenment concept of self-determination, which makes it possible for 'benefit' to be conceived as both individual and social at the same time, which ultimately results in the shift from taxation as 'payment for benefit' to taxation as 'ability to pay'. Where taxation is perceived as payment for government services from which the individual benefits, the problem lies in quantifying the tax base for individual taxpayers. The number or volume of benefits received from the state will likely differ from person to person and will fluctuate for a single person from year to year. Some benefits may have higher monetary value than others insofar it is possible to determinatively adhere such a value to government output. If we want to utilize the benefits principle as a basis for taxation, the problem lies in measuring and valuating individual benefits from government services. There is no practical way to do this on an individualized basis. Adam Smith solved this problem by suggesting measuring not the benefits provided by, i.e., the output of, the government but, instead, to base taxation on the earnings a person has been able to realize under the protection of the state, i.e., the input of the individual. In Smith's words a subject should contribute "in proportion to the revenue which they respectively enjoy under the protection of the state" (Smith [1776] 1981). That is a smart approach because where it is impossible to individualize government output, individual input is a knowable and measurable quantity. Hobbes and Locke were entirely focused on the protection or security provided by government as a basis for taxation, a view shared by some libertarians, concluding to equal taxation. Smith's reasoning would allow for proportional taxation of earnings: if you make twice as much, you pay twice as much, which is in itself a form of progressive taxation.

It is a small step from Smith's philosophical basis for taxation, i.e., that what one has been able to earn, to arrive at the ability to pay principle, in particular where the focus shifts from exclusive individual self-preservation to an individual connected to a society of other human beings and taxation serves to contribute to the long-term welfare of the individual and society at large. The 'ability to pay' approach understands the individual as connected to society and, thus, shifts to the nature of economic activity as analyzable through distribution and the division of labor. 'Ability to pay' does not provide much in terms of justification for taxation, but for acknowledging that those who have no ability to pay should not be taxed at all, providing a rationale for not taxing income below at least the poverty threshold. The question is, given different levels of earnings, how much one should pay under this principle relative to other individuals. The modern welfarist approach applies the premise that we should structure property rights so as to maximize efficiency under the assumption that this will lead to larger prosperity for all. Utilitarian reasoning calls on the ability to pay as a justification for graduated taxation. However, prima facie, 'ability to pay' fails to convince as a justification for progressive taxation, simply because the sole possession of monetary and investments funds, or wealth, does not explain or justify the level or method of taxation. If income were to be taxed proportionally, taxation would inflict equal hardship on all, it would seem. However, an additional argument for justifying graduated taxation is found in the premise of diminishing marginal utility, the idea that with rising income the use or utility of that income would decrease. Therefore, to warrant equal sacrifice by all to the fiscal needs of the state, higher incomes should pay a larger percentage of their income in tax, ideally inversely proportional to the diminishing grade of utility. I find that premise unconvincing on its merits because additional income translates into additional purchase power. In other words, the utility of an additional monetary unit is the same for everyone, regardless of whether the receiver is a millionaire of a minimum wage earner, as it provides the same additional purchasing power. Given scarcity of means, however, an economic actor will prioritize his wants and satisfy them according to his preferences, using additional monetary units to satisfy wants lower and lower on the scale. As a result, additional income obtained by a minimum wage earner will likely be used to accommodate wants higher on his scale than the wants the millionaire would satisfy with the same additional income. The idea that additional increments of income provide less satisfaction to the well-off than to lower income groups is, so it seems, mostly a psychological assumption that cannot be verified nor measured. Even if one were to accept the premise on its face value, the practical problem lies in the inability to determine the curve of marginal utility, rendering it equally impossible to determine income brackets and associated tax rates on the basis of this theory (Brederode 2020, 7).

1.4 Conservatism

Conservative thinkers offer distinctive commentary on the normative and empirical dimensions of taxation and their connections to wider philosophical debates about social order and public prosperity. Their views on taxation are fused with a number of key themes: an opposition to imposing rigid economic formulas on the complexity of social life; a sensitive awareness of the inverse relationship between the modern state's growth in taxing powers and the displacement of voluntary associations; and a deep unease over the negative impact of wide-scale taxing schemes on social order. Collins, in Chap. 6, starts with a foundational subsection dealing with a few premises that conservatives over the centuries seem to share. Firstly, they recognize that man is a social creature by nature. Rather than conceiving human beings as free and equal individuals bound together only by political consent, the conservative view sees man as part of a broader weave of associations, groups, and institutions that cannot be reduced to mere contractual relations. Secondly, and in additional to the first premise of sociability, conservatives recognize that individuals and social groups hold many differences in terms of experiences, talents, abilities, skills, knowledge, social status, and family pedigree. While all individuals are equal under God, this does not mandate equality of condition or outcome, an approach very different from the one egalitarians support, and the acceptance of human variety explains conservatives' attitude towards taxation. The sociability premise allows conservatives to resist assessing the merits of taxation through the lens of a doctrinaire form of individualism and prevents the development of a hardened individualistic ideology. Conservative thinkers imagine the goals of public policy, such as taxation, through the broader framework of what consequences it generates for society as well as for the individual. In other words, their attitudes toward taxation are not determined solely by whether taxes enhance or diminish individual autonomy, an aspect that receives more emphasize from libertarian thinkers. Given the human variety and the complexity of societies, thirdly, conservatives harbor a great distrust in the powers of rationalism to legislate the intricate dimensions of human affairs. Fourthly, conservatives' attention to the limits of rationalism is part of their deeper moral and religious understanding of man as a fallible and sinful creature, which makes utopian society an illusion. Finally, conservatives view private property as sacrosanct that warrants special protection by the rule of law.

Collins then distinguishes and discusses two common principles of taxation, namely that taxation should be limited and non-excessive, and not serve non-fiscal purposes, i.e., social engineering.

The second half of the chapter contains a treatise of three different conservative schools of thought, demonstrating areas of tension over the appropriate range of the taxing power, the connection between revenue and the state, and the purpose of the state in general.

The first, represented most powerfully by Burke, Churchill, and Kirk, understands taxation to be a necessary part of civilized society and an instrument, when used wisely, to promote the common good. Burke realized, as demonstrated by his opposition to arbitrary taxes and property confiscation, that the power to tax could be utilized as an instrument for tyranny and for mass wealth redistribution schemes. On the other hand, he recognized that taxation could be used to promote the public welfare and to finance projects that could imbue a sense of reverence in state establishments and traditions. Burke's approach to taxation did not call for a radically minimalist state but for prudential management pursuant to the ends of a commonwealth grounded in justice and religion. Churchill attempted to negotiate a delicate balance between encouraging the free enterprise system and supporting tax-funded social insurance programs that could alleviate the negative consequences of modern industrial capitalism. Russell Kirk's position on taxation is situated between Burke's and Churchill's positive conception of the state and Robert Nisbet's antagonism toward it. Apart from his opposition to the graduated income tax, which he perceived as a dangerous tool for utilitarian social reformers, Kirk was contemptuous in regard of the inheritance tax, which he considered to be harmful due to its negative impact on familial social and economic life and its discriminating effect against family enterprises and partnerships. For Kirk the social struggle is between traditional society, with its religious and moral and political inheritance, and collectivism, similarly to Nisbet's framing of modernity as a blunt confrontation between social groups and the state. He has strong objections against collectivist approaches that undermine human bonds historically secured through voluntary associations, such as social security which is essentially a form of collective coerced saving.

The second, represented by Oakeshott, Will, Buckley and Sowell, views taxation in theory as necessary to finance the minimal duties required to administer a state. Taxation in accord with this Oakeshottian framework could be appropriate insofar as it provided revenue for the administering of the civil association, such as a state, and insofar as it was employed in a neutral manner free of explicit or implicit incentives, and without coaxing taxpayers into making particular decisions in pursuit of substantive aims. Sin taxes, to take but one specific example, might violate this principle of tax neutrality. The limited nature of the civil association would thus preclude attempts by the state to use taxation for shared substantive aims such as equality or justice, or to accommodate other social changes.

The third, represented by Nisbet, questions the very credibility of a state's taxing powers in general. His major concern is the trend of the modern state to assume responsibilities that were previously met by voluntary associations and local communities, financed by tax revenues.

Areas of tension prevail among the various conservative thinkers regarding specific questions about taxation, such as whether to utilize taxes to advance common purposes of society, whether to grant priority to taxes on inherited wealth or active wealth, and whether the very power of taxation itself lacked credibility. Such differences can be attributed both to the particular political theories of each thinker and to the distinctive set of constraints, incentives, and audiences they confronted as thinkers and statesmen.

What ultimately unites the different conservative 'schools' in their approach to taxation is an awareness of the limits in imposing rigid economic formulas on the complexity of social life, as well as the collective impact of secularism and rationalism on the augmentation of the modern state and the subsequent decline in voluntary associations, and the potential danger embodied in the state's taxing power to unsettle the social order of communities in pursuit of abstract ideals.

1.5 Liberalism and Libertarianism

1.5.1 General

Contemporary libertarianism finds its origin in the natural rights theory of John Locke, but libertarian thought is much older and not limited to the West. McGee and Block in Chap. 7 point to Lao Tzu (sixth century BCE) as the first libertarian philosopher. Ibn Kaldūn formulated in the fourteenth century economic free market principles and was the first to formulate a theory of the optimum rate of taxation ([1377] 2015, 2: 89–90), in the twentieth century presented in a graph by supply-side economist Arthur Laffer:[8]

> When tax assessments and imposts upon the subjects are low, the latter have the energy and desire to do things. Cultural enterprises grow and increase, because the low taxes bring satisfaction. When cultural enterprises grow, the number of individual imposts and assessments mount. In consequence, the tax revenue, which is the sum total of the individual assessments, increases.

According to Locke, individuals have a right to life, liberty and property and they join into civil society for the purpose of protecting these rights. Life is the primary right, and liberty and property are instrumental rights, necessary for individuals to actually further and protect their lives. There exist different branches of libertarian though with further subdivisions. McGee and Block distinguish four varieties: anarcho-capitalists (Spooner, Rothbard), who see no role for government at all and posit that the functions of government can be exercised through cooperation between individuals; minarchists (Mises, Rand, Nozick) who support only small governments with narrowly defined authority required for the protection of individual rights to life, liberty and property, the so-called nightwatchman state; libertarian constitutionalists (Ron and Rand Paul) who center their philosophy around a narrow interpretation of the U.S. Constitution; and classical liberals (Hayek, Friedman) who allow for a small state that also offers a modest level of welfare for the poor, some anti-trust laws, and some public goods. In this book, we deal with classical liberals separately in Chap. 4. Classical liberalism has been influenced by the social contract approach where it finds justification for the state in the interests of its citizens. Beyond, it is a theory that provides what Delmotte and Nientiedt in Chap. 4 call a methodology for the justification of legal-political systems. The social contract origin requires that political power be justifiable, not to the rulers, but instead to those who are subject to it; government's purpose is to serve the individual interests of its citizens.

Classical liberals conceive the social contract as an instrumental perspective on political power. It is essentially a model to reconstruct political institutions as the outcome of a voluntary agreement whereby law and policy making authority is delegated to agents (the state) with the understanding that individuals maintain their sovereignty and, therefore, act as the principals in the relationship. The justification of the state as agent of society depends on its success in achieving universal benefit, i.e., rule-making that benefits all citizens. Delmotte and Nientiedt describe the contours of that minimum contract with the state in its protective and productive capacities. The protective capacity of the state is responsible for creating a legal framework to protect property rights, to enforce compliance with private contracts, and to

---

[8]At a restaurant dinner in 1974 that included Arthur Laffer, then professor at the University of Chicago, journalist Jude Wanniski, Donald Rumsfeld, then Whitehouse chief of staff to President Gerald Ford, and his deputy Dick Cheney, according to the story, Arthur Laffer sketched a curve on his napkin illustrating the trade-off between tax rates and tax revenues. Wanniski (1978) named the trade-off "The Laffer Curve."

support the functioning of markets. This is referred to as the rule of law criterion which has three components: generality, the law applies to all; equality, the law does not discriminate; certainty, the law is predictable in its application. The productive capacity of the state tailors towards providing those goods and services which are not adequately provided by the market, which requires a mechanism for collective decision-making. Taxation is justified insofar it serves to maintain the state in both its protective and productive capacity. Classical liberals from Smith to Viti de Marco to Wicksell and Epstein base taxation on the benefits principle. Because the exact benefit from government services cannot be determined for each individual, a proportional levy on income or consumption would be used as a practical proxy. Classical liberals pertain that such a tax would be accepted as adequate and fair from the perspective of individual citizens as it mimics voluntary exchange: individuals buy public goods from the government. The contrast with utilitarians, who also apply the benefits principle, becomes manifest. Utilitarians, especially in their contemporary welfarist form, are not concerned with the perspective of the individual; rather they focus on maximizing general welfare, i.e., welfare at the aggregate. The benefits theory, supported by classical liberals, establishes a direct link between taxation and government expenditure. Shifting the tax burden to future generations by borrowing is rejected in relation to consumption expenditure (which should be borne by those benefitting from it in the present) and acceptable only for investment expenditure to the extent that future generations benefit therefrom. Classical liberalism generally does not support progressive taxation, contrary to utilitarian welfarists, to prevent the inherent cost shifting by taxpayers under a progressive rate system, which lead to special deductions, credits and exemptions aimed to benefit a small list of industries, economic groups, or types of income. Progression of one tax is only accepted as a tool to counter the regressivity of another individual tax, but the overall tax system should remain proportional. Tax policy, in the classic liberal view, should be constitutionalized to prevent majoritarian changes influenced by lobby and pressure groups.

These branches of libertarian thought, distinguished by McGee and Block, take different approaches to certain topics and subjects but share common values. First of all, the acceptance of the theory of natural rights as postulated by John Locke, in particular the right to life, liberty and property already mentioned. There are only negative rights and no positive rights to any form of entitlements, although classical liberals allow for modest welfare. Economic freedom is central as well because it is a precondition for the protection of property rights, and for political freedom. Taxation, at least beyond the level necessary to fund the minimal state, is considered to be equivalent to theft.

McGee and Block do not support and argue convincingly against the thesis that taxation would constitute slavery but contend that it is an act of theft. They illustrate the size of the theft by presenting a comparative overview, comprised of 17 countries, of the popular notion of Tax Freedom Day, i.e., the first day of the year individuals work for themselves rather than for the government, assuming that income were taxed at 100% until total tax liability for the year is collected. For the U.S. they include data from 2000 in 20-year intervals to 2019 showing the gradual increase of the taking.[9]

The authors further discuss a number of topics, fairness, efficiency and value issues, and redistribution, from the perspective of the distinguished schools of libertarian thought to demonstrate their respective approaches.

In Sect. 7.6 they evaluate a number of taxes to determine whether and, if so, to what extent such taxes are acceptable from a libertarian perspective: the flat tax, consumption taxes such as the retail sales tax and value added tax, income tax, social security taxes, estate and inheritance taxes, gasoline taxes, poll taxes. In this context, they also discuss fairness, ability to pay, the virtue of visible over hidden taxes, and pro and cons of regressive, proportional, and progressive taxes. In the next section they reflect on moral justification of tax and the moral obligation to pay.

Because libertarians are either fully opposed to taxation or see room only for financing of a government with very limited functions, the question arises how libertarians seek to organize and fund the many functions and tasks currently fulfilled by government in absence of such government. The authors address this in the final section and make a number of suggestions in that respect. Unsurprisingly, privatization of many government functions is at the core of libertarian approach while funding for the few remaining tasks of the nightwatchman state would come from voluntary contributions (which, I think, may trigger a free rider problem), lotteries, or a consumption tax.

Libertarianism has a long tradition based on the liberty principle but has also run into opposition, in particular from those who are communitarian, egalitarian, or socialist in their philosophical leanings. Early in this century, two New York University professors published a book targeting the foundations of the libertarian view on taxation. I discuss and evaluate their reasoning in the next section.

1.5.2 Private Ownership: Myth or Truth

Egalitarians Murphy and Nagel object strongly to what they call the "everyday libertarian" view that taxation constitutes a taking, a view widely supported in general opinion. In fact, their book "The Myth of Ownership" (2002)[10] reads like a political pamphlet arguing that taxation is not a taking at all. Their book is an effort to change the dynamics of the debate by denying the existence of natural rights and establishing the state as the origin of any rights. Echoing Bentham (see Sect. 1.4 *supra*), they assert that property rights are simply post-institutional conventions. Free market distributive outcomes, therewith, lose their moral credentials and become irrelevant: "... pre-tax distribution of welfare is both entirely imaginary and morally irrele-

---

[9] For a critical note on the idea of Tax Freedom Day, see Buchanan (2014).

[10] For reviews of their book, see inter alia, Kordana and Tabachnick (2003); Gosseries (2005); Schoenblum (2003); Gordon (2002); Sterba (2004); and Waltman (2002).

vant …" (Murphy and Nagel 2002, 99). In other words, individuals do not have *a priori* rights to private property (Graetz 1983, 275–76). Thus, the moral basis of libertarianism and classical liberalism with its reliance on natural rights, private property, free markets, and small government, is effectively eliminated, i.e., if Murphy and Nagel are correct.

I will discuss their approach at some length here because it provides an opportunity to show the contrast between egalitarianism and libertarianism. Moreover, while diametrically opposing the philosophical basis of libertarianism, they also appear to provide within their reasoning three arguments to justify taxation: (1) As the originator of property rights the state reserved a retainer right, (2) Taxation does not constitute a taking because the state owns part of someone's gross income, (3) Taxation is part of the private property system. Thus, taxation cannot be evaluated by its impact on private property rights because it is a constituting factor in defining these same property rights.

I assess the validity of their positions in the next three subsections.

1.5.2.1 Taxation Is a Retainer Right on Property

Murphy and Nagel posit that taxation should not be considered constituting appropriation because property rights originate with the state. The state, they say, created property rights and, therefore, the state retains a claim on the property and can take part of it away through taxation without violating individual rights. They formulate their position as follows:

> Private property is a legal convention…The conventional nature of property rights is both perfectly obvious and remarkably easy to forget… We cannot start by taking as given…some initial allocation of possessions-what people originally own, what is theirs, prior to government interference (Murphy and Nagel 2002, 8).

Your income is only yours because the state created laws instituting property rights. Therefore, if correct, there apparently existed no concept of ownership before the state made property laws. This reasoning gives to the state a form of divine status: all law originates with the state; and what the state giveth it can taketh away. I am paraphrasing Job 1:21, of course, where Job after he loses everything says: 'Naked came I out of my mother's womb, and naked shall I return thither: the Lord gave, and the Lord hath taken away; blessed be the name of the Lord.' However, God – in the Abrahamic traditions – is truly sovereign and the origin of creation; God is unique in that he has no origin in anything or anybody else.[11] The state, however, is not the origin of human relations, nor is it sovereign out of itself. Rather, since Hume and Smith (see Chap. 3), we perceive the state as a tool or an institution, created by, or emerged from, a society of humans to rule over them for the benefit of all. If it were true that the concept of ownership originates with the state, primitive

[11] The same notion is found in the Indian *Ṛgveda* where Prajāpati is the creator-God, equivalent to Allah in the Qur'ān and Elohim/Yahweh in the Torah or Hebrew Bible.

societies in existence before the first form of government and state emerged, would lack any notion of private ownership. If a hunter, assume twenty thousand years ago, killed a bison, then cut and dried the meat, processed the bones into tools, preserved the skin and made it into a coat, all the products of his labor must have been owned either by everybody or by nobody. There is no evidence that such a society ever existed. If we look closer at societies without a state of the near past, for example, the tribal societies of the indigenous peoples in North America – who have a concept of kinship, tribe, even society perhaps, but not of state – we conclude that private ownership was common but diverse and heterogenous in concept, often quite complicated, and included property rights in land (Bobroff 2001, 1571).[12] These property rights originated from before European contact (Hoebel 1954, 67–256, 316–17; referenced by Bobroff 2001, 1572).

So, the first premise of Murphy and Nagel that the notion of and rights to ownership are created by the state, i.e., are post-institutional, is false (see also Sect. 1.5.2.2 *infra*). Instead, the state has codified existing communal concepts of ownership and developed these further into legal doctrines.[13] By claiming we should not start with ownership prior to government interference, they essentially ask to ignore historic facts because – I suspect – these are inconvenient to the outcome they prefer.

Even if the premise were true, it does not follow automatically that if the state creates ownership rights for the benefit of individuals within the state, it retains rights to take (part of) that property back. That appears to be Murphy and Nagel's position. But why would that be the case? If I buy a bicycle and give it to my neighbor as a present, i.e., I bestow ownership rights of the bicycle on my neighbor, can I demand its return a week or so later to use it to go shopping, arguing that I retained that right? The answer is negative because the retainer right is not inherent. God's sovereignty arises from himself and as the creator of the universe, by implication, he has ownership of the hunter, the bison, the meat, tools, and coat. That is the foundation for divine rights. The state cannot make such a claim, simply because it is not its own origin; state sovereignty is derived from the community it serves. When the Lord exercised his rights, Job may have had reason to bless the Lord as recognition of His majesty; but we certainly do not have to bless the state when we are taxed on those grounds. For conventionalists, property rights exist only within a particular legal system, i.e., they are created by law. If we extrapolate from this view on property rights and apply the same premise to laws and legal concepts in general, the fallacy becomes more apparent. "Many laws have a moral foundation, containing rules of appropriate behavior to be applied to human interaction… That is obviously the case with criminal law, forbidding theft, murder, rape, etc., but it is essential to realize that these legal norms derive from moral standards and not the other way around. These moral standards exist regardless of whether they have found

[12] Bobroff presents an overview of the New England, Algonquian, Iroquois, Inuit property rights regimes and those of the Five 'Civilized' Tribes, tribes of the Southwest, of the West coast, and the Great Plains.

[13] Therewith I confirm Locke's conclusion that property rights pre-date the institution of the state (Epstein 2011, 99).

reflection in written laws. Murder, theft and adultery were already considered morally wrong by the Hebrews before Moses carved the Commandments in stone" (Brederode 2020, 1). For Murphy and Nagel, it seems, there exist no moral rights and obligations *in se* but only those that arise from law, i.e., rights and obligations *in legem*. This approach denies that the origin of laws – in particular, the basics ones – lies in the customs of society; laws are the codification of existing moral rules.[14] The Ten Commandments would not prohibit theft if the Hebrews had no pre-existing concept of ownership, i.e., property rights. If property rights can only arise from law, as Murphy and Nagel seem to posit, then that would be true for all rights, including crucial civil rights as, for example, enshrined in the U.S. Bill of Rights, and the state could remove these rights at will as their originator.[15] As a result, not one person would have personal autonomy or sovereignty and we would all live under arbitrary state law.

When the state formulates ownership rights, it does so, ideally, as the steward of society; not to vest rights for the state itself, but to ensure through regulation the proper furtherance of human affairs. The state should demonstrate an altruistic attitude as its purpose is to serve the society that created it, comparable perhaps to the charge of humankind to serve God as their creator. Unfortunately, where humans often fail in their mission, so does the state when it usurps authority and wrestles for power with the people whose ultimate sovereignty is the source of the state's existence. Even if one were to concede that rights are created by the state (and not developed from pre-existing concepts held by the people), in doing so, the state would only act as agent of society. For these reasons, Murphy and Nagel's premise cannot be accepted: ownership rights do not originate with the state but with the people and mutatis mutandis the state has no claim on private property as a retained right. The role of the state is to protect property rights, not to usurp these rights as a justification for taxation.

1.5.2.2 Taxes Partially Define Private Property Rights

As to the role of taxation in the context of property rights, Murphy and Nagel state the following:

> "Private property is a legal convention, defined in part by the tax system; therefore, the tax system cannot be evaluated by looking at its impact on private property, conceived as something that has independent existence and validity. Taxes must be evaluated as part of the overall system of property rights that they help to create" (Murphy and Nagel 2002, 8). "Since there are no property rights independent of the tax system, taxes cannot violate those rights" (Murphy and Nagel 2002, 58).

[14] That does not mean that laws are unchangeable, of course. Moral views change and that may trigger a change in laws. But the fact that a law is changed or repealed does not mean that the original law was deprived of a moral basis or societal acceptance.

[15] Their position echoes utilitarian Jeremy Bentham's assertion that natural rights are "nonsense upon stilts" (Bentham 1973, 269).

The notion, postulated by Murphy and Nagel in the quote above, that 'taxes are part of the overall system of property rights that they help to create' alleges that taxes are a constituting factor in the creation of property rights. That would require tax law to be developed simultaneously with the initial system of property rights and not later.[16] However, historically, property rights precede the institution of taxes. Most of our current taxes are relatively young and developed during the twentieth century.[17] Even the oldest taxes, such as Customs duties, tolls, market taxes,[18] and tithing[19] emerged long after the societal recognition of individual property rights. In other words, taxes are not part of the original concept of property rights, limiting their scope, but arose later and, thus, constitute an infringement of those property rights, regardless the legitimacy of that infringement.

Libertarians may idealize market outcomes, which they consider to be just; Murphy and Nagel similarly idealize the outcomes of the state regulatory process. For them, it appears, the state is the origin of everything. Their argument is not limited to denying the moral basis of free market distributive outcomes but includes the supporting position that pre-tax markets do not exist. One has no entitlement to one's gross or pre-tax income, in their reasoning, because without markets no one would be able to earn an income; and there exist no functioning markets without state regulation; and there exist no state without funding via taxes. So, taxes have priority over property rights, as funding the state is what enables us in the end to earn a living (Murphy and Nagel 2002, 32–33). This reasoning is flawed as it requires something to be the cause of itself like the impossible perpetuity of M.C. Escher lithograph depicting a waterfall driving the waterwheel, which recycles the water to create the waterfall.[20] In essence, they suggest a series of consecutive actions where the last action is the cause of the first: A is the cause of B which is the cause of C which is the cause of D which is the cause of A. According to Murphy and Nagel, the state (A) is needed to create a marketplace (B) in which an

[16] Obviously, taxes cannot be levied on property before the concept of property was developed.

[17] The personal income tax in the U.S. was enabled by the passage of the 16th Constitutional Amendment on June 2, 1909, ratified February 3, 1913. Sales and turnover taxes were introduced as an emergency measure in times of economic distress and war in the early twentieth century. West Virginia was the first in the U.S. to introduce a gross receipts tax in 1921; in Europe such turnover taxes started in 1916 in Germany, followed by France and Belgium in 1920 and 1921 respectively. Turnover taxes go back in concept to the Spanish Alcabala, first impose in 1342. VAT started its proliferation in Europe in 1948 in France as a single stage manufacturer's tax. Excise taxes are typically levied on commodities and go back 5000 years (Boesen 2021), but the first excise tax in the U.S. was introduced in 1791 and levied on the manufacture of whiskey.

[18] Tolls for passage across bridges and roads were common in medieval Europe. Rome, e.g., under Julius Caesar had a 1% sales tax (*centesima rerum venalium*), land taxes and a direct tax in the form of a head tax. Ancient Egypt and China had taxation, see Keen and Slemrod (2021, Ch. 2).

[19] All three Abrahamic religions have thithing traditions going back to Abraham himself (Gen. 14:20), but likely rooting in the Temple states of Mesopotamia and Syria-Palestine in the second millennium BCE, see Chodorow (2006, n. 2).

[20] M.C. Escher, 'The Waterfall' (lithograph 1961).

individual can make earnings (C), necessary to pay taxes (D) to fund the state (A) which depends on tax revenue to be able to create a marketplace, etc.

Thus, they put the state on the same footing with the neo-platonic Demiurge who believes to be the true god. They confuse the state with society. Society created the state for the purpose to rule for the benefit of all. Markets are as old as the first interaction between groups of early humans dating back 300,000 years ago,[21] clearly before the emergence of the state around 5000 BCE and before the development of taxes (Carneiro 1970). Trade is not possible without the acceptance of private property, so the idea of private property also predates taxation and the emergence of the state. At some point, trade and other human interactions became more complex and required regulation and intervention, and the state was born.[22] However, the state acts on behalf of society not for its own purposes. The fact that modern markets may have difficulties functioning without the regulatory framework provided by the state, and to that extent are dependent on the state,[23] may lead to a necessity – and even moral duty perhaps – to fund the cost of government, providing a justification for taxation, but does not constitute an independent right or entitlement of the state to funding nor does it justify the state's priority claim on national income at the detriment of individual property rights. It is generally accepted as a legal adage that a moral obligation of one towards another does not in itself create a moral right of the other towards the one. Likewise, participants in society may have a moral obligation to contribute to its costs, but such an obligation by itself does not create a right for society to be compensated. Therefore, society has no *per se* claim on a person's earnings, regardless of whether society has been an enabling factor in generating these earnings.

One can concede that the state contributes to the creation of the conditions under which wealth can be produces and preserved. However, it does not follow, logically, that the state has exclusive entitlement to control all of the wealth thus created, as Murphy and Nagel suggest, because that would ignore the substantial contributions of the private sector to the wealth creation (Schoenblum 2003, 562–63).

[21] Scientist have discovered artefacts at Middle Stone Age sites at the Olorgesailie Basin in Southern Kenya indicating that hominins at that time (300,000 years ago) exchanged goods with others (Potts et al. 2018; Deino et al. 2018; Brooks et al. 2018).

[22] Modern markets are just a temporary end point in a long historical development, and we cannot reach conclusions on the functioning of markets and the intervening role of the state in isolation, i.e., without considering the historical roots and future direction of markets and the continued changing role of governments in these markets. If the state were to disappear tomorrow, markets would either continue their existence or emerge anew.

[23] Libertarians will argue, though, that other solutions than government regulation, such as consensual private ordering, are feasible and more appropriate.

1.5.2.3 The State as Co-owner of Individual Income

The crucial and preconditional role of the state in society is the reason Murphy and Nagel allocate direct rights to the state to some (not all) of the national income earned. On an individual level this seems to mean that one is not entitled to gross income earned, because part of that belongs to the state out of its requirement to be funded. In other words, the difference between gross and net income always belongs to the state and never to the income earner. Taxation, thus, cannot be a violation of property rights because the part of one's income that is 'taxed' is actually not owned by the taxpayer, but belongs rightfully to the state. This is essentially a return to seventeenth and eighteenth century absolutism under which levies were not tributary, "rather they were the appropriation by the king of resources the property in which was in a sense *already his*" (Snape 2017, 17).

Stated differently, because part of your income belongs to the state, taxation is in essence a manner of allocating ownership of income between the individual and the state. This would transform individual-owned property into joint-ownership, like a partnership between the state and the individual. This is of course not reality: a labor contract is not a tripartite agreement vesting an independent right with the state to part of the earnings of the employee; otherwise, if the employer were to default, the state would have a claim in bankruptcy to part of the unpaid earnings separate from the employee. Neither becomes my town a proportional co-owner of my home or car just because it levies an annual tax on the value of these items. Rather, this is an appeal to change our attitude towards taxation, or a moral argument – we should see taxes as an entitlement of the state. In essence, under this approach, the state becomes our feudal lord. Regardless the state's 'joint-ownership' of my income, it still depends on my labor to reap the fruits: if I for whatever reason am unable to work, the state is derived of its proportional share of the now-missed earnings. One could wonder whether Murphy and Nagel with vesting a priority claim with the state on earned income do not, unintentionally for sure, reinforce Nozick's position (1974, 169) that 'taxation of earnings is on a par with forced labor'?

The forced labor argument should be understood in conjunction with the thesis of self-ownership. Every person has full autonomy over himself both as a moral and a legal right. Each person fully owns herself, a right that cannot be usurped by someone else nor can be alienated.[24] If I own my body and my brain, then I also own the fruits of my labor when I put my body and brain to work. Thus, if I exchange my labor for money, that money must be fully mine as it is the equivalent of my fully owned labor that I have provided in return. Where the state creates entitlements for its citizens (certain services and/or share of the aggregate wealth), each taxpayer labors partially for the purposes of the state and of those who benefit from the state's

[24] Nozick's view that one could voluntarily enter into slavery (Nozick 1974, 331) is incorrect in that (1) such an alienation is not acceptable under the conception of self-ownership and (2) where an individual certainly could enter into a condition in which he would act in a slave-like manner, this would logically not constitute slavery simply because of the voluntary character of the arrangement (Feser 2000, 227).

largess (Feser 2000, 224). At a tax rate of 25%, one would labor 2 hours of a standard 8-hour workday for the benefit of others. Taxation of earnings, therefore, amounts to an enforceable claim of the state on an individual's labor. Where a person owns her labor as a derivative of owning herself, taxation does not only lead to her forced labor but, indeed, would vest partial ownership rights for the state in that person, violating the conception of self-ownership. Murphy and Nagel's position that part of someone's gross income belongs to the state, essentially acknowledges that our labor is partially owned by the state and, thus, establishes the state as our part owner and master.

1.6 Marxism

Marxism originates in the nineteenth century as a particular version of socialist theory. With ups and downs, it has remained influential throughout the twentieth century to the present in various forms including the Western European social-democratic model. Marxist and socialist ideas remain active in current political and academic debate. In its purest form, Marxism strives to socialize the means of production and abolish private property. It presents a form of radical egalitarianism (see Sect. 1.7 *infra* and Chap. 9) which is appealing to many, given the level of inequalities present in the world. Marxists argue that capitalism exploits workers and alienates the result of their labor. Marx developed the labor theory of value that perceives the value of any good to be the result of the labor that was put into making it. The labor theory of value goes back to John Locke's idea that by mixing one's labor with physical objects, one acquires rights to the fruits of that work. Capitalist profits come from alienating the 'surplus value' from the workers who created it. This theory is not without criticism. It ignores that goods are produced not solely by labor but through the managed cooperation of labor with capital. Workers receive compensation for their contribution during the manufacturing process in the form of wages. However, the contributors of capital are compensated only if the enterprise is successful, i.e., turns out a profit, and only at that delayed time, through the distribution of dividends. The contributors of capital take a risk that workers are able to avoid: if an enterprise fails, capital contributions may be lost, while workers have received payment for their input. Thus, the profits that an enterprise is able to realize do not arise from the exploitation of workers under capitalism.

Marx believed that socialism was a scientific theory, and as such amoral, and he rejected liberal moralism which he saw as ideology (Solt 2004, 9). Central to Marxist thought is the theory of historical materialism that holds that ideas and social institutions (such as religion, morality, law) develop only as the superstructure of a material economic base. Marx was strongly influenced by the dialectical method as developed by the German philosopher Georg Hegel. While Marx agreed with Hegel's basic dialectical thesis of social change, he rejected abstract ideas as the engine for that change. It his view, the dialectic of change is driven by material, economic forces, and our relationship to the natural world. Solt characterizes the theory of historical materialism as reductionistic. Marx should be honored for his recognition of the importance of economic factors, but ideas are as important factors to the constitution and change of society.[25] In fact, Marxism itself offer an argument for the power of ideas (Solt 2004, 9).

Marx' view of the working class as agent of social change triggered as capitalism evolved by its continuing impoverishment seems outdated; instead, workers have been 'coopted into the capitalist system' (Solt 2004, 9). Moreover, as McCloskey posits (see Sect. 1.7.2 *infra*), today the most important form of capital is human capital, i.e., skills and knowledge, which is largely held by workers.

Picciotto, in Chap. 5, traces the philosophical, political, sociological, and economic underpinning for the advocacy by socialists of progressive taxation, linked with the aim of socialisation of the ownership of the means of production, from the Communist Manifesto to recent supporters of tax justice campaigns. It shows how their attitudes to taxation have reflected their views on how capitalism rests on private property and state power, and how it could be transcended, including through progressive taxation. It discusses the views of Marx and Engels, from the revolutions of 1848 to the Paris Commune, and their influence on and the debates among German socialists (Liebknecht, Kautsky, Bernstein and Luxemburg), and the Austro-Marxists (Renner, Hilferding). It examines Goldscheid's arguments for a social science of the state centering on fiscality, leading to Schumpeter's different concept of the 'fiscal state', and how this was taken up in the 1970s and later by O'Connor and other Marxists.

The theories are examined in the context of the practical political engagement of their advocates, both struggling against autocratic capitalist states, notably the German socialists' dilemmas over welfare and warfare budgets, and then in government, including Lenin and the Bolsheviks, Hilferding as finance minister in Germany, and Schumpeter in Austria. It discusses socialist variants of Keynesianism, arguing that disparities of wealth generate growing inequality, and proposing tax measures for social ownership and equalization of property, notably James Meade, and most recently Anthony Atkinson and Thomas Piketty (who is also discussed in Chap. 9).

It concludes with reflections on what socialists can learn from these debates about transcending capitalism and the role and nature of progressive taxation in relation to the accumulation of capital particularly through large transnational corporations. This chapter focuses on socialism in this sense, especially the strand developed by Marx and Engels and their followers, and while it discusses revisionism it does not deal with social-democratic theories that defend private ownership of the means of production.

---

[25] Solt mentions the emergence of Christianity ending classical civilization, and humanism that concluded the Middle Ages.

1.7 Egalitarianism as Basis for Distributive Justice and Taxation

1.7.1 Introduction

Egalitarianism has its roots in the enlightenment (see Chap. 2), and we can distinguish between the Scottish and French schools. In the Scottish or Lockean tradition, equality means equal treatment both before the law and in interpersonal relationships, i.e., the recognition of our fellow human beings as equal in value regardless of social position. Adam Smith described as follows: "allowing every man to pursue his own interest his own way, upon the liberal plan of equality, liberty and justice" (Smith [1776] 1981, IV, 9, 664). Inspired by Rousseau ([1762] 1963) and under influence of the French Revolution (1789–1799), the concept of equality of the political left has evolved into equality of material outcomes. The latter philosophical approach is reflected in then-U.S. President Obama's speech in which he stated: "you didn't build that", referring to the legal and physical infrastructure upon which business owners are dependent, and used as an argument against unequal outcomes and pro taxation to fund public goods.[26]

Pedersen in Chap. 9 examines egalitarianism (taken in the French tradition's meaning) with a focus on how the tax system in combination with other measures and mechanisms can be instrumental in achieving egalitarian justice. He concentrates first on the egalitarian objective of eliminating relationships of domination and establishing a democratic form of power distribution as championed by John Rawls and in his footsteps Liam Murphy and Thomas Nagel, as well as Thomas Piketty, all influenced by the ideas of James Meade for a property-owning democracy. This form of egalitarianism seeks to find ways to mitigate repression, inherited status hierarchies, class privilege, and to ensure that political power is shared equally regardless of economic and relational differences. As these differences, to a large extent, are caused by inequalities in wealth and income, taxation is a key tool for arriving at a just society.

Pedersen points to the crucial role of the Liberty principle in Rawls' thinking, which ascribes to each individual an equal right to basic liberties, such as liberty of conscience and freedom of association, freedom of speech and liberty of the person, the right to vote and to hold public office, and, crucial to our argument here, the right to influence national elections. Rawls is aware of the distinction between formal liberties and factual liberties, which goes back to Karl Marx observation that formal liberties could be offset by inequalities produced by society/capitalism (see Chap. 5), an important thesis underlying feminist studies as well (see Chap. 10). Rawls was quite aware that the wealthy can exercise disproportional political influence simply because of their wealth.[27]

---

[26] *Election campaign speech* delivered in Roanoke, VA on July 13, 2012.

[27] To focus on the United States, where Rawls lived and worked, donations by the wealthy have enormous influence, directly or indirectly on the election process. Either through donations directly

Equality of opportunities is important to Rawls, which means that opportunities, such as a job or scholarship, are assigned to the best qualified person. For Rawlsian philosophers, this approach has to go further and include that people with comparable innate abilities and motivation have equal prospects of becoming best qualified. As Pedersen notes, Rawls tries to find a compromise between the idea of equal outcomes and the economist's view that the wealth of society as a whole will increase if those who produce more are allowed to earn more. That compromise is the difference principle: differences in outcome are acceptable only to the extent these provide benefits for the worst off. We notice here an important difference between utilitarians (see Chap. 3) and egalitarians: the former focus on realizing aggregate benefits for society as a whole, while the latter gear towards elevating the position of the worst off.

1.7.2 Egalitarianism and Taxation

The egalitarian approach to society has, of course, consequences for the types of taxation it allows. Beyond funding the cost of government, for egalitarians taxation must also serve to realize egalitarian goals of justice. Progression of income taxes serves primarily to prevent accumulation of wealth. Egalitarians widely support inheritance tax. Surprisingly to some perhaps, they agree in principle with libertarians that one should be allowed to bequeath money that is rightfully earned. However, egalitarians, following the lead of utilitarian Mill, want to limit the amount a single person is allowed to receive, taxing the excess inheritance at steep rates to prevent capital concentration. Egalitarians are critical of the modern welfare state model as being unjust because it continues to allow for concentrations of capital. Egalitarians endorse progressive income, wealth, and inheritance taxes for the single purpose of realizing a just society but would have less or no need for these taxes once the egalitarian utopia is realized. For example, high inheritance taxes of up to 80% will only be levied on extreme wealth transfers and with only a few intergenerational transfers the private wealth would be effectively diminished, i.e., the accumulated private wealth would be transferred from the private sector to the public sector. Taxes are purely instrumental to the ultimate goal, i.e., achieving distributive justice. Preventing accumulation of wealth is accommodated by a thin theory of property rights that allows individuals to hold personal property rights but not

---

to favorite candidates or donations to organizations that utilize funds to enhance partisan voter turnout, i.e., of voters that support the preferred cause or candidate. For example, Michael Bloomberg supports candidates and policies aligning with his gun control preferences; Charles and David Koch support libertarian (and Republican) politicians and causes, and Facebook's Mark Zuckerberg in 2020 donated hundreds of millions of dollars to one-sidedly increase Democratic party turnout in certain counties, i.e., that more Democratic votes would be casted relative to Republican votes, putting his foot on the scale of electoral outcome (In re of the 2020 election, see Hemingway 2021).

control over means of production or natural resources. This is a fundamental difference with the deontological approach of libertarians. Piketty (2014) claims that ownership is temporary; in my interpretation, he seems to opine that property rights essentially belong to society and are only held by individuals insofar allowed by society. Rawls and Piketty do not support an individual's right to bequeath in sharp contrast to libertarians who hold that ownership, logically, must include the right to give that what is owned away. In Piketty's view, taxation (particularly income and inheritance taxation) is not sufficient to realize equality and flanking measures are required to that end, such as universal basic income – an idea that harks back to Thomas Paine (cf. Chap. 2), labor representation on company boards, and equal access to education.

Piketty's focus is on the growing wealth disparity in society, i.e., the rich are getting richer, which he sees as problematic. In essence, his argument is that capitalism leads to inequality. It appears to me that Piketty mainly tries to sell European style social-democrat solutions, essentially state interventions in the economy and in the personal lives of citizens, to arrive at a utopian egalitarian society. Piketty, however, never substantiates why it is likely that his proposals will actually work and bring the desired results. An important critique of Piketty is that he is mistaken by viewing capitalism only through the prism of capital accumulation or concentration while ignoring its undeniable success in terms of betterment. The driving force of capitalism is not capital accumulation but innovation. Over the last two centuries, the position of all in capitalist society has significantly improved to the extent that the relatively poor of today in, for example, the U.S. are better off than the middle class in the 1970s measured in the quantity of consumption goods owned and the labor time needed to acquire these (Horwitz 2013, 2 cited by McCloskey 2014, 102). Defenders of capitalism will likely agree that capitalism does not lead to equal outcomes but may argue, utilitarianistically, that under capitalism everyone is better off and the aggregate level of prosperity, much higher than under any egalitarian, Marxist, or socialist economic system. As McCloskey points out, economists claiming that the economy is malfunctioning and requires massive state intervention, never show that the malfunctioning matters in the aggregate. Capitalism is not perfect, but it is also most certainly not defective. When we seek to reach perfection, we will fail because perfection is not an attainable commodity. Instead, she argues, referencing John Mueller (1999), we should be satisfied with reaching the stage of "pretty good" (McCloskey 2014, 80). In her view, there is little reason to be pessimistic about the functioning of capitalism – regardless of its imperfections and inadequacies – given "the largest enrichment per person humans have ever witnessed" (McCloskey 2014, 81). The rich getting richer is true only in a relative sense. It is not that the poor are getting poorer, or the middle class are facing reduced prosperity; on the contrary, the middle class and the poor are getting richer too. A fact ignored by the critiques of capitalism on inequality grounds is that inequality goes up and down over time. McCloskey (2014, 84) argues that government, the selected institution to solve inequality, is often the cause of wealth concentration in modern times and not capitalism. Inheritance is not the primary source of wealth, but entrepreneurial profit and trade-tested betterment that allows the poor to climb the social ladder and claim their own riches (McCloskey 2014, 87). Absolute poverty has disappeared in the West and will also vanish over time in the rest of the world. Piketty excludes human capital, being the main form of capital in today's world, from his definition of wealth. His argument for exclusion is that human capital cannot be owned (Piketty 2014, 46), which implies that he either does not understand or finds invalid (without explaining why) the Lockean concept of self-ownership. However, most important today are a worker's skills and knowledge and, thus, most of a nation's capital is actually held by workers (McCloskey 2014, 88–89).

The egalitarian tradition, presented in this chapter by discussing Piketty, Murphy and Nagel, relies on the state and government for social and economic action and change. Libertarians are sceptic of that reliance. Hayek, for example, recognizes the limitation of human rationality and therewith the limitations of grand government and central planning that ignores or reduces the role of the market. The market, in Hayek's view, is a form of government institution superior to government itself, because it allows humans to make choices and incorporates their myriad choices into an evolutionary process of perpetual improvement.[28] This does not mean that the outcome of market forces is always just, but it also does not follow that the outcome is unjust solely because it is the result of market forces instead of government intervention. Markets are not always subtle in their movements and may at times bring unjust results, but markets have an enormous capability for adapting to changing environments and demands, thus offering a more spontaneous, flexible, and immediate response to societal needs than bureaucratic institutions and political decision-making processes are able to offer. Markets are, thus, more effective. Moreover, markets react to grassroots demands, which are bottom-up, where governments actions are mostly top-down in approach; in addition, markets allow for individual differentiation while governmental decisions are mostly majoritarian, one fit for all, in nature. These observations support the argument that markets are likely more susceptible to democratic forces than representative forms of government.

Another objection to the approach of ideal theories, as postulated notably by John Rawls, is the internal contradiction in reasoning. If in the Original State we all agree to an egalitarian model of justice, we may assume all members of society would support it and to voluntarily work towards realizing that ideal. Consequently, there would be no need for government or the state to intervene and take action to redistribute wealth and income. Nevertheless, Rawls and other egalitarians such as Murphy and Nagel exactly call for state intervention and forced redistribution of wealth and income, which should be completely unnecessary if all were truly committed to realizing that purpose on a voluntary basis. It appears that egalitarians idealize the state and simply assume that the state will always act justly, operating like a machine programmed for justice, and overlook that the state by necessity employs humans to exercise its authority and, thus, operates within the realm of

[28] Hayek (1945).

human behavioral dynamics. Egalitarians are wrong in dismissing the free market systems as vehicles for realizing justice (Freiman 2017).

1.7.3 Luck Egalitarianism

1.7.3.1 Introduction

Although we may agree that all are equal in an abstract or moral sense, we are certainly all different in physical and mental capabilities, talent, intelligence, endurance, persistence, and social and economic background. To overcome these differences and ensure equal participation in society for all is the objective of egalitarians. The reasoning of this school of thought, generally referred to as luck-egalitarians or desert theorists, is that in an egalitarian society a person should be rewarded for what she deserves, i.e., what she has earned through her own efforts, not on the basis of qualifications and circumstances outsides one's control, received through "good luck" or "bad luck" (Dworkin 2000). Dworkin's abstract egalitarian principle that government must improve the lives of those it governs and "must show equal concern for the life of each" (Dworkin 2000, 128), is a normative ideal under which the government must determine which differences between individuals constitute morally relevant inequalities that must be mitigated. Differences in share of resources that are the consequence of an individual's choices (work hard/work less, study, saving or spending) are acceptable, but differences caused by circumstances are morally irrelevant in this respect.

Intelligence, good looks, talent for sports or arts, bad parents, illness, etc., are not earned or deserved, so any advantage or disadvantage derived from these endowments should be neutralized. In other words, these natural and social endowments are not received on the basis of merit or virtue or lack thereof, so there should be no (positive or negative) consequences in terms of any distribution to the extent that accomplishments can be attributed to these random endowments.

Not all will agree with the premise that those endowments are the result of mere "luck". Luck can be defined as a force that causes things to happen by chance.[29] Since the dictionaries describe it as a "force", the question arises whether "luck" has a source or a cause. We call something "luck" simply because we have no other available explanation for something happening, but if "luck" indeed has a source or cause, its attribution may not be coincidental at all. Two theories that can be seen as alternative for "luck" or that explain "luck" in this context are divine attribution and karma. The Declaration of Independence of the United States claims that we all have been endowed with inalienable rights by our Creator, and similarly one may argue that our natural and social endowments are also given to us by the same Creator and, therefore, they have not arisen from chance but are purposefully attrib-

[29] Cambridge Dictionary: dictionary.cambridge.org/us/dictionary/English/luck; Merriam Webster Dictionary: merriam-webster.com/dictionary/luck

uted to us, and we rightfully and justifiably own them. Consequently, we are entitled to the advantages derived from these endowments as they are bestowed on us by the highest authority. Indian philosophers may reason that our current natural and social endowments are the result of the aggregate of our actions (good and bad) in previous lives. Consequently, they are not coincidental or caused by chance but earned and deserved, and therefore, just.[30] Luck is a hypothesis as much as attribution and karma are hypotheses. All three of these approaches (luck, attribution, and karma) to the existence of natural and social endowments are equally valid as none of them can be either proven or falsified; but only when "luck" is considered the attributing factor of endowments, the issue of justice arises, providing reason for corrections.

The argument that the randomness deprives individuals of the entitlement to endowments is unconvincing, in my opinion, because it remains unclear why the state, society, or the 'collective' would have a stronger claim to these individual endowments than the individual actually endowed. If I own my body and my brain, I must by extension own the physical, intellectual, and emotional talents that are inseparably connected thereto, regardless their ultimate source (luck, God, or karma). Reversely, if I am denied ownership of my talents, by consequence I am denied ownership of my body and brain and, logically, must live in servitude to the collective which exercises authority over me through the agency of the state. One could argue that egalitarians do not deny an individual the ownership of her talents but claim the earnings they generate (Lister 2017). That difference is mostly semantic as these two are immediately related. If I own my talent, then I also own the earnings that my talents allow me to generate in the marketplace. Randomness, essentially, disputes the idea of merit and deserve and, thus, undermines individual self-worthiness and strengthens government's claim of authority over private property and individuals, in the end establishing the state as the all-controlling master over existence itself (cf. Schoenblum 2003, 568).

1.7.3.2 Desert Theory

If merit or desert should be the basis for distributional justice, under the egalitarian approach, these natural and social endowments should be negated when deciding on the distribution of rewards among community members. There are three related elements in desert theory: the subject (the deserving person), the object (the reward), and the virtue/merit on the basis of which the subject is entitled to receive the reward (Baiasu 2007, 180–182). In order to measure credit for a certain achievement, the extent to which these natural and social endowments have contributed to the overall

[30] Karma is not a single concept and different schools within Hinduism, Buddhism, and Jainism derive different definitions from the ancient texts. Conceptually it is first discussed in the *Upaniṣad* and is also discussed in the epic *Mahābhārata*. For a deeper understanding of the many theories of karma, see, e.g., Karl Potter (2001). Karma is based on the notion of cause and effect – you reap what you sow – which in that sense (and that sense only) is also found in the Christian tradition, see *Galatians* 6:7.

result must be determined and then subtracted from that achievement to arrive at the true merit of the performing person. Identifying the natural and social circumstances of each person may be a challenge but is not impossible (Moriarty 2005, 216). Baiasu (2021) suggest using Roemer's theory of equality of opportunity (Roemer 1993, 1998) to measure an individual's merit for a certain reward. He applies that, as an illustration, to the admission process for higher education. If we assume that the natural and social factors influencing success in secondary education can be determined (e.g., IQ, teacher quality, classroom size, and parental encouragement), students are categorized in groups or classes, each comprised of students who are equally impacted by these factors. Achievements are then scored on a scale of 100. Within the same class, the person with the highest score is the most deserving. If competing students are in different classes, their respective percentile rank within their own class will determine who is most deserving. For example, if Patricia and Peter are in the same class with scores of 90 and 85 respectively, Patricia would be more deserving. However, if Patricia and Peter are in different classes and Patricia's score lands her in in the 80th percentile in her class while Peter's score puts him in the 90th percentile in his class, Peter would be the most deserving for admission to higher education, regardless Patricia's superior intellectual faculty. Prima facie this approach seems to offer a good degree of fairness as a model to compare apples to oranges. Essentially, however, this method come down to a norm of comparative effort or, at least, effort under this method is the dominant factor for establishing the degree of merit as basis for the distribution of a particular reward. *In extremis*, this approach could also lead to the advancement of those with less ability at the detriment of the more talented ones. Imagine that Scottie Pippen and Michael Jordan were in high school competing with 75 other students nationwide for two basketball scholarships at UConn. Scottie and Michael are categorized in the same class of most talented players and their respective scores are 90 and 89, which lands them in the upper 80th percentile. A much less talented player from the class of mediocre talents ends up in the 90th percentile of his group, and neither Michael Jordan nor Scottie Pippen ever plays professional basketball.

An obvious challenge of this method of measuring comparative merit or desert is to identify adequately and completely all relevant factors in relation to the reward to be distributed, which is no sinecure, and the main objection to this method of allocating comparable bases of merit or desert to individuals for the purpose of equitable distribution of resources is the lack of practicability, not the use of desert itself as a criterion. It will require adequate tools to segregate properties of choice from those of luck. Scheffler (2010, 187) claims that it is almost impossible to make such a distinction because every choice "is routinely influenced by unchosen features of their personalities, temperaments, and the social contexts in which they find themselves." Society with some degree of precision must be able to determine who is deserving to the distribution of a certain resource and to what extent. The distinction between choice and luck may also lead to both excessive harshness, for example, by denying medical treatment to a person who chose not to take insurance (cf. Voigt 2007, 391), and excessive leniency by offering compensation not just for serious damaging conditions caused by let's say a crippling disease, but for any form of bad luck including, for example, physical unattractiveness (cf. Halliday 2013, 129). These objections are generally countered by proposing government programs that cover basic needs for all, such as a national healthcare system, free education, and a universal basic income (see, e.g., Barry 2006, 99–101; Knight 2009; Segall 2010). Meeting citizens' basic needs is perceived as a precondition for citizens to exercise their rights and liberties (Rawls 1993, 7; Tan 2012, 102). By doing so, the worst off do not suffer from deprivation, regardless the degree of responsibility they carry for their misfortune. Such an approach will likely lead to an increase in entitlement programs with on-going demands to expand coverage. Free education may start with kindergarten and elementary school, but voices will be raised to expand to secondary and then higher education; and pressure will build to widen the scope of medical services included in free healthcare.

A related question is who will set the criteria and will perform the measuring, i.e., what institution? I would assume a government funded, bureaucratic Office of Endowment Assessment. Next, questions arise as to procedure, appeal, and other due process guarantees, accountability and oversight.

1.7.3.3 Endowment Taxation

Another approach among egalitarians is to simply accept the existing allocation of resources; and then mitigate the advantages one individual has over the other due to the imbalance of their respective natural and social endowments by taxing these endowments. These taxes are then used for redistribution from those with above average earnings potential to those with below average faculties.[31] The mathematical result is equal income for all at the level of earnings produced by the average talented person.

Jonathan Swift's *Gulliver Travels* reports a proposal to tax female beauty where the tax base would be determined by the tax subject herself under the assumption that voluntary compliance would be optimum and predicting a high revenue yield.[32] Gulliver's travel is a satire, of course, and does not contain genuine tax policy proposals. But the idea, attractive to egalitarians, to tax individuals on the basis of their natural endowments has been proposed by serious economists, first by Francis Walker in 1888, later by Nobel-prize winner Jan Tinbergen (1970), and David Bradford (1984, 1986) to name a few.

Walker proposed to replace tax bases such as wealth, income, and consumption with what he called "faculty", i.e., the power of production. An equitable distribution of the tax burden could more accurately be achieved on the basis of what someone could earn than on actual earnings, the latter inviting indolence and waste of opportunities.

---

[31] Redistribution of the faculties itself, i.e., in kind, is of course not possible, so the compensation must take place in monetary form.

[32] Swift [1726] 1900, 233/4.

> …[A] faculty tax constitutes the only theoretically just form of taxation, men being required to serve the state in the degree in which they have ability to serve themselves (Walker 1888, 14–15).

Tinbergen was an influential economist who was a member of the Dutch social-democratic party and their leading economic policy advisor. He could be qualified as a non-dogmatic socialist because science was his starting point and frame of reference (Blok 1988, 36). An egalitarian, he believed that equal opportunities alone were insufficient and should be paired with equality of outcomes to arrive at an acceptable level of social or distributive justice. That premise, however, did not lead him to conclude that all should have the same income because he recognized that some jobs are more demanding. One of the instruments to achieve distributive justice he suggested was a tax on talents in the form of a lump sum payment. He realized that at the time talents could not be quantified but was hopeful that future research would make such a tax operational (Tinbergen 1970; Pen 1988, 57).

Bradford believes that taxes should vary depending on a person's opportunities rather than on an individual's choices. He prefers a tax based on an individual's potential earnings to separate someone's tax from his choice of what to do (Bradford 1986, 156). In his view, a person would be subject to a one-time tax at the beginning of his working years, the tax base being the present value of "his initial endowment of financial wealth and of future earning power" (Bradford 1984, 36). Alternatively, and economically equivalent, an annual tax would be feasible based on the maximum income that could be earned in the current year.

Endowment taxes avoid the deadweight loss of the substitution effect but allow for utility gains from redistribution.[33] The tax is degressive, and thus encourages productivity, as additional income generated beyond the estimated earnings potential remains untaxed. The endowment tax is attractive for egalitarians because it would allow for redistribution based on differences in luck rather than differences in choices. This last point is important for liberal egalitarians. Welfarist egalitarians are focused on accommodating distributive concerns and ignore the causes of inequality. Liberal egalitarians distinguish between acceptable and unacceptable inequalities, the former caused by free will choices made by an individual, an approach based on the notion of self-responsibility. If someone makes the choice to work less hours, then the outcome of lower earnings is acceptable and should not be compensated for through redistribution (cf. Cappelen and Tungodden 2018). The endowment of talent tax fits well in their philosophical approach.

There exist a number of objections against the endowment tax which we will briefly discuss below.

The first objection to taxing potential earnings is that it does not capture all differences in endowments between individuals but only those that translate into earnings. That is in itself true but is also unavoidable when taxation is chosen as a tool to mitigate advantages. Taxation, by its nature, requires a monetary base. If an

---

[33] Zelenek 2006, 1150.

endowment would consist of fame or prestige, which do not translate into a monetary reward, then taxation is simply not possible.

The second objection lies in the practical impossibility to accurately identify, assess, and value those endowments that lead to potential future earnings. This objection is valid only to a degree. Although currently we may not be able to identify and measure all endowment factors, it seems reasonable to assume that our capabilities in that respect will grow in the future with the advancement of social sciences. Moreover, measuring and assessing more and more factors will not necessarily lead to a significant different outcome.

The third objection relates to the possibility of cheating, i.e., a tax incentive arises if one were able to appear less endowed for the purpose of reducing the tax burden. However, this is not a convincing argument, because cheating would result in self-injury as intelligence, skills and capability testing would also determine access to higher education or other forms of talent training. By faking reduced faculties, one would indeed avoid higher taxes but, at the same time, one would slam the door of advancement in one own's face. One would be assessed a lower tax but also would be denied access to more lucrative professions as the result of failing the tests; in other words, as a result of cheating one would not be able to generate the higher earnings for which one has the talent.

Although the tax offers the advantage from a utilitarian perspective that it forces individuals to develop their most valuable talent, herein also lies its main risk and disadvantage, our fourth objection: the loss of individual freedom to choose one's own professional career, often referred to as talent slavery.

What if Michael Jordan had called it quits after high school basketball, and told his parents and the Office of Endowment Assessment that he wanted to pursue a nursing career? Where the purpose is to mitigate any advancements due to talent disparity through taxation, logically earning potential is the core determinant factor in deciding which talent is most valuable. Obviously, the earning potential of a professional basketball player is much higher than that of a nurse. The lowest paid NBA player since 2017 earned $925,000 annually.[34] Even at a low 20% tax rate, the taxes due on that income are more than double the average salary of $73,550 a registered nurse made in that year.[35] At the top of his career, Michael Jordan made over $33 million at the Chicago Bulls in the 1997/98 season;[36] the taxes at 20% over that year's income are over twice the life-time earnings of the nurse.[37]

If Michael's tax assessment would remain to be based on his anticipated basketball career income, a nursing career would be preempted. That may seem acceptable from a utilitarian perspective as Michael would be forced to develop his most

---

[34] Source: https://www.statista.com/statistics/minimum-nba-salary

[35] Source: registerednursern.com/rn-salary/

[36] Which is over $53 Million in today's dollars. Source: hoopshype.com/player/Michael-Jordan/salary.

[37] Assuming a 40-year career making an average salary of $73,000 each year, it would take a nurse 89 years and 284 days to earn enough to pay the $6.6 million in taxes owed on the $33 million salary.

valuable talent, but he would have lost his freedom to decide what professional career to pursue. Developing his basketball talent may be most financially beneficiary from a communal or societal perspective but would neglect his personal preference for the deeper gratification of caring for others, offered by nursing. This is the disutility dilemma associated with endowment taxation. Factoring in the disutility is possible but would effectively change the endowment tax into an income tax (Zelenek 2006, 1166).

Assume the situation that a person does not have a single outstanding talent but is, instead, endowed with two equally strong talents. She would face what I will call the Jayne Mansfield dilemma. Jayne Mansfield was an actress, singer, performer, and Playmate, starring in the 1950–1960ies as the then popular curvaceous dumb blond bombshell stereotype, while in reality blessed with a high IQ.[38] Given her intelligence and her talent for entertainment, how would the Office of Endowment Assessment rank her faculties? What would deserve priority, her beauty or intelligence, and why? If earnings potential is the determining factor, Jayne would be forced into the entertainment career. One might object to the chosen criterium and suggest that she would potentially make a more meaningful contribution to society as a scientist, but where taxation is the mitigating instrument, only earning potential would count. If Jayne would oppose an entertainment career, resisting to become a lust object, would her acceptance of a solid middle-class college professor income, liberate her from the obligation to pay taxes on the basis of her potential earnings as an entertainer?

These examples serve to demonstrate that egalitarianism can easily become totalitarian in application when ignoring personal preferences and, as a result, communal interests would always supersede individual interests, thus sacrificing freedom altogether for the advantage of equality and distorting the balance required for a well-functioning society. Perhaps the problem of talent slavery can be mitigated or reduced by assessing tax on someone's basket of talents, assuming that we all have more than a single talent. That would restore the freedom of choice to some degree but not completely. We would measure each talent and arrive at a weighted market value of all talents by affording each talent a score of its strength relative to the other talents combined with the market value of each talent. However, the weighted market value thus established and taxed would be lower than that of the most valuable talent but more than the least valuable talent, so taxation would still push for development of any of the more valuable endowments and make a choice for developing the less valuable talents financially infeasible. Moreover, although the weighted system would reduce the pressure to develop the most valuable talent and, thus, restore freedom of choice to some degree, it would of course also reduce the utilitarian optimum.

[38] She claimed an IQ of 163 but other sources mention an IQ of 149. Legacy.com/news/celebrity-deaths/jayne-mansfield-33facts; salon.com/2001/08/06/jayne_mansfield; projects.latimes.com/Hollywood/star-walk/jayne-mansfield; crfashionbook.com/celebrity/g26041893.jayne-mansfield-secret-moments/?slide=23

It has been argued that a very talented person could spend just enough time in the profession for which she is talented to pay the endowment tax bill, and then spend the rest of her time doing what she prefers to do. Both the lowest paid basketball player in 2017 and Michael Jordan in 1997–1998 had only to appear in 16.4 games out of 82 seasonal games to pay their endowment taxes of respectively $185,000 and $6.6 Million. The underlying assumption is twofold, first that a given occupation is available on a part-time basis, and second that the labor market would allocate the same hourly wages if a person is only available for sporadic work hours or only full time for a short period of the year. In many instances, however, part-timers are paid less per hour than full-timers in the same profession, and the issue of talent slavery remains. Even where true, it would not change the moral dynamic that someone would be forced into work she does not want to do. "[I]t would interfere with their liberty to conduct their life within the scope of the principles of justice" (Rawls 2001, 158). Musgrave (1974) has proposed to modify the endowment tax into a welfare tax, i.e., redistribution would take place to ensure equal welfare, measured as a combination of leisure and monetary units of consumption. Musgrave's proposal depends on a single standardized utility function and ignores differences in individual utility functions, including disutility associated with work. Therefore, the stated goal of equalized welfare is not truly realized. Moreover, combined with a lumpy labor supply, the talent slavery problem would also not be solved (Zelenek 2006, 1165).

The final objection against the endowment tax is found in its fundamentally illiberal nature. Applying Rawls' 'original position' methodology, David Hasen (2007, 1079) argues that the social contract would include a strong demand for "autonomy, understood as the right to posit and realize one's own ends with minimal interference from others." Constraints on autonomy in his view are allowed only to the extent needed to generate the benefits of social cooperation. Because only actual income is produced through social cooperation, only actual and not potential earnings can be taxed. Zelenek's main critique of Hasen is that his version of the social contract is not an exclusive one, i.e., under a different version of the social contract people in the original position might have agreed to an endowment tax (Zelenek 2006, 1171), for example as a Dworkinian low-endowment insurance. I agree but the same is true for Dworkin's version of the social contract. In this context it is worthwhile being reminded that the 'social contract' and Rawls' 'original position' are both fictional. Combined, they serve only as a theoretical method of reasoning to arrive at a model of distributive justice. If applying this method leads to a wide variety of outcomes, in other words: if people in the original position may give substantially different contents to the social contract, the validity and usefulness of Rawls' methodology itself becomes questionable.[39]

[39] There is no actual social contract every signed historically or contemporarily. It is a theoretical construct based on what free people might agree to if they were in the original position ignorant to their endowments. The original position has no historical basis either and the closest we can come to imagining the state of ignorance is Adam and Eve in the Garden of Eden, which is an allegory not history, and even there we see immediately differences in endowment between the happy couple, with Adam showing tardiness and Eve curiosity and initiative; endowments they would not have ignored if called to negotiate a social contract between them.

In my opinion, Hasen makes a valid assumption that autonomy is something people value and expect in a society, regardless of their endowment, although the preferred degree of autonomy may differ between individuals. Where he is correct, in my view, is that social cooperation does not produce income-earning capacity, simply because that capacity is derived from our natural endowments. From the libertarian viewpoint, as argued above, these endowments are personally owned, and the utilization of our endowments falls within the realm of our autonomy, reason why society or the state has no inherent right to tax the associated potential income, but only earned income which is the actual result of social cooperation. In contrast, egalitarians reason that in the original state we would likely give up most of our autonomy and agree to a social contract including an endowment tax. Dworkin's assumption of low-endowment insurance is not convincing, because it goes against human nature. Even if participants in the social contract negotiations are unaware of the relative strength of their faculties, they will realize that most of them are average and few below and above average. A social contract dividing the cake equally is only beneficiary to those with below average endowments. Those with above average faculties are worse off than under a regime of free exchange, and those with average faculties are neutral but may take their changes with a free exchange system because of the potential up-side it offers. People prefer to pursue their own interests. Even when they do not know what these interests are when starting negotiations, they will likely prefer a free exchange system that allows them to discover their talents and interests and bring these to full fruition for their own benefit than settling for an equal piece of the cake, regardless of contribution to the baking process. Empirical proof for a preference for autonomy is the USSR's failed experiment with collective farming through kolkhozy and sovkhozy where after 1937 the workers resigned from their duties and returned to individual farming which "held out the promise once again to be able to determine their own fate" (Merl 2016, §39). Collective agriculture failed in the Soviet Union because of the use of compulsion and the lack of material incentives for producers (Merl 2016, §44), and homestead farming proved to be far more productive than collective farming.[40]

At its core, egalitarianism is collectivism, because the differences between individuals are monetized (by estimating earning potential) and then distributed equality among all members of society. The weak point of the egalitarian reasoning is that it is exclusively based on speculation of what people might agree to if they had to forge a fictitious social contract in an imaginary original state.

The illiberal objection deserves some support, in my opinion. Under our current system, giving greater rewards to scarce talents serves to encourage the most productive uses of those talents. Earnings are used as an enticement; nevertheless, economizing talents remains an individual's choice. However, under an endowment tax regime, individuals are no longer enticed but forced towards the most productive

[40]The 2–3% of arable land held privately contributed 25% of total agricultural production in 1970–1980ies. See https://en.wikipedia.org/wiki/Agriculture_in_the_Soviet_Union

use of their talents as they are taxed on the assumed income these talents can produce. At the same time, because earning above those of an average talented person are taxed away, all rewards for developing talents are removed and what rests is sole coercion. The coercive character and the lack of liberty are, in my mind, convincing moral objections to egalitarianism.

1.8 Taxation Through Feminist Eyes

Feminist thought is heterogenous and broader in range of opinions even than Marxism, libertarianism, or egalitarianism. The only agreement between them is that the status of women relative to men should be improved (Solt 2004, 11). There are different schools, offering varying perspectives of the same social phenomena, and Davis in Chap. 10 focuses on three crucial areas of feminine thought as related to tax: dominance feminism, which sees gender differences through the lens of power; difference feminism, searching for remedies of different treatment between the genders; and intersectional feminism, which emphasizes the position of persons subject to multiple or combined discriminations, e.g., race and gender. Feminism, therewith, offers a rich variety of perspectives on tax. Moreover, feminism is not abstract but essentially focused on realizing practical equitable outcomes; thus, it provides valuable insights for developing more just tax policy. For feminism, equal economic and political rights are the ultimate goals, and the tax system serves to help achieve these.

Feminine tax scholarship is relatively young, making inroads only since the 1980ies, and relatively scarce even where feminine scholarship flourished in other disciplines.[41] Feminist tax scholarship borrowed three key insights from general feminist thought: (a) all legal categories and doctrines can reflect and reify gender division and bias; (b) law is often an agent of gendered power; and (c) legal theory and reform often fail to account for the ways in which gender intersects with other aspects of identity such as class, sexuality, and ability.

Feminist thought does not translate into a prescription of a specific feminist tax code. Feminism makes clear that factual neutrality in tax is a myth; rather, the Tax Code[42] is gendered in the sense that the choice for tax is the extent to which it will passively reflect, actively reify, or work to rectify such inequity.

Tax laws over the last decades have focused on economic growth detached from social justice and against gender equality (Gunnarsson 2020). Domestic tax laws are mostly legally neutral and meet standards of formal equality but may often have a substantial indirect impact on gender-related socio-economic inequalities, thus

---

[41] For an historic overview of feminist tax scholarship in the U.S., see Infanti and Crawford (2020).

[42] Davis refers to the U.S. Tax Code, but this is likely correct for the tax codes of almost all countries.

leave factual inequality intact.[43] Moreover, a neutral tax standard can receive biased interpretation from the courts. Tax law generally does not discriminate on the basis of ethnicity, gender, religion, etc., with few exceptions, such as the *Jizyah*, an annual tax which used to be levied on non-Muslim permanent residents in lieu of military service in countries governed by *Sharia* law,[44] and the *Fiscus Iudaicus*, the Roman Imperial tax on Jews.[45] Economic gender equality may be a general government objective or even a constitutional obligation in many countries, but tax policies and laws are seldom directed to addressing these goals. Tax law can be used as a tool to resolve factual inequality issues (outside of tax law) but, I would caution, that may over time lead to reverse inequality. If B suffers from a significant economic disadvantage compared to A, it makes the most sense to remove the cause of the economic inequality. Changing the tax law to mitigate the disadvantage would succeed in creating factual equality but would do so at the expense of creating formal inequality as B would receive preferred tax treatment to achieve socio-economic parity between B and A. If, over time, the socio-economic gap would be bridged by other factors, the formal inequity to which A remains subjected would re-create factual inequality but now at the detriment of A. Using tax law to mitigate socio-economic problems unrelated to tax has, therefore, its limitations and risks. Only if formally equal tax law leads to factually inequal outcomes, i.e., when the tax law is the cause of the de facto inequality, should amendment of the law be considered. Tax law could, e.g., affect the choice between paid work and unpaid care giving in several ways. Assume Joyce and John plan to marry and start a family contemplating having three children. John generates an annual income of 100 and Joyce of 60. They are discussing the choice between hiring a nanny and house cleaner for 40, or for Joyce to become a stay-at-home caregiver. Outsourcing the care services seems to make financially sense since Joyce's income is higher than the cost of care. They recognize the benefit of taking care of their own children, but Joyce would also like to further her career. Their accountant informs them that before their marriage each was taxed at 20%, the rate applicable to income up to 100, but as a married couple their incomes are joint, and Joyce's income is now subject to 35%. So, John and Joyce paid 20 and 12 in taxes before marriage, but after their marriage they do not pay 32 in tax but 41. By working, Joyce adds gross income of 60 to the household, but after paying tax of 21 and the cost of outsourced care at 40, the outcome is negative: (1). Given the financial implications, Joyce decides to become a stay-at-home

[43] The distinction between formal equality and factual equality has its roots in Karl Marx and can also be found in Rawls' philosophy.

[44] Jizyah is based on Qur'ān 9:29. It was paid by non-Muslims in return for protection and the right to practice their own religion. Certain categories, such as monks, religious functionaries, the elderly, women, the mentally ill, and the poor were exempt as well as those non-Muslims serving in the military. The tax was generally a fixed amount per income group.

[45] See, Couzin (2017). After the Jewish rebellion in Judea was defeated, emperor Vespasian imposed a head tax on the Jews wherever resident (in the empire) as a replacement (appropriation) of the religious Temple tax paid previously. On the Temple tax, see, inter alia, Chodorow (2007–2008, 62–65).

mom. Progressive income tax rates combined with joint filing status for married couples, as demonstrated with this example, de facto reduces the scope of the choice between care giving and paid work for women, and in outcome it discourages women to choose paid work and, therewith, it confirms traditional roles and, feminists argue, solidifies the patriarchal power structure of society. Now, compare John and Joyce with Jack and Janice. The latter generate the same incomes but live in a state where all income taxes are assessed on an individual basis only. Obviously, the outcome of the same scenario is different because both incomes are now taxed at 20% and they pay 20 and 12 respectively, or 32 in total. After tax and the cost of outsourced care services, Janice is left with discretionary income of 8. Now, assume that care giving cost are tax deductible. Jack and Janice can each deduct half the cost for income tax purposes. Jack has now a taxable income of 80, paying 16 in taxes; Janice has a taxable income of 40 also taxed at 20%, or 8. After payment for the care giving services, this would leave 12 in additional discretionary income for the household. Due to the taxation of individual incomes instead of combined incomes, Janice and Jack pay total of 32 in taxes where John and Joyce after their marriage pay 41. The additional deduction of care giving cost lowers the total combined tax for Janice and Jack to 24. If John and Joyce were to move to the other state, they would reduce their household tax burden to 32. However, if Joyce would become a stay-at-home mom, they would have no caregiving cost to deduct because they do not procure these services from a third party. As a result, comparing both households, Jack and Janice retain their gross income of 160, pay 24 in tax and 40 in care giving services, leaving 96 in remaining income; John and Joyce would forgo the latter's income to enable her to give care and have thus 100 in gross income, pay 20 in tax, which would leave 80 in remaining spendable income. This is clearly an unfair outcome and would discourage parents from caregiving to their own child, thus reducing their autonomy to make choices for their families, due to taxation. To bring both sets of parents on equal footing, insourced care giving should be treated the same as outsourced care giving, which can be realized either by also allowing Jack and Janice a flat rate deduction, or instead by providing a tax credit for each child, regardless of whether care services are insourced or outsourced, and disallowing any deduction of real costs incurred.

This example demonstrates inequality triggered by tax law which by necessity must be resolved by amending the tax law. I am hesitant for reasons explained afore to go so far as to use taxation as a tool to counter inequality caused by factors outside tax law. Davis mentions the proposal to compensate women for the wage gap by taxing their income at lower rates than men, basically ensuring that net pay is the same. *Ceteris paribus*, there exist no moral justification for paying women less than men, so the goal deserves support. But the means carry the risk of reversed discrimination when at some point in the future the gross wage gap is closed by other factors. Using tax for this purpose is disingenuous because it only provides compensation for the injustice but does not remove the injustice itself. Likewise, under this proposal, the underlying socio-economic causes of the wage gap would not be addressed but only softened through lower taxation.

Feminist studies gives us a fresh look at the impact of tax in the real world and demonstrates that the facially neutral tax code has substantial different outcomes for certain groups of people. Although income tax law is technically neutral as it measures taxpayers only by income, ignoring the particularities that distinguish taxpayers from one another – elevating the economic position of taxpayers as the only objective standard for tax policy – feminist studies show that this assumption forces all taxpayers to conform to a norm (Bird-Pollan 2019, 1, referencing Livingston 1998). Feminist thinkers have written little on tax. Given the diversity of feminine thought, feminist prescriptions for tax naturally lack consistency. Nevertheless, there are unifying threads in feminist thought on tax that make feminism an essential voice in the conversation on tax justice and the capacity of tax to shape society.

1.9 Lessons from Legal Positivism for Taxation Law

Legal positivism is an outlier because regardless its strong influence on legal theory in the last century, it is not truly a philosophical school. As Prebble and Shanske explain in Chap. 8, legal positivism is primarily a description of what law is or not and is to be distinguished from morality by certain formal structures which are characteristic of law. As such, legal positivism does not engage in questions about the nature of the state, the relationship between the state and its citizens, or the justification of taxation. In fact, the two leading positivist legal scholars of the last century discussed in the chapter, Herbert Hart and Hans Kelsen, have written hardly anything on taxation. What the authors in Chap. 8 do is applying some of the theoretical findings of these scholars to taxation. They start with a short general introduction to legal positivism and its meaning to tax law, in which they first observe that as a descriptive theory, legal positivism does not directly address questions of distributive justice. However, the topics discussed in the chapter touch larger and related issues of justice associated with tax law in two ways. Firs, if tax law as law is (partially) defective, this suggests possible rule of law issues; and if tax law fails from a positivist description of law, this might indicate limitations as to the value of positivism as a descriptive theory. Second, anti-abuse rules need to remain consistent with the rule of law, otherwise they may lose their effectiveness in advancing the distributive justice objectives for which they were implemented. The rest of the chapter is divided in two parts, one with focus on Kelsen and the other on Hart.

Kelsen's fundamental distinction between "is" and "ought" is the conditional syllogism underlying the legal norms. "If fact X exist, then consequence Y ought to follow." To be valid, laws must follow this paradigm. The chapter compares certain fundamental rules of income tax law, in particular the capital/revenue distinction, with some of the criteria for judging the quality of law propounded by Kelsen and concludes that income tax law suffers from shortcomings in meeting Kelsen's criteria, which explain tax law's incoherence and resistance to reform.

Although Hart did not specifically write about tax, his central contributions to jurisprudence might be relevant to philosophical discussions of taxation and this is demonstrated with the focus on general anti-avoidance rules (GAARs). In particular, the authors focus on the question whether GAARs violate the rule of law and, if so, whether that renders them illegitimate, to which end they analyze four different approaches with varying results. They conclude that GAARs are not a violation of the rule of law, but a different kind of rule of law for situations that do not lend themselves to rules.

1.10 Finally

An ideal society does not exist, and it is a metaphysical concept only. People have different values, and although some values may complement others, often however values conflict with one another. Compromise is possible to some extent, for example: one could agree to sacrifice a degree of liberty to realize another degree of equality. However, one cannot have complete liberty simultaneously with full equality. Therefore, choices between values need to be made and that is also true for one's approach to the role of government in society and the function and modalities of taxation. Several of these theories have been touched in this chapter and are dealt with in far more detail in the remaining chapters of this volume. It is important to realize, that there exists no separate political theory of taxation; rather taxation is a derivative of a general political theory. Hume's wise observation that our problems are connected to the abstract principles on which their solution depends, is often ignored in contemporary politics. Instead, we observe a tendency to quickly fix problems through an instrumental use of taxation, often directed at changing corporate or individual behaviors. However, to be effective and morally binding, tax policy should be driven by an underlying political philosophy. Insofar taxes are levied without consideration for political philosophy, i.e., on an ad hoc basis, the resulting tax system will be ill-designed, loaded with inconsistencies and contradictions, and lack structural soundness. What, whom, and how to tax should not be based on impulsive determination, driven by the perceived political need of the day, but instead follow logically from the underlying political philosophy adhered to by the legislature and the populace at large. In the absence of the desired structural consistency, taxation will be perceived as arbitrary and lacking moral standing. Taxation applied consistent with an underlying political philosophy would benefit from enhanced societal acceptance which, in turn, would positively affect compliance.

References

Baiasu, Sorin. 2007. Institutions and the Normativity of Desert. *Contemporary Political Theory* 6: 175–195.

———. 2021. Distributive Justice and the Epistemological Argument Against Desert. *Academia Letters*: Article 127. https://doi.org/10.20935/AL127.

Barry, Nicholas. 2006. Defending Luck Egalitarianism. *Journal of Applied Philosophy* 23: 89–107.

Bentham, Jeremy. 1973. A Critical Examination of the Declaration of Rights. In *Bentham's Political Thought*, ed. Bhikhu Parekh [1791], 257. London: Croon Helm.
Berlin, Isaiah. 1990. The Pursuit of the Ideal. In Isaiah Berlin, *The Crooked Timber of Humanity: Chapters in the History of Ideas*, ed. H. Hardy. London: John Murray.
Bird-Pollan, Jennifer. 2019. Taxing the Brave New World: A Comment on Professor Tessa Davis's Article 'Freezing the Future: Elective Egg Freezing and the Future of the Medical Expense Deduction'. *Kentucky Law Journal Online* 107: 1–6. Available at SSRN https://ssrn.com/abstract=3440861.
Blok, Aad. 1988. Jan Tinbergen en de Nederlandse Sociaaldemocratische Ideologie. In *Distantie en Engagement: J. Tinbergen Autobiographisch*, ed. Gerard Alberts and Pieter Weeder, 9–36. Eindhoven: Technische Universiteit Eindhoven.
Bobroff, Kenneth H. 2001. Retelling Allotment: Indian Property Rights and the Myth of Common Ownership. *Vanderbilt Law Review* 54 (4): 1559–1623.
Boesen, Ulrik. 2021. *Excise Tax Applications and Trends*, Fiscal Fact No. 753. Washington, DC: Tax Foundation.
Bonaham, O. Michael. 1953. Moral and Ethical Considerations in Tax Practice. *Marquette Law Review* 37 (1): 85–91.
Bradford, David F. 1984. *Blueprints for Basic Tax Reform*. Arlington: Tax Analysts.
———. 1986. *Untangling the Income Tax*. Cambridge: Harvard University Press.
Brooks, Alison S., et al. 2018. Long-Distance Stone Transport and Pigment Use in the Earliest Middle Stone Age. *Science* 360 (6384): 90–94.
Buchanan, Neil H. 2014. Freedom, Taxes, and Forced Labor: A Strange Brew of Libertarianism and Marxism. *Verdict*. Available at https://verdict.justia.com/2014/04/28/freedom-taxes-forced-labor.
Bushyhead, D.W., P. N. Blackstone, and George Sanders, Cherokee Delegation to Congress of the United States (Jan. 17, 1881), in SEN. DOCS., 49th Cong., 1st Sess., Serial 2362, vi.
Cappelen, Alexander W., and Bertil Tungodden. 2018. Tax Policy and Fair Inequality. In *Taxation: Philosophical Perspectives*, ed. Martin O'Neill and Stephen Orr, 111–123. Oxford: Oxford University Press.
Carneiro, Robert L. 1970. A Theory of the Origin of the State. *Science* 169 (3947): 733–738.
Chodorow, Adam. 2006. *God's Income Tax: What Jewish Tithing Practices Can Teach Us About Tax Reform*. Available at SSRN https://ssrn.com/abstract=889960 or https://doi.org/10.2139/ssrn.889960.
———. 2007–2008. Biblical Tax Systems and the Case for Progressive Taxation. *Journal of Law and Religion* 23(1): 51–96.
Couzin, Robert. 2017. A Modern Look at the Roman Imperial 'Jewish Tax'. *Canadian Tax Journal* 65 (2): 333–352.
Cowan, Edward J. 2020. *The Declaration of Arbroath: 'For Freedom Alone'*. East Linton: Birlinn.
Deino, Alan L., et al. 2018. Chronology of the Acheulean to Middle Stone Age Transition in Eastern Africa. *Science* 360 (6384): 95–98.
Dworkin, Ronald. 1973. The Original Position. *The University of Chicago Law Review* 40 (4): 500–533.
———. 2000. *The Theory and Practice of Equality*. Cambridge, MA: Harvard University Press.
Epstein, Richard A. 2011. *Design for Liberty: Private Property, Public Administration, and the Rule of Law*. Cambridge, MA: Harvard University Press.
Fergusson, James. 1970. *The Declaration of Arbroath 1320*. Edinburgh: Edinburgh University Press.
Feser, Edward. 2000. Taxation, Forced Labor, and Theft. *The Independent Review* 5 (2): 219–235.
Freiman, Christopher. 2017. *Unequivocal Justice*. London: Routledge.
Gordon, David. 2002. Property: Convention or Right? *The Mises Review* 8 (2).
Gosseries, Alex. 2005. Book Review, the Myth of Ownership: Taxes and Justice. *Disputatio* 1 (19): 271–277.
Graetz, Michael J. 1983. To Praise the Estate Tax, Not to Bury It. *The Yale Law Journal* 93: 259–286.

Gray, John. 1995. *Liberalism. 2nd Edn. Minneapolis: University of Minnesota Press.*

Gunnarsson, Åsa. 2020. *Gender Equality and Taxation: International Perspectives*. Copenhagen Business School [wp]. CBS Law Research Paper No. 20–29. Available at https://ssrn.com/abstract+3688899.

Halliday, Daniel. 2013. Review Essay of Kok-Char Tan, Justice, Institutions, and Luck. *Utilitas* 25 (1): 121–132.

Hasen, David. 2007. Liberalism and Ability Taxation. *Texas Law Review* 85: 1057–1113.

Hayek von, Friedrich A. 1945. The Use of Knowledge in Society. *American Economic Review* 35 (4): 519–530.

Hemingway, Mollie. 2021. *Rigged: How the Media, Big Tech, and the Democrats Seized Our Elections*. Washington, DC: Regnery Publishing.

Hobbes, Thomas. 1991. *Leviathan. Or the Matter, Forme, & Power of a Common-Wealth Ecclesiastical and Civill* [1651], ed. Richard Tuck. Cambridge: Cambridge University Press.

Hoebel, E. Adamson. 1954. *The Law of Primitive Man: A Study in Legal Comparative Dynamics*. Cambridge: Harvard University Press.

Horwitz, Steven. 2013. *Inequality, Mobility, and Being Poor in America*. Unpublished Paper, Department of Economics, St. Lawrence University, Presented to Conference on "Equality and Public Policy," Ohio University, Athens, OH, November 14–16, 2013.

Huemer, Michael. 2017. *Is Taxation Theft?* Available at https://www.libertarianism.org/columns/is-taxation-theft. Accessed 28 May 2021.

Ibn Khaldūn. 2015. *The Muqaddimah: An Introduction to History* [1377]. Trans. Franz Rosenthal. Princeton: Princeton University Press.

Infanti, Anthony C., and Bridget J. Crawford. 2020. A Taxing Feminism. Forthcoming in *The Oxford Handbook of Feminism and Law in the United States*, ed. Deborah L. Brake, Martha Chamallas, and Verna Williams. University of Pittsburgh Legal Studies Research Paper No. 2020-24. Available at https://ssrn.com/abstract=3659884.

Keen, Michael, and Joel Slemrod. 2021. *Rebellion, Rascals, and Revenue: Tax Follies and Wisdom Through the Ages*. Princeton: Princeton University Press.

Klieforth, Alexander L., and Robert J. Munro. 2004. *The Scottish Invention of America, Democracy and Human Rights: The History of Liberty and Freedom from the Ancient Celts to the New Millennium*. Lanham: University Press of America.

Knight, Carl. 2009. *Luck Egalitarianism: Equality, Responsibility, and Justice*. Edinburgh: Edinburgh University Press.

Kordana, Kevin A., and David H. Tabachnick. 2003. Tax and the Philosopher's Stone. *The Virginia Law Review* 89: 647–678.

Lister, Andrew. 2017. Markets, Desert, and Reciprocity. *Politics, Philosophy & Economics* 16: 47–69.

Livingston, Michael A. 1998. Radical Scholars, Conservative Field: Putting 'Critical Tax Scholarship' in Perspective. *The North Carolina Law Review* 76: 1791.

Locke, John. 2008. *Two Treatises of Government*, ed. P. Laslett [1689]. Cambridge: Cambridge University Press.

Lounissi, Carine. 2016. Thomas Paine's Reflections on the Social Contract: A Consistent Theory? In *New Directions in Thomas Paine Studies*, ed. Scott Clearly and Ivy L. Stabell, 175–193. New York: Palgrave Macmillan.

McCloskey, Deirdre. 2014. Measured, Unmeasured, Mismeasured, and Unjustified Pessimism: A Review Essay of Piketty's Capital in the Twenty-First Century. *Erasmus Journal of Philosophy and Economics* 7 (2): 73–115.

McGee, Robert W., ed. 2012. *The Ethics of Tax Evasion: Perspectives in Theory and Practice*. New York: Springer.

Merl, Stephan. 2016. Why Did the Attempt Under Stalin to Increase Agricultural Productivity Prove to be such a Fundamental Failure? *Cahiers du Monde Russe* 57 (1): 191–220.

Moriarity, Jeffrey. 2005. The Epistemological Argument Against Desert. *Utilitas* 17 (2): 205–221.

Mueller, John. 1999. *Capitalism, Democracy, and Ralph's Pretty Good Grocery*. Princeton: Princeton University Press.

Murphy, Liam, and Thomas Nagel. 2002. *The Myth of Ownership*. Oxford: Oxford University Press.
Musgrave, Richard. 1974. Maximin, Uncertainty, and the Leisure Trade-Off. *The Quarterly Journal of Economics* 88: 625–632.
Nagan, Winston P., John A.C. Cartner, and Robert J. Munro. 2017. Ideological Contributions of Celtic Freedom and Individualism to Human Rights. In *Human Rights and Dynamic Humanism*, 92–134. Leiden: Brill/Nijhoff.
Nozick, Robert. 1974. *Anarchy, State, and Utopia*. Basic Books.
Oliver, Neil. 2009. *A History of Scotland*. London: Weidenfeld & Nicolson.
Pen, Jan. 1988. Tussen Elite en Egalitarisme. In *Distantie en Engagement: J. Tinbergen Autobiographisch*, ed. Gerard Alberts and Pieter Weeder, 55–63. Eindhoven: Technische Universiteit Eindhoven.
Phillips, E.D. 1972. The Scythian Domination in Western Asia: Its Record in History, Scripture and Archaeology. *World Archaeology* 4 (2): 129–138.
Piketty, Thomas. 2014. *Capital in the Twenty-First Century*. Trans. Arthur Goldhammer. Cambridge: Harvard University Press.
Potter, Karl. 2001. How Many Karma Theories Are There? *Journal of Indian Philosophy* 29 (1/2): 231–239.
Potts, Richard, et al. 2018. Environmental Dynamics During the Onset of the Middle Stone Age in Eastern Africa. *Science* 360 (6384): 86–90.
Rawls, John. 1971. *A Theory of Justice*. Cambridge, MA: Harvard University Press.
———. 1993. *Political Liberalism*. New York: Columbia University Press.
———. 2001. *Justice as Fairness: A Restatement*. Harvard: Harvard University Press.
Roemer, John E. 1993. A Pragmatic Theory of Responsibility for the Egalitarian Planner. *Philosophy and Public Affairs* 22 (2): 146–166.
———. 1998. *Equality of Opportunity*. Cambridge, MA: Harvard University Press.
Rousseau, Jean-Jacques. [1762] 1963. *Du Contrat Social ou Principes du Droit Politique*. Paris: Union Général d'Éditions.
Scheffler, Samuel. 2010. *Equality and Tradition: Questions of Value in Moral and Political Theory*. New York: Oxford University Press.
Schoenblum, Jeffrey A. 2003. Myth of Ownership/Myth of Government. *The Virginia Tax Review* 22: 555–587.
Segall, Shlomi. 2010. *Health, Luck, and Justice*. Princeton: Princeton University Press.
Seto, Theodore P. 2016. *A Forced Labor Theory of Property and Taxation*. Legal Studies Paper No. 2016-04. Los Angeles: Loyola Law School. Available at https://ssrn.com/abstract2727378. Also published in *Philosophical Foundations of Tax Law*. 2017, ed. Monica Bhandari, 193–216. Oxford: Oxford University Press.
Smith, Adam. [1776] 1981. *An Inquiry into the Nature and Causes of the Wealth of Nations*. Glasgow edition, ed. Campbell, Skinner, and Todd, 2 Vols. Indianapolis: Liberty Classics.
Snape, John. 2017. The 'Sinews of the State': Historical Justifications for Taxes and Tax Laws. In *Philosophical Foundations of Tax Law*, ed. Monica Bhandari, 9–33. Oxford: Oxford University Press.
Solt, Roger. 2004. *The Handbooks of Moral and Political Philosophy Two: Contemporary Political Philosophies*. Denton: Paradigm Research.
Sterba, James P. 2004. Book Review: Liam Murphy and Thomas Nagel, the Myth of Ownership: Taxes and Justice. *Ethics* 114 (3): 628–631.
Swift, Jonathan. [1726] 1900. *Gulliver's Travels into Several Remote Nations of the World*. Boston: D.C. Heath & Co.
Tan, Kok-Chor. 2012. *Justice, Institutions, and Luck: The Site, Ground, and Scope of Equality*. Oxford: Oxford University Press.
Tinbergen, Jan. 1970. Belastingen op Bekwaamheid. *Intermediair* 6: 1–3.
van Brederode, Robert. 2020. Introduction: Why Ethics Matter in Taxation. In *Ethics and Taxation*, ed. Robert van Brederode, 1–19. Singapore: Springer.

Voigt, Kristin. 2007. The Harshness Objection: Is Luck Egalitarianism Too Harsh on the Victims of Option Luck? *Ethical Theory and Moral Practice* 10: 389–407.
Walker, Francis A. 1888. The Basis of Taxation. *Political Science Quarterly* 3 (1): 1–16.
Waltman, Jerry. 2002. A Review of The Myth of Ownership: Taxes and Justice by Liam Murphy and Thomas Nagel. *Journal of Lutheran Ethics* 2 (12).
Wanniski, Jude. 1978. Taxes, Revenues, and the 'Laffer Curve'. In *A New Look at Taxation: I. The Public Interest*, 3–16.
Wolff, Jonathan. 2016. *An Introduction to Political Philosophy*. 3rd ed. Oxford: Oxford University Press.
Zelenak, Lawrence A. 2006. Taxing Endowment. *Duke Law Journal* 55: 1145–1181.

Robert F. van Brederode (LL.M., Utrecht University, 1985; PhD Tax law, Amsterdam University, 1993) is University Professor at the Global Humanistic University, Curaçao, name partner of a niche tax consultancy firm, and an independent legal scholar. He is a former Big 4 partner, practicing in Europe and the U.S., and former in-house tax counsel to a Fortune 100 company. Previously, he served as assistant professor at Maastricht University, School of Law, professor of tax law at the Erasmus University, School of Economics, and adjunct professor at New York University, School of Law, Graduate Tax Program. His research area is public law and tax law both from a legal and economic perspective with concentration on International Tax and Global Indirect Taxes and particular interest for comparative studies, tax law interpretation, tax policy, and normative aspects of taxation. Robert published dozens of journal articles and 10 books on tax topics. His most recent books are *Virtues and Fallacies of VAT: An Evaluation after 50 Years* (Kluwer Law International, 2021), *Ethics and Taxation* (Springer, 2020), and both with Richard Krever *Legal Interpretation of Tax Law* (Kluwer Law International, 2nd ed., 2017) and *VAT and Financial Services: Comparative Law and Economic Perspectives* (Springer, 2017).

Chapter 2
The Enlightenment and Influence of Social Contract Theory on Taxation

Hans Gribnau and Jane Frecknall-Hughes

Abstract This chapter considers some of the most important political philosophers of the Enlightenment (taken as broad concept) – thinkers whose reflections on the idea of a social contract we relate to their views on taxation. Hobbes argues for an (almost) absolute political sovereignty and legal authority and corresponding obedience of citizens constituted by the social contract. For Hobbes, taxes are justified as the price of security. He advocates the benefit theory of taxation, best measured by consumption. The same goes for Locke, although for him the social contract serves to guarantee the individual's property rights which embody his liberty. Taxes are the price of the protection of the right to property. Both Montesquieu and Hume do not have need for a social contract: man living in societies is a fact of life. Their focus is on legitimate government rather than sovereignty and obedience. Hume inherently adheres to the benefit theory of taxation as paying tax is contributing to society on which one depends to survive. Montesquieu is a proponent of indirect taxation, though he considers progressive taxation and a subsistence minimum which must not to be taxed. For him, tax fairness is a contextual affair, since taxation should be relative to a given form of government. Rousseau radicalises the notion of the social contract which is a device to protect an equal freedom for all. He transposes the emerging new ideal of equality to taxation which not only is to enable government to protect its citizens, but also to consider their subsistence. Taxes should enhance liberty and equality (distributive justice). Thus, progressive taxation based on the ability to pay is put on the agenda. Rousseau's popular sovereignty was self-evident for Paine, the Federalists and Anti-Federalists alike. Paine argued for a more radical redistribution as taxes should pay for welfare provision which was part of his proposals for reform. Both the Federalists and Anti-Federalists elaborated on Montesquieu's plea for the separation and distribution of powers, but unlike

H. Gribnau (✉)
Tilburg University, Tilburg, The Netherlands

Leiden University, Leiden, The Netherlands
e-mail: J.L.M.Gribnau@tilburguniversity.edu

J. Frecknall-Hughes
Nottingham University Business School, Nottingham, UK

R. F. van Brederode (ed.), *Political Philosophy and Taxation*,
https://doi.org/10.1007/978-981-19-1092-0_2

Montesquieu, their take focus was on multi-level governance. Like the other theorists, they approached taxation from their political-philosophical perspective.

Keywords Hobbes · Locke · Hume · Montesquieu · Rousseau · The Federalists and Anti-Federalists · Paine · Social contract theory · Tax/political philosophy · Benefit theory · Justice · Equity · Equality · Liberty · Separation of powers

2.1 Introduction

Not all scholars agree that there was an Age of Enlightenment but see the development of ideas it particularly embodied as an on-going process. However, men were aware of it at the time. Porter (2000, 3) cites a letter[1] from Antony Ashley Cooper, third Earl of Shaftesbury, to a comrade in The Netherlands in 1706:

> There is a mighty Light which spreads it self all over the world, especially in those two free Nations of Holland and England … [If peace comes] it is impossible but Letters and Knowledge must advance in greater Proportion then ever … I am far from thinking that the Cause of Theisme will lose anything by fair Dispute. I can never … wish better for it than when I wish the Establishment of an intire Philosophicall Liberty.

Old, long-established ideas were re-examined and demystified, with a new freedom from the religious restrictions of previous centuries (Halévy 1928, 5; Israel 2002, 24). It was a long-lasting phenomenon, and while its dates are disputed depending on the various aspects considered, it is often taken to be synchronous with the period 1688 to 1799, the so-called 'long' eighteenth century, although some see Enlightenment attitudes emerging as early as the late sixteenth century (at least in England – see Hampson 1968, 15). As societies develop and adopt ideas at their own rates, it is very difficult to be definitive about the dates of such a phenomenon, or its precise meaning in different contexts (see Outram 2005). No form of thinking or set of hitherto accepted facts was free from examination under this new light of thinking – including taxation. As Locke so aptly put it in *An Essay Concerning Human Understanding* (Book I, II: 24):

> So much as we ourselves consider and comprehend of truth and reason, so much we possess of real and true knowledge. The floating of other men's opinions in our brains, makes us not one jot the more knowing, though they happen to be true. What in them was science, is in us but opiniatrety; whilst we give up our assent only to reverend names, and do not, as they did, employ our own reason to understand those truths which gave them reputation.

The aim of this chapter, then, is to examine the theories developed in regard to taxation by Enlightenment theorists, especially the school of thinkers who have become known, broadly speaking, as social contract theorists – as well as those who paved their way – individuals such as Hobbes, Locke, Hume, Rousseau, Montesquieu,

[1] The cited letter is *Letter to Jean Le Clerc* (1706), quoted in Rand (2010 [1900], 353).

Paine, and certain other European and American writers. The Enlightenment saw the occurrence of events such as the Seven Years' War (1756–1763), the American Revolution (1775–1783), the French Revolution (1789) and the Napoleonic Wars (1793–1815), wherein taxation played a significant role, and which influenced the views of many thinkers of all kinds worldwide, whether political, legal, economic or philosophical. The relationship between governments and their subjects was a key focus as was the development of various kinds of rights. We will take a thematic approach to the writers considered here, teasing out in reference to taxation their views on the role of the state and its relationship with its citizens, private property rights and the fairness of taxation. We will consider their approaches justifying taxation and the immanent values that make taxation just. Many theorists developed new ideas during the Enlightenment, some of whom are considered elsewhere in this book with reference to more particular aspects of their thinking.

Moreover, these writers responded in different ways to the major political issues of the particular political society and time in which they lived. The concepts of the state of nature and the social contract, for instance, key to early modern political theory, gradually became less central to overall discussions. Owing to their diverging assumptions and analysis of the major (often overlapping) political issues they faced, it is hardly possible to categorise neatly the divers and diverse elements of their ensuing theoretical approaches to, and elaboration of, taxation issues so as to fit them neatly under the same headings.

In a work of this kind, it is always difficult to decide who should be included and who not, and space constraints permit consideration of only the main protagonists. Individuals considered here belong to various different schools of philosophical and political thought: there is no over-arching 'Enlightenment School', so to speak, but a pervasive theme underlying their writings is radicalism in its most basic meaning of starting from the roots of ideas and developing them, often in ways that were also radical in a more political sense and possibly reflected the turmoil they experienced in their own lives. In presenting these ideas it may suffice to give an extended citation but sometimes an analysis in more detail is needed.

2.2 Thomas Hobbes (1588–1679)[2]

2.2.1 Introduction

Thomas Hobbes was witness to turbulent years of English history. The political upheaval of the mid-seventeenth century meant the disintegration of the early modern polity. The civil war fought between the king, Charles I, and parliament in 1642–1646 was disruptive. Charles's problems were not confined to England. Events in Scotland and in Ireland contributed to the collapse of his authority.

[2] This section summarises Gribnau and Dijkstra (2019) and Gribnau and Dijkstra (2020).

Dramatic transformations thus occurred. A commonwealth and military rule replaced the abolished monarchy and the House of Lords. The behaviour of parliament did probably strengthen Hobbes's belief that democracy was prone to collapse into chaos and factionalism (Ryan 1996, 235). Hobbes started to develop his theories in the context of this political upheaval (Sommerville 2012, 3). The Thirty Years Wars, the last international religion-inspired conflict in Europe, certainly also contributed to the development of Hobbes's insights (Martinich 1999, 38, 84–85).

Hobbes viewed human life as "perpetuall and restlesse desire of power after power, that ceaseth onely in Death" (*Leviathan* XI, 70). If men are not restrained "by fear of a common power, they will distrust and fear each other" (*On the Citizen, Preface to the Readers* 10). This natural inclination fuelled conflict and civil war. This explains the pervasive need for security which drives Hobbes's political thinking. Moreover, Hobbes held that the behaviour of human beings is strongly determined by their education or training, which generates conflict (*Leviathan* XI, 73; cf. *On the Citizen, Preface to the Readers*). Unlike in the more optimistic Humean view, it is inadequate moral upbringing rather than fundamental human nature that animates civil conflict (*Leviathan* VI, 41–42). The point Hobbes drives home is that other-regarding human traits are an inadequate basis on which to build a workable political theory. Hobbes's perception of people's lack of viable sociability accounts for his focus on security which should be provided by a strong sovereign.

In the natural condition all men are equal, having an unlimited but rather useless natural right to preserve themselves. Because of this equality, there is no natural authority among men. All authority has to be instituted "by the consent of those who authorize a sovereign to make law and to permit his will to stand for theirs" (Riley 1982, 25). For Hobbes, virtually any government would be better than a civil war (*Leviathan* XVIII, 128). To assure stability and prevent dissolution into civil war, people ought to submit themselves to a government with almost unlimited power.

The origin of the sovereign authority to command (and the obligation to obey) has roots in a social contract that institutes sovereignty. The people in the state of nature are presumed to confer their power to a common authority. The duty to obey the law is created by the social contract – itself depending on trust (Riley 1982, 26). By entering into this contract, people agree to give up their right to act solely on their private judgment, and "to act instead on the judgment of the sovereign, as expressed by the civil law" (Steedhar 2012, 192). The main thrust of Hobbes's argument throughout his moral and political writings is the necessity of making private judgment take second place to public judgment wherever the two come into conflict.

To justify the establishment of sovereign authority and the obedience to its laws, Hobbes paints the picture of life in a state of nature, that is, an imaginary condition without government (no person was ever actually in the state of nature). For Hobbes, the natural condition is "one of liberty, equality, and the most extensive individual rights imaginable" (Hoekstra 2007, 122). However, exactly because of this liberty and equality, the state of nature is a "dissolute condition of masterlesse men, without subjection to Lawes, and a coercive Power to tye their hands from rapine, and revenge" (*Leviathan* XVIII, 128). Each person in the state of nature has a right to preserve himself, which Hobbes terms "the right of nature" (*jus naturale*) (*Leviathan*

XIV, 91). However, the right of each to all things invites conflict and even war, with men competing for resources. Therefore, nobody will be secure in the state of nature. Self-preservation is permanently at risk.

In this condition everyone is equally vulnerable to violence and uncertainty and no one can expect to be able to dominate the others. Absent a supreme authority that can lay down and enforce rules to govern human interaction, unrestricted competition for scarce goods between people makes enemies of them. Competition, diffidence and glory, all rooted in scarcity, are the three principal causes of quarrels – or the war of all against all (*Leviathan* XIII, 88, 90; Ryan 1996, 219–222 and Newey 2014, 85–88). Such an ungoverned condition is devoid of sociability and civilisation (*Leviathan* XVIII, 128).

2.2.2 Social Contract: Security Justifies Obedience

The desire to preserve their own lives is very strong in most people. Under pressure of necessity, their passions and reason make men choose a sovereign-making covenant. The natural laws, being dictates of reason, prescribe men to seek peace and give up part of their natural liberty – as much as others will do (first and second law of nature; *Leviathan* XIII, 90–92; Jaume 2007, 202–203 and Ryan 1996, 222–224). They agree to leave the state of nature by establishing the civil state. This can be done only by submitting to some mutually recognised public authority, by using a legal device, the social contract, which marks the transition from the state of nature to the civil state. The contract or covenant is concluded by self-interested individuals driven by the fear of death (*Leviathan* XIII, 90).

The contract consists of a mutual agreement among the many to submit to one or a few, who are expected to lay down the rules that will enable the many to coexist peacefully with one another. Thus, this pact is aimed at establishing rule and premised upon the idea of human equality: an agreement by a multitude of equally free individuals (Sorell 2007, 147). More specifically, the original contract is a combination of conferring of power, consenting to be governed, and mutual transfer of right to the sovereign who is not a party to this contract (*Leviathan* XVIII, 122).

The citizen's obligation to obey the law, the command of the sovereign, is thus rooted in the social contract. However, the obligation to obey the commands of the sovereign is not established by a contract between governors and governed, but a covenant "of every man with every man" whereby each gives up his right of governing himself to one man or assembly of men, on condition that the others do so too (*Leviathan* XVII, 120). There is no obligation to observe the laws of nature in practice unless one has sufficient security that the others will observe the "same Lawes towards him" (*Leviathan* XV, 110).

Since the sovereign is given authority by covenant to which he is not a party, he cannot forfeit the authority given to him by covenant "by breach of covenant" (*Leviathan* XVII, 110). This is Hobbes's almost absolutist theory of the state (Harrison 2012, 33; May 2013, 65). The sovereign can do no wrong (*On the Citizen*

VII, 14, 97). Laws can be unfair, but Hobbes argues, they must be complied with. After all, the sovereign power of command came about through the social contract. That is an agreement, and one should observe such agreements into which one has voluntarily entered. The exception to the far-reaching duty to obey is based on the right to self-preservation, which indeed is the very ground of the social contract, and therefore the (civil) state. Self-preservation is an inalienable right (*Leviathan* XXI, 153).

The wise sovereign has certain duties, nonetheless, derived not from contract, but from the law of nature (Lobban 2012, 53). These duties derive from the fundamental duty to procure the safety of the people: "the safety of the people is the supreme law" (*On the Citizen*, XIII, 2, 143; *Leviathan* XXX, 231). Safety, for instance, requires that justice "be equally administred to all degrees of People [...] For in this consisteth equity" (*Leviathan* XXX, 237). However, Hobbes adds, the sovereign is accountable to God and to no one else. The duty is not a (binding) legal obligation.

Submitting to the sovereign authority does nothing to subvert people's liberty. Liberty is the capacity of doing something in the absence of external impediments (*Leviathan* XXI, 145). Liberty is defined by the sovereign's commands (*Leviathan* XXI, 148). For Hobbes, arbitrary power within a civil association does not undermine its freedom. Liberty is only undermined by overt actions of interference (so-called negative liberty; Berlin 1958, 122). Government's interference with its subjects' liberty must basically aim to preserve the life and health of the state and "hence the common good or public interest of its subjects" (Skinner 2009, 348). Liberty in the civil state is for Hobbes the liberty to decide for ourselves in circumstances not regulated by the civil law (*Leviathan* XXI, 148). The laws also protect citizens from incursions by fellow citizens. For Hobbes it is apparently sufficient that subjects enjoy their "civic rights and liberties as a matter of fact; the mere presence of arbitrary power within a civil association does nothing to subvert our liberty" (Skinner 2008, 212). Hobbes's negative liberty depends on the "Silence of the Law" (*Leviathan* XXI, 152) which seems to leave the subject entirely at liberty without any public-spirited self-restraint.

As taxation is generally seen as an infringement of the right to property, the question is whether Hobbes sees the right to property as an inalienable right. The answer is simply no: since there is no such thing as a natural right to property in the natural condition, it follows that the right to property is created by the civil law and dependent on the sovereign will (*Leviathan* XXIV, 171). The sovereign has the authority to dispose of his subjects' properties as he sees fit. There is no right to property he has to respect. For Hobbes, even the belief that one can invoke a right to property against an all-powerful sovereign authority is a seditious opinion which should be rooted out (*Human Nature* and *De Corpore Politico* XXVIII, 176).

2.2.3 Law as Command

Hobbes's conception of law reflects the notion of (nearly) absolute sovereign power (*Leviathan* XV, 111). Importantly, the sovereign who issues a command "intends his expressions of intention to be taken as a reason for doing them [...] independent of the content or character of the actions to be done" (Hart 1982, 254). This fits well in with legal positivism (Goldsmith 1996, 275). The validity of laws is therefore a matter of form, not content. Hobbes does not require the laws (sovereign commands) to comply with principles of justice or substantive moral values, for example a fair distribution of the tax burden. On the contrary, distributive justice is not natural but conventional, and it is up to the sovereign to determine justice. Justice and morality are an effect of the law issued by the sovereign (*Leviathan* XIII, 90. Cf. *Dialogue Between a Philosopher and a Student of the Common Laws of England* (henceforth *Dialogue*), 72–73). To argue that some tax or tax assessment violates the 'higher' value of distributive justice therefore does not make any sense.

The sovereign (an assembly or one man) who has the power to make, change and repeal laws is not even bound by his own laws (*Leviathan* XXVI, 184). This also goes for tax laws. In principle no law can be unjust, since the law-making sovereign represents the subjects who therefore are considered to be the author of the laws. Hence, a good law has little to do with justice content-wise. "By a good law I mean not a just law, for no law can be unjust" (*Leviathan* XXX, 239). Moreover, statute law is primary since the law emanates from the sovereign's law-making authority. This legislation is the embodiment of reason (*Dialogue* 58; Goldsmith 1996, 91).

2.2.4 Tax Principles and Benefit

For Hobbes, taxation is a necessary part of any commonwealth. Taxation in intimately linked to security and the enjoyment of life. His main focus is on public security and need for public revenue to provide for the payment of the armed forces. Taxes are "the wages, due to [the sovereign], to defend private men in the exercise of several trades and callings" (*Leviathan* XXX, 238). As all subjects benefit from the peace, they all should pay taxes. Circumstances determine the amount of taxation required, but it must be limited to the maintenance of civil peace and national security (*Leviathan* XXIV, 172–173; Shapiro 1986, 32–33).

Actually, there are virtually no limitations to the tax system to be established by the sovereign. As long as taxation does not threaten the self-preservation of the subjects, it is justified. Citizens have a natural right to resistance if the exercise of sovereign power affects their self-preservation and security. The subjects, therefore, retain a right to disobey commands when their lives are at stake (*Leviathan* XXI, 151).

The subjects have no property rights against the sovereign and can therefore legitimately be taxed. Law interferes with subjects' liberty but, outside the interferences authorised by a law, individuals possess a sphere of autonomy. Taxes, therefore, should be imposed by laws; if the sovereign has not issued a command to pay tax, no such obligation exists. The obligation to pay tax – an interference with subjects' liberty – has to be laid down in a command. It is up to the sovereign to determine this obligation. This obligation should be codified, prescribed by law, that is, a command.

As shown above, the wise sovereign has certain duties that follow from the law of nature. In his earlier work, *De Corpore Politico*, Hobbes says: "For the duty of a sovereign consisteth in the good government of the people" (XXVIII, 172). He continues, "*salus populi suprema lex* must understood not to refer to the mere preservation of the lives of the subjects, but "generally their benefit and goods".

This must have consequences for tax. Hobbes offers certain principles the sovereign should follow in determining the tax burden. Equality is a very important one. The burden of tax should be equally borne. Citizens often complain about taxes which they find too easily oppressive, he says. However, "it is not so much the burden itself that men object to, as the inequality" (*On the Citizen* XIII 10, 147. Cf. *Leviathan* XXX, 238). Therefore, he considers complaints justified when burdens are imposed on the citizens unequally (cf. *De Corpore Politico* XXVIII, 174).

Tax exemptions are thus very sensitive matters which lead to much envy. It is in the interest of public quiet to remove all just complaints, and therefore it is a duty of the sovereign authority to ensure that public burdens are equally borne. According to Hobbes, tax exemptions should be avoided because they fly in the face of equality.

Equal taxation is not only in the interest of public peace, for it is also a matter of natural law. For Hobbes, since what subjects contribute to the community is nothing else but the price they pay to purchase peace, it is logical that those who equally share in the peace should pay an equal part – either by contributing money, or service to the commonwealth. It is a law of nature that in assessing others' rights every man should treat himself as equal to every other man. Hence, sovereigns are obliged by natural law to impose the burdens of the commonwealth upon the citizens equally (*Leviathan* XIII, 10, 147).

Of course, the question is: equality of what? Hobbes elaborates on equal taxation. It is not about monetary equality, so he does not advocate a head tax. Rather, equal taxation refers to equality of burden, that is to say, proportionate equality between burdens and benefits. Tax is a contribution to the community paid to purchase peace and, of course, all citizens equally enjoy peace. Yet the benefits springing from this peace are not equally distributed among the citizens, for some acquire more property and others less. That would suggest taxing wealth.

Taxing wealth is a bad idea, however, because people who possess equal wealth need not have acquired equal property – because consumption diminishes personal wealth. Some may be thrifty and keep what they have, says Hobbes, but others may waste their money on luxury goods. Paying taxes in proportion to wealth thus implies that people do not bear the burdens of the commonwealth equally – while equally enjoying the benefit of peace. He argues that this method "of exacting money is against equity, and likewise against the duty of sovereigns, and that [citizens being taxed in proportion to their consumption] is consistent with reason, and with their duty" (*On the Citizen* XIII, 10, 148). Subjects thus should contribute to the public purse, in proportion to their consumption, which implies that "things should be taxed, so that each man contributes in proportion to consumption" (*On the Citizen* XIII 10, 148).

So, to Hobbes, government benefits were to be best measured by consumption. Indeed, it was "the heyday of the benefit theory of taxation, according to which a person should pay for what he gets" (Groves 1974, 14). Moreover, Hobbes's suspicion of luxury shows. This aversion and the willingness to see luxury consumption curtailed, was another commonplace of Hobbes's time (Groves 1974, 15).

2.3 John Locke (1632–1704)

2.3.1 Introduction

Undoubtedly affected by the upheaval of the times in England through which he lived, and during which he himself was a politically active figure (especially in the English Civil War, the restoration of the monarchy and the 'Glorious Revolution'), Locke was an influential figure, with a varied career, ranging from being an Oxford don, later doctor and medical researcher, and friend of, assistant to, physician to and political ally of Anthony Ashley Cooper (later Lord Shaftesbury). He himself was embroiled with Shaftesbury in what became known as the exclusion crisis, whereby James II was ultimately barred from the throne of England because of his Catholicism. Locke's chief work was as Secretary to the Board of Trade and Plantations and secretary to the Lords Proprietors of the Carolinas, being involved in drafting the fundamental constitution of the Carolinas. He also served as a Commissioner of Appeals for Excise in 1689, on his return to England after leaving because of his involvement in the exclusion crisis.

Locke was a friend of Robert Boyle, Robert Hooke and Isaac Newton, and was greatly influenced by Boyle's scientific method of starting from first principles. He himself had seen many established institutions eradicated and replaced by something new – the monarchy, the House of Lords, the Anglican Church and the Cromwellian Protectorate – and this idea of starting from first principles pervades much of his writing. For instance, in *An Essay Concerning Human Understanding (Epistle to the Reader)* (1690a, 9–10), he saw himself as "clearing the ground a little, and removing some of the rubbish that lies in the way to knowledge", and throughout *Book I* of the *Essay* uses the term *tabula rasa* ('blank slate') to describe the state of the mind before experience writes upon it. More exactly, a *tabula rasa* is not so much a 'blank slate' as one which has been 'scraped clean' (the basic meaning of *rasa*) of earlier contents for reuse.[3]

[3]The term is derived from the Roman use of a wax tablet (*tabula*), which was made of wood and covered with a layer of wax for writing on, which could be scraped and smoothed for reuse, getting

Locke's political thoughts are contained predominantly in his *Second Treatise of Government, Part I* (1690b) and *Part II* (1690c) in which he develops his theories from first principles. In his *Part II* (1690b, Chapter 2.4), for instance, he aims to define political power "from its original". Adams and Dyson (2003, 66) comment that "Locke's political theory is, above all, a theory of resistance … a theory of revolution, published after all, to defend or in some sense celebrate the removal of James II from the throne of England". This point about Locke's radicalism is seldom made, but it is supported by the fact that the *Two Treatises* were written about ten years before they were published, as "they would have been treasonable beyond doubt had they been published at the time when they were written" (Adams and Dyson 2003, 66), with Waldron (2003, 182) making the point that they were "not an apology for a revolution that has succeeded, but a call for a revolution to take place".[4]

2.3.2 *Taxation and Property*

While Locke actually wrote very little on taxation, the meaning and nuances of what he did write are still debated. Snape and Frecknall-Hughes (2017) have considered in detail past and more recent scholarship[5] on Locke and taxation (e.g., Voegelin 1999; Woolhouse 2007; Knights 2011; Andrew 2012, 2015), examining the four key tropes: "the legitimacy of property rights, the contractarian nature of government, just and unjust taxation and the need for majoritarian consent to taxation and other levies" (Snape and Frecknall-Hughes 2017, 1). Opinions on Locke's work are often themselves controversial, and there are, for instance, many different interpretations of Locke's theory of property (see, for instance, Tully 1980, 1993a, b, 1994, 1995; Vaughn 1980; Arneil 1996; Buckle 2001), which is key to his view on taxation.

The essence of Locke's taxation thought appears in the *Second Treatise,* Chapter 11.140 – a key passage:

> 'Tis true that Governments cannot be supported without great charge, and 'tis fit every one who enjoys his share of the Protection should pay out of his estate his proportion for the maintenance of it. But still it must be with his own Consent – *i.e.* the Consent of the Majority, giving it either by themselves or their Representatives chosen by them. For if any one shall claim a *Power to lay* and levy *Taxes* on the People by his own authority, and without such consent of the People, he thereby invades the *Fundamental Law of Property*, and subverts the end of government. For what property have I in that which another may by right take when he pleases himself?

---

rid of what had gone before. Given the political situations through which Locke lived, this fundamental underlying meaning of the term adds a further dimension.

[4] Ashcraft (1994, 258), however, comments on "the radical nature of Locke's moves against contemporary arguments for political, epistemological, and religious authority".

[5] The scholarship on Locke is extensive, and many works are of great value. See, for instance, Gough (1956); Grant (1987).

As the passage cited immediately above shows, for Locke, tax and property rights were inextricably linked. However, the exact meaning of many of the terms Locke used has been much debated. 'Estate' or 'property',[6] for instance, might mean particular assets (land, chattels) or rights/obligations in respect of those assets. This has led some to suggest that Locke envisaged that landowners only would have to pay tax, rather than everyone, as the possession of land at this time conferred the right to vote – the holding of a 40-shilling freehold in the shires, for instance (see Cohen 1986, 301). Indeed, in his pamphlet, *Some Consideration of the Consequences of the Lowering of Interest, and Raising the Value of Money* (1691) (cited by Dome 2004, 12, n. 6), Locke does suggest that the "publick charge" of government must be borne by landholders, not merchants or labourers. Similarly, the use of the words "proportion for the maintenance of it" ("it" being "protection", by reference to the earlier part of the sentence) has caused debate. Some form of equity or fairness is innately suggested by the use of "proportion", which may or may not mean progressive or proportionate taxes (in the modern sense of these terms – see Byrne 1999), but the linking of the concept to the "maintenance" of protection leaves the way open for debate on whether tax should be paid in relation to income/assets or on some consumption basis.[7] Still less do we know how the state might provide protection, and whether that might include welfare for the needy. While there is, perhaps, the seed of a benefit principle in Locke's thinking, it took Paine to develop this more fully (see later). It may be that we are trying to read too much into Locke's words and that he was doing no more than trying to establish a broad tax framework, with a philosophical underpinning.

Snape and Frecknall-Hughes (2017, 13) comment that Locke's theory of property – one of the most famous of all property theories – identifies with privacy, and is in opposition to the public realm of the state. Locke's work (*Part I*) was a response, in part, to counter the views and theories of Sir Robert Filmer in support of the divine right of kings, whereby property belonged to the monarch. In developing his theory of property, Locke again goes back to first principles: God gave the earth "to Mankind in common" (*Part II* Chapter 5.25). He bases his argument on man's development from a state of nature where he could take freely what he needed – and if he mixed his labour with something, then that more definitely confirmed his ownership. For example, ploughing land might confer the right to own land as the ploughing mixes labour with something left in a certain state by nature (*Part II* Chapter 5.27).[8] This is the basis of his natural right to property, which is inalienable (*Part II* Chapter 11.140):

---

[6] See the discussion by Macpherson (1951), Rapaczynski (1981) and Arneil (1996, 132–167).

[7] It should be remembered that 'taxes' at the date of Locke's writing would primarily mean land tax and hearth tax, not excise or customs duties, the latter only predominating from the late 1690s, most probably reflecting their popularity in The Netherlands and the influence of William III, although the English were familiar with excises and customs duties, which generated substantial revenues.

[8] It is fair to comment that Locke's justification of the right to private property on these principles continues to be the subject of academic debate (see Snape and Frecknall-Hughes 2017, 13–15).

> The supreme power cannot take from any man any part of his property without his own consent. For the preservation of property being the end of government, and that for which men enter into society, it necessarily supposes and requires that the people should have property, without which they must be supposed to lose that by entering into society which was the end for which they entered into it; too gross an absurdity for any man to own … For I truly have no property in that which another can take from me when he pleases against my consent. Hence it is a mistake to think that the supreme of legislative power of any commonwealth can do what it will, and dispose of the estates of the subject arbitrarily, or take any part of them at pleasure.

This is the basis of Locke's social contract.

2.3.3 Locke's Version of the Social Contract

According to Locke, men are born "free, equal and independent" (*Second Treatise* Chapter 5.48), which rights no one can take away. In the same passage, he says that no one should be subject to another's political power unless he consents, with consent meaning that men agree with one another "to join and unite into a community for their comfortable, safe and peaceable living … in a secure enjoyment of their properties". This is the body politic, and the individual hands over power to majority rule as the only lawful means of government – and it is a tacit consent.[9] As Locke says:

> And thus every Man, by consenting with others to make one Body Politick under one Government, puts himself under an Obligation to every one of that Society, to submit to the determination of the *majority*, and to be concluded by it; or else this original Compact, whereby he with others incorporates into one Society, would signifie nothing, and be no Compact, if he be left free, and under no other ties, than he was before in the State of Nature. (*Second Treatise* 7.97)

In Chapter 12 of the *Second Treatise*, Locke expounds more fully on the benefits of community membership, namely, the protection of life, health, liberty and the right to own private property. How, then, does the concept of taxation – which involves taking away part of an individual's property – sit with the idea of the primary purpose of the state being to protect private property ownership?

The idea that an individual voluntarily alienates his property rights in respect of tax seems much at odds with the idea of Locke's right to private property. The notion that a government's primary function is the protection of property is inherently contradicted by its simultaneous right to take it away. Thomas Hobbes, Locke's forerunner, also felt that levying taxes was justifiable as the price of protection (see Jackson 1973, 176–177). However, the implicit tension in these concepts remains with us to this day. The distinguished American legal scholar, Richard Epstein,

---

See also the thorough analysis of Locke's basic argument/tenets by Shrader-Frechette (1993), McClelland (1996, 229–248) and Haworth (2004, 117–133).

[9] Much has been written on the nature and meaning of this 'tacit' consent, and also of the consent of the majority. See, for example, Dunn (1967), Bennett (1979) and Russell (1986).

when considering the U.S. tax system from a Lockean viewpoint, comments on this fundamental contradiction. Taxation is (Epstein 1986, 49):

> … the power to coerce other individuals to surrender their property *without* their consent. In a world – a Lockean world – in which liberty is regarded as good and coercion an evil, then taxation authorizes the sovereign to commit acts of aggression against the very citizens it is supposed to protect.

While governments cannot exist without taxation, taxation is "institutionalized coercion", the dilemma being "how to preserve the power of taxation while curbing its abuse" (Epstein 1986, 50). Locke, when read in context, was aware of this dilemma, hence his stress on the need to adhere to a majority decision, although this could mean that a sizeable minority might disagree. Locke explicitly says (*Part II* Chapter 11.138), that a legislative power cannot act wilfully or arbitrarily, so the power to tax must be regarded as limited. Locke explicitly says (*Part II* Chapter 19.222) that in such cases, revolt by the people is justified (Seliger 1963), although where there is an issue specifically requiring justice in other circumstances, Locke does not seem to have envisaged a judiciary to deal with it (*Second Treatise* Chapter 7.91). Taxation is therefore justified as the means to provide benefits in return for surrender of individual rights, as a result of a (tacit) bargain or contract between the state and the individual.[10]

In Locke's version of the social contract, consent may be given in person or by means of an elected representative (implicit in *Part II* Chapter 11.140). Where men have "*consented to make one Community* or government … and make *one Body Politick* … the *Majority* have a Right to act" (*Part II* Chapter 8.95), though it is not clear from Locke's text whether he refers to a majority of the nation or of elected representatives. In *Part II*, Chapter 8.99, Locke expressly states that uniting into such a community means that power is handed over to the majority. However, it must be realised that, in reality, this did not mean that the right to have a say in government was available to all, but was limited to those holding the relevant property qualification: women, children, the poor and, of course, colonial subjects, with no vote, could not actually give any consent. Moreover, taxation at this time was different in concept, being raised especially in times of war rather than on any regular basis.

2.3.4 *Tax and Justice*

Returning to the idea of an individual handing over power to a body politic, it is reasonable that he should be willing to contribute to maintaining that body, as he will also be contributing to the protection of himself and his property (a state can

[10] It is commonly remarked that such a bargain or contract was never explicit. However, Pollock (1908, 108) makes the point that there is historical evidence to support such contracts being formal compacts between rulers and subjects, not least in the case of the *Magna Carta*, and notes as well that the Pilgrim Fathers, for instance, made a formal covenant for a body politic. Pollock cites the latter example from Hobbes, but does not give the reference to Hobbes's work for this.

protect them if required, against anyone attacking them, at law or in war). However, this raises questions about the inherent justice of a tax system based on this concept of benefit. Locke's system does not appear distributive at state level, as already noted. To cite Snape and Frecknall-Hughes (2017, 31):

> As Peter Laslett [1988] writes, "[i]n his published works he [Locke] showed himself the determined enemy of beggars and the idle poor, who existed, he thought, because of 'the relaxation of discipline and the corruption of manners'". Andrew [2015, 26] notes that, "following a long correspondence pressing his reluctant agent, Cornelius Lyde, to evict a widow from one of Locke's properties, Locke cited the Pauline dictum that those who do not work do not deserve to eat".

Charity, and supporting the needy were thus personal, not a state's, obligations. Locke chiefly focuses on the incidence of taxation on landowners, making this clear in *Some Consideration of the Consequences of the Lowering of Interest, and Raising the Value of Money* (1691, 55–56):

> This by the way, if well considered, might let us see, that taxes, however contrived, and out of whose hands soever immediately taken, do, in a country, where their great fund is in land, for the most part terminate upon land. Whatsoever the people is chiefly maintained by, that the government supports itself on: nay, perhaps it will be found, that those taxes which seem least to affect land, will most surely of all other fall the rents. This would deserve to be well considered, in the raising of taxes, lest the neglect of it bring upon the country gentleman an evil, which he will be sure quickly to feel, but not be able very quickly to remedy. For rents once fallen are not easily raised again. A tax laid upon land seems hard to the landholder, because it is so much money going visibly out of his pocket: and therefore, as an ease to himself, the landholder is always forward to lay it upon commodities. But, if he will thoroughly consider it, and examine the effects, he will find he buys this seeming ease at a very dear rate: and though he pays not this tax immediately out of his own purse, yet his purse will find it by a greater want of money there, at the end of the year, than that comes to, with the lessening of his rents to boot: which is a settled and lasting evil, that will stick upon him beyond the present payment.

Locke himself had been a Registrar of the Excise at one point in his career, so would have known that excise duties, along with customs duties, raised more than the land tax, which he believed were passed along by labourers as higher wages and merchants as higher prices (see Andrew 2015, 27). It is protection received that should determine the amount to pay, not the ability to pay. The amount of land tax a landowner paid was known in advance, but those buying commodities do not know how much of the price is taxation, so Locke's system might be viewed as inherently unfair. As remarked, the idea of paying out of one's 'estate' and how this may be 'fit' have been the subject of much debate in terms of the meaning of 'estate' (land, goods, property, money, etc.) and fairness. Laslett, when commenting on Locke's *Second Treatise* (1690c, 104), notes that Locke's "object seems to be to guarantee secure and quiet possession, however large the estate and whatever it contained", and "while the whole tenor of his argument is in favour of those with a great deal to lose" (1690c, 105), he finds a hint (ibid.) in *Part II*, Chapter 7.94 that even the poorest of men would have sufficient property to merit society's protection for it. This is not to say that Locke should be interpreted as favouring, for example, a capitalist society (in the modern sense), or indeed, any other. Given that the individual has agreed to majority rule, "[i]f not complete communism, certainly redistributive taxation, perhaps nationalisation could be justified" (Laslett 1988, 105), provided that the majority consented – even if "all the property-owners were in the minority" (ibid.). While it is clear that Locke followed Hobbes in some of his thinking, the two diverge on these issues. Hobbes thought that taxation was justified as the price of security and that it should be equally imposed on all citizens to equate to benefits received. These are conceptual tensions which remain with us to this day.

2.4 Montesquieu (1689–1755)

2.4.1 Introduction

Charles-Louis de Secondat, Baron de La Brède et de Montesquieu, was born into a noble and prosperous family. He studied law at the University of Bordeaux. In 1716 he inherited from his uncle the office of président à mortier in the Bordeaux Parlement which was chiefly a judicial and administrative body. To satisfy his scientific interest, he joined the Academy of Bordeaux, and wrote papers on physics, physiology, geology and other natural sciences. In 1721 Montesquieu published the *Persian Letters*, an epistolary novel. In 1728 Montesquieu left France for a long voyage abroad. He also went to England (1729). He attended meetings of the House of Commons and corresponded with Hume. He was greatly impressed with the English constitution and political institutions. It proved to him that "the rule of law and political freedom were practical possibilities," (Shklar 1987a, 21). In 1731 he resettled in La Brède and began work on his master work, *The Spirit of the Laws* (henceforth, *Spirit*), which was published in 1748. Among the famous contemporary authors who reacted to this treatise were D'Alembert, Rousseau, Voltaire, Burke, Beccaria, Bentham, and across the Atlantic, Madison, Jefferson and Adams.

Montesquieu lived in a monarchy. However, during the eighteenth century the ground shifted under the French monarchy, the 'Old Regime'. Montesquieu was obviously aware of the frailty of the *ancient régime*, and he attributed it to the decline of countervailing powers. In the previous century Louis XIV had created a massive, heavily centrist bureaucratic modern state, which had become a major world power. The actual administrative power of the government was, however, limited by an ever-growing body of laws and an ever-expanding number of officials (Koenigsberger 1994, 319). The perpetual need for money to pay for the wars resulted in the permanent increase in taxes. However, the tax system was highly complex and inefficient. There were several kinds of taxes and the system was shot through with special exemptions and privileges "at the level of individuals, institutions, social orders, towns, and provinces" (Elster 2020, 216). The peasants bore the greatest burden of highly regressive tax system (Hoffman 1994). Adam Smith later gave a trenchant critique of the "extraordinary privileges [but also] extraordinary restraints and "the arbitrary and degrading taxes" (*Wealth of Nations* IV.ix, 3, 663–664).

2.4.2 Irrelevance of the State of Nature and Social Contract

For Montesquieu, men living in society seems to be the natural state of affairs. This explains why he shows little interest in the transition to (civil and political) society and the notion of social contract. In the *Persian Letters*, Usbek finds it "absurd" that any discussion of political right starts with a preliminary inquiry into the origin of society. Men do not live outside society (*Persian Letters* 94, 175). Man's feeling of inferiority and weakness and of his needs are important drivers to "approach one another" (*Spirit* I, 2, 6). In contradistinction with Hobbes, who starts with the state of nature to argue for absolute sovereignty which equals despotic power, Montesquieu seems to maintain that without any principles of equity or justice, men cannot form any sustainable political society.

A social contract is not the only valid basis for political legitimacy, as evidenced in Usbek's story in the *Persian Letters* of the futile attempt to form a social contract among the Troglodytes (*Persian Letters* 11, 53–56). Men's social embeddedness cuts against the association between individual identity and the autonomous exercise of will. Moreover, Pangle says, the notion of a social contract is "a kind of legalistic reconstruction of a process which must have been considerably less rational" (Pangle 1973, 41). Montesquieu seeks to found liberty on bases other than the concepts of nature and sovereignty. In doing so, he abandons the language of absolute rights, in Hobbes the sovereign's, in Locke the individual's (Manent 1994, 53).

Man's natural sociability enables Montesquieu to shift the focus of political discourse to the conditions of good governance and the institutions necessary to guarantee political liberty. Montesquieu's chief concern was to criticise 'despotism' which he saw "as a symbol of corruption which threatened every type of government" (Kawade 2003, 220). Despotism is contrary to justice and undermines the general spirit of a political society. He rejects the despotic power of absolute sovereignty with concentration and centralisation of power, as found in Hobbes, and argues for a plurality of politic powers.

Montesquieu criticises Hobbes for picturing the state of nature as a state of war and argues that Hobbes imported features of the civil state of humanity back into the pre-civil state (*Spirit* I, 2, 6; Rousseau also makes this point). The desire to live in societies, the human disposition to sociability, is a natural law. This desire is not threatened by the desire of domination, which develops only with competition for social advantages, that is, after "the establishment of societies" (*Spirit* I, 2, 6). However, as soon men enter into a state of society, they lose the sense of their weakness and equality ceases. Individuals begin to feel the superiority of their minds or talents and seek to appropriate to themselves the advantages of society, and "the state of war begins" which in turn "brings about the establishment of laws among men" (*Spirit* I, 3, 7). Society is thus "founded on mutual advantage" and the implicit consent of its members (*Persian Letters* 76, 153).

2.4.3 Theory of Law

Montesquieu's theory of law reflects his critique of despotic law-making power. His concern is the fundamental moral norms behind human positive law. Unlike Hobbes, good legislation cannot be reduced to a command of a sovereign will (Shklar 1987a, 71). Legislation has, for example, to conform to relations of justice or "fairness prior to the positive law" (*Spirit* I, 1, 4). To explain this, Montesquieu starts *The Spirit of the Laws* with a definition of law in general, drawing our attention to the relational character of law. "Laws, in their most general significance, are the necessary relations deriving from the nature of things, and in this sense all beings, have their laws" (*Spirit* I, 1, 3). This definition includes physical laws, the laws governing animal behaviour, "the moral law which defined justice and injustice, and the human positive law" (McClelland 1996, 321). The legislator has to respect these prior relations.

For Montesquieu law and justice are inseparable: one implies the other (Shklar 1987a, 72). His concern is justice in human relations, which must be grounded in the sociability of reasonable human beings. Nature is not only ruled by physical laws, "but also includes the invariable and necessary relations of fairness" (*Spirit* I, 1, 4). Positive laws, that is, human law, "must therefore be derived from 'the nature of things', not from the arbitrary command of the legislator" (Kawade 2003, 224). Laws define relationships and they are just to the extent that they define relationships properly.

Montesquieu's conception of human law is both general and particular. "Law in general is human reason insofar as it governs all the peoples of the earth" (*Spirit* I, 3, 8). This declaration echoes natural law theory which maintains that positive law has to fulfil certain moral requirements. However, he immediately particularises that reason: "the political and civil laws of each nation should be only the particular cases to which human reason is applied" and laws should fit "the people for whom they are made" (*Spirit* I, 3, 8). Montesquieu actually advances a kind of legal 'relativism' – the notion of 'spirit of the laws' featuring as main figure. Thus, Montesquieu's relational conception of law rejects the idea of some immutable precepts by which to measure regimes and legislation.

The French term *esprit* has many meanings which are not easy to translate. As Rahe (2009, 11) shows, it can mean "the spirit, the mindset, the motive, the impetus, the intention, the object, as well as the logic". Montesquieu uses the term not only to refer to "the deeper meaning as opposed to the surface meaning (the 'letter') of the laws, but takes the 'spirit of the laws' in a sociological sense as the "driving force' of a system, as a principle that animates people and organizes social and political orders" (Witteveen 2006, XV).

Montesquieu argues that "laws must relate to the nature and the principle of the government that is established" and adds another list of relations which together form, Montesquieu says "the spirit of the laws" (*Spirit* I, 3, 9):

> The laws should be related to the physical aspect of the country; to the climate (...); to the properties of the terrain, its location and extent; to the way of life of the peoples (...); they

should relate to the degree of liberty that the constitution can sustain, to the religion of the inhabitants, their inclinations, their wealth, their number, their commerce, their mores and their manners; finally, the laws are related to one another, to their origin, to the purpose of the legislator, and to the order of things on which they are established".

The laws must be considered from all these points of view.

Thus, the "general spirit" of nations is an extra-juridical normativity to which the legislator must adapt (De Dijn 2008, 21). "It is for the legislator to follow the spirit of the nation, when it is not contrary to the principles of government; for we do nothing better than what we do freely and following our natural genius" (*Spirit* XIX, 5, 310). The legislator should therefore not try to correct everything (*Spirit* XIX, 6, 311). Montesquieu would therefore probably oppose government micro-managing citizens' behaviour – for instance by using tax incentives.

2.4.4 *Liberty*

Without laws, there is no liberty. In *Spirit*, Book XI Montesquieu distinguishes liberty in a state (political liberty), from the 'independence' one would enjoy in the state of nature (Rahe 2001, 18). Liberty in a state, that is, in a society where there are laws, definitely does not consist in doing what one wants, but having the power to do what one should want to do and not be constrained or forced to do otherwise. Montesquieu apparently does not equate liberty with negative liberty – the absence of interference from other persons or institutions. Laws empower citizens and protect them against constraints. He establishes a particular relationship between a citizen's liberty and the law. Montesquieu advocates a conception of freedom as non-domination: the condition of the individual of being free from any threat of domination – or dependence on the arbitrary will of other individuals or institutions. As Viroli (2002, 37) explains, there is interference without domination when we are subjected to the restraints and restrictions of law.

Indeed, Montesquieu goes on to explain his claim: "Liberty is the right to do everything the laws permit; and if one citizen could do what they forbid, he would no longer have the liberty because the others would likewise have this same power" (*Spirit* XI, 3, 155). Others would obstruct his freedom to do what the laws allow. According to Manent (1994, 55), Montesquieu thus determines the definitive language of liberalism by framing the heart of the political problem, that is, the form under which men's social and political life should be organised, as "the conflict between *power* and *liberty*".

Not every government is capable of guaranteeing a citizen's liberty, since political liberty is only found in moderate states. More precisely, it is only when power is not abused that one actually has the right to do everything the laws permit. In order to prevent abuse of power, "power must check power by the arrangement of things" (*Spirit* XI, 4, 155). Montesquieu believes that a well-designed constitution will constrain no one to acts the law does not oblige him/her to do or kept from doing the things the laws permit him/her to do.

Moderate governments thus protect and enhance political liberty; it "must be such that one citizen cannot fear another citizen" (*Spirit* XI, 6 1, 157). Governments have to establish laws that constrain the citizens, enhancing liberty defined as absence of fear. For this second kind of political liberty also means that (in moderate states) it depends on the constitutional distribution of power: again, power must check power. Without limits on political power, there is no political liberty.

2.4.5 Separation and Distribution of Powers

For Montesquieu the antagonist of liberty is power, because any man who has power is led to abuse it. He therefore abhors despotic government in which all the powers are concentrated in one person or institution. He distinguishes three kinds of power: legislative, executive and judicial power. Liberty would "be lost if the same man, or the same body of principal men, either of nobles, or of the people, exercised these three powers" (*Spirit* XI, 6, 157). Indeed, where all power is one, a despotic ruler "is felt at every moment" (*Spirit* XI, 6, 158). (Cf. Locke, *Second Treatise* (*Part II*, Chapter 5.91), who says: "For wherever any two men are, who have no standing rule and common judge to appeal to on earth, for the determination of controversies of right betwixt them, there they are still in the state of Nature…".)

In the French absolute monarchy the previously existing balance of power had been thrown off balance. Montesquieu strove to restore this balance (Shklar 1987a, 80). Law had become an instrument of the monarch. He argued that this meant that in essence law was not formed by the will of the legislator, but was seen as command issued by the sovereign. Law was not to be made by one central body, but there should be several authorised lawmakers. There should be a functional separation between the legislative, executive, and judicial branches of the state (unlike Locke who "insists on the essential subordination of the executive to the legislative" (Manent 1994, 54).

The legislature, administration and judiciary are partners in the business of law making. "These three powers […] as they are constrained to move by the necessary motion of things, they will be forced to move in concert." (*Spirit* XI, 6, 164).

Montesquieu's focus on the limitation of political power reflects his chief concern: his criticism of despotism, a form of government characterised by pervasive corruption and injustice. He therefore distinguishes between moderate and despotic regimes where power is unchecked. Montesquieu further distinguishes between two forms of moderate government, the republican and the monarchical. The legal system and, a fortiori, the tax laws should be relative to the different forms of government but also, for instance, to "the principles forming the general spirit, the mores and the manners of the nation" (cited from the title of *Spirit* XIX, 308–333).

Every form has its own nature, that is, its particular structure, and its own principle, that is, "the human passions that set it in motion" (*Spirit* III, 1, 21). For the republic (democracy or aristocracy), the monarchy and the despot, the principles are respectively virtue, honor and fear. These principles are normative: when a form of government does not live up to its characteristic principle, for example, when a particular republic is not virtuous, this means that "the government is imperfect" (*Spirit* III, 11, 30). In each society, the mutually dependent institutions are thus ordered in their own characteristic way.

Montesquieu defines republics as forms of government in which "the people, or only a part of the people, have sovereign power" (*Spirit* II, 1, 10). There is need for much integrity, since the person who has to execute the laws "feels that he is subject to them himself and that he will bear their weight" (*Spirit* III, 3, 22). This requires virtuous citizens, which is possible only in a state characterised by special equality and frugality (De Dijn 2008, 21). Political equality therefore presupposed social equality: "Love of the republic in a democracy is love of democracy; love of democracy is love of equality" (*Spirit* V, 3, 43).

In both monarchical and despotic governments, power is exercised by a sovereign ruler rather than the people. Despotism is a form of government where "one alone, without law and without rule, draws everything by his will and his caprice" (*Spirit* II, 1, 10). A monarch's rule, however, is not unfettered because of a structural feature of monarchy: his power is always checked by 'intermediary powers'. Montesquieu sees the *parlements*, that is, an independent judiciary, as "a depository of laws" channeling the monarch's power and ensuring the stability of the law (*Spirit* II, 4, 18–19). However, the primary barrier preventing abuse of power is the nobility (*Spirit* II, 4).

The structural features of despotic governments are social equality and atomisation – it dissolves the social tissue (De Dijn 2008, 23). Men are equal because "they are nothing" (*Spirit* VI, 2, 75). There is no social hierarchy and aristocracy. "In despotic states, each household is a separate empire" (*Spirit* IV, 3, 34). There are no laws. "In despotic states there is not law; the judge himself is the rule" (*Spirit* VI, 3, 76). In despotic governments there is domination without law, injustice, cruelty, and corruption that will spread from the ruler to the subjects.

2.4.6 Taxation

For Montesquieu, taxes and political liberty are intimately linked: "The revenues of the state are a portion each citizen gives of his goods in order to have security or the comfortable enjoyment of the rest" (*Spirit* XIII, 1, 213). Reciprocity, give and take, is the normative underpinning of the imposition of taxes; an 'implicit', semi-contractualist argument according to Goyard-Fabre (1979, 274). Taxes are seen as an insurance premium (Mann 1978, 214–215).

The raising of public funds, a fortiori, the levying of taxes, is the legislator's prerogative and it is the "most important point of legislation" (*Spirit* XI, 6, 164). Taxation requires "wisdom and prudence" to determine the proper proportion between "the necessities of the state and the necessities of the citizens" (*Spirit* XIII, 1, 213). It is all about moderation and political prudence (Shklar 1987a, 91). With regard to tax administration, Montesquieu prefers tax collection by government officials rather than revenue farming, which boils down to impoverishing the treasury and often implied the use of brutal methods (*Spirit* XIII, 19, 226).

The amount of taxes to be paid by the citizens relates to the form of government of the state and political liberty. They should pay in proportion to their liberty. The 'general rule' is that the more liberty citizens enjoy the greater the public revenue that could be extracted (*Spirit* XIII,12, 220–221). He points at England and Holland (the Dutch Republic) that were heavily taxed. As political liberty declined, as in the Ottoman empire, the fiscal burden becomes lower, he thinks (Bonney 1995, 193). He subsequently argues that taxes can be increased in most republics – the citizen is willing to pay because "he believes he is paying to himself" – and in monarchies as a "kind of reward to the prince for his respect of the laws" (*Spirit* XIII, 13, 221). However, heavy taxes are not a good thing in themselves, they are unlikely to make people work harder (*Spirit* XIII, 2, 214).

Montesquieu distinguishes between taxes on persons, on lands and on commodities, the latter being "the ones the least felt by the people, because no formal request is made for them" (*Spirit* XIII, 7, 217). He advocates limited progressive taxation. With regard to a tax on persons "an unjust proportion would be one that followed strictly the proportion of goods" (*Spirit* XIII, 7, 216). Each one has a physical necessity (subsistence minimum) which should not be assessed. Only, the "useful" that comes next to the basic physical need should be taxed. This "superfluity" surplus of goods should be assessed, but at less than in proportion to the superfluous (*Spirit* XIII, 7, 217). He notes the egalitarian effect of this regressive rate (even a regressive rate for the superfluity may make the rich pay more than the poor). The same principle seems to apply to land taxes. Thus, Montesquieu made a huge contribution to the public opinion embracing these social political measures (Mann 1978, 160). Progressive taxation, and considering the subsistence minimum, were crucial to a new ideal of equality (to be radicalised by Rousseau in his *Discourse on Political Economy*).

Every form of government has its own nature and principles to which institutions like the legal system and taxation must relate. The nature of taxation is therefore also relative to the form of government. A poll tax, or head tax, is more natural to despotic regimes (without political liberty), where a tax on commodities (or indirect tax) fits in moderate states with political liberty because it less related to the person (*Spirit* XIII, 14, 222). The latter can be so wisely designed such "that the people will be almost unaware that they pay them" (*Spirit* XIII, 7, 217). The seller of commodity should pay the duty, for if the consumers would have to pay, a "perpetual searching" of their houses would be required. "Nothing is more contrary to liberty" (*Spirit* XIII, 7, 218).

Political and social equality and frugality are the hallmarks of democracy. The laws should establish equality, although "extreme precision in this regard would not always be suitable" (*Spirit* V, 5, 47), and sustain frugality. In monarchies, however, there is a great deal of luxury and inequality (*Spirit* VI, 4, 99). Inequality helps "to safeguard liberty in the monarchical system rather than to undermine it" (De Dijn 2008, 30–31). Consequently, democracies allow for higher taxes than monarchies. As Montesquieu says, frugality in a democracy consists in keeping "the necessaries for one's family" and giving all the superfluities to one's homeland (*Spirit* V, 3, 43).

Taxes should be an instrument to curtail luxury and "achieve as equal a distribution as possible of basic commodities and benefits" (sumptuary taxation; Gross 1993, 91). Taxes should be used to redistribute wealth, preventing the rich from being too rich (Snape 2012, 86). Montesquieu does not advocate any extreme form of levelling but rather the "spirit of equality", that is the desirability of "a reduction of inequality" (Gross 1993, 91). To conclude, for Montesquieu taxation (and tax fairness) is very much a contextual affair. Taxes should be attuned to different political societies and their general spirit. He puts progressive taxation on the agenda.

2.5 David Hume (1711–1776)

2.5.1 Introduction

The development of Hume's thoughts is difficult to unravel as he frequently revised his works, which makes it hard to detect any sequential evolution. He was born near Berwick into a minor landed gentry family, and became a leading figure of the Scottish Enlightenment. His experience of the turmoil affecting that country – especially the financial turmoil – undoubtedly coloured his views. As Frecknall-Hughes (2014, 93) notes:

> Scotland had been involved in the disastrous Darien schemes, to set up colonies in the late 1690s on the Isthmus of Panama, which had lessened resistance to its formal political union with England in 1707, though there was still protest against this; there were the various Jacobite rebellions (1689–1692, 1715, 1719 and 1745); the South Sea Bubble had burst in 1720; the Bank of England had been established (1694) and the National Debt to fund Britain's wars, notably the War of the Spanish Succession (1702–1713) and the War of the Austrian Succession (1740–1748) (see Dome 2004, 1).

Hume's world was very different from Locke's, especially in financial terms, with the introduction of the National Debt being considered a significant part of what was termed the 'Financial Revolution' (Dickson 1967). This latter was regarded as a means of raising money other than by taxes, but tax revenues were required to fund the interest due, which Hume thought onerous to the people. In his essay *Of Public Credit* (1742), he considered the issues of public debt and the threat they posed – including the possibility of national bankruptcy (see Dome 2004, 1–2). Notably also, Hume was a friend of Rousseau, and was instrumental in providing him with refuge in England at one point, although the two men quarrelled and Rousseau alleged that Hume plotted to destroy his character (see Zaretksy and Scott 2009). Despite slower methods of communication in the eighteenth century than we are accustomed to see today, ideas spread rapidly, and leading thinkers often knew each other's ideas from travelling and meeting each other, intellectual 'salons', correspondence, reading works, etc. Hume was also a friend of Benjamin Franklin (Werner 1972, 448). During his own lifetime, Hume was better known as a historian than as a philosopher, as a result of his six-volume work, *The History of England*, which he wrote between 1754 and 1761 during his tenure as librarian at the

University of Edinburgh, a post he took when attempts to secure an academic university post met with lack of success.

2.5.2 Property and the Destruction of the Social Contract

Hume's body of works on moral and political philosophy is extensive and often repetitive. The destruction of the Lockean concept of the social contract and natural rights is widely attributed to Hume (Sabine 1961, 597–606; Werner 1972, 439), although many scholars have rejected these ideas, especially Jeremy Bentham, to whom the idea of natural rights was an anathema (see Frecknall-Hughes 2019). For rights to exist, they have to be given by law (see Molivas 1999), and the law protects the individual's rights. There is no natural right to property, as Hume says in Section 3, Part II of *An Inquiry Concerning the Principles of Morals*:

> [A]ll questions of property are subordinate to the authority of civil laws, which extend, restrain, modify, and alter the rules of natural justice, according to the particular CONVENIENCE of each community. The laws have, or ought to have, a constant reference to the constitution of government, the manners, the climate, the religion, the commerce, the situation of each society.

He continues later in the same section:

> But farther, though it seems a very simple proposition to say, that nature, by an instinctive sentiment, distinguishes property, yet in reality we shall find, that there are required for that purpose ten thousand different instincts, and these employed about objects of the greatest intricacy and nicest discernment. For when a definition of PROPERTY is required, that relation is found to resolve itself into any possession acquired by occupation, by industry, by prescription, by inheritance, by contract, &c. Can we think that nature, by an original instinct, instructs us in all these methods of acquisition?

For Hume, the idea of property originates from man's natural condition, which is beset by competition and conflict. Common or mutual interest therefore leads to the notion of property rights, to protect the public interest, create stability and consent in respect of property transfer, but these are artificial rules, based on human practice and serve a function (see Kelly 2003, 208).Riker and Sened (1991, 252) usefully summarise this perspective:

> Governments have existed throughout recorded history, and all primitive societies today display at least a judicial system enforcing a customary law. Since, in known history, government of some sort has always existed, social contracts cannot have created governments and thus rights. In fact … the causal relation probably runs the other way: rulers themselves (legislatures, executives, judges) have generated property rights, hoping to encourage efficiency, and doubtless, also, to increase tax income.

That this is also Hume's view is very clear in his essay *Of the Original Contract* (1748a), in which he examines the differing Tory and Whig philosophical stance on the genesis of government. He concurs with the Tory view that political authority derives from divine right. Locke was regarded by the Whigs as the mainstay of their political theory, and counter to Locke's argument for government stemming from a social contract, Hume argued that government is most commonly established by violent means (because of shortages in resources), a topic to which he often returns (see, for example, *Of the Origin of Government* (published in 1777). In Book 2 (3:1) of his *Treatise of Human Nature* (1739–1740), he comments:

> Men cannot live without society, and cannot be associated without government. Government makes a distinction of property, and establishes the different ranks of men. This produces industry, traffic, manufactures, law-suits, wars, leagues, alliances … and all those other actions and objects, which cause such a diversity, and at the same time, maintain such an uniformity in human life.

In *Of the Original Contract* (1748a) Hume is critical of social contract ideas, particularly objecting to their inherent notions of tacit consent, as the latter ignores the fact that many people may live under a government simply because they cannot leave (Adams and Dyson 2003, 76). Hume sees feeling/emotion as predominant over logical thought: men reason in the way they do because of the feelings that they have. Thus "government and political obligation are to be understood as originating not in some such abstraction as a social contract or law of nature, but in the practical responses of human beings to felt needs and desires" (Adams and Dyson 2003, 74). Hume has no truck with natural law. In his *Treatise of Human Nature* (Book 3, 3:1), a fact or law of nature, for example, such as a man needing food without which he would die, does not confer a 'natural' right to food: there is a gap between 'is' and 'ought', in Humean terms.

In his work, *Of the First Principles of Government* (1741a), Hume bases the foundation of government on two needs: to protect public interest and the rights to property and justice (see Kelly 2003, 211), also arguing for government maintenance of justice in *Of the Origin of Government* (published in 1777). Human weakness, especially the tendency towards conflict, prevents individuals from acting justly, so a government is needed to help establish a duty of obedience, to maintain law – but such authority must also be balanced against the need to maintain liberty. Hume did not understand why the origin of government itself was of importance to philosophers. The answer to this question was unknown and it was "probably best to regard government as having evolved over time and become established by the authority of custom" (Adams and Dyson 2003, 75), and he had no preference for any particular kind:

> I look upon all kinds of subdivision of power, from the monarchy of France to the freest democracy of the Swiss cantons, to be equally legal if established by custom and authority (Hume, *New Letters*, 1954, 81).

2.5.3 Taxation, and the Relevance of Custom

In Lockean theory, the concept of the social contract was key in underpinning the legitimacy of imposing taxation, so without this, how does Hume justify the imposition of taxes by a government, given his views on maintaining liberty? This presents a philosophical dilemma. It is one which he does not directly address. His thoughts on taxation are found disseminated among his many writings. He did write one work on taxation (*Of Taxes*, 1752), but this is not theoretically based (see later). although there are indications of his thinking scattered throughout his work, especially in his moral theory, in Book 3 of the *Treatise of Human Nature* (1739–1740) and in *An Inquiry Concerning the Principles of Morals* (1751), where he discusses the nature of justice and man's motivation to act justly, especially in relation to property. A sense of justice is not innate, but is derived from self-interest, convention and education. If man depends on society to survive, it is in his interest to respect others' property so that society remains stable and intact. Such behaviour imbues man with a common interest, and anticipation that others will behave similarly, thus engendering a respect for rules and a sense of civic duty. It is a not a huge leap in thinking to suggest that imposing and paying tax might be an anticipated part of civic duty and support for a desired society.

The idea of convention or custom permeates Hume's work (see Kelly 2003, 206ff). In *An Inquiry Concerning Human Understanding* (1748b), Hume says (with some similarity to Locke's ideas) that human knowledge is based on impressions and ideas, which then become bound together. As Werner (1972, 440) notes:

> Any attempt to find some reality underlying these impressions is useless. Reality can be found only in a continuously changing aggregate of feelings bound together by a psychological or social force known as custom. Custom thus replaces a priori reason as the subjective basis of beliefs about causation in external and human nature.

In the context of taxation, this might mean that man accepts taxation simply because it has been customarily developed. One deals with what exists, and there is no need to speculate why it exists, although this does not mean that things cannot be changed, as Hume makes clear in his work *Of the Original Contract* (1748a, 275–276):

> When a new government is established, by whatever means, the people are commonly dissatisfied with it, and pay obedience more from fear and necessity, than from any idea of allegiance or of moral ... Time, by degrees, removes all these difficulties, and accustoms the nation to regard, as their lawful or native princes, that family, which, at first, they considered as usurpers or foreign conquerors.

This may explain Hume's view of taxation as shown in his essay *Of Taxes* (1752). As noted, this does not consider taxation theory in any way: rather, it is strongly practical, although somewhat inconsistent. Gribnau and Dijkstra (2020, 81) comment that Hume's ideas about taxation "resemble more an assemblage of separate thoughts than a consistent exposition on taxation". He discusses, for example, how workers should increase their labour so as to deal with any increase in taxation, rather than by seeking higher wages: a man who works more will earn more. Snape (2015, 453) considers this as part of Hume's purpose "to analyse the mercantilist proposition that people will absorb higher taxes by working harder". Hume compares this situation to the greater effort required, for instance, by a worker to prevail over a harsher climate if travailing in a country other than Great Britain. In *Of Taxes*, he "divides taxes into consumption taxes, taxes on possessions and poll taxes" (Snape 2015, 453).

Hume is aware, nonetheless, that not all customs are beneficial, particularly in reference to taxation. Well established governments, notably monarchies, can degenerate because of excessive debts and taxes, and he cites in this regard in *Of Civil Liberty* (1741b, 54), the instance of France:

> The greatest abuses … proceed not from the number or weight of taxes, beyond what are to be met with in free countries; but from the expensive, unequal, arbitrary, and intricate method of levying them, by which the industry of the poor, especially of peasants and farmers, is, in great measure, discouraged, and agriculture rendered as beggarly and slavish employment.

It would take a superior leader to break through these "ancient customs" (*Of Civil Liberty* 1741b, 54). Although Hume does not offer specific recommendations for developing a tax system, despite his concern with the public debt (Dome 2004, 3), he acknowledges that it is better to tax luxury goods rather than the necessities of daily life. Purchase of luxury goods is often a matter of choice whereas buying daily necessities is not.

> The best taxes are those which are levied on consumptions, especially those of luxury: because such taxes are least felt by the people. They seem to be, in some measure, voluntary; since a man may chuse how far he will use the commodity which is taxed: They are paid gradually and insensibly: They naturally produce sobriety and frugality, if judiciously imposed: And being confounded with the natural price of the commodity, they are scarcely perceived by the consumers. Their only disadvantage is, that they are expensive in the levying. (Hume, *Of Taxes* (1752, 205), cited by Dome (2004, 3))

Though expensive to levy, taxes on consumption, are "nonetheless convenient for the subject to pay" (Snape 2015, 453–454). Similarly, Hume was opposed to arbitrary taxes ("bad because they are uncertain" and are inequitable (Snape 2015, 453)), including land taxes, disagreeing with Locke that all taxes would ultimately be borne by landowners.

> [T]he most pernicious of all taxes are the arbitrary. They are commonly converted, by their management, into punishments on industry; and also, by their unavoidable inequality, are more grievous, therefore, than by the real burden they impose. It is surprising, therefore, to see them have place among any civilised people. (Hume, *Of Taxes* (1752, 205), cited by Dome (2004, 3))

As Dome (2004, 5 comments), Hume left "to future generations the problem of how to establish a system of public finance compatible with liberal and commercial society".

2.6 Jean-Jacques Rousseau (1712–1778)

2.6.1 Introduction

Rousseau was born in the independent Calvinist city-state of Geneva and, as son of Isaac Rousseau, enjoyed the rank of citizen of Geneva, a status inherited by Jean-Jacques. His mother, Suzanne Bernard Rousseau, was from an upper-class family.

He received a haphazard education from his father and a pastor. His father's stories of the brotherhood of all Genevans fostered in his son an ideal of republican virtue and patriotic identification. In Paris, in his early thirties, he mixed freely with Diderot and other intellectuals. In 1749 he had the transformative experience that society ruins everything. He subsequently left the salons of Paris, and became a criticaster of modern civilization. In 1765 he travelled to England as the guest of David Hume, but he quickly fell out with him because he believed Hume to be implicated in some kind of plot against him. He published works on many topics such as music, nature (botany) and (political) philosophy, and was one of the contributors to the famous *Encyclopédie* of Diderot and d'Alembert – both leading *philosophes*.[11] He offers an autocritique of Enlightenment (Hulliung 1994), forcing the *philosophes*, to rethink their thoughts and work time and again.

The eighteenth century showed an increased optimism about the permanence of human societies and saw ordered society and government fuelled by the widespread idea that religious disputes with all their disruptive consequences should be confined to the private sphere and "the ideal of at least limited religious toleration" (Outram 2005, 32). Rousseau takes civil society as given, rather than providing a theory of the origins of civil society (unlike Hobbes). His theory aims to give an account of the form political association should have to qualify as legitimate (McClelland 1996, 257–258; Cohen 2010, 24).

Rousseau sees a close connection and interplay between conceptions of sovereignty, law, taxation and citizenship. In the *Discourse on Political Economy*, which contains first sketches of some key themes of *The Social Contract*, he says that "[t]he body politic, taken individually, may be considered as an organised, living body, resembling that of man". He subsequently explains this image.

> The sovereign power represents the head; the laws and customs are the brain, [...] the public income is the blood, which a prudent economy, in performing the functions of the heart, causes to distribute through the whole body nutriment and life: the citizens are the body and the members, which make the machine live, move and work; and no part of this machine can be damaged without the painful impression being at once conveyed to the brain, if the animal is in a state of health. (*The Social Contract* 131–132)

2.6.2 Relation Between the State, Society and Citizens/Subjects

Rousseau's political thought is rich but difficult and may seem even contradictory – giving rise to very diverging interpretations – for instance totalitarian, liberal and republican (Boucher 2003, 239–240). In Rousseau the idea of social contract itself

[11] The multi-volume *Encyclopédie* aimed to present a comprehensive overview of "all aspects of human endeavour and achievement, showing the progress of man in the newly liberated environment of universal reason and Enlightenment" (Dent 1992, 111). The philosophes were a new phenomenon. They represented a new force in history: men of letters acting in concert, who wanted to put their ideas "to use, to persuade, propagandize, and change the world" around them (Darnton 1997).

does not explain the origins of human societies. Rousseau argued that Hobbes's conception of the state of nature imported features of the civil state back into the pre-civil state (Montesquieu shared this critique). Natural law philosophers play a trick on us by granting almost arbitrary social conventions the status of 'timeless' laws (Lee 2010, 26–27).

Rousseau is concerned about individual freedom – but also social inequality in the sense that it may never "cause any one person to become dependent on the will and favour of some (specific) other person" (Dent 1992, 115). The famous first sentence of *The Social Contract* reads: "Man is born free, but is everywhere in chains." He maintains that civilisation does not guarantee freedom. In order to understand Rousseau's view on society we have to go back to his earlier *Discourse on Inequality*. His goal was to understand human nature and the nature of society itself (*Preface*). He actually offers a natural history of inequality in the framework of a natural history of civil society. He imagines life as it might have been like before society existed, and reconstructs the evolution of humanity. This reconstruction provides a view of human nature quite unlike Hobbes and Locke: human beings are far less rational that they assume.

2.6.3 State of Nature, Civil Society and Property

Consequently, Rousseau's conception of human nature is very different from Hobbes's and Locke's. His point of departure is "to distinguish properly between what is original and what is artificial in the actual nature of man" (*Discourse on Inequality*, *Preface* 44). From the conjunction of two principles (passions) that drive human beings, *amour de soi* and *pitié*, all the rules of natural right flow inherently to human nature, without the necessity of introducing the principle of natural sociability (*Discourse on Inequality*, *Preface* 47). What are these rules of natural right? First of all, Rousseau argues early in *The Social Contract* that all people have a natural right to provide for their self-preservation and that they are the sole judge of the proper means of preserving themselves. Free from interference or control of others, they become their own master. Rousseau equates the right to provide for one's own self-preservation with liberty, inherent in the nature of man (*The Social Contract* 1, 2, 2; Dent 1992, 210).

Rousseau then turns to the evolution of humanity. In the first evolutionary stage, human beings live basically solitary lives, wandering in the woods. Unlike in Hobbes, man is not naturally evil – lacking the motive of domination. The state of nature is an asocial condition since humans have little need of each other's company or support. The 'noble savage' has "an unlimited right to everything that tempts him and that he can get" (*The Social Contrac*t 1, 8, 2).

As human populations grow, humans are subsequently drawn into more frequent interaction and develop some technical skills and simple forms of co-operation with one another evolve around activities like deer hunting. They cooperate together but there is no real sense of belonging or loyalty to a group. Next, in small, settled communities, human beings start "to value themselves as others see them" (Bertram

2004, 37). This is the emergence of *amour propre*, the feeling that one merits 'consideration' (*Discourse on Inequality* 90). This passion leads human beings to seek recognition by others and to be treated with dignity and respect, "as equal members in our association with others" (Dent 1992, 35). However, there is a competitive side to *amour propre*, leading to the demands for precedence and domination over others (Dent 2005, 70–71).

The next stage features the invention of agriculture and metallurgy and the institution of private property. According to Rousseau: "The first man who, having enclosed a piece of ground, bethought himself of saying 'This is mine', and found people simple enough to believe him, was the real founder of civil society" (*Discourse on Inequality* 66). However, with civil society comes justice and misery, as property is the source of inequalities of power and reputation, exacerbating and perverting the *amour de soi*. This 'self-interested drive', the need for recognition that makes people compare themselves with others, is inflamed and, in the destructive form of *amour propre*, drives competition and the excessive pursuit of status, and consequently becomes the root of conflict, frustration and misery. The more powerful among the inhabitants of the state of nature claim the property of others and their (usurped) property is backed by law and state power. Society's institutions thus "compound artificial inequalities that are social in origin; honor, prestige, power, and privilege" (Boucher 2003, 243). Consequently, "emerging society gave way to the most horrible state of war" (*Discourse on Inequality* 97). Society is to blame, but society is also a fact of life. This view may reflect Rousseau's quest to understand his own contradictions (Damrosch 2005, 207, 397).

Although Rousseau calls this society *société civile*, it is civil society with a negative connotation – a far cry from the Enlightenment ideology of progress. Men are living in an unequal society, in a semi-socialised state (Shklar 1987b, 51). Nonetheless, inequality still entails mutual dependency as there arises "the multiplicity of new wants, brought into subjection [...] to one another". Moreover, the rich, being used to luxury and slaves, are more vulnerable (*Discourse on Inequality* 95, 101).

Hobbes was therefore in a way perfectly right about human selfishness. However, Rousseau disagrees with his assumption that it is inherent in human nature. He holds that man is naturally good, but society made man selfish and wicked. Moreover, unlike Hume, Rousseau's theory is not premised upon human sociability. Another society is conceivable. This requires the redirection of *amour propre* "toward civic self-esteem, and the replacing of opinions that tends to inequality with those that prevent it" (Shklar 1987b, 187).

The foregoing shows that private property plays an important role, because in its improper enlargement private ownership causes natural man to fall into the state of moral corruption and inequality (Hulliung 1994, 65). Rousseau dismisses the claims to proprietorship of individuals who have been enriched by their own industry, bringing down misery, servitude or dispossession on others. However, he sees nothing wrong in the nature of private ownership as such, after all it is a means to self-preservation (*Discourse on Inequality* 97). Rousseau is concerned about the extent of ownership by some, rather than arguing for the complete abolition of private property (Dent 1992, 199). Locke too was concerned about individuals creating more property than was enough for their needs or use (*Second Treatise* 5.31).

2.6.4 Renewing Social Contract Theory: Liberty and Equality

The outcome of Rousseau's story of the evolution of humanity is a fierce criticism of received social contract theory that not only aims at explaining the origins of society but actually tries to attribute legitimacy to a society few of its members would consent to (McClelland 1996, 258).

Man must leave a corrupt form of political society, which has become an instrument of the domination of man over man rather than the state of nature as in Hobbes and Locke, and establish a republic based on the social contract, that is, "on the unanimous agreement of each with all" (Bobbio 1989, 39), not unlike Locke in many respects. An equality that is moral and legitimate should be substituted for men's natural inequality of mere strength or intelligence. Equality is not be hypostasised, though, at the expense of private property. Rousseau does not advocate the abolishment of private property.

Liberty is therefore central to Rousseau's conception of a legitimate state, but "equality is indispensable for the attainment of liberty" (Wokler 1995, 62). The key question of how to devise a legitimate society, then translates into a question of how to ground political authority so as to enable men to experience their fullest freedom through living in civil society. That is exactly the task Rousseau undertakes in *The Social Contract*. He aims to justify the terms of political association ("principles of political right", according to the sub-title of *The Social Contract*). He shows that a certain form of political association is legitimate because interdependent individuals would themselves agree to that form (Cohen 2010, 24). As citizens, Wokler (1995, 61), explains, they "acquire moral responsibilities and cooperative interests". Unlike social contract thinkers before him, Rousseau portrays a pact of association which is a vehicle for the fulfilment of ambitions "unimaginable to solitary savages" (ibid.).

The social contract is the device for men to aggregate their forces, to constitute themselves as a people, and create the basis of a legitimate civil order. The communal life grounded in a common agreement increases their liberty far beyond that of the mere physical independence of solitary savages. To preserve liberty and enhance self-preservation, Rousseau grounds the individual's duty to submit to an authority in a voluntary act.

By virtue of the pact, individuals become political equals – the precondition of the formation of a single will, that is, the sovereign authority (Loughlin 2010, 114). Hence, the social contract involves "a form of association" in which each citizen, "uniting with all, nevertheless obeys only himself and remains free as before" (*The Social Contract* 1, 6, 4). According to Rousseau, the clauses of the contract amount to "the total alienation of each associate with all the rights, to the whole community" ("pactum unionis" or "pactum sociale"; *The Social Contrac*t 1, 6, 6). This 'alienation' can be best understood as "an exchange of natural liberty for civil liberty" (Loughlin 2010, 116). Unlike Hobbes, Rousseau does not envisage a transfer of political authority to a sovereign, with men giving away their freedoms. Legitimacy is only possible if sovereignty is retained by the people. The sovereign must therefore be identical with the citizens themselves (Hampsher-Monk 1992, 177).

2.6.5 *Social Contract: Grounding a Legitimate Political Society*

The essence of the social compact is that each individual, "contracting with himself so to speak" (*The Social Contract* 1, 7, 1), has entered into two reciprocal agreements. First, since he is member of the sovereign body, as a citizen he shares with other individuals in the sovereign authority. Secondly, as a subject he is under the laws, of which he is author in his capacity of citizen, of the state (ibid.). Hence, one also has to obey a law with which one disagrees but which is procedurally the expression of the general will.

The individual becomes citizen and subject, whose liberty takes on a profoundly different form in the civil state. Rousseau gives an account of positive liberty in such a legitimate state (Viroli 1987). Citizens are recognised as persons of equal moral standing which involves "equal protection by the public force of the person and goods of each individual" (Dent 1992, 211). Rousseau's focus is on a feeling of the common good – an artificial feeling to be fostered by laws (Riley 2005, 365–366). This form of association does not involve a loss of liberty, but rather an exchange of natural liberty for civil liberty, the latter being limited by the general will (*The Social Contract* 1, 8, 2; Dent 1992, 211). True liberty is to be found in rules that we impose on ourselves (self-government).

The sovereign will is declared in legislation, that is, the fundamental laws which lay down the whole structure and organisation of the civil association. They are acts of the general will (*volunté générale*), which alone makes legitimate law. The general will is distinct from the will of all which "takes private interest into account, and is no more than a sum of particular [self-interested] wills" (*The Social Contract* 2, 3, 2). The general will can be understood as an expression of freedom, protecting an equal freedom for all. Nonetheless, some interpret Rousseau's idea of popular sovereignty translated into a seemingly absolute obedience to the general will as a covert plea for totalitarian dictatorship.

The primary purpose of civil association is procuring justice for each and every person. If the fundamental laws are an expression of the general will, "then those laws are just and legitimate, laws in nature as well in name" (Dent 2005, 135). Each person is thus recognised by others as an equal and is consulted in matters that affect him and contributes as legislator to common affairs (Dent 1992, 138–139). This conjunction of both liberty and equality with sovereignty comprises a strikingly original approach to social contract theory (Wokler 1995, 63). Nonetheless, Rousseau realised the general will would never amount to more than a theory unless reinforced by civic virtue. This requires, inter alia, that citizens develop a sense of duty and motivational supports for it, complementing the general will.

The object of the general will is liberty and equality – "the greatest good of all, which should be the end of every system of legislation" (*The Social Contract* 2, 11, 1). The law is an instrument to advance (a measure of) substantive equality to secure each citizen "against personal dependence" (*The Social Contract* 1, 7, 8). Rousseau also advocates equality before the law since the general will is oriented to formal equality. To be general, laws must be created and obeyed by all; the general will must "both come from and apply to all" (*The Social Contract* 2, 4, 5; Hampsher-Monk 1992, 183). This general (and abstract) law is opposed to any kind of individual command: it does not refer to individually nominated persons or their particular actions.

The requirement of generality fits in with a republican conception of political liberty. Generality of law is to be seen in opposition to an arbitrary will imposing commands on others. Republican theorists consider behaviour regulated by law to be free, when the law is not arbitrary, that is, when it is applied equally to all citizens or to all members of the group in question (Viroli 2002, 42–43). The 'faceless' general will protects us from being subject to the arbitrary will of other persons, such as arbitrary taxation. Thus, the requirement of generality protects us from arbitrary taxation, from dependence on other persons, and from domination in the sense of the constant possibility of interference (Hulliung 1994, 196–197).

2.6.6 Taxation

Rousseau's republican conception of political liberty guides his approach to taxation. Citizens should not pay for public services and troops in order to escape their civic duties. "Men surrender a part of their profits in order to have time to increase them at leisure" (*The Social Contract* 3, 15,1). In no way should tax payments replace the fulfilment of civic duties. Unlike for Hobbes, taxes are not reduced to the price for security to be paid by passive subjects. Citizens should have their share in public governance and participate in law-making so as to perceive the laws as their laws, which guarantee the "common liberty" (*Discourse on Political Economy* 146). Rousseau's republican understanding of citizenship emphasises active participation in politics, which he considers essential for the strength of a democracy. Citizens substituting tax payments for civic duties undermine their liberty. In this context, Rousseau holds "enforced labour to be less opposed to liberty than taxes" (*The Social Contract* 3, 15,1).

This is not an argument against taxation as such. Taxation provides the state with public income. Rousseau has no doubts about the importance thereof. The duty of government is not only to protect its citizens, but also to consider their subsistence. This comes as no surprise as the purpose of general will is the greatest good of all, that is, both liberty and equality (*Discourse on Political Economy*, 151). Nonetheless, Rousseau warns that taxes often cause great inequality. Tax collectors "hand out a few small amounts to those bands of slaves and rascals who surround them and would pocket the rest" (*Political Fragments*, IV:9 30). Absent effective accountability and control mechanisms, taxes impoverish people without enriching the treasury (*Political Fragments*, VII:7, 52). In his *Confessions* Rousseau described an incident when he met a peasant who had hidden bread, ham, and wine in his cellar, afraid of government spies looking for evaders of a tax known as the *taille* (1789, 137). This kind of injustice inspired his thoughts on taxation. The French tax system was deeply flawed. Especially the salt tax (*gabelle*) and the wine tax, both indirect taxes, were deeply unpopular. The tax on salt which was vital for preserving food, and consuming less was hardly a way to pay less tax, since the purchase of a stipulated quantity of salt was obligatory. Consequently, Elster (2020, 80) writes the salt tax "could cut deeply into the consumption budget". Tax collectors, viz., tax farmers and state administrators, enjoyed considerable discretionary powers of assessment and collection, and much tax "went in the pockets of the tax officials" (Webber and Wildawsky 1986, 282). The latter often used brutal methods and punishments, such as "fines, whipping, branding, sentencing to the galleys and execution", to enforce the tax payment (Elster 2020, 80).

The right of taxation is one of the main attributes of sovereignty (*The Social Contract* 2, 2, 2). Ideally, the people would govern themselves and there would be no intermediary between the administration of the State and the citizens. These citizens would assess themselves occasionally, "in proportion to the public needs and the abilities of individuals" (*Discourse on Political Economy*, 152–153) and because of full transparency of the assessment and the subsequent spending process, no fraud or abuse could occur. Moreover, says Rousseau, the people would be never "over-burdened with taxes; or at least the knowledge of how the money would be used would be a consolation for the severity of the tax" (ibid., 153). Perfect self-government, distributive justice based on the ability to pay, full compliance and transparency with regard to public spending, are, unfortunately, Utopian ideals.

Rousseau argues that the obligation to pay tax follows from the social contract (*Discourse on Political Economy*, 159). Rousseau speaks the language of fiscal equality which had become stronger in eighteenth-century political-economic French literature. There was a call for "some sort of social contract between rulers and subject [that] rendered tax privilege illegitimate" (Kwass 2000, 231). According to Rousseau, all who contribute should clearly recognise the need for this encroachment upon their property rights. Such assessment should be lawful, and therefore voluntary; it must depend on the general will rather than a particular will. This requires the consent of the (majority of the) people or its representatives. Arbitrary taxes are thus avoided if legislated in conformity with the general will, and, Rousseau immediately adds, if they are levied at a proportional rate. With regard to the application and enforcement of the tax laws, Rousseau argues that the spirit of the law ought to decide in every particular case that it could not anticipate. Additional guidance is provided by the sense of justice inherent in the general will, "the source and supplement of all laws" (*Discourse on Political Economy* 138).

Truly equitable and proportionate taxation entails that taxes should not be levied in "simple ratio to the property of the contributors" (*Discourse on Political Economy*, 160). Rousseau advocates the benefit principle, but he adds that taxes should be proportional to the difference in circumstances of individuals: the amount of property, of 'superfluities' (superfluous commodities) and "the advantage that every person derives from the social confederacy" (*Discourse on Political Economy* 160). Thus, he changes the traditional idea of proportionality considerably (Mann 1978, 163). He actually advocates something like the ability to pay principle, leaving the subsistence minimum untaxed. "He who possesses only the common necessaries of life should pay nothing at all, while the tax on him who is in possession of superfluities may justly be extended to everything he has over and above mere necessaries"

(*Discourse on Political Economy* 160, cf. 153). Rousseau's plea for progressive taxation resonated with contemporary French political and economic axioms the logic of which demanded a redistribution of the tax burden in order to rebuild the impoverished French economy. Louis XIV's fiscal policies which overburdened the poor and relieved the rich could not produce economic growth (Gross 1993, 79–87; Kwass 2000, 225–231). Progressive taxation became a matter of both tax justice and social reform (Mann 1978, 165).

Rousseau gives the example of the French *capitation*, a direct tax (*Discourse on Political Economy*, 159; he thus disagrees with Montesquieu). Thus, Rousseau calls for the imposition of high taxes on wealth and luxuries by which "the poor are eased, and the burdens are thrown on the rich", making it possible to "prevent the continual increase of inequality of fortune" (ibid. 165). There is no need to be concerned as to "these taxes being arbitrary, because they are laid on things not absolutely necessary" (ibid. 166). An individual who buys articles, the use of which he can deny himself, actually consents to this progressive consumption tax. Therefore, as "the individual is under no absolute necessity to pay, his contribution may count as voluntary". His consent thus substitutes "the general consent of the whole people" (ibid. 167).

High taxes on wealth and luxuries are a matter of distributive justice but may also safeguard the integrity of the legislative process and legislation. Extreme inequality of fortunes should be prevented as the rich will use their power to bring about biased legislation at the expense of the 'common liberty'. Groups should be relatively equal in power and resources widely distributed (Cohen 2010, 164). Rousseau emphasises, however, that extreme inequality of fortunes should be prevented "not by taking away wealth from its possessors, but by depriving all men of means to accumulate it" (*Discourse on Political Economy* 147).

2.7 Thomas Paine (1737–1809)[12]

2.7.1 Introduction

Thomas Paine is, arguably, one of the most radical thinkers there has been, and his contribution to taxation theory is often overlooked, although tax is frequently mentioned in his revolutionary writings. He actively participated in much of the political upheaval he helped to instigate. He initially started on a career as an exciseman, although he was dismissed for involvement in agitation to increase excisemen's pay. In that role, he would have experienced at first hand practical issues in regard to taxation, notably smuggling to avoid high taxes on luxury goods such as tea, textiles, etc. At the suggestion of his friend, Benjamin Franklin, he moved to America and became actively involved in the struggle for independence from Great Britain, and published pamphlets in support of this cause, notably *Common Sense* (1776)

[12] This section follows closely Frecknall-Hughes (2007).

and *The American Crisis* (a series published between 1776 and 1783, and sometimes just referred to as *The Crisis*). He returned to England in 1787. His best-known work, however, is *The Rights of Man*, published in two parts in 1791 and 1792 respectively. Paine moved to France when he heard he was about to be arrested for sedition, as a result of publishing *Part I*. He remained in France and was an active participant in the Revolution, becoming a member of the Convention. However, his opposition to the execution of Louis XVI saw him imprisoned and narrowly escaping execution. He returned to America in 1802, dying there in penury in 1809 (see also Dorfman 1947, 447–459).

2.7.2 Paine's Version of the Social Contract

Part I of *The Rights of Man* was primarily a response to Edmund Burke's *Reflections on the Revolution in France* (1790), in an attempt to defend the French Revolutionaries. Paine was frequently at political loggerheads with Burke. His work contains many references to Burke's writings, and the two men never wasted any opportunity to attack each other verbally. While supporting the 'Glorious Revolution' and the grievances of the American colonists, Burke was opposed to the revolution in France, and his apparently contradictory views caused contemporaries to doubt his sincerity. However, as Adams and Dyson (2003, 91) point out, Burke was not necessarily inconsistent[13] in his thinking:

> The Glorious Revolution, even while getting rid of a king, had left the traditional institutions of government untouched. The Americans were defending the traditional right of Englishmen not to be taxed without representation. The French, by contrast, were sweeping away an immemorial order in favour of the unhistorical and contextless dogma of the 'rights of man'.

The ways in which human beings live, according to Burke, are based on tried and tested means, which experience over time has shown to work, and any changes are implemented slowly in a complex and intricately linked societal order that has developed gradually: it is not based on any kind of contract. To sweep all that away in favour of untried revolutionary doctrines denies the reality of human association and is an offence against nature. This is the basis of Burke's disagreement with Paine. Rather like Hume, Burke is content with things that work (although he does not refer to this as 'custom'), and would leave them well alone.

Paine's particular innovation was to set out the role of government in a society where morality took precedence over economics (Christian 1973, 367), his idea being to reform governments that had become tyrannical and corrupt with the passage of time. Reform, for Paine, involved three stages – political education, then political action, and finally changing social and economic conditions for the better.

[13] Indeed, Cobban (1960, 39) comments that many other thinkers can be charged with inconsistency. See also, for example, Day (1966) and Cherno (1957, 51) on Locke.

Political action encompassed revolution, which was a means to end oppression and burdensome taxation. He would sweep away the problems of the past and start anew.

Much like Locke, Paine saw society as based on natural rights, with a kind of social contract giving rise to government, but Christian (1973) sees this as based on economic need, as men cannot be self-sufficient and need state protection to combat economic aggression. As Paine writes in *Part II* of *The Rights of Man*,[14] Chapter 1 (7):

> As nature created him for social life, she fitted him for the station she intended. In all cases she made his natural wants greater than his individual powers. No one man is capable, without the aid of society, of supplying his own wants, and those wants, acting upon every kind of individual, impel the whole of them into society, as naturally as gravitation acts to a centre.

Paine considered that all men should participate in government and have the right to provide some input into public affairs: they were given this right because they paid tax, remarking (in *Part I,* 23) that all men in France, under its new constitution, who paid a tax of 60 sous were electors. Paine would have been familiar with the slogan of the American colonists – 'no taxation without representation' – which he has re-shaped into 'taxation means representation'.

2.7.3 Extension of the Idea of Benefit

Paine speaks extensively about taxation in *The Rights of Man*, specifically saying in *Part II*, Chapter 1 (9):

> Excess and inequality of taxation, however disguised in the means, never fail to appear in their effects. As a great mass of the community are thrown thereby into poverty and discontent, they are constantly on the brink of commotion.

He comments frequently on the oppressiveness of taxation, notably taxes on consumption, which he feels have become extremely onerous, especially to the industrial and agricultural poor (see Ayer 1988, 103).

> Before the coming of the Hanoverians, the taxes were divided in nearly equal proportions between the land and articles of consumption, the land bearing rather the largest share: but since that era nearly thirteen millions annually of new taxes have been thrown upon consumption. The consequence of which has been a constant increase in the number and wretchedness of the poor, and in the amount of the poor-rates.
>
> Several of the most heavy and productive taxes are so contrived, as to give an exemption to this pillar, thus standing in its own defence. The tax upon beer brewed for sale does not affect the aristocracy, who brew their own beer free from this duty.[15] It falls only on those

[14] The text referred to from *Part I* and *Part II* is an online edition, freely available. While it does not have page numbers per se, it is easy to identify specific page numbers from the online version.

[15] A tax on the raw ingredients which were used in brewing beer, most typically malt, would have meant that all brewers of beer, regardless of whether they sold the end product or not, could have borne the tax alike, but this does not seem to have been thought of at the time.

> who have not conveniency or ability to brew, and who must purchase it in small quantities. But what will mankind think of the justice of taxation, when they know that this tax alone, from which the aristocracy are from circumstances exempt, is nearly equal to the whole of the land-tax, being in the year 1788, and it is not less now, £1,666,152, and with its proportion of the taxes on malt and hops, it exceeds it.– That a single article, thus partially consumed, and that chiefly by the working part, should be subject to a tax, equal to that on the whole rental of a nation, is, perhaps, a fact not to be paralleled in the histories of revenues. (*The Rights of Man, Part II* 38)

Significantly, in *Part II*, Paine gives a great many details and statistics about English taxation, reminiscent of his approach in earlier writing on taxation (*Pamphlet 9b The Crisis Extraordinary. On The Subject of Taxation*, written in Philadelphia in 1780), but the source of this information is not provided. Ayer (1988, 104–108) summarises Paine's narrative. Starting with William the Conqueror, Paine informs us that £400,000 per annum were raised in taxes, decreasing to £100,000 by 1466, then rising to £500,000 in 1566, £1,800,000 in 1666 and £17,000,000 in 1791, with the increases being driven by extravagance, corruption and foreign wars. Steep increases in tax led to inflation, with the Bank of England suspending payment in gold in 1797, which Paine predicted. Of the £17,000,000, he estimates that £9,000,000 would be needed to service the interest on the National Debt, with the remaining £8,000,000 left to cover other annual costs, including £1,000,000 set aside for the army and navy.

Paine assumes that out of a population of seven million, about one fifth would be so poor as to need financial support: 140,000 over 50 or 60 years of age would need pensions (£6 for those over 50; £10 for those over 60); and 630,000 children under age fourteen would require support for their education. He would obtain the funds for this by abolishing window and house taxes, and the commutation tax[16] and replacing them with a graduated income tax. A call for an income tax had been a particular grievance of the Revolutionaries in France, so he was very familiar with the concept. The proposed income tax rates were 3d[17] per £1 on incomes up to £500 per annum and 6d on incomes from £500 to £1,000, with increments of 3d up to £2,000 and £3,000, 6d to £4,000 and £5,000, and then 1s on each additional £1,000 up to £23,000. The most a person could retain from annual income would be £12,370. Hence a man with £50 of earned income would pay 12s 6d in income tax and a man with £1,000 would retain £979.

It is not surprising to find that Paine also sets out in *Part II* particular uses of tax revenues. In addition to the pensions referred to above, he would make provision for 350,000 poor families and for the education of 1,030,000 children overall; donations of 20s each for 50,000 births and 20,000 marriages; allowance of £20,000 for those who travelled for work purposes and died away from home; and employment

---

[16] The commutation tax was so named after the *Commutation Act* of 1784, whereby William Pitt the Younger reduced the tax on tea from 119% to 12.5%, to end the punitive rates, which had promoted smuggling.

[17] These rates are expressed in the pre-decimal currency used in the UK before 1971 – pounds (sterling, denoted by £), shillings (denoted by s) and pence (denoted by d), with 20 shillings to £1 and 12 pennies (or pence) to 1 s.

for the casual poor in London and Westminster (seemingly via some sort of workhouse). Ayer notes (1988, 107) that some groups are left without provision – poor bachelors and spinsters who are not children but not yet 50 years of age, but assumes this is an oversight. Paine also proposes to support 15,000 disbanded soldiers and sailors with an allowance of 3 s per week for life, and to increase pay rates for the rest of army and navy personnel. An omission from Paine's programme is any mention of death duties – but he did revisit this later, in 1795, in his pamphlet, *Agrarian Justice*, in which he proposed death duties of 10% on most estates.

Paine's writings went a long way in the development of tax theory, and extended the idea of natural rights to include the rights of citizens to education, old-age pensions and other financial benefits. For him, paying tax meant that men had a right to have their say in public affairs, and this was not governed by how much they paid. His detailed proposals for taxation contain the beginnings of benefit theory – and Ayer (1988, 109) feels justified in calling his ideas a 'blueprint' for a Welfare State, the main difference between Paine's ideas and the scheme introduced in the UK in 1945 being the absence of a National Health Service. Despite his unpopularity with the British Government, it is not hard to see the influence of his ideas on Pitt's income tax introduced in the 1798 Budget – but, of course, this would never be acknowledged. However, while an energetic proponent of welfare provision, Paine does not seem to be aware that it could not be supported without the substantial imposts by government which he condemned as oppressive.

2.8 America, *The Federalist Papers* and *The Anti-Federalist Papers*

2.8.1 Introduction

The theme of the development of America and the United States is evident in the work of a number of the philosophers considered earlier – Locke, Hume, Burke and Paine – although as a nation state it was at different stages of its development during their respective lives. Indeed, their own writings and actions had considerable influence on the country's political evolution, as noted earlier, with Paine taking an active part in the American and French Revolutions, as mentioned. The sequence of events leading up to the American War of Independence and the impact of taxes are well known (see Adams 1958, 86–106; Greene and Pole 2000, passim). While tax played a significant role in the French Revolution, the resentment felt was at its unevenness and unfair impact: in essence, an income tax was desired which would apply to all citizens, regardless of status and not exempt the rich, who could afford most but paid the least tax, if any at all. In contrast, when Great Britain decided that American colonists should contribute to their own protection, a series of taxes followed – the 1765 *Stamp Act*, which colonial riots forced to be cancelled, with the 1767 *Townshend Acts* introducing additional duties and generating further riots, culminating in the 1773 tea duties and the famous 'Boston Tea Party' and subsequent *Coercive Acts* in 1774. Initially the colonists did not want independence, but greater control over their own affairs, especially taxes, but Thomas Paine's *Common Sense* of 1776 was instrumental in promoting the view that the colonists owed nothing to Britain. *Common Sense* was a radical, reasoned polemic, arguing convincingly against British monarchical rule and for separation of America from Great Britain, and was enormously influential in turning public opinion towards independence:

> Everything that is right or natural pleads for separation. The blood of the slain, the weeping voice of nature cries, 'TIS TIME TO PART. Even the distance at which the Almighty hath placed England and America is a strong and natural proof that the authority of the one over the other was never the design of Heaven. (*Common Sense*, 12)

By the time of the 'Boston Tea Party', the amount of tax payable was actually minimal, but the principle of it being imposed without the consent of those taxed was the issue. The War of Independence ended in 1781, with a peace treaty being formally signed at Versailles in September 1783 – leaving the 13 newly independent states in need of a constitution.

2.8.2 *The Influence of the Philosophers*

It was to earlier theorists that many of the U.S. Founding Fathers turned for political guidance in their search for principles on which to found a new state with a written constitution. Arguably, the influence of Locke was the most predominant. It is not surprising to find this, given the circumstances pertaining. After all, a new nation was being forged, and all of the old institutions had been swept away, so who better as an inspiration than Locke who had had similar experiences, and whose view of America was one that would resonate with those descended from American pioneers?

Locke, of course, died before these cataclysmic events: even the union of Scotland with Britain to form Great Britain occurred after his death. However, his body of work is generously laced with mentions of America, with Lebovics (1986, 567) commenting that the *Second Treatise* is "filled with references to the world across the Atlantic, which was … just coming under systematic colonization and settlement". Locke knew a great deal about America, his knowledge being obtained from reading about travel, geography and explorations, from his investments in colonial ventures and from his public service. Via Shaftesbury's patronage, from 1673–1675 he served as Secretary to the Lords Proprietors of Carolina (and was involved in drafting the state's constitution) and to the Council of Trade and Plantations, serving on its successor body, the Board of Trade, from 1696 to his retirement in 1700 (see Lebovics 1986, 575–576). Locke used America to provide key examples in the development of his political theories, particularly the right to private property – a use which has always been considered controversial and has generated much debate (notably by scholars such as Macpherson, Tully and Arneil – see Buckle (2001)) on the positions of the Amerindians, English, European and other colonists. Buckle (2001, 274) summarises Locke's basic tenets (as being from a domestic and English perspective):

> His political message is that property is acquired by natural right, and so not freely disposable by political authorities; his economic message is that the prosperity enjoyed by Englishmen is due to the benefits which flow from a system where the fruits of value-adding labour, compounded by the investment and trade made possible by the invention of the money economy, are thus guaranteed against arbitrary incursions.

It is easy to be critical of Locke's use of America, but it must be remembered that many of his contemporary readers would not have known much, if anything, about America. It is often the case that a far away, largely unknown country is used to provide cautionary or illustrative examples. Medieval maps, for instance, often bore the legend 'here be dragons' to denote unchartered or dangerous territories. While the territories were known to exist, it is doubtful if anyone believed dragons lived there, but the uncertainty and lack of knowledge about them meant that they could be used for various purposes. It is not unreasonable to suggest that Locke's readers may have similarly interpreted his use of American examples. It is equally easy to point to inconsistencies and omissions, for example, that the concept and practice of slavery could not be encompassed within his theories.

Dienstag (1996a, b) shows that of the American Founding Fathers, Jefferson and Adams alike were particularly influenced by Locke's political thinking in the *Second Treatise*, which resonates in Jefferson's original drafting of the Declaration of Independence:

> We hold these truths to be self evident: that all men are created equal; they are endowed by their Creator with inherent and inalienable rights; that among these are life, liberty, and the pursuit of happiness; that to secure these rights, governments are instituted among men, deriving their just powers from the consent of the governed; that whenever any form of government becomes destructive of these ends, it is the right of the people to alter or abolish it, and to institute new government, laying its foundation on such principles, and organizing powers in such form, as to them shall seem most likely to effect their safety and happiness. (Jefferson 1903, 1, 29)

Dienstag (1996a) makes very clear, however, that the exact nature of Locke's influence has been extensively debated. Many writers also consider Hume and other, ancient Greek and philosophers had their part to play (evident in Alexander Hamilton's thinking – see below).

2.8.3 The Move to an Explicit Contract

Likewise, Locke's *Second Treatise* influenced the writers of *The Federalist Papers* (Madison et al. 1788). *The Federalist Papers* are a set of essays and articles written by Founding Fathers James Madison, Alexander Hamilton and John Jay, and published collectively under the pseudonym 'Publius', although the various pieces have subsequently been attributed to specific authors. Their purpose was to promote acceptance of the Constitution developed in 1787 after the War of Independence, and explain and justify the political principles it embodied. The use of a pseudonym was to emphasise that the identity of the writer was not important, but that the ideas expressed were. Key – and highly controversial – issues were the separation of powers between the judiciary, the legislature and the executive, and the concept of federalism. Weaver (1997, 422), in looking at the influence of Locke, comments that, while he would not contend, in respect of *The Federalist Papers*, that "Locke's influence was monolithic and stood alone as a dominant influence", and accepts that "other influences were at work as well", his influence was nonetheless significant. Wootton (2018, 140–141) comments, for instance:

> The English war was fought to curb the power of the state, at the time identified with monarchy. In the early years of the eighteenth century the emphasis was still on curbing the power of the executive. … it was indeed still Tom Paine's concern in Common Sense, the text that more than any other inspired the American Revolution. But as debt and taxation rose, the key issue for many became limiting the power not of the executive but of the legislature.

The works of many philosophers had influence, and as Werner (1972) notes, if is often very difficult to trace the influence of particular ideas. Sometimes the Founding Fathers explicitly acknowledged a writer, as Hamilton did, when speaking out "against a proposal to attach legal penalties against corruption on the part of office-holders" and insisting that "this was unnecessary by referring to Hume" (Werner 1972, 451). Wootton (2018, 141) comments that "[n]otoriously, Hume approved of Robert Walpole's policy of buying votes in the Commons by distributing government pensions, since it helped redress the growing imbalance between legislature and executive". Hamilton, in reference to Hume's opinion of the British Constitution, expressed the view that a body of patriots would always exist who could deal with corruption in the administration (Werner 1972, 451). This shows a familiarity with Hume's work on English history. Indeed, Wills (1981) considers that Hume is the major intellectual source for *The Federalist Papers.*

The Federalist Papers, numbers 30 through to 36, attributed to Alexander Hamilton, concern taxation, so are of particular relevance to this chapter. Overall, Hamilton aimed to persuade readers that there should be federal taxation, at a national level – that there should be a general power of taxation (No. 30) to provide public necessities – a concept that was repeated in other articles, although he was not opposed to individual state taxation (Nos. 32 and 33). This, of course, was an issue with which Great Britain (and, indeed, Locke) never had to contend. Until relatively recently, the separate nations which comprise Great Britain/the United Kingdom have not had separate taxes or taxing rights. A particularly vexing issue was the nature of the relationship between state tax law and any federal imposition and their respective standing. Again, this is something which should not be surprising, given the U.S. states had clear individual identities and any federal tax could possibly be viewed in the same way as the colonists had viewed impositions from Great Britain. Moreover, there was the history of tax impositions made during the War, and immediately after, to contend with as well (see Edling and Kaplanoff

2004). Hamilton was concerned to point out that two sets of tax laws could co-exist harmoniously, drawing on examples from ancient Rome (No. 34) and would exist to serve different purposes. For example, federal revenue would be necessary to deal with future contingencies of a national character, such as war, as well as national government administration.

The views of the Federalists were countered by the Anti-Federalists, who were opposed to the ratification of the Constitution (see Ball 2003). They too were in favour of federalism, but wanted a 'small republic' (a weak central government), as opposed to a 'big republic', fearing that a national government would have too much power and would be a threat to individual liberties. To counter this latter threat, they wanted a bill of rights. They were concerned especially about the effect on state government if a national government were too powerful, the potential for a president to have monarch-like powers and a congress to seize too much power, as well as having concerns about a system of federal courts. In general too, they considered that the actual size of the combined U.S. states would mean that a republican-style government could not operate effectively. They favoured direct election of government officials with limited terms and accountability by office holders. Their views are contained in collection of writings known as *The Anti-Federalist Papers* (Bailey, undated). As with *The Federalist Papers*, the authors of *The Anti-Federalist Papers* use pseudonyms, but there remains debate about their individual identities. Their views are representative of the landowners, small farmers, merchants and workmen who comprised this body. In general, their views are coloured more by Montesquieu's works than Locke's (see Dry 2000, 486).

The Anti-Federalist Papers are liberally peppered with detailed arguments about taxation, with numbers 30 to 36 being devoted entirely to tax. A particular concern was about the federal power to tax, which they wanted limited to taxing imports from overseas. As Dry (2000, 489) comments:

> Thus they attempted to reply to Hamilton's great challenge, expressed in *The Federalist*, no. 23, that one not embrace the contradiction of, on the one hand, supporting union and entrusting certain national objectives to the federal government, and, on the other hand, refusing to grant ample powers for the attainment of those objectives.

While the Constitution was ratified, albeit by a very narrow margin, taxation continued to be contentious, with Edling and Kaplanoff (2004) noting that the government had to resort to arms to extinguish the Whiskey Rebellion in 1794 and Fries's Rebellion in 1798, although these were regarded as 'one-off' events.

It is, perhaps, not easily appreciated today just how radical and contentious the U.S. Constitution was when it was first drafted, as the countries of the known world were still predominantly governed by monarchical powers, sometimes absolute. There was no frame of reference for such a written document: hitherto just philosophical ideas. The Founders had indeed started with a *tabula rasa*, scraped clean of past ideas and associations. What they did was move from the tacit social contract idealised by Locke and develop an explicit, written version (particular to the circumstances of 13 states which had fought a war to achieve independence) which defined government power, specific rights, obligations and expectations in a way that had not been done before – and particularly as regards taxation.

2.9 Concluding Remarks

In this chapter we have considered some of the most important political philosophers of the Enlightenment (taken as broad concept) – thinkers whose reflections on the idea of a social contract we have related to their views on taxation. In conclusion we will bring together the various, emergent themes. Their ideas, however, often only show a partial overlap since these political theorists reflected in different ways on the major political issues of the particular political society they lived in. Moreover, we did not deal in depth with the diverging approaches and arguments which allows for an over-arching comparison only.

To begin with, Hobbes's argument is grounded in an (almost) absolute political sovereignty and legal authority and corresponding obedience of citizens. The social contract is a device to replace the lack of natural sociability by a strong state which creates and maintains an artificial sociability. Subsequent authors are less pessimistic about human nature. Rousseau holds that man is naturally good, but corrupted by society. Human sociability is taken for granted by, for example, Montesquieu and Hume: they do not have need for the state of nature and a social contract. Hume even assumes that all primitive societies have a judicial system enforcing a customary law. However, Locke, in the *Second Treatise* (7.91) says that in the state of nature, there is no actual judge to enforce the law.

In Hobbes, absolute rights are conferred on the sovereign, the subjects' liberty depending on the silence of the law. Unlike Hobbes, Locke argues that the social contract serves to guarantee the individual's property rights which embody his liberty. Montesquieu is also concerned with citizens' liberty but abandons the language of absolute rights. To complicate matters further, Rousseau's radical conception of the social contract entails the total alienation of rights to a whole community, which boils down to an exchange of natural liberty for civil liberty and equality. Sovereignty is retained by the people, and men do not give away their freedoms. For Hume, society and even government are a fact of life to maintain liberty and the right to property. Much like Locke, Paine sees the social contract as being grounded in men's need for cooperation in order to survive. The contract gives rise to government, the sole purpose of which is to provide security, that is, negative liberty. However, his innovative proposals on economic, social and political reform show Paine's additional concern for positive liberty. Nonetheless, reform was very much a white masculine affair, as many groups of the population were still excluded from emancipation.

The Federalist Papers followed Locke in asserting certain inalienable rights to be secured by government. Moreover, they replaced Locke's tacit social contract by an explicit, written version, that is, a written constitution. They elaborated on Montesquieu's doctrine of separation and distribution of powers as a safeguard against law as a despotic instrument, violating the general spirit of society, and consequently an indispensable device for the protection of liberty. The Anti-Federalists, for their part, argued for a bill of rights, a kind of supplement to the written contract, to protect individual liberties against federal government's power. Popular sovereignty and the idea that liberty in civil society consists in one's authorship of the laws to which one adheres, as advocated by Rousseau were self-evident to Paine, the Federalists and anti-Federalists alike.

These political philosophers all developed new political ideas and arguments which account for changing views on taxation. A gradual shift in the justification of taxation occurred. For Hobbes, taxes are the price of security, while for Locke it is the price of the protection of the right to property. Hume seems to see the legitimacy of imposing and paying tax in a sense of civic duty to contribute to society on which one depends to survive. Paying taxes is a customary habit in a given society. Montesquieu, however, offers a normative underpinning. Paying tax is based on reciprocity, give and take. Taxation provides the state with public income. Rousseau argues that taxation is to enable government not only to protect its citizens, but also to consider their subsistence, enhancing liberty and equality. Paine followed suit as taxes should pay for welfare provision. The Federalists and Anti-Federalists alike grasped the principle that tax revenue was needed for running states and provision of defence, etc., but their particular difference concerned the distribution of the power to tax, with the Anti-Federalists having a fear of conferring too much power on the State (with a capital 'S') as opposed to leaving it in the hands of states (with a lower case 's'). Given that the 13 states forming a new nation had emerged from a war in which the power to tax had played such a dominant role and had lain in the hands of a distant sovereign nation, this debate was both terrifying and familiar at the same time as being novel: a case both of what might be seen as customary (per Hume) and starting with a *tabula rasa* (as per Locke). Moreover, taxation is a matter of the separation and distribution of powers but unlike in Montesquieu, from the perspective of multi-level governance.

The principle underpinning the distribution of the tax burden evolves with the views by the different theorists on the type of government advocated. The emphasis seems to shift from the grounding of political authority and obedience on the need for security and the protection of property, to the preconditions for legitimate government and governance: legitimate government and governance should be capable of protecting and enhancing individual liberty and equality. This development clears the way for more egalitarian notions of taxation, going beyond the distribution of the tax burden based on the benefits secured by government. As principles of equity or justice come to the fore as preconditions for any sustainable political society, tax becomes instrumental to social justice. The benefit principle is past its peak and the ability to pay principle, embodying the concept of distributive justice (along with a different conceptualisation of rights), enters the scene. Nevertheless, it will be a long, long way to go towards legitimate governance, a just, inclusive political society and a corresponding tax system.

References

Adams, Randolph G. 1958. *Political Ideas of the American Revolution*. 3rd ed. New York: Barnes & Noble Inc.

Adams, Ian, and R.W. Dyson. 2003. *Fifty Major Political Thinkers*. London: Routledge.

Andrew, Edward. 2012. Possessive Individualism and Locke's Doctrine on Taxation. *Good Society* 21 (1): 151–168.

———. 2015. Locke on Consent, Taxation and Representation. *Theoria* 62 (2): 15–32.

Arneil, Barbara. 1996. *John Locke and America: The Defence of English Colonialism*. Oxford: Clarendon Press.

Ashcraft, Richard. 1994. Locke's Political Philosophy. In *The Cambridge Companion to Locke*, ed. Vere Chappell, 223–269. Cambridge: Cambridge University Press.

Ayer, A.J. 1988. *Thomas Paine*. London: Secker & Warburg.

Bailey, Bill. (ed.) undated. The Antifederalist Papers, at https://www.thefederalistpapers.org/wp-content/uploads/2012/11/The-Anti-Federalist-Papers-Special-Edition.pdf. Accessed 30 Sept 2020.

Ball, Terence. 2003. The Federalist Papers. In *Political Thinkers: From Socrates to the Present*, ed. David Boucher and Paul Kelly, 235–252. Oxford: Oxford University Press.

Bennett, John G. 1979. A Note on Locke's Theory of Tacit Consent. *Philosophical Review* 88 (2): 224–234.

Berlin, Isaiah. [1958] 1969 Two Concepts of Liberty. In *Four Essays on Liberty*, ed. Isaiah Berlin, 118–172. Oxford: Oxford University Press.

Bertram, Christopher. 2004. *Rousseau and The Social Contract*. London: Routledge.

Bobbio, Norberto. 1989. *Democracy and Dictatorship: The Nature and Limits of State Power*. Minneapolis: University of Minnesota Press.

Bonney, Richard. 1995. Early Modern Theories of State Finance. In *Economic Systems and State Finance*, ed. Richard Bonney, 163–229. Oxford: Oxford University Press.

Boucher, David. 2003. Rousseau. In *Political Thinkers: From Socrates to the Present, David Boucher*, ed. Paul Kelly, 235–252. Oxford: Oxford University Press.

Buckle, Stephen. 2001. Tully, Locke and America. *British Journal for the History of Philosophy* 9 (2): 245–281.

Burke, Edmund. [1790] 2019. *Reflections on the Revolution in France*. Dumfries and Galloway: Anodos Books.

Byrne, Donna M. 1999. Locke, Property and Progressive Taxes. *Nebraska Law Review* 78 (3): 700–738.

Cherno, Melvin. 1957. Locke on Property: A Reappraisal. *Ethics* 68 (1): 51–55.

Christian, William. 1973. The Moral Economics of Tom Paine. *Journal of the History of Ideas* 34 (3): 367–380.

Cobban, Alfred. 1960. *Edmund Burke and the Revolt Against the Eighteenth Century*. 2nd ed. London: George Allen & Unwin Ltd.

Cohen, Joshua. 1986. Structure, Choice, and Legitimacy: John Locke's Theory of the State. *Philosophy and Public Affairs* 15 (4): 301–324.

———. 2010. *Rousseau: A Free Community of Equals*. Oxford: Oxford University Press.

Damrosch, Leo. 2005. *Jean-Jacques Rousseau: Restless Genius*. Boston and New York: Houghton Mifflin Company.

Darnton, Robert. 1997. *George Washington's False Teeth*. New York Review of Books, 27 March, at https://www.nybooks.com/articles/1997/03/27/george-washingtons-false-teeth/. Accessed 8 Nov 2021.

Day, J.P. 1966. Locke on Property. *The Philosophical Quarterly* 16 (64): 207–220.

De Dijn, Annelien. 2008. *French Political Thought from Montesquieu to Tocqueville: Liberty in a Levelled Society?* Cambridge: Cambridge University Press.

Dent, Nicholas J.H. 1992. *A Rousseau Dictionary*. Oxford and Cambridge, MA: Blackwell Publishers.

Dent, Nicholas. 2005. *Rousseau*. London: Routledge.

Dickson, P.G.M. 1967. *The Financial Revolution in England. A Study in the Development of Public Credit 1688–1756*. London, Melbourne and Toronto: Macmillan.

Dienstag, Joshua F. 1996a. Serving God and Mammon: The Lockean Sympathy in Early American Political Thought. *American Political Science Review* 90 (3): 497–511.

———. 1996b. Between History and Nature: Social Contract Theory in Locke and the Founders. *Journal of Politics* 58 (4): 985–1009.
Dome, Takuo. 2004. *The Political Economy of Public Finance in Britain 1767–1873*. London and New York: Routledge.
Dorfman, Joseph. 1947. *The Economic Mind in American Civilization 1606–1865*, Vol. 1. London: George G. Harrap & Ltd.
Dry, Murray. 2000. The Debate Over Ratification. In *A Companion to the American Revolution*, ed. Jack P. Greene and J.R. Pole, 482–494. Massachusetts: Blackwell Publishers.
Dunn, J. 1967. Consent in the Political Theory of John Locke. *The Historical Journal* 10 (2): 153–182.
Edling, Max M., and Mark D. Kaplanoff. 2004. Alexander Hamilton's Fiscal Reform: Transforming the Structure of Taxation in the Early Republic. *William and Mary Quarterly* 61 (4): 713–744.
Elster, Jon. 2020. *France before 1789: The Unraveling of an Absolutist Regime*. Princeton and Oxford: Princeton University Press.
Epstein, Richard A. 1986. Taxation in a Lockean World. *Social Philosophy and Policy* 4 (1): 49–74.
Frecknall-Hughes, Jane. 2007. The Concept of Taxation and the Age of Enlightenment. In *Studies in the History of Tax Law*, ed. John Tiley, vol. 2, 253–286. Oxford and Portland, Oregon: Hart Publishing.
———. 2014. Locke, Hume, Johnson and the Continuing Relevance of Tax History. *eJournal of Tax Research* 12 (1): 87–103.
———. 2019. Jeremy Bentham: Developing Ideas About Taxation and Law. In *Studies in the History of Tax Law*, ed. Peter Harris and Dominic de Cogan, vol. 9, 1–15. Oxford and Portland, Oregon: Hart Publishing.
Goldsmith, M.M. 1996. Hobbes on Law. In *The Cambridge Companion to Hobbes*, ed. Tom Sorell, 274–305. Cambridge: Cambridge University Press.
Gough, J.W. 1956. *John Locke's Political Philosophy*. Oxford: Clarendon Press.
Goyard-Fabre, Simone. 1979. *La Philosophie du Droit de Montesquieu*. Paris: Librairie C. Klincksieck.
Grant, Ruth W. 1987. *John Locke's Liberalism*. Chicago: University of Chicago Press.
Greene, Jack P., and J.R. Pole, eds. 2000. *A Companion to the American Revolution*. Massachusetts: Blackwell Publishers.
Gribnau, Hans, and Carl Dijkstra. 2019. Contractualism and Tax Governance: Hobbes and Hume. In *Studies in the History of Tax Law*, ed. Peter Harris and Dominic de Cogan, vol. 8, 17–54. Oxford and Portland, Oregon: Hart Publishing.
———. 2020. Social Contract and Beyond: Sociability, Reciprocity and Tax Ethics. In *Ethics and Taxation*, ed. Robert F. van Brederode, 47–90. Singapore: Springer Nature Pte Ltd.
Gross, Jean-Pierre. 1993. Progressive Taxation and Social Justice in Eighteenth-Century France. *Past & Present* 140: 79–126.
Groves, Harold. 1974. *Tax Philosophers: Two Hundred Years of Thought in Great Britain and the United States*. Madison: WUP.
Halévy, Elie. [1928] 1972. *The Growth of Philosophical Radicalism*. London: Faber and Faber.
Hampsher-Monk, Iain. 1992. *A History of Modern Political Thought*. Oxford and Cambridge, MA: Blackwell Publishers.
Hampson, Norman. 1968. *The Enlightenment*. London: Penguin.
Harrison, Ross. 2012. The Equal Extent of Natural and Civil Law. In *Hobbes and the Law*, ed. David Dyzenhaus and Thomas Poole, 22–38. Cambridge: Cambridge University Press.
Hart, Herbert L.A. 1982. Commands and Authoritative Legal Reasons. In *Hart, Essays on Bentham*, ed. L.A. Herbert, 243–268. Oxford: Oxford University Press.
Haworth, Alan. 2004. *Understanding the Political Philosophers*. London: Routledge.
Hobbes, Thomas. [1640] 1994. *Human Nature and De Corpore Politico*, ed. J.G.A. Gaskin. Oxford: Oxford University Press.
———. [1642–1651] 1998. *On the Citizen*, ed. Richard Tuck. Cambridge: Cambridge University Press.

———. 1651. In *Leviathan. Or the Matter, Forme, & Power of a Common-Wealth Ecclesiastical and Civill*, ed. R. Tuck. Cambridge: Cambridge University Press (1991).

———. [1681–1682] 1971. *A Dialogue Between a Philosopher and a Student of the Common Laws of England*, ed. J. Cropsey. Chicago: University of Chicago Press.

Hoekstra, Kinch. 2007. Hobbes on the Natural Condition of Mankind. In *The Cambridge Companion to Hobbes's Leviathan*, ed. Patricia Springborg, 109–127. Cambridge: Cambridge University Press.

Hoffman, Philip T. 1994. Early Modern France, 1450–1700. In *Fiscal Crises, Liberty, and Representative Government*, ed. Philip T. Hoffman and Kathryn Norberg, 226–252. Stanford: Stanford University Press.

Hulliung, Mark. 1994. *The Autocritique of Enlightenment*. Cambridge, MA and London: Harvard University Press.

Hume, David. 1739–1740. *Treatise of Human Nature*, ed. L. H Selby-Bigge and P.H. Nidditch. Oxford: Clarendon Press (1978).

———. [1741a] 1875. Of the First Principles of Government. Essay 1. In *Essays, Literary, Moral, and Political*, 9–11. London: Ward, Lock, & Co.

———. [1741b] 1875. Of Civil Liberty. Essay 11. In *Essays, Literary, Moral, and Political*, 49–55. London: Ward, Lock, & Co.

———. [1742] 1987. Of Public Credit. Essay 9. In *Part 2, Essays, Moral, Political, and Literary*, E.F. Miller (ed.). Indianapolis, In: Liberty Fund, Inc., at http://www.econlib.org/library/LFBooks/Hume/hmMPL32.html. Accessed 18 Feb 2014.

———. [1748a] 1875. Of the Original Contract. Essay 34. In *Essays, Literary, Moral, and Political*, 270–283. London: Ward, Lock, & Co.

———. [1748b] 1875. An Inquiry Concerning Human Understanding. Essay 39. In *Essays, Literary, Moral, and Political*, 308–385. London: Ward, Lock, & Co.

———. [1751] 1875. An Inquiry Concerning the Principles of Morals. Essay 41. In *Essays, Literary, Moral, and Political*, 407–501. London: Ward, Lock, & Co.

———. [1752] 1875. Of Taxes. Essay 30, in *Essays, Literary, Moral, and Political*, 203–207. London: Ward, Lock, & Co.

———. [1754–1761] 1983. The History of England. USA: Liberty Fund, Incorporated.

———. [1777] 1875. Of the Origin of Government. Essay 5. In *Essays, Literary, Moral, and Political*, 25–28. London: Ward, Lock, & Co.

Hume, David. [various] 1954. In *New Letters of David Hume*, ed. Raymond Kilbansky and Ernest C. Mossner. Oxford: Clarendon Press.

Israel, Jonathan I. 2002. *Radical Enlightenment. Philosophy and the Making of Modernity 1650–1750*. Oxford: Oxford University Press.

Jackson, Dudley. 1973. Thomas Hobbes' Theory of Taxation. *Political Studies* 21 (2): 175–182.

Jaume, Lucien. 2007. Hobbes and the Philosophical Origins of Liberalism. In *The Cambridge Companion to Hobbes's Leviathan*, ed. Patricia Springborg, 199–216. Cambridge: Cambridge University Press.

Jefferson, Thomas. 1903. In *The Writings of Thomas Jefferson*, ed. Andrew Lipscomb and Albert E. Bergh, Memorial ed. Washington DC: The Thomas Jefferson Memorial Association.

Kawade, Yoshie. 2003. Montesquieu. In *Political Thinkers: From Socrates to the Present*, ed. David Boucher and Paul Kelly, 217–234. Oxford: Oxford University Press.

Kelly, Paul. 2003. Hume. In *Political Thinkers: From Socrates to the Present*, ed. David Boucher and Paul Kelly, 198–216. Oxford: Oxford University Press.

Knights, Mark. 2011. John Locke and Post-Revolutionary Politics: Electoral Reform and the Franchise. *Past & Present* 213 (1): 41–86.

Koenigsberger, Helmut Georg. 1994. *Early Modern Europe 1500–1789*. London/New York: Longman.

Kwass, Michael. 2000. *Privilege and the Politics of Taxation in Eighteenth-Century France*. Cambridge: Cambridge University Press.

Laslett, Peter. 1988. The Social and Political Theory of 'Two Treatises of Government'. In *John Locke, Two Treatises of Government*, ed. Peter Laslett, 2nd ed., 93–122. Cambridge: Cambridge University Press.

Lebovics, Herman. 1986. The Uses of America in John Locke's Second Treatise of Government. *Journal of the History of Ideas* 47 (4): 567–581.

Lee, Natasha. 2010. Making History Natural in Rousseau's Discourse on the Origins of Inequality. In *Rousseau and Freedom*, ed. Christie McDonald and Stanley Hoffman, 24–43. Cambridge: Cambridge University Press.

Lobban, Michael. 2012. Thomas Hobbes and the Common Law. In *Hobbes and the Law*, ed. David Dyzenhaus and Thomas Poole, 19–67. Cambridge: Cambridge University Press.

Locke, John. [1690a] 1975. *An Essay Concerning Human Understanding*, ed. Peter H. Nidditch, Oxford: Oxford University Press.

———. [1690b] 1988. The First Treatise of Government. In *John Locke Two Treatises of Government*, ed. Peter Laslett, 2nd ed. Cambridge: Cambridge University Press.

———. [1690c] 1988. The Second Treatise of Government. In *John Locke Two Treatises of Government*, ed. Peter Laslett, 2nd ed. Cambridge: Cambridge University Press.

———. [1691] 1824. Some Consideration of the Consequences of the Lowering of Interest, and Raising the Value of Money. In *The Works of John Locke in Nine Volumes*, vol. 4, 12th ed. London: Rivington. http://oll.libertyfund.org/title/763. Accessed 12 Feb 2014.

Loughlin, Martin. 2010. *Foundations of Public Law*. Oxford: Oxford University Press.

Macpherson, C.B. 1951. Locke on Capitalist Appropriation. *Western Political Quarterly* 4 (4): 550–566.

Madison, James, Alexander Hamilton, and John Jay. [1788] 1987. *The Federalist Papers*, ed. Isaac Kramnick, London: Penguin.

Manent, Pierre. 1994. *An Intellectual History of Liberalism*. Princeton: Princeton University Press.

Mann, Fritz Karl. 1978. *Steuerpolitische Ideale*. Darmstadt: Wissenschaftliche Buchgesellschaft.

Martinich, Aloysius P. 1999. *Hobbes: A Biography*. Cambridge: Cambridge University Press.

May, Larry. 2013. *Limiting Leviathan: Hobbes on Law and International Affairs*. Oxford: Oxford University Press.

McClelland, J.S. 1996. *A History of Western Political Thought*. London and New York: Routledge.

Molivas, G.I. 1999. A Right, Utility and the Definition of Liberty as a Negative Idea: Richard Hey and the Benthamite Conception of Liberty. *History of European Ideas* 25 (1–2): 75–92.

Montesquieu. [1721] 1973. *Persian Letters*. Trans. C. J. Betts. Harmondsworth: Penguin Books.

———. [1748] 1989. *The Spirit of the Laws*. Transl. and eds. Anne M. Cohler, Basia C. Miller, and Harold F. Stone. Cambridge: Cambridge University Press.

Newey, Glen. 2014. *The Routledge Guidebook to Hobbes' Leviathan*. London: Routledge.

Outram, Dorinda. 2005. *The Enlightenment*. 2nd ed. Cambridge: Cambridge University Press.

Paine, Thomas. 1776. *Common Sense*, at http://americainclass.org/wp-content/uploads/2014/07/Common-Sense-_-Full-Text.pdf. Accessed 8 June 2021.

———. 1776–1783. *The American Crisis*, ed. Steve Straub, at https://thefederalistpapers.org/wp-content/uploads/2013/08/The-American-Crisis-by-Thomas-Paine-.pdf. Accessed 8 June 2021.

———. 1780. Pamphlet 9b The Crisis Extraordinary. *On The Subject of Taxation*, at http://www.vlib.us/amdocs/texts/crisis9b.html. Accessed 8 June 2021.

———. 1791. *The Rights of Man, Part I*, at https://infidels.org/library/historical/thomas_paine/rights_of_man/. Accessed 8 June 2021.

———. 1792. *The Rights of Man, Part II*, at https://infidels.org/library/historical/thomas_paine/rights_of_man/. Accessed 8 June 2021.

———. 1795. *Agrarian Justice*, at http://piketty.pse.ens.fr/files/Paine1795.pdf. Accessed 8 June 2021.

Pangle, Thomas L. 1973. *Montesquieu's Philosophy of Liberalism, A Commentary on the Spirit of Laws*. Chicago and London: The University of Chicago Press.

Pollock, Frederick. 1908. The Social Contact in English Political Philosophy. *Journal of the Society of Comparative Legislation, New Series* 9 (1): 107–112.

Porter, Roy. 2000. *Enlightenment: Britain and the Creation of the Modern World*. London: Penguin.
Rahe, Paul A. 2001. Forms of Government: Structure, Principle, Object, and Aim. In *Montesquieu's Science of Politics: Essays on The Spirit of Laws*, ed. David W. Carrithers, Michael A. Mosher, and Paul A. Rahe, 69–108. Lanham: Rowman and Littlefield.
———. 2009. *Soft Despotism, Democracy's Drift: Montesquieu, Rousseau, Tocqueville, and the Modern Prospect*. New Haven and London: Yale University Press.
Rand, Benjamin (ed.). [1900] 2010. *The Life, Unpublished Letters and Philosophical Regimen of Anthony, Earl of Shaftesbury*. Whitefish: Kessinger Publishing, LLC.
Rapaczynski, Andrzej. 1981. Locke's Conception of Property and the Principle of Sufficient Reason. *Journal of the History of Ideas* 42 (2): 305–315.
Riker, William H., and Itai Sened. 1991. A Political Theory of the Origin of Property Rights: Airport Slots. *American Journal of Political Science* 35 (4): 951–969.
Riley, Patrick. 1982. *Will and Political Legitimacy: A Critical Exposition of Social Contract Theory in Hobbes, Locke, Rousseau and Hegel*. Cambridge MA: Harvard University Press.
———. 2005. Social Contract Theory and its Critics. In *The Cambridge History of Eighteenth-Century Political Thought*, ed. Mark Goldie and Robert Wokler, 347–375. Cambridge: Cambridge University Press.
Rousseau, Jean-Jacques. [1754] 1973. A Discourse on the Origin of Inequality (Second Discourse). In *Jean-Jacques Rousseau, The Social Contract and Discourses*, ed. G.D.H. Cole, J.H. Brumfitt, and J.H. Hall, 2nd ed. London and Melbourne: J.M. Dent & Sons.
———. [1755] 1973. Discourse on Political Economy. In *Jean-Jacques Rousseau, The Social Contract and Discourses*, ed. G.D.H. Cole, J.H. Brumfitt, and J.H. Hall, 2nd ed., 128–168. London and Melbourne: J.M. Dent & Sons. Originally in *Encyclopédie Volume V*, ed. Denis Diderot, and Jean Le Rond D'Alembert.
———. [1762] 1994. On the Social Contract or Principles of Political Right. In *The Collected Writings of Rousseau*, ed. Roger D. Masters and Christopher Kelly, vol. 4, 129–244. Hanover and London: University Press of New England.
———. [1789] 1995. *Confessions. The Collected Writings of Rousseau, Volume 5*, ed. Roger D. Masters and Christopher Kelly. Hanover/London: University Press of New England.
———. 1994. Political Fragments. In *The Collected Writings of Rousseau*, ed. Roger D. Masters and Christopher Kelly, vol. 4, 16–75. Hanover/London: University Press of New England.
Russell, Paul. 1986. II. Locke on Express and Tacit Consent. *Political Theory* 14 (2): 291–306.
Ryan, Alan. 1996. Hobbes's Political Philosophy. In *The Cambridge Companion to Hobbes*, ed. Tom Sorell, 208–245. Cambridge: Cambridge University Press.
Sabine, George H. 1961. *A History of Political Theory*. 3rd ed. London: George G. Harrap & Co. Ltd.
Seliger, Martin. 1963. Locke's Theory of Revolutionary Action. *Western Political Quarterly* 16 (3): 548–568.
Shapiro, Ian. 1986. *The Evolution of Rights in Liberal Theory*. Cambridge: Cambridge University Press.
Shklar, Judith N. 1987a. *Montesquieu*. Oxford: Oxford University Press.
———. 1987b. Men and Citizens. In *A Study of Rousseau's Social Theory*. Cambridge: Cambridge University Press.
Shrader-Frechette, Kristin. 1993. Locke and Limits on Land Ownership. *Journal of the History of Ideas* 54 (2): 201–219.
Skinner, Quentin. 2008. *Hobbes and Republican Liberty*. Cambridge: Cambridge University Press.
———. 2009. A Genealogy of the Modern State. *Proceedings of the British Academy* 162: 325–370.
Smith, Adam. [1776] 1976. *An Inquiry in the Nature and Causes of the Wealth of Nations II*. Indianapolis: Liberty Fund.
Snape, John. 2012. Montesquieu – 'The Lively President' and the English Way of Taxation. In *Studies in the History of Tax Law, Volume 5*, ed. John Tiley, 73–90. Oxford and Portland, Oregon: Hart Publishing.

———. 2015. David Hume: Philosophical Historian of Tax Law. In *Studies in the History of Tax Law, Volume 7*, ed. Peter Harris and Dominic de Cogan, 421–464. Oxford and Portland, Oregon: Hart Publishing.
Snape, John, and Jane Frecknall-Hughes. 2017. John Locke: Property, Tax and the Private Sphere. In *Studies in the History of Tax Law, Volume 8*, ed. Peter Harris and Dominic de Cogan, 1–35. Oxford and Portland, Oregon: Hart Publishing.
Sommerville, Johann. 2012. Life and Times. In *The Bloomsbury Companion to Hobbes*, ed. Sharon A. Lloyd, 1–28. London: Bloomsbury.
Sorell, Tom. 2007. Hobbes's Moral Philosophy. In *The Cambridge Companion to Hobbes's Leviathan*, ed. Patricia Springborg, 128–153. Cambridge: Cambridge University Press.
Steedhar, Susanne. 2012. Obligation. In *The Bloomsbury Companion to Hobbes*, ed. Sharon A. Lloyd, 192–193. London: Bloomsbury.
Tully, James. 1980. *A Discourse on Property: John Locke and his Adversaries*. Cambridge: Cambridge University Press.
———. 1993a. *An Approach to Political Philosophy: Locke in Contexts*. Cambridge: Cambridge University Press.
———. 1993b. Placing the Two Treatises. In *Political Discourse in Early Modern Britain*, ed. Nicholas Phillipson and Quentin Skinner, 253–280. Cambridge: Cambridge University Press.
———. 1994. Rediscovering America: The Two Treatises and Aboriginal Rights. In *Locke's Philosophy: Content and Context*, ed. G.A.J. Rogers, 165–196. Oxford: Clarendon Press.
———. 1995. *Strange Multiplicity: Constitutionalism in an Age of Diversity*. Cambridge: Cambridge University Press.
Vaughn, Karen I. 1980. John Locke's Theory of Property. *Literature of Liberty: A Review of Contemporary Liberal Thought* 3 (1): 5–37.
Viroli, Maurizio. 1987. The Concept of *Ordre* and the Language of Classical Republicanism of Jean-Jacques Rousseau. In *The Languages of Political Theory in Early-Modern Europe*, ed. Anthony Pagden, 159–178. Cambridge: Cambridge University Press.
———. 2002. *Republicanism*. New York: Hill and Wang.
Voegelin, Eric. 1999. The New Order and Last Orientation. In *History of Political Ideas: New Order and Last Orientation, Volume 7 (Collected Works of Eric Voegelin, Volume 25)*, ed. Jurgen Gebhardt and Thomas Hollweck. Columbia: University of Missouri Press.
Waldron, Jeremy. 2003. Locke. In *Political Thinkers: From Socrates to the Present*, ed. David Boucher and Paul Kelly, 181–197. Oxford: Oxford University Press.
Weaver, David R. 1997. Leadership, Locke and the Federalist. *American Journal of Political Science* 41 (2): 420–446.
Webber, Carolyn, and Aaron Wildavsky. 1986. *A History of Taxation and Expenditure in the Western World.* New York: Simon and Schuster.
Werner, John M. 1972. David Hume and America. *Journal of the History of Ideas* 33 (3): 439–456.
Wills, Gary. 1981. *Explaining America*. London: The Athlone Press.
Witteveen, Willem. 2006. The Montesquieu Connection. In *The Perils of Pervasive Instrumentalism. Tilburg Law Lectures Series, I-XVII*, ed. Brian Z. Tamanaha. Nijmegen: Wolf Legal Publishers.
Wokler, Robert. 1995. *Rousseau*. Oxford: Oxford University Press.
Woolhouse, Roger. 2007. *Locke: A Biography*. Cambridge: Cambridge University Press.
Wootton, David. 2018. *Power, Pleasure, and Profit: Insatiable Appetites from Machiavelli to Madison*. Cambridge, MA and London: The Belknap Press of Harvard University Press.
Zaretsky, Robert, and John T. Scott. 2009. *The Philosophers' Quarrel: Rousseau, Hume and the Limits of Human Understanding*. New Haven and London: Yale University Press.

Hans Gribnau is professor of Tax Law at Tilburg University, The Netherlands and at Leiden University, The Netherlands. He has been a visiting professor at Antwerp University. He is an external member of the Board of Professors of University of Bologna Law School. He published more than 150 articles. His research focus is taxation, tax methodology, philosophy of tax law, procedural tax law, tax law principles and tax ethics. Recent publications dealt with topics such as corporate tax governance, corporate social responsibility and voluntary compliance beyond the letter of the law, codes of conduct, public tax governance, cooperative compliance, tax transparency, reciprocity, trust, and fair play.

Hans is a member of the editorial board of the *Journal of Tax Administration* (JOTA) and of various Dutch tax journals. In 2007 he received the Jan Giele-award for his 'substantial contribution to just taxation in the Netherlands.' He is a member of the advisory board of the Dutch Taxpayers Association. Hans is a guest lecturer for tax ethics within Oxford University's MSc in Taxation Program and teaches 'Ethics and Taxation' in the Doctoral Program in International Business Taxation of Vienna University of Economics and Business (WU). His publications are available at http://ssrn.com/author=441648 and https://www.researchgate.net/profile/Hans_Gribnau/contributions?ev=prf_act

Jane Frecknall-Hughes is Professor of Accounting and Taxation at Nottingham University Business School, which she joined on 1 November 2016. After graduating from the University of Oxford, she became a chartered accountant and chartered tax consultant with KPMG. In 1992 she joined the University of Leeds, gaining postgraduate teaching qualifications and a PhD (in Revenue Law and Tax Practice) and was awarded a master's degree (with distinction) in Commercial Law from the University of Northumbria in 2007. She is a fellow of the Higher Education Academy. After moving to the University of Sheffield in 2005, she then joined The Open University in 2008 as Professor of Accounting, later holding the posts of Professor of Law and Head of the Open University Law School and then Professor of Revenue Law. She joined Hull University Business School in September 2014 as Professor of Accounting and Taxation and Head of the Accounting and Finance Subject Group. Jane's research focuses on taxation, especially from an interdisciplinary perspective. She has gained an international reputation for her work in this area, which is reflected in her publication record. She has taught a wide range of subjects in the accounting and business law area, including taxation, and her textbook, entitled *The Theory, Principles and Management of Taxation: An Introduction*, was published by Routledge in October 2014.

Chapter 3
Taxation and Utilitarianism: The Historical Evolution

Jennifer Bird-Pollan and Stefan Bird-Pollan

Abstract We propose to investigate the history of the relation between the concept of utility and utilitarianism and the need for taxation, specifically as it relates to Anglo-American political thought from the seventeenth century in Hobbes to the nineteenth century in Mill. During this period, the justification for taxation gradually shifted from a taxation model of 'payment for benefit' to taxation as 'ability to pay'. Specifically, we show that it is the enlightenment concept of self-determination, arising in one form or another in Locke, Hume, Smith and even Bentham, which makes it possible for 'benefit' to be conceived as both individual and social at the same time, which ultimately results in the shift from taxation as 'payment for benefit' to taxation as 'ability to pay'. We first examine the concept of the idea of utility (here often understood as self-interest) as it forms the basis of the social contract. Because of the individualistic notions of benefit, Hobbes and Locke both argue that taxation should fall on all equally since the fundamental benefit of each is security. In the eighteenth century, however, we find an emphasis on 'fellow feeling' (Smith) which modifies the agent's self-interest. While Hume is the first theorist to use the concept of utility systematically, Smith retreats from it out of concern that it would result in some deciding for others in matters of personal happiness. Bentham, the founder of utilitarianism, somewhat surprisingly also emphasizes critique of received opinion and personal autonomy, arguing that the concept of utility is compatible with utility maximization. This ambiguity continues in Mill, whose *Utilitarianism* and *On Liberty* have often been seen as at odds. In Hume through Mill it is the attention to autonomy conceived of socially which mitigates the idea of taxation as 'payment for benefit' since the benefit is understood as accruing to society as a whole.

Keywords Liberalism · Utilitarianism · Taxation · Enlightenment · Bentham

---

J. Bird-Pollan (✉)
College of Law, University of Kentucky, Lexington, KY, USA
e-mail: jbirdpollan@uky.edu

S. Bird-Pollan
Department of Philosophy, University of Kentucky, Lexington, KY, USA

R. F. van Brederode (ed.), *Political Philosophy and Taxation*,
https://doi.org/10.1007/978-981-19-1092-0_3

> To point out subjects of taxation is but a thankless office: without any other intention but to alleviate, or any motive in prospect but the hope of alleviating, the mass of public burthen, a man [who suggests new sources of public revenue] may be looked upon as the author of it (Bentham 2004a, 379).

3.1 Introduction

It is perhaps a truism that every age interprets its history in its own light. What is not a truism is that this interpretation constantly threatens to make invisible the particular elements of history which do not fit so easily with the age's self-conception. In taking up the question of utilitarianism and taxation it might be thought that since theories of taxation are intertwined with economics and since economics is the study of efficiency as based on perceived preference, that to claim that utilitarianism and taxation belong together is nearly a tautology. However, in this chapter we undertake to demonstrate that, rather to the contrary, the concept of utility has a complex history which again and again resists a simple equation with economic efficiency. Taxation too has its history. One can see in a society's tax systems the expression of its conception of how social obligations should be distributed. The modern usage of the term 'utility' arrives through a complex history of the idea of subjectivity from the reductivist conception of self-preservation in Hobbes, through Hume and Smith's conception of subjects as ineluctably tied to each other through fellow-feeling, to the theory of liberal autonomy as articulated in Bentham and Mill. In each instance the corresponding theory of taxation provides important insights into the received view of each author.

This chapter tracks the development of the concepts of utility and utilitarianism through the historical development of ideas about taxation from Hobbes to John Stuart Mill. It will come as no surprise that as ideas about taxation changed, so did ideas about utility and vice versa. For some of the philosophers discussed here, the attitude about taxation will reveal what they considered to be the proper understanding of utility and, for others, utility will be the key to understanding their views of taxation. In order to best elucidate the critical relationship between theories of utility and taxation, we have chosen figures who concerned themselves with both utility and taxation.

3.2 Some Preliminary Remarks About Utilitarianism and Taxation

Before embarking on the historical path, it is perhaps useful to make some general distinctions as a matter of orientation. We take the paradigm that will now be elaborated to capture the general features of all the figures and issues discussed in this Chapter. Utilitarianism is a wide field, but taxation is even wider. Neither are sui generis and both have complex historical and conceptual trajectories. In this section we will flag only a few central themes.

3.2.1 *Utilitarianism*

Utilitarianism is itself a species of the larger theory of consequentialism, which suggests that an action's value is to be measured by its consequences, as opposed, for instance, to deontology which derives an action's value by reference to whether or not it conforms to the actor's duties (or in the Kantian sense, duty itself).[1] Consequentialism is thus a successor concept to older teleological approaches attempting to make sense of cause and effect.[2] Utilitarianism naturalizes the idea of an ultimate cause.

If we take utilitarianism in its broadest sense to be concerned with the *maximization* of utility, we can distinguish several discrete issues:

(1) Who is the *subject* of the utility, i.e., who is it who maximizes: individual, group or society at large, the government etc.?
(2) What is the object of the maximization, i.e., who is the beneficiary of the maximization, again: individual, group or society at large?
(3) The type of utility to be generated, i.e., *what* is to be maximized: pleasure or higher order values?
(4) At the theoretical level, what sort of decision procedure applies to the utility maximization, i.e., act or rule utilitarianism?

We now consider each of these matters in turn.

(1) The *subject* of utility: the idea of maximizing utility in accordance with the principles of utilitarianism requires that there be a subject who seeks to maximize. In ethics, the subject is often taken to be the rational agent who maximizes utility either on her own or some other entity's behalf (usually assumed to include the subject herself). At the level of social policy, by contrast, the 'subject' who maximizes utility is the government in charge of making decisions about the welfare of the inhabitants of the state (Amartya and Williams 1982a, 1–2).
(2) The *object* of utility concerns the beneficiary of utility maximization. Here the question is whether to think of, say, the individual's utility maximization as concerned only with her own utility or whether the object is greater than the individual, for instance society at large or some subgroup of society. While it is often assumed that the object of the benefit will include the agent who produces

[1] Consequentialism ref. Deontology ref. Kant defines duty as what is objective accord with the moral law (Kant 1996a, 5: 81).

[2] In questions of teleology it is customary to distinguish between Aristotle's four causes: material cause, formal cause, efficient cause and final cause (Aristotle 1993, Ch. 2, 1013a–b).

the utility maximization, this may not be the case when the agent of utility maximization is, for instance, a government that works *for* the people. Thus, in some circumstances it may maximize utility to exclude lawmakers from benefiting from any tax benefits they design for the people.

(3) One central problem in the history of utilitarian thought is what constitutes utility and how to measure it. Bentham (1962, 1) famously advocates the principle of pleasure and displeasure as the ultimate criterion for utility, while Mill (1998a, 124) argues for a hierarchy of utility. Smart (1987, 12–13) identifies the dispute as ranging from hedonism to ideal utilitarian with Bentham occupying the place of hedonist and G. E. Moore, who believes that certain states of mind – such as that of acquiring knowledge – have intrinsic value independent of their pleasurableness, as ideal utilitarian. Mill, Smart argues, falls somewhere in the middle. This question of the constitution of utility is central to any theory of taxation, which concerns itself with money, but not only so, as we shall see. The problem with hedonism, as Smart (1987, 23) notes, is that it reduces to a state of affairs in which the only question is the enjoyment of the subject, which makes it unworkable as a model for tax theory.

(4) Next comes the important question of what model of utilitarianism is applied. In the period discussed here, the chief distinction is between act and rule utilitarians. Act utilitarians – generally associated with the classical school of Bentham, Mill, and Moore – hold that the rightness or wrongness of an action depends on the goodness or badness of the action itself. Rule utilitarians hold that the rightness or wrongness of an action is to be judged by the goodness or badness of the consequences of a rule that everyone should perform the action in like circumstances (Smart 1987, 9). Rule utilitarianism is often touted as being more compatible with individual rights and personal obligation (Harsanyi 1982a, 235). For this reason, rule utilitarianism is often also connected to rational choice theory (Harsanyi 1982b, 55). As Smart (1987, 14) has observed, the dispute over what type of utilitarianism is best is actually a dispute about the principles for arriving at what is in most cases a fairly similar set of moral beliefs about how things should be. As such, it will be of only tangential concern in this Chapter and is mentioned here only for completeness' sake.

(5) Finally, we must ask whether, on utilitarian grounds, it is even right to *be* a utilitarian. In some sense this question reduces something of a psychological question. For instance, utilitarian utility maximization generally appears cold and calculating and hence detracts from the very benefit it seeks to achieve. Most people are happier being offered something out of (perhaps irrational) spontaneous generosity rather than from the rational calculation of future benefit for the giver. Mill, in particular, believed this to be an important question, as we shall see. It is also the source of Bernard Williams' famous criticism of utilitarianism, which observed that, to be a utilitarian, I must implausibly strive to acquire preferences that I do not have or want to acquire.

3.2.2 Taxation

Taxation has historically been motivated both by redistributive goals as well as taxpayers' own self-interest in things like security or other social goods that can best be provided by the government. Our tour through the history of the intersection between utilitarianism and taxation must acknowledge that the government-imposed collection of tax as we recognize it today was not widely instituted until the nineteenth century, with the first income tax imposed in the United States in 1861, but the current broad form of the tax not imposed until 1913 (Ratner 1967). Similarly, Britain's first broad system of taxation first appeared in the late eighteenth century. Thus, utilitarian thinking about these matters predates most of the world's actual tax systems.

When considering a system of taxation imposed and administered by a government, one can evaluate the system according to the following criteria (1) to what end or purpose a tax is paid, (2) who is taxed, (3) what is the tax base, (4) how the tax is implemented and collected and, (5) how much tax is imposed.

(1) The theory of taxation varies widely with regard to the purpose of the tax. Classical authors such as Hobbes and Locke, and modern authors like Robert Nozick, argue that taxation is justified when the revenue collected is used to provide security.[3] Others believe taxation should mainly be used in the service of redistribution, of creating a more level playing field. Rawls' difference principle, for instance, is an example of a redistributivist theory of taxation (Rawls 1999, 54). Still others, like Hume, think that taxation can serve as a stimulus to economic production.
(2) Who should be taxed also varies widely, from the view, found in Hobbes, that everyone should be subject to tax, since everyone benefits equally from the security the state provides (the so-called "benefit principle of taxation"), to Bentham and Mill's proposals that the lowest earners be exempt in a progressive income tax scheme (more of an "ability to pay" theory of tax). Bentham also advocates a variety of special taxes, such as taxes on bankers and stock traders comparable perhaps to the Tobin tax on international financial transactions (Tobin 1978).
(3) Determination of the proper tax base features also as a central topic in early philosophical treatments of taxation. Smith, for instance, distinguishes four possible bases for the imposition of tax: rent, profit, wages and universal taxation. Tied into this debate are discussions of valuation and its difficulties, which, in some of these thinkers' perspectives, leads to the conclusion that ease of valuation makes real property the best tax base.
(4) Thinking about the method of tax collection and imposition raises a variety of questions connected to the implementation of any particular theory of tax. For instance, should an annuity be taxed yearly or taxed once as the whole? In the

[3] Nozick (1975) understands the state exclusively as a security firm.

same vein, one must answer questions about withholding obligations, taxing authorities, and other instrumental elements of a tax system.

(5) Finally there is the amount of tax imposed, with a special focus on the question of tax rates, with various authors proposing different schemes for determining the appropriate rates. Early theorists contemplated in this Chapter did not typically advocate for graduated tax rates, although some did support exemptions for individuals with less wealth or income. Alternatively, some thinkers proposed different rates based on the source of income subject to tax. For instance, Bentham (2004a, 386) proposes to tax land at twice the rate of income.

3.2.3 *Utility and Taxation*

We will use the paradigms outlined above to chart a path through the many different theories of taxation with regard to concerns for utility. With respect to utility or utilitarianism, our exploration concerns chiefly the question of who is the beneficiary of the maximization of utility, (utilitarianism point (2)) and *what* is maximized (utilitarianism point (3)). On the tax side, the question in the classical period revolves principally around the purpose or end of taxation (taxation point (1)) and what is the proper tax base (taxation point (3)).

3.3 Historical Overview of Utility and Taxation

The historical section of this Chapter can be divided into three more or less discrete sections in both the development of taxation theory and of the theory of utility. The first period concerns the founders of social contract, Hobbes and Locke, and the justification of taxation on social contract grounds. The second period, coinciding with the development of classical economic theory in Smith, concerns the entrance of utility as a concept into philosophical discourse in Hume. Finally, there is the period from Bentham to Mill in which utilitarianism as a philosophical doctrine is elaborated and tax policy is theorized to accord with explicitly utilitarian principles, first as the minimization of burden on the population in Bentham and then as the minimization of suffering in Mill.

This periodization reflects the gradual development of utility as a free-standing philosophical principle, culminating in the work of Bentham and Mill. Rather than treating utilitarianism as a philosophical entry point to the theory of taxation, this historical approach offers more insight into the relationship between utility and tax, since concepts have histories which are often hidden when treated solely from a systematic perspective. Indeed, given the obviousness with which the principle of utility is treated today, one might ask why the concept had to wait until the late eighteenth century to be formulated as such. The answer lies in the problematic nature of treating utility as separated from social life in general. While self-interest, a concept prior to and related to utility, has played a central role in the conceptualization of the relation between individual and society since the seventeenth century, many theorists have been resistant to it, as we shall show, preferring to see utility in dialectic with the concept of autonomy.[4]

Examining what each theorist has to say about taxation provides an important perspective on the thinker's overall theory, since it demonstrates *in concreto* the author's general theoretical orientation. For instance, while Hobbes' remarks on taxation seem to follow directly from his concern for the subject's survival, Hume's remarks on the subject introduce an important ambiguity into his conception of how humans interact. Therefore, while the subject of this Chapter is the interplay between taxation and utilitarianism, we believe this work also provides insight into larger observations about utilitarian theories more generally.

Each of the three periods to be examined reveal a particular problem with the principle of utility as maximization. The social contract tradition with its emphasis on security acts as a *reductio* of the principle of utility in the sense that utility is simply equated with the value of life itself. The Scottish enlightenment perspective of Hume and Smith resists utility as a free-standing principle for the opposite reason, namely that it provides too much space for interpretation when treated on its own. What is useful to whom, Hume and Smith agree, is best left to the individual subject. And finally, Bentham and Mill show themselves to be much more concerned with individual autonomy than the more radical twentieth century versions of utilitarianism would accept. Working through these three approaches to utilitarian theories of tax provides additional insights beyond what a study of any of the thinkers in isolation would reveal.

3.3.1 Social Contract Theory and Taxation: Hobbes and Locke

The utility calculations attributed to the founders of social contract theory might be best characterized as a reduction of all preferences to one (Sen and Williams 1982a, 8). The preference which Hobbes singles out as the basis for his social contract is, of course, the preference for life.[5] For Hobbes, we are driven into society by recognizing that while we might be capable of surviving on our own, the expectations of life alone are much dimmer than if we join forces with others. Since the continuation of life is the ultimate goal of life itself, the agent is rationally constrained to seek the conditions through which life can be prolonged or, to put it differently, through which life is itself maximized.

By joining with others to implement a social contract, the subject achieves the conditions which are most favorable to the extension of life. Yet for Hobbes, since

[4] For a study of self-interest in the period we are concerned with, see Hirschman (1997).

[5] "The Law of Nature is a precept, or general Rule, found out by reason, by which a man is forbidden to do, that, which is destructive to his life, or taketh away the means of preserving the same" (Hobbes 1991, Book 1, Ch XVI, 91).

joining the social contract is the *only* way in which life can be maximized, the subject is now also entirely dependent on the social contract and with it on the laws which follow from its implementation. Famously, Hobbes takes the view that the sovereign who is constituted by the social contract must be obeyed in all things since the sovereign is the guarantor of peace or the likely continuation of life, and to oppose the sovereign would be also to oppose the conditions allowing for the continuation of one's own life.

Hobbes' view of taxation follows directly from the commitment the individual has made to the sovereign for her security. Since the subject has no claims on the sovereign other than the general benefit of security, Hobbes holds that the sovereign also retains ultimate authority over the right to tax (Hobbes 1991, 172). And because all subjects are reduced to one single utility function – the maintenance of life – all benefit equally from the security the state provides. This leads Hobbes to the conclusion that all should be taxed equally.

> To Equall Justice, appertaineth also the Equall imposition of Taxes; the Equality whereof dependeth, not on the Equality of riches, but on the Equality of the debt, that every man oweth to the Common-wealth for his defence (Hobbes 1991, 238).

Hobbes thus bases the justification of taxation on the benefit the individual will receive (Jackson 1973; Frecknall-Hughes 2007, 262).[6] Since for Hobbes, in the last analysis, all benefit is reduced to the maintenance of life, all must pay equally for that benefit since it accrues equally to each member of the society. A correlate of this view, Hobbes argues, is that commodities should be taxed, since a tax on these will ultimately be the least disruptive to the security of the state: "when the Impositions, are layd upon those things which men consume, every man payeth Equally for what he useth" (Hobbes 1991, 238–239). In other words, a consumption tax is the most fair, because it focuses the burdens of taxation in a way that distributes the burdens evenly across all participants in a society – everyone who purchases goods.

Locke's theory, like Hobbes', is a benefits theory except that Locke's account introduces a complication into the justification of taxation by grounding the social contract on the acquisition of property rather than on the maintenance of life, as in Hobbes (Gray 1995, 14). This has implications for Locke's theory of taxation as well.

Locke famously argues that in the state of nature property is acquired by mixing one's labor with nature: "Whatsoever then he removes out of the State that Nature hath provided, and left it in, he hath mixed his Labour with, and joyned to it something that is his own, and thereby makes it his *Property*" (Locke 1988). Yet in order to secure one's property, it is rational, Locke argues, to join with others into a social contract "for their comfortable, safe, and peaceable living one amongst another, in a secure Enjoyment of their Properties, and a greater Security against any that are not of it" (Locke 1988, Ch. VIII, para 95).

---

[6] See also Nozick's claim that society should be conceived as a mutual protection association (Nozick 1975, 12–13).

The difficulty with taxation arises since the funds the state requires for its maintenance depend on the people *giving up* (part of) the very thing they joined the state to maintain, namely their property.[7] Taxation then, for Locke, constitutes a sort of contradiction in terms. In partial remediation of this contradiction, Locke is quite clear that taxation cannot proceed unilaterally from the government, but must only be done with the consent of those ultimately subjected to the tax. Yet Locke follows Hobbes in claiming that taxation is ultimately payment for security, that it is "fit every one who enjoys his share of the Protection, should pay out of his Estate his proportion for the maintenance of it" (Locke 1988, Ch. XI, para 140). This constitutes the entirety of Locke's explicit discussion of taxation, but provides useful insight into the role of government in Locke's model.

Both Hobbes and Locke, then, operate on an implicitly reductive form of utility, if that term can be imputed to them at all. A reductive conception of benefit produces a reductive or at least limited system of taxation similar to a capitation tax. Taxation is here conceived of as a matter of safeguarding productivity. Participation is expected only because payment of taxes allows the individual to receive the protection of the group. Nevertheless, Hobbes' conception of taxation as tied to consumption seems to mediate this minimal notion of tax, building into the tax for security a variable which looks toward ideas about distribution we find more thoroughly articulated in the mid eighteenth century in Hume and Smith.

3.3.2 *Utility, Sympathy and Taxation*

There is considerable disagreement about whether Hume ought to be classed as a utilitarian *avant la lettre.*[8] However one falls on that question, it is nevertheless clear that Hume represents an important moment in the conceptual history of utility, standing as he does between the social contract tradition with its reductive conception of utility and the more complex notion of utility we later find in Smith, Bentham, and Mill.

As we enter the eighteenth century, the social contract tradition gives up its hard Hobbesian edge under the influence of moral sense theories. Here it is particularly the influence of Lord Shaftsbury (whose private secretary was, for a time, Adam Smith) and Francis Hutcheson on Hume and Smith that is usually noted.[9] While Hobbes and Locke sought to reduce the individual to a function of the just state,

---

[7] Locke (1988, Ch. XI, para 138) writes: "*Men* therefore in Society having Property, they have such a right to the goods, which by the Law of the Community are theirs, that no Body hath a right to take their substance, or any part of it from them, without their own consent; without this, they have no *Property* at all."

[8] Rosen (2003, Ch. 3) and Raphael (1972–1973, 88), for instance, argue for Hume's status as a utilitarian, Sayre-McCord (1996), argues against. On Smith, see again Rosen (2003, Ch. 4) who argues for, while Raphael (1972–1973, 88) argues against.

[9] For a compelling account of this period see Robertson (2020), Ch. 6.

moral sense theory, we might say, sought to understand the state as a function of the feeling individual as she relates *socially* to other individuals, for instance in Smith's concept of "fellow feeling". This shift in paradigm from the individualistic-political to the mediate realm of the social allowed the state to become a function of the social or society with all its nuances rather than merely a collection of rationally consistent actors.

The notion of utility which operates in this context might be characterized as 'idealization' rather than reduction.[10] The idealization we find in Hume and Smith also leads to a more extensive notion of the purposes of taxation (taxation point (1)) and a determination of who is to be taxed (taxation point (2)). The expanded notion of society, in other words, allows individual members of society to be evaluated according to their position within the social matrix as a general function of an overall social utility. As an example of the application of this thinking, on this model, it might not make sense to tax the poorest, since this would have adverse effects on the overall balance of society. Ultimately, in other words, having the rich pay more in taxes is preferable to social unrest.

Like Hobbes and Locke, Hume and Smith begin from the conflict between self-interest and the interests of society. What distinguishes them from the earlier theorists we have considered is that, to a certain extent, they leave behind the rationalistic paradigm of the social contract and understand human interaction as grounded in a certain natural fellow-feeling which simply does not admit of further investigation, as Hume puts it.[11] Hume and Smith both seem to accept some version of a social contract, though they attribute it more to providence than to mere human ratiocination.[12] Reason is thus displaced from the central role it plays for Hobbes and Locke with important consequences for the conception of society.

The Theory of Moral Sentiments, for instance, begins with the programmatic claim:

> How selfish soever man may be supposed, there are evidently some principles in his nature, which interest him in the fortune of others, and render their happiness necessary to him, though he derives nothing from it except the pleasure of seeing it.[13]

And Hume, referring to our sometimes insensibility to the interests of others, writes:

---

[10] Basing themselves on a formulation by R. M. Hare, Sen and Williams (1982a, 9) characterize the idealization view of utility as "perfectly prudent preferences".

[11] "It is needless to push our researches so far as to ask, why we have humanity or a fellow-feeling with others. It is sufficient, that this is experienced to be a principle in human nature. We must stop somewhere in our examination of causes; and there are, in every science, some general principles, beyond which we cannot hope to find any principle more general. No man is absolutely indifferent to the happiness and misery of others" (Hume 1983, sec. V. 43).

[12] Hume (1985a, 468) argues that though the source of all society is divine providence, he acknowledges that the origin of government must have been founded in contract. Smith (1981, Ch. I, Part II, 710–11), by contrast, seems to think it plausible.

[13] Smith (1985, Part I, Sec. I, Ch. I. 9).

> Let a man's insensibility be ever so great, he must often be touched with the images of RIGHT and WRONG; and let his prejudices be ever so obstinate, he must observe, that others are susceptible of like impressions.[14]

For Hume, as for Smith, the underlying condition of humanity is thus that of fundamental benevolence between humans. It is based on an only lightly theorized teleological conception of the human species as developing through mutual benefit.[15] This light teleological conception is at the core of the central problematic both Hume and Smith diagnose in society: the fact that the individual seems to show a marked preference for doing what benefits them in particular but at the same time harbors strong feelings about the order of society and what it takes to get along. For both, it is custom which greases the wheels of society.

The teleological conception shared by Hume and Smith is both what seems to push them toward utilitarianism but also what prevents them from becoming fully so. The idea of teleology per se has the right form in the sense that teleology assumes that things are done to achieve a certain consequence, i.e., it is consequentialist. However, the belief in a teleology also means that humans do not see themselves in charge of the end that is to be achieved, at least not as intentional agents. Rather, the teleological conception of the benefit of humanity somehow proceeding at the level of the species and behind the back of the individual introduces a tension into any conception of utilitarianism which might arise out of Hume and Smith.

Yet we also find in Hume and Smith the first gestures toward a naturalization of teleology into a social science. Montesquieu's *The Spirit of the Laws* (1848), the first attempt at an empirical social science, is positively referred to by Hume (1983, 29). Smith, of course, is credited with developing the social science of economics. Yet the question remains to what extent the teleological has been replaced by the social scientific, the idea of providence by the idea of utility. An additional issue presents itself in the fact that in the shift from teleological conceptions of nature to social scientific conceptions, this general transition was, in the eighteenth century, conceived of as a shift from final cause to efficient cause. In other words, thinkers believed that only relative connections between cause and effect could be studied. Such a shift, however, left space for the final cause or the purpose of life to persist (Haakonson 1981, 77). The theory of utilitarianism is radical in that it wants to replace the teleological view of the final end as well.

In the following two subsections we will consider first Hume's theory, which can be linked to thinking of utility both in terms of this moral theory and in terms of the few remarks he makes about taxation. The difficulty in Hume's view has to do with the perspective the subject is supposed to take on her own actions. In fact, Hume articulates three distinct perspectives: the perspective of the philosopher who notices

---

[14] Hume 1983, sec. I, 13.

[15] Hume writes, for instance, "Upon the whole, then, it seems undeniable, that nothing can bestow more merit on any human creature than the sentiment of benevolence in an eminent degree; and that a part, at least, of its merit arises from its tendency to promote the interests of our species, and bestow happiness on human society" (Hume 1983, sec. II, 20). For Smith's similar position, see Smith (1985, Part II, Ch. V, Sec. I. 77–78).

the underlying teleological dimension of social life from an external perspective, the internal perspective of the agent quasi-unconsciously swept along by the tension between private gains and public good, and the morally self-conscious agent who ultimately does everything from the principle of utility awkwardly caught between the two.

The second subsection will consider Smith's moral theory as a way of overcoming these tensions in Hume. In particular we will see that Smith's "invisible spectator" theory emphasizes the subject's ability to see herself from the internal perspective of a certain subjective selfishness and from the external perspective of the larger public good. The subject is thus conceived of as fundamentally unified through a capacity to rise above the desire for individual yet still at times driven by private gain.

3.3.2.1 Hume

Hume's sentimental empiricism proceeds from a basis of feelings of being "sociable, good-natured, humane, merciful, grateful, friendly, generous, beneficent" which are so self-evidently estimable, says Hume, that they need no philosophical proof. These feelings are subjective in nature, requiring close contact with others to be appreciated.[16] They may be treated as the semi-unconscious internal perspective referred to earlier.

Alongside these exists the virtue of justice, the social virtue *par excellence*. Our entrance into larger society requires adopting, or at least acknowledging, this more clear cut virtue. Justice, for Hume, acts as a backstop to society upon its creation out of the state of nature which, for Hume like for Hobbes, is a state of war: "The laws of war, which then succeed to those of equity and justice, are rules calculated for the *advantage* and *utility* of that particular state, in which men are now placed" (Hume 1983, Sec. III, Part I, 23). Thus laws, which are the expression of justice, serve both to delimit and to encourage the fundamental benevolent attitude of the members of society toward each other.

> The necessity of justice to the support of society is the SOLE foundation of that virtue; and since no moral excellence is more highly esteemed, we may conclude, that this circumstance of usefulness has, in general, the strongest energy, and most entire command over our sentiments (Hume 1983 #1758, Sec. III, Part II, 34).

Hume develops the concept of justice out of an account of the useful. The useful functions as a common denominator, which connects the ties of friendship with the master-servant relationship, private feeling with public merit. All human interactions are, Hume argues, assessed with regard to the common project of sociability. Hume asks "may it not thence be concluded, that the UTILITY, resulting from the social virtues, forms, at least, a part of their merit, and is one source of that approbation and regard so universally paid to them?" (Hume 1983, Sec. II, Part II, 18) Since

---

[16] On the less formalized virtues, see, Hume (1983, Sec. II, part I, 16–17).

we are now irrevocably members of society, society itself needs to develop in an orderly manner which only laws can ensure. Both the civil sphere of property and the political sphere itself must be maintained.

Yet despite this talk of utility, it would be a mistake to see Hume's use of the concept of utility as equivalent to the conception of utility as understood by later utilitarians. For utility is here conceived of as connected to the overall moral universe, which includes not only the strictly ethical but also the aesthetic and the epistemic. Hume, following Shaftsbury, argues that utility is part of the larger structure of the social whole which perpetuates itself by the harmonizing interactions between people benevolently disposed to one another, writing that "the social virtues must, therefore, be allowed to have a natural beauty and amiableness, which, at first, antecedent to all precept or education, recommends them to the esteem of uninstructed mankind, and engages their affections".[17] So, for Hume, utility is conceived of as an expression of the overall teleological or providential character of the moral universe. It is not yet, in the moral theory at least, the expression of an instrumental calculus. This can be seen in the fact that, for Hume, laws themselves are ultimately of no use if customs do not develop in order to support them (Hume 1983, Sec. III, Part II, 29–30). It is precisely because it is rooted so deeply in a conception of humans as benevolently disposed toward each other, utility cannot be pried out of its social context in order to be made into a meta-principle. Hume's universe is a delicate balance of advantage, utility and unforced benevolence (Mackie 1980, 153/4).

Yet there is a dimension in which utility does seem to make an appearance in a more classically utilitarian form, namely when it comes to social engineering through tax policy. Here we find the perspective of the social scientist observing but also manipulating society. The social scientist's perspective appropriates the teleological position which stands outside the fray and is usually attributed to god. Such a perspective is now an explicit one which claims to know what the people want and is willing to help them secure it, even if it occurs without their knowledge.

Thus, taxation is understood by Hume as a method to encourage people to make themselves useful to society. Such taxes, Hume says, work best when "taxes are moderate, [and] laid on gradually" (Hume 1985b, 343). Like Hobbes, Hume argues that the appropriate means of taxing is through a tax on commodities, not, perhaps, because that way they reach everyone but because they "are paid gradually and insensibly" and, Hume goes on, because they "naturally produce sobriety and frugality" (Hume 1985b, 345). So, taxation functions for Hume as a means of cultivating certain beneficial social relations within an already existing society. Luxuries are to be taxed to encourage savings, for instance (Frecknall-Hughes 2007, 270).

Yet Hume's position is ambiguous since, like Locke, he is wary of the arbitrary power to impose taxes. However, Hume's concern seems to arise out of apprehension for general social cohesion, rather than as the result of seeing an inherent

[17] Shaftsbury writes that "beauty and truth are plainly joined with the notion of utility and convenience" (Shaftsbury 2000, 415). See also Hume (1983, sec. V, part I, 40).

problem with the concept of property (Hume 1985b, 346). So, Hume suggests here that an external perspective, the perspective of even an enlightened despot perhaps, would itself be deleterious to mutual benefit because it would undermine people's understanding of themselves as agents.

Hume's position on the burden of taxation adumbrates Smith's concept of the indelible hand when he maintains that it is false to think of any tax falling on any particular part of the population, for instance, if all tax falls upon landowners. For, as Hume astutely observes:

> Every man, to be sure, is desirous of pushing off from himself the burden of any tax, which is imposed, and of laying it upon others: But as every man has the same inclination, and is upon the defensive; no set of men can be supposed to prevail altogether in this contest (Hume 1985b, 347).

So here again it is the underlying teleological conception of parts and individuals working together which allows Hume to see taxation as just one social function among many in which a public benefit of safety comes not at the expense of any particular set of individuals but as a result of the whole working more or less in harmony. Utility thus remains overall social utility rather than being susceptible to reduction for Hume. The idealized conception of utilitarianism thus remains very idealized indeed, so much so that it is hard to think of articulating the conception in a way that could reduce it to something which could be operationalized numerically.

So, we find in Hume three different positions: the observer of society who understands society according to a teleological concept of what we may now term economic behavior, the participant in society who seeks her own benefit, and the more rationalized social actor who articulates her own moral conception according to a principle, that of the social virtue of utility and justice.

3.3.2.2 *Teleology* and Social Science

Smith's contributions to the question of utilitarianism and taxation are at once more specific – since he has rather a lot to say about taxation – and more vague since, for Smith much more than for Hume, utility as a term seems to disappear into an even more thorough conception of the individual as mediated by the social. Like Hume, Smith incorporates various perspectives into his work: the perspective of the self-interested agent, the perspective of the virtuous agent interested in the benefit of society at large and the perspective of the social scientist. These different perspectives have given rise to the so called "das Adam Smith Problem" which sees a conflict between the theory of virtue articulated in *A Theory of Moral Sentiments* and the theory of economics articulated in *The Wealth of Nations*.[18] The problem seems in part to stem from Smith's refusal to formulate his theory of morality in anything resembling even Hume's virtue-oriented concept of utility. While it goes well

[18] The perceived mismatch between these two texts has long been noted and debated as "das Adam Smith Problem". For an overview, see Keith Tribe (2008).

beyond the scope of this Chapter to solve the problem, we would like to suggest that what was a rather free-floating constellation of these different perspectives in Hume is given a more robust formulation in Smith through the theory of the "impartial spectator" which orders the different perspectives under a conception of autonomy.

Why is Hume's position in need of a solution? The problem can be stated in terms of a slippage which occurs in Hume between the teleological or philosophical perspective (which could remain merely descriptive) and the perspective of the social scientist or legislator (which is normative). The problem is that while Hume himself seems to avoid the problem to a certain extent by equivocating in his usage of utility, using it in a descriptive sense in his ethical theory, his comments on taxation commit him to a more robust and normative notion of utility such as will indeed be found in latter utilitarians.

So, what is the problem with the normative notion of utility? As we noted at the outset, utility, to the extent that it proposes some sort of action, necessarily presupposes a *utility maximizer* and a *beneficiary of the utility maximization*. (Our utilitarianism points (1) and (2)). While there are significant problems in the intra-psychic case, let us stick with the problem as it results in interactions between different people. There is a significant possibility of a mismatch between the maximizer's conception of utility and the beneficiary's conception. Take the perspective of the social scientist who advocates taxation on commodities so that taxes are not felt as much. This policy assumes that it is best for the consumer not to know how much they are being taxed. Moreover, this position assumes that the consumer is *not* a social scientist who, like the social scientist implementing the policy, would like to know how much they are being taxed.

The problem lies in the fact that the utility maximizer must always make a normative assumption about what will be most useful for the beneficiary. And because utility is understood to be a sui generis quality, the Archimedean point of the decision process, the utilitarian calculus will maintain its independence or objective perspective with regard to the beneficiary. So, it turns out to be a prerequisite for the utility maximizer's pursuit of the beneficiary's utility in the previous example for the beneficiary *not* to care about knowing how much they are being taxed. But this introduces certain restrictions on the sort of subject the beneficiary can be, which may sit poorly with how the beneficiary actually feels. The point, as Bernard Williams (1973, Ch. 5) famously formulated it, is that utilitarianism requires us to give up our personal integrity, the fact that we happen to have the sorts of desires and beliefs we actually have.[19] This objection has become known as the "integrity objection" and will be referred to as such in this Chapter.

The more general point that can be made from the perspective of the history of the relation between utilitarianism and taxation is that, in Hume, the teleological perspective, which remains mostly descriptive, begins to be taken up in the perspective of the social scientist who is concerned not only with describing a state of affairs but also with influencing it. But because the social scientist wants influence,

[19] For a critique of the inter-psychic version of this critique, see Robert Merrihew Adams (1976).

she must also make assumptions about the actual particular utility of an activity rather than seeing it simply operate impersonally without direct influencing it, as in the teleological perspective. Or, put another way, the replacement of teleology with a theory of efficient cause necessarily spills over into postulating a final cause which the efficient cause serves. And this requires positing a concrete final end to the beneficiary of legislation on the part of the social scientist. So, the decisive difference between deontology and consequentialism is that, while deontology can rely on process, the activity of self-determination, utilitarianism requires a determinate benefit to be known in advance of rational action.

3.3.2.3 Smith

Like Hume, Smith countenances a variety of perspectives within social life – that of the social scientist, that of the individual who is out for her own gain, but also that of the virtuous person who sympathizes with the condition of others and who disapproves of their ill treatment. However, unlike in Hume, these perspectives are all unified by what Smith calls the perspective of the "impartial spectator" which allows us to inhabit in turn each of these perspectives, but from a fundamentally unified first personal perspective. It is this unified first personal perspective which avoids the integrity objection to utilitarianism and which underlies what Smith says about taxation but which also makes Smith turn away from the sort of impersonal utility talk that Hume engaged in.

Let us begins with Smith's most famous statement of self-interest: "It is not from the benevolence of the butcher, the brewer, or the baker, that we expect our dinner, but from their regard to their own interest" (Smith 1981, Book I, Ch. 2, 27). It is indeed tempting to understand this statement as already the expression of *homo economicus*, the rational economic actor we find in twentieth century libertarian treatments of writers like Hayek, Friedman and Nozick.[20]

We find implicit support for the claims to self-interest in what appears as a pithy formulation of Smith's macro-economics, namely the famous metaphor of the "invisible hand":

> [People] are led by an invisible hand to make nearly the same distribution of the necessities of life, which would have been made, had the earth been divided into equal portions among all its inhabitants, and thus without intending it, without knowing it, advance the interest of the society, and afford means to the multiplication of the species (Smith 1985, Part IV, Sec. I, 183).[21]

[20] Thus Hayek (2002) speaks of the spontaneity of the interaction between the individual and the market. Or Friedman's idea that economic freedom promotes political freedom (Friedman 1962, 9).

[21] See also the very similar use of the term in *The Wealth of Nations*:

> By preferring the support of domestiek to that of foreign industry, he intends only his own security; and by directing that industry in such a manner as its produce may be of the greatest value, he intends only his own gain, and he is in this, as in many other eases, led by an

Hayek (1990), for instance, has interpreted this metaphor to be suggesting that, for Smith, the individual responds to invisible signals from the market. Again, we see here the tendency in later interpreters to make of Smith more of a normative social scientist than he intended to be. Rather, as Rothschild (1994, 319) has argued, the metaphor of the invisible hand was intended by Smith to be ironic. Smith, as a serious empiricist, disdained talk of invisible forces. Indeed, as Rothschild points out, the invisible hand is un-Smithian precisely *because* it seems to presuppose the existence of a theorist who sees more than any other ordinary individual, and for whom the hand is, in fact, *not* invisible (Rothschild 1994, 320). In Rothschild's interpretation, then, Smith refuses to liken social interactions to an invisible hand precisely because this would imply just the sort of perspective Hume's position adumbrates and which poses a serious problem for later utilitarians.

Indeed, rather than supposing the individual to be essentially driven by self-interest, Smith's view of human nature is, as we have already seen, fundamentally the same as Hume's in that he believes humans to be both self-interested *and* always concerned with the benefits of society. But Smith, unlike Hume, offers us a model through which to understand how these two work together, the idea of the "impartial spectator". For Smith then, the impartial spectator has a capacity to stand outside of her own interests. As Smith (1985, Part II, Sec. II, 83) puts it:

> Though it may be true, therefore, that every individual, in his own breast, naturally prefers himself to all mankind, yet he dares not look mankind in the face, and avow that he acts according to this principle. [...] When he views himself in the light in which he is conscious that others will view him, he sees that to them he is but one of the multitude in no respect better than any other in it. If he would act so as that the impartial spectator may enter into the principles of his conduct, which is what of all things he has the greatest desire to do, he must, upon this, as upon all other occasions, humble the arrogance of his self-love, and bring it down to something which other men can go along with.

The impartial spectator should then be read as a capacity to abstract from the concerns of the present, a space to reflect akin to Bishop Butler's claim that the passions, though in some sense equally strong, can be given order by reflection (Butler 1983, Sermon II). So, not only does the capacity for reflection unify our different feelings with regard to ourselves and individuals, it also orders them. While self-interest is understood to be natural, it is not thereby deemed to be normatively orienting, as it was in Hobbes or in Hayek. Rather, it is subsumed under the larger social capacity which we become aware of as we consider the social virtues of priority, for instance, or gratitude.

The principle at work in the impartial spectator and which orients us morally is reciprocity:

> To judge of ourselves as we judge of others, to approve and condemn in ourselves what we approve and condemn in others, is the greatest exertion of candour and impartiality. In order

---

invisible hand to promote an end which was no part of his intention (Smith 1981, Book IV, Ch. 2, 456).

> to do this, we must look at ourselves with the same eyes with which we look at others: we must imagine ourselves not the actors, but the spectators of our own character and conduct, and consider how these would affect us when viewed from this new station, in which their excellencies and imperfections can alone be discovered (Smith 1985, Part III, Sec. 1, 111).

The idea of reciprocity with the power of imagining ourselves in someone else's position remains for Smith a fundamentally first personal experience. We can indeed try to attain the perspective of other subjects but only in the limited sense of *imagining* ourselves in their place. There can be no hard knowledge of others' perspectives. Smith thus avoids taking up the position of the social scientist who knows better than the ordinary individual. Smith's moral theory is thus not to be classed as utilitarian and even as preemptively offering some criticisms of utilitarianism in his refusal to violate the idea of personal integrity.[22]

The related principles of impartiality and reciprocity underlie Smith's remarks on taxation, especially the famous four principles enumerated at the beginning of the discussion. Smith has been criticized for not having ranked the preferability of one form of taxation over another in a properly utilitarian manner, yet this is to some degree a virtue since it allows a certain pragmatism in the service of the overall project of impartiality and reciprocity.[23] The general orientation of *The Wealth of Nations* is descriptive not normative with regard to its view of economic. This is not to say that Smith does not have a normative conception, but that normative conception stems from the teleological view of humanity as articulated in *The Theory of Moral Sentiment*.

Smith articulates four broad maxims of taxation, (1) that taxes should fall on those who are able to pay for society's upkeep, (2) that taxes should not be arbitrary, i.e., in conformity with the expectations of a rationalized society, (3) that they should be levied in a form that is convenient for the payer, and (4) taxation should be efficient, i.e., levied on those sources which can be most rational assessed for tax purposes.

Of these it is clearly the first, the most normative, which is most relevant to our discussion.

> The subjects of every state ought to contribute towards the support of the government, as nearly as possible, in proportion to their respective abilities; that is, in proportion to the revenue which they respectively enjoy under the protection of the state (Smith 1981, Book V, Ch. II, 825).

Here we transition from the benefit approach to the ability to pay approach (O'Brien 1975, 241).[24] Recall that the basis for the justification of taxation in Hobbes and Locke comes down to payment for security which all are held to require equally, which justifies asking for all to pay equally. In those theories, protection is primarily

---

[22] Here we are in agreement with Raphael (1972–1973, 88) who argues that "Adam Smith is an anti-utilitarian, indeed a natural-law theorist, but his natural law is natural law with a difference, a genuinely empiricist natural law." For a similar assessment see Witztum and Young (2013),

[23] For such a criticism see Dome (1999, 337).

[24] Somewhat surprisingly, however, O'Brien seems to group Smith in the 'benefits' approach.

concerned with the continued ability of the individual to produce for herself. The 'ability to pay' approach, by contrast, understands the individual as connected to society in a more comprehensive way. We thus shift to the nature of economic activity as analyzable through distribution and the division of labor.

For Smith, the individual is not just the beneficiary of equal security but connected to others through a thick notion of intersubjectively grounded moral feelings.[25] *The Theory of Moral Sentiment* consists almost entirely of the different ways in which individual desires are at bottom mediated by social virtues. It should come as no surprise that Smith's conception of taxation would thus include considerations of these intersubjective ties in determining who should pay what for the necessities of society. Nor should it be surprising, given Smith's recognition of human self-interest, that it should itself be conducive to the cohesion of society that whatever revenue must be collected should be collected through a tax system that operates in the most economically pragmatic way, i.e., predictably, conveniently and efficiently.

From the first maxim certain progressive tax policies follow (Groves 1974, 19). Concerning taxation on rent, for instance, Smith argues that since rent is a larger part of the budget of the poor "it is not very unreasonable that the rich should contribute to the publick expence, not only in proportion to their revenue, but something more than in that proportion" (Smith 1981, Book V, Ch. II, 842). Smith goes so far as to contemplate a proportional tax for rent since "there is not perhaps, any one article of expence or consumption by which the liberality or narrowness of a man's whole expence can be better judged of, than by his house rent" (Smith 1981, Book V, Ch. II, 843). Yet it is the owners of ground and buildings who are singled out as the best source of government revenue since, as Smith points out, the government is actually part owner of the enterprise since ultimately the government retains at least partial responsibility for the ground and only entrusts it to the owner (Smith 1981, Book V, Ch. II, 844). Smith also rejects what we now call regressive taxation such as capitation taxes and Windows taxes which, though easy to tax, are inequitable (Smith 1981, Book V, Ch. II, 846).

Smith acknowledges certain limits on what can be done in the service of equality given the administrative limitations that prevail. Here it is point (4), which has here been abbreviated as efficiency, which is of greatest interest. Smith's point is simply that taxation should involve as little waste as possible. And, perhaps more importantly, should not discourage industry. For Smith this means that certain types of taxation are to be rejected because they are too complicated to administer, for instance. In theory, then, Smith favors a variable tax on rent, i.e., one that rises with the increase the landowners receive from their tenants, but deems it ultimately too difficult to implement (Smith 1981, Book V, Ch. II, 830), thus settling for a non-variable tax (Smith 1981, Book V, Ch. II, 834). Smith also worries that a tax on stocks driving away investors (Smith 1981, Book V. Ch. II, 849).

[25] This is a point also noted by Groves (1974, 16) who argues that Smith disagreed strongly with Mandeville's conception of self-interest.

Ultimately then, Smith's tax proposals are concerned to uphold or extend equality based not on some ultimate principle but on the reasonable expectation of people to be treated fairly by others. The expectation of fairness does not envision a social scientific administration which judges what is right and wrong for individuals but rather seeks to allow individuals to pursue their own projects in ways that also provide the means to the state to facilitate these projects. In classical liberal manner, Smith is thus concerned with the ability of individuals to pursue their socially constituted but nevertheless individually constituted interests. He is not a utilitarian in the sense that he does not believe there is a higher level of insight than can be found in the individual who reflects on her projects with a cool head and an open heart.

3.3.3 Utilitarianism

As we approach the theory of utilitarianism proper it is necessary to keep in mind that even utilitarianism proper has a history. Bentham and Mill themselves are merely the waystations in the history of an idea which has taken many turns. What principally distinguishes the philosophies of both Bentham and Mill from the thinkers of the Scottish enlightenment is that the principle of utility such as Bentham develops it and Mill modifies it, brings to a head a certain ambiguity which Smith, for instance, was happy to leave be. The central problem is that Smith's teleological conception allowed the working together of self-interest and social responsibility to be conceived of as compatible since the teleological conception simply *is* a conception of the working together of these two strands in human behavior under the perspective of the invisible hand. The principle of utility which replaces the teleological conception in Bentham and Mill, however, not only opens up but makes necessary the perspective of the social scientist who knows better than the individual how human life should best be lived (Gray 1995, 51).

Yet as will emerge in this section, neither Bentham nor Mill, political reformers both, were willing to dismiss the idea of individual autonomy which is required to fully embrace the perspective of social engineering. It is perhaps their unwillingness to reject autonomy which qualifies them as classical utilitarians, as distinct from modern utilitarians who are willing to reject the concept. What characterizes modern utilitarianism, we can say, is a certain relation in which they stand to the problem of liberty which must be reconciled with the system in various ways. Thus, for instance, G. E. Moore's rejection of the sort of hedonistic maximization which occurs in classical theory. The crucial distinction introduced by Moore is that between the hedonistic utility calculation of the Benthamite sort and the claim that pleasure must have an *intrinsic* relation to right and wrong (Moore 2005, 29–30; Smart 1987, 12–13). This distinction, in some modern utilitarians like Smart (1987, 14), leads to the claim that utility can be grasped as an assessment of value, or as an expression of approval. Classical utilitarianism of the sort considered here must also be distinguished from efforts like those of Harsanyi (1982b) to connect utilitarianism and rational choice theory.

In sum, then, classical utilitarianism, though it operates at a high level of rationality, has not yet attained the philosophical or mathematical formulation it receives in the twentieth century and hence has not yet as forcefully come into conflict with the idea of liberty. The limitation of utility by liberty, of course, makes it somewhat vague what, exactly, utility maximization means. Yet these are not merely shortcomings since, as we will seek to show, the vagueness of utility maximization allows utilitarianism to coexist relatively unobtrusively with a liberal theory of freedom which sits much more uneasily with stricter conceptions.

3.3.3.1 Bentham

If he is to be understood not merely as the originator of the principle of utility, Bentham must be appreciated as a reformer and a radical. Indeed, as Bentham makes clear, the target of the principle of utility is the *ancien regime* of received morality: asceticism, sympathy and antipathy as the principle of morality, and all theological principles (Bentham 1996, 18–19). Bentham was also an early feminist and opponent of slavery, as were many of his contemporaries, though the opposition to slavery was far more widespread than opposition to women's oppression (Williford 1976; Boralevi 1984). Central to Bentham's program stands the enlightenment ideas of self-determination and critical examination. Says Bentham:

> to justify every thing at any rate, and to disapprove of nothing, is a resolution which, pursued in future, must stand as an effectual bar to all the *additional* happiness we can ever hope for; pursued hitherto would have robbed us of that share of happiness which we enjoy already (Bentham 2009, 400).

Bentham's writings, beginning in 1776 with the just quoted *A Fragment on Government*, can quite plausibly be read as a reaction against the more tranquil mid-century of Hume and Smith. In Bentham's age of revolutions, his predecessors common sense philosophies may seem to justify rather than to improve society. Bentham's enlightenment spirit is expressed in the maxim "To obey punctually; to censure freely (Bentham 2009, 400)." No matter that the phrase endures today in Kant's more famous formulation: "Argue as much as you will and about what you will; only obey!" (Kant 1996b, 8:42)[26] Just as Kant's revolutionary gesture lay in championing autonomy over heteronomy, Bentham must be read as seeking to provide foundation for individuals to decide how to live their lives.[27]

While Kant sought to give an a priori grounding to the moral law as the principle of autonomy, Bentham sought to ground the ability to think for oneself on the principle of utility. Bentham, operating in the empiricist tradition, sought to construct his first principle from experience. Given the scientific background of his time and

[26] Kant's essay was published in 1784, three years after the *Critique of Pure Reason* first appeared.

[27] For an account of Bentham and the enlightenment, see De Champs (2015, Part I).

especially the avowed influence of the materialist Helvetius, whose work *De l'esprit* (1758, Essays on the Mind, into English 1807) provided the early formulations of the principle of utility, Bentham formulated his universal principle along the lines of what he saw as the lowest common denominator of human life, that of pleasure and pain.

> By the principle of utility is meant that principle which approves or disapproves of every action whatsoever, according to the tendency which it appears to have to augment or diminish the happiness of the party whose interest is in question: or, what is the same thing in other words, to promote or to oppose that happiness. I say of every action whatsoever; and therefore not only of every action of a private individual, but of every measure of government (Bentham 1996, 12–13).

A chief characteristic of this principle is its self-evidence. For surely what is pleasurable or painful to an individual must be known to them directly. Pleasure and pain can be verified subjectively. The idea that pleasure and pain is self-evident to the subject who experiences it means that Bentham is usually referred to as a hedonist (Smart 1987, 15). What this hedonistic outlook entails more exactly will be taken up below when we come to Bentham's ideas about tax policy.

It is this self-evidence which makes the principle fit for autonomy. This self-evidence requirement leads Bentham to assume that utility encompasses a variety of concepts which subsequently become the subject of much contestation: "By utility is meant that property in any object, whereby it tends to produce benefit, advantage, pleasure, good, or happiness, (all this in the present case comes to the same thing)" (Bentham 1996, 13).

Autonomy requires universality. Indeed, as Harsanyi (1982b, 39) has pointed out, Bentham and Kant both formulated their principles in universal terms, something that has perhaps been implied by Hume and Smith but had not been formulated as such. It is the idea of universality that gives the principle of utility its ability to guide individual decision making but crucially also provides it with its political force. The principle thus reaches all the way down to the core of the individual's ability to act and becomes a *rational* principle which allows the individual to act on her own *authority*. It constitutes a principle of action.

Importantly, and again like Kant, Bentham maintains the autonomy principle even in the face of those who would pretend to know better, writing that with regard to monarchy that no "man now [is] so far elevated above his fellows, as that he should be indulged in the dangerous licence of cheating them for their good" (Bentham 2009, 441). Thus the individual's authority is in no way secondary to the authority of the state. This is also the ground for Bentham's criticism of the social contract tradition, if not in principle, then at least in what it has become: a way of subordinating the people to a king and hence to laws not of their own making. Accordingly, Bentham champions the principle of utility as a principle of legislation since it alone "furnishes us with that reason, which alone depends not upon any higher reason, but which is itself the sole and all-sufficient reason for every point of practice whatsoever" (Bentham 2009, 449).

Like Hobbes, who begins *Leviathan* with an extended discussion of the nature of mind as it is rooted in a naturalistic psychology, Bentham too begins his account of morality and legislation with an account of the natural condition of mind, that is, its attraction to pleasure and repulsion by pain. It is no small historical irony that Bentham's elevation of the principle of utility to the status of sole principle which can ground the founding of a society is precisely how later interpreters have interpreted Hobbes' social contract theory Gauthier 1969; Hampton 1998). These interpreters are indeed right to find in Bentham the same sort of naturalized thinking mixed with the rather un-naturalistic thinking of autonomy. What is rational for Hobbes and Bentham, what constitutes the freedom of the individual, is really only the ability to determine oneself according to one's fundamental natural condition, which for Hobbes is fear of death and for Bentham is the quest for pleasure. These are rightly seen as effectively the same. For the point of the principle of utility as empirically verifiable is that it is able to cut through the fiction of morality and religion and to offer the subject a position from which to evaluate social life from her own proper perspective.

We thus arrive at an ambiguity in Bentham's thought. We have found that Bentham's political radicalism commits him to interpreting the principle of utility as a principle of autonomy, that is, as a principle through which the individual can gain authority over herself and participate in the creation of laws. The commitment to autonomy also means that for Bentham there is no position from which the social scientist can stand over and above the individual, dictating to them what is properly useful to them. At the same time, however, Bentham seems to be committed, via the naturalistic description of pleasure, to a view in which all humans are identically motivated by pleasure and pain and which turns out, after all, to make it possible to offer determinate legislation which would facilitate their welfare. These two strands can coexist with relative ease because, in an important sense, the idea of autonomy which we have been imputing to Bentham had not yet been invented by Kant. For it is only with Kant's notion of autonomy as both free and determinable that the conflict between utility and self as we have seen it in Williams' critique of utilitarianism properly appears.

Nevertheless, even if it was not obvious to Bentham, psychological hedonism carries with it an important ambiguity. On the one hand, the fact of pleasure and pain's self-evidence seems to suggest strongly that the individual's experience should be conceived of as the ultimate standard of what is good for them since only the individual knows what feels pleasurable to them. This is hedonism's first personal dimension. On the other hand, the empiricist conception of pleasure and pain as biological determinants of subjectivity per se suggest that empirical science ought to be able to determine what is objectively good for an individual and ought on the basis of these biological laws be able to prescribe to the individual certain norms which it makes sense to follow, no matter whether the individual feels like it or not. This is the third personal perspective. The ambiguity becomes fatal when the first personal conception of the final cause is taken to be generalizable to the third person perspective and thus prescribed to all, regardless of their actual experience.[28]

[28] On this point see the important critique of Adorno & Horkheimer (2002).

This ambiguity can also be found Bentham's theory of taxation. As a function of distributive law, taxation is in the ultimate service of "subsistence, abidance, security and equality" (Bentham 1989, 158). Or, as he puts it when discussing taxation directly, taxation is necessary for the maintenance of justice and for the maintenance of security against foreign adversaries (Bentham 1996, 152). These lofty goals, however, must, for Bentham, be made compatible with his psychological hedonistic commitments. Accordingly, Bentham must balance the long-term benefits of taxation for the maintenance of justice and security with the immediate perspective of the person who does not want to pay taxes because it reduces her pleasure. The trick is then to determine a form of taxation that is not only acceptable contingently, i.e., what would be acceptable for whatever reason in the moment, but one that contributes to the long-term welfare of the individual and society at large.

The object of the present Chapter is to enquire, not what would *go down*, but what ought to go down: "what [would] go down, not merely with least disturbance from the outcry of the moment, [...] but with least suffering at the long run, with the slightest wound to the feelings of individuals, and that which promises to be the soonest closed" (Bentham 2004a, 379).

Bentham, like his immediate predecessors, favors taxation based on the ability to pay. This suggests that an equal system of taxation would take a *relatively* equal share from each (Bentham 2004a, 380). So here the principle of autonomy triumphs. Bentham's advocacy of a consumption tax might seem to be in conflict with that principle since, as is regularly claimed now, consumption taxes are typically regressive, falling more on those who expend a larger portion of their income on consumption.[29] Yet Bentham's reason for a consumption tax lies not in its fair distribution but rather in the way it is administered. For while a tax on possession seems to Bentham unacceptable because it means taking away what already belongs to an individual, a tax on consumption seems to him to be voluntary and hence less painful (Bentham 2004a, 380). In a gesture toward a progressive system of taxation, Bentham argues that it is right for the rich to be taxed at twice the rate of the poor. Perhaps as a function of Bentham's view of the difference between the subjective satisfaction generated by the activity of labor and the passive receipt of income, Bentham advocates that income from industry should be taxed at half the rate of that of property income (Bentham 2004a, 380, 386).

Concretely, Bentham makes two proposals to limit the impact of tax on the population in general by taxing those who would least feel it: distant relatives in a more widespread application of the escheat tax, and bankers and stock dealers. Bankers and stock dealers would be given a monopoly in exchange for paying higher taxes (Bentham 2004a, 388). Bentham's more famous proposal is an escheat tax whereby in the case of the death of a landowner with no close relatives, half of the property

[29] Of course, most of the world's countries have a Value Added Tax ("VAT"), which permits a broader offering of publicly funded goods. As a result, the progressivity or regressivity of any particular tax should be considered within a larger context.

would be reappropriated by the state.[30] Bentham's proposal focuses heavily on the psychological aspect of the proposed tax, emphasizing the dimension of expectation. He argues that since distant relatives have no rational expectation of inheritance (since they stand in line behind children) they do not organize their lives around an expected inheritance (Bentham 2004a, 284). In such circumstances, receiving half of the deceased relative's property would count as a real benefit. This too would encourage the owner of the property to improve it, another social benefit (Bentham 2004a, 285).

Thus, Bentham seeks to hold together the general need for taxation in order to provide funds for the state, a need the individual may or may not be happy about, and the perceived happiness of the individual subject who is to be burdened as little as possible. As in Hume and Smith, and later in Mill, the unity of autonomy and hedonism within the principle of utility are ultimately held together by the assumption of a certain 'reasonableness' which characterized enlightenment assumptions in the eighteenth century, a reasonableness which sits uneasily between the idea that humans are all different and that they are really fundamentally the same.

3.3.3.2 Mill

The unreflective assumption about the unproblematic unity of the science of the legislator and of individual hedonism in Bentham's conception of utilitarianism begins to come apart in Mill's conception of utilitarianism. Mill inherited many of the radical ideas advocated by Bentham, including the fundamental equality of women and opposition to slavery. But whereas these ideas had not been thematized in Bentham's conception of utility, the connection between individual rights to self-determination and the principle of utility began to strain the theory of utilitarianism proper in Mill. This leads to the same question that had dogged the interpretation of Smith almost 100 years earlier: what is the relation between Mill's two most famous works *Utilitarianism* and *On Liberty*?[31] Yet while in Smith the issue could be resolved from a general teleological perspective in which the two sides were simply not, ultimately, resolvable, the new language of utilitarianism and its stronger demands for consistency make Smith's light touch difficult to repeat within the framework Mill demands for his theory. Nevertheless, as we shall see, the attempt to connect utilitarianism and the concept of liberty will here too require an Aristotelian conception of human flourishing to succeed and is not ultimately fully successful.

Before we get into the details of the conflict between the two sets of principles most closely associated with Mill, it will be good to lay them out one at a time. Mill's definition of liberty proceeds, as one might expect from someone schooled in

[30] For pragmatic reasons or not, Bentham proposes to exempt the peerage from such a tax (Bentham 2004, 284).

[31] For an overview of some of the controversy, see Riley (1998a, Ch. 7).

Benthamite empiricism as Mill was, from the idea of complete self-authorization through the principle of utility:

> I regard utility as the ultimate appeal on all ethical questions: but it will be utility in the largest sense, grounded on the permanent interests of man as a progressive being. Those interests, I contend, authorize the subjection of individual spontaneity to external control, only in respect to those actions of each, which concern the interests of other people (Mill 1998b, 14).

Leaving aside the social scientific or third personal aspect of utility, we can see that for Mill too, what is attractive about utility, in distinction from natural rights which Mill explicitly rejects, is that it is a standard which is immediately evident to the subject.[32]

Mill acknowledges that there are interests which are wider than the subject and which can therefore not be left completely up to them. Liberty, for Mill as for Hobbes, begins where law ends. Yet,

> there is a sphere of action in which society, as distinguished from the individual, has, if any, only an indirect interest; comprehending all that portion of a person's life and conduct which affects only himself, or if it also affects others, only with their free, voluntary, and undeceived consent and participation. [...] This, then, is the appropriate region of human liberty (Mill 1998b, 15).

Liberty comprise three essential areas: (1) the "inward domain of conscience" which includes the liberty of thought, (2) the "liberty of tastes and pursuits, of framing our own plan to suit our own character" and, (3) the freedom to unite "for any purpose not involving harm to others" Mill 1998b, 15). The text of *On Liberty* is a defense of each of these areas of liberty as essential to self-determination. For our purposes of understanding Mill as a theorist of autonomy, it is perhaps worth mentioning the sort of pragmatism which Mill articulates as a way of understanding the second point, the liberty to pursue one's own plans. This is Mill's famous claim about 'experiments in living':

> As it is useful that while mankind are imperfect there should be different opinions, so is it that there should be different experiments of living; that free scope should be given to varieties of character, short of injury to others; and that the worth of different modes of life should be proved practically, when any one thinks fit to try them. It is desirable, in short, that in things which do not primarily concern others, individuality should assert itself (Mills 1998b, 56).

Mill's point seems to be explicitly directed against any sort of paternalism which might propose that one way of doing things is intrinsically superior to another for all individuals. We can then say that in general *On Liberty* seems to adopt the tone of autonomy or what we have referred to as the first personal perspective.

Yet Mill seems to strike a different tone in *Utilitarianism*. Here he proposes to understand humans from a third person perspective, positing a final cause: "All action is for the sake of some end, and rules of action, it seems natural to suppose,

---

[32] "It is proper to state that I forgo any advantage which could be derived to my argument from the idea of abstract right, as a thing independent of utility" (Mill 1998b, 14).

must take their whole character and colour from the end to which they are subservient" (Mill 1998a, 116). For Mill it follows from this what is needed for right action is a test of what is right or wrong to orient us in advance of undertaking the action.

Adopting the third person perspective allows Mill to formulate the principle of utility as follows:

> The creed which accepts as the foundation of morals, Utility, or the Greatest Happiness Principle, holds that actions are right in proportion as they tend to promote happiness, wrong as they tend to produce the reverse of happiness. By happiness is intended pleasure, and the absence of pain; by unhappiness, pain, and the privation of pleasure (Mill 1998a, 121).

So, the principle of utility or greatest happiness principle gives us a determinate way of ascertaining the goal of our actions: pleasure turns out to be the final cause. If the principle of utility is the ultimate standard of all human action, then it also subsumes morality (Mill 1998a, 126).

So far, then, Mill is in agreement with Bentham's conception. Where he diverges is in his famous attempt to defend Bentham from the charge that pleasure is base. Rather, Mill says, there are different sorts of pleasures, writing in a much misquoted passage:

> It is better to be a human being dissatisfied than a pig satisfied; better to be Socrates dissatisfied than a fool satisfied. And if the fool, or the pig, is of a different opinion, it is because they only know their own side of the question. The other party to the comparison knows both sides (Mill 1998a, 124).

The problem is that the distinction between different types of pleasure introduced here seems to depart from the central achievement of Bentham's principle of utility: its absolute empirical self-evidence. For though Mill asserts that the difference is self-evident by claiming that those are fools who do not see it, it is precisely the fools who need convincing on the basis of the principle's self-evidence, as Bentham well knew.

Mill's introduction of higher and lower pleasure points to a significant problem within utilitarian theory which that distinction is meant to address: what are the conceptual parameters which modify the principle of utility as the pursuit of pleasure. Bentham too was not immune from this criticism since he assumed that hedonism would at least be temporally deferred. So, if pleasure necessarily requires some sort of conceptual modification what form will such a modification take? The history of utilitarian thinking, as already suggested, contains a variety of answers to this question. Thus, act utilitarians, whom Mill is usually counted among, think of the action as the proper unity of pleasure. Yet action, of course, remains a rather vague term. Can getting a PhD be considered an action? Rule utilitarians consider pleasure to be modified by a universal rule (Smart 1987, 9). But either such a conception will subordinate utilitarianism to deontology, as, for instance, in Rawls, or rule utilitarianism will collapse back into act-utilitarianism since the rule is itself supposed to be the expression of utility.[33]

The problem with pleasure's conceptual modification leads also to a problem with the idea of liberty: should liberty be understood as a constraint on utility or should utility be understood as a constraint on liberty? If it is the former, then we have the Rawlsian view in which utilitarianism is subsumed under a deontological or better, procedural, conception of justice. To do so would effectively to give up on utilitarianism as a theory.[34] So the relation must be the other way around, liberty must be understood as ultimately modified by utility. This is more in line with Mill's claim that "I regard utility as the ultimate appeal on all ethical questions" (Mill 1998b, 14).

Gray has argued that Mill's attempt to unify liberty or autonomy with utility must be understood as an attempt to articulate an indirect utilitarianism, one in which reasoning does not directly concern itself with the idea of utility maximization but is nevertheless framed by it. This is so, in part, for reasons that have become evident through Williams' integrity objection: it is psychologically problematic to regard oneself as having general desires which one does not feel one has but which are prescribed on the grounds of a utility maximizing calculation (Gray 1983, 15). Rather, Gray suggests, Mill should be understood as advocating an Aristotelian conception of happiness or flourishing in which autonomy requires a particular conception of happiness for it to be *about* something (Gray 1983, 81–82). Yet Gray also suggests that in formulating this conception Mill departs in significant ways from the social scientific perspective upon which the principle of utility is supposed to be based and thus fails to bring the project of combining utilitarianism and liberty to fruition (Gray 1983, 83).

More generally the problem between utility and liberty arises for Mill in a way it had not arisen in Smith because Smith recognizes that the relation between economic and political life can never be fully reconciled since they are in a certain sense always artificial. The contingent connection between the economic and the political in Smith prevents Smith (and to some extent Hume too) from thinking that society could be fully rationalized by means of the knowledge provided us by the new social sciences, in particular economics. Utility maximization, in its strong Benthamite version, however, *does* postulate a theory in which the social sciences, reduced to the principle of utility, can tell us how to live in the manner of a social engineer (Gray 1995, 25, 29–30).

---

[33] In Rawls, the difference principle which concerns itself with efficiency and thus utility is subordinated to the principle of justice (Rawls 1999, §11. 53. For the criticism that rule utilitarianism collapses back into act-utilitarianism, see Lyons (1965).

[34] Kant too subordinated instrumental reason, taking the means to one's ends, under the moral law (Kant 1996c, 4:417).

3.3.3.3 Taxation

Mill's account of taxation exists within this somewhat unreflective balance between the autonomy and principle of utilitarianism. In his economic theory Mill builds on Ricardo in the service of implementing a more autonomous theory of the economic individual than the one Bentham conceived of (Riley 1998b, 296). Bentham and Mill decisively shift away from the idea that economic activity is to be understood in terms of production and toward the idea that economic activity is to be understood in terms of distribution (Mill 1965a, 199; Groves 1974, 28). Since distribution is purely artificial, it is a fit subject for legislation and hence alteration. Indeed, Mill's conception goes so far as to countenance socialism (Mill 1965a, 207). Yet Mill's theory of taxation does not extend to a radical redistribution since for Mill the possession of property is an essential part of every individual's life plan and hence necessary for their autonomy.

Citing the four maxims which begin Smith's account, Mill states that the principle of taxation consists in the "equality of sacrifice":

> If any one bears less than his fair share of the burthen, some other person must suffer more than his share, and the alleviation to the one is not, *ceteris paribus*, so great a good to him, as the increased pressure upon the other is an evil. Equality of taxation, therefore, as a maxim of politics, means equality of sacrifice (Mill 1965b, 807).

Again, we find here the notion of responsibility for payment distributed not according to benefit but rather according to how payment fits with the ability to bear the burden of financing society. All must be subject to the same pressures relative to their ability to maintain a flourishing and autonomous life. So, Mill favors an overall progressive tax schema. Yet, Mill also links the tax burden to the amount of effort expended in the accumulation of wealth, arguing that we must not relieve the prodigal at the expense of the industrial (Mill 1965b, 810). Rather, those fortunes which are unearned, i.e., income from rent or by bequest, which should be taxed Mill 1965b, 811–12).

And like Bentham, and befitting his own model of human flourishing, Mill understands taxation as affecting not only an individual's pocketbook but also their general attitudes and feeling. Indeed, he goes so far as to suggest that it is "manifestly absurd" to seek to resolve arguments in favor of one type of taxation over another merely on numerical grounds (Mill 1965b, 814). Faced with a subject as open to social engineering suggests how important the principle of autonomy is to Mill, perhaps so important that it would be correct to speak of Mill's conception of utility as after all being tempered by the idea of individual autonomy.

3.4 Conclusions

Modern theories of taxation are founded on assumptions that have evolved from historical utilitarianism. In this Chapter we have laid out the development of the theories of utilitarianism in order to enrich the understanding of these underlying assumptions. A careful reflection on the history makes clear that those assumptions should perhaps be disrupted more than they currently are. Considering the interactions between autonomy and utility or efficiency as they are currently understood provides rich and important insights into the development of the current thinking that underlies many legislative decisions. While the priority of efficiency or the welfare economic theory that undergirds most contemporary tax policy does not seem at risk of serious disruption any time soon, we hope this Chapter contributes to efforts to think critically about that work in the future.

References

Adams, Robert M. 1976. Motive Utilitarianism. *The Journal of Philosophy* 73 (14): 467–481.

Amartya, and Williams. 1982a. *Utilitarianism and Beyond.*

Adorno, Theodor W., and Max Horkheimer. 2002. *Dialectic of Enlightenment: Philosophical Fragments*. Gunzelin Schmid Noerr, Transl. Stanford: Stanford University Press.

Aristotle. 1993. *Metaphysics Books Gamma, Delta and Epsilon*. Christopher Kirwan Transl. Oxford: Oxford University Press.

Bentham, Jeremy. 1962. *An Introduction to the Principles of Morals and Legislation*, ed. John Bowring. New York: Russell and Russell.

———. 1989. *First Principles Preparatory to Constitutional Code*, ed. Philip Schofield. Oxford: Clarendon Press.

———. 1996. *An Introduction to the Principles of Morals and Legislation*. Oxford: Clarendon Press.

———. 2004a. Proposal for a Mode of Taxation in Which the Burthen May Be Alleviated or even Balanced by an Indemnity. In *Jeremy Bentham's Economic Writings*, ed. Werner Stark. London: Routledge.

———. 2004b. Supply without Burthen, or Escheat Vice Tax. In *Jeremy Bentham's Economic Writings*, ed. Werner Stark. London: Routledge.

———. 2009. A Fragment on Government. In *The Collected Works of Jeremy Bentham: A Commentary and A Fragment on Government*, ed. J.H. Burns and H.L.A. Hart. Oxford: Oxford University Press.

Boralevi, Lea C. 1984. *Bentham and the Oppressed*. New York: De Gruyter.

Butler, Joseph. 1983. *Five Sermons, Preached at the Rolls Chapel and A Disserattion upon the Nature of Virtue*. Stephen L. Darwall (ed.). Indianapolis: Hackett Publishing Company.

De Champs, Emmanuelle. 2015. *Enlightenment and Utility: Bentham In French, Bentham In France*. Cambridge: Cambridge University Press.

Dome, Takuo. 1999. Bentham and Mill on Tax Reform. *Utilitas* 11 (3): 320–339.

Frecknall-Hughes, Jane. 2007. The Concept of Taxation and the Age of Enlightenment'. In *Studies In the History of Tax Law*, ed. John Tiley, vol. 2, 253–286. Oxford: Hart Publishing.

Friedman, Milton. 1962. *Capitalism and Freedom*. Chicago: University of Chicago Press.

Gauthier, David P. 1969. *The Logic of Leviathan*. Oxford: Oxford University Press.

Gray, John. 1983. *Mill on Liberty: A Defense*. London: Routledge & Paul Kegan.

———. 1995. *Liberalism*. 2nd ed. Minneapolis: University of Minnesota Press.

Groves, Harold. 1974. *The Tax Philosophers*. Madison: University of Wisconsin Press.

Haakonson, Knud. 1981. *The Science of Legislator*. Cambridge: Cambridge University Press.

Hampton, Jean. 1998. *The Authority of Reason*. Cambridge: Cambridge University Press.

Harsanyi, John C. 1982a. Rule Utilitarianism, Rights, Obligations and the Theory of Rational Behavior. In *Papers In Game Theory*, 235. Dordrecht: Springer.

———. 1982b. Morality and the Theory of Rational Behavior. In *Utilitarianism and Beyond*, ed. Amartya Sen and Bernard Williams, 39–62. Cambridge: Cambridge University Press.

Hirschman, Albert. 1997. *The Passions and the Interests*. Princeton: Princeton University Press.
Hobbes, Thomas. 1991. *Leviathan*. Cambridge: Cambridge University Press.
Hume, David. 1983. In *An Inquiry Concerning the Principles of Morals*, ed. J.B. Schneewind. Indianapolis: Hackett Publishing Company.
———. 1985a. Of the Original Contract. In *Essays Moral, Political, and Literary*. Indianapolis: Liberty Classics.
———. 1985b. Of Taxes. In *Essays Moral, Political, and Literary*. Indianapolis: Liberty Classics.
Jackson, Dudley. 1973. Thomas Hobbes' Theory of Taxation. *Political Studies* 21 (2): 175–182.
Kant, Immanuel. 1996a. *Critique of Practical Reason*. Mary J. Gregor (ed., and transl.). Cambridge: Cambridge University Press.
———. 1996b. An Answer to the Question: What is Enlightenment? In *Practical Philosophy*, ed. Mary J. Gregor. Cambridge: Cambridge University Press.
———. 1996c. *Groundwork for the Metaphysics If Morals*, ed., and transl., Mary J. Gregor. Cambridge: Cambridge University Press.
Locke, John. 1988. Second Treatise of Government. In *Two Treaties of Government*, ed. Peter Laslett. Cambridge: Cambridge University Press.
Lyons, David. 1965. *Forms and Limits of Utilitarianism*. Oxford: Oxford University Press.
Mackie, J.L. 1980. *Hume's Moral Theory*. London: Routledge.
Mill, John Stuart. 1965a. *Principles of Political Economy*, Books I-II § II. University of Toronto Press.
———. 1965b. *Principles of Political Economy*, Books III-V § III. University of Toronto Press.
———. 1998a. *Utilitarianism*, ed. John Gray. Oxford: Oxford University Press.
———. 1998b. *On Liberty*, ed. John Gray. Oxford: Oxford University Press.
Moore, G.E. 2005. *Ethics*. Oxford: Oxford University Press.
Nozick, Robert. 1975. *Anarchy, State, and Utopia*. Oxford: Blackwell.
O'Brien, D.P. 1975. *The Classical Economists*. Oxford: Clarendon Press.
Raphael, D.D. 1972–1973 "Hume and Adam Smith on Justice and Utility." 73(1) *Proceedings of the Aristotelian Society* 87-104.
Ratner, Sidney. 1967. *Taxation and Democracy in America*. New York: Wiley.
Rawls, John. 1999. *A Theory of Justice*. Harvard: Harvard University Press.
Riley, Jonathan. 1998a. *Mill On Liberty*. London: Routledge.
———. 1998b. Mill's Political Economy: Ricardian Science and Liberal Utilitarian Art. In *The Cambridge Companion to John Stuart Mill*, ed. John Skorupski, 293–337. Cambridge: Cambridge University Press.
Robertson, Ritchie. 2020. *The Enlightenment: The Pursuit of Happiness, 1680–1790*. London: Allen Lane/Penguin.
Rosen, Frederick. 2003. *Classical Utilitarianism from Hume to Mill*. London: Routledge.
Rothschild, Emma. 1994. Adam Smith and the Invisible Hand. *The American Economic Review* 84 (2): 319–322.
Sayre-McCord, Geoffrey. 1996. Hume and the Bauhaus Theory of Ethics. *Midwest Studies* 20: 280–298.
Sen, Amartya, and Bernard A.O. Williams. 1982a. Introduction. In *Utilitarianism and Beyond*, ed. Amartya Sen and Bernard Williams. Cambridge: Cambridge University Press.
———, eds. 1982b. *Utilitarianism and Beyond*. Cambridge: Cambridge University Press.
Shaftsbury, Third Earl of. 2000. *Characteristics of Men, Manners, Opinions, Times*. Cambridge: Cambridge University Press.
Smart, J.J.C. 1987. An Outline of a System of Utilitarianism. In *Utilitarianism: For and Against*, ed. J.J.C. Smart and Bernard Williams. Cambridge: Cambridge University Press.
Smith, Adam. 1981. *An Inquiry Into the Nature and Causes of the Wealth of Nations*. Indianapolis: Liberty Classics.
———. 1985. In *The Theory of Moral Sentiments*, ed. A.L. Macfie and D.D. Raphael. Indianapolis: Liberty Fund.
Tobin, James. 1978. A Proposal for International Monetary Reform. *Eastern Economic Journal* 4: 153.

Tribe, Keith. 2008. 'Das Adam Smith Problem' and the Origins of Modern Smith Scholarship. *History of Europen Ideas* 34 (4): 514–525.
von Hayek, Friedrich A. 1990. Adam Smith's Message in Today's Language. In *New Studies In Philosophy, Politics, Economic and the History of Ideas*, ed. Friedrich A. Hayek. Chicago: The University of Chicago Press.
———. 2002. Competition as a Discovery Procedure. *The Quarterly Journal of Austrian Economics* 5 (3): 9–23.
Williams, Bernard A.O. 1973. A Critique of Utilitarianism. In *Utilitarianism: For and Against*, ed. J.J.C. Smart and Bernard Williams. Cambridge: Cambridge University Press.
Williford, Miriam. 1976. Bentham on the Rights of Women. *Journal of the History of Ideas* 36 (1): 167–176.
Witztum, Amos, and Jeffrey T. Young. 2013. Utilitarianism and the Role of Utility in Adam Smith. *European Journal of the History of Economic Thought* 20 (4): 572–602.

Jennifer Bird-Pollan is the Associate Dean of Academic Affairs and the Judge William T. Lafferty Professor of Law at the University of Kentucky J. David Rosenberg College of Law. She earned a B.A. in Philosophy and French Literature at Penn State University, a J.D. at Harvard Law School and an M.A. and Ph.D. in Philosophy at Vanderbilt University. Before joining the U.K. faculty, she practiced tax law at Ropes and Gray in Boston. Bird-Pollan's research lies at the intersection of tax law and philosophy, specifically with regard to the taxation of wealth transfers and issues of sovereignty in international taxation. Her publications include articles published in the Maine Law Review, Boston College Law Review, Arkansas Law Review, Pepperdine Law Review, Notre Dame Journal of Law, Ethics and Public Policy, as well as several book chapters. She teaches a variety of tax law courses, including Federal Income Tax, Corporate Tax, and Partnership Tax.

Stefan Bird-Pollan (D.Phil. Oxford, in German Literature; Ph.D. Vanderbilt, in Philosophy) is associate professor at the University of Kentucky. His research focuses on how the notion of subjectivity is related to intersubjectivity in modern moral and political philosophy as well as in aesthetics. His book *The Dialectic of Emancipation; Hegel, Freud and Fanon* which places Frantz Fanon's social critique in the tradition of German idealism appeared in 2015 (Rowman and Littlefield). He has published articles on Kant, Hegel, Rawls, Marcuse, Adorno, Benjamin, Freud, John McDowell and Stanley Cavell as well as on the topics of the relation between populism and liberalism, intersectionality, and the unconscious. He has also edited (with Vladimir Marchenko) a volume on the relation between Hegel's aesthetic and Hegel's political thought, *Hegel's Political Aesthetics* (Bloomsbury, 2021). He is working on two book projects. One concerns Kant's theory of the subject and its relation to Kant's ethics. His second book project concerns the role of emotion in political life as seen through the lens of psychoanalytic theory and German idealism.

Chapter 4
Classical Liberalism: Market-Supporting Institutions and Public Goods Funded by Limited Taxation

Charles Delmotte and Daniel Nientiedt

Abstract The chapter outlines the classical liberal perspective on taxation. From the point of view of classical liberalism, the legitimacy of all legal-institutional arrangements depends on the voluntary agreement of the people who live under them. This contractarian criterion implies a positive (if limited) role for government, namely, to engage in activities that further the common interests of the citizens. In this context, classical liberals emphasize that taxes should be viewed as payment for government services received ("benefit principle"). Regarding the specification of the tax system, classical liberal scholars point to two problems. First, the administrative and compliance costs associated with complex tax rules, and second, the incentives for interest groups to influence tax policy in their favor. The chapter discusses institutional remedies for these issues, including the reliance on simple rules in the sense of Richard Epstein (Simple rules for a complex world. Harvard University Press, Cambridge, MA, 1995) and the constitutionalization of tax rules to constrain government behavior.

Keywords Classical liberalism · Constitutionalism · Philosophy of taxation · Benefit principle of taxation · Rule of law · Flat taxes

4.1 Classical Liberal Political Philosophy

Classical liberalism is a political theory of limited government. There are many strands of classical liberalism, yet many classical liberals will agree that the state should secure a limited number of legal institutions such as private property,

---

C. Delmotte (✉)
College of Law, Michigan State University, East Lansing, MI, USA

School of Law, New York University, New York, NY, USA
e-mail: Charles.Delmotte@nyu.edu

D. Nientiedt
Department of Economics, New York University, New York, NY, USA

R. F. van Brederode (ed.), *Political Philosophy and Taxation*,
https://doi.org/10.1007/978-981-19-1092-0_4

freedom of contract, and the rule of law – an operation that justifies the imposition of taxes on its citizens (Epstein 1985). Classical liberalism is more than this institutional proposal, it is also a theory of justifiability of specific rules and governmental institutions. The classical liberal research program offers a *methodology* for the justification of legal-political systems (Cowen 2021). Political power must be justifiable not to those who exercise it, but solely to those who are subject to it (Vanberg 2014). Rules and governmental institutions do not have some supra-individual goal such as "the nation," "god," or "tradition"; the framework that constructs the state must be solely in the interest of the separate individuals who live under it (Sugden 2018).

Classical liberalism locates the justification of the state in the interests of the citizens – a theory that's historically closely connected with the model of "the social contract" (Brennan and Buchanan 2000a; Dold 2018). The social contract is a metaphor to symbolize an instrumental perspective on political power. Political institutions are not a goal in themselves – they are a means to serve "the people". The conceptualization of the state as an agreement between its participants is a way to prioritize the interests of all those involved. The modeling of politics as a contractual agreement does not entail actual consent from every individual. As Delmotte and Dold (2021) phrase it: legal-political institutions must be *reconstructible* as the outcome of a social contract, meaning they should not be imposed on but chosen by the individuals that live under them.[1] James Buchanan (1999, 288) contends as follows:

> The legitimacy of social organizational structures is to be judged *against the voluntary agreement* of those who are to live or are living under the arrangements that are judged. The central premise of individuals as sovereigns does allow for delegation of decision-making authority to agents, so long as it remains understood that *individuals remain as principals*.

Although the delegation of power to political agents is principally allowed, the exercise of power can be solely justified by reference to the sovereign individuals that make up society (Vanberg 2014). Legal-political institutions are justified – i.e., "reconstructible" as the outcome of a contract – if they generate beneficial effects for all participants in society (Gaus 2012; Epstein 1985). This "universal benefit requirement" is a tool employed to operationalize the (untenable) test of voluntary agreement: when all individuals benefit from a specific rule, can we reason that this rule would be backed by the agreement of the contractors (Buchanan 2000, 44; Delmotte 2020).[2] The requirement traces back to Hobbes, who justified the state through an individualistic calculus: all individuals within the social order benefit

[1] In the language of Geoffrey Brennan and James Buchanan (2000a, 26) the political institutions of the state can be legitimized "as if" they emerged contractually, i.e., were chosen by individuals.

[2] We use the term "benefit requirement" and not "Pareto norm" because the latter is sometimes interpreted as Pareto optimality, meaning no one can be made better off without anyone being made worse off. The benefit requirement is a much weaker and dynamic form of the Pareto principle and allows for improvements that do not have to "reach" optimality straight away, but rather can hinge to the "Pareto frontier."

from the movement from the state of nature to the establishment of government (Hobbes 1996).

The universal benefit requirement of classical liberalism can also be justified on grounds of rule consequentialism: the rules and enforcement that make up the state are legitimate based on their consequences (Buchanan 2000; Epstein 1985; von Hayek 2011).[3] Often, explicit recourse to "the contract" disappears, and theorists evaluate the acceptability of rules and institutions by gauging their acceptability towards the individuals that live under them. Friedrich von Hayek (1979, 6) refrained from using the metaphor, but argues nonetheless that "the ultimate justification of the conferment of a power to coerce is that such a power is required ... and that *all have therefore an interest* in the existence of such a power."

As we will see below, we can identify several rules and institutions that are beneficial to all individuals, yet that *cannot* be achieved through voluntary exchange (Epstein 1994). While all individuals benefit under a legal system in which private property is protected and contracts are enforced, transaction costs to set up such a system voluntarily are too high (Gaus 2012). So, individuals benefit from a coerced "contract" by which every single individual contributes in return for the protection against predation, and the security that contracts will be executed (Buchanan 2000). And so, we need the state to establish a number of institutions and enforce taxes, to set up a network of "forced exchanges" – i.e., adherence to the rules and taxes to enforce them – that leaves everyone better off (Epstein 1994).

4.2 Classical Liberal Institutions

As discussed in the previous section, classical liberalism offers, among other things, a normative justification for the coercive apparatus of the state. The source of justification is the voluntary consent of citizens. With the contractarian criterion as a starting point, what exactly should the state do? This brings us to the kind of institutions recommended by classical liberalism. Institutions are the "rules of the game" of a society, the formal and informal constraints that shape human interactions (North 1990). Most importantly for our purposes, the term refers to the legal framework in which economic interactions take place.

To begin with, self-interested individuals will consent to an initial contract that establishes the state. In a Hobbesian state of nature, individuals use some of their resources to either defend themselves or attack others. Each individual would benefit if these resources were instead used for the production of goods. Thus, an initial contract emerges that assigns property rights and creates an agency, the state, that enforces compliance with contractual agreements. The initial constitutional contract

[3] The alternative tradition within classical liberalism is natural rights theory. This chapter will not discuss this tradition since it was less prominent in the last 100 years and provides a less articulate framework for economic and tax analysis. For an excellent reanimation, see Christmas (2021).

establishes what is called the "protective" state, or the institutions of law (Buchanan 2000).

In its protective role, the state creates and maintains the legal framework required for the functioning of markets. One feature of the constitutional contract is that it defines the rights of the individual against the state. They guarantee a free sphere of action for every individual, which is the basic prerequisite for voluntary economic exchange. Important economic rights include the aforementioned principle of private property as well as the freedom of contract and the freedom of trade. The state's commitment to these rights reduces uncertainty, stimulates investment and provides incentives for competitive market processes (von Hayek 2011; Olson 2000).

Another feature of the constitutional contract is that it imposes restrictions on behavior that would undermine the functioning of markets. Concerning private actors, legal provisions are needed to counteract anti-competitive practices (e.g., the formation of cartels) and regulate natural monopoly. With regard to the state, the constitutional contract determines the range of economic policy options. Perhaps most importantly, a stable currency becomes "constitutionalized" – i.e., part of the constitution – if the central bank is shielded from political influence (Buchanan 2010). Similarly, constitutional provisions may be used to constrain fiscal policy, thus ensuring the sustainability of public spending (Feld and Kirchgässner 2008).

In contrast to the protective state, the "productive" state is responsible for providing those goods and services which, according to the citizens, are not adequately provided by the market. This function of the state inevitably requires a mechanism for collective decision-making. The decision-making rules are specified in the constitution. Self-interested individuals will find it expedient not to require unanimity for decisions made on the post-constitutional stage. Instead, they will choose rules with lower decision-making costs, i.e., some kind of majority rule (Buchanan and Tullock 1999).

Why should the state act in a productive capacity? Firstly, some goods and services are more efficiently provided by the state. Typical examples include national defense, pandemic prevention or fire services. In these cases, it is assumed that the incentive to free ride makes the voluntary private provision of the service unsustainable. Secondly, the state can counteract some of the negative effects (externalities) that individual actions have on third parties. Of course, due to the preferences of electorates, public goods provision is usually not limited to those two categories. Among the public goods that have been advocated by classical liberals are a guaranteed minimum income, subsidized education and regulation of environmental pollution (von Hayek 1979).

When evaluating individual policy measures, classical liberals often turn to the rule of law criterion. There are three attributes which a law must possess in order to conform to the rule of law: Generality, equality and certainty. This means that the law does not discriminate in favor of or against any person or group, that it applies equally to all, and that individuals are able to predict whether the law affects them (von Hayek 2011; Delmotte 2020). From a normative point of view, it seems plausible that people would consent to laws that comply with the rule of law criterion. The positive argument in favor of general laws is that they enable the coordinating principle of spontaneous order, which is associated with better economic performance (von Hayek 1945). As can be seen from the above description, the protective state embodies the rule of law ideal particularly well.

The actions taken by the state to maintain the institutions of a free society – whether in its protective or productive capacity – are necessarily costly. Thus, the existence of such institutions is contingent on the state's ability to raise funds to pay for them. The following section will explore questions related to the funding of public expenditures, i.e., the issue of taxation.

4.3 Taxation Within the Classical Liberal Tradition

4.3.1 The Benefit Theory of Tax

As the previous sections show, classical liberal political and economic theory proposes a *specific* set of institutions that the state should enforce. Taxation comes into the picture as the system that organizes the funding of these activities and public services. It is important to note that classical liberal tax theory is distinct from mainstream welfare economics. In the latter theory, the expenditure side of government and the taxing side are separated (Buchanan 1949; Salanié 2012). This connects to the purpose of the state: the goal is to maximize an "over-arching social objective or aggregate of individuals' welfares" (Sugden 1990). Taxation and government expenditure are two different ways to maximize *overall* utility. In the classical liberal tradition, the fundamental test for the justification of rules governing a society is whether they could be backed by an *individual* calculus (Brennan and Buchanan 2000a, 26).

This gives rise to an essentially different normative test for tax policy in classical liberal political economy *versus* welfare economics (Scherf and Weinzierl 2020). Concerning the latter, in the theory of optimal taxation, which has its origins in the works of Francis Edgeworth, Frank Ramsey (1927), and later A.C. Pigou (1932), the tax rules are "imperfect" when there are ways to amend them that increase overall utility. The point of the tax code is to raise revenue for the government in a way that minimizes welfare loss (Hindriks and Myles 2013; Marciano and Khalil 2012). Welfare economics produced the "least-aggregate-sacrifice" principle that *a priori* does not focus on the respective positions of different individuals under different sets of rules (Buchanan 1949, 497–98).[4] Rather the idea is to minimize the "excess burden" induced by taxation. To that end, tax theorists work out taxes that do *not* alter individuals' behavior and that will typically build on private responses to various taxes (Boadway 2012, 34). In their search for taxes that sacrifice the least wel-

[4] In application of standard utilitarianism, what matters is to maximize the economic outcome. It is for instance allowed to "sacrifice the few for the many" and tax specific groups harsher if this enhances overall utility.

fare, optimal tax theorists have argued for deferring rates based on the elasticity in demand of the taxed good (Ramsey 1927), type of income (see, for instance, Chamley 1986; Lucas 1990); level of income (Diamond and Saez 2011), or the taxpayer's height (Mankiw and Weinzierl 2010).

This welfarist approach stands in stark contrast to the "old school" theories of public finance – that go back to Knut Wicksell (1992) and Viti de Marco (1936). Here, the task is not to tweak the tax rules to maximize some objective welfare function. The goal of the entire system is to mimic an individual *exchange* where individuals buy public goods voluntarily (Viti de Marco 1936, 112; Wicksell 1992). The forced exaction by the state is but one side of a transaction, with the other side denoting the receipt of services in return (Wagner 2006, 243). The tax system intends to impose prices for the benefits individuals enjoy from public goods (Viti de Marco 1936, 113; Epstein 1994, 1404). And so, the classical liberal credo has been the "benefit theory of tax": taxes are involuntary prices that "correspond to what individuals would voluntarily contribute to the funding of the activities they have democratically decided to pursue collectively (through the state) rather than privately" (Scherf and Weinzierl 2020, 4).[5] The benefit theory of tax resonates with the *quid pro quo* ideal that undergirds the justification of the state (Buchanan 1949, 499): every individual should benefit from the state, and taxes should be calculated to reflect benefits consumed (Epstein 1994, 1405).

The connection between payments and benefits is particularly close in the case of special assessment taxes, which in the United States can be imposed for street improvements and similar works. The basic idea is that individuals who receive a direct and unique benefit from a certain public project should be made to contribute to the project's financing. This practice leads to the problem of distinguishing between local improvements that should be financed out of general revenues and those that warrant special taxes (see Epstein 1985, 286–89).

An important implication of the benefit theory is that taxes and expenditures should be considered together. While the welfarist approach asks how a certain level of tax revenue can be raised in an optimal way, the contractarian perspective suggests that taxation is inextricably linked with the provision of government services. The reason for this is that the contractarian approach looks for tax arrangements that could potentially garner unanimous support. Taxpayers are expected to consent to taxation only if they receive services that are more valuable in return.

Thus, from the contractarian point of view, the question of optimal taxation encompasses not only the issue of raising taxes, but also the issue of how tax revenue is spent. The latter issue, in turn, leads proponents of the benefit theory to be interested in the collective choice processes that determine the behavior of political agents (see Sects. 4.3.2 and 4.3.3 below).

In a multi-period setting, the taxpayer's choice calculus is altered by the possibility of shifting the tax burden onto future generations. As emphasized by Buchanan

[5] To illustrate the intellectual divide, standard welfarist approaches such as Salanié (2012) and Boadway (2012) don't mention the benefit theory of taxation.

(1958), public expenditures can be financed either by taxation or borrowing, where the second option is paid for by future taxation. Individuals of the current generation may finance their spending by issuing debt and rely on future taxpayers to pick up the bill. The benefits of future generations depend on the specific kinds of expenditures undertaken by the current generation. A distinction must be drawn between short term or "consumption" public spending on the one hand and long-term public investment projects on the other hand. Only investment type expenditures confer (some) benefits upon future taxpayers.

4.3.2 The Problem of Administration: The Need for a Simple Rule

The nineteenth-century founding fathers of classical liberal public finance, such as Wicksell and Viti de Marco, understood that the benefit principle cannot be operationalized accurately: the state cannot calculate how much public services each taxpayer individually consumes (Viti de Marco 1936, 110). To make the tax system administrable, we need to find rules that don't require heroic efforts to be executed.

The insight that the purpose of legal rules is not to execute (economic) ideals, but rather to find workable ways of regulating behavior while minimizing operational costs, was phrased more recently by Richard Epstein (1995). According to Epstein, rules that entail high compliance costs for individuals and high inspection and supervision costs for governments, are a recipe for welfare destruction (Epstein 1995). The more complex the rules, the bigger the margin for mistakes in running the system and thus for outcomes that are contrary to legislative intent (Epstein 1995, 31). Classical liberal legal theory does not aspire to perfection but tries "to seek rules that minimize the level of imperfections" (Epstein 1995, 32), meaning we rely on "the use of crude proxies (…) to reach second-best solutions" (Epstein 1994, 1407).

The pragmatic search for simple rules also marked the efforts of nineteenth-century theorists. Chief Justice Thomas Cooley (1873, 495) stated: "Taxation is the equivalent for the protection which the government affords to the persons and property of its citizens; and as all are alike protected, so all alike should bear the burden, in proportion to the interests secured." More than simply phrasing the benefit principle of taxation, Cooley insisted that the burden be proportional to the general economic benefits that taxpayers enjoy in society. This is consonant with Viti de Marco (1936, 114) who proposed that "our income has been the index by which we measure our consumption" of public goods (Viti de Marco 1936, 114). More specifically his axiom was that "the consumption of public services is *proportional* to the income of each citizen" (Viti de Marco 1936, 116). He hereby echoes Adam Smith, who already insisted that one's income is a measure of one's benefit from the state (Smith 1991, 498). If the state produces public goods such as the protection of private property, the enforcement of contracts, the construction of highways, railroads, the creation of national defense, etc.; generally speaking, rich people tend to consume proportionally more of these goods than poor people (Viti de Marco 1936, 114). To simplify the task of measuring the consumption of public goods, the assumption that the gains taxpayers experience from the state moves in lockstep proportion with their measurable income (Epstein 1994, 1408).

Being a realist rather than a perfectionist, Viti de Marco (1936, 116), was aware that this principle wasn't a pure description of economic reality, but an approximation – on average and over a lifetime.[6] While at any moment in time, the benefits from public goods are randomized, imbalances between individuals tend to balance out in the long run (Epstein 1995, 138). Across individuals and, in aggregate, more income leads to proportionally more consumption of public goods (Viti de Marco 1936, 114). This assumption explains why taxes should be taken as a proportion of one's income (Viti de Marco 1936, 114): "Ever since Public Finance has existed, the income of each citizen has been taken as an index for measuring his demand for general public services, and it is on the basis of this presumption that taxes have been fixed as a percentage of income."

So, the classical liberal ideal to match taxes and benefits leads to the defense of proportional taxes on income. Each unit of income earned carries with it a claim by the state for the publicly supplied productive services that made the income possible (Buchanan 2008). Under a single – i.e., uniform – rate structure, every income earned gives back a proportion to the state, which is, in turn, used to produce future public goods that will facilitate new income. The background philosophy is that we engage in a constant beneficial exchange with the state – which ideally operates through a simple, certain, and easily administrable "flat" rate.

This overall philosophy transcends the question of choice of tax base: the very same principle can also be operationalized through a general consumption tax (Delmotte and Dold, 2021). This is because a consumption tax is an income tax that fully deducts expenses and investments, and exempts capital gains (Hall and Rabushka 2007; Delmotte 2021). So, the general idea is that a fraction of your economic benefits – measured through income or consumption – needs to be repaid for benefits conferred by the government.

The pragmatic reflex for simple rules will often favor consumption taxes (Hall and Rabushka 2007). A tax that only targets consumption, say a flat rate on all purchases of goods, causes less administrative costs for government and taxpayers than a tax that targets all income (Bankman and Weisbach 2006.) A general income tax has to deal with the taxation of capital gains – and thus the occurrence of income unrelated to economic exchange. Moreover, capital yields income as it accrues, meaning the tax system ought to install some measurement system that estimates the market value of capital. Cowen and Delmotte (2019) have shown that tax

[6]Lindahl (1958) developed a more sophisticated measure of one's benefits for public goods that calculates individuals' marginal willingness to pay for public goods. His approach intends to assign different taxes for the same public goods to different individuals, based on their subjective valuation. This departs from the pragmatic search for simplicity and second bests that characterizes classical liberalism.

authorities will lack information to effectively calculate the market value of assets at any given point in time. The alternative of a realization-based tax on capital gains has been said to lead to much of the distortions and complexity that marks the income tax system today – which explains why leading tax scholars defend consumption taxes (Bankman and Weisbach 2007; Shaviro 2004). Discussions about how to operationalize a general consumption tax, for instance, via a retail tax or a VAT like in the European Union, pertain in the literature (Mclure 1993). Debates also revolve around the fact that a failure to tax returns to savings requires some progressivity within consumption taxes (Shaviro 2004).

This point enables us to nuance the choice for flat rates: not all classical liberals dislike progressive taxation, which has been a contested issue among classical liberal thinkers. von Hayek (2011) put forward the idea that a progressive income tax can be justified as compensation for other taxes that are regressive with regard to income, such as certain forms of consumption taxes (e.g., value added tax and sales tax). Regressive taxes impose a harsher burden on low-income households. Hayek was, however, opposed to the notion that the tax system as a whole should be progressive in nature.

As argued by Brennan and Buchanan (2000b), progressive income taxation may also be used to constrain government behavior. This argument is based on the model of a "Leviathan" type government that maximizes tax revenue. Brennan and Buchanan assume that taxpayers want to limit the revenue-raising potential of Leviathan, at least to a certain degree. At the constitutional level, they have two possibilities to achieve this. First, by imposing limits on the tax base. Second, by imposing limits on the tax rate structure for a given tax base.

Regarding the second option, Brennan and Buchanan show that moving from a proportional to a progressive schedule can actually decrease the government's tax revenue. Consider the case of a proportional income tax. The easiest way to make the rate structure progressive is to exclude parts of the income from taxation, while the remaining income is still taxed at the same proportional rate. This simple "progressive" rate structure limits the revenue potential of Leviathan and reduces the burden of taxpayers. Thus, from the point of view of Brennan and Buchanan, there are good reasons to favor progressive tax schedules even if one is not concerned with the aspect of redistribution.

4.3.3 The Problem of Opportunism: The Need for a General and Constitutionalized Rule

There is an additional reason why the classical liberal political economy defends a uniform rate on a broadly defined tax base – whether income or consumption. This reason is an extra argument for flat rate taxes – and against possible more accurate ways to operationalize the benefit principle, or against other principles like the "least-aggregate-sacrifice" principle, or the connected "ability to pay" principle.[7] Apart from the fact that a uniform "flat" tax on all income or consumption is a pragmatic way to execute the benefit principle (see Sect. 4.3.2), a flat tax holds specific *incentive aligning* qualities.

When the tax system is used to fund the production and distribution of public goods, every individual is expected to benefit under the system of proportional taxation. However, while all parties could benefit from cooperation, everyone could benefit maximally by shifting the costs of the public goods onto the other individuals (Buchanan and Tullock 1999). In classical liberal political economy, the assumption is that individuals and the political associations they form will be opportunistic and will invest resources to shape tax rules in those ways that yield private gain (Buchanan and Tullock 1999; Pennington 2011). The intimate nexus between the operationalization of tax rules and the net revenue of taxpayers explains why the empirical literature observes that tax policy is highly vulnerable to pressures exerted by lobby groups and voters (Richter, Samphantharak, and Timmons 2009; Alexander, Mazza, and Scholz 2009). Hindriks and Myles (2013, 413) and Olson (2000) show that in democratic systems there is an incentive for narrow interest groups to capture benefits while at the same time little incentive exists for diffuse voters to oppose the marginal cost of every additional targeted tax rule. These efforts will typically result in "targeted tax rules": special deductions, credits, and tax exemptions, aimed at well-defined economic groups, industries, or types of income (Delmotte 2021). This incentive structure at least partially explains the emergence of tax law as a laundry list of itemized deductions, special credits, and exemptions (Rabushka 1988; Wagner 2006, 142).

The classical liberal ideal that each member should contribute in accordance with what they take out (as measured through income or consumption) will be undermined by the tendency of majoritarian democracy to hand out tax benefits to various interest groups (Lehto and Meadowcroft 2021). Departures of the principle of proportional taxation lead to situations where groups of taxpayers internalize benefits yet transfer costs onto others. The nineteenth-century economist J. R. McCulloch (von Hayek 2011, 433) predicted: "The moment you abandon the cardinal principle of exacting from all individuals the same proportion of their income or their property, you are at sea without rudder or compass, and there is no amount of injustice and folly you may not commit." The abandonment of the proportional tax system, in favor of differential tax burdens, risks violating the universal benefit requirement. Dominant groups will transfer the tax burden onto others, and groups that are taxed disproportionally experience net losses after the exchange with the government, a phenomenon that Delmotte (2020, 67) and Buchanan and Tullock (1999, 133–49) call "fiscal exploitation". The principle "you pay for what you receive" here degrades into "you take and let others pay", and as Delmotte (2020, 62) observes that currently "tax policy, at least in the United States and

[7]These two normative principles of taxation are (historically) connected: asking more from those who are less hurt from paying more (ability to pay), is a way to minimize utility loss caused by taxation (least-aggregate-sacrifice principle).

Europe, embodies an 'anything goes' regime, a political jungle in which well-organized subgroups of society are successfully fighting for controversial privileges at the expense of (the welfare of) their fellow citizens."

The proposal of proportional taxes on a broadly defined tax base is an institutional remedy against political opportunism and fiscal exploitation – and pressure groups trying to decrease their tax liabilities. To reconcile taxation and public finance with the universal benefit requirement, taxation should follow the precepts of generality, meaning that a proportional share of all income or consumption returns to the state (Delmotte 2020, 63). Under a single proportional rate, no dominant player can abuse its political power by shifting the burden onto the relatively powerless. Under a proportional rate, moreover, when groups propose new expenditures and thus taxes, they inevitably call for increased taxes on their own income. Any rise in taxes on other groups of voters will be paralleled by an equal proportionate rise in tax shares on one's own group. Due to this incentive-aligning quality, proportional taxation promotes (Delmotte 2020, 76) "a rudimentary form of fairness: those decisive in the fiscal process will treat others in ways they would like to be treated themselves".

Although flat-rate taxes are the most robust response to voters and lobby groups trying to shift the tax burden onto others, Delmotte (2020, 82) argues that "progressive rates on all income would be a step toward more generality and represents a reasonable account of generality." Compared to current tax codes, which are characterized by a myriad of tax exemptions, with different types of revenue facing different tax rates and deduction rules (Delmotte 2021), a move toward progressive rates that apply generally, would be a significant improvement. Such a progressive tax system discriminates based on one criterion – income levels. Current tax systems, to quote Richard Wagner (2016, 142) are "so large that no one can read it … and create(s) a nearly unique tax liability for each taxpayer." In other words, a progressive income tax system that applies its rates and brackets universally to all taxpayers would deal better with fiscal opportunism and align closer to the generality norm than current tax systems.

Generally, classical liberalism generates the belief that various forms of rules should be "constitutionalized" and be left outside the hands of simple majority. This also applies to tax policy. As illustrated by the American experience of tax reform, for such a system to be politically stable, uniformity would need to be enforced at the constitutional level (Rabushka 1988). Otherwise, majorities and the powerful interest groups that support them, will overturn any general rule – progressive or flat – and create exemptions and credits to their benefit. We can distinguish the constitutional from the non-constitutional setting. The basic constitutional contract encompasses only those tax rules that all citizen-taxpayers can agree upon. The defining characteristic of constitutional rules is that they are more permanent than other rules. While constitutional reform is generally possible, constitutional rules are treated as "quasi-permanent arrangements" (Brennan and Buchanan 2000b, 222) that enable individuals to adjust their behavior and engage in long-term economic planning.

By contrast, tax rules that are not part of the constitutional contract will frequently be changed. The taxpayers will be faced with tax obligations determined by the current political coalition, which may or may not coincide with an individual's own interests. In this non-constitutional setting, interest groups have clear incentives to engage in the opportunistic or "rent-seeking" behavior outlined above. Frequently changing rules also make it easier for Leviathan type governments to maximize tax revenue.

Given the ideal of voluntary exchange implicit in the benefit theory of taxation, classical liberals take a constitutional attitude towards tax reform. That is, they are interested in proposing quasi-permanent arrangements that could appeal to all citizen-taxpayers. While such proposals naturally limit the scope of democratic decision-making in day-to-day politics, it is important to note that their declared aim is to align policies with the actual wishes of taxpayers. In the words of Brennan and Buchanan 2000b, 226

> The desire to limit government constitutionally, to define in advance the range and scope for the subsequent implementation of the taxing authority, arises only from a presumption-prediction that government may, at least on some occasions, act in ways that are not within the interests of taxpayers.

4.4 Conclusion

Classical liberalism should be carefully distinguished from libertarianism. Although classical liberals are nowadays often associated with a call for fewer taxes and less government (Murphy and Nagel 2002), its philosophical origins formulate a more constructive message on government than libertarianism (Rothbard 2009). Thinkers like Smith, Viti De Marco, and later Hayek and Buchanan certainly did not think that all state action was unjustified. Rather, they made a positive case for government, and stressed the conditions in which human societies should rely on government. Classical liberal theory can be understood as a theory on the justified use of coercion, namely when coercion leads to outcomes that benefit us all. Because of this focus, classical liberalism is particularly useful to inspire a theory of taxation – which in essence is the coerced extraction of money from citizens.

This coercive mechanism is justified under several conditions. Generally, the tax money should be used to maintain the state in both its protective capacity (the maintenance of the legal framework) and its productive capacity (the production of public goods such as national defense). The protective functions of the state are set down in the initial constitutional contract, which derives its legitimacy from the voluntary consent of the citizens. The constitution also contains decision-making rules for determining the state's productive tasks. This way, classical liberal institutions are supposed to reflect the common interests of all citizens rather than private interests. If people are taxed to fund the private goods of other people, this violates the classical liberal theory of tax.

The way the money is levied is also subject to constraints. The first principle is that taxes are prices for benefits received. The role of the tax system is to mimic market transactions and align individual taxes with individual consumption of public goods. Taxing individuals to satisfy other goals like redistribution or overall efficiency creates tensions with the classical liberal perspective on taxation. Second, classical liberals are pragmatics and will look for the least burdensome way to administrate the benefit principle. This search for simple rules can be seen as a principle in and of itself (Epstein 1995). The standard way to measure one's consumption of public goods has been by assuming it is a fraction of one's income or one's general consumption. Public goods are a factor of production and so, for every unit of income or consumption, there is a fraction that represents the use of government services. Hence, a proportion of your income or consumption should go back to the government. Thus, it is, warranted to impose a proportional (or "flat") rate. As the last principle, classical liberals tend to adhere to a very realistic image of government that considers the occurrence of opportunism within the legislative process. This underscores the case for a simple flat-rate tax: the presence or possibility of exemptions and deviations from general taxation hosts opportunities for interest groups to put the burden onto others. Completeness requires mentioning that many classical liberals see a general regime of progressive rates on a broadly defined income as a good alternative as well.

Given their realistic image of democratic politics, classical liberals will want to see the most essential parts of tax design located at the constitutional level. To avoid that interest groups or voting blocs bend the rules to their benefit, the basic tax rules should be part of a "fiscal constitution", which gives them a quasi-permanent character.

References

Alexander, Raquel, Stephen Mazza, and Susan Scholz. 2009. Measuring Rates of Return for Lobbying Expenditures: An Empirical Case Study of Tax Breaks for Multinational Corporations. *Journal of Law and Politics* 25 (401): 401–458.

Bankman, Joseph, and David Weisbach. 2006. The Superiority of an Ideal Consumption Tax over an Ideal Income Tax. *Stanford Law Review* 58: 1413–1458.

———. 2007. Consumption Taxation is Still Superior to Income Taxation. *Stanford Law Review* 60: 789–802.

Boadway, Robin W. 2012. *From Optimal Tax Theory to Tax Policy: Retrospective and Prospective Views*. Cambridge, MA: MIT Press.

Brennan, Geoffrey, and James M. Buchanan. 2000a. *The Reason of Rules: Constitutional Political Economy*, The Collected Works of James M. Buchanan, v. 10. Indianapolis: Liberty Fund.

———. 2000b. *The Power to Tax: Analytical Foundations of a Fiscal Constitution*, The Collected Works of James M. Buchanan, v. 9. Indianapolis: Liberty Fund.

Buchanan, James M. 1949. The Pure Theory of Government Finance: A Suggested Approach. *Journal of Political Economy* 57 (6): 496–505.

———. 1958. *Public Principles of Public Debt: A Defense and Restatement*. Homewood: Richard D. Irwin.

———. 1999. The Foundations for Normative Individualism. In *The Logical Foundations of Constitutional Liberty*, The Collected Works of James M. Buchanan, v. 1, 281–291. Indianapolis: Liberty Fund.

———. 2000. *The Limits of Liberty: Between Anarchy and Leviathan*, The Collected Works of James M. Buchanan, v. 7. Indianapolis: Liberty Fund.
———. 2008. Italian Fiscal Theorists. In *The Encyclopedia of Libertarianism*, ed. Ronald Hamowy, 258–260. Los Angeles: Sage.
———. 2010. The Constitutionalization of Money. *Cato Journal* 30 (2): 251–258.
Buchanan, James M., and Gordon Tullock. 1999. *The Calculus of Consent: Logical Foundations of Constitutional Democracy*, The Collected Works of James M. Buchanan, v. 3. Indianapolis: Liberty Fund.
Chamley, Christophe. 1986. Optimal Taxation of Capital Income in General Equilibrium with Infinite Lives. *Econometrica* 54 (3): 607–622.
Christmas, Billy. 2021. *Property and Justice: A Liberal Theory of Natural Rights*. London: Routledge.
Cooley, Thomas. 1873. *A Treatise on the Constitutional Limitations Which Rest Upon the Legislative Power of the States of the American Union*. 2nd ed. Boston: Little, Brown & Co.
Cowen, Nick. 2021. *Neoliberal Social Justice. Rawls Unveiled*. Cheltenham: Edward Elgar.
Cowen, Nick, and Charles Delmotte. 2019. The Mirage of Mark-to-Market: Distributive Justice and Alternatives to Capital Taxation. *Critical Review of International Social and Political Philosophy*. (Published online and forthcoming in print).
Delmotte, Charles. 2020. Tax Uniformity as a Requirement of Justice. *Canadian Journal of Law & Jurisprudence* 33 (1): 59–83.
———. 2021. Simple Rules and the Political Economy of Income Taxation: The Strengths of a Uniform Expense Rule. *European Journal of Law and Economics*. (Forthcoming). https://doi.org/10.1007/s10657-021-09693-7.
Delmotte, Charles, and Malte F. Dold. 2021. Dynamic Preferences and the Behavioral Case Against Sin Taxes. *Constitutional Political Economy*. (Forthcoming). https://doi.org/10.1007/s10602-021-09328-8.
Diamond, Peter, and Emmanuel Saez. 2011. The Case for a Progressive Tax: From Basic Research to Policy Recommendation. *Journal of Economic Perspectives* 25 (4): 165–190.
Dold, Malte. 2018. A Smithian critique of James M. Buchanan's constitutional contractarianism. In *Interdisciplinary Studies of the Market Order*, ed. Don Boudreaux, Chris Coyne, and Bobbi Herzberg, 17–40. New York: Rowman & Littlefield.
Epstein, Richard A. 1985. *Takings: Private Property and the Power of Eminent Domain*. Cambridge, MA: Harvard University Press.
———. 1994. The Ubiquity of the Benefit Principle. *Southern California Law Review* 67: 1369–1409.
———. 1995. *Simple Rules for a Complex World*. Cambridge, MA: Harvard University Press.
Feld, Lars P., and Gebhard Kirchgässner. 2008. On the Effectiveness of Debt Brakes: The Swiss Experience. In *Sustainability of Public Debt*, ed. Reinhard Neck and Jan-Egbert Sturm, 223–256. Cambridge, MA: MIT Press.
Gaus, Gerald F. 2012. *The Order of Public Reason: A Theory of Freedom and Morality in a Diverse and Bounded World*. Cambridge: Cambridge University Press.
Hall, Robert E., and Alvin Rabushka. 2007. *The Flat Tax*. 2nd ed. Stanford: Hoover Institution Press.
Hindriks, Jean, and Gareth D. Myles. 2013. *Intermediate Public Economics*. Cambridge, MA: MIT Press.
Hobbes, Thomas. 1996. *Leviathan*. Revised Student ed. Cambridge: Cambridge University Press.
Lehto, Otto, and John Meadowcroft. 2021. Welfare Without Rent Seeking? Buchanan's Demogrant Proposal and the Possibility of a Constitutional Welfare State. *Constitutional Political Economy* 32 (2): 145–164.
Lindahl, Erik. 1958. Just Taxation: A Positive Solution. In *Classics in the Theory of Public Finance*, ed. Richard A. Musgrave and Alan T. Peacock, 168–176. London: Macmillan.
Lucas, Robert E. 1990. Supply-Side Economics: An Analytical Review. *Oxford Economic Papers (New Series)* 42 (2): 293–316.

Mankiw, N. Gregory, and Matthew Weinzierl. 2010. The Optimal Taxation of Height: A Case Study of Utilitarian Income Redistribution. *American Economic Journal: Economic Policy* 2 (1): 155–176.

Marciano, Alain, and Elias L. Khalil. 2012. Optimization, Path Dependence and the Law: Can Judges Promote Efficiency? *International Review of Law and Economics* 32 (1): 72–82.

Mclure, Charles Jr. 1993. Economic, Administrative, and Political Factors in Choosing a General Consumption Tax. *National Tax Journal* 46 (3): 345–358.

Murphy, Liam B., and Thomas Nagel. 2002. *The Myth of Ownership: Taxes and Justice*. Oxford: Oxford University Press.

North, Douglass C. 1990. *Institutions, Institutional Change and Economic Performance*. Cambridge: Cambridge University Press.

Olson, Mancur. 2000. *Power and Prosperity: Outgrowing Communist and Capitalist Dictatorships*. New York: Basic Books.

Pennington, M. 2011. *Robust Political Economy: Classical Liberalism and the Future of Public Policy*. Cheltenham: Edward Elgar.

Pigou, A.C. 1932. *The Economics of Welfare*. 4th ed. London: Macmillan.

Rabushka, Alvin. 1988. The Tax Reform Act of 1986: Concentrated Costs, Diffuse Benefits – An Inversion of Public Choice. *Contemporary Economic Policy* 6 (4): 50–64.

Ramsey, Frank P. 1927. A Contribution to the Theory of Taxation. *Economic Journal* 37 (145): 47–61.

Richter, Brian K., Krislert Samphantharak, and Jeffrey F. Timmons. 2009. Lobbying and Taxes. *American Journal of Political Science* 53 (4): 893–909.

Rothbard, Murray N. 2009. *Man, Economy, and State: A Treatise on Economic Principles; with Power and Market: Government and the Economy*. Auburn: Mises Institute.

Salanié, Bernard. 2012. *The Economics of Taxation*. 2nd ed. Cambridge, MA: MIT Press.

Scherf, Robert, and Matthew Weinzierl. 2020. Understanding Different Approaches to Benefit-Based Taxation. *Fiscal Studies* 41 (2): 385–410.

Shaviro, Daniel. 2004. Replacing the Income Tax with a Progressive Consumption Tax. *Tax Notes* 103: 91–131.

Smith, Adam. 1991. *Wealth of Nations*. Buffalo: Prometheus Books.

Sugden, Robert. 1990. Rules for Choosing Among Public Goods: A Contractarian Approach. *Constitutional Political Economy* 1 (2): 63–82.

———. 2018. *The Community of Advantage: A Behavioural Economist's Defence of the Market*. Oxford: Oxford University Press.

Vanberg, Viktor J. 2014. James M. Buchanan's Contractarianism and Modern Liberalism. *Constitutional Political Economy* 25 (1): 18–38.

Viti de Marco, Antonio. 1936. *First Principles of Public Finance*. New York: Harcourt Brace & Co.

von Hayek, Friedrich A. 1945. The Use of Knowledge in Society. *American Economic Review* 45 (4): 519–530.

———. 1979. *Law, Legislation and Liberty, Volume 3: The Political Order of a Free People*. Chicago: University of Chicago Press.

———. 2011. *The Constitution of Liberty*, The Collected Works of F. A. Hayek, v. 17. Chicago: University of Chicago Press.

Wagner, Richard E. 2006. Choice, Catallaxy and Just Taxation: Contrasting Architectonics for Fiscal Theorizing. In *Taxation, Economic Prosperity, and Distributive Justice*, ed. Ellen F. Paul, Fred D. Miller Jr., and Jeffrey Paul, 235–254. Cambridge: Cambridge University Press.

———. 2016. *Politics as a Peculiar Business: Insights from a Theory of Entangled Political Economy*. Northampton: Edward Elgar.

Wicksell, Knut. 1992. *Finanztheoretische Untersuchungen: Nebst Darstellung und Kritik des Steuerwesens Schwedens*. Bristol: Thoemmes Press.

Charles Delmotte is an assistant professor of Law at Michigan State University College of Law. Charles has BA and MA degrees in philosophy, in Law, and earned his PhD from Ghent University, Belgium. He was a visiting researcher at the Center for the Philosophy of Freedom (Arizona), King's College Department of Political Economy (London) and Max Planck Institute for Tax Law (Munich). He was twice an Adam Smith Fellow in Political Economy at George Mason University and was an Edison Fellow in Innovation Law and Policy at George Mason University. He published a dozen articles that investigate tax law through the lens of political philosophy, political economy and empirical research.

Daniel Nientiedt is a postdoctoral research fellow at the Department of Economics at New York University. His areas of interest include public choice, constitutional economics, and the history of economic thought. Before coming to NYU, he was a research associate at the Walter Eucken Institute in Freiburg, Germany, and a research fellow at the Center for the History of Political Economy at Duke University. He received his PhD in Economics from the University of Freiburg in 2020.

Chapter 5
Marxism and Socialism: Progressive Taxation and Socialisation of Property

Sol Picciotto

Abstract This chapter traces the philosophical, political, sociological, and economic underpinning for the advocacy by socialists of progressive taxation, linked with the aim of socialisation of the ownership of the means of production, from the Communist Manifesto to recent supporters of tax justice campaigns. It shows how their attitudes to taxation have reflected their views on how capitalism rests on private property and state power, and how it could be transcended, including through progressive taxation. It discusses the views of Marx and Engels, from the revolutions of 1848 to the Paris Commune, and their influence on and the debates among German socialists (Liebknecht, Kautsky, Bernstein and Luxemburg), and the Austro-Marxists (Renner, Hilferding). It examines Goldscheid's arguments for a social science of the state centring on fiscality, leading to Schumpeter's different concept of the 'fiscal state', and how this was taken up in the 1970s and later by O'Connor and other Marxists. The theories are examined in the context of the practical political engagement of their advocates, both struggling against autocratic capitalist states, notably the German socialists' dilemmas over welfare and warfare budgets, and then in government, including Lenin and the Bolsheviks, Hilferding as finance minister in Germany, and Schumpeter in Austria. It discusses socialist variants of Keynesianism, arguing that disparities of wealth generate growing inequality, and proposing tax measures for social ownership and equalisation of property, notably James Meade, and most recently Anthony Atkinson and Thomas Piketty. It concludes with reflections on what socialists can learn from these debates about transcending capitalism and the role and nature of progressive taxation in relation to the accumulation of capital particularly through large transnational corporations.

Keywords Tax · State theory · Capitalism · Transcendence · Socialisation · Property · Corporation

---

S. Picciotto (✉)
Lancaster University, Lancaster, UK
e-mail: s.picciotto@lancaster.ac.uk

R. F. van Brederode (ed.), *Political Philosophy and Taxation*,
https://doi.org/10.1007/978-981-19-1092-0_5

5.1 Introduction

For over two centuries, since the emergence of capitalism, its socialist critics and opponents have advocated 'progressive taxation', as a means for transforming it to an egalitarian system, by replacing private with social or common ownership of the means of production. The term socialism originated due to its advocates' support for this socialisation of ownership, while 'communism' generally came to refer to the type of society which was its aim; in the classic formulation: 'socialism … is communism in course of construction' (Bukharin and Preobrazhensky 1919, 334). This chapter focuses on socialism in this sense, especially the strand developed by Marx and Engels and their followers, and while it discusses revisionism it does not deal with social-democratic theories that defend private ownership of the means of production.[1]

In the *Communist Manifesto* of 1848, Karl Marx and Friedrich Engels included 'a heavy progressive or graduated income tax' as the second on their list of measures to be adopted in the 'radical rupture with traditional property relations' of the communist revolution (Marx and Engels 1968, 52). This was based on Marx's post-Hegelian view of the need to transform and transcend the state and end its autonomisation from civil society. However, wide differences emerged within socialism, especially in the first decades of the twentieth century, on the aims and means for revolutionary transformation, in which the form and role of progressive taxation continued to be viewed as ancillary.

Views coalesced around the two poles of communism and social democracy, which were rooted in divergences underlying the philosophical, economic, and political perspectives of different strands of socialism. The gap between these perspectives grew very wide. Marxists prioritised revolutionary transformation based on the socialisation of property, but this became focused on state ownership and planning. They viewed social-democratic taxation programmes as ameliorative reformism, while social democrats retreated from viewing socialism as an alternative system, especially with the retreat from state ownership under neo-liberalism and with the collapse of the Soviet bloc.

The recent emergence of new anti-capitalist movements has reopened debates about progressive taxation on the left, challenging both perspectives. A few Marxists have begun to re-examine the arguments for progressive taxation made by the founding fathers (Ireland 2019), and others have begun to attempt analyses of contemporary tax issues, although hampered by the lack of any developed Marxist perspective on the forms of taxation (Prokla 2009). Meanwhile, social democrats have begun to focus more on 'pre-distribution', and the ways in which state policies, including taxation, have generated increasingly wide and structural economic

[1] There is some overlap with Chap. 9 on Egalitarianism, particularly relating to some versions of the idea of a 'property-owning democracy'. The linking of taxation with the socialisation of property also merges into the much broader issues raised by debates about 'market socialism', that were revived in the 1990s after the demise of the USSR, and are not treated here.

inequalities, rooted in private ownership. Indeed. it is now increasingly recognised that taxes not only help to legitimise the acceptance of private property as natural, the tax system also helps to create and define private property, as Murphy and Nagel have pointed out (Murphy and Nagel 2002, 8). These shifts were strengthened by the impact of the great financial crash of 2009 and the ensuing austerity policies in the main capitalist countries, which gave momentum to the nascent campaigns around the world for 'tax justice'.

5.2 Socialism, Communism and Marxism

5.2.1 The Revolutions of 1848

The *Communist Manifesto* was written collaboratively by Karl Marx and Friedrich Engels. Indeed, the first draft came from Engels, based on his *Principles of Communism* of late 1847. This argued that democracy would bring the victory of the proletariat, which should then implement a list of measures, the first of which was '[l]imitation of private property through progressive taxation, heavy inheritance taxes, abolition of inheritance through collateral lines (brothers, nephews, etc.) forced loans, etc.'.

In composing the Manifesto in January 1848, Marx made some revisions, so that the final version referred more specifically to 'a heavy progressive or graduated income tax', and separately to the 'abolition' of both 'property in land' and of 'all rights of inheritance'. Thus, the call for restricting private property through taxation was replaced by one for its direct abolition, and a separate demand for progressive taxation of income (Hollander 2011, 64). A fuller analysis of these formulations must be situated in a wider understanding of their thinking at this time.

Marx and Engels had met in 1844, 'the year in which German socialism was born' (Stedman Jones 2016, 208). Both were deeply engaged in socialist and communist politics, and with the critiques of Hegel among the 'young' Hegelians,[2] notably Feuerbach. These critiques centred on Hegel's abstract view of 'history', and argued that Hegel's approach should be rethought and placed on a materialist perspective, viewing history as the activity of human beings. Marx adapted Feuerbach's 'transformative' approach to turning Hegel's philosophy 'upside down'. As he later explained it:

> the process of thinking, which, under the name of "the idea" he [Hegel] even transforms into an independent subject, is the demiurgos of the real world, and the real world is only the external, phenomenal form of "the Idea". With me, on the contrary, the ideal is nothing

[2] The term originated from a derogatory reference by the ex-Hegelian Heinrich Leo, to 'die Hegelingen', sometimes translated as 'new', although more accurate would be 'little' (Stedman Jones 2016, 78).

> else than the material world reflected in the human mind, and translated into forms of thought.[3]

Hence for Marx

> legal relations, as well as forms of state are to be grasped neither from themselves nor from the so-called general development of the human mind, but rather have their roots in the material conditions of life, the sum total of which Hegel, following the example of the Englishmen and Frenchmen of the eighteenth century, combines under the name of "civil society", that however the anatomy of civil society is to be sought in political economy. (Marx and Engels 1968, 181)

Marx applied this critical approach also to Hegel's modification of Aristotle's concept of *praxis*, arguing for a philosophy that integrates theory and practice. Thus, 'praxis means for Marx both a tool for changing the course of history and a criterion for historical evaluation [it is] … man's conscious shaping of the changing historical conditions' (Avineri 1968, 138). In other words, ideas are shaped by the life experiences and practices of those who formulate them, and in turn shape the world through their practical application.

Like most of the socialists of the nineteenth century, he and Engels worked in this way, as their theories interacted with their practical political activity, as well as being based on examination of empirical evidence of both historical development and contemporary socio-economic conditions. Recent historiography has done much to situate the development of their work in the context of their lives and political engagement: from their involvement with the formation of the Communist League and the revolutions of 1848, to work with trade unionists in England in the 1860s in creating the International Workingmen's Association (IWA, known as the First International), and their support of the Paris Commune of 1870.[4] Marx's practical role was not on the barricades, but drafting statements and manifestos, which commanded authority because of the way they marshalled and presented evidence and data collected through extensive reading and research. In his view revolution would come primarily through democratisation of the state, although the organised proletariat might have to take to arms to defend the revolution, as occurred in Paris in 1870.

It was Engels who first shifted this analysis to political economy. Marx studied law and philosophy at the university in the period of ideological and political ferment of the aftermath of the French revolution and the Napoleonic spread of republicanism in Europe. Meanwhile, Engels' vocation to work in his family's business gave him a more practical formation, though he also plunged into the post-Hegelian philosophical debates during his time in Berlin in 1841. His move to Manchester to work in his father's textile firm in 1842 led to his first major work, *The Condition of the Working Class in England* (1844), and the more analytical *Outlines of a Critique of Political Economy*, written in late 1843 and published in 1844 in the *Deutsch-Französische Jahrbücher,* edited by Marx. This work strongly influenced Marx's

[3] Afterword to the second German edition of *Das Kapital*, 1873, cited in Avineri 1968, 40.

[4] See notably Stedman Jones (2016).

own 1844 *Manuscripts*, which paved the way for his more extended work on the critique of political economy leading to his masterwork *Capital*, the first volume published in 1867, but the second and third not until 1893 and 1894, after his death, in a form edited by Engels.

Applying the transformative approach derived from Feuerbach, Marx also criticised Hegel, and diverged from some of the other post-Hegelians, for the view that the modern state represents a universality that transcends the conflicts of civil society, and that the state's bureaucracy is the universal class. Instead, Marx insisted that the separation or autonomisation of the state is a specific historical process resulting from the separation of political from economic power in the emergence of capitalism, which he anatomised in terms of class struggles rooted in the social relations of production. For him the state embodies the domination of the ruling class and is the political manifestation of its rule.

Taxes are therefore instruments of class rule, which can be seen in the forms they take. He outlined the link between taxes and the form of the state in the *Eighteenth Brumaire of Louis Bonaparte* of 1852, as follows:

> Taxes are the source of life for the bureaucracy, the army, the priests and the court, in short, for the whole apparatus of the executive power. Strong government and heavy taxes are identical. By its very nature, small-holding property forms a suitable basis for an all-powerful and innumerable bureaucracy. It creates a uniform level of relationships and persons over the whole surface of the land. Hence it also permits of uniform action from a supreme centre on all points of this uniform mass. (Marx and Engels 1968, 174)

For Marx and Engels, the purpose of gaining state power by the proletariat is not simply to secure its rule, but to use that power to realise the transformation of social relations as a whole to establish communism, which they saw as already immanent in the development of the social conditions of production. This was boldly outlined in the *Communist Manifesto*:

> When, in the course of development, class distinctions have disappeared, and all production has been concentrated in the hands of a vast association of the whole nation, the public power will lose its political character. Political power, properly so called, is merely the organised power of one class for oppressing another. If the proletariat during its contest with the bourgeoisie is compelled, by the force of circumstances, to organise itself as a class, if, by means of a revolution, it makes itself the ruling class, and, as such, sweeps away by force the old conditions of production, then it will, along with these conditions, have swept away the conditions for the existence of class antagonisms and of classes generally, and will thereby have abolished its own supremacy as a class.

This explains what might be regarded as the contradictory pronouncements of Marx and Engels on tax policies, since they were generally contingent on analysis of the political conjuncture. However, in practical political contexts they consistently advocated direct taxes on the wealthy and on capital, and attacked indirect taxes and levies that were generally regarded by socialists as oppressing the poor (Ireland 2019). Their views on tax were expressed first in their writings during their involvement in the revolutions of 1848–9 in Europe, mostly in the *Neue Rheinische Zeitung (NRZ)*, founded by a group prominent in the Communist League, and edited by Marx.

The need to seek approval for taxes had long been a key issue in the development of sovereign states, and this need for consent was used by nobles and clergy to protect their privileges from centralising royal power. It had again become a focus at the time of the French revolution in the struggles over ending feudal rights and the move to representative government. In the political reform attempts in Prussia in 1807 and 1810 an income tax was favoured by the King's reformist ministers because, applying to all residents, it could help create a sense of common interest and national unity, as well as to pay the war tribute to France. However, the attempt to extend it beyond East Prussia failed, due to opposition from aristocrats to losing tax exemptions and other privileges (Levinger 2000, 60–61). Some other governments succeeded in introducing income taxes at this period to help pay for the wars, notably England in 1798, but it was resented as 'against freedom', repealed in the short period of peace of 1802–3, then re-enacted with a new method of assessment, but abolished as soon as the war was over (Seligman 1914, 57–114; Webber and Wildavsky 1986, 338–9). In France itself, the direct taxes introduced in the first phase of the revolution in 1790–1 (the 'quatre vieilles') applied to indices of wealth rather than income as such, and were not progressive (Piketty 2001, 234; Piketty 2020, 143–7). A much more radical plan for public finance, effectively a progressive tax on wealth to finance education and a kind of basic income for all, had been proposed by Thomas Paine (*Rights of Man* Part II 1792, Paine and Foner 1945, esp. 431–60).

It was with the rise of socialism that direct taxes on wealth became a clear political demand. A progressive income tax was viewed in this light, since at that time a direct right to income was predicated on wealth.

The revolutions of 1848 were again struggles for democracy and over the control of state power, focusing in Germany on the first all-German elected parliament, the Frankfurt Assembly of May 1848. The German movement was outmanoeuvred within a few months by the King with a combination of concessions and repression by the army. The response of Marx and his group was to call for a tax strike, and the *Neue Rheinische Zeitung* masthead for a month in late 1848 was *No More Taxes!!!* The campaign targeted the regressive and widely unpopular indirect taxes, such as the Milling and Slaughter Tax, as well as the Class Tax (Klassensteuer). Although this was a direct tax, it was a flat tax on different social categories, so was closer to a poll tax, and was lambasted in the *NRZ* by Wilhelm Wolff (Ireland 2019, 200–212). The Assembly rejected a motion to support the civil disobedience championed in the NRZ, but it did resolve that the government had no right to raise or spend taxes so long as it suspended the Assembly's meetings. The illegitimacy of taxation in these circumstances was a central plank of Marx's defence when he and others were prosecuted for sedition, helping to secure his acquittal (Stedman Jones 2016, 291).

Marx and Engels also criticised what they regarded as reformist perspectives on tax. In April 1850 they reviewed the book *Le Socialisme et l'Impot*,[5] by Emile de

[5] In the monthly *Neue Rheinische Zeitung Politisch-ökonomische Revue*, which was published in Hamburg after Marx was exiled and moved to London, and later republished by Engels among the

Girardin, a journalist and member of the French Legislative Assembly, who distinguished 'good' from 'bad' socialism, characterised as 'harmony' or 'war' between labour and capital. The review outlined and dissected Girardin's analyses showing that the burden of the diverse French taxes was economically detrimental and contrary to the republican constitutional principle that 'every Frenchman shall contribute to the upkeep of the state in proportion to his wealth'. The review concluded simply that 'his criticism is as shallow as it is correct'. However, it attacked the book's thesis that 'taxation should be an *insurance premium* paid by those who have property, *to insure themselves against all risks which might disturb them in the possession and enjoyment of it*', so that '[e]veryone who has an interest in payment pays, and pays only to the extent of his interest'.

In reply to this version of the 'benefit' principle of fairness in taxation, the review argued:

> Tax reform is the hobby-horse of every radical bourgeois, the specific element in all bourgeois economic reforms. From the earliest medieval philistines to the modern English free-traders, the main struggle has revolved around taxation. … Tax reform has as its aim either the abolition of traditional taxes which impede the progress of industry, or less extravagant state budgets, or more equal distribution. The further it slips from his grasp in practice, the more keenly does the bourgeois pursue the chimerical ideal of equal distribution of taxation. The distribution relations, which rest directly upon bourgeois production, the relations between wages and profit, profit and interest, rent and profit, may at most be modified in inessentials by taxation, but the latter can never threaten their foundations. All investigations and discussions about taxation presuppose the everlasting continuance of these bourgeois relations. Even the abolition of taxes could only hasten the development of bourgeois property and its contradictions. … The reduction of taxes, their more equitable distribution, etc., etc., is a banal *bourgeois reform*. The *abolition* of taxes is *bourgeois socialism*.… Behind the abolition of taxation lurks the abolition of the state. The abolition of the state has meaning with the Communists, only as the necessary consequence of the abolition of classes, with which the need for the organised might of one class to keep the others down automatically disappears.

Here Marx and Engels are clear that the liberal principle of equality in taxation is a chimera, so long as private property remains; but equally, the abolition of taxes (and of the state) would do nothing to change private property. The aim should be to use state power, including taxation, to achieve the transformation of property from private to social rights, which would abolish class conflict and hence end the class character of the state.

---

essays he titled Class Struggles in France (*MECW* Volume 10, 326–337, available at https://marxists.info/archive/marx/works/1850/04/girardin.htm)

5.2.2 *The Paris Commune and the Transcendence of the State*

Marx's views on the 'abolition of the state' were profoundly affected by the second major revolutionary moment in which he was involved, the Paris Commune of 1870. His analysis of these events, written for the General Council of the IWA,[6] argued that this short-lived experience showed how the self-organisation of working people could overturn 'the centralised State power, with its ubiquitous organs of standing army, police, bureaucracy, clergy and judicature', and replace it with a social and democratic Republic, with a people's militia, and public officials 'elective, responsible and accountable' to 'municipal councillors elected by universal suffrage' acting as both an executive and legislative body. This model was to be adopted throughout France, with district assemblies sending deputies to the National Delegation in Paris. Thus, 'While the merely repressive organs of the old governmental power were to be amputated, its legitimate functions were to be wrested from an authority usurping pre-eminence over society itself, and restored to the responsible agents of society' (Marx and Engels 1968, 288–9).

Hence, Marx and Engels did not support progressive taxation as a means of financing extensive state expenditures on either a standing army or on social programmes run by the state. Their view of the state was dialectical: the process of universalisation that Hegel saw in the very idea of the state depended on the power of social action led by the proletariat to conquer state power and use it to transform society as a whole, achieving the transcendence (*Aufhebung*) of both state and civil society so that, in the words of the *Manifesto*, 'public power would lose its political character'. For them, it was not dramatic events such as the fall of the Bastille that constituted the revolution, they were merely historical moments expressing the need for and an opportunity to realise the potential for transformation already evident in civil society. The basis for a new society would emerge from the development of capitalism itself ('in the womb'), and with the extension of democracy, the transition could be relatively peaceful (Stedman Jones 2016, 468).

Marx himself identified as the main element of this maturing the increasingly socialised nature of the processes of production. He argued that this sharply contradicts the individualisation imposed by the alienated appearance of social actors as individual legal persons, subjects (and objects) of exchange in the economic sphere, and citizens in the political sphere. Since this contradiction hampers the potential for human development, capitalism paves the way for its own negation, with the revolutionary class (the proletariat) acting as the agent of the transformation.

Furthermore, he identified the forms of socialisation immanent within capitalism. In particular, in volume three of Capital (*The Process of Capitalist Production as a Whole*) he presciently outlined the implications of the formation of stock companies as well as worker cooperatives:

[6] Published as *The Civil War in France*.

1) An enormous expansion of the scale of production and of enterprises, that was impossible for individual capitals. At the same time, enterprises that were formerly government enterprises, become public.
2) The capital, which in itself rests on a social mode of production and presupposes a social concentration of means of production and labour-power, is here directly endowed with the form of social capital (capital of directly associated individuals) as distinct from private capital, and its undertakings assume the form of social undertakings as distinct from private undertakings. It is the abolition of capital as private property within the framework of capitalist production itself.
3) Transformation of the actually functioning capitalist into a mere manager, administrator of other people's capital, and of the owner of capital into a mere owner, a mere money-capitalist.

... This is the abolition of the capitalist mode of production within the capitalist mode of production itself, and hence a self-dissolving contradiction, which *prima facie* represents a mere phase of transition to a new form of production.

... The co-operative factories of the labourers themselves represent within the old form the first sprouts of the new, although they naturally reproduce, and must reproduce, everywhere in their actual organisation all the shortcomings of the prevailing system.[7]

Marx seems also to have identified fertile ground for the socialisation of property in the persistence of communal land rights in village communities across Europe, including Germany. This led him, late in his life, to accept that a revolution could also aim to restore such communal forms in countries that had not undergone a full transition to capitalism, such as Russia, and colonised countries (Stedman Jones 2016, 583). Both these perspectives have been a continued strand in socialist thinking, revived again recently in arguments, not confined to Marxists, for reframing corporations as cooperatives or collectives of workers (Hayden and Bodie 2021), and for rethinking property in terms of a commons.

Hence, Marx's and Engels' views of tax were closely tied to their view of the state, and its relationship to social relations as a whole ('civil society'). Rejecting Hegelian idealism about the state, they stressed the class character of state activities and of the taxes used to fund them. They saw demands for measures such as progressive taxation as part of the process for the proletariat to gain state power through democratisation, and a means for ending private ownership of the means of production, which would end class conflict, so that 'public power will lose its political character'.

[7]Capital vol. III, chapter 27. This was written in 1864–5, but Marx published only volume I of *Capital* in 1867; Engels edited and published it in 1894, with additions about later developments (chronic overproduction and cartelisation), which obscured its methodological and political implications (Avineri 1968, 179; Stedman Jones 2016, 467). Subsequent Marxist commentators have also largely ignored or downplayed this argument, focusing instead on capitalism's tendency to crisis (see, e.g., Harvey 2018, Ch. 7; Heinrich 2012, 83), which provides little guidance on what should replace it.

5.3 The Parliamentary Road and the Dilemma of State Socialism

5.3.1 The German Socialists Under Bismarck

The limits of this perspective began to emerge with the development of electoral politics, creating complex interactions between an increasingly institutionalised and professionalised political sphere and wider social struggles. This became evident in Marx's lifetime as the growing size and power of an industrial working class in Germany facilitated the formation in 1875 of the first mass membership socialist party.[8] It was led by August Bebel and Wilhelm Liebknecht,[9] and formed through a process of political manoeuvring and compromises, particularly with the Lassallean strand of socialism. Marx's position on this is best known through his *Critique of the Gotha Programme* of 1875, which lambasted the fledgling party's proposed programme, based on a detailed dissection. The critique culminated by attacking the document for seeing the state not as a reflection of society but 'rather as an independent entity that possesses its own intellectual, ethical, and libertarian bases', stating that this 'is shown by the words "the German Workers' party demands as the economic basis of the state: a single progressive income tax", etc.' (Marx and Engels 1968, 327–8).

This attacks not the demand for a progressive income tax itself, but such taxation 'as the basis of the state', maintaining Marx's position of 25 years earlier. It was directed at what he regarded as an acceptance of Lassalle's essentially Hegelian perspective that the way to socialism was by using universal manhood suffrage to democratise the existing state and achieve state power. Lassalle had been a member of the Communist League and a friend (but increasingly a rival) of Marx, until he helped create the General German Workers' Association (*Allgemeiner Deutscher Arbeiterverein*, ADAV) in 1863, shortly before his abrupt death in a duel (Stedman

[8] They called it the Socialist Workers Party of Germany; in 1890, when the anti-socialist law had ended, it was renamed *Sozialdemokratische Partei Deutschlands* (SPD), which continues to this day, though after great changes in political orientation.

[9] Liebknecht studied theology and philosophy at Giessen and Marburg, becoming a 'conscious socialist' during 6 months studying in Berlin in 1845–6 (when he read Engels' *Condition of the Working Class in England*), but became a disciple of Marx only after they met in London in 1850, after a tumultuous period of direct involvement in the insurrections of 1848–9, particularly in south Germany (Dominick 1982). He did not write any substantial theoretical work, but was a prolific journalist and a political strategist. Bebel was an artisan and trade unionist, whose organisational skills complemented Liebknecht's. With the growth of the party from 1875 both went from penury to being well paid, party finances enabling them to be paid some 300 marks a month in 1876, while Bebel estimated Liebknecht's income in 1885 as 7000 marks a year; this led to a hot debate in the party in 1892 on a proposal to cap the salaries of its officials (Dominick 1982, 251, 331, 385–6). In the same period, many of them experienced recurring periods of imprisonment, Liebknecht himself seven times between 1877 and 1897, of between 1 and 12 months each (Dominick 1982, 408). Only after 1906, however, did the party become bureaucratised, under Friedrich Ebert, 'the Stalin of Social Democracy' (Schorske [1955] 1983, 124).

Jones 2016, 437–448). The Gotha programme resulted from the merger of the ADAV with Liebknecht's and Bebel's Social Democratic Labour Party formed at Eisenach in 1869. It blended Marx's approach with the Lassallean perspectives of ADAV members, while also echoing 'people's state' ideas that had influenced Bebel and others. However, Lassalle's unashamedly Hegelian view of the state extended to bargaining even with Bismarck, a 'statist cult' that was anathema to the Eisenachers (Lidtke [1966] 2015, 26, 52).

Marx's critique was directed at the argument that tax receipts should fund the government machinery to fulfil functions such as a standing army, or even education for all. Instead, '[g]overnment and church should rather be equally excluded from any influence on the school … the state has need, on the contrary, of a very stern education by the people' (Marx and Engels 1968, 329). In response, Liebknecht conceded that the programme could be better worded, but he pointed out that they had made similar compromises earlier with Lassalleans which Marx or Engels had not criticised – indeed the Gotha programme was broadly similar to that adopted at Eisenach (Dominick 1982, 239).

Two key intervening events had caused the change in Marx's position. First, the Paris commune of 1870 had sharpened Marx's faith in the possibilities of collective organisation of public functions in communal rather than state forms. Secondly, there had been a fierce conflict with Bakunin over opposition to the state, leading to the disintegration of the IWA. Hence, Marx was now concerned to deflect continuing anarchist criticism that he favoured a Lassallean path of reforming existing states. The concept of a 'people's state' nevertheless retained its appeal, particularly with those such as Bebel who fought for democracy, although as a stage towards the creation of a socialist society (Lidtke 2011, 788–794).

This tension was resolved through a restatement by Engels of the Marxist view on the transition to socialism, particularly in polemical articles against Eugen Dühring in the party's paper *Vorwärts* in 1877, later published in edited form as *Socialism, Utopian and Scientific.* This text strongly influenced a generation of Marxists, including Bernstein, Kautsky and Plekhanov (Riazanov 1927, 209–10). Engels presented Marxism as a scientific theory:

> Whilst the capitalist mode of production more and more completely transforms the great majority of the population into proletarians, it creates the power which, under penalty of its own destruction, is forced to accomplish this revolution. Whilst it forces on more and more the transformation of the vast means of production, already socialised, into state property, it shows itself the way to accomplishing this revolution. *The proletariat seizes political power and turns the means of production in the first instance into state property.* But, in doing this, it abolishes itself as proletariat, abolishes all class distinctions and class antagonisms, abolishes also the state as state. … State interference in social relations becomes, in one domain after another, superfluous, and then dies out of itself; the government of persons is replaced by the administration of things, and by the conduct of processes of production. The state is not "abolished". *It dies out.* This gives the measure of the value of the phrase "a free people's state", both as to its justifiable use at times by agitators, and as to its ultimate scientific insufficiency; and also of the demands of the so-called anarchists for the abolition of the state out of hand. (Marx and Engels 1968, 423–4, italics in the original)

However, this 'scientific' version over-simplifies Marx's dialectical approach to Hegel. While Engels refers to *Absterbung* (dying out or withering away), Marx generally preferred the Hegelian term *Aufhebung*, the transcendence or transformation of the state, which has very different implications (Avineri 1968, 202–207).

Engels' formulation upheld the vision of revolutionary transformation, while suggesting a strategy of waiting until conditions were ripe. This largely succeeded in maintaining ideological unity within the SPD for a significant period, enabling it to remain Marxist, with a strategy of combining parliamentary and extra-parliamentary action. However, it was severely tested by Bismarck's carrot-and-stick approach, enacting anti-socialist legislation criminalising socialist extra-parliamentary activity between 1878 and 1890, while introducing welfare reforms funded by social insurance in the 1880s (Lidtke 2011, 797–8). There was continuing interest among party members in the ideas of 'state socialists' such as Rodbertus, which had some affinity with Lassalle's perspective on achieving change through democratisation of the state (Lidtke [1966] 2015, 171–2).

This became a practical political question as the extension of the franchise led to the election of socialist members of regional assemblies and the Reichstag. A dilemma arose when Bismarck introduced legislation for sickness and accident insurance in 1881–4, and then for old-age and invalidity in 1888. The party decided to view these proposals as tactical concessions to the working class, and they tabled amendments to strengthen them while voting against the legislation when the amendments were rejected. They supported the alternative of tax-funded social insurance, arguing that the scheme should be run by the central, Imperial, state and subsidised by an income tax (Lidtke [1966] 2015, 167–8, 175).

Based on this rationale, the party continued to maintain its 'ambivalent parliamentarism' (Lidtke [1966] 2015, 286): opposition to the state, while continuing to participate in legislatures, even tabling legislative proposals, particularly in Saxony, such as bills for free education, a progressive income tax and exemptions for state employees from contributing to the sickness and old age funds (Lidtke [1966] 2015, 276). The party continued this strategy even after the ending of the anti-socialist law and Bismarck's fall in 1890, heading off an anti-parliamentary movement by a radical group '*Die Jungen*' (Lidtke [1966] 2015, 310–315).

5.3.2 Kautsky, the Erfurt Programme and Scientific Socialism

The scientistic rationale reached its apogee in the party's Erfurt programme of 1891, drafted by Karl Kautsky. A first version had been prepared by Liebknecht, working with Bebel, but Kautsky had published a counterproposal which was eventually preferred by the leadership, and which Liebknecht then endorsed at the congress (Dominick 1982, 363). Like the Gotha programme, its first part outlined the party's general orientation, while the second part put forward specific programmatic demands, including progressive taxation. Kautsky's draft diverged most sharply on the first part, though there were also some differences on policy.[10] The earlier version argued that the separation of workers from the means of labour and their monopolisation by a class of owners was the cause of exploitation, growing misery and class conflict, as well as planlessness and crises. It stated clearly that the Party 'has nothing in common with the so-called state socialism: the system of fiscal nationalisation which puts the state in the place of the private entrepreneur but allows the dual yoke of economic exploitation and political repression to oppress the worker' (Dominick 1982, 416).

This rejection of 'fiscal state socialism' was omitted in Kautsky's version, approved as the Erfurt programme, which presented a significantly different argument:

> The economic development of bourgeois society leads by natural necessity to the downfall of the small industry, whose foundation is formed by the worker's private ownership of his means of production [so that] the powers of production of contemporary society have grown beyond measure, and that private ownership of the means of production has become incompatible with their intended application and their full development. ... Only the transformation of capitalistic private ownership of the means of production ... into social ownership and the transformation of production of goods for sale into socialistic production managed for and through society, can bring it about, that the great industry and the steadily growing productive capacity of social labour shall for the hitherto exploited classes be changed from a source of misery and oppression to a source of the highest welfare and of all-round harmonious perfection.

The bold assertion in the opening sentence of the 'natural necessity' of the transformation of capitalism reflects the 'scientistic' and Darwinist turn towards the transition to socialism, already signalled by Engels, who's *Anti-Dühring* had been published in the party's main journal *Vorwärts*.

Kautsky had since 1883 been editor of the Party's theoretical journal *Die Neue Zeit*, which became the main vehicle for interpreting 'scientific socialism'. He was a theorist, not a politician, and under him the journal focused on the economic crises and changes in the character of capitalism such as the growth of concentration (Lidtke [1966] 2015, 280–1). He was interested in and influenced by Darwin's work from an early age, arguing for its congruence with Marxism, which he also considered a scientific theory. However, this was within the broad German concept of *Wissenschaft*, and he distinguished the 'blind' laws of nature from the analysis of social relations as the processes by which humans shape their own history (Steenson 1989). His emphasis on the view that the contradictions of capitalism would lead to its inevitable downfall has been criticised as overly deterministic and leading to

[10] The surviving version drafted by Liebknecht is in Dominick (1982, 415), and the approved Erfurt programme is in Lidtke ([1966] 2015, 335). The final version included a proposal for the 'abolition of all laws which are prejudicial to women', not present in the earlier version. Its tax proposal was similar to that in the earlier version, but slightly more elaborated: 'Graduated taxes on income and property, to meet all public expenses as far as these are to be covered by taxation. Obligatory self-assessment. A tax on inheritance, graduated according to the size of the inheritance and the degree of kinship. Abolition of all indirect taxes, customs, and other politico-economic measures which sacrifice the interests of the whole community to the interests of a favored minority.'

political passivity. However, his argument can more fairly be said to be for democratic socialism, reconciling Marxism's goal of revolutionary transformation with the view that this could be accomplished through democracy, and the practical parliamentary engagement this involved.[11] Kautsky wrote prolifically, and his main publications were translated into many languages, so he became widely influential, although later denounced by Lenin as a 'renegade'.

In the book he wrote to explain the Erfurt programme in 1892,[12] the increasing tax burden under capitalism is argued to result from the growth of an army of state officials, police and the military, due to both its increased need for internal repression and wars caused by international competition. In the chapter on *The Class Struggle*, he also argues that 'Like every other class, the working-class must strive to influence the state authorities, to bend them to its purposes', and that in 'the modern state' this is by increasing its power in parliament through elected representatives, particularly as the parliament must approve tax levies. The demands socialists should make of parliament are to advance and improve the conditions of the proletariat as well as of other groups with common interests, including 'such reforms as an income tax, the initiative and referendum, freedom of press and speech, election of judges, etc.'.

The word 'tax' does not appear in its chapter on *The Commonwealth of the Future*. Instead, in its section on *Social Reform and Social Revolution*, he wrote:

> When we declare the abolition of private property in the means of production to be unavoidable, we do not mean that some fine morning the exploited classes will find that, without their help, some good fairy has brought about the revolution. We consider the breakdown of the present social system to be unavoidable, because we know that the economic evolution inevitably brings on conditions that will compel the exploited classes to rise against this system of private ownership.

Its emphasis is on the need to end 'private ownership by the individual in the means of production used by co-operative labour', and '*To substitute common, for private, ownership in the means of production*' (italics in the original). However, there is no further elaboration of the possible forms of common ownership.

Guided by the approach reflected in the Erfurt programme, the party continued to treat parliament mainly as a political platform, rather than a means of achieving gains for the proletariat. When its members in the Prussian assembly voted for a state budget which contained some measures favourable to workers, the party's national congress reacted strongly and in 1894 confirmed the policy of voting against state budgets, a position maintained until 1913 (Schorske [1955] 1983, 8).[13]

---

[11] For an excellent recent survey of Kautsky's work, and of the views of various commentators on it, see Ben Lewis's introduction to Kautsky (Kautsky and Lewis 2019).

[12] *Das Erfurter Programm in seinem grundsätzlichen Theil erläutert von Karl Kautsky,* published in English as *The Class Struggle*, and available online in the Marxists Internet Archive. It was admired by Lenin, who translated it into Russian in 1894.

[13] Schorske points out that although the Erfurt synthesis acted as a brake on radical action in this period, when it was readopted in 1917 by the Independent Social Democratic Party formed by the leftists and centrists (from Luxemburg through to Kautsky and even Bernstein), the opposition to

5.4 Revisionism and the Great Schism

5.4.1 Bernstein and 'Back to Kant'

However, the Erfurt synthesis quickly met a direct ideological challenge, and from an unexpected source: Eduard Bernstein, long a follower of Marx, a close friend of Engels, and a leading party theorist. Indeed, he had led the battles against both Lassalleans and anarchists, arguing in the 1880s that the aim should be to seize state power in order to replace the state by 'a communistic society' (Tudor and Tudor 1988, 46). Nevertheless, he began to modify his views even as the Erfurt programme was approved, and in 1896 he started publishing his articles in *Die Neue Zeit* on "Problems of Socialism", which broke open the fissures in the party. The position he laid out, published in 1899 as *Voraussetzungen des Sozialismus* (*The Preconditions of Socialism*) eventually split the socialist movement.

Bernstein's argument was based on the empirical grounds that both economic and political developments had disproved Marx's view that the achievement of revolutionary change is a 'historical necessity'. He rejected the dialectical method, considering that it was not essential to Marxism, and substituted a linear view of historical progress as 'organic evolutionism' (Gay 1979, 146). For him, economic development had resulted in a 'greater scope for independent activity' of 'ideological and especially ethical factors'. This had curtailed the 'historical necessity' of socialism, a view which he saw as rooted in an economic determinism, arguing that adopting a more amplified version of Marxism would make it 'more scientific' (Bernstein [1899] 1993, 19–20). Bernstein was also influenced by the more pragmatic and empiricist approach of the Fabians, with whom he had socialised and debated while living in London (Gay 1979, 104–109), and his critique of Marx's theory of value cited Jevons and Böhm-Bawerk, although his analysis remained rooted in Marxism.

Bernstein's thesis was that the 'modern economy' had shown an ability to adapt, evidenced by an empirical analysis of capitalism's contradictions and tendency to crisis as an 'economic' process. He presented data to show that the joint stock company form had not led to concentration but to an increase in the number of property owners, and that there had been a growth in the number of income-tax payers, arguing that 'the prospects of socialism depend not on the decrease but the increase of social wealth' (Bernstein 1899, 61). Given the increase in capitalists 'of many degrees' and of some better-off workers, socialists should seek allies, and aim to achieve even partial gains, short of socialism, that could improve the position of workers.

He cited, for example, the spread of cooperatives, and the role of trade unions, including their provision of unemployment insurance and participation in municipal labour exchanges. He accepted that these did not constitute socialism, but 'as

---

the existing order which it expressed lined the party up in favour of the mass strike movements and revolutionary wave of 1917–18 (Schorske [1955] 1983, 320).

workers' organisations they have in them enough of the socialist element for them to be developed into valuable and indispensable instruments of socialist emancipation' (Bernstein 1899, 179). Similarly, the creation of municipal and state enterprises should not be dismissed with 'such mindless slogans as "state capitalism"'. They might be described as 'fiscal enterprises' if 'kept aside from private profiteering for reasons which have nothing to do with their economic and political functions', especially when administered by a privileged minority bureaucratically for its own benefit; but with the growing democratisation rooted in the working class 'the principles of industrial management will be modified along democratic lines' (Bernstein 1896, in Tudor and Tudor, 76).

Bernstein's thinking converged with the revival of interest in Kant, which he further fuelled by calling for a 'back to Kant' movement (Bernstein 1898, 229; Gay 1979, 153). However, his own contribution to this remained in the realm of commonsense philosophy, closest to naturalism (Gay 1979, 160–2). A response to the Kant debates came from Kautsky, who elaborated his views on the relation of scientific socialism to Darwin, in his *Ethik und materialistische Geschichtsauffassung* (*Ethics and Historical Materialism*) of 1906. His analysis was not unlike Marx's critique of Hegel, aiming to place the 'categorical imperative' of ethics and morality on a materialist basis. He argued that, since Kant's ethics 'spring from the wish of a harmonious society' a socialism based on this perspective aimed to tone down and reconcile class antagonism, rather than 'overcoming them through struggle' (Kautsky 1907, 56). To counter this, he argued that Darwin had made a great advance by showing 'that the altruistic feelings formed no peculiarity of man, that they are also to be found in the animal world' (Kautsky 1907, 71), pointing in particular to the 'social impulse'. He concluded that 'An animal impulse and nothing else is the moral law' (Kautsky 1907, 97; see Stedman Jones 2016, 564). This reinforced the scientistic interpretation of Marxism, while adding an ethical element.

A more radical counterblast came from Rosa Luxemburg, comprehensively expressed in her book *Reform or Revolution?* (1910, in Scott 2008). She argued that what Bernstein described as capitalism's adaptation, particularly concentration and cartelisation, only ripened and sharpened its internal contradictions. She accepted that 'Capitalist development modifies essentially the nature of the state, widening its sphere of action, constantly imposing on it new functions (especially those affecting economic life), making more and more necessary its intervention and control in society. In this sense, capitalist development prepares little by little the future fusion of the state to society' (Scott 2008, 61). However, she argued that even interventions that improve the conditions of the working class, such as labour legislation, are enacted in the interests of the bourgeoisie, and the state remains 'a class state'. She returned to Marx's dialectic, urging that reform and revolution should not be seen as opposites, but should be combined as a unity through social action (Scott 2008, 41). This meant that demands should not be aimed at piecemeal improvements, but should be formulated and fought for with the final aim of social transformation in view. She emphasised extra-parliamentary action, particularly the political general strike ('mass strike'), although its timing depended on the political situation.

Bernstein, Kautsky and Luxemburg, all avowed Marxists, expressed the three main divergent theoretical perspectives that led to the disintegration of the German party, and have continued to divide socialism. The cracks grew and widened, particularly due to the effects of growing inter-imperialist rivalries, culminating in the outbreak of war in 1914 and the schism between communism and social democracy.

5.4.2 *Socialists and the Welfare-Warfare State*

These positions crystallised during the 1890s, in a period of increasing fiscal pressures on states, due to a combination of rapidly growing military expenditures and demands for welfare provision resulting from widening of the franchise in many countries. It was in this period that tax reforms spread in the main capitalist states, generally introduced under acute fiscal pressure, and proposed or supported by left liberals. These included the introduction of graduated income taxes based on the concept of 'ability to pay', underpinned by the rise of marginalist economics (Mehrotra 2013). However, this was far from an attack on capital or wealth, the aim was rather to mitigate the increasing burden from indirect taxes, which also generally rose, while welfare measures were often funded through social insurance provisions (Seligman 1908; Seligman 1915). Nevertheless, the growth in taxation sparked political conflicts in many countries, due to resistance particularly from often aristocratic landowners.

In Germany, the rapid increase in military spending had plunged the Federal government into deficit by 1904, which a rise in indirect taxes only partly remedied, resulting in growing state debts and a fall in the value of its bonds. The government's proposals in 1908 were to raise M500m, 80% through indirect taxes, but 20% by introducing the first federal direct tax, an inheritance tax. Despite its modest reach, the Conservatives opposed this on the principle that the power to tax property should not be vested in a body elected by equal suffrage (Schorske [1955] 1983, 149). In alliance with the Centre parties, they passed an alternative bill funding the same sum entirely through indirect taxes, including some on business credit instruments, resulting in the resignation of Chancellor Bülow. His successor split the package into two, hoping to ensure passage of the indirect taxes by the centre and Conservatives, and of the direct taxes by the left liberals with the support of social democrats. This gave the SPD its first chance to achieve its long-standing demand of direct taxation, as well as to combine with left liberals to defeat the right, both prospects attractive to the revisionists. In parliament its representatives, even the radicals, followed the traditional line of voting for direct taxes in the initial stages; and the party was saved from a split on the whole package by the defeat of the inheritance tax proposal.

The internal party debate continued. While Bernstein supported the general policy of rejection of all new taxes and a stance against militarism, he called for flexibility in decisions on parliamentary votes (Bernstein 1909). Kautsky, who had warned of rising nationalism, gave stronger priority to anti-militarism, anticipating that the government might before long resort to more direct taxation to finance its armaments drive, quoting the British example (Kautsky 1909, 231). The party congress failed to reach agreement on either its stance on tax or an alliance with the liberals, leaving it to its parliamentarians and leadership to resolve the differences (Schorske [1955] 1983, 159–170). In the election of 1912 the leadership, under Bebel, stressed domestic issues, including opposition to indirect taxes, and dropped its previous condition of anti-militarism for electoral pacts with other parties (Schorske [1955] 1983, 227). Despite the additional seats this brought for the liberals, attempts at alliance after the election failed, and the SPD became increasingly divided, over both militarism and the primacy of gaining state power through parliamentary alliances. Both issues came into play when the government again proposed new taxes as well as increased military spending in 1912 and 1913. Finally, with the rising tide of nationalism and the rush to war in 1914, on 4 August the SPD parliamentarians decided by majority to vote in support of the war credits.[14]

The party majority's ensuing decision to collaborate with the government and the army in the conduct of the war led to the expulsion of both the centre and the radicals (now named Spartacists), who together established the Independent Social Democratic Party, again at Gotha and readopting the Erfurt programme, albeit on an interim basis. Formed just a month after the Russian revolution, the Independents supported the great mass strike movements of 1917–18 and rode the revolutionary wave (Schorske [1955] 1983, 320), but again split when the Spartacists opted for a soviet-style insurrection, and the centrists for a parliamentary republic.

5.5 Marxists in Government

In the ensuing period, Marxists attained access to state power, although by two very different means: by revolution and civil war in Russia, and through a combination of mass movements and the ballot box in Austria and in Germany. However, the thinking of all these strands had been strongly influenced by the German socialists, particularly as formulated by Kautsky and in the Erfurt programme. They accepted in particular Kautsky's central thesis, that the growth of large capitalist firms paved the way to the socialisation of the means of production, and that this could be achieved by socialists once in power through a combination of means, including both state ownership and progressive taxation. However, these theories worked out very differently when they did achieve political power, largely because of the very different paths taken by the process.

[14]The left accepted the majority vote, but by December Liebknecht broke with this position, to be quickly followed by Kautsky, Bernstein and other centrists.

5.5.1 Lenin and the Bolsheviks

Writing in *Pravda* in 1913, Lenin had analysed in detail the proposed U.S. income tax, criticising its 'exceedingly slow rate of progression … so that the owner of a million dollar income generally pays less than three per cent'. He went on:

> We see that the demand put forward by the Social-Democrats – the *complete* abolition of all indirect taxes and their replacement by a real progressive income tax and not one that merely plays at it – is *fully* realisable. Such a measure would, without affecting the foundations of capitalism, give tremendous immediate relief to nine-tenths of the population; and, secondly, it would serve as a gigantic impetus to the development of the productive forces of society by expanding the home market and liberating the state from the nonsensical hindrances to economic life that have been introduced for the purpose of levying indirect taxes. (Lenin 1963, 199)

Lenin also agreed with and followed Kautsky's analysis of the implications of the concentration of capital for a transition to socialism, but he broke decisively with him on the political strategy. In *State and Revolution*, written in the summer of 1917 while taking temporary refuge in Finland, Lenin attacked the leaders of the Second International, singling out Kautsky as the leading figure, for 'socialism in words and chauvinism in deeds' (Lenin 1918, in Chretien 2015, 37–8). Quoting from the writings of Engels and Marx on the state, he argued that the 'withering away' of the state referred to 'the remnants of the *proletarian* state *after* the socialist revolution' (Chretien 2015, 53). For him, achieving socialism inevitably entailed a violent revolution and the creation of a new and powerful state expressing the dictatorship of the proletariat. However, the key to this was to ensure political control and accountability: 'the scientifically trained staff of engineers, agronomists, and so on [who]… are working today in obedience to the wishes of the capitalists … will work even better tomorrow in obedience to the wishes of the armed workers' (Chretien 2015, 140). This viewed the state apparatus and its personnel, as well as state measures such as taxation, as a neutral mechanism that can be directed politically.

The Bolsheviks' application of their theories as practical policies was strongly moulded by the headlong trajectory of events in 1917, from the spontaneous creation of the Petrograd Soviet in February, and the growth of the soviets into a counter-power of the provisional government dominated by liberals, to the October revolution, and thereafter the period of 'war communism'.

In April, the Bolsheviks proposed state ownership only of capitalist syndicates and the banking system. Writing in *Pravda* in May, Lenin explained that nationalisation of the banks would enable indirect control over capital, as well as facilitating the gradual introduction of progressive taxation of incomes, through access to information on bank accounts (Malle 2002, 35, 46; Kotsonis 2016, 400). By September, Lenin was advocating state ownership of firms also in key industrial sectors, although not 'general expropriation'. Bukharin favoured more rapid nationalisation particularly of large firms, also to provide centralised control and planning, building on Kautsky's view that the growth of large firms was an advanced stage of capitalism, and that they were more efficient.

The rapid shift towards nationalisation was accelerated by a number of factors outside the Bolsheviks' control, including the spontaneous occupations of workplaces and the formation of factory committees, from which demands came by January 1918 for state ownership of all the means of production (Malle 2002, 55). Again in response to these direct actions by workers, one of the first actions of the Bolshevik government was a decree of 27 November 2017 on Workers' Control. However, this aimed at ensuring a political check on managers particularly of the remaining private firms, and not the replacement of managerial hierarchies (Malle 2002, 47). Indeed, by the end of 1920 the role of factory committees or managerial councils was overridden in favour of central appointment of 'one-man managers' and party control, strongly argued for by Trotsky based on his experience of the need for discipline in the Red Army (Malle 2002, Ch. 3).

The Bolsheviks attempted to implement the policy of shifting to direct taxes, introducing an extraordinary income tax in 1918 aiming to raise about two-thirds of the government's estimated revenue needs. However, revenues from both direct and indirect taxes reached less than 20% of state revenues in 1919, and the rising civil and military spending needs could only be met by printing money, which fed rising inflation (Malle 2002, 160). Under the New Economic Policy initiated in 1921 non-state-owned business operated under a system of licensing; but due to the extensive nationalisations particularly of large enterprises, the non-state sector peaked in 1925 at around half total recorded trade, while privately earned income never surpassed 55% of total national income (Kotsonis 2016, 433).

A personal income tax was reintroduced in 1921, described as a Universal Citizens' Tax, revised in 1923 with schedules for different occupations. The taxes were designed by Pavel and Nikolai Kutler, who had performed the same role for the imperial government (Kotsonis 2016, 434), as had 90% of officials in the Commissariat of Finances and two thirds of tax inspectors (Kotsonis 2016, 387). Kotsonis argues that this continuity confirms that the primary role of taxes was similar under both the late empire and the communists: to secure state control over the people and identification of citizens with the state. Lenin's view of a state under political control through the party was implemented by Stalin in much more extreme ways.

5.5.2 The Austro-Marxists

The distinctive strand of Marxism that emerged in Austria before the first world war steered a line between Bolshevism and social-democracy, from the founding of the journal *Marx Studien* by Max Adler and Rudolf Hilferding in 1904, to the dispersion of its leading members after the outlawing of the Austrian Social Democratic Party in 1934. They came together as students, many of them under Carl Grünberg, who became professor of political economy in Vienna in 1895, at a time when the Austrian School of economics was also influential with Böhm-Bawerk returning to teach there in 1904. Max Adler was strongly influenced by the Neo-Kantian revival, and the positivism of Ernst Mach, and was credited by Grünberg with having made the 'necessary distinction between "historical materialism" as a systematic, empirical, historical discipline, and "philosophical materialism" as a metaphysical doctrine' (Bottomore and Goode 1978, 10–11). Although philosophically and methodologically the Austro-Marxists were closer to Bernstein, politically they aligned with Kautsky. Trotsky became acquainted with the group during his stay in Vienna between 1907–14, and found their ideas interesting, but later recalled that in his view they were 'not revolutionaries' (Bottomore and Goode 1978, 14).

5.5.2.1 Hilferding and Weimar Germany

A leading figure of this group, particularly on economic issues, was Rudolf Hilferding, who moved to Germany in 1906. There he became a leading theorist and politician in the SPD, although spending much of the war as a conscript in the medical corps of the Austro-Hungarian army. He was part of the SPD's centrist group, which later formed the Independent party, and then rejoined the main party in 1922. His first major work resulted from the students' debates over Eugen von Böhm-Bawerk's critique of Marx's explanation of the transformation of values into prices of 1896, two years after the publication of *Capital* volume III by Engels. Hilferding's response was squarely on the epistemological grounds that Böhm-Bawerk's 'subjective' approach to the theory of value, starting from the individual, was 'unhistorical and unsocial' and based on 'natural and eternal categories', whereas Marx's theory of value viewed labour as 'the constitutive element in human society' (Hilferding [1910] 1981; Hilferding and Sweezy 1949, 133). This robust response by a neophyte economist has continued to be Marxism's central rejoinder to the marginalist school of which Böhm-Bawerk was already a leading exponent.[15]

Hilferding's masterwork *Finance Capital* (1910) presented Marxism as a 'theory of the laws of motion of society', which a person could accept without being a socialist, a view based on Max Adler's discussion of causality published in *Marx Studien* (Hilferding [1910] 1982, 23).[16] It aimed to build on and develop Marx's analysis in volumes II and III of Capital on money and finance, and the emergence of large-scale capitalist enterprises based on the joint stock company. He argued that the growth of the system of credit 'socialises other people's money for use by the few',[17] and pointed to its increasing monopolisation by banks, as well as their close

[15] Hilferding had studied medicine at Vienna University, and was only 25 when he wrote this critique, while Böhm-Bawerk was one of the founders of Austrian marginalism, with Menger and Wieser (Hilferding and Sweezy 1949).

[16] Adler and Otto Bauer had reacted to Kautsky's response to Bernstein's appeal to Kant by arguing for a sharp differentiation between knowledge of facts and values, influenced by Marburgian neo-Kantianism (Czerwinska-Schupp 2016, 73–84).

[17] Hilferding ([1910] 1982, 180); this phrase was later used by the U.S. liberal jurist and eventually Supreme Court Associate Justice Louis D. Brandeis (Brandeis 1914), again echoed after the financial crisis of 2007–9 by others.

organisational and personal links to large industrial firms. It was this that he termed finance-capital, 'the latest phase of capitalist development'.

The work impressed and influenced the leading Marxists of the time, including Kautsky and Lenin. Bukharin went even further, arguing that, especially due to war, the dictatorship of finance had resulted in a merger of politics and economics in the form of 'state capitalism', so that with the revolution 'the *political* dictatorship of the working class must inevitably entail its *economic* dictatorship too' (Bukharin 2003, 48–9). Hilferding's analysis also influenced later theorists, notably Paul Sweezy, who however criticised the view that finance and banking had become dominant (Sweezy 1970, 266–7), and with Paul Baran formulated an alternative version, mixing Marxism and neo-Keynesianism, termed 'monopoly capitalism' (Baran and Sweezy 1966). However, the institutional intertwining of finance and industry pointed to by Hilferding was indeed characteristic of Austria and Germany, and more recent neo-Marxist work has returned to the concept of 'financialised' capitalism (e.g., Krippner 2005).

Hilferding himself later went further in his analysis, arguing that finance capital had become 'organised capitalism', with greater state intervention in the economy, thus moderating capitalism's tendency to produce immiseration and crisis, although the reliance on states also drove inter-imperialist rivalry (Smaldone 2008, 84). By the time he was in a position to put his theories into practical effect, the disruption caused by the war meant that in his view priority should be given to restoring orderly capitalist growth (Smaldone 2008, 73).

His first practical opportunity came in December 2018 with his appointment as a member of the Socialisation Commission, which was chaired by Kautsky and included as an independent economist Joseph Schumpeter (see further below). The Commission was established to fulfil the long-standing socialist commitment to this policy and respond to popular pressure, though with a purely advisory role, since key SPD members in the government fiercely opposed the idea of socialisation of industry, on the grounds that it would damage economic recovery. The Commission was given an impetus by the wave of spontaneous factory occupations and creation of revolutionary workers' councils, and in February 1919 it produced a majority report on coal and steel. To avoid the creation of a state bureaucracy,[18] this proposed a new legal framework, a Community governed by a Council of one hundred representatives, twenty-five each of workers, managers, consumers and the state, with a five-person Executive Directorate (Winkler 1984, 191).

However, the responsible SPD minister took the view that socialisation did not mean expropriation, and opted for a 'social economy' approach, derived from the liberal industrialist Walther Rathenau, who had been involved in coordinating the war economy. Based on a Kantian moral imperative, this concept preserved private ownership and self-governing corporations within a framework for coordination and regulation by government. It had been introduced in key industries to help

[18] A key issue also was that state property could be subject to the war reparations imposed at Versailles.

secure support from the SPD and workers during the war and was enacted in the Coal Industry Act of March 1919 (Winkler 1984, 194). Despite a further impetus for socialisation following the Kapp putsch in 1920, these two perspectives could not be reconciled (Winkler 1984, 338), and the government again opted to preserve private property and follow the 'social economy' approach. Hence, the main achievement of the workers' council movement was the enactment of the Works Councils Act (Betriebsrätegesetz) 1920, giving worker's representatives 'codetermination' rights of consultation and seats on company boards; it was abrogated during the Nazi period, but revived after the second world war (Bartolke and Kappler 1989, 200; Dukes 2005; McGaughey 2016).

After rejoining the SPD, Hilferding was twice appointed as Finance Minister in coalition governments. The first was a short period lasting only 2 months under Stresemann, who needed to appoint cabinet members from the SPD to defuse the general strike of August 1923 sparked by the devastating impact on wages of the hyperinflation (Fowkes 1984, 100). Based on his view that orthodox policy should be used to restore capitalism's stability and growth, he supported establishing a new currency based on gold (Smaldone 2008, 89). In an SPD-led coalition in 1928–9 he again followed a 'sound money' policy in the face of deteriorating government finances, adopting a budget that cut expenditures and exempted industry and banks from tax on earnings from their loans to the government. Under pressure to produce a plan to reform government finances particularly for the funding of unemployment insurance, his proposal to cut income tax while increasing indirect taxes on beer and tobacco met opposition within his own party, precipitating his resignation (Harsch 1993, 54–5).

In the crisis of 1931–2, SPD economists diverged over its nature and the appropriate response. A plan for anti-cyclical government spending was proposed by a former Russian Menshevik, Wladimir Woytinsky, who had been following Keynes's work. This was opposed by Hilferding and his supporters, in fear of inflation, and Hilferding's rejection of it as 'un-Marxist' carried the day (Harsch 1998, 156–166). Thus, Hilferding's reliance on orthodox methods of managing state finances to restore 'organised capitalism' led him to neglect new economic theories on the management of capitalist economies and public finance.

5.5.2.2 A Fiscal Sociology of the State: Goldscheid and Schumpeter

Internationalism was central to Austro-Marxism, as it emerged among primarily German speakers at the heart of a multi-cultural empire, posing intractable problems, which it struggled to overcome. The declaration of principles of the Austrian Socialdemocratic Workers' Party (SDAP) agreed at its founding congress in Hainfeld in 1889 was drafted by Victor Adler and revised by Karl Kautsky, adopting a centrist position to reconcile divergent views that had hindered unity for 15 years (Loew 1979, 17). It advocated obligatory, free and secular schooling, replacing the standing army by arming the people, and 'the elimination of all indirect taxes and the introduction of a *single, direct, and progressive income tax*' (Blum and Smaldone

2017, 20). The SDAP maintained unity through ambivalence even during the war, initially inclined to supporting Karl Renner's defence of the fatherland but adopting an anti-war and leftist stance at its congress of 1917, with the rise to prominence in its leadership of Otto Bauer (Loew 1979, 23).

At the collapse of the Habsburg empire in autumn 1918 the SDAP was the dominant political force in German Austria, with mass movements among workers and soldiers creating a revolutionary situation. However, it rejected as premature the calls from communists and the workers' councils to create a soviet-style Republic, following the examples in Hungary and Bavaria. Instead, the SDAP aimed to channel the workers' movement towards parliamentary democracy, joining with the Christian Social and Greater German Peoples parties in November to convene the first National Assembly and officially declare German-Austria a republic, with Renner as Chancellor, and Bauer becoming Foreign Minister on the death of Victor Adler (Czerwinska-Schupp 2016, 20–21).

The public debts amassed during the war placed the issue of state finances onto the political agenda. A novel approach to this issue had been proposed during the war by Rudolf Goldscheid, who was anti-war, a socialist and an SDAP member. He had studied philosophy and sociology in Berlin and become a writer, later developing a humanistic sociology based on the concept of 'organic capital' (Exner 2004). He argued for the need for a social science of the state, which he rightly said had been neglected by historical materialism, and asserted that 'the history of the state is first and foremost tax history and national debt history' (Goldscheid 1917a, 258). He regretted that finance had become a technical issue driven by short-term politics, while sociology thought it could discern deep causes, neglecting the key issue of fiscality (Goldscheid 1917b, 3). His argument was that historically war had resulted in the 'expropriation of the state', as the war needs of princely states had turned public finances into a cashbox for the bourgeoisie and an extraction pump for the people (Goldscheid 1917a, 256–8). He recalled Marx's analysis that public debts were the lever of original capital accumulation, and argued that 'it was advanced capitalism which became the creator of the poor State, or … the State which is poor on principle' (Goldscheid [1925] 1994, 204).

Based on this analysis, he put forward an ambitious plan aiming to both restart the economy and deal with state debt after the war, by 'repropriation of the state and expropriation of the expropriators' (Goldscheid 1917b, 56). In *State Socialism or State Capitalism*, he argued that instead of burdening the economy with high taxes to repay war debts, the state should acquire around one-third of 'active assets' (werbende Vermögen), especially of the shares of large joint stock companies (Goldscheid 1917b, 44). Compensation should be provided through state bonds, and although the proposal would no doubt nevertheless be seen as infringing the sanctity of private property, safeguarding income from work and public property were higher values, especially for forms of property that should be regarded as social rather than private (Goldscheid 1917b, 61). He conceded that in the current political situation no existing parliament would likely approve the proposal but argued that the war had bound the state and the people tightly together, and any state that adopted this measure would gain an enormous boost to its development (Goldscheid 1917b, 40).

Goldscheid strongly criticised the approach that the SDAP had adopted to the state budget, separating minimalist demands for a shift to direct taxes to reduce the burden on workers from its maximalist aims of socialisation of the means of production. He argued that the impact of indirect and direct taxes is ultimately much the same, and there should be no rejoicing if owners are hit first by a tax if the whole economy suffers. Here he was addressing the dilemma identified in Karl Renner's short two-volume work on taxation published in 1909, to support the SPD's position on the budget (Renner 1909).

Renner's analytical first volume rejected the simple assumption that indirect taxes were bad and direct taxes good. He presented a detailed categorisation of different types of taxes, as well as state expenditure, attempting to analyse their impact on different classes and effects on private and public capital accumulation, social production and reproduction. On his analysis, as long as the economy remains capitalist, 'if we tax not just the rate of consumption but also the rate of accumulation of surplus-value we directly hinder social development' (Renner 1909, 40). However, the risk of overtaxation could be moderated by using progression, and differentiating between types of income. Tax should be very high on rents, but low or zero on loan interest, to avoid raising the cost of credit; taxes should generally be higher on public (corporate) debt than on private loans, higher on mortgages than on personal credit, higher on dividends than on personal business profits (Renner 1909, 46). The second volume was a polemical analysis of the government's proposed budget, culminating in a call on parliament to ensure a fair, equal and social tax reform and to voters to support the SPD if they wished to reduce the tax burden of the poor and end the tax privileges of the rich. A report based on Renner's work was presented at the party congress in Jena in 1913 by Emanuel Wurm, who himself had written a book on the history of taxes in Germany, although Wurm's proposals had some variations from Renner's (SPD 1913, 20–487, Krätke 1986, 50–52).

In a later paper, Goldscheid explicitly cited Renner's 'little book' as making 'one of the best socialist contributions' (Goldscheid [1925] 1994, 209) but he repeated his strong criticisms of the SDAP's tax policies, which had continued along the same lines in the 1920s, with little political success (Krätke 1986). In his view, Renner's position essentially agreed with bourgeois economic and financial theory 'that tax reform and public finance reform can by and large alter nothing in the existing social and economic order and that fiscal policy can contribute little or nothing to a solution of the social question' (Goldscheid [1925] 1994, 209).

Goldscheid argued that socialists should recognise that the budget is 'the state's skeleton stripped of all deceptive ideologies' and 'the state cannot be significantly different from its budget' (Goldscheid 1917b, 129). He saw the root of the problem as being the social-democrats' disdain for the role of the state in the socialisation of the means of production, originating in anarchistic ideas. For him, the state should be seen as the expression of organised society (Goldscheid 1917b, 131), the socialisation of the means of production could only be achieved through the state, and 'the science of public finance must culminate in a theory of public property' (Goldscheid [1925] 1991, 213).

This direct linking of the fiscal crisis and the issue of private property proved prescient in Austria's revolutionary situation at the end of the war. The socialisation of property had been a central demand of the workers' movement, and was a plank of the SDAP programme for the elections of February 1919, from which it emerged as the biggest party, and hence formed a government with the Christian socialists. In January Otto Bauer had expanded on the election slogans in a series of articles outlining his approach to socialisation, published as *The Road to Socialism* (Bauer 1919; Seidl 1994, 43). While he held out an enticing vision for the future, he cautioned that the revolution could not be won by simply chasing away the capitalists and their managers, which with a weakened economy faced by hostile powers would 'ruin our productive apparatus even more', and that socialism should be constructed by 'planned organising activity, proceeding step by step toward a clearly conceived goal' (Bauer 1919, in Bottomore and Goode 1978, 149–50).

His blueprint for socialisation was that industry should not be run by government, which would be both undemocratic and inefficient,[19] but that company boards should be composed equally of representatives of workers, consumers, and the state. In parallel, there should be works committees in all enterprises with more than 20 employees, to participate in managing all labour issues. The process should begin with heavy industry, then large estates and banks, merging the major banks into one Central Bank to ensure public control over the credit system, and later extending to other sectors as they became more concentrated. Compensation should be paid in the form of state bonds to the shareholders of the expropriated enterprises, but financed by a progressive levy on all capital and property to ensure fairness, while inheritance taxes should be used to prevent the bondholders from transmitting their assets to future generations. Thus, taxation should promote the socialisation of enterprises, which would be more efficiently managed, enabling the profits to reduce general taxation and hence stimulate the economy (Bauer 1919; Seidl 1994, 45).

The new parliament passed enabling legislation laying down general principles by 14 March, and a Commission on Socialisation was created to develop more detailed provisions, chaired by Bauer. In less than a month four draft laws based on his approach were produced, dealing with the procedures and institutional arrangements for socialisation. To appease the workers' movement, the law on works councils (Betriebsräte) was passed by the end of April. However, the procedural law was revised, first to require prior parliamentary approval for each expropriation, and then to identify in advance which industries could be affected, limiting these to coal, iron and steel, electricity and water, and large forests and timber; also, the law on management of socialised entities was watered down (Seidl 1994, 57–60). In this period the parliament also approved some significant social and labour protection legislation, which the SDAP regarded as a step forward, though well short of socialism (Czerwinska-Schupp 2016, 213–8). However, once the coalition government

[19] The idea that this was counter to the view of state ownership 'insisted upon by Marx' suggested by Czerwinska-Schupp (2016, 211) wildly misunderstands Marx's views on the state and socialisation, as discussed above. It perhaps reflects the extent to which the mythology of 'Marxism' has eclipsed knowledge of Marx, pointed out by Stedman Jones (2016, Prologue).

fell in October 1919 the prospects for its gradualist policies for socialisation evaporated, and the works' council law remained the only legacy.

A notable factor in the failure of the socialisation programme was a conflict over the financing of the expropriation, between Bauer and Joseph Schumpeter, who had been appointed finance minister on 15 March 1919. He owed this appointment to Bauer and Hilferding, who had known him in their university days, when he had participated in the debates on Böhm-Bawerk's critique of Marx (Swedberg 1991, 7), and they had also nominated him to serve on the German Socialisation Commission a few months earlier, as mentioned above.

Like Hilferding, Schumpeter treated Marx's work as social science, regardless of its political implications. He himself was a political conservative, but was personally very ambitious, and his writing at this time, which combined journalism and academic works, could be taken as 'political positioning' (von Blumenthal 2008, 650). Although he was not part of Marxism as a political movement, his theoretical approach can be regarded as Marxian,[20] as much so as Kautsky's or Hilferding's, particularly his view that capitalism would create the conditions for socialism through its own success, preparing the ground for its transcendence. However, he disagreed with Hilferding's view that the growth of large-scale firms would make capitalism more stable (Schumpeter [1943] 1976, 42), and emphasised a dynamic view of capitalism based on a restless search for competitive advantage particularly through entrepreneurship and innovation. As he put it later, 'objective and subjective, economic and extra-economic factors, reinforcing each other … make not only for the destruction of the capitalist but for the emergence of a socialist civilization', although he immediately corrected himself to say that 'transformation' might be a better term than 'destruction' (Schumpeter [1943] 1976, 162). The capitalist process itself 'takes the life out of the idea of property' (Schumpeter [1943] 1976, 142), and 'the very success of capitalist enterprise', with the emergence of large-scale firms, means that the 'giant unit of control tends to oust the bourgeoisie from the function to which it owed that social weight' (Schumpeter [1943] 1976, 139).

In 1918 Schumpeter had followed up on Goldscheid's arguments for a fiscal sociology with an essay on 'The Crisis of the Tax State' (Schumpeter [1918] 1991). Like Goldscheid, he saw taxation as central to the 'modern state', emerging from its feudal and princely antecedents, so that '[t]axes not only helped to create the state … [t]hey helped to form it' (Schumpeter [1918] 1991, 108). In contrast to Goldscheid, he considered that the tax state rests on the existence of a private or 'free' economy, and 'a socialistically organized people would have no state' (Schumpeter [1918] 1991, 109). He also differed from Goldscheid's view that taxes inevitably damage the economy, though he did think that taxes lose their effectiveness if they damage or destroy their 'tax object'. As regards direct taxes, he distinguished between different types of income, arguing that taxing entrepreneurial income would sap the dynamism of capitalist development, whereas monopoly profit, ground rent and

[20] On this distinction see Stedman Jones 2016, Prologue.

windfall profits 'may be almost completely taxed away without any unfavourable repercussions' (Schumpeter [1918] 1991, 114).[21]

His view was that the survival of the tax state depends on the vitality of capitalism itself, and in the long run he anticipated its demise:

> If the will of the people demands higher and higher public expenditures, if more and more means are used for purposes for which private individuals have not produced them, if more and more power stands behind this will, and if finally all parts of the people are gripped by entirely new ideas about private property and the forms of life – then the tax state will have run its course. (Schumpeter [1918] 1991, 116)

However, in the context of Austria at the war's end, he considered that the tax state could and should survive, since '[t]he social form of the society of the future cannot grow out of an impoverished economy thrown backward in its development' (Schumpeter [1918] 1991, 130). As a member of Germany's Socialisation Commission, he voted with the more radical majority (and against Hilferding), because he thought that if socialisation were to be tried it should be done 'integrally' (Swedberg 1991, 14). However, Bauer's gradualist strategy for socialisation in German Austria raised the question of its relation to taxation.

For Schumpeter, the immediate problem was how to resolve the state's financing of the war, which called for 'an adjustment of money values which would return them to harmony with the world of goods, that is to say, a large-scale writing-down of book values' (Schumpeter [1918] 1991, 119). He advocated that the state should aim to restart the 'free' economy, by repaying its bank loans and most of the war bonds through a broad-based one-off capital levy, for which war bonds could be accepted in payment (Schumpeter [1918] 1991, 119–126). This would need 'a strong government on the broadest political base' (Schumpeter [1918] 1991, 122).

On appointment as finance minister, Schumpeter immediately began publicly campaigning for this capital levy, to 'serve the reduction of the war burden and the spirit of the age, socialisation' (cited in von Blumenthal 2008, 652). However, the financial plan that he presented directed the proceeds of the capital levy to repaying the war debts (Seidl 1994, 62–3). This contradicted Bauer's proposal, which was closer to Goldscheid's approach, that prioritised the acquisition of shares in companies, retaining those of companies on the socialisation list, only the remaining revenue from the levy being used to redeem war debts (Bauer 1919). Thus, the two came into direct conflict, particularly as Schumpeter also opposed Bauer's idea for an inheritance tax and insisted that socialised firms should be responsible for the costs of their acquisition (Seidl 1994, 65). Since he also doubted that they would be more efficient, he was erecting an insuperable obstacle. Although he did not openly oppose the socialisation programme itself, he clearly thought it should wait until the time was ripe.

[21] Inheritance taxation was only briefly mentioned, but dealt with in a later article, which criticised it as detrimental to capital formation; he objected to taxes on savings, and later suggested a consumption-based income tax, on similar grounds (von Blumenthal 2008, 659).

Schumpeter's view agreed with Renner and others that taxes should be geared to the taxable capacity of the 'free' economy. However, his analysis of the dynamism and limits of entrepreneurship led to different tax design proposals, notably by favouring entrepreneurial profits and advocating heavy taxation for monopoly profits and rents. Despite considering that the growth of large firms would pave the way for socialism, he did not propose policies for socialisation. Here he concurred with Hilferding, that a transition to socialism would occur on the full maturation of capitalism. Hence, his approach differed from that of Goldscheid in one crucial respect: his concept of the 'tax state' was linked to the continuation of capitalism. In sharp contrast, Goldscheid argued that the primary aim of taxation and public finance should be to facilitate socialisation.

5.6 Socialism, the Mixed Economy and Neoliberalism

State expenditures grew rapidly, especially with the New Deal in the 1930s and the post-war expansion of welfare states, from 5–10% of GDP at the start of the twentieth century to 30–50% or higher by its end (Tarschys 2001, 28). Together with the extension of state ownership in many countries especially of infrastructure industries, this created the 'mixed economy', with a substantial state sector providing social and public services alongside the private economy, which became increasingly dominated by large corporations. This growing role for state spending was underpinned by the rise of Keynesianism to economic orthodoxy and eclipsing the approach of fiscal sociology of which Schumpeter had said 'much may be expected' (Schumpeter [1918] 1991, 101).

5.6.1 Keynesianism and Socialism

Keynesianism led to a further refinement of economics as a technical discipline excluding 'moral' considerations, and hence it could be used to support a range of policy ideas. In the period of critique of capitalism sparked by the depression and the War, this could feed into socialism or radical liberalism (White 2009). A good exemplar was James Meade. Meade's expertise was primarily in economic modelling, and he combined 'radical sympathies but an iron detachment' (Atkinson and Weale 2000, 474). In the 1930s he prepared policy ideas for the Labour Party that combined Keynesian counter-cyclical expenditures with policies for a National Investment Board to regulate public and private investment, as well as nationalisation. Compensation should be paid to ensure continued private investment, but '[l]ater, "once ... the main body of capitalists are rentiers the Government can make drastic use of the instrument of taxation to buy them out", particularly by inheritance taxes and possibly a capital levy' (Howson 2000, 125). These proposals were in the same vein as those made by Goldscheid in 1917 for Austria.

He later published a study, based on lectures given in Stockholm in 1964, showing logically that where property is unequally owned (under capitalism), economic efficiency widens inequalities. Hence, he argued that 'to combine efficiency in the use of resources with equity in the distribution of income would … cry out for measures to equalise the distribution of the ownership of private property and to increase the net amount of property which was in social ownership' (Meade [1964] 2012, 75). He therefore analysed two main alternatives to capitalism,[22] a 'property owning democracy', with equal distribution of property among all citizens, and a 'socialist state', with property socially owned (by the state or public bodies). These, especially the first, were essentially ideal types, but he also discussed measures to achieve them, including progressive inheritance and gift taxation, a progressive annual tax on wealth to be used for investment in public property, the encouragement of small property ownership, and egalitarian education policies.

With the changing political climate his policy proposals became more utopian and social-democratic or left-liberal. He put forward a vision for a 'partnership economy' based on a form of cooperative he called a 'discriminating labour-capital partnership' in which labour and capital shares would receive the same rate of dividend, which he termed 'agathopia' (Atkinson and Meade 1993; Howson 2000, 140, White 2009, 179). These ideas have underpinned employee share-ownership and profit-sharing plans in many capitalist countries. However, he continued to assert the importance of social ownership of a substantial part of the economy, differing clearly from Rawls, who later took up the term 'property-owning democracy' (Jackson 2012, 46). In 1974 he chaired a committee set up by the Institute of Fiscal Studies on direct taxation, mainly known for advocating Kaldor's concept of consumption-based direct taxes, and also argued for progressive taxes on wealth (on transfers, inheritance, and an annual wealth tax). In his preface to the report, Meade expressed the hope that it would provide 'a reasonable basis of consensus for our mixed economy' (Meade 1978, xvi).

5.6.2 Neo-Marxist State Theories and the 'Fiscal Crisis of the State'

The rise of a 'new left', spurred by decolonisation, the movements for civil rights and against the Vietnam war, and the 'events' of May 1968, included the emergence of neo-Marxist theories of the state. These generally criticised views of the state as a neutral instrument wielded by the group or class holding political power, and aimed to show how the capitalist nature of the state is inscribed in its forms and functions (Jessop 1982). The perspectives were mainly general and abstract, but a

[22] He also very briefly and critically discussed the role of trade unions (or legislation) in setting a minimum real wage, and a 'welfare state', by which he meant using taxation to subsidise the incomes of the poor.

few theorists did address the issue of state budgets and taxation, which had clearly become very important given the scale of state spending. These harked back to the concept of the tax state, although relying more on Schumpeter's notion of it as inherently linked to capitalism, and doing little to develop the fiscal sociology pioneered by Goldscheid.

The concept of the fiscal state was taken up by James O'Connor, who had worked on public finance at Columbia with Carl Shoup, but also become a Marxist. His *Fiscal Crisis of the State,* appearing at the apogee of Keynesianism in 1973, argued that fiscal crisis 'is the inevitable consequence of the structural gap between state expenditures and revenues' (O'Connor 1973, 221), due to 'growing needs which only the state can meet' (O'Connor 1973, 2). O'Connor's analysis reflected the enormous expansion of the state's role, going well beyond military or policing and basic social services such as primary education, so understandably he focused mainly on the nature of expenditure in what he described as 'American state capitalism'.

His analysis was that the state 'must try to fulfil two basic and often mutually contradictory functions – *accumulation* and *legitimisation*' (O'Connor 1973, 6). The support of accumulation requires spending on 'social capital', including both social investment (in physical and human capital) and social consumption (e.g., urban projects and unemployment insurance). Both increase the rate of profit, whereas the social expenses of the 'warfare-welfare state' needed to maintain legitimisation are not even indirectly productive. However, he stressed that these are analytical distinctions which do not correspond to budget categories, and state agencies generally fulfil both functions. The transition from competitive to monopoly capitalism meant profound changes in the fiscal system, as the state budget was no longer simply a drain on the private economy, but was now supporting private accumulation in many ways, and it had to try to balance spending on the accumulation and legitimation functions. Although '[t]he fiscal crisis of the capitalist state is the inevitable consequence of the structural cap between state expenditures and revenues', ways could be found to ameliorate it. A society's tax and expenditure structures are determined politically, but it is hard to mount political movements around tax and the state budget because of the extensive and complex issues raised. The class issue of state finance takes new forms, of interest group and sectional politics, and popular resistance to tax has been neutralised by progressive taxation (O'Connor 1973, Ch. 9).

O'Connor provided only a few pages of analysis of the 'tax state' which stressed the exploitative class character of the tax system, concealed through the ideological concepts of incentives, ability to pay, and equal treatment. He pointed out that the justification of incentives generally overrides ability to pay, so that income from capital is lightly taxed, and the emphasis is on taxing income not wealth, while 'a tax system that "treats equals equally" merely reinforces existing inequalities' (O'Connor 1973, 205). He suggested that the wealthy have generally preferred taxation of corporate income, because the monopoly sector can control prices, so such taxes are absorbed by their customers, as are commercial property taxes, while payroll taxes are shifted to workers, and gift and inheritance taxes are minimal and easy to avoid or evade (O'Connor 1973, 206). Only in times of national crisis or war has there been any serious attempt to tax income from capital. The shift of personal taxation from indirect taxes to the individual income tax was 'ideally suited to the needs of monopoly capital' because it cannot be shifted to profits, and is 'progressive in form, although regressive or proportional in content', thus preserving the myth of tax equity (O'Connor 1973, 209).

In some respects, O'Connor's analysis agreed with Goldscheid, particularly the view that in capitalism the tax state is 'poor in principle'. However, his prognosis aligned more with Schumpeter's perspective, since he argued that political pressures leading to increasing state expenditures would create a crisis of the tax state. He provided little discussion of what progressive tax policies might be, and did not follow Goldscheid in proposing ways in which they could support socialisation. Much of his analysis continues to have relevance, particularly his critique of the justifications for income tax as egalitarian, which amplify Marx's attack on the 'chimerical ideal of equal distribution of taxation'. He himself admitted that his central prediction of fiscal crisis failed to anticipate the rise of neoliberalism, and underestimated the ability of macroeconomic techniques to balance the budget (O'Connor 1973, xviii), although fiscal crises have indeed subsequently returned. Indeed, despite the widespread privatisation of state enterprises under neoliberalism, state expenditures as a proportion of GDP have remained much the same in most countries even after the neoliberal period.

A similar approach to O'Connor's was adopted by some German Marxists, viewing the tax state 'as the specific form taken by the state in a society in which the social creation of value is basically organised in private capitalist forms … [so that] securing and promoting this is a designated aim embedded in its basic structure' (Grauhan and Hickel 1978, 8). This seems both an over-expansion of the concept of a tax state, and at the same time a narrowing of it (Gerstenberger 1978, 57), since it identifies the concept with capitalism, and yet provides no perspective on how it could be transcended. Subsequently, Krätke provided a survey of the historical Marxist debates over taxation, reaffirming that from this perspective the only long-term solution to inequality is the socialisation of property, while presenting a Marxist analysis of the extensive social transfers of income and public goods in the welfare state based on an analysis of 'tax exploitation'. He suggested that the aim should be democratisation of tax, but meantime an immediate way to dispel the 'fiscal illusion' could be earmarking taxes to specific purposes, to make more visible citizens' share in public institutions (Krätke 1986).

These critiques of the state lost political traction under neoliberalism, as socialists felt the need to defend rather than criticise the gains of the Keynesian period, the mixed economy, and the welfare state. Tax again became technicised, despite the efforts of a few scholars to revive the concept of fiscal sociology (Musgrave 1992; Campbell 1993; Martin et al. 2009), but this was mainly derived from Schumpeter, and the earlier socialist debates were largely forgotten. This continued even after the emergence of a new fiscal politics and a global tax justice movement, as the financial crash brought sharply to view how the fiscal and financial system enables the private appropriation of profits while losses are borne by the public purse. In this context, Marxists were only able to point out the key role of taxation in the formation and maintenance of the capitalist state, and recognise the structural limits to state spending, while arguing for policies that level social inequalities even if they do not create socialism (Himpele and Recht 2009, 12).

5.6.3 The Financial Crash and the Revival of Progressive Taxation

The aftermath of the financial crash of 2009 gave a great impetus to campaigns for 'tax justice', as well as public concerns about inequality. This mood was caught by a book that became an unexpected best-seller, Thomas Piketty's *Capital in the Twenty First Century* (2014). Piketty is concerned with the distribution of income, but he focuses squarely 'on the respective shares of global income going to labour and capital' (Piketty 2014, 39). However, he uses the term 'capital' interchangeably with 'wealth' (Piketty 2014, 47), and not in a Marxist sense. He disavows any partisan stance on class struggle, asserting that his aim is 'to gain as clear as possible a view on reality' (Piketty 2014, 40). His central concern is with the political and social consequences of the inequalities generated by the more rapid rate of return on capital, which he considers 'less apocalyptic than those implied by Marx's principle of infinite accumulation and perpetual divergence' but 'not heartening' (Piketty 2014, 27).

The concept of 'wealth' enables him to deploy an enormous accumulation of data, much of it drawn from tax records, to demonstrate that the 'rate of return' on capital has exceeded the rate of growth of output and income, during the nineteenth century, and again since the 1980s. Like others, such as Branko Milanovic,[23] he aims to reverse the optimistic prognosis of the pioneer in this field, Simon Kuznets, which underpinned the 'trickle-down' theory that economic growth reduces inequality, which Piketty argues ignored historical realities and led economists to neglect inequality of outcomes (Piketty 2014, 11–15). Much of this work on data has been in collaboration with others, particularly Emmanuel Saez in France and the U.S., and Anthony Atkinson in the UK (Atkinson and Piketty 2010).

Atkinson who studied under Frank Hahn at Cambridge, was also influenced by James Meade (Atkinson and Meade 1993), and worked with Joe Stiglitz on the economics of public finance and optimal taxation (Aaberge et al. 2017). Prompted by the success of Piketty's book, Atkinson summed up his own views in *Inequality:*

---

[23] Milanovic is more sceptical about the role of taxation, since 'capital is hard to tax because it is so mobile', and emphasises 'reduction in the equality of endowments, especially inequality in the ownership of assets and education' (Milanovic 2016, 218). Hence, he supports de Soto's advocacy of a greater extension of private property rights particularly to the poor, and policies encouraging the poor and middle classes to have financial assets, although he also follows Piketty in supporting high inheritance taxes, and corporate tax policies encouraging distribution of shares to workers 'moving towards a system of limited workers' capitalism' (Milanovic 2016, 221).

What Can be Done (2015), published not long before his death. Unlike Piketty, Atkinson notes the distinction between wealth and capital, especially in relation to home ownership and personal savings, pointing out that 'it is necessary to keep distinct the beneficial ownership of wealth and the control conveyed by capital over economic decisions' (Atkinson 2015, 155). Harking back to Thomas Paine, Atkinson follows others such as Le Grand in proposing a 'capital endowment' for all on reaching adulthood, as well as increasing the progressivity of personal income tax to a top rate of 65% with preferential treatment of earned income, a progressive lifetime capital receipts tax, and consideration of an annual wealth tax (Atkinson 2015). While acknowledging a link to Rawls, he preferred to draw on Amartya Sen's 'capability' approach to 'social justice in terms of opportunities open to people according to their functioning' (Atkinson 2015, 13–14).

Piketty similarly acknowledges Rawls and Sen, although he places them in the Republican heritage of a 'logic of rights' that should underpin 'modern redistribution' for the 'social state' needed for the twenty-first century, providing the fundamental socio-economic rights to which access should be guaranteed to all, and funded through taxation (Piketty 2014, 479–480). At least in Europe, he asserts, they are education, health and retirement, although they cannot be deduced from general principles but should be decided by democratic deliberation. He argues that, although there is no reason in principle why the range of such collectively supplied goods should not be expanded, so that public financing could extend to two-thirds or even three-quarters of national income, first 'it would be good to improve the organisation and operation of the existing public sector' (Piketty 2014, 479–481).

Piketty also urges a rethinking of the progressive income tax, which should be set at very high rates for the top incomes: he proposes, based on research (Piketty 2014), that the rate should be 80% on incomes above $0.5 m or $1 m, with corresponding (unspecified) increases down the scale (Piketty 2014, 508). His argument for the very high top rate is not to provide revenue, but to remove the incentives for high remuneration of corporate executives by 'dissuasive taxation'. In a state with such extensive social provision that state expenditure is as much as 50% of GDP, taxes must be broad based. So, for him, the steeply progressive income tax is 'an ideal compromise between social justice and individual freedom', respecting free competition and private property while modifying private incentives 'according to rules thrashed out in democratic debate' (Piketty 2014, 505). To complement this, he also sketches out proposals for a 'global tax on capital', to 'regain control over the globalised financial capitalism of this century' (Piketty 2014, 515). At least as a 'useful utopia', the aim should be 'a progressive annual tax on individual wealth – that is, on the net value of assets each person controls' (Piketty 2014, 516). This could raise substantial revenues, even at a low rate – he suggests that in the EU a tax at 1% for fortunes between 1 and 4 million euros, and 2% above 5 million would raise 2% of the EU's GDP (Piketty 2014, 528). It would also perhaps improve allocation of investments by wealth owners, since some may have to sell assets to pay it (Piketty 2014, 527).

Spurred by Atkinson, Piketty followed with a more ambitious volume, *Capital and Ideology* (2020), providing a broad theoretical and historical perspective and much wider proposals, more clearly in the socialist tradition. This time his focus is on property, and the bulk of the book provides a sweeping historical account of the creation of the 'ownership societies' which became dominant in the nineteenth century, their crisis after 1914, and the 'great transformation' in the twentieth century. His broad geographical and historical approach counterposes 'ternary' to 'ownership' societies, drawing on historians including some of the Annales school such as Georges Duby, and covers colonialism and slavery, from India to Haiti, to show how the concept and system of private property emerged and became entrenched. The view of the 'great transformation' is drawn from Polanyi (Piketty 2020, 417), and Piketty regards it as an incomplete process. On the one hand, social democracy 'did not succeed in building new transnational federal forms of shared sovereignty or social and fiscal justice' (Piketty 2020, 486). On other hand, the failure of 'the most radical challenge to the proprietarian ideology' from communism, as implemented in the USSR's replacement of private property with state ownership has 'inspired a new kind of disillusionment, a pervasive doubt about the very possibility of a just economy, which encourages identitarian disengagement' (Piketty 2020,578).

In this much broader perspective, Piketty revises his proposals for progressive taxation, so that they take on a much wider scope, and are supplemented by more extensive measures. In his summary:

> New forms of social ownership will need to be developed, along with new ways of apportioning voting rights and decision-making powers within firms. The notion of permanent private ownership will need to be replaced by temporary private ownership, which will require steeply progressive taxes on large concentrations of property. The proceeds of the wealth tax will then be parceled out to every citizen in the form of a universal capital endowment, thus ensuring permanent circulation of property and wealth. (Piketty 2020, 967)

He provides only a sketchy outline of some proposals, in a few pages at the end of a lengthy work, with the aim of contributing to what he hopes might be a democratic deliberation. Their general substantive aim is 'the transcendence of capitalism and private property' (Piketty 2020, 971), a clearly Marxian formulation. He describes his approach as 'participatory socialism', and as 'building on the largely positive results of democratic socialism and social democracy in the twentieth century'.

Aiming to 'transcend capitalism and private property and bring participatory socialism into being' he proposes measures combining the socialisation of private property rights and progressive taxation. To enhance social ownership, he suggests building on the Germanic and Nordic models of workers' codetermination or co-management in firms, strengthening their position by capping the voting rights of large shareholders. However, he accepts the need for a role for private property especially in small and medium firms, subject to measures to prevent the concentration of ownership in a wealthy elite. Thus, Piketty's approach to the socialisation of property involves a combination of social ownership and shared voting rights in firms, and tax measures to ensure the 'temporary ownership and circulation of capital' (Piketty 2020, 989).

His outline blueprint for a tax system would dispense with indirect taxes, except for dealing with an 'externality', particularly a carbon tax. There would be three direct taxes: (i) a progressive income, social security and carbon tax, yielding around 45% of national income, to fund social and public spending, particularly on health, education, pensions and a basic income; (ii) a progressive annual property tax (yielding roughly 4% of annual income), and (iii) a progressive inheritance (including lifetime gifts) tax (1% of national income).[24] The yield from these taxes on capital should fund an annual 'capital endowment', an extension of Atkinson's proposal – Piketty proposes a payment to each young adult at age 25 of roughly 60% of the average wealth of adults (in rich countries around €120,000). He suggests that it should also be linked to an ambitious plan for a basic income, harking back to Thomas Paine, as well as referring to other contemporary proposals for a basic income.

Generally, Piketty's focus is on individual and family wealth and inequality, and for him 'concentration' means ownership of an increasing share of assets by a smaller proportion of people. It is only in relation to his support for workers' co-management that the importance of the corporation itself as a manifestation of the concentration of capital is glimpsed. Although he does consider that the corporate income tax is a tax on income from capital (Piketty 2014, 494), he provides no analysis of profits taxation or proposals for its progressivity.[25] Nor does he consider other such taxes such as capital gains tax. He rightly criticises Marxists for having paid little attention to the implications of the abolition of private property in and socialisation of the means of production, but his solution relies as much on equalisation of private ownership among individuals as on exploring possibilities and forms of social ownership.

Although not utopian, Piketty's proposals are speculative, explicitly advanced to stimulate and contribute to a debate. His work clearly shows that historically significant shifts in taxation and inequality have been precipitated only due to crises such as war or revolution. However, as we have seen above, the tax provisions actually adopted have built on previous measures and techniques and implemented ideas and approaches that were previously been put forward and debated. Hence, it is important to aim for continuous improvement as well as preparing the ground for a paradigm shift that might become possible due to a crisis.

[24] A table suggests 'illustrative' rates geared to multiples of the average annual wealth or income: income tax starts relatively high at 40% on twice the average income, 50% for five times, 60% for 10 times, and on up to 90% for 10,000 times; the annual property tax starts much lower, but rises to 10% on 100 times average wealth, 60% on 1000 times and 90% on 10,000 times; while inheritance tax rises more evenly from 20% on twice average wealth, 50% on five times, 60% on 10 times, 70% for 100, 80% for 1000 and 90% for 10,000 (Piketty 2020, 982).

[25] In the context of international cooperation, he proposes apportionment of the profits of large multinational corporations 'in a transparent manner … with minimal [sic] tax rates compatible with the general level of taxation' (Piketty 2020, 1032).

5.7 Conclusion: Taxation in the Transformation and Transcendence of Capitalism

In taking up Piketty's challenge to rethink the role of taxation in the transcendence of capitalism, socialists and Marxists should also reflect on the strengths and limitations of earlier contributions in this tradition. Goldscheid's plea for the development of a social science of the state should begin by rethinking Marx's conceptualisation that the merger of civil society and the state, resulting from the socialisation of property, entails the transcendence of both civil society and the state. The experience of the socialist movement suggests that this is not a single stage but a much longer process of merger, with successive stages in which capitalism becomes more 'socialised'. As Marx himself recognised in his third volume of *Capital*, the joint-stock company was already a form of socialisation of ownership of the means of production. Its counterpart, which escaped Marx's attention, has been the growth of social provision by the state funded through increased and broad-based taxation.

While the vision of the 'overthrow' of capitalism has long inspired radicals and revolutionaries, it has also impeded serious consideration of the nature of the transformations undergone by capitalism itself. Piketty rightly points out that, although major changes have generally been sparked by crises, both wars and revolutions, they have been shaped by prior ideologies. The Marxian dialectical perspective goes further, arguing that ideas spring from the new social forms that emerge 'from the womb' of the old society itself (Marx and Engels 1968, 182).

As Goldscheid also argued, the issue of the fiscal nature of the state is in many ways central to such consideration. The assumption in Schumpeter's version of the concept of the 'tax state' that it is necessarily capitalist is unhelpful, as it begs the question of transformations of the capitalist state and assumes that there would be no fiscal transfers under socialism. However, they share a concept of the 'fiscal state' that encompasses not only the forms of taxation, but also state expenditure, as well as the power of the state to issue debt, and the need to consider these in historical perspective (Whiteside 2021). The enormous growth of taxation and state expenditure in the twentieth century reflects major transformations in both the state and its relationship with civil society. This is not merely a quantitative matter, but also qualitative.

Most visible is the growth of the 'social state', which must be regarded as an achievement of the socialist movement, even if its forms frequently compromise with left liberalism. This reflects the lack of a logical rationale for determining which activities should be 'socialised' and how. 'Social justice' arguments are essentially ethical, and provide little guide for determining this, as Piketty recognises in proposing that the scope of the social state should be decided democratically, and could be much more extensive. However, he also accepts the common assumption that such provision is through the state, and financed by taxation, hence in his view the scope would also depend on the efficiency of state organisation. This, as noted above, was not at all the perspective of Marx, who insisted that activities such as education should be independent of both government and church.

Marxist critiques of 'fiscal state socialism' point to the structural problems of tax-funded social provision through the state. As Goldscheid put it, reliance on taxes makes the state 'poor on principle', creating continual threats of austerity and underfunding, while also creating a 'cash-box for the bourgeoisie'. The condition of 'fiscal crisis' seems to be an enduring characteristic of the 'mixed economy' in corporate capitalism, in which taxes reflect the tension between the increasing socialisation of provision, particularly of services, and the continued preservation of private property rights. For example, the delivery of health services is generally through public or state owned facilities and substantially funded through taxation, but a major role in the health sector is played by privately owned corporations, notably pharmaceutical companies. This not only means that they can derive substantial profits from sales to tax-funded public services, they also shape the nature of health provision, creating continual pressure towards prescribing pills rather than wider public health strategies. The battles over the state's role in healthcare particularly in the U.S. are a stark reminder of the complexity of these interactions.

In all sectors, the significant proportion of public budgets directed at purchasing from private corporations has made public procurement an endemic source of bribery and corruption around the world. The separation between state-owned and private enterprises has been succeeded by their intertwining through new forms of 'public-private partnership'. The justification is that the private sector can supply capital and manage risk, but more often it is the state budget that pays the bills for cost overruns and corporate failures. Where services that are vital to social life have been privatised, for example railways or utilities such as water or energy, extensive public subsidies are generally provided either directly or through favourable tax treatment.

Marxism points to the key role of taxation in capital accumulation. The concept of the 'fiscal state' goes beyond taxation, to encompass the state's centrality in the monetary and financial system. This means not only that the state's expenditure rests on its capacity to borrow as well as to tax, but also that tax and finance are closely tied together in capital accumulation. This can be seen clearly in the methods of tax 'planning' of both wealthy families and large transnational corporations that have shaped the current international tax and financial system. These have used strategies of 'offshoring' to exploit disjunctures and differences between the tax and financial rules and regulations of different countries and their loose international coordination. These techniques originated early in the twentieth century, at the time of and in reaction to the shift to direct taxation in major capitalist states, were extended under the partial liberalisation of the Bretton Woods system, and boomed due to the financial liberalisation of the 1980s. Only in periods of politicisation, particularly after the financial crisis of 2009, have there been any serious attempts to rein in this process (Picciotto 2020).

Hence, a socialist approach to 'progressive taxation' should entail designing appropriate taxes to restrict and phase out the control by a small ruling class of the increasingly socially coordinated processes of production. This goes beyond the introduction of graduated rates of tax on income, as well as on 'wealth', even the steeply rising ones proposed by Piketty. Indeed, both these categories need to be reconsidered, and different distinctions made, for example between earned and unearned income as proposed by Atkinson, and between small savings and personal assets such as housing, and assets amounting to some control over means of production or consumption. The rationale for graduation of tax rates on income should be underpinned by a clearer analysis of the distinction between income needed for an acceptable standard of living and income amounting to an accumulation of capital.

More centrally, there is need for a rationale for taxation of profits, which are also often lumped together in the general category of 'income'. In the general perspective of neo-classical economics profits are seen as resulting from investment, and tax as increasing the costs of financing such investment, hence restricting growth. A specific tax on corporate profits is analysed also on the basis of such a 'general equilibrium' model, in terms of its 'incidence' on the company's 'factors of production', labour and capital, assuming perfect competition and constant returns to scale (Harberger 1962), thus concluding that such a tax falls on either the company's employees or shareholders or a combination of the two. Despite the weaknesses of this approach, it has been surprisingly little challenged even by socialists.

The dominance of the economic argument that high taxes on capital income impede investment and growth has underpinned the reduction of taxes, especially on income from capital and on wealth, that has resulted in the growing inequalities demonstrated by Piketty. Yet he provides no analysis of corporate taxation. His collaborators Emmanuel Saez and Gabriel Zucman, who also focus their arguments for progressive taxation on taxing 'the rich', do venture a critique of the received wisdom that taxing corporate profits deters investment. However, they accept that 'only people pay taxes', and that a tax on corporate profits must fall on either labour (employees) or capital (shareholders); their critique is on the empirical grounds that the decline in corporate tax rates since the 1980s has had little effect on investment or savings (Saez and Zucman 2019, Ch. 5). Although they also show how international tax avoidance and tax competition have boosted the profits of large multinationals, and argue for an internationally coordinated minimum tax on them of 25%, this is not supported by economic arguments, but by moral outrage. Piketty's case for progressive taxation of both income and wealth also depends on the ability of moral arguments about inequality advanced in a process of in 'democratic deliberation' to prove convincing.

Marxists who have taken account of the importance of the corporate form in enabling the concentration of capital have been ambivalent about taxation of corporate profits. Hilferding's perspective, that large-scale 'organised capitalism' paves the way for socialisation, suggested that the process should be encouraged rather than penalised through taxation. Schumpeter in contrast favoured higher taxes on monopoly profits and rents and the encouragement of entrepreneurialism, although he thought that in the long run the success of large-scale enterprises would eclipse the appeal of private property. O'Connor took the view that the power of monopoly capital enabled it to pass tax costs on to consumers through higher prices.

It seems that the analysis of taxation has posed difficult challenges to socialists precisely because of its centrality to the much wider range of issues raised by the visions of socialist transformation. As the concept of the fiscal state brings out, taxation is key to both the functions and form of the state, and a prime vector of its political power over social and economic relations. This was recognised by the prominence given to demands for progressive taxation in socialist political programs beginning with the Communist Manifesto. Marxism went further in insisting that progression was not just a matter of formal equal treatment of citizens, even taking into account 'ability to pay'. However, tying taxation to the fundamental claim that social justice and emancipation requires socialisation of property has been both essential to the socialist perspective, and particularly difficult in practice. This can be seen as symptomatic of the sweeping scope of Marxism's epistemology, spreading from its post-Hegelian philosophical roots to base itself on a materialist critique of political economy both grounded in and providing a perspective for practical social and political action.

References

Aaberge, Rolf, François Bourguignon, Andrea Brandolini, Francisco H.G. Ferreira, Janet C. Gornick, John Hills, Markus Jäntti, Stephen P. Jenkins, Eric Marlier, John Micklewright, Brian Nolan, Thomas Piketty, Walter J. Radermacher, Timothy M. Smeeding, Nicholas H. Stern, Joseph Stiglitz, and Holly Sutherland. 2017. Tony Atkinson and his Legacy. *Review of Income and Wealth* 63: 411–444.

Atkinson, Anthony B. 2015. *Inequality: What Can Be Done?* Cambridge, MA: Harvard University Press.

Atkinson, Anthony B., and J.E. Meade. 1993. *Alternatives to Capitalism: The Economics of Partnership*. New York/Basingstoke: St. Martin's Press in Association with the International Economic Association.

Atkinson, Anthony B., and Thomas Piketty. 2010. *Top Incomes. A Global Perspective*. Oxford: Oxford University Press.

Atkinson, Anthony B., and Martin Weale. 2000. James Edward Meade 1907–1995. *British Academy Lectures and Memoirs* 105.

Avineri, Shlomo. 1968. *The Social and Political Thought of Karl Marx*. Cambridge: Cambridge University Press.

Baran, Paul A., and Paul M. Sweezy. 1966. *Monopoly Capital: An Essay on the American Economic and Social Order*. New York/London: Monthly Review.

Bartolke, Klaus, and Ekkehard Kappler. 1989. Institutional Reform: The Future of Codetermination. In *Codetermination: A Discussion of Different Approaches*, ed. H.G. Nutzinger and J. Backhaus, 199–222. Berlin/Heidelberg: Springer.

Bauer, Otto. 1919. *Der Weg zum Sozialismus*. Berlin. Available at: https://www.marxists.org/deutsch/archiv/bauer/1919/weg/; excerpt in Bottomore and Goode 1978, 146–151.

Bernstein, Eduard. 1896. General Observations on Utopianism and Eclecticism. *Neue Zeit*, 28 October. Reprinted in Tudor and Tudor (1988), 73–81.

———. 1898. The Realistic and the Ideological Moments in Socialism. *Neue Zeit* nos. 34 and 39. Reprinted in Tudor and Tudor (1988), 244.

———. [1899] 1993. The Preconditions of Socialism. Cambridge: Cambridge University Press.

———. 1909. Zur Reichsfinanzaufbesserung. *Sozialistische Monatshefte* 12: 767–773. http://library.fes.de/cgi-bin/somo_mktiff.pl?year=1909&pdfs=1909_0767x1909_0768x1909_0769x1909_0770x1909_0771x1909_0772x1909_0773&verz=1909/1909_12.

Blum, Mark E., and William Smaldone. 2017. *Austro-Marxism: The Ideology of Unity, Volume 2: Changing the World: The Politics of Austro-Marxism*. Leiden: Brill.

Bottomore, Tom, and Patrick Goode. 1978. *Austro-Marxism: Texts Translated and Edited by Tom Bottomore & Patrick Goode*. Oxford: Clarendon Press.
Brandeis, Louis D. 1914. *Other People's Money, and How the Bankers Use It*. New York: Frederick A. Stokes.
Bukharin, Nikolai. 2003. *The Politics and Economics of the Transition Period*. London/New York: Routledge.
Bukharin, Nikolai, and Yevgeniy Preobrazhensky. 1919. *The ABC of Communism: A Popular Explanation of the Program of the Communist Party of Russia*. Trans. Eden and Cedar Paul. The Communist Party of Great Britain.
Campbell, John L. 1993. The State and Fiscal Sociology. *Annual Review of Sociology* 19: 163–185.
Chretien, Todd, and Vladimir Il'ich Lenin. [1918] 2015. State and Revolution. Chicago: Haymarket Books.
Czerwinska-Schupp, Ewa. 2016. *Otto Bauer 1881–1938: Thinker and Politician*. Leiden: Brill Academic Publishers.
Dominick, Raymond H. 1982. *Wilhelm Liebknecht and the Founding of the German Social Democratic Party*. Chapel Hill: The University of North Carolina Press.
Dukes, R. 2005. The Origins of the German System of Worker Representation. *Historical Studies in Industrial Relations* 19: 31–62.
Exner, Gudrun. 2004. Rudolf Goldscheid (1870–1931) and the Economy of Human Beings. *Vienna Yearbook of Population Research* 2: 283–301.
Fowkes, Ben. 1984. *Communism in Germany Under the Weimar Republic*. London: Palgrave Macmillan.
Gay, Peter. 1979. *The Dilemma of Democratic Socialism: Eduard Bernstein's Challenge to Marx*. New York: Octagon Press.
Gerstenberger, Heide. 1978. Kritische Anmerkungen zum Begriff des Steuerstaats. In *Krise des Steuerstaats? Widersprüche, Perspektiven, Ausweichstrategien. Leviathan Sonderheft 1/1978*, ed. R.R. Grauhan and R. Hickel, 51–57. Opladen: Westdeutscher Verlag.
Goldscheid, Rudolf. 1917a. Finanzwissenschaft und Soziologie. *Weltwirtschaftliches Archiv* 9: 253–263.
———. 1917b. *Staatssozialismus oder Staatskapitalismus. Ein finanzsoziologischer Beitrag zur Loesung des Staatsschulden-Problems*. Wien/Leipzig: Anzengruber. Available at: https://www.digitale-sammlungen.de/de/view/bsb11124275?page=9.
———. [1925] 1994. A Sociological Approach to Problems of Public Finance. In *Classics in the Theory of Public Finance*. 202–213. R. A. Musgrave and A. T. Peacock (eds.). Basingstoke: Macmillan. (Extracts from "Staat, Oeffentlichcher Haushalt und Gesellschaft. Wesen und Aufgaben der Finanzwissenschaften vom Standpunktc der Soziologie". *Handbuch der Finanzwissenschaft*, ed. W. Gerloff and F. Meisel, Vol 1, 146–155. Tübingen, 1925)
Grauhan, Rolf Richard, and Rudolf Hickel. 1978. Krise de Steuerstaats? – Widersprüche, Ausweichstrategien, Perspektiven staatlicher Politik. In *Krise des Steuerstaats? – Widersprüche, Ausweichstrategien, Perspektiven staatlicher Politik*, ed. R.R. Grauhan and R. Hickel, 7–33. Opladen: Westdeutscher Verlag.
Harberger, Arnold C. 1962. The Incidence of the Corporation Income Tax. *Journal of Political Economy* 70: 215–240.
Harsch, Donna. 1993. *German Social Democracy and the Rise of Nazism*. Chapel Hill: University of North Carolina Press.
———. 1998. The Iron Front. Weimar Social Democracy Between Tradition and Modernity. In *Between Reform and Revolution. German Socialism and Communism from 1840 to 1990*, ed. David E. Barclay and Eric D. Weitz, 252–291. New York/Oxford: Berghahn Books.
Harvey, David. 2018. *A Companion to Marx's Capital – Complete Edition*. London/New York: Verso Books.
Hayden, Grant M., and Matthew T. Bodie. 2021. *Reconstructing the Corporation. From Shareholder Primacy to Shared Governance*. Cambridge: Cambridge University Press.

Heinrich, Michael. 2012. *An Introduction to the Three Volumes of Karl Marx's Capital*. New York: Monthly Review Press.
Hilferding, R. 1910/1981. Finance Capital. A Study of the Latest Phase of Capitalist Development. London: Routledge.
Hilferding, Rudolf, and Paul M. Sweezy. 1949. *Karl Marx and the Close of His System and Böhm-Bawerk's Criticism of Marx*. New York: Augustus Kelley.
Himpele, Klemens, and Alexander Recht. 2009. Moglichkeiten und Grenzen von Steuerpolitik. *Prokla* 39: 9–26.
Hollander, Samuel. 2011. *Friedrich Engels and Marxian Political Economy*. Cambridge: Cambridge University Press.
Howson, Susan. 2000. James Meade. *The Economic Journal* 110: 122–145.
Ireland, David. 2019. What Marxist Tax Policies Actually Look Like. *Historical Materialism* 27: 188–221.
Jackson, Ben. 2012. Property-Owning Democracy – A Short History. In *Property-Owning Democracy: Rawls and Beyond*, ed. Martin F. O'Neill and Thad Williamson, 33–52. Chichester: Wiley-Blackwell.
Jessop, Bob. 1982. *The Capitalist State: Marxist Theories and Methods*. Oxford: Robertson.
Kautsky, Karl. 1907. *Ethics and the Materialist Conception of History*. Chicago: Charles H. Kerr.
Kautsky, K. 1909. Sozialdemokratische Finanzreform. *Die neue Zeit: Wochenschrift der deutschen Sozialdemokratie* 2: 229–233.
Kautsky, Karl, and Ben Lewis, eds. 2019. *Karl Kautsky on Democracy and Republicanism*. Leiden: Brill.
Kotsonis, Yanni. 2016. *States of Obligation: Taxes and Citizenship in the Russian Empire and Early Soviet Republic*. Toronto: University of Toronto Press.
Krätke, Michael. 1986. Sozialistische Steuerpolitik -gestern und morgen. *Prokla* 65: 34–70.
Krippner, Greta R. 2005. The Financialization of the American Economy. *Socio-Economic Review* 3: 173–208.
Lenin, V.I. 1963. *Collected Works: Volume 19, March – December 1913*. Moscow: Progress Publishers.
Levinger, Matthew. 2000. *Enlightened Nationalism: The Transformation of Prussian Political Culture, 1806–1848*. New York: Oxford University Press.
Lidtke, Vernon L. [1966] 2015. The Outlawed Party: Social Democracy in Germany 1878–1890. Princeton: Princeton University Press.
———. 2011. German Socialism and Social Democracy 1860–1900. In *The Cambridge History of Nineteenth-Century Political Thought*, ed. Gareth Stedman Jones and Gregory Claeys, 780–810. Cambridge: Cambridge University Press.
Loew, Raimund. 1979. The Politics of Austro-Marxism. *New Left Review* 118: 15–51.
Malle, Silvana. 2002. *The Economic Organization of War Communism 1918–1921*. Cambridge: Cambridge University Press.
Martin, IsaacW, Ajay K. Mehrotra, and Monica Prasad. 2009. *The New Fiscal Sociology: Taxation in Comparative and Historical Perspective*. Cambridge: Cambridge University Press.
Marx, Karl, and Friedrich Engels. 1968. *Selected Works*. Moscow: Progress Publishers.
McGaughey, Ewan. 2016. The Codetermination Bargains: The History of German Corporate and Labor Law. *The Columbia Journal of European Law* 23 (1): 135.
Meade, James E. [1964] 2012. Efficiency, Equality and the Ownership of Property. London: Routledge.
———. 1978. *The Structure and Reform of Direct Taxation*. London: Allen & Unwin for the Institute of Fiscal Studies.
Mehrotra, Ajay K. 2013. *Making the Modern American Fiscal State: Law, Politics, and the Rise of Progressive Taxation, 1877–1929*. New York: Cambridge University Press.
Milanović, Branko. 2016. *Global Inequality: A New Approach for the Age of Globalization*. Cambridge, MA: The Belknap Press of Harvard University Press.
Murphy, Liam, and Thomas Nagel. 2002. *The Myth of Ownership*. Oxford: Oxford University Press.

Musgrave, Richard A. 1992. Schumpeter's Crisis of the Tax State: An Essay in Fiscal Sociology. *Journal of Evolutionary Economics* 2: 89–113.

O'Connor, James. 1973. *The Fiscal Crisis of the State*. New York: St. Martin's Press.

Paine, Thomas, and Philip S. Foner. 1945. *The Complete Writings of Thomas Paine; With a Biographical Essay, and Notes and Introductions Presenting the Historical Background of Paine's Writings; Complete in Two Volumes*. New York: The Citadel Press.

Picciotto, Sol. 2020. Technocracy in the Era of Twitter. Between Intergovernmentalism and Supranational Technocratic Politics in Global Tax Governance. *Regulation & Governance* 15. https://doi.org/10.1111/rego.12351.

Piketty, Thomas. 2001. *Les Hauts Revenus en France au XXe siècle*. Paris: Grasset.

———. 2014. *Capital in the Twenty-First Century.* Trans. Arthur Goldhammer. Cambridge: Harvard University Press.

———. 2020. *Capital and Ideology*. Cambridge: Harvard University Press.

Prokla-Redaktion. 2009. Editorial- mit Steuern steuern. *Prokla* 39 (1): 2–6.

Renner, Karl. 1909. *Das arbeitende Volk und die Steuern: zum Kampfe gegen die Steuervorlagen der Regierung Bienerth-Bilinski*. Wien: Brand. Available at: https://digi.landesbibliothek.at/viewer/toc/AC03959009/1/.

Riazanov, David. 1927. *Karl Marx and Friedrich Engels*. New York: International Publishers.

Saez, Emmanuel, and Gabriel Zucman. 2019. *The Triumph of Injustice: How the Rich Dodge Taxes and How to Make Them Pay*. WW Norton.

Schorske, Carl E. [1955] 1983. German Social Democracy, 1905–1917: The Development of the Great Schism. Cambridge: Harvard University Press.

Schumpeter, Joseph A. [1918] 1991. "The Crisis of the Tax State." In *The Economics and Sociology of Capitalism/Joseph A. Schumpeter.* 99-140. Richard Swedberg (ed.). Princeton: Princeton University Press.

Schumpeter, Joseph. [1943] 1976. Capitalism, Socialism and Democracy. London: Routledge.

Scott, Helen. 2008. *The Essential Rosa Luxemburg. Reform or Revolution? and The Mass Strike*. Chicago: Haymarket Books.

Seidl, Christian. 1994. The Bauer-Schumpeter Controversy on Socialization. *History of Economic Ideas* 2: 41–69.

Seligman, Edwin R.A. 1908. Progressive Taxation in Theory and Practice. *American Economic Association Quarterly* 9 (4): 1–334.

———. 1914. *The Income Tax*. New York: Macmillan.

———. 1915. *Essays in Taxation*. New York: Macmillan.

Smaldone, William. 2008. *Confronting Hitler: German Social Democrats in Defense of the Weimar Republic, 1929–1933*. New York: Lexington Books.

SPD. 1913. *Protokoll des Parteitages der Sozialdemokratischen Partei Deutschlands zu Jena vom 19*. bis 20. September 1913, Berlin. Available at: http://library.fes.de/parteitage/index-pt-1910.html.

Stedman Jones, Gareth. 2016. *Karl Marx. Greatness and Illusion*. Cambridge: Harvard University Press.

Steenson, Gary P. 1989. Karl Kautsky: Early Assumptions, Preconceptions, and Prejudices. *International Journal of Comparative Sociology* 30 (1-2): 33–43.

Swedberg, Richard. 1991. *The Economics and Sociology of Capitalism/Joseph A. Schumpeter*. Ithaca: Cornell University Press.

Sweezy, Paul M. 1970. *The Theory of Capitalist Development*. New York/London: Monthly Review.

Tarschys, Daniel. 2001. Wealth, Values, Institutions: Trends in Government and Governance. In *Governance in the 21st Century*, 27–41. Paris: OECD.

Tudor, H., and J.M. Tudor. 1988. *Marxism and Social Democracy. The Revisionist Debate 1896–1898*. Cambridge: Cambridge University Press.

von Blumenthal, Karsten. 2008. Economic Theorist and 'Entrepreneur of Popularisation': Schumpeter as Finance Minister and Journalist. *The European Journal of the History of Economic Thought* 15: 641–671.

Webber, Carolyn, and Aaron Wildavsky. 1986. *A History of Taxation and Expenditure in the Western World*. New York: Simon and Schuster.

White, Stuart. 2009. 'Revolutionary liberalism'? The Philosophy and Politics of Ownership in the Post-war Liberal Party. *British Politics* 4 (2): 164–187.

Whiteside, Heather. 2021. Beyond Death and Taxes. Fiscal Studies and the Fiscal State. *Economy and Space* (Early access).

Winkler, Heinrich August. 1984. *Von der Revolution zur Stabilisierung. Arbeiter und Arbeiterbewegung in der Weimarer Republik 1918 bis 1924*. Berlin/Bonn: J.H.W. Dietz.

Sol Picciotto (BA Oxford, JD Chicago) is emeritus professor of Lancaster University, visiting professor at the Centre for Law, Regulation & Governance of the Global Economy (GLOBE) of Warwick University, Senior Fellow at the International Centre for Tax and Development, and Senior Research Fellow of the Institute of Advanced Legal Studies, University of London. He has taught at the Universities of Dar es Salaam (1964–8), Warwick (1968–1992), and Lancaster (1992–2007); and was Scientific Director of the Oñati International Institute for the Sociology of Law (2009–2011). He was joint founding editor and continues as an editor of *Social & Legal Studies*. He is the author of *International Business Taxation* (1992), *Regulating Global Corporate Capitalism* (2011), several co-written books, and many chapters and articles on various aspects of international business and economic law, and social theories of law and the state.

Chapter 6
The Conservative Approach to Taxation: The Complexity of Society, the Displacement of Voluntary Associations, and the Growth of the State

Gregory M. Collins

Abstract Although conservatives have harbored a variety of views on taxation, their approaches are interwoven by a number of key themes: an opposition to imposing rigid economic formulas on the complexity of social life; a sensitive awareness of the inverse relationship between the growth of the modern state's taxing powers and the displacement of voluntary associations; and a deep unease over the negative impact of wide-scale taxing schemes on social order. The spiritual vacuum created by the dissolution of a belief in a God-centered transcendent order and the decline in organized religion and traditional morality, combined with the rise of modern rationalism and its managerial and technocratic tendencies, has encouraged the modern state to practice social engineering in pursuit of abstract ideals, of which the power to tax was one of its most potent accomplices.

Keywords Conservatism · Taxation · Edmund Burke · Michael Oakeshott · Winston Churchill · Russell Kirk · Robert Nisbet · William F. Buckley · George F. Will · Thomas Sowell · Property · Voluntary associations · French revolution · Revenue · Socialism · Capitalism · Agricultural economy · Freedom · Wealth redistribution · Social engineering · Rationalism · Utopianism · Equality

The author would like to thank Ben Dormus, Dominic de Cogan, Annette Kirk, Felicia Kirk Flores, Cecilia Kirk Nelson, the Russell Kirk Center for Cultural Renewal, Lee Trepanier, Jason Jewell, Marjorie Jeffrey, Steven Hayward, and Luke C. Sheahan for their research support for this chapter.

G. M. Collins (✉)
Yale University, New Haven, CT, USA
e-mail: gregory.collins@yale.edu

R. F. van Brederode (ed.), *Political Philosophy and Taxation*,
https://doi.org/10.1007/978-981-19-1092-0_6

6.1 Introduction

Conservative political thinkers are not normally considered to be shrewd tax policy analysts. The purpose of this chapter, however, is to demonstrate that these thinkers have in fact offered distinctive commentary on the normative and empirical dimensions of taxation and their connections to wider philosophical debates about social order and public prosperity. The conservative approach to taxation is rooted in a number of shared assumptions about human nature and the role of the state in shaping fiscal policy. These include: man is a naturally social creature; society is marked by a rich variety in talents, experiences, and interests; the human mind is constrained by the limits of individual rationalism in penetrating the complex dimensions of society; man is a fallible being; utopian projects are hopeless and dangerous undertakings; and private property is a sacred institution that warrants sturdy protection by the state.

Conservative views on tax policy contain shades of difference, however, and may be classified in the following sense. The first strand of thought is exemplified by Edmund Burke and Winston Churchill and reflects a blend of Aristotelian political philosophy with Oliver Wendell Holmes' famous dictum that "[t]axes are what we pay for civilized society."[1] Because man is a social creature, he was best understood as part of a whole, such as a political community or a state; and this community, and the individuals who comprised it, existed for some teleological purpose, which for Aristotle was happiness grounded in virtue. The aim of a state was to promote conceptions of public virtue to help its subjects reach this final condition. Taxation, if carefully implemented, was therefore an important tool to both finance the state's administrative responsibilities and facilitate the well-being of its members.

The second strand adheres more closely to the classical liberal strand of conservatism and is represented by Michael Oakeshott. Although he embraced many of Burke's presuppositions about political life, Oakeshott endorsed a conception of the state that cautioned against the collective pursuit of a telos in a commonwealth. He articulated this view most powerfully in his theoretical distinction between civil association, a mode of social organization in which individuals and groups were bound by shared procedural rules, and an enterprise association, a different mode that aspired as a unified body to achieve a substantive aim. A civil association embodied Oakeshott's ideal vision of a political community. Hence the purpose of taxation was to generate the financial resources necessary to ensure the basic administrative functions of this form of association and little more.

The third conservative strand of taxation communicates a stronger antagonism toward the basic idea that a state should possess the authority to extract wealth from private individuals and institutions. Represented by Robert Nisbet, this school lays the sharpest emphasis on the close connection between the growth in a government's taxing powers and the expansion of the modern state, a trend that in Nisbet's

[1] See Holmes' dissent in *Compañia General de Tabacos de Filipinas v. Collector of Internal Revenue,* 275 U.S. 87 (1927).

judgment led to at least two dreadful consequences: the government's displacement of voluntary associations as the primary custodian of the people's welfare, and the symbiosis between taxation and war. The Nisbettian school also flows from the Aristotelian tradition because it stresses the importance of human association as the embodiment of the natural sociability of man, but it departs from Aristotelianism by holding that associations are gravely threatened by the very existence of the state—a state that for Aristotle served as the essential political unit of a society.

Such typologies overlap to a certain extent, for each has conveyed deep apprehensions over the aggrandizement of the modern state. Yet it would be misguided to collapse any qualitative distinctions between them. Consequently, the following analysis will examine the schools' common principles before drawing out their areas of intellectual tension.

We should be reminded of the following provisos before proceeding. First, the views of these thinkers (and the political calculus in the case of statesmen) may have evolved over time. Oakeshott, for instance, exhibited socialist and rationalist sympathies in his youth before shifting to conservatism later in his life; and Churchill was a member of the Liberal Party for two decades. "Conservative" as a political classification did not even exist in Burke's day. Second, the cultural, economic, and political contexts in which each thinker wrote varied in important ways, and sometimes considerably so; Burke expressed his thoughts on taxes during an epoch before the full burst of mass industrialization, while the rest of the thinkers discussed in this chapter witnessed its widespread effects. Third, the primary vocation of the thinkers ranged from statesmen (Burke and Churchill) to university professors (Oakeshott and Nisbet) to independent scholars and journalists (Russell Kirk and William F. Buckley Jr.). At various times, they possessed different responsibilities, faced different audiences, and bore different institutional restraints and pressures commensurate with the demands of their professions.[2] Fourth, because these men did not write systematic treatises on taxation, one is inevitably compelled to merge together their scattered passages and remarks on the subject in order to distill their underlying themes.[3]

Nevertheless, such thinkers were all united in their attempt to guide public opinion toward their most cherished convictions on politics and society, a mission that naturally intersected with tax policy. What ultimately threads together their approach to taxation is a sensitive awareness of the limits in imposing rigid economic formulas on the complexity of social life; the collective impact of secularism and rationalism on the augmentation of the modern state and the subsequent decline in voluntary

[2] It is plausible that such institutional restraints influenced the pragmatic substance of their views on taxation. If Kirk, Oakeshott, or Nisbet had been elected representatives in the national legislature, for instance, perhaps they would have supported particular tax policies similar to the ones endorsed by Burke or Churchill, or perhaps not. Similarly, if Burke or Churchill had never served in government, perhaps they would have framed their views on taxation in a different manner.

[3] This chapter will avoid discussion of the thinkers' personal finances. In addition, please consult biographies of these thinkers for greater detail on the historical context behind their thoughts on taxation and public affairs discussed herein.

associations; the dissolution of a belief in a God-centered transcendent order; and the latent dangers in the state's power of monetary extraction to unsettle the social equipoise of communities in pursuit of abstract ideals. From the perspective of conservatives, commonwealths were imbued with many layers of institutions, experiences, and aims that escaped the narrow comprehension of the legislator and tax collector.

6.2 Foundations

6.2.1 Man as a Social Creature and the Importance of Community

The chief premise connecting the various schools of conservative thought on taxation is that man is a naturally social creature. Rather than conceiving human beings as free and equal individuals bound together only by political consent, the conservative view sees man as part of a broader weave of associations, groups, and institutions that cannot be reduced to mere contractual relations.

Burke (1730–1797) offered a vigorous defense of this idea in the *Reflections on the Revolution in France*, his famous epistle that attacked the French Revolution's war on custom and privilege. In contrast to French revolutionaries, who in his interpretation framed man as disconnected individuals in an abstract state of nature who joined together to form a political community to secure their pre-political natural rights, Burke painted men as possessing inherent social natures who held deep attachments to their kinship networks in political society. "One of the first symptoms they discover of a selfish and mischievous ambition, is a profligate disregard of a dignity which they partake with others," Burke remarked in the *Reflections*, referring to the revolutionaries. "To be attached to the subdivision, to love the little platoon we belong to in society, is the first principle (the germ as it were) of public affections. It is the first link in the series by which we proceed towards a love to our country and to mankind" (Mitchell 2007, 97). According to Burke, French ideologues yearned to rupture the embedded social connections, institutions, and traditions that had built up French civilization throughout the centuries and in their place manufacture a new conception of atomistic man free from any prior allegiances to kin, community, and nation.

Robert Nisbet (1913–1996) laid a sharp accent on this insight in post-World War Two America, during a time when the global conflict between capitalism and communism engendered a powerful libertarian conception of society that pitted the state against the individual. Unlike libertarians, however, Nisbet framed the key division as the state against group association. "The real conflict in modern political history has not been, as is so often stated, between State and individual," he observed in *The Quest for Community*, "but between State and social group" (Nisbet 2010, 100). Even more, "Unlike the State, which rests upon force, the social groups in society rest upon the reciprocal principle of friendship (*amicitia*). The principle of mutual responsibility is the very structure of these associations. Man is a social being by nature and these associations are but manifestations of his instinct for sociability" (Nisbet 2010, 118). The release of man from his traditional associations and the consecration of individual autonomy in modernity fueled debilitating psychological and social consequences, such as isolation, alienation, and disenchantment (Nisbet 2010, 7).

Conservatives have therefore observed that *community*, whose elemental unit was the family, was the social structure that gave men and women a sense of purpose and belonging, material welfare, and firm protection against state encroachment. Describing Nisbet's insights into the loss of community in modernity, Russell Kirk (1918–1994) wrote, "The most conspicuous result of the revolutionary destruction of traditional society—a result, too, of mass industrialism—has been the creation of the Lonely Crowd: a mass of individuals without real community, aware that they matter to no one, and often convinced that nothing else matters" (Kirk 2001, 483). Shorn from the ties of local community, this mass of faceless individuals could then be manipulated by enterprising rulers to serve their self-serving aims clothed in benevolent rhetoric. As Kirk counseled, "Free community is the alternative to compulsive collectivism" (Kirk 2001, 473).

Because conservative thinkers have assigned great weight to the idea that man is naturally sociable, they have resisted the temptation to assess the merits of taxation through the lens of a doctrinaire form of individualism. Whereas conservatives have sympathized with the idea of the individual to some extent—through conceptions of constitutional liberty, rational agency, and the ethical primacy of character formation—they did not transform a respect for the individual into a hardened ideology unto itself. Such thinkers imagined the goals of public policy, such as taxation, through the broader framework of what consequences it generated for society as well as for the individual. In other words, their attitudes toward taxation were not determined solely by whether taxes enhanced or diminished individual autonomy.

Moreover, as we shall see, conservatives were quite conscious of the tendency of governments in modernity to leverage their taxing powers to take on crucial social obligations that were previously fulfilled by voluntary associations and groups in local communities, including, most importantly, the family. Kirk lamented the collectivist desire to "have the political state assume nearly all the responsibilities which the family once possessed" (Kirk 1957a, 46). Consequently, conservatives' appreciation for the natural sociability of man and their stress on community were closely related to their deep unease over the covetous tentacles of the modern state, as manifested in its vast powers of taxation.

6.2.2 Variety and Complexity of Man and Society

Although conservatives have discerned in human beings an instinct for sociability, they have also recognized that individuals and social groups hold many differences. The importance of *variety* is thus integral to the conservative disposition toward taxation. According to this view, while all individuals were equal under God, they were unequal in many other respects, including in experiences, talents, abilities, skills, knowledge, social status, and family pedigree. "In all societies, consisting of various descriptions of citizens, some description must be uppermost," Burke wrote in the *Reflections*, defending the idea of an aristocracy. "The levellers therefore only change and pervert the natural order of things" (Mitchell 2007, 100). It followed that differences in wealth, among a myriad of social and economic indicators, were reflections of naturally forming distinctions among human beings. Robert Nisbet gave voice to this keystone of conservative sociology in the twentieth century. "Variations among individuals, in strength, intelligence, age, aspiration, ability of whatever kind, and aptitude, will always tend toward the creation of inequality of result," he insisted in *Twilight of Authority* (Nisbet 2000, 191). Equality under God for conservatives did not mandate equality of condition.

Similarly, the many distinctions among man disclosed the *complex nature* of society. "The nature of man is intricate; the objects of society are of the greatest possible complexity; and, therefore, no simple disposition or direction of power can be suitable either to man's nature, or to the quality of his affairs," Burke observed in the *Reflections* (Mitchell 2007, 112). More than a century later Winston Churchill (1874–1965) delivered this classic Burkean argument when highlighting the chasm between British Prime Minister H.H. Asquith's rationalist certitudes and the ambiguities of reality:

> The world, nature, human beings, do not move like machines. The edges are never clear-cut, but always frayed. Nature never draws a line without smudging it. Conditions are so variable, episodes so unexpected, experiences so conflicting, that flexibility of judgment and a willingness to assume a somewhat humbler attitude towards external phenomena may well play their part in the equipment of a modern Prime Minister (Churchill 1991, 83).

As a practicing statesman, Churchill, like Burke, was keenly aware that the mysteries of complex society often transcended the boundaries of rulers' cognitive faculties.

Conservatives have not only recognized the layered and impenetrable divisions of complex society. They have also conveyed an "[a]ffection for the proliferating variety and mystery of human existence…", as Russell Kirk wrote in *The Conservative Mind* (Kirk 2001, 8). The variations among individuals in experience and interest, preference and vocation, should not simply be tolerated but valued, as long as they remained within the moral parameters of civilized conduct. Because society was not a detached monolith but a textured community of men and women embedded in a web of associations, social groups were diverse as well, encompassing religious, educational, industrial, civic, and philanthropic institutions. Attempts by the state to equalize society by eliminating or threatening these structures of social attachment militated against the vast complexities of man and association—complexities that were constituent to the human condition.

From the conservative point of view, then, differences among individuals, including social and economic differences, did not necessarily denote injustice. Such differences might simply reflect the mixed variety of tastes, preferences, and interests of human beings, rather than the effects of systematic mistreatment or political malfeasance. "If some social categories of people are not equally represented in particular occupations, institutions or income brackets, that is regarded as someone's fault that the supposedly natural equality of outcomes has been thwarted," Thomas Sowell wrote. "This is the seemingly invincible fallacy behind much that is said and done" to correct imbalances in the distribution of resources and outcomes (Sowell 2019, 216). The exercise of arbitrary power is anathema to the conservative disposition, but the distinctions that have emerged among human beings cannot all be attributed to unfairness.

6.2.3 The Limits of Rationalism

Because human beings possessed many differences in preference, experience, skills, and background, and because society was a complex organism irreducible to simplistic precepts of knowledge, conservatives have harbored a great distrust in the powers of rationalism to legislate the intricate dimensions of human affairs. Logical precision thus bore heavy limitations in governing men and women compared to the steady diffusion of wisdom built up throughout generations. This connection between rationalism and taxation is fundamental to understanding the epistemic assumptions behind the conservative disposition toward taxation.

The most destructive type of rationalism conservatives have castigated is not the Aristotelian-Thomistic conception of the rational man but rather Enlightenment rationalism and its radical strands. Burke levelled a tenacious attack on this philosophical school in his commentary on the French Revolution, in which he excoriated the rationalist pretensions of French revolutionaries seeking to socially engineer French society in accord with their utopian visions. As he wrote in *Appeal from the New to the Old Whigs* (1791):

> An ignorant man, who is not fool enough to meddle with his clock, is however sufficiently confident to think he can safely take to pieces, and put together at his pleasure, a moral machine of another guise importance and complexity, composed of far other wheels, and springs, and balances, and counteracting and co-operating powers. Men little think how immorally they act in rashly meddling with what they do not understand (Marshall and Bryant 2015, 472).

Burke detected this blind faith in rationality in the minds of French ideologues, which in his view tempted them to dismiss the distilled insights of the many and overstate their level of comprehension of society. "They have no respect for the wisdom of others; but they pay it off by a very full measure of confidence in their own," he quipped in the *Reflections*, referring to the revolutionaries (Mitchell 2007, 138).

Michael Oakeshott (1901–1990) amplified this criticism of Enlightenment rationalism in the twentieth century. In his famous essay "Rationalism in Politics," he wrote that the modern rationalist believed in "unhindered human 'reason'" as the "infallible guide in political activity" (Oakeshott 1991, 8). The seeming infallibility of reason inspired the rationalist to embrace the "politics of perfection" and the "politics of uniformity" (Oakeshott 1991, 9). The rationalist did not seek the best remedy in imperfect circumstances but a utopian solution for all social ills, sanctioning rigid formulas for the various segments of complex society regardless of time or place. As he explained, "Political activity is recognized as the imposition of a uniform condition of perfection upon human conduct" (Oakeshott 1991, 10). Oakeshott identified "a single tax"—referring to the land value tax, an idea closely associated with Henry George—as one of a number of policies that exemplified this rationalist mindset (Oakeshott 1991, 11).

The rationalist outlook therefore disregarded the collective reason that slowly accreted throughout generations, as embodied in immemorial customs, traditions, and institutions. Burke captured this insight in his praise of the prescriptive traditions of the British constitution. The "individual is foolish…but the species is wise, and, when time is given to it, as a species it always acts right," he observed (Burke 1869, 147). Similarly, Oakeshott averred that the rationalist is the "*enemy* of authority, of prejudice, of the merely traditional, customary or habitual" (Oakeshott 1991, 6). The rationalist did not necessarily renounce experience *in toto*, but the experience he did rely on was exclusively his own (Oakeshott 1991, 6).

The modern rationalist's exploded confidence in his own intellect, combined with his repudiation of accumulated wisdom, reflected an impulse to concoct new schemes for remaking society and reject gradual alterations to existing institutions. His "disposition makes both destruction and creation easier for him to understand and engage in," Oakeshott wrote, "than acceptance or reform." For he "always prefers the invention of a new device to making use of a current and well-tried expedient" (Oakeshott 1991, 8). Political innovation without self-restraint could gravely disturb the settled foundations of a prosperous society.

According to the conservative orientation, prudence, which Burke called the "first of all virtues" (Mitchell 2007, 113), was the essential guide in steering this process of reform. Prudence was not synonymous with a sluggish meliorism or opposition to change. It was rather a quality of disposition keen on weighing social complexities and competing alternatives, and then arriving at a firm moral judgment that sought to reform—or preserve—existing institutions in pursuit of an aim without disrupting social order. This judgment typically required moderate and selective approaches to public policy rather than sweeping and absolutist changes to the underlying political and social structures of the commonwealth. "Society must alter, for prudent change is the means of social preservation…" Kirk taught in the *Conservative Mind*, "but a statesman must take Providence into his calculations, and a statesman's chief virtue, according to Plato and Burke, is prudence" (Kirk 2001, 9). Prudence served as an indispensable check against the temptations of rationalist design.

6.2.4 Man as a Fallible Being and the Impossibility of Utopian Society

Conservatives' attention to the limits of rationalism is part of their deeper moral and religious understanding of man as a fallible and sinful creature. Although men and women were created in the image and likeness of God, they were nevertheless prone to error, folly, and misjudgment. They were therefore required to obey a divinely inspired moral order. Because this sinful nature was universal and inescapable, attempts to perfect man through grand utopian schemes were bound to fail and would often lead to despotism.

Burke's censure of the French Revolution rested on this conception of man and his belief that the Revolution's canonization of reason positioned man above God as the final source of morality. And reason released from divine judgment degenerated into tyranny. "...[I]f no supreme ruler exists, wise to form, and potent to enforce, the moral law, there is no sanction to any contract, virtual or even actual, against the will of prevalent power," he asserted in *Appeal from the New to the Old Whigs* (Marshall and Bryant 2015, 442). During the impeachment proceedings of Warren Hastings, Burke recognized the authority of "one great, immutable, pre-existent law" that did "not arise from our conventions or compacts." For "[e]very good gift is of God; all power is of God; and He who has given the power and from whom it alone originates, will never suffer the exercise of it to be practised upon any less solid foundation than the power itself" (Marshall 1991, 350).

Consequently, schemes to perfect the human condition and establish a utopian society were fanciful and had to be curbed by firm restraints. As Burke wrote in October 1789 to French correspondent Charles-Jean-François Depont, to whom he would later address the *Reflections*:

> There is, by the essential fundamental constitution of things, a radical infirmity in all human contrivances; and the weakness is often so attached to the very perfection of our political mechanism, that some defect in it,—something that stops short of its principle,—something that controls, that mitigates, that moderates it,—becomes a necessary corrective to the evils that the theoretic perfection would produce (Fitzwilliam and Bourke 1844, 117).[4]

Human artifice necessarily bore imperfections because of the sinfulness and frailty of man. From Burke's point of view, however, French revolutionaries vowed to introduce a new conception of man and society that casually disregarded this enduring truth of classical and Judeo-Christian thought.

It is this devilish appeal of perfectionism that has motivated twentieth-century conservatives to caution intellectuals and statesmen against attempting to create heaven on earth, or what William F. Buckley (1925–2008) liked to describe as "immanentizing the eschaton" in the spirit of Eric Voegelin (Buckley 2015, 237).[5] The founding mission statement of Buckley's conservative publication *National Review* in 1955 declared that the "profound crisis of our era" was "the conflict between the Social Engineers, who seek to adjust mankind to conform with scientific utopias, and the disciples of Truth, who defend the organic moral order." For the "century's most blatant force of satanic utopianism" was "communism" (Buckley 1955).

[4] Note that Burke observed in the *Reflections* that insofar as man can be perfected, it was through God, not social engineering. See Mitchell (2007, 148).

[5] For Voegelin, see his essay "The New Science of Politics" in Henningsen (2000, 75–241).

A closely related species of immanentization, socialism, was the object of Churchill's wrath spanning his political life. Although he supported selective schemes of national social insurance as a statesman, Churchill loathed the oppressive manner in which socialist economies suffocated the entrepreneurial capacities of private individuals and advanced a wholly unrealistic vision of society. In his infamous "Gestapo Speech" during the 1945 general election, he thundered, "There is to be one State to which all are to be obedient in every act of their lives. This State is to be the arch-employer, the arch-planner, the arch-administrator and ruler, and the arch-caucus-boss." For socialism was "inseparably interwoven with Totalitarianism and the abject worship of the State" (Cannadine 1989, 273). In a later address he drew attention to the campaign by Socialists to "drag their long-term fads and wavy Utopias across the practical path of need and duty" (Gilbert 1991, 847). Such resistance to the hazardous seduction of socialism in post-World War Two Europe captured his animus toward utopianism.

Socialism, then, was one of the ways that fallible human beings aspired to substitute a God-centered society with a human one based on the false promise of unassisted reason. In order to preserve this God-centered society, Russell Kirk affirmed that the first pillar of conservatism was a "[b]elief in a transcendent order, or body of natural law, which rules society as well as conscience. Political problems, at bottom, are religious and moral problems" (Kirk 2001, 8). From the conservative point of view, socialism and communism repudiated this idea of transcendent order by replacing the eternal compass of divine authority with the potent pretensions of secular rationalism.

We may compare this insight with Oakeshott's celebrated conception of conservatism as a "disposition" rather than a "creed" or a "doctrine." Even though Oakeshott, unlike Kirk, held that conservatism—specifically the conservative disposition—did not necessarily prescribe a faith in a providential order or natural law (Oakeshott 1991, 423), he, like Kirk, thought it was marked by a keen sense of human finitude:

> To be conservative…is to prefer the familiar to the unknown, to prefer the tried to the untried, fact to mystery, the actual to the possible, the limited to the unbounded, the near to the distant, the sufficient to the superabundant, the convenient to the perfect, present laughter to utopian bliss. Familiar relationships and loyalties will be preferred to the allure of more profitable attachments; to acquire and to enlarge will be less important than to keep, to cultivate and to enjoy; the grief of loss will be more acute than the excitement of novelty or promise (Oakeshott 1991, 408/9).

The elements of preservation and restraint in conservatism cooled legislative or administrative urges to fundamentally alter society. The conservative disposition was not against reform, as long as it was executed in a gradual and deliberate manner and did not unsettle existing social order. Yet change for the sake of novelty and in pursuit of utopian objectives was a futile and perilous endeavor.

Oakeshott underscored this principle in his broader moral philosophy. In his essay "The Tower of Babel,"[6] Oakeshott warned against attempts to find a "short cut to heaven" (Oakeshott 1991, 465). The utopian mission to reify abstract ideals in society threatened the settled habits of moral life. As he explained, the "penalty" of the "pursuit of perfection" is "a chaos of conflicting ideals, the disruption of a common life, and the reward is the renown which attaches to monumental folly" (Oakeshott 1991, 466). According to the conservative perspective, the drive for perfection on earth—whether accelerated by extensive taxing programs or by any other state mechanism—was not a noble undertaking; it was a license for bloody oppression.

6.2.5 Sanctity of Property

Finally, the conservative disposition has cherished property as a sacrosanct possession that warrants special protection by the rule of law. Applying this belief to both mobile and immobile property, but especially to the latter, conservatives have understood landed property to meet crucial functions in a political community: it provided stability and moderation to the vagaries of society, particularly commercial society; it was the traditional source of inherited wealth and thereby served to strengthen families; it was the repository of ancient moral values; its proprietors were less likely to support political schemes that would upset social order and defy the common good; and the security of estates served as a necessary check against encroachment by the central state on the people's constitutional liberties.

Burke's appreciation for the sanctity of property was illustrated by his vehement attack on the French Revolution's expropriation of Gallican Church property, which was part of the movement's financial scheme to pay off the national debt. "...[I]t is to the property of the citizen, and not to the demands of the creditor of the state, that the first and original faith of civil society is pledged," he wrote in the *Reflections*. "The claim of the citizen is prior in time, paramount in title, superior in equity" (Mitchell 2007, 157). For the "property of the nation is the nation," Burke asserted in *First Letter on a Regicide Peace*, a precept he thought was placed in the crosshairs by French ideologues (McDowell 2005, 252). This act of usurpation violated the principle of prescription Burke treasured in his thought: settled possessions acquired an authority over time and merited a presumption of legitimacy against innovative schemes seeking to confiscate them (Lucas 1968).

According to Burke, then, the protection and accumulation of property—particularly inherited property, as exemplified by his defense of primogeniture (Marshall and Bryant 2015, 433)—performed a number of vital functions in a nation: it served as an essential pillar of social order and commercial activity; it preserved continuity

[6] This essay was first published in 1948. He wrote another paper with the same title that was published later.

from generation to generation; it built up a leadership class of aristocrats prepared to pursue the public welfare in government; and it prevented the concentration of political power in the Crown (Mitchell 2007, 102/3; Collins 2020, chs. 11 and 12).

Kirk endorsed a similar conception of property in his political and economic thought in the twentieth century. In *The Intelligent Woman's Guide to Conservatism* (1957), he wrote that the "rights of property are ancient and essential human rights." Kirk continued: "Unless property is secure, there can be no civilized life; for without the right to keep what is one's own, and to add to that if possible, there can be no leisure, no material improvement, no culture worthy of the name" (Kirk 1957a, 67/8). Property therefore must be safeguarded from the grasping hands of the state. "The existence of property, above the most meagre personal possessions, is possible only when some form of political order ensures that a man may keep what is his own," he maintained (Kirk 1957a, 68).

The possession of property served both material and moral purposes. Kirk remarked that the institution of private property

> has been one of the most powerful instruments for teaching men and women responsibility, for providing motives to integrity, for supporting religion and general culture, for raising mankind above the level of a simple drudge, for giving us leisure to think and freedom to act with moderation and prudence (Kirk 1957a, 69).

Property not only held a sacred status but also provided indispensable utilities, such as the encouragement of moral conduct and the liberty for leisure.

Michael Oakeshott, representing the classical liberal school of conservatism,[7] similarly affirmed the importance of property in a political community. The "freedom enjoyed in the right to own private property" (Oakeshott 1991, 391), as well as freedom of association, he stated in "The Political Economy of Freedom," were two of the most prized freedoms of a commonwealth.[8] The "institution of property most favourable to liberty is, unquestionably, a right to private property least qualified by arbitrary limits and exclusions," he wrote, "for it is by this means only that the maximum diffusion of the power that springs from ownership may be achieved" (Oakeshott 1991, 393).

Even though the conservative mindset has cherished the sanctity of property rights, it has not gone as far as strands of libertarian thought in denouncing any taking of property consistent with the rule of law as legalized theft. The baseline conservative attitude may rather be framed in the following sense: if the taking of property was necessary to discharge some critical function of government, such as to generate revenue to finance its basic administrative duties, the state should do so in the least intrusive way possible and without causing disruption to the broader body politic. In the end, the conservative outlook is governed by the commitment to protect property rights against schemes to redistribute property in the name of

---

[7] Paul Franco has characterized Oakeshott's political philosophy as a distinctive kind of liberalism blending Hegelianism and Hobbesianism. See Franco (1990).

[8] Oakeshott reviewed Professor Henry C. Simons' book *Economic Policy for a Free Society* in this essay.

promoting abstract conceptions of the social welfare.[9] Public prosperity and public justice were not possible without a society rooted in good order—and good order was made possible in large part by the stability and security of property rights.

6.3 Two Common Principles of Taxation

6.3.1 Taxation Should Be Limited in Scope and Remain Free of Excess

Aware of these intellectual foundations of the conservative mindset on the subject of taxation, we may now draw out two of the most important principles of tax policy that are shared by the thinkers discussed in this chapter: first, taxes should be limited in scope; and second, tax policy should not be implemented for the purpose of social engineering. The following two subsections will explore these common principles before probing the tensions in conservative thought regarding a state's permissible range of the taxing power.

Insofar as taxation was necessary for civilized society, writers sharing the conservative disposition have stressed that taxes must be limited in scope in order to prevent excessive and arbitrary taxing schemes. This attitude stemmed from many of the shared insights into human nature and the fallibility of man outlined earlier. Because society was a complex organism that involved a great multitude of individuals, abilities, preferences, and stations in life, stretching the net of tax policy over all segments of civil society overlooked their many shades and variations. The powers of rational cognition therefore faced inherent limitations in fully comprehending such complexities, making it even more difficult for the legislator and administrator to enact taxes that would bring about commensurate fairness and justice—not to mention ensure that goods would flow as vigorously and efficiently as they would under a system of free enterprise.

Even if civilized society required taxes, then, it also required the preservation of a wide zone of constitutional and economic liberty. This environment would allow consumers and producers to satisfy their particular market preferences and to balance the shifting proportions of stock and want in society. According to this line of reasoning, taxing regimes guided by selection rather than sweeping arbitrary meddling could promote public virtue while still reserving a capacious sphere of agency for individuals and groups in a political community.

Burke's defense of a free internal grade in *Thoughts and Details on Scarcity* (1795), his primary economic tract, illustrated these canons of the conservative mindset on taxation. Written at a time of social and economic dislocation in agricultural England, Burke cautioned against state interference in the domestic grain

[9] Do note that even this formulation contains exceptions. Consider the Housing Act 1980, passed under Margaret Thatcher and the Conservative Party.

market, a particularly fragile sector of Britain's economy, to mitigate the struggling condition of the laboring classes. "Of all things, an indiscreet tampering with the trade of provisions is the most dangerous," he admonished in *Thoughts and Details*, "and it is always worst in the time when men are most disposed to it: that is, in the time of scarcity" (McDowell 2005, 120). Burke believed that the voluntary employment contracts and the competitive price system would facilitate the circulation of grain throughout England with greater effect than interventionist measures proposed at the time, such as the enhanced regulation of labor contracts, the implementation of new minimum wage laws and price controls, and the establishment of new public granaries.[10]

Burke criticized such proposals through his conception of taxation:

> There is an implied contract, much stronger than any instrument or article of agreement, between the labourer in any occupation and his employer—that the labour, so far as that labour is concerned, shall be sufficient to pay to the employer a profit on his capital, and a compensation for his risk; in a word, that the labour shall produce an advantage equal to the payment. Whatever is above that, is a direct *tax*; and if the amount of that tax be left to the will and pleasure of another, it is an *arbitrary tax* (McDowell 2005, 123).

The combination of direct taxes and arbitrary taxes—such as those decreed by magistrates—inflicted extraneous financial burdens on employers and laborers that suppressed the spirit of equity that naturally emerged from this implied contract.

Yet in Burke's judgment, the suggested regulations would induce precisely this outcome by empowering justices of the peace to enact a levy on labor contracts according to their personal discretion. The crucial question, then, was whether private employment arrangements should be determined by public officials or by those actually engaged in the art of husbandry:

> The questions arising on this scheme of arbitrary taxation are these—Whether it is better to leave all dealing, in which there is no force or fraud, collusion or combination, entirely to the persons mutually concerned in the matter contracted for; or to put the contract into the hands of those, who can have none, or a very remote interest in it, and little or no knowledge of the subject (McDowell 2005, 123).

Burke answered in the former by anticipating Hayekian insights into the limits of rationality: private market participants possessed a treasure of knowledge about their particular preferences and circumstances that lied far beyond the comprehension of the magistrate. Arbitrary taxation fueled by the discretionary judgment of public officials would threaten the virtue of mutual advantage inherent in free labor contracts.

This principle carried particular importance in Burke's age because the agricultural economy included many variations of labor, spanning from able-bodied men to infirm men to women with domestic responsibilities to children. Such diversity exposed how rigid rules and arbitrary taxes "never can provide the just proportions between earning and salary on the one hand, and nutriment on the other..."

[10] Consult Collins (2020) for discussion of *Thoughts and Details on Scarcity* and other aspects of Burke's economic thought.

(McDowell 2005, 128). Rather, "interest, habit, and the tacit convention, that arise from a thousand nameless circumstances, produce a *tact* that regulates without difficulty, what laws and magistrates cannot regulate at all" (McDowell 2005, 128).

These comments marked Burke's belief that legislators and administrators were hampered by the constraints of knowledge and power; and that state interventions in private market activity, if not tempered by institutional restraints and legislators' own awareness of the fallibility of man, could lead to schemes ruinous to society. "My opinion is against an over doing of any sort of administration, and more especially against this most momentous of all meddling on the part of authority; the meddling with the subsistence of the people," he concluded in *Thoughts and Details* (McDowell 2005, 145).

Living in a post-agricultural age, Winston Churchill, on a theoretical level, advocated a similar measure of tax restraint throughout his political life. In 1908 he pronounced that "taxation…is a gross and unredeemed evil." Churchill continued:

> …what are the root principles of British taxation…? They are very simple. A child can learn them; only a fool can misunderstand them. Here they are. First, no more taxes than are necessary; secondly, what taxes you have let them be substantial and effective taxes; thirdly, change them as seldom as possible; fourthly, let the taxes be such that the whole yield of them goes to the public Exchequer, and that there is no opportunity at any point for private persons to get an advantage or profit out of those taxes (James 1974a, 923).

Spanning to his post-World War II years, Churchill was arguing to constrain the scope of government regulations and stimulate the free market. Fighting the socialist temptations of the Labour Party as leader of the Conservative opposition, he declared in 1947, "Destroy the free market, and you create a black market; you overwhelm the people with laws and regulations, and you induce a general disrespect of law..." Furthermore, "You may try to destroy wealth, and find that all you have done is to increase poverty."[11]

In his more philosophical ruminations, Churchill thus believed that the range of tax policy should be tightly bound and avoid grand social experimentation. As we shall see, however, Churchill in practice did make strategic use of tax policy as Chancellor of the Exchequer to serve humane and political objectives, which demonstrated how his aversion to meddlesome taxing schemes in theory was disciplined by the empirical realities of British politics and industrial society.

Like Burke and Churchill, Russell Kirk expressed opposition to intrusive taxes. In his high school economics textbook *Economics: Work and Prosperity* (1989), he listed "[e]xcessive taxation" as the first negative consequence of the manifold ways that governments have "done harm" to economic systems (Kirk 1989a, 243). When taxes on property, income, and real property become "too heavy," he wrote, they initiate a cascade of repercussions: individuals and companies are discouraged from saving money that would otherwise be used to replace capital goods or invest in new capital goods; production of goods and services slows down; and the diminished

[11] "Economic Situation," vol. 434, Hansard, UK Parliament, 12 March 1947, 1349. Available at https://api.parliament.uk/historic-hansard/commons/1947/mar/12/economic-situation, accessed March 11, 2021.

supply of goods triggers a rise in prices and creates more difficulties for consumers to meet their needs. Kirk continued:

> Then, perhaps…the government, to satisfy public demands, tries to provide for people's wants by furnishing food and other goods to the poor at low prices or free. To do this, taxes must be raised. When taxes are increased, there is still less saving of capital. The economy continues to spiral downward, perhaps toward national bankruptcy (Kirk 1989a, 243).

Kirk observed soon thereafter that "excessive regulation" could "kill an economy" by employing a "host of inspectors, tax collectors, and government regulators" to tinker with the free enterprise system (Kirk 1989a, 244).

Kirk was a resilient defender of private property rights, particularly landed property rights; and he grew to appreciate the virtues of the free market system, while always remaining alert to its imperfections, throughout his intellectual life (Jewell 2020). Hence he concludes *Work and Prosperity* by reminding readers that the American market economy "has put a cornucopia into most households in the United States." The threats to this material abundance included "[c]rushing taxation, imprudent meddling, malicious envy, or revolutionary violence" (Kirk 1989a, 368).

Michael Oakeshott championed the principle of government restraint, including tax restraint, with perhaps an even greater intensity than Burke and Kirk. As Oakeshott wrote in "On Being Conservative," the "conservative disposition" is informed by the belief that governing "is a specific and limited activity, namely the provision and custody of general rules of conduct," that would enable individuals to satisfy their particular preferences free of unnecessary burdens (Oakeshott 1991, 424). He did not include broad-based taxation within this conception of government, a view he underscored by outlining his distinction between civil association and enterprise association, as we shall discuss in Section Five.

William F. Buckley adopted a parallel conception of government that demanded restraint in private economic activities and low levels of taxes (Buckley 1973, 51–83). "…[I]t is never too soon to muse on the pleasures of the simple tax, and the end to the grotesqueries of justice by taxation," he wrote in *Four Reforms*, his 1973 book offering a detailed program of political reforms, including tax reform (Buckley 1973, 82). Furthermore, controlling the growth of taxation and the state's regulatory power would empower individual initiative and autonomy. "Let the individual keep his dollar…and he can indulge his taste…in houses, in doctors, in education, in groceries, in entertainment, in culture, in religion…" he wrote in *Up from Liberalism* (Buckley 2016, 180). State interference in markets would pose a threat to the satisfaction of consumers' particular preferences. "Direct politically the economic activity of a nation," Buckley insisted, "and the economy will lose its capacity for that infinite responsiveness to individual tastes that gives concrete expression to the individual will in material matters" (Buckley 2016, 201). Not only did an excess of tax law—replete with deductions and exemptions—restrict individual freedoms, but it also created much confusion and uncertainty throughout the populace, thereby undermining the rule of law (Buckley 1973, 51–83).

It is important to note that with the exception of Nisbet, the conservative thinkers examined in this chapter, unlike elements of libertarian and anarchist thought, never questioned the credibility of taxation in itself. Nor did they deny that particular taxes were necessary to fulfill some legitimate government purpose. The activity they did denounce was public officials' abuse of the taxing system for broadening its horizon far beyond the reasonable aims of the state—such as to bring about a state of perfect equality.

6.3.2 *Taxes Should Not Be Enacted for the Purpose of Promoting Abstract Equality, Facilitating Mass Wealth Redistribution, and Advancing Other Forms of Social Engineering*

Clogging the flow of goods, raising the price of labor, diminishing public prosperity, and infringing on private employment contracts were noxious enough consequences of excessive taxation. What has haunted the conservative disposition even more, however, is the exploitation of taxing schemes *for the purposes of promoting equality of condition and levelling society through mass wealth redistribution programs and other forms of social engineering.* Their opposition to such schemes derived from the conservative recognition of the natural variety and diversity of human beings. Because individuals were equal under God but unequal in experiences, interests, and pedigrees, state attempts to thrust abstract conceptions of equality on unequal people ignored such rich variations of the human condition. Yet the dangers of equalizing society surpassed ignorance of variety. From the conservative point of view, a system of taxation designed to further the cause of equality without compromise would violate the sanctity of property, lead to mass social disorder, and condemn all men and women to poverty rather than lift them up to opulence.

Burke's reckoning with the French Revolution cast light on all of these conservative concerns about the menace of social engineering. "...[T]hose who attempt to level, never equalize," he flatly declared in the *Reflections* (Mitchell 2007, 100). There was no more brazen attempt to level society in his judgment than the French revolutionary assembly's expropriation of Gallican Church property and the subsequent selling of *assignats*, which were first sold as bonds and then became legal tender throughout France. The revolutionaries' seizure of church property to use as collateral for the *assignats* was part of their scheme to pay down the national debt.

This attack on the Gallican Church, as part of the French Revolution's swift program of dechristianization, struck hardest at the religious sentiments of the French people and their attachment to private possessions. But it also precipitated destructive economic effects. By effectively imposing a universal and unlimited tax on ecclesiastical property, revolutionaries drained value from the Church's estates; and by disseminating *assignats* without tact, they debased the currency. These *de facto* taxes generated tumultuous consequences on French markets, such as inflation, price instability, and widespread distrust among the French people, and led to additional state seizures of private property and grain.[12]

In effect, the scheme launched a massive redistribution of wealth from ancient, landed proprietors to monied men of new wealth, who had increasingly gained sway over French politics throughout the eighteenth century and were suddenly thrust into positions of great influence during the revolution. As Burke pronounced in *First Letter on a Regicide Peace*, Jacobinism was the "revolt of the enterprising talents of a county against it's property" (McDowell 2005, 241). While the possession of traditional forms of land ownership ensured stability and constancy in a nation, the proliferation of mobile property could wreak social havoc in Burke's judgment—and in fact did wreak social havoc, as demonstrated by the crippling consequences of the *assignats* and the unchecked rise of monied men—if not tamed by the calm presence of landed property.

The impulse behind this contrivance to redistribute wealth according to Burke was the French Revolution's abstract notions of equality and rights. Men "have equal rights; but not to equal things," he observed in the *Reflections* (Mitchell 2007, 110). Burke held that the Revolution flouted this principle. Informed by the principles of the Declaration of the Rights of Man and of the Citizen, revolutionaries craved for the eradication of odious social distinctions in order to bring about an egalitarian state inhabited by free and equal individuals. The expropriation of the property and wealth of the Gallican Church, which owned around one-tenth of the land surface in France (Jones 1995, 53), as well as the abolition of all remaining feudal privileges, embodied the attempt by the new French state to accomplish this task.

Yet the state's urge to determine the amount of property an individual or family should possess based on this abstract conception of equality endangered the sacredness of property, defied justice and prudence, and provoked stratagems of social experimentation. "Too much and too little are treason against property," Burke wrote in the *Reflections* (Mitchell 2007, 153). Rather than bend the strata of society to the will of speculative conceptions of equality, rulers, he maintained in the text, should preserve the beauty and richness of their many layers.

The French Revolution's expropriation of church land and eradication of feudalism in the name of egalitarianism violated each of the cherished maxims of the conservative outlook with regard to taxation: it offended the social nature of man that gained expression in social organizations such as religious institutions and landed estates; it sweepingly dismissed the notion that society was a complex artifact consisting of men and women from different backgrounds, responsibilities, pedigrees, and interests; it imposed a corrupted form of rationalism, abstract equality, on this complex society; it profaned the truth that man is fallible and that utopias are fanciful dreams; and it threatened the very sacredness of property.

Burke communicated his alarm over the wealth redistribution of the French Revolution in *Thoughts and Details* as well, which he composed in the backdrop of the French revolutionary schemes to impose price controls over France's grain markets. In Burke's judgment, the massive transfer of property and wealth from the rich

[12] Consult Collins (2020), chapter 11 for elaboration on these consequences.

to the poor, whether through coercive taxation, usurpation of property, or plain riots, would provoke social disorder and fail to satisfy the needs of the laboring classes. "That class of dependant pensioners called the rich is so extremely small," Burke remarked, "that if all their throats were cut, and a distribution made of all they consume in a year, it would not give a bit of bread and cheese for one night's supper to those who labour, and who in reality feed both the pensioners and themselves" (McDowell 2005, 121).

Similarly, state interventions in employment contracts—such as arbitrary taxation, minimum wage raises, and price controls—for the purpose of levelling conditions between the rich and the poor would generate poverty for all, not affluence for the lower orders. "A perfect equality will indeed be produced;—that is to say, equal want, equal wretchedness, equal beggary…" Burke insisted (McDowell 2005, 127). He continued: "Such is the event of all compulsory equalizations. They pull down what is above. They never raise what is below: and they depress high and low together beneath the level of what was originally the lowest" (McDowell 2005, 127).

Other conservatives have retained this deep trepidation about mass wealth redistribution for reasons similar to those voiced by Burke: they ignored the complex dimensions of man, ignited social confusion, were plainly ineffectual, and augured despotism. The most flagrant manifestation of wealth redistribution in Churchill's political life was socialism, which in many ways was the offspring of the French Revolution. "Socialism is, in its essence, an attack not only upon British enterprise," Churchill declared in his Gestapo speech in June 1945, "but upon the right of the ordinary man or woman to breathe freely without having a harsh, clumsy, tyrannical hand clapped across their mouths and nostrils" (Cannadine 1989, 273). Later that year he averred, "The inherent vice of capitalism is the unequal sharing of blessings. The inherent virtue of Socialism is the equal sharing of miseries."[13]

The relentless pursuit of abstract equality therefore revolted against true human equality. "Ultimate equality in the judgment of God, and equality before courts of law, are recognized by conservatives…," Kirk counseled in the *Conservative Mind*, "but equality of condition, they think, means equality in servitude and boredom" (Kirk 2001, 8/9). For "economic levelling" was "not economic progress" (Kirk 2001, 9). Oppressing the rich to empower the poor would do neither. Kirk's opposition to inheritance taxes and the death tax, as will be described below, captured his disgust over taxing schemes intended to reduce wealth disparities in the name of egalitarianism.

Oakeshott's conception of government reflected a similar opposition to the notion that the state should attempt to reorganize society in a systemic fashion, whether through wealth redistribution programs or other alternative measures. As he wrote in his essay "On Being Conservative":

> …[T]he office of government is not to impose other beliefs and activities upon its subjects, not to tutor or to educate them, not to make them better or happier in another way, not to direct them, to galvanize them into action, to lead them or to co-ordinate their activities so

[13] "Demobilisation," vol. 414, Hansard, UK Parliament, 22 October 1945, 1703–04, https://api.parliament.uk/historic-hansard/commons/1945/oct/22/demobilisation, accessed February 22, 2021.

> that no occasion of conflict shall occur; the office of government is merely to rule (Oakeshott 1991, 427).

Social engineering was a blunt attack on this Oakeshottian canon of conservatism.

More recently, Thomas Sowell has drawn sharp attention to the perils of forcing upon reality abstract conceptions of equality, or what he called "the mirage of equality" (Sowell 1999, 49–95). "…[T]o equate the attractiveness of [equality] is to assume that politicizing inequality is free of costs and dangers," he asserted in *The Quest for Cosmic Justice*, "when in fact such politicization can have very high costs and very grave dangers" (Sowell 1999, 51). Sowell highlighted the estate tax, as well as criticisms of the Reagan tax cuts, as examples of the reckless attitude that yearned to manufacture a false sense of equality by correcting disparities in the distribution of wealth (Sowell 1999, 82). Yet, as he quipped, "…[U]nlike God at the dawn of Creation, we cannot simply say, 'Let there be equality!' or 'Let there be justice!'" (Sowell 1999, 8).

Conservatives have thus embraced a strand of consequentialist reasoning in their objection to taxation for the purpose of promoting equality: massive taxing programs to redistribute wealth from the rich to the poor would spawn universal indigence and introduce far more hardships than they intended to combat. The more important philosophical consideration in their opposition to such schemes, however, was drawn from their deepest convictions about man. Because individuals and groups possessed varying aims, skills, and beliefs, and because natural differences emerged in societies overflowing in complexity, state campaigns to press uniform equality on all persons and institutions through wide-scale taxing schemes was a trespass against human nature itself.

6.4 Tensions

6.4.1 The First School of Thought: Taxation as Necessary for a Civilized Society Yet Prone to Rationalist Excess

Although conservatives have shared such principles informing their views on taxation, their political and economic thought suggests areas of tension over the appropriate range of the taxing power, the connection between revenue and the state, and the purpose of the state in general. These differences can be organized as a heuristic under the following conservative schools of thought: the first, represented most powerfully by Burke and Churchill, understands taxation to be a necessary part of civilized society and an instrument, when used wisely, to promote the common good; the second, represented by Oakeshott, views taxation in theory as necessary to finance the minimal duties required to administer a state; and the third, represented by Nisbet, questions the very credibility of a state's taxing powers in general. This section will discuss the first school of thought before examining the additional schools in the subsequent two sections.

6.4.1.1 Burke

Burke's thought and statesmanship conveyed the belief that taxation and revenue were necessary ingredients of civilized society and a flourishing nation. As demonstrated by his stern objections to arbitrary taxation and property confiscation, Burke was well aware that the power to tax could be utilized as an instrument for tyranny and for mass wealth redistribution schemes. Yet he also maintained that the tool of monetary extraction, when used legally, selectively, and effectively, could be harnessed to promote the public welfare and to finance projects that could imbue a sense of reverence in state establishments and traditions. Burke's approach to taxation, in short, did not call for a radically minimalist state but for prudential management pursuant to the ends of a commonwealth grounded in justice and religion.

Burke's recognition of the credibility of taxation originated in his divinely inspired conception of the state in general. "...He who gave our nature to be perfected by our virtue, willed also the necessary means of its perfection—", he wrote in the *Reflections*. "He willed therefore the state..." (Mitchell 2007, 148). One vital function of the state was to serve as a restraint on man's passions and a bulwark of social order (Mitchell 2007, 110/11; McDowell 2005, 120).

Yet a second function was to foster corporate reverence and fealty among the people from all social ranks, as manifested in "buildings, in musick, in decoration, in speech, in the dignity of persons, according to the customs of mankind, taught by their nature; that is, with modest splendour, with unassuming state, with mild majesty and sober pomp." Burke described this notion of reverence, which was aided by the use of national wealth to support such causes, as thus: "It is the publick ornament. It is the publick consolation. It nourishes the publick hope" (Mitchell 2007, 148).

Burke elaborated on this theme later in a key passage in the *Reflections*, which shall be quoted from at length because it provided perhaps the most comprehensive statement in his political life on the role of revenue in a nation:

> ...[R]evenue, which is the spring of all power, becomes in its administration the sphere of every active virtue. Public virtue, being of a nature magnificent and splendid, instituted for great things, and conversant about great concerns, requires abundant scope and room, and cannot spread and grow under confinement, and in circumstances straitened, narrow, and sordid. Through the revenue alone the body politic can act in its true genius and character, and therefore it will display just as much of its collective virtue, and as much of that virtue which may characterize those who move it, and are, as it were, its life and guiding principle, as it is possessed of a just revenue. For from hence, not only magnanimity, and liberality, and beneficence, and fortitude, and providence, and the tutelary protection of all good arts, derive their food, and the growth of their organs, but continence, and self-denial, and labour, and vigilance, and frugality, and whatever else there is in which the mind shews itself above the appetite, are no where more in their proper element than in the provision and distribution of the public wealth (Mitchell 2007, 274).

He continued:

> It is therefore not without reason that the science of speculative and practical finance, which must take to its aid so many auxiliary branches of knowledge, stands high in the estimation not only of the ordinary sort, but of the wisest and best men; and as this science has grown

> with the progress of its object, the prosperity and improvement of nations has generally increased with the increase of their revenues; and they will both continue to grow and flourish, as long as the balance between what is left to strengthen the efforts of individuals, and what is collected for the common efforts of the state, bear to each other a due reciprocal proportion, and are kept in a close correspondence and communication (Mitchell 2007, 274).

In Burke's view, a state in many ways derived its nourishment from the collection and distribution of revenue for purposes of the common good. The dissemination of public wealth both met the demands of public administration and promoted public virtue in its various manifestations, all of which relied on the conscious decisions of statesmen to determine which undertakings merited investment by the state. These decisions for Burke did not embody mere acts of fiscal policy but, more fundamentally, the moral priorities of a nation.

The specific context of Burke's comments here related to the French Revolution's schemes to reform its revenue system. Burke concluded that its schemes, imposed rashly with little foresight or discipline, were failing miserably and disrupting existing revenue streams, not to mention intensifying political and social disorder. This disorganization portended a fateful doom for the new French state, since the prudential custodianship of a government's financial resources shaped its long-term fortunes. "The revenue of the state is the state," he declared in the *Reflections*. "In effect all depends upon it, whether for support or for reformation" (Mitchell 2007, 273).

Burke's political activities translated into practice his belief in the importance of the state to sustain and fortify social and political attachments among the people. In 1775, for example, he supported an increase in public funding to finance the transformation of the Somerset House into a new building of public offices. He hoped that this "new edifice may be rendered an ornament" to the flourishing London metropolis (Elofson and Woods 1996, 169/70). As Burke explained in Parliament, "When the public money is spent on public works, the public spend it on themselves; they enjoy those works when elegant and magnificent; they pride themselves on the glory of their country possessing such" (Elofson and Woods 1996, 170).

Is there a tension between Burke's support for public revenue in the *Reflections* and his endorsement of government restraint in *Thoughts and Details*? Based on his rebuke of the expropriation of church property and French ideologues' commitment to abstract equality, his reference to "the provision and distribution of the public wealth" above clearly is not a sanction for a similar scheme of massive wealth redistribution.

The best way to frame Burke's thoughts on this matter is to first observe that a flourishing revenue in his view did not stem from a meddlesome system of taxation but one that was selective in approach, orderly in execution, and consistent in application. It was further fostered by a steady government and a stable market environment that invigorated the springs of industry. If French revolutionaries had met these standards by carrying out prudential reforms that grew out of France's ancestral traditions, they "would have had an unoppressive but a productive revenue" and a "flourishing commerce to feed it" (Mitchell 2007, 87). Revenue withered if based on short-term political contrivances, yet it prospered if grounded in long-term and stable fiscal systems and guided by the hand of moderation.

Accordingly, Burke's conception of taxation and revenue brought forward a distinction between the legitimate public responsibilities of the state and the private activities of men and women. As he wrote in *Thoughts and Details*, "the state ought to confine itself to what regards the State, or the creatures of the State..." This included "revenue," as well as religious establishments, the magistracy, the military, and chartered corporations—"in a word, to every thing that is *truly and properly* public, to the public peace, to the public safety, to the public order, to the public prosperity" (McDowell 2005, 143).

We can detect from this analysis of Burke the general principles of the first conservative approach to taxation. The state was a natural reflection of the social nature of man and his divine origins.[14] It followed that government required revenue to finance projects that would help inspire public morality and instill in the people a heightened sense of reverence for its institutions. In other words, the state should help promote the well-being of the commonwealth. Taxes were the most effective way to generate such revenue—but they must be implemented with discrimination and caution in order to demonstrate due appreciation for the variety of man and the complexity of society.

6.4.1.2 Churchill

Winston Churchill, like Burke, whom he quoted often (Roberts 2019), was a practitioner of statecraft in the dense medium of politics as well as an independent thinker in private study.[15] Churchill similarly applauded market competition as an engine of commercial affluence. As a statesman who served as Chancellor of the Exchequer (1924–1929) and as a member of both the Conservative Party and Liberal Party at various times throughout his political life, he also grasped that civilized society required taxation up to a certain point to finance the expenditures of the state. His political life and policy programs illustrated this recognition of the necessary presence of a taxing system in a commonwealth.

Yet Churchill in many ways went beyond Burke by actively supporting state-backed taxing schemes to help fund various initiatives of welfare reform to aid struggling laborers and the poor. Churchill's general attitude toward taxation, then, attempted to negotiate a delicate balance between encouraging the free enterprise system and supporting tax-funded social insurance programs that could alleviate the negative consequences of modern industrial capitalism. This confidence can possibly be attributed to his greater faith than Burke in the capacity of the national government to provide for the welfare of the people; to his expedient attempt to

[14] Even on this note, Burke's conception of the state is not precisely defined. In various contexts, including those above, it encompassed public administration and the wider social relations of a people in a political community.

[15] This section on Churchill is indebted to the scholarship of Martin Gilbert and Martin Daunton.

ward off grander socialist experiments threatening the British people in the interwar period; or, more cynically, to careful consideration of the political benefits such programs would generate for the Conservative Party in the 1920s (or to a combination of all three possibilities).[16] In addition, Churchill's vision of taxation and welfare reform could be interpreted as a response to the distinctive set of social complications introduced by modern industrialization. These complications were only beginning to be grappled with in Burke's age, which had remained a largely agricultural-based economy at the time he passed away in 1797.

We begin with Churchill's tribute to capitalist enterprise. Early in his tenure as Chancellor of the Exchequer, he remarked to Lord Salisbury that the "existing capitalist system is the foundation of civilisation, and the only means by which great modern populations can be supplied with vital necessities" (Gilbert 1991, 468). Reflecting on his first visit to the United States in 1895, Churchill poured lavish praise on the nation's free-market economy for generating public riches without arbitrarily seizing property or imposing burdensome taxes on the Americans. He observed:

> When we reflect that such benefits have been secured to the people not by confiscation of the property of the rich or by arbitrary taxation but simply by business enterprise—out of which the promoters themselves have made colossal fortunes, one cannot fail to be impressed with the excellence of the active system (Gilbert 1981, 2).

Churchill struck a similar tone in 1903, when he commented that "light taxation," as well as education reform and a stable and peaceful society, rather than import duties, were the "best means of stimulating the commercial prosperity of our country" (Gilbert 1991, 156).

Furthermore, the voluntary exchange of services in an environment of market competition gifted benefits to both parties. "If the railway makes greater profits, it is usually because it carries more goods and more passengers," Churchill remarked in 1909, applying the same principle to the services rendered by doctors and lawyers (Churchill 1909, 321/2). In this atmosphere of mutual exchange, "There is constant service, there is constant competition; there is no monopoly, there is no injury to the public interest, there is no impediment to the general progress" (Churchill 1909, 322).

Churchill's instinct for market economies coincided with his bitter antipathy to socialism. "Socialism seeks to pull down wealth; Liberalism seeks to raise up poverty," he said in his speech on the Dundee election in 1908. In addition:

> Socialism would kill enterprise; Liberalism would rescue enterprise from the trammels of privilege and preference. Socialism assails the pre-eminence of the individual; Liberalism seeks, and shall seek more in the future, to build up a minimum standard for the mass. Socialism exalts the rule; Liberalism exalts the man. Socialism attacks capital; Liberalism attacks monopoly (Churchill 1909, 155).

Churchill would harbor this attraction to the spirit of enterprise, and this enmity toward socialism, throughout his entire political life.

---

[16] Consult Martin Daunton (2002) for a review of the politics of British taxation during this period and throughout the twentieth century.

Churchill's suspicions of intricate taxing schemes flowed from his general affinity for market economies, which oftentimes included a level of admiration for free trade reminiscent of Richard Cobden, the famous nineteenth-century foe of protectionism. During a parliamentary debate in 1907, Churchill, a member of the Liberal Party at the time who was serving as Under-Secretary of State for the Colonies, urged restraint on the part of the British government before interfering with the reciprocal trade agreements between colonial dependencies within the British Empire. "Taking the simple position of the orthodox Cobdenite Free Trader," he said, "I am of opinion that taxes are an evil, a necessary evil, but still an evil, and the fewer we have of them the better."[17] Although this remark was made in the context of foreign trade policy rather than domestic trade policy, it does hint at Churchill's distaste for the intrusive meddling of a central ruler in the voluntary economic affairs of transacting parties.[18]

One year later he amplified this criticism in a speech to the Financial Reform Association (FRA) at Liverpool, which addressed tariff reform:

> ...all taxation is an evil, and so far as taxation itself is concerned as a mere process of raising money, it is an evil 'harsh, unmingled, and unmitigated.' When the State takes from the earnings of the community money which it needs for national purposes, however vital, it withdraws that money from the healthy fructification of industry, it diminishes the consuming and productive energies of the people, and it rests with the State to prove at every moment that the employment of the money which it raises conduces to a greater commercial profit than if it had been left to private persons to use, or else that the money is needed for purposes which have to be justified on grounds of necessity quite apart from economic ones (James 1974a, 922/3).

Later in his speech, he contended that there was "only one justification for taxation, and only one advantage to be got out of taxes, and that is revenue." Furthermore, "...it is wrong and unjust to tax any person, however rich, with the object of making him poorer" (James 1974a, 925).

Such comments, punctuated by Churchill's repeated denunciations of taxation as "evil," imply at first glance an unwavering fidelity to a minimalist state. Yet he did not pledge allegiance to a rigid form of laissez-faire economics, as subtly suggested by his references to "a minimum standard" in his Dundee speech and "revenue" in his FRA speech. Indeed, in the same FRA speech he conceded the possible merit of "sensible and substantial increases in direct taxation" that were broadly and gradually applied (James 1974a, 925).

As a practicing statesman, then, Churchill supported various forms of social insurance that would guard the most vulnerable members of society against the unpredictable nature of capitalist enterprise. "I do not want to see impaired the vigor

[17] *The Parliamentary Debates*, vol. CLXIX (London: Wyman and Sons, 1907), 133.

[18] In 1902, as a member of the Conservative Party, Churchill was charged with a breach of consistency in endorsing free trade while also supporting the sugar tax and corn tax. Churchill defended himself by insisting that the primary aim of the taxes—which were intended as emergency proposals to help finance the costs of war—was to generate revenue, not to protect colonial goods from foreign markets. Consult Gilbert (1991, 152).

of competition," he said as a member of the Liberal Party in a 1906 speech in Glasgow, "but we can do much to mitigate the consequences of failure." Therefore,

> We want to draw a line below which we will not allow persons to live and labour, yet above which they may compete with all the strength of their manhood. We want to have free competition upwards; we decline to allow free competition to run downwards. We do not want to pull down the structures of science and civilisation: but to spread a net over the abyss… (Churchill 1909, 82/3).

Churchill looked "forward to the universal establishment of minimum standards of life and labour, and their progressive elevation as the increasing energies of production may permit" (Churchill 1909, 81). The most appropriate path forward was to strike a balance between unbridled capitalism and command-and-control socialism that could secure the fruits of industry while protecting the most classes from economic deprivation.

6.4.1.3 Churchill's Tenure as Chancellor of the Exchequer

Churchill's preference to blend free enterprise with social insurance in the conduct of statecraft steered his policy program as Chancellor of the Exchequer from 1924 to 1929, a time in his political life that offers a tantalizing glimpse into his approach to taxation. The governing principles behind what Martin Gilbert has called Churchill's "philosophy of wealth" (Gilbert 1981, 54) as Chancellor included: spread the spirit of enterprise and industry; give priority to the creation of new wealth over the preservation of old wealth; and mold the tax system to support moderate income earners. These principles were complemented by Churchill's approval of social insurance as security against extreme want.

Churchill presented this integrated vision of fiscal and social policy in a speech on his first budget of 1925, which has endured as one of the most distinctive such orations in the history of industrial England (Daunton 1997, 1068). Churchill proclaimed:

> I cherish the hope that by liberating the production of new wealth from some, at least, of the shackles of taxation, the Budget may stimulate enterprise and accelerate industrial revival; and that, by giving a far greater measure of security to the mass of the wage-earners, their wives and children, it may promote contentment and stability, and make our island more truly a home for all its people.[19]

Informed by these guiding tenets as Chancellor, Churchill sought to reduce both the income tax by ten percent for lower income earners and the super tax (which imposed an additional tax on incomes over £2000) on active earners in the middle class. This consideration represented a pillar of his fiscal strategy and marked his instinctual appreciation for market competition: in Churchill's view, the vitalizing

[19] "Financial Statement," vol. 183, Hansard, UK Parliament, 28 April 1925, 89, https://hansard.parliament.uk/Commons/1925-04-28/debates/b2d498aa-4e33-443c-8f89-f2f3e8f7238c/FinancialStatement, accessed February 22, 2021.

tonic of public prosperity was the wealth generated by entrepreneurs, including those from modest circumstances. Departing from the Treasury's prevailing priority to redeem the government's debt and preserve its financial solvency, Churchill channeled his efforts toward unleashing the industrious capacities of businessman, merchants, and the professional classes.

Churchill united his focus on lowering the tax liability of modern income earners with his sympathy for expanding the tax burdens for the rich, in particular by raising the death duty on estates ranging from £12,500 to £1 million. This aspect of Churchill's fiscal program—which introduces a point of friction with Russell Kirk's views on the death tax, as will be explained below—underlined what he called an "increasing distinction" (Gilbert 1991, 467) in his approach to taxation as Chancellor: although he opposed campaigns to "hunt down the 'idle rich'" (Gilbert 1991, 467), Churchill believed that the state should favor the encouragement of active wealth over old wealth because the former in his judgment conferred greater advantages to society. "The process of the creation of new wealth is beneficial to the whole community," he wrote in 1924. "The process of squatting on old wealth though valuable is a far less lively agent" (Daunton 1997, 1072). Placing the British government's finances on a steadier foundation and generating public prosperity following the First World War depended greatly on the "energetic creation of new wealth." Therefore, "A premium on effort is my aim and a penalty on inertia may well be its companion" (Daunton 1997, 1072). Churchill held that the creative energies of the entrepreneur, rather than the sluggish nature of possessors of inherited wealth, were the trigger for economic revitalization, suggesting his proto-supply-side inclinations. In addition, he hoped that the increased revenue from the new death duties could mitigate the loss in revenue from the reduction in the super tax.

Churchill was keen on combining this program of fiscal reform with welfare reform. As Home Secretary, he had helped to facilitate the passage of the National Insurance Act of 1911; and three years prior, as President of the Board of Trade, he had endorsed non-contributory old age pensions. Churchill retained this proclivity for social reform as Chancellor by proposing pension plans for widows and orphans, lowering the age of eligibility for pensions from 70 to 65, and expanding old age insurance. He also envisioned a program for inexpensive housing and approved of coal miners' proposition for a national minimum wage during the coal strike of 1926 (Gilbert 1991, 178/9), which was sparked in part by the harsh economic consequences of his controversial decision to return to the gold standard in his 1925 budget. Churchill's support for welfare reform disclosed a humane outlook that called for the state to ensure social stability and to aid those stranded at the margins. "It is to the stragglers, to the exhausted, to the weak, to the wounded, to the veterans, to the widow and the orphans that the ambulances of the State and the aid of the State should, as far as possible, be directed," he declared in his speech on the 1925 budget.[20]

[20] "Financial Statement," vol. 183, Hansard, 28 April 1925, 72, *supra* n. 20.

Churchill's four subsequent budgets embodied this attempt to meld his interest in welfare reform with a pragmatic fiscal program intended to stimulate industry and secure public revenue. Churchill's ideas for his second budget, introduced in 1926, included taxes impacting petrol, luxury cars, heavy lorries, all bets, and imported American films (Gilbert 1991, 474). His third budget in 1927 called for new levies on imports of wine and motor-car tires and hikes in existing taxes on tobacco and matches. Churchill further rejected Cabinet arguments to reduce death duties, preserving his attraction to their utility as a source of revenue and an alternative to taxes on active wealth (Gilbert 1991, 481).

Yet Churchill was also intent on extinguishing local rates of taxation on real estate in order to spur the industrial and agricultural sectors of Britain's economy, a plan that would potentially leave local governments in a financially precarious position (Daunton 1997, 1080). He aimed to substitute these rates for a profits tax and petrol tax to generate government receipts (Gilbert 1991, 481/2). Churchill later scrapped the former and retained the latter as the primary impetus for revenue. Winning approval from the Cabinet Policy Committee, the derating scheme was included in the budget of 1928 (Churchill's fourth budget), which Churchill insisted would "revive industry and create new jobs" (Gilbert 1991, 485). His fifth budget, introduced in April 1929, pledged to abolish the tea duty, a move criticized as an election ploy (Gilbert 1991, 489).

We should pause and note that Churchill's speech on June 5, 1928 in support of the petrol tax indicated a sharp shift away from his prior embrace of a land value tax that Henry George had famously endorsed in his 1879 book *Progress and Poverty*. In a 1909 speech Churchill had advocated for the tax, observing that the land monopoly was the "mother of all other forms of monopoly" (Churchill 1909, 320) and that the land monopolist "renders no service to the community" (Churchill 1909, 323; see also Gilbert 1991, 174). Yet he argued in his 1928 speech that George's theory had become progressively outdated due to the increasing variety of methods to generate and sustain wealth beyond the possession of landed property, and to the transformation in the ways that taxes had been raised within the prior two decades years (James 1974b, 4420/1).

This brief review of Churchill's budgets, as framed by the vision behind his budget of 1925, illustrated a number of economic tenets that governed his attitude toward taxation. First and most important, the easing of income taxes lights a spark for capitalist enterprise and releases the entrepreneurial spirit from regulatory burden. Second, light taxation on income for the middle classes in particular encourages private savings and personal responsibility. Third, the additional economic activity inspired by this fiscal program, combined with selective taxation on luxury goods and the death duty, can produce sufficient revenue for the state to strengthen its financial solvency. Fourth, the state is capable of supporting both industry and social welfare in order to soften the consequences of economic dislocation. Churchill maintained that this approach provided a more disciplined alternative to fiscal management than the one put forth previously by the Labour Party, which had proposed a levy on accumulated capital as part of an effort to target the wealth of the idle *rentier* class. Nevertheless, we must not forget that Churchill's program, by granting relief to the middle class and not to the rich, was modifying but retaining the progressive system of taxation that had predated his tenure as Chancellor.

Churchill's budgets evinced a calculated political strategy as well. They represented his effort to curry favor with moderate yet enterprising wage-earners to augment the political support of the Conservative Party. Churchill also sought to win acceptance from key electoral constituencies for additional levels of extraction and expenditure by government.

In the end, Churchill believed that this fiscal program would renew the social contract spanning different social classes and restore confidence in the national government. The "'fiscal sociology' of Winston Churchill meant that interwar Britain came to terms with an unprecedented level of extraction and a further shift to progressive, direct taxation," Martin Daunton concludes. "Consent and the legitimacy of the state were preserved" (Daunton 1997, 1083). As a statesman with sympathies for both capitalism and social insurance, Churchill imparted a vision of tax policy that could serve in theory as an inducement for enterprise, a lever for electoral self-interest, and an instrument for the common good. Taxation indeed was necessary for civilized society, brimming with both social complexities and political considerations.

6.4.1.4 Kirk, Civilized Society, and the Farming Community

Russell Kirk's thoughts on taxation occupy a sort of middle ground between Burke's and Churchill's positive conception of the state and Robert Nisbet's antagonism toward it. As suggested in his critical comments on taxation in *Work and Prosperity*, Kirk firmly opposed taxing schemes for the purposes of mass wealth redistribution and levelling society. His later writings in particular revealed a growing fondness for the free enterprise system. Yet even more important for Kirk was the negative impact of taxes on the aristocracy, small businesses, and farming communities, reflecting his agrarian inclinations and allegiance to traditional moral values.

Perhaps the tax for which Kirk professed his greatest contempt was the inheritance tax. Kirk's attitude toward this tax was rooted in his recognition of the crucial role of the aristocracy in a commonwealth, a class he maintained promoted the common good and served as exemplars of moral leadership. "A society so rich as ours," he wrote in the *Intelligent Woman's Guide*, "can afford to tolerate rich men and women—and can afford to encourage, indeed, the bequest and inheritance of large properties" (Kirk 1957a, 110). Kirk continued: "No social institution does more to develop decent leadership and a sense of responsibility than does the inheritance of large properties, and of the duties that accompany those properties" (Kirk 1957a, 110). The possession of property, and the commensurate responsibilities that came with stewardship, motivated the landowner to act with probity, support religion and culture, and nurture a social environment of leisure (Kirk 1957a, 69).

Kirk accordingly communicated sharp revulsion toward what he believed were high rates of taxation on inherited property. "Little serious thought seems to be given to the consequences...of continuing inheritance-taxes at their present rate; yet they now constitute confiscation, and are a levy upon capital, not a voluntary contribution out of income toward the maintenance of our Republic," he explained (Kirk 1957a, 109/10). Inheritance taxes both burdened the aristocracy by discouraging capital accumulation and investment and diminished their broader social influence in serving as patrons of high culture (Kirk 1957a, 110). Kirk did not go so far to insist that abolishing the tax would cure all social ills, but he did issue a public plea to reassess its supposed benefits to wider society.

Kirk connected the harmful influence of the inheritance tax to its negative impact on familial social and economic life. The tax discriminated "against family enterprises and partnerships" and placed in danger "family farms of any extent," he warned in *The Wise Men Know What Wicked Things Are Written on the Sky* (Kirk 1987, 51). In this sense the inheritance tax struck at the traditional conception of economics as household management. For it was one of the "deliberate or quasi-deliberate techniques of the mass-state for undermining the family," he wrote in the *Intelligent Woman's Guide*, and left "small margin for family saving" (Kirk 1957a, 47/8). Furthermore, because the family for Kirk was the essential structure of civilized society, any impediment to strengthening the family was a hindrance to the preservation of social order. "The conservative feels that the family is the natural source and core of any good society…" he stated (Kirk 1957a, 45).

The unsettling nature of the inheritance tax on families introduces an additional dimension to Kirk's analysis of inheritance taxes, and of taxation in general: his sensitivity to their damaging effect on the immemorial habits and customs of a culture. Rejecting George Bernard Shaw's—and *a fortiori* contemporary libertarians'-portrayal of modernity as a binary contest between capitalism and socialism, Kirk maintained that the "real struggle" was "between *traditional society*, with its religious and moral and political inheritance, and *collectivism*…with its passion for reducing humanity to a mere tapioca-pudding of identical producers and consumers" (Kirk 1957a, 106). Traditional society was characterized by "old motives of integrity," which he concluded were absent in modern collectivist societies (Kirk 1957a, 107). This reasoning was similar to Nisbet's framing of modernity as a blunt confrontation between social groups and the state.

Kirk indicted the inheritance tax in this section of the *Wise Men Know* as a glaring example of the modern impulse toward collectivism and a cause of the dissolution of the traditional social order. "Certain measures of taxation…most conspicuous in Britain but differing only in degree in America," he asserted, "operate to destroy private enterprise in the old sense, to abolish the inheritance of property and the sense of responsibility that accompanies inheritance, and to substitute, in the long run, state compulsion for the ancient motives to integrity" (Kirk 1957a, 109).

We can detect in this insight and Kirk's prior comments an echo of Burke's observation in the *Reflections* that society was a sacred partnership between past, present, and future generations, which in Burke's time was sustained in large part by the hereditary nobility. Kirk's outlook on taxation, and his broader historical and philosophical commentary, radiate a similar conviction that the aristocracy stood as the bedrock of a stable political and social order throughout the ages. Yet public policy, such as the inheritance tax, imposed heavy burdens on this class by provoking the fragmentation of families of traditional wealth. But it also, and necessarily, imposed heavy burdens on society writ large by draining influence from a group of men and women who provided composure to the whims of the day, exhibited civic leadership, and served as philanthropists for charitable endeavors and as sponsors of the arts and letters. The inheritance tax, in other words, pressed against the common good and disturbed social stability.

Kirk was similarly critical of additional taxing schemes that typified this ethos of collectivism and frayed the bonds of human affection historically nourished in voluntary associations. Social Security, which Kirk branded "remorseless collectivism" (Kirk 1962, 160), was the prototype of such schemes in his view. Describing the system in *A Program for Conservatives* (1962) as "disguised taxation" (Kirk 1962, 161), Kirk preferred voluntary charity over coercive wealth transfers as a remedy for social ills. He appended in this section an interesting remark that signaled his awareness of the ontological shift in the idea of taxation: throughout history it was considered a "free grant from the citizens for the general welfare"—not "extortion by a central political authority," a practice he believed characterized Social Security (Kirk 1962, 161). Armed with this novel taxing power that generated a flow of money and credit for public coffers, the state suppressed the spirit of free association and local philanthropy that had served as the time-honored cure for social and economic dislocation (Kirk 1962, 160/1).

Kirk's portrayal of Social Security in *Work and Prosperity* projected a more disinterested mood, presumably because it was written as a textbook. In the book, he did emphasize in italics that many Americans "*pay more in Social Security taxes than they pay in federal and state income taxes*" (Kirk 1989a, 190). Kirk further spotlighted the increasingly unstable nature of the system and the "heavy financial burden" it placed on the American economy (although, he adds, not as burdensome as similar systems in European nations).

Yet the more important insight Kirk proffers in this section in *Work and Prosperity* related to the tight connection between savings and national social insurance programs. Savings in Kirk's judgment were essential not only for capital investment and economic development but also for the habituation of thrift and the postponement of gratification. As he explained, "thrifty habits" were the foundation for "[a]ny person's prosperity and any nation's prosperity" (Kirk 1989a, 192). The voluntary saving of private wealth, for individuals, families, and businesses, was the most efficacious means to practice such habits.

But Social Security, according to Kirk, was a "form of compulsory saving" that required Americans to pay into the system, even if they opposed the program (Kirk 1989a, 189). The implicit message running throughout his discussion of savings announces itself most forcefully at the conclusion of the chapter: while schemes of compulsory saving such as Social Security, funded by coercive taxation, discouraged the practice of voluntary saving, a more lightly regulated market economy encouraged voluntary savings, which "keeps a people free, as well as fed" (Kirk 1989a, 193). As Kirk stated with emphasis, "*Without saving, there can be no security and little liberty*" (Kirk 1989a, 193). Tax-funded social insurance programs—not to mention the inheritance tax—melted away the market incentives of thrift and responsibility for both individuals and families, which thwarted the growth in public prosperity and imperiled freedom.

In addition, Kirk directed harsh criticisms toward the graduated income tax for being a symptom of modern industrialization, a dangerous tool for utilitarian social reformers, and a symbol of the levelling humanitarian tendencies of modernity. "As an instrument for deliberate social alteration," he wrote in the *Conservative Mind*, referring to the establishment of the federal income tax in the United States in 1913 (which, he remarked, was intended as a temporary measure), "the income tax soon would supplement that unconscious force, the second industrial revolution" (Kirk 2001, 374). The potent combination of this tax with the inheritance tax was "irresistibly tempting to social reformers, almost impossible to restrain within the strict necessities of ordinary government…" (Kirk 2001, 453). For the "power to tax certainly is the power to destroy; humanitarians confidently believed it was the power to create, as well" (Kirk 2001, 453).

Kirk also denounced the steady increase in the graduated income tax, along with the introduction of death duties, in late nineteenth-century Britain. As he explained, the growth in social welfare legislation, the expansion of the civil service, and the rise in army and navy estimates all demanded abundant government revenue. With reference to the death duties, Kirk approvingly cited William Lecky's remark that the "first principle of taxation" according to orthodox political economy was that it should tax income and not capital.[21] Yet "one of the two largest direct taxes annually raised is now a highly graduated tax falling directly upon capital," which in consequence amounted to "absolute confiscation" if successive owners of a large property died quickly (Kirk 2001, 332).

Kirk indicated that the most deleterious effect of this escalation in British taxation was the painful demise of agrarian communities: "higher death duties, two great wars to slaughter the sons of country families, more income taxes, the addition of taxes upon 'unearned' income—so the end of the whole pattern of rural Britain begins to take shape in 1894" (Kirk 2001, 332). Kirk's lament here preserved a line of reasoning consistent with his comments in his other writings on tax policy: promiscuous taxation not only frustrated the accumulation of capital and the free enterprise system but also corroded the social foundations of a political community, the landed aristocracy and rural communities, both of which served as its calm anchors.

Kirk conveyed particular regret over the impact of taxation on the fading presence of small businesses embedded in their local communities. In *Confessions of a Bohemian Tory* (1963), Kirk highlighted "high rates of taxation," along with the monopolistic practices of trade unions, as ruinous to the traditional, property-owning entrepreneur (Kirk 1963, 267). Both in Britain and America, he wrote, one of the most "conspicuous" causes of the "decline of small enterprise" was "taxation, especially death duties or inheritance tax…" For the "'[p]rogressive' income tax makes it extremely difficult, at best, to build up a new small or local business out of personal savings; while British death duties, or American inheritance taxes, make it

[21] Note that this formulation does not necessarily reflect the actual history of taxation in England.

almost impossible to pass on a successful family business, or private proprietorship, to one's heirs" (Kirk 1963, 272). One of Kirk's proposed remedies to stem this trend was to undertake a "careful and impartial survey" of the effect of the capital gains tax on spurring the consolidation of firms (Kirk 1963, 268). He concluded in this chapter of *Confessions of a Bohemian Tory* that "[p]robably nothing will save variety in commerce, and local character, but a sweeping revision of the tax-structure, and the applying of antitrust laws to labor unions" (Kirk 1963, 273).

Similarly, in Kirk's telling, the local entrepreneur was increasingly crowded out by economic development and urban renewal projects backed by the perilous alliance of government and big business, a coalition that illustrated the repercussions of mass commercial and financial capitalism on traditional forms of social life. He wrote that the "chief promoter of bigness in business is government itself, with its heavy-handed tax policies" (Kirk 1963, 272). In addition, Sweden's system of "[s]ocialist taxation prevents the emergence of new competing firms, and destroys small family businesses; but it is allied with the impersonal 'private' corporations that produce a high degree of standardized prosperity" (Kirk 1963, 267). Rather than pitting capitalism and socialism as bitter foes, then, Kirk conceived them as economic systems based on overlapping premises: they both epitomized efforts by the state to engineer industrial and commercial expansion to the detriment of the local proprietor.

Kirk's reckoning with the harmful consequences of tax policy on family businesses and local community informed a number of his proposals in the *Wise Men Know* to strengthen the family. First was his support, consistent with the preferences of the Reagan administration, for the "virtual abolition of the inheritance tax." The tax worked to the "heavy disadvantage of family enterprises" while promoting the concentration of wealth in corporations, institutions that were largely unaffected by the tax. Kirk also called to revise the practice of assessing real property based on speculative market values, which in his view "encouraged the destruction of farmland and of farm families in the neighborhood of growing cities and towns" (Kirk 1987, 51). Because agrarian localities represented traditional values, the inheritance tax and tax assessments based on speculation threatened to destroy the moral compass of a political community.[22]

Whereas many writers and thinkers have highlighted the consequences of taxation on the social fabric of commonwealths, it is this sensitivity to the impact of taxes on local businesses in both urban and rural communities that is perhaps the most distinctive quality of Kirk's commentary on taxation. Excessive taxes from his perspective did not simply obstruct the flow of economic resources and depress capital investment. It also imposed throbbing burdens on the local proprietor to the benefit of big business and speculators, seeking to strike a profit from developing urban areas; and it unsettled the balance between the city and the country that had

[22] As an aside, Kirk also endorsed the idea of tax credits to provide support to independent colleges and a school voucher system in which the state would provide tax relief or a rebate to the school, see Kirk (1971a, b).

traditionally stabilized the vicissitudes of a commonwealth and reconciled the mercantile interest with the rural interest.

Note also Kirk's inversion of the progressive argument that taxation is necessary to restrain the nefarious influence of big business. In his judgment, the most destructive consequences of taxation were not borne by the rich and powerful but by the modest entrepreneur and his family living in communities less affluent than highly clustered urban areas. In short, Kirk's reflections on taxation took into account the wider effects of heavy taxation on the scale of enterprise, the delicate homeostasis between different geographical areas, the leadership class in a political community, ancestral social institutions such as the family, and the moral character of a people.

While Kirk was a cautious proponent of market economies, such traits exude a different tone than the individualistic and utilitarian mood associated with arguments in favor of capitalism today, which often place a sharp accent on personal autonomy, profit maximization, and wealth accumulation as a means to happiness. As John Attarian (1996) shrewdly observes, however, Kirk's comprehension of the more profound implications of tax policy on the social texture of a people reflected his humane conception of economics. Kirk in this context was following in the tradition of, and sought inspiration from, Wilhelm Röpke, the German-born professor of economics who was the chief intellectual influence behind the revitalization of Germany's economy following World War II (Kirk 1989b).

Kirk's notion of a humane political economy was predicated on his belief in a transcendent moral order, ordained by God, that governed all human beings. A political community was best grasped not as a dispersed collection of atomized rational actors but as "a community of souls" (Kirk 2001, 8) that yearned for meaning and purpose beyond the momentary sparkle of material gratification. A prosperous society included what Kirk, in the spirit of T.S. Eliot, called the "permanent things" (see Kirk 2013, 2016)—such as beauty and love and charity—as well as commercial affluence. The permanent things were not the product of profit but of the deeply rooted moral values Kirk believed were fundamental to the human condition and present in the ethos of agrarian communities and small family shops. This is why Kirk's commentary on tax policy drew particular attention to its impact on these local structures of social and economic organization. In his view, a morally and religiously grounded state should devise its system of taxation to favor these pillars of social order and embodiments of the permanent things.[23]

In a larger sense, Kirk's apprehensions about the growing burdens of excessive taxation in modernity was part of his broader economic diagnosis of the modern mass state, as manifested in its collectivist and democratic forms. A free society depended in great part on a free economy: "a free economy is essential to the preservation of freedom in general," he averred in the *Intelligent Woman's Guide* (Kirk 1957a, 106). Yet the modern state gave birth to a collectivist economy—as

[23] For Kirk's writings on humane political economy and its moral and religious underpinnings, see Kirk (1957b, 1982, 1989a, b, 1992). Consult Attarian (1996, 1998).

exemplified by the inheritance tax, income tax, and Social Security—in which individuals remained servile to rulers in power:

> Men and women must eat. If they are dependent upon a solitary power or a solitary individual for their subsistence, they are slaves. They can act in any external respect only upon the sufferance of that master. If that master is the state, they have no alternative employment; they must obey, or live on air; and the state, because of its impersonality, can be a harder master, more devoid of charity and generosity, than any medieval lord (Kirk 1957a, 107).

In sum, Kirk's thoughts on taxation were intimately connected to his notion of social freedom for both individuals and groups. The taxing of inherited wealth and the coercion of national wealth transfer schemes laid bare the heartless detachment of the modern state, threatening the moral exercise of economic liberty and the nourishment of social bonds that had traditionally tied local communities together. If taxes were in fact necessary for civilized society, they should not torment these ancient sources of meaning and purpose.

6.4.2 *The Second School of Thought: The Limited State and Civil Association*

Because the first and second strands of conservative thought overlap to some extent, we should be careful not to impose rigid distinctions between them. Indeed, that the thinkers discussed in this particular section do not wholly reject the utility of taxes implies a measure of assent to the notion that taxes were necessary in some way to civilized society. Yet this proviso should also not deter us from shedding light on conservatives' gradations of support and varying philosophical justifications for taxation. The most important gradation for our purposes regards differing conceptions of the aim of a state: while the first strand, represented by Burke and Churchill, accommodated the use of taxation to promote affirmative notions of the common good, the second strand calls for a more constrained view of government that resists teleological approaches to the crafting of tax policy.

6.4.2.1 Oakeshott

Michael Oakeshott represents this second school.[24] Most famous for arguing that conservatism was a disposition rather than an article of faith, Oakeshott integrated this idea with a suspicion of modern rationalism to offer a collection of important insights into the appropriate range of a state's regulatory powers. Applied to the domain of taxation, Dominic de Cogan has characterized this Oakeshottian outlook as a "conservative disposition" of tax law (de Cogan 2017), which was broadly

[24] This account of Oakeshott is indebted to Dominic de Cogan (2017).

rooted in a "conservative disposition in politics" (Oakeshott 1991, 423) toward governing and in his abhorrence of rationalism. Governing, Oakeshott wrote in *Rationalism in Politics*, was a

> specific and limited activity, namely the provision and custody of general rules of conduct, which are understood, not as plans for imposing substantive activities, but as instruments enabling people to pursue the activities of their own choice with the minimum frustration, and therefore something which it is appropriate to be conservative about (Oakeshott 1991, 424).

The end of government was not to establish and pursue teleological objectives in a commonwealth but to facilitate a civil system of generally applicable rules that allowed individuals to attain their particular life goals.

The specific content of this system can be grasped by considering Oakeshott's famous distinction between enterprise association and civil association. As described in greatest detail in his essay "On the Civil Condition," an enterprise association ("*universitas*") was a mode of relationship "in terms of the pursuit of some common purpose, some substantive condition of things to be jointly procured, or some common interest to be continuously satisfied" (Oakeshott 2003, 114). What bound people in an enterprise association together was a substantive aim, an idea Oakeshott traced back to the idea of a corporation aggregate in medieval Europe. Yet the distinctive quality of this form of association was not merely the existence of a shared aim but the "'management' of its pursuit" (Oakeshott 2003, 115). Joint purposes needed to be consciously identified and consciously sought in an enterprise association.

A civil association ("*societas*"), on the other hand, was an association of people who were united by common rules of living but not by a substantive aim. It was an "intermittent transactional association of reciprocity" in which individuals desired the "satisfaction of their wants" (Oakeshott 2003, 112) under a universally recognized system of law that prescribed conditions of human conduct. The authority of this legal system, rather than a shared teleological purpose, was the salient feature of a civil association. The duty of the ruler in a civil association was not to manage individuals' activities in pursuit of a single shared aim—for there existed no single shared aim to pursue—but to serve as the responsible custodian of the legal and political system that permitted men and women to fulfill their individual preferences.[25] Whereas Oakeshott imagined the civil association to be an ideal (though not perfect) type of association in theory, drawn out from the contingencies and fluxes of human life (Oakeshott 2003, 109), he understood both the limits of translating this concept into practice and its permanent tension with enterprise association.[26]

The civil association, rather than decreeing a shared objective, created what Oakeshott (2003, 113) called "adverbial conditions" under the rule of law: the purpose of law was not to set forth specific substantive ends but to establish

[25] Consult Oakeshott's essays "On the Civil Condition" (*On Human Conduct*, 108–84) and "On the Character of a Modern European State" (*On Human Conduct*, 185–326).

[26] I thank Dominic de Cogan for alerting me to this key point.

acknowledged rules of procedural behavior to which individuals must subscribe in the exercise of their specific activities. He noted, for instance, that the law does not ban individuals from lighting a fire but from lighting it "arsonically" (Oakeshott 2003, 58 n1). Laws, Oakeshott explained in "The Rule of Law," were "unavoidably indeterminate prescriptions of general adverbial obligations" (Oakeshott 1999, 156).

In his lectures at the London School of Economics, Oakeshott sharpened this distinction between enterprise association and civil association by exposing a similar divergence between telocracy and nomocracy. Telocracy was the act of governing for the realization of a "single, premeditated end"; as he wrote, "nothing but the chosen end or purpose is regarded as being valuable in itself" in this type of government (Oakeshott 2006, 491). The rule of law in a telocracy possessed no "independent virtue" but held value to the extent that it aided in the fulfillment of this premeditated end (Oakeshott 2006, 492). Nomocracy, on the other hand, served as a "custodian of a system of legal rights and duties" in which individuals could pursue their individual "ends and purposes" within a single civil association (Oakeshott 2003, 504). Arguing that a nomocracy had a positive character, Oakeshott stated that under this system of government, "*how* a government acts is a more important consideration than *what* it does," while these conditions were reversed for a telocracy (Oakeshott 2003, 505).[27]

On a theoretical level, the blend of Oakeshott's notions of the conservative disposition, the disharmony between civil association and enterprise association, the distinctions between telocracy and nomocracy, the rule of law, and adverbial conditions hint at some provisional conclusions about the application of his views to tax law. As de Cogan (2017, 110) explains, taxation in accord with this Oakeshottian framework could be appropriate insofar as it provided revenue for the administering of the civil association, such as a state, and insofar as it was employed in a neutral manner free of explicit or implicit incentives, and without coaxing taxpayers into making particular decisions in pursuit of substantive aims. Sin taxes, to take but one specific example, might violate this principle of tax neutrality. The limited nature of the civil association would thus preclude attempts by the state to use taxation for shared substantive aims such as equality or justice.

What further informed this view of taxation was an inborn trait of the conservative disposition: a fondness for incremental reform over transformative change. Although Oakeshott recognized that the conservative must adjust to the inevitability of change, the conservative still preferred "small and slow changes" over "large and sudden" (Oakeshott 1991, 410). Large and sudden changes were those that were inspired by the spirit of "innovation"—a word that Oakeshott, like Burke, understood to suggest negative and socially disruptive qualities. For Oakeshott and Burke, innovation was not synonymous with "improvement," nor did it mean automatic gain (Oakeshott 1991, 411).

[27] See Oakeshott's comments on Aristotle's teleology and its connection to notions of the common good in Oakeshott (2003, 118/9 n1).

We may reasonably conclude that taxing programs seeking systemic social changes were the kinds of policies Oakeshott thought should be met with extreme caution. To such extent that innovation was necessary, the man with the conservative temperament "considers the most favourable occasion for innovation to be when the projected change is most likely to be limited to what is intended and least likely to be corrupted by undesired and unmanageable consequences" (Oakeshott 1991, 412). It follows from this principle that legislation such as tax policy should be devised in a manner that is prudent, selective, and targeted.

This window into the application of Oakeshott's political thought to the subject of taxation can be made more transparent by considering his remarks on wealth redistribution schemes designed by the state. In his essay "The Rule of Law," in which Oakeshott described his conception of law as "the recognition of the authority of known, noninstrumental rules" (Oakeshott 1999, 148), he criticized the pretension that the law should be used to ensure the "equal or differential distribution of reputed benefits or opportunities" (Oakeshott 1999, 153). Similarly, *jus* (justice) in the rule of law was not to be equated with the provision of benefits, particularly in the guise of "fairness," or with ensuring the enjoyment of such benefits by everyone in the general population (Oakeshott 1999, 153). *Jus* rather connoted moral discourse about legal values inherent in the prescription of conditional obligations absent any motive of instrumentality (Oakeshott 1999, 152–56). These comments smoothly reconcile with his notion of the civil association as a mode of relationship whose modest responsibilities included prescribing adverbial codes of conduct but not establishing substantive ends—such as equality of wealth.

Even more, Oakeshott's commentary on the rise of the modern European state exhibited an underlying disdain for the expansion of its administrative powers, including the power to tax for a myriad of purposes. He identified this phenomenon as evidence of the trend toward telocracy spanning the eighteenth to the twentieth centuries. As he explained in his essay "On the Character of a Modern European State," civil rulers in the modern state, equipped with new powers of custodianship—such as the power to raise revenue, marking a shift from the sacerdotal authority to tax (Oakeshott 2003, 222–25)—were lured by the trappings of *universitas* to seek substantive purposes for citizens. These purposes included, most glaringly, national objectives fueled by war, which Oakeshott called "the enemy of civil association" (Oakeshott 2003, 273).

It also included the rise of the managerial state, presaged in many ways by Francis Bacon's exhortation for government to exploit natural resources for the satisfaction of human wants (Oakeshott 2003, 287–93). Reminiscent of Voegelinian and Nisbettian theories of modernity, Oakeshott rendered the managerial state as an attempt to relieve the miseries of the masses through the promise of salvation from self-alienation. These masses were characterized by the individual *manqué*, the unfulfilled and displaced soul, who required shelter by the state to gain purpose and enjoy welfare. "The emergence of the individual *manqué*, then, and of what may be called in the broadest sense the problem of the 'poor'," he wrote, "invited the government of a modern state to a managerial engagement in respect of the lives of at least some of its subjects in some important respects…" (Oakeshott 2003, 276/7).

The appearance of the managerial state "called for a command of resources which was gradually reflected in a modification of the idea of taxation," while "civil law was modified in having to make room for rules for awarding substantive benefits to assignable persons..." (Oakeshott 2003, 277).

Additionally, the ascent of the modern European state helped to midwife the "enlightened state" in the eighteenth century, which "identified itself as a development corporation in which virtue and cupidity were to constitute a single engagement directed or managed by a lord and his agents" (Oakeshott 2003, 299). The enlightened state was characterized by a meddlesome network of administrative and bureaucratic councils, managers, officials, and directors, all of whom were invested in promoted its substantive aims. This commitment entailed, among a string of administrative activities:

> substantial command over the resources of the estate, including the energy and the talents of its inhabitants; the directions of productive activity controlled by agreements, subsidies, exemptions, licences, penalties, man-power budgets, or orders, etc.; full employment or a guaranteed income; taxation transformed into a means of acquiring direct control over a large part of a 'national income' to be expended in favoured projects or distributed in the form of 'truck' or notionally tied income..." (Oakeshott 2003, 300/1).

For Oakeshott, tax policy in modernity that engineered the massive redistribution of wealth typified this managerial trend and defied the modest procedural aims of the rule of law in a civil association.

Oakeshott's thoughts on private property in general suggested a contempt for government experiments to extract private wealth from individuals. As discussed, he defended a vigorous conception of property rights in "The Political Economy of Freedom" that was "least qualified by arbitrary limits and exclusions" (Oakeshott 1991, 393). This essay conveyed a number of additional tenets of Oakeshott's economic thought, including the virtues of competition, the dangers of monopoly, collectivism, and syndicalism, and the importance of a strong and stable currency. The common trait of these principles was the diffusion of power, which in Oakeshott's view served as the palladium of a free society. "In short," he declared, "we consider ourselves to be free because no one in our society is allowed unlimited power..." (Oakeshott 1991, 388). Similar to his prior remarks on enterprise civil association distinctions and the telocratic aims of the modern European state, it is exceedingly difficult to square such comments in defense of freedom and private property and against wealth redistribution schemes with heavy taxation.

Oakeshott's commentary on civil and enterprise associations, rationalism, and the rule of law therefore insinuate several conclusions about an Oakeshottian approach to tax policy. Taxes should be limited in scope and enacted only to the extent that they provide sufficient revenue to the administration of the civil association. They should be general rather than specific and applied transparently and consistently throughout the commonwealth. Legislators and bureaucrats should not impose taxes patterned after their own rationalistic conception of the ideal society, nor pursuant to common aims of the state. They should rather implement them in a provident manner that preserves the traditions and temper of a people.

The promise of applying Oakeshott's idea of civil association to tax policy lies in its emphasis on simplicity in aim and consistency in execution. Attempting to mold tax policy in a multiplicity of ways to advance many and oftentimes conflicting aims—equality, happiness, justice—would create much confusion and irregularity. The outcome would be an incoherent patchwork of many laws. Tax law embedded in a civil association, on the other hand, would establish a code of rules that would, in theory, be equally applied and resist the inclination to create specialized rules, privileges, and exceptions that in Oakeshott's view marred contemporary tax policy. Under this framework, tax policy would be guided by regularity, predictability, and steadiness. It would also reduce the technocratic influence of managerial elites in government by diminishing their power to manipulate the tax code for seemingly benevolent or self-interested purposes.

We can see how this vision of taxation overlaps with but is not synonymous with the first conservative view outlined in this chapter. Whereas Oakeshott held a similar conservative appreciation for tradition and continuity, his conception of the state—a conception in which he included the power to tax—was more limited and accorded with the classical liberal strand of conservatism with regard to the purpose of government: the role of taxation, as was the role of all government policy, was to ensure the minimal conditions for the perpetuation of the state, and in particular for the administration of the rule of law. Indeed, Oakeshott wrote that the conservative believes that the "main (perhaps the only) specifically economic activity appropriate to government is the maintenance of a stable currency" (Oakeshott 1991, 431).

Consequently, Oakeshott did not offer a robust notion of the state in general, for he displayed deep misgivings over the idea that rulers should use governmental power to pursue shared political and moral ends. Oakeshott rather imagined the ideal ruler to be a detached arbiter: "The image of the ruler is the umpire whose business is to administer the rules of the game, or the chairman who governs the debate according to known rules but does not himself participate in it" (Oakeshott 1991, 427).

It was not that government should not act; on the contrary, by recognizing and permitting individuals to hold divergent opinions and preferences in the commonwealth, government shouldered the responsibility to "keep its subjects at peace with one another in the activities in which they have chosen to seek their happiness" (Oakeshott 1991, 430). For "governing is recognized as a specific and limited activity; not the management of an enterprise, but the rule of those engaged in a great diversity of self-chosen enterprises" (Oakeshott 1991, 429).

Although Oakeshott assailed the managerial state, his thought, de Cogan argues, could accommodate the activity of government reformers tapping into historical experience and knowledge to suggest incremental alterations to existing policies, a belief harmonious with Oakeshott's attraction to prudential reform over wide-scale change. The British government's Office of Tax Simplification, established in 2010, offered one possible application of uniting this idea with Oakeshott's modest notion of taxation. As de Cogan writes, "…[F]or a highly regarded group of experts to embark on limited examinations of important questions, to draw on established political traditions, to make a range of feasible recommendations, but to leave the ultimate decisions to government, is about as close as a programme of tax reform could approach to our Oakeshottian story" (de Cogan 2017, 123).

In our final analysis, Oakeshott's minimalist conception of the state reinforced his belief, as articulated in "The Political Economy of Freedom" that "the most general condition of our freedom" was "the absence from our society of overwhelming concentrations of power" (Oakeshott 1991, 388). Elsewhere he declared that "the rule of law is the greatest single condition of our freedom" (Oakeshott 1991, 391). Oakeshott's constrained vision of the civil association and taxation was ultimately inspired not by the prospect of sparking capitalist enterprise but by securing the most delicate and valuable of possessions in a commonwealth: liberty under law.

6.4.2.2 Buckley, Will, and Sowell

It is worth mentioning a number of modern American conservative thinkers who can reasonably be located in this Oakeshottian school for communicating a similar vision of the modest state and a corresponding aversion to meddlesome taxation. Among these prominent thinkers was William F. Buckley, founder of the conservative opinion magazine *National Review* and the television series *Firing Line* and considered by many to be the most influential figure in the post-World War II conservative movement in the United States. Spanning from his undergraduate years at Yale University to his later life, Buckley was a proponent of limited constitutional government. The first prong in the credo of *National Review*'s mission statement (1955) stated that it was "the job of centralized government (in peacetime) to protect its citizens' lives, liberty and property." For "[a]ll other activities of government tend to diminish freedom and hamper progress" (Buckley 1955).

Buckley, who was moved by the economic ideas of Milton Friedman, wed this constrained notion of government with a celebration of free enterprise and competitive capitalism. *National Review*'s mission statement declared that the "competitive price system is indispensable to liberty and material progress" (Buckley 1955). Lee Edwards (2010, 108) writes that "capitalism," along with Communism and faith, were the three "central themes" of *Firing Line* in its three decades of existence. Buckley's advocacy of free enterprise was complemented by his sharp criticism of Social Security and other sprawling national welfare programs for generating economic costs, providing disincentives for responsible behavior, and being compulsory and redistributionist, among various reasons (see Buckley 2016, 168–88; 1973, 17–50). Insofar as state welfare was defensible, he preferred it to be administered on a local level (Buckley 2016, 202).

Buckley, perhaps more so than any other thinker discussed in this chapter besides Thomas Sowell, examined taxation with an abiding interest throughout his intellectual life. Guided by his support for limited constitutional government and free enterprise, Buckley consistently called for the reduction in tax rates in his writings and television appearances. In his first book, *God and Man at Yale*, Buckley rebuked the income tax and inheritance tax, which were championed by the economics textbooks assigned at Yale when he was an undergraduate, for spreading the collectivist mentality he believed was permeating the university's campus. Buckley further attacked wealth redistribution and offered a resolute defense of private property rights in the book (Buckley 1977, 49–62).

Buckley maintained this opposition to burdensome taxation throughout his adult life. In *Four Reforms*, a book in which he cited Oakeshott multiple times (Buckley 1973, 4–5, 150), Buckley formulated a thorough program of tax reform for the 1970s that included, among various proposals, a flat tax of fifteen percent on all income, the abolition of the progressive income tax and corporation tax, and the elimination of most deductions and all exemptions (Buckley 1973, 63/4).[28] Buckley in general was disgusted by the winding labyrinths of the modern U.S. tax code. "The incomprehensibility of modern IRS language challenges the dignity of self-rule," he bitterly observed in 2005 (Buckley 2005a).

Moreover, Buckley provided dynamic public platforms for free-market thinkers and supply-sider economists to advertise the virtues of capitalism and tax cuts. According to Edwards, after Buckley hired economist Alan Reynolds to write for *National Review*, the publication became the "first journal of public opinion to have a writer with a supply-side perspective on staff" (Edwards 2010, 125). Fond of the Laffer curve, Buckley invited supply-siders such as Arthur Laffer and George Gilder on *Firing Line* to spar with Keynesians such as John Kenneth Galbraith (Edwards 2010, 125).

One tax that Buckley did approve of was the land tax. Echoing the logic of Henry George, Buckley noted in 2000 that there was an "infinite capacity to increase capital and to increase labor, but none to increase land, and since wealth is a function of how they play against each other, land should be thought of as common property." He said, "I've run into tons of situations where I think the single-tax theory would be applicable."[29] Such reasoning, we recall, bears a resemblance to Churchill's initial support for the tax.

In general, Buckley, similar to many of the conservative thinkers mentioned in this chapter, did not fetishize free enterprise like influential strands of classical liberal and libertarian thought. Late in his life, he was quoted as saying, "The trouble with the emphasis in conservatism on the market, is that it becomes rather boring. You hear it once, you master the idea" (Robin 2018, 202). And he did not shy from criticizing the extreme effects of capitalism (Buckley 2005b), nor repudiate the notion that selective regulations of the market might at times be necessary (Buckley 2016, 193).

In addition to Buckley, we may add George F. Will, a former editor of *National Review* and long-time *Washington Post* columnist, and Thomas Sowell, professor of economics affiliated with The Hoover Institution, as influential American conservative thinkers who reside most comfortably within this second school on taxation. Both thinkers shifted their thinking over time on economics and the role of

[28] See also Buckley's many comments on Reaganomics and taxation in Buckley (1985).

[29] "In Depth: William F. Buckley Jr.," C-SPAN, April 2, 2000, https://www.c-span.org/video/?156252-1/depth-william-f-buckley-jr, accessed March 13, 2021.

government. Will moved from an Aristotelian understanding of politics and a theoretical endorsement of the welfare state in the 1980s to a more libertarian conception of government later in his intellectual life. Sowell held Marxist sympathies in his youth before emerging as a firm proponent of market economies. Their settled political philosophies placed heavy weight on the notion that intrusive governmental regulations, including onerous taxes, would create counterproductive social and economic consequences such as the suffocation of entrepreneurial activity, the discouragement of personal responsibility, and the decline in public prosperity.[30] Will and Sowell, we should add, have identified as a libertarian in some variant, as has Buckley.[31]

It is this brief snapshot of Buckley, Will, and Sowell that suggest a closer adherence to the Oakeshottian school than to the other two schools explored in this chapter. Their fully matured political and economic beliefs conveyed a vigorous defense of limited constitutional government, free enterprise, private property rights, and minimal taxes, a creed that illustrated their broader philosophical observations on the limits of rationality and the primacy of individual liberty. They also embraced elements of moral and social traditionalism in their thought. To some extent the beliefs of Buckley, Will, and Sowell overlapped with the other two schools, but the thinkers also imparted varying degrees of emphasis on important matters. They expressed a deeper suspicion than the first school over the efficacy of taxes to advance the public welfare, for instance. Nor did Buckley, Will, and Sowell lay as much stress as Kirk did on the impact of taxation on agrarian communities. Furthermore, unlike the third school, they did not display a Nisbettian hostility to the very credibility of the state.

There are certainly tensions within the Oakeshottian school, such as differences regarding religious faith. Yet its thinkers are ultimately bound by the judgment that government efforts to promote hardened conceptions of the common good, or what Oakeshott called a "substantive aim", through taxation and other invasive schemes were dangerous enterprises that were likely to fail and destined to tyrannize.

6.4.3 The Third School of Thought: Taxation, the Modern State, and the War Economy

Robert Nisbet, a twentieth-century sociologist associated with the University of California, Berkeley and Columbia University, represents the third school of conservative thought. This school harbors grave doubt about the very credibility of taxation in the modern state. The support granted by the previous thinkers to some

---

[30] For Will, consult, among many, Will (1984, 2011, 2019). For Sowell, consult, among many, Sowell (1996, 1999, 2004, 2007, 2012).

[31] Will said in 2019 that he embraced "soft libertarianism." See Nordlinger (2019). Sowell said in 1999 that "libertarian" was the best way to describe him, even though he held differences with the movement regarding the military. See Sawhill (1999). For Buckley, see Buckley (2008).

forms of tax policy effectively conveyed implicit or explicit recognition of the legitimacy of a central government to extract money from its subjects. Nisbet, however, expressed an uncommon hostility within the conservative tradition to the elemental notion that the state should possess this power to tax in the first place—and to the validity of the state in general. Nisbet's thoughts on this matter can best be framed by understanding his conception of the modern state and his description of the relationship among the state, voluntary associations, and the individual.

First and foremost, however, Nisbet, more so than most other philosophers and statesmen in the conservative tradition, questioned the fundamental existence and legitimacy of the state. "…[T]he Western state's very existence in the ancient world and in the modern since the Reformation," he wrote in *Twilight of Authority*, "has represented a kind of built-in war against traditional society and its ingrained authorities" (Nisbet 2000, 186/7). The level of intensity in Nisbet's attack on the state, as demonstrated by this comment, is not matched in the writings of Burke, Kirk, Churchill, Oakeshott, Buckley, Sowell, and Will. These thinkers, like Nisbet, were quite aware of the dangerous augmentation of the modern state, the treacherous marriage between taxation and war, and the displacement of local authority by the national government. Ranging from Oakeshott's minimal state to Churchill's more expansive one, however, such conservatives accepted, if not promoted, the legitimacy of the state as a necessary and potentially salutary instrument to fulfill the basic demands of public administration and to serve the common good.

Nisbet's unease over modernity therefore derived from the emergence of the all-encompassing state and its effect on the wider social order. As he wrote in his most important work, *The Quest for Community*:

> …[T]he single most decisive influence upon Western social organization has been the rise and development of the centralized territorial State. ...The conflict between the central power of the political State and the whole set of functions and authorities contained in church, family, guild, and local community has been, I believe, the main source of those dislocations of social structure and uprootings of status which lie behind the problem of community in our age (Nisbet 2010, 91).

Nisbet proceeded to quote Walter Lippman to highlight what he believed were the boundless powers accumulated by the state in modernity:

> A State is absolute in the sense which I have in mind when it claims the right to a monopoly of all the force within the community, to make war, to make peace, to conscript life, to tax, to establish and disestablish property, to define crime, to punish disobedience, to control education, to supervise the family, to regulate personal habits, and to censor opinions (Nisbet 2010, 95).

Nisbet retained this conception in his own description of the state in the *Quest for Community*: "The modern State is monistic; its authority extends directly to *all* individuals within its boundaries" (Nisbet 2010, 95). The character of politics in modernity, then, was defined by a relentless contest among various parties grasping for power. "The extraordinary unity of relationship in the contemporary State, together with its massive accumulation of effective functions," he observed, "makes the control of the State the greatest single goal, or prize, in modern struggles for power" (Nisbet 2010, 95).[32]

Nisbet did in fact recognize "some resplendent gains in liberty and welfare," such as the abolition of slavery, as the product of the centralizing forces of the modern state (Nisbet 2000, 187). Yet he suggested that these advantages were vastly outweighed by their pernicious consequences, the most important of which was the steady encroachment of government on the liberty of social associations. Such associations that Nisbet often praised in his writings—such as the church, the guild, and the family—were fundamental to civilized society in his judgment because they offered spiritual and material support for individuals: associations gave them a sense of belonging and purpose, furnished religious and moral instruction, and granted welfare to those in times of need. Social groups promoted friendship and shaped the character of their members as well, reflecting the spirit of association Alexis de Tocqueville eloquently described in *Democracy in America*, a book Nisbet frequently quoted.

Nisbet captured all of these themes in the *Quest for Community*. As he explained in the book, social associations provided "affection, friendship, prestige, recognition" (Nisbet 2010, 44). Furthermore:

> This is the area of association from which the individual commonly gains his concept of the outer world and his sense of position in it. His concrete feelings of status and role, of protection and freedom, his differentiation between good and bad, between order and disorder and guilt and innocence, arise and are shaped largely by his relations within this realm of primary association (Nisbet 2010, 44).[33]

This theory of association was rooted in Nisbet's Aristotelian belief, as discussed in Section Two, that men and women were best understood as naturally social creatures rather than as scattered atoms. Associations thus brought out their full humanity when they lived in affectionate communion with others.

More important for the purposes of this chapter, these institutional associations *did not derive from the cold mandate of a centralized and bureaucratized government*. They were diffuse, organic, and local—not centrally planned, coerced, and national, as were the edicts of the modern state. The "revolutionary role of the State in history," Nisbet lamented in the *Quest for Community*, has been manifested, among many occurrences, by "the whole development of an administrative bureaucracy that gradually absorbed functions and authorities formerly resident in other associations" (Nisbet 2010, 109/10). In addition, these associations traditionally served as checks against the aggrandizement of the state. "The very prestige and functional importance of church, family, guild, and local community as allegiances limited the absoluteness of the State's power," he wrote (Nisbet 2010, 96).

[32] Consult also Nisbet's essay "Cloaking the State's Dagger," *Reason* (October 1984), https://reason.com/1984/10/01/cloaking-the-states-dagger/, accessed March 11, 2021.

[33] For a recent discussion of Nisbet's thoughts on associations and their application to First Amendment law, see Sheahan (2020).

According to Nisbet, the false hope of redemptive power in the modern state, and the modern state's muscular intrusion into these social associations, represented the most vicious effect of the expansion of government authority in the twentieth century. While Nisbet did not outline his thoughts on taxation in a systematic fashion, we can begin to tease out the connection between his social and political philosophy and taxation: the modern state's displacement of voluntary associations and assumption of control over the functions conventionally fulfilled by such associations—such as moral and religious guidance and material succor—were fueled, in great part, by the broad extension of its taxing power over all aspects of social life. Nisbet never *explicitly* wrote that taxes, in theory, were wholly illegitimate. But he did maintain that the taxing power was one of the consequential ways that the modern state spawned the bureaucratization and centralization of power in one plenary authority, in turn foisting a rigid formula of uniformity on complex society and inducing a rise in tyranny.

This analysis of Nisbet is rooted in a number of his statements on taxation. In *Twilight of Authority*, he first reminded readers, in the spirit of Rousseau, that the traditional power exerted by kings and princes represented by the "tax collector and the military" was "very weak" compared to the power wielded by a government dependent on the general will. Yet modernity had ushered in an age characterized by "the almost incessant growth in power over the lives of human beings" (Nisbet 2000, 177), or what Nisbet called "the new despotism" (Nisbet 2000, 180).[34] This despotism signified the dark denouement of the national regulatory state, among which its taxing schemes were a central feature. "In the name of education, welfare, taxation, safety, health, and environment, to mention but a few of the laudable ends involved," he observed, "the new despotism confronts us at every turn" (Nisbet 2000, 180).

Nisbet's ambivalent attitude toward capitalism—a term he believed was outdated (Nisbet 2000, 193)—also implied a measure of deep regret over the ascent of the modern state's taxing power. On the one hand, Nisbet criticized laissez-faire capitalism for intensifying the harmful consequences of individualism (Nisbet 2010, 218–22). On the other hand, he hinted at the virtues of free enterprise. In *Twilight of Authority*, for instance, Nisbet singled out the "modern radical mind" with an "invariably negative reaction to private enterprise, profit, and competition." Moreover, the modern state widened its bureaucratic powers "by virtue of the controls and restraints it has placed upon capitalist enterprise," a trend that was further fanned by the regulatory capture of federal agencies by influential industry leaders (Nisbet 2000, 193).

Three additional notes on Nisbet's economic thought are necessary here. First, Nisbet blamed "social equalitarianism" and the prioritization of "economic or material values" as the chief causes of inflation (Nisbet 2000, 88), in effect ascribing the indirect taxation of consumers' purchasing power to the allure of modern equality

[34] For the origins of this phrase, see Hewart (1929).

and the rise of materialism. Second, Nisbet criticized minimum wage laws for increasing unemployment among inexperienced youth (Nisbet 2000, 86).

Third, and more significant, Nisbet objected to modern social welfare schemes financed by the "fresh infusion of large public monies," such as wars against poverty, urban renewal, and public housing (Nisbet 2000, 82). Nisbet also attacked Christopher Jencks' proposal for wealth redistribution in the name of equality, arguing that this plan would lead to even greater social controls over all aspects of human life (Nisbet 2000, 194/5). In addition, social insurance programs created a perverse incentive structure that discredited the traditional value of labor. "…[T]he ethic of work cannot for very long have the compulsion it has immemorially had in a society now politically committed to unemployment compensation, food stamps, Social Security, and Medicare," he explained (Nisbet 2000, 85). Acknowledging that a minimum amount of security would appear to be an indispensable standard of a community, Nisbet still remained uncertain whether such security was possible without undermining the motivation for industry (Nisbet 2000, 85).

Nisbet in *Twilight of Authority* went so far as to insinuate a harmonious relationship between the family and capitalism. Citing Joseph Schumpeter, Nisbet noted that "the household" was "the main engine of modern capitalist development." He continued: "Not economic man but, quite literally, the head of the household working for the present *and future* of the members of his family, and hence saving and investing in however small degree, is the central figure in the capitalist drama, as in all earlier forms of economy" (Nisbet 2000, 199).[35] Without probing too deeply into Nisbet's general economic thought, we may reasonably conclude that his capitalist sympathies, like Kirk's, lay with small-scale enterprise immersed in local communities and not with the modern corporation and its bureaucratic tendencies. It bears reminder that such comments about national insurance programs, regulatory meddling, wealth redistribution, and the enlargement of government's taxing powers marked Nisbet's greatest anxiety about the modern age: the national government had dislodged voluntary associations as the primary source of spiritual meaning and social welfare.

One compelling implication of Nisbet's insights here is that in many ways they veered toward the libertarian conception of the state. For both parties, the state represented the menacing fusion of monopoly and coercion that was congenitally disposed to smothering the people's liberties, such as through various taxing schemes. Yet there are also crucial differences in their approaches to taxation. The traditional libertarian—or at least its radical variant—has treated taxation as a form of theft: according to this view, it was the legalized coercion of wealth transfers that would otherwise be unlawful if engineered by a private party.[36] For Nisbet, however, taxation was not the theft of money; it was the theft of the autonomy of corporate associations.

---

[35] Of course, Schumpeter was more praiseworthy than Nisbet of the contributions of large firms to society.

[36] Variations of this argument can be found, among many, in Bastiat (2018); Rothbard (2002); and Nozick (2013).

There are other important differences, of course. Nisbet, for instance, did not adopt libertarians' binary framework that pitted the individual against the state, instead identifying the key contest in modernity to be the social group versus the state (Nisbet 2010, 100). He was also far more adamant than most libertarians in defending traditional moral values, and conveyed deeper suspicions over efforts to maximize individual autonomy, particularly at the expense of these values. On the subject of tax policy and the state, however, Nisbet's kinship with libertarianism exposes an antipathy toward the legitimacy of government taxation sharper than the attitudes of the other conservative thinkers studied in this chapter.

Perhaps the most glaring repercussion of the frightful convergence between the modern state and the taxing power in Nisbet's view was what he called the "war economy" (Nisbet 2010, 35). Similar to Oakeshott's observation that war was the enemy of civil association, Nisbet wrote in the *Quest for Community*:

> More than one historian has observed that it is in time of war that many of the reforms, first advocated by socialists, have been accepted by capitalist governments and made parts of the structures of their societies. Equalization of wealth, progressive taxation, nationalization of industries, the raising of wages and improvements in working conditions, worker-management councils, housing ventures, death taxes, unemployment insurance plans, pension systems, and the enfranchisement of formerly voteless elements of the population have all been, in one country or another, achieved or advanced under the impress of war. The tremendous urge toward unity and the resolution of group differences, which is a part of modern war, carries with it certain leveling and humanitarian measures not to be omitted from the full history of modern warfare. For all the horrors of contemporary war and the genuine abhorrence of war which still exists among populations, its incidental benefits in the realm of social reform cannot be overlooked (Nisbet 2010, 34).

These manifold reform efforts underscored Nisbet's grave concern, once again, that the trend of the modern state was to swallow up responsibilities that were previously met by voluntary associations and local communities. Notice that many of the reforms Nisbet listed here were coterminous with the taxing power or financed by tax revenues.

The menace of modern war for Nisbet was thus characterized by a variety of cruel features. First, this form of war was waged in the name of some sort of ideological crusade (Nisbet 2010, 32–34). Second, organized warfare required mass-scale public financing (a reality, we should add, that is not distinctive of modern war). Third, war could be used as a pretext to enact a maze of novel social and economic programs, including those involving new forms of taxation.[37] Fourth, these programs inevitably led to centralization, bureaucratization, and uniformity.

These three consequences touched the most sensitive nerves of Nisbet's social and political thought: they exposed the muscular enhancement of the modern state; they swept away the authority of voluntary associations and local communities; and they embodied the modern state's attempt in the wake of the war economy to engineer innovative schemes that slammed down the inflexible principle of equality on

[37] One could offer as an addendum to Nisbet's list the U.S. Congress' Revenue Act of 1861, which introduced the first federal income tax in U.S. history to help finance the Union's war against the Confederacy.

the various shades and complexions of social life. As Nisbet expounded in *Twilight of Authority*:

> If we plot the development of social equality in Western society over the past few centuries, we find that it follows almost perfectly the development of centralization and bureaucratization in the political sphere. Even more strikingly, the development of equality follows the trajectory of war. It is in periods of national, mass warfare that we observe the greatest advances of the egalitarian ethic in many areas. The point is that even if no egalitarian ethic existed, if there were not the vein of equality in the modern Western mind that there so plainly is, the mere existence of political and military centralization in the modern world would have brought about pretty much the same patterns of equality we see around us.
>
> My own estimate is that a good 75 per cent of all the national programs which have been instituted in Western countries during the past two centuries to equalize income, property, education, working conditions, and other aspects of life have been in the first instance adjuncts of the war state and of the war economy. Equality is far from least among the qualities which go with social and economic programs of nationalization during times of war (Nisbet 2000, 200/1).

Accordingly, the rapid growth of the taxing power in times of war did not simply represent the swelling of the modern state and the vanishing of local authority. It also signified a new conception of man in modernity defined by the theme of equality, or what Nisbet called "mass equalitarianism" or the "New Equality," an aim he believed was the product of the new despotism (Nisbet 2000, 180). The vanguards of these ideas, the "New Equalitarians" (whose founder, according to Nisbet (2000, 194), was Rousseau), sought to impose not equality under the law or equality of opportunity but "*equality of condition, equality of result*" (Nisbet 2000, 181).

Therefore, in an echo of Burke's insight into the symbiosis of revolution, war, and the drive for equality during the French Revolution, Nisbet wrote in *Twilight of Authority*, "There is nothing paradoxical in the fondness of equalitarians for centralized power, the kind that the military best evidences, and the fondness of centralizers for equality" (Nisbet 2000, 181). Organizing small communities, such as monastic orders, based on these forms of equality were noble undertakings. When engineered by the state, however, they led to the violent strengthening of the government's powers of war and its national bureaucracy (Nisbet 2000, 181). And the strive toward equality, unlike the preservation of local community, knew no boundaries (Nisbet 2000, 184).

This conception of equality militated against an enduring motif of Nisbet's thought and a cornerstone of conservatives' views on taxation: there were a variety and complexity of social life, overflowing with diffuse associations, institutions, and groups, that could not—and should not—be squared into uniformity by public authorities. Although the Christian faith taught that all human beings were equal in the eyes of God, they were different in countless other ways with regard to rank, wealth, pedigree, education, and privilege, religion, and personal preference, among many variables. Inequalities and distinctions were thus natural and inescapable expressions of the human condition.

In addition to its practical endangerment of voluntary associations, then, the taxing power in the modern state posed an existential threat to man. Taxing schemes with the aim of pressing equality on unequal people embodied a futile attempt to eliminate these distinctions and inequalities—and thereby embodied a revolt against the human condition.

In order to recover a proper sense of man and restore the primacy of local community, Nisbet at the end of the *Quest for Community* actually communicated an implicit measure of approval of the state—but of one that was far more restrained than the bulging governments he believed characterized modernity. Urging readers to resist the state that was bureaucratic, administrative, and centralized, he praised a second conception of the state that would "maintain a pluralism of functions and loyalties in the lives of its people" (Nisbet 2010, 261), which would be inspired by what Nisbet called a "new philosophy of laissez faire" (Nisbet 2010, 256). This new state would "not spurn the demands of human security," he explained, but it would "seek means by which such demands can be met through spontaneous association and creation rather than through bureaucratic rigidities of formal law and administration" (Nisbet 2010, 262). The logical consequence of this general principle would be the dramatic reduction—but not necessarily the complete elimination—of the central state's taxing powers that had aspired to fulfill social responsibilities previously met by local associations. For Nisbet, the traditional sources of meaning, purpose, and affection in society could be crushed, not enhanced, by the distant and faceless tax collector.

6.5 Conclusion: When Is Taxation Just?

As demonstrated throughout this chapter, areas of tension prevail among the various conservative thinkers concerning specific questions about taxation, such as whether to utilize taxes to advance common purposes of society, whether to grant priority to taxes on inherited wealth or active wealth, and whether the very power of taxation itself lacked moral credibility. Such differences can be attributed both to the particular political theories of each thinker and to the distinctive set of constraints, incentives, and audiences they confronted as thinkers and statesmen.

In addition, conservatives' commentaries on taxation —due to their intellectual substance and their incomplete nature— remain vulnerable to criticisms and call out for additional clarification. With regard to the first school, where exactly can one draw a line between the use of tax policy to serve the public welfare and the use of tax policy to restrict individual freedoms? From the perspectives of the thinkers in this school, the state financing of public buildings or national insurance programs through taxation may appear to promote the common good. But to others—especially classical liberals and libertarians—these initiatives may undermine it by coercing individuals into giving money to government to underwrite extravagant and inefficient projects unsupported by a sizable number of subjects or citizens.

Although Oakeshott embraced Aristotelian principles about the *social* nature of man, the second school he represents is open to the charge that the idea of civil association flouts the *teleological* nature of man. Indeed, he more or less acknowledged this implication in his attack on telocracy. But if a state is not helping to facilitate a final end through taxation or other public instruments, is this second school not prone to the conservative and communitarian indictment of deontological liberalism, namely that it is not guided by ultimate moral objectives and simply reduces man to the imperatives of self-preservation and the maximization of autonomy?

Observers could also find fault with the third school. Did Nisbet's praise of voluntary associations and his hostile opposition to the state insufficiently account for the maltreatment of individuals within *local* structures of social and economic organization? The modern state has certainly been responsible for varying degrees of political misconduct and persecution, ranging from financial corruption to totalitarianism. But have not the church, the guild, and the clan throughout history also oppressed men and women and denied to them their individual rights? If so, does not the state hold some duty to safeguard these rights if local organizations cannot?

This point introduces additional lines of criticism directed at all three schools: do most taxes in fact generate the level of despotism that conservative thinkers have implied? Is it true that incremental increases in a state's taxing power will naturally lead to unbounded tyranny? Moreover, does not the state bear at least *some* obligation to ensure that the people do not fall below a certain social and economic threshold? (Churchill's support for national insurance leaves him protected from this criticism.) Does taxation, even burdensome taxation, amount to the heights of social engineering practiced by the most oppressive of twentieth-century regimes? When is a tax a form of social engineering, and when is a tax prudent? Can one draw a meaningful distinction between tax administration on a local level and that on a national level? If the conservative disposition is to conserve the underlying social order, what if this social order was built up in part by taxation? One can, of course, imagine conservatives' responses to these challenges. At the very least, we may conclude that many opportunities remain for conservative thinkers to more fully explicate the principles and policies animating a coherent vision of conservative tax policy.

Even with such areas of ambiguity in their thought, conservatives have enriched our understanding of taxation by harmonizing the subject with their distinctive insights into human nature, society, and the state. Their thought has given rise to a number of key themes that suggest a general guiding theoretical framework[38] for just taxation from the conservative point of view:

- First, the tax must provide sufficient revenue to secure the basic administrative functions of a state, such as to pay judicial officers and ensure the operation of the courts. Even Nisbet, the most suspicious among this chapter's thinkers of the

[38] In practice, of course, conservative statesmen and governments have not always heeded these principles.

very legitimacy of a state, acknowledged the rule of law as a necessary underpinning of a functioning society in modernity.
- Second, the tax must *not* be used to equalize wealth, a tenet stemming from conservatives' observations on the unavoidable inequalities of human beings in experience, preference, knowledge, and many other factors.
- Third, a tax must not be used to finance national programs that displace the functions, responsibilities, and purposes of voluntary associations that lie between the individual and the state. Churchill came the closest among the thinkers to granting legitimacy to wide-scale insurance programs, although even he recognized that they could not replace the family as a source of aid and comfort.[39]
- Fourth, taxation must be selective in application and modest in aim, reflecting conservatives' awareness of the limits of rationalism and the complexity of society. Even those who were more favorable to tax policy for the purpose of funding public works and programs, such as Burke and Churchill, were keenly aware of the dangers of promiscuous taxation.
- Fifth, the tax must not be promulgated arbitrarily and suddenly. Rather, it must be prudentially enacted through deliberative institutions within a constitutional structure.
- Sixth, the tax must be transparent and consistently enforced.
- Seventh, all things being equal, the state should avoid progressive income taxes (again, Churchill departed from this principle in some sense) and minimize taxes on capital.
- Eighth, because society was a sacred partnership connecting the past, present, and future, a government's tax policy should not impose heavy financial burdens on generations to come.

The final common principle, and perhaps the one that best captures these prior tenets, is that a just tax must not seek to socially engineer society to meet abstract moral and social objectives. The conservative mindset is acutely conscious of the disruptive effect of widespread taxing schemes on the social order of the state. Any proposed policy that seeks to change this order—and all of the conservative thinkers discussed in this chapter desired some kind of social reform to varying extents—must attempt to minimize such dislocation to the fullest extent possible.

All of these principles illustrate conservatives' most important philosophical conception of the link between taxation and the modern state: the spiritual vacuum created by the dissolution of a belief in a God-centered transcendent order and the decline in organized religion and traditional morality, combined with the rise of modern rationalism and its managerial and technocratic tendencies, have fueled the ascent of radical ideologies. These ideologies have yearned to create heaven on earth in its various manifestations—equalize wealth, level society, eliminate social distinctions, establish equality, achieve immanent perfection—by leveraging and abusing the powers of the modern state, including the power to tax.

[39] Consult "Family Man," *International Churchill Society*, https://winstonchurchill.org/the-life-of-churchill/life/family-man/, accessed March 9, 2021.

According to the conservative outlook, this was a futile and perilous endeavor. The limited uses of taxation to meet the basic needs of a state, or to finance selective public monuments or insurance programs, were prudential measures to preserve order or promote a modest conception of the common good and were tempered by conservatives' anti-utopian notions of man and society. Yet taxes used to finance sweeping programs for the purpose of fundamentally altering the nature of man and the settled texture of society were not only doomed to fail but marked a rebellion against the human soul.

Compañía of Case Law

United States.

Compañia General de Tabacos de Filipinas v. Collector of Internal Revenue, 275 U.S. 87 (1927).

References

Attarian, John. 1996. Russell Kirk's Economics of the Permanent Things. *Foundation for Economic Education*. Available at https://fee.org/articles/russell-kirks-economics-of-the-permanent-things/.

———. 1998. Russell Kirk's Political Economy. *Modern Age* 40: 87–97.

Bastiat, Frederic. 2018. *The Law*. Revised by David M. Hart. Indianapolis: Liberty Fund. Available at https://oll.libertyfund.org/title/the-law-revised-lf-ed.

Buckley, William F., Jr. 1955. Our Mission Statement. *National Review*. Available at https://www.nationalreview.com/1955/11/our-mission-statement-william-f-buckley-jr/.

———. 1973. *Four Reforms: A Program for the 70's*. New York: G.P. Putnam's Sons.

———. 1977. *God and Man at Yale: The Superstitions of 'Academic Freedom'*. South Bend: Gateway Editions.

———. 1985. In *Right Reason*, ed. Richard Brookhiser. Boston: Little, Brown and Company.

———. 2005a. Whither Taxes? *National Review Online*, January 4, 2005. Available at https://www.nationalreview.com/2005/01/whither-taxes-william-f-buckley-jr/.

———. 2005b. Capitalism's Boil. *National Review Online*. Available at https://www.nationalreview.com/2005/04/capitalisms-boil-william-f-buckley-jr/.

———. 2008. In *Happy Days Were Here Again: Reflections of a Libertarian Journalist*, ed. Patricia Bozell. New York: Basic Books.

———. 2015. *The Unmasking of a Mayor*. New York: Encounter Books.

———. 2016. *Up from Liberalism*. Mansfield Center: Martino Publishing.

Burke, Edmund. 1869. *The Works of the Right Honourable Edmund Burke*. Vol. VI. London: Bell & Daldy.

Cannadine, David, ed. 1989. *Blood, Toil, Tears and Sweat: The Speeches of Winston Churchill*. Boston: Houghton Mifflin Company.

Churchill, Winston. 1909. *Liberalism and the Social Problem*. New York: Hodder and Stoughton.

———. 1991. *Great Contemporaries*. New York: W.W. Norton & Company.

Collins, Gregory M. 2020. *Commerce and Manners in Edmund Burke's Political Economy*. Cambridge: Cambridge University Press.

Daunton, Martin. 1997. Churchill at the Treasury: Remaking Conservative Taxation Policy, 1924–1929. *Revue Belge de Philologie et d'Histoire* 75 (4): 1063–1083.
———. 2002. *Just Taxes: The Politics of Taxation in Britain, 1914–1979*. Cambridge: Cambridge University Press.
de Cogan, Dominic. 2017. Michael Oakeshott and the Conservative Disposition in Tax Law. In *Philosophical Foundations of Tax Law*, ed. Monica Bhandari, 101. Oxford: Oxford University Press.
Demobilisation. 22 October 1945. Vol. 414, Hansard. UK Parliament, 1703-04. https://api.parliament.uk/historic-hansard/commons/1945/oct/22/demobilisation.
Economic Situation. 12 March 1947. Vol. 434, Hansard. UK Parliament, 1349. https://api.parliament.uk/historic-hansard/commons/1947/mar/12/economic-situation.
Edwards, Lee. 2010. *William F. Buckley Jr.: The Maker of a Movement*. Wilmington: ISI Books.
Elofson, Warren M., and John A. Woods, eds. 1996. *The Writings and Speeches of Edmund Burke. Vol. 3, Party, Parliament, and the American War 1774–1780*. Oxford: Clarendon Press.
Family Man. *International Churchill Society*. https://winstonchurchill.org/the-life-of-churchill/life/family-man/.
Financial Statement. 28 April 1925. Vol. 183, Hansard. UK Parliament, 89. https://hansard.parliament.uk/Commons/1925-04-28/debates/b2d498aa-4e33-443c-8f89-f2f3e8f7238c/FinancialStatement.
Fitzwilliam, Charles W., and Richard Bourke, eds. 1844. *Correspondence of the Right Honourable Edmund Burke*. Vol. III. London: Francis & John Rivington.
Franco, Paul. 1990. Michael Oakeshott as Liberal Theorist. *Political Theory* 18: 411–436.
Gilbert, Martin. 1981. *Churchill's Political Philosophy*. Oxford: Oxford University Press.
———. 1991. *Churchill: A Life*. New York: Henry Holt and Company.
Hewart, Gordon. 1929. *The New Despotism*. London: Ernest Benn Limited.
In Depth: William F. Buckley Jr. 2000. C-SPAN. https://www.c-span.org/video/?156252-1/depth-william-f-buckley-jr.
James, Robert R., ed. 1974a. *Winston S. Churchill: His Complete Speeches 1897–1963. Vol. 1, 1897–1908*. New York: Chelsea House Publishers.
———. 1974b. *Winston S. Churchill: His Complete Speeches 1897–1963. Vol. 5, 1928–1935*. New York: Chelsea House Publishers.
Jewell, Jason. 2020. The Extent of Russell Kirk's Support for the Free Market. *Journal of Markets & Morality* 23: 61–75.
Jones, Peter M. 1995. *Reform and Revolution in France: The Politics of Transition, 1774–1791*. Cambridge: Cambridge University Press.
Kirk, Russell. 1957a. *The Intelligent Woman's Guide to Conservatism*. New York: The Devin-Adair Company.
———. 1957b. Ideology and Political Economy. *America* 96: 388–391.
———. 1962. *A Program for Conservatives*. Chicago: Henry Regnery Company.
———. 1963. *Confessions of a Bohemian Tory: Episodes and Reflections of a Vagrant Career*. New York: Fleet Publishing Co.
———. 1971a. "No Hope for Independent Schools?" To the Point, *Los Angeles Times Syndicate*—General Features Corp. Division, July 14.
———. 1971b. "Tax Credit: One Way to Save Independent Colleges." To the Point, *Los Angeles Times Syndicate*—General Features Corp. Division, September 13/14.
———. 1982. Is Capitalism Still Viable? *Journal of Business Ethics* 1: 277–280.
———. 1987. *The Wise Men Know What Wicked Things Are Written on the Sky*. Washington, DC: Regnery Gateway.
———. 1989a. *Economics: Work and Prosperity*. Pensacola: A Beka Book.
———. 1989b. *The Humane Economy of Wilhelm Roepke*. The Heritage Foundation, July 3, 1989, republished on *The Imaginative Conservative* website, January 27, 2012. Available at https://theimaginativeconservative.org/2012/01/humane-economy-wilhelm-roepke-russell-kirk.html.
———. 1992. Capitalism and the Moral Basis of Social Order. *Modern Age* 35: 99–105.

———. 2001. *The Conservative Mind: From Burke to Eliot*. Washington, DC: Regnery Publishing.
———. 2013. *Prospects for Conservatives: A Compass for Rediscovering the Permanent Things*. Houston: Imaginative Conservative Books.
———. 2016. *Enemies of the Permanent Things: Observations of Abnormity in Literature and Politics*. Providence: Cluny Media.
Lucas, Paul. 1968. On Edmund Burke's Doctrine of Prescription; Or, an Appeal from the New to the Old Lawyers. *The Historical Journal* 11: 35–63.
Marshall, P.J., ed. 1991. *The Writings and Speeches of Edmund Burke. Vol. 6, India: The Launching of The Hastings Impeachment 1786–1788*. Oxford: Clarendon Press.
Marshall, P.J., and Donald C. Bryant, eds. 2015. *The Writings and Speeches of Edmund Burke. Vol. 4, Party, Parliament, and the Dividing of the Whigs 1780–1794*. Oxford: Clarendon Press.
McDowell, R.B., ed. 2005. *The Writings and Speeches of Edmund Burke. Vol. 9, I: The Revolutionary War 1794–1797; II: Ireland*. Oxford: Clarendon Press.
Mitchell, L.G., ed. 2007. *The Writings and Speeches of Edmund Burke. Vol. VIII, The French Revolution 1790–1794*. Oxford: Clarendon Press.
Nisbet, Robert. 1984. Cloaking the State's Dagger. *Reason*. https://reason.com/1984/10/01/cloaking-the-states-dagger/.
———. 2000. *Twilight of Authority*. Indianapolis: Liberty Fund.
———. 2010. *The Quest for Community: A Study in the Ethics of Order and Freedom*. Wilmington: ISI Books.
Nordlinger, Jay. 2019. A Conservative in the World. *National Review Online*, June 3, 2019. Available at https://www.nationalreview.com/corner/a-conservative-in-the-world/.
Nozick, Robert. 2013. *Anarchy, State, and Utopia*. New York: Basic Books.
Oakeshott, Michael. 1991. *Rationalism in Politics and Other Essays*. Indianapolis: Liberty Fund.
———. 1999. *On History and Other Essays*. Carmel: Liberty Fund.
———. 2003. *On Human Conduct*. Oxford: Clarendon Press.
———. 2006. In *Lectures in the History of Political Thought*, ed. Terry Nardin and Luke O'Sullivan. Exeter: Imprint Academic.
Roberts, Andrew. 2019. Churchill's Debt to Burke. *The New Criterion*. Available at https://newcriterion.com/issues/2019/5/churchills-debt-to-burke.
Robin, Corey. 2018. *The Reactionary Mind: Conservatism from Edmund Burke to Donald Trump*. Oxford: Oxford University Press.
Rothbard, Murray. 2002. *The Ethics of Liberty*. New York: New York University Press.
Sawhill, Ray. 1999. Black and Right. *Salon*. Available at https://www.salon.com/1999/11/10/sowell_2/.
Sheahan, Luke C. 2020. *Why Associations Matter: The Case for First Amendment Pluralism*. Lawrence: University Press of Kansas.
Sowell, Thomas. 1996. *Knowledge and Decisions*. New York: Basic Books.
———. 1999. *The Quest for Cosmic Justice*. New York: The Free Press.
———. 2004. *Basic Economics: A Citizen's Guide to the Economy*. New York: Basic Books.
———. 2007. *A Conflict of Visions: Ideological Origins of Political Struggles*. New York: Basic Books.
———. 2012. *Trickle Down' Theory and 'Tax Cuts for the Rich'*. Stanford: Hoover Institution Press.
———. 2019. *Discrimination and Disparities*. New York: Basic Books.
The Parliamentary Debates. 1907. Vol. CLXIX. London: Wyman and Sons.
Voegelin, Eric. 2000. The New Science of Politics. In *The Collected Works of Eric Voegelin. Vol. 5, Modernity Without Restraint*, ed. Manfred Henningsen, 75–241. Columbia: University of Missouri Press.
Will, George F. 1984. *Statecraft as Soulcraft: What Government Does*. New York: Simon & Schuster.
———. 2011. Declaration of Independents. *Washington Post*. Available at https://www.washingtonpost.com/opinions/declaration-of-independents/2011/07/29/gIQAJrUAiI_story.html.
———. 2019. *The Conservative Sensibility*. New York: Hatchette Books.

Gregory M. Collins is a Lecturer in the Program on Ethics, Politics, and Economics at Yale University. He is the author *Commerce and Manners in Edmund Burke's Political Economy* (Cambridge University Press, 2020) and has published articles on Edmund Burke, Adam Smith, Aristotle, Britain's East India Company, Leo Strauss, Friedrich Hayek, and Frederick Douglass. Greg was the 2020 recipient of the Novak Award, awarded annually by The Acton Institute to one young scholar conducting research on the intersection of markets and morals. He received his Ph.D. from The Catholic University of America.

Chapter 7
Taxation: The Libertarian View

Robert W. McGee and Walter E. Block

Abstract Libertarianism is a "many splendored" philosophy, with various dimensions contending with one another. Included is anarcho-capitalism, minarchism or limited government libertarianism, constitutionalism, and classical liberalism. Each category has a different perspective on taxation. This chapter explores all of them. But they all have something in common, otherwise they could not all be included in a chapter devoted to libertarianism and taxation. And what is that: all such viewpoints want to minimize taxes to a far greater degree than any other political economic philosophy.

Keywords Taxation · Libertarianism · Coercion

JEL Category: H00 · H20

7.1 Introduction

> A libertarian is committed to the principle that liberty is the most important political value. Liberty means being free to make your own choices about your own life, and that what you do with your body and your property ought to be up to you. Other people must not forcibly interfere with your liberty, and you must not forcibly interfere with theirs. (Libertarianism.org 2021)

The libertarian philosophy is based upon a rich and interesting body of literature, going back to at least 384 BCE in the West (Mises Institute 2021), and as far back as the late sixth century BCE in China. Rothbard (2005) asserts that the Chinese philosopher Lao Tzu, the founder of Taoism and the author of the *Tao Te Ching*, was

R. W. McGee (✉)
Broadwell College of Business and Economics, Fayetteville State University, Fayetteville, NC, USA

W. E. Block
College of Business, Loyola University, New Orleans, LA, USA

R. F. van Brederode (ed.), *Political Philosophy and Taxation*,
https://doi.org/10.1007/978-981-19-1092-0_7

the first libertarian intellectual. According to this ancient philosopher, government must be drastically limited in order for individuals to flourish.[1]

There are several varieties of libertarians. If one were to divide them into two categories, one might choose the labels anarchists and minarchists. Anarchists, also referred to as anarcho-capitalists, believe that there is no legitimate role for government to play (Raimondo 2000; Spooner 2008a). In this view, governments are just bands of gangsters and thieves (Hoppe 2006; Rothbard 2009). However, unlike a robber, who merely robs you, then leaves you alone, a government will rob you, then lecture you on how it will use the money it has just taken from you for your own benefit, then visit you again from time to time to repeat the robbery and lecture (Spooner 2008b). Anarcho-capitalists believe that individuals are capable of organizing society without government interference. The free market and cooperation can solve problems better than governments, and they can do it without initiating violence.[2]

Minarchists are advocates of the night watchman state, believe that governments are necessary, but that their realm of authority should be limited to the protection of life, liberty and property. Governments that go beyond these limited roles by engaging in redistribution of income or preventing individuals from engaging in non-rights-violating activities are engaged in illegitimate functions. Governments have no funds of their own. Whatever funds they have must first have been taken from someone.

There are eminent libertarian philosophers in both of these camps. Ludwig von Mises was one of the most eminent libertarian philosophers, economists, historians and sociologists of the twentieth century. He was a minarchist. His friend and intellectual colleague, Murray Rothbard, was also one of the most eminent libertarian philosophers, economists, historians and sociologists of the twentieth century. He was an anarcho-capitalist.

It is possible to further divide the minarchists into subcategories. Scholars who give the most credence to the libertarian principles of non-aggression and private property rights would be those who would limit government to armies, courts and

[1] The Libertarianism.org website goes into some detail about his brand of libertarianism.

[2] In the view of Rothbard (1973): "For centuries, the State (or more strictly, individuals acting in their roles as 'members of the government') has cloaked its criminal activity in high-sounding rhetoric. For centuries the State has committed mass murder and called it 'war'; then ennobled the mass slaughter that 'war' involves. For centuries the State has enslaved people into its armed battalions and called it 'conscription' in the 'national service.' For centuries the State has robbed people at bayonet point and called it 'taxation.' In fact, if you wish to know how libertarians regard the State and any of its acts, simply think of the State as a criminal band, and all of the libertarian attitudes will logically fall into place." For more in this vein see: Anderson and Hill (1979); Benson (1989, 1990); Block (2007b, 2010, 2011f, 2016a, b, c); Casey (2010, 2018); DiLorenzo (2010); Friedman (1989); Gregory (2011); Guillory and Tinsley (2009); Hasnas (1995); Heinrich (2010); Higgs (2009, 2012); Hoppe (2008, 2011a); Huebert (2010); King (2010); Kinsella (2009); Long (2004); McConkey (2013); Molyneux (2008); Murphy (2005); Paul (2008a, b, c); Rockwell (2013); Rothbard (1973, 1975, 1977, 1998); Salerno (2012); Smith (2017); Spooner (2008a, b); Stringham (2007); Tannehill (1984); Tinsley (1998–1999); Wenzel (2013, 2016); Woods (2014).

police. But these philosophers only favor armies to protect the country from foreign aggression, not to go gallivanting all over the globe, exporting U.S. style "democracy" at the point of a gun.[3] Similarly, the sole function of the police would be to stop murderers, rapists, thieves, arsonists, kidnappers, etc., not victimless "criminals" who engage in consensual adult behavior, such as involving drugs or sexual activity. The libertarians most closely associated with this variety of libertarianism include Rand (1956) and Nozick (1974).

One step down from this position would be libertarian constitutionalists.[4] The U.S. constitution is their lodestar. But not as interpreted by any actual Supreme Court, even the present conservative members. Rather, as strictly and very narrowly interpreted by the likes of judge Andrew Napolitano (2011) and former Congressman Ron Paul (2000, 2008a, b, c), perhaps the highest profile libertarians associated with this position.

The lowest level of libertarianism, furthest removed from the anarcho-capitalist position, is that of the Classical Liberals. The most prominent scholars who adhere to this viewpoint are Milton Friedman (1962) and Friedrich Hayek (1944).[5] Proper functions of government, here, include all the aforementioned, plus a very modest level of welfare for the poor, limited anti-trust legislation, and a plethora of other institutions such as those dealing with education, libraries, museums, parks, etc., but on a modest level. Many of them would make room for government action to quell market "failures" such as externalities, public goods and monopoly.[6] The classical liberals are indeed libertarians, at least assuming a "big tent" vision of this philosophy, for most supporters favor full free trade, and oppose such regulations as minimum wages, rent control, licensing, tariffs and quotas, etc.

How do tax levels correlate with these four positions? The anarcho-capitalists are the easiest to pigeon-hole in this regard. Their answer to this question would be zero, nada, zilch. No taxes at all. The other three are not as easy to characterize, but rates would increase as we move away from this strict libertarian position. Possibly, these are our rough estimates, the very limited government minarchist position would limit tax revenues to 5% of GDP and the constitutionalists to no more than 10%. The classical liberals would presumably be comfortable with a ceiling of 20% of the total product of the nation.[7]

---

[3] The United States has some 800 military bases located in almost 200 foreign countries. This is not defense. This is offense. How would citizens like it if soldiers from Brazil or Burundi or Belgium were prancing around on our shores?

[4] It justifies governmental post roads and post offices and in other ways goes beyond the armies, courts and police of the previous position.

[5] Others include Epstein (2003, 2014); Murray (1997) and Buchanan and Tullock (1962).

[6] For the Austrian economic perspective according to which there is no such thing as a "market failure" see Anderson (1998); Barnett et al. (2005); Block (2002a); Callahan (2000); Cowen (1988); DiLorenzo (2011); Guillory (2005); Higgs (1995); Hoppe (2003); MacKenzie (2002); Rothbard (1985); Simpson (2005); Westley (2002); Woods (2009a, b).

[7] Milton Friedman once articulated his position on this matter at 10% (source: personal conversation with one of the present authors). However, in our estimation, the functions he would allow government would amount to significantly more than that. Hence, our 20% estimate in the text.

Libertarian philosophers have many common values, but they take different approaches to the subject. Ludwig von Mises was a utilitarian. He believed that an act or policy was justified if the result was an increase in social harmony and prosperity (Mises 1998). Murray Rothbard approached philosophical questions from a rights perspective (Rothbard 1978, 1998). Acts and policies that do not violate anyone's rights should be permitted, even if some people view them as unethical or immoral. An act or policy that violates even one person's rights is problematic and should be punished.[8] These different approaches to resolving philosophical disputes and questions can lead to interesting conversations. Utilitarians and rights theorists often, but not always, arrive at the same conclusion while following different philosophical paths (McGee 2004).

If one believes that government should not exist, then

Taxation = Theft, and

Fair Share of taxes = 0.

If one believes that government has some legitimate role to play, then some kind of taxation might be needed to support the legitimate functions of government. Interestingly, the public finance literature does not even attempt to justify taxation. The authors of such books merely assume that taxation is justified (Block 1989, 1993). Their arguments center around issues such as which tax is best or worst in a given situation, and why.

Taxation is the forcible confiscation of someone's property. There is nothing voluntary about it. Merely remaining in a particular tax jurisdiction does not imply consent. One must always be physically present somewhere. The only option one has is voting with one's feet to move from one tax jurisdiction to another. If slaves had the option of voting with their feet to move from one plantation to another, they would still be slaves regardless of which plantation they chose. The same might be said of taxpayers. It cannot be said that someone consents to be taxed just because that individual decides to remain in a certain tax jurisdiction.

Suppose you were a judge, gentle reader. The authors of the present chapter sue someone for $1000. The defendant (D) claims he doesn't owe us a penny. You ask us to give you evidence to back up our claim that D owes us this money. You expect something like a bill of sale (we sold him something, and he agreed to pay us $1000), or a bet that he lost, and there are witnesses who will back us up, or maybe he is our tenant, and his monthly rent is $1000. You expect us to give you *something* along these lines. We offer you nothing, zilch, nada. You throw our lawsuit out of court and maybe accuse us of bringing you a frivolous lawsuit.

[8] For example, in the movie "Dr. Strangelove" it was necessary to shoot a Coca Cola machine in order to save the world from a nuclear conflagration. This act was a clear violation of property rights. Libertarians were in effect criticized for wanting to prohibit this deviation from deontology, even though all of humanity would perish. Perish the thought. The libertarian analysis would be of course to destroy this bit of private property, but, then, to pay (a relatively very slight) penalty for so doing.

Here is the next case. The government comes to D with a tax bill for $1000. It is going to use this money to support a safety net for the poor, or for some other good cause such as the military or the police. Again, you are the judge. You ask the government, this time, for some proof that D really owes this $1000. Does it have a contract that D signed, agreeing to pay taxes? They do not. Does it have any evidence whatsoever that D owes it this money? Not a bit of it; nothing, zilch, nada.

How do you rule in this case? If you are logically consistent, your finding is exactly the same as before: you throw out the plaintiff's argument. There is no more evidence here, than there was in the preceding case. But is there not an implicit contract that we all in effect "signed?" requiring all of us to pay taxes? This is a circular argument. It assumes to be correct the very issue under debate. To wit; the government is a just organization, and is entitled to assume, or presume, that everyone in "its" territory has agreed to its rule, and hence to pay it taxes to support its efforts in our behalf. We can say with far more justification[9] that there is an implicit contract we all "sign" with one another to the effect we will all adhere to the libertarian non-aggression principle (NAP) according to which no one may demand money with threats and menaces from anyone else, unless the other has *explicitly* agreed to do so.

It has been argued that voting constitutes consent to be taxed. However, as Lysander Spooner pointed out (2008b), many people vote for politicians who promise to reduce or abolish certain taxes. In such cases, the individuals who vote for them are actually trying to protect their property from confiscation. In no way are they consenting to be taxed.

Suppose the slave master allows his human property to vote between overseer Goody, who will beat them, viciously, once per month, and Baddy, who will do so every single day. The slaves all vote for Goody. Are we entitled to deduce that they agreed that Goody should engage in violence against them on a monthly basis? Of course not.

7.2 Taxation as Slavery

A common element in the philosophical toolbox of libertarian philosophers is the Body as Property Doctrine (McGee 2013). Basically, this doctrine states that my body belongs to me, and I can do anything I want with it, provided I do not violate the rights of others. I can ingest substances that harm me, I can rent it out for sex, I can kill it. If I use my body, including my brain, to sell products or services, I should

[9] Hans-Hermann Hoppe argues that the only way to get to the truth of any matter is to allow discussion, argumentation, back and forth disagreement, etc. He then asks what are the prerequisites for this to occur? He answers, in a nutshell, respect for the NAP and private property rights. Thus, we can derive an implicit contract to adhere to libertarianism on the part of at least those who value the truth. See on this Block (2004a, 2011g); Eabrasu (2009); Gordon (1988); Hoppe (1988a, b, c, d, 1993a, 1995); Kinsella (1996, 2002); Meng (2002); Rothbard (1988); Van Dun (2009).

be able to keep the fruits of my labor. The fruits of my labor are merely extensions of my body. My claim to the fruits of my labor is superior to anyone else's claim to those fruits. Anyone who confiscates some or all of those fruits is violating my property rights. They are committing an act of theft.

Some commenters extrapolate fallaciously from this eminently reasonable doctrine. They reason from this major premise to a false conclusion. They aver that to the extent that the government confiscates a portion of the fruits of my labor, I am a slave. For example, if some government confiscates 40% of my income in the form of taxes, in substance it is the equivalent of being forced to work for government 2 days a week. It is a form of forced labor (Nozick 1974).

Prior to the end of slavery, slaves picked cotton or harvested tobacco or other crops, and the slave master confiscated 100% of the fruits of the slaves' labor, while providing food, clothing, shelter and some medical care to the slaves. Although the slaves received benefits, it was forced labor. They didn't have a choice. In modern times, individuals work to earn a living so that they can provide food, clothing, shelter and medical care for themselves and their families, and the state takes its "cut." The percentage of this "cut" establishes the degree to which the individual is a slave of the state. To that extent, the state owns your body and the fruits of its labor. Under such a tax regime, the state has a property interest in people and thus enslaves them.

On the other hand, it is possible to criticize this claim that taxation amounts to slavery. One can do so on the ground that that this thesis fails to properly distinguish between mere robbery and kidnapping – forced labor, legal rape and murder, and other vicious accoutrements of actual slavery. Suppose the slave owner gave the slaves one day off per week. They could not run away on that day, but he would require no work from them at all. Nor would he abuse them in any way. Now, along comes the government and seizes 6/7, or 86% of their salaries in the form of taxes. From one perspective, the two scenarios are identical. The government steals as much labor from the taxpayers, enslaves them to the same degree, in both cases. From another viewpoint however, there is all the world of difference between the two scenarios. In one we have slavery; in another, we have mere theft. It is crucially important to distinguish between the two.

Consider another example. If the government is an enslaver due to taxation, what about the ordinary thief? He also steals labor, just like the state, and must, then, also, be considered as a slave master. If the government robs you of your labor, why, then, so does the "private enterprise" criminal. But if all robbers are also enslavers, it is impossible to engage, merely, in ordinary burglary. If a criminal does that, he also becomes an enslaver. So, when a child steals some bubble gum from a grocery store, has he also engaged in an act of enslavement? This seems like nothing as much as a serious misuse of language; and pointing it out appears as a powerful reductio ad absurdum.

Here is yet another reductio. As we have seen, only the anarcho-capitalist libertarians favor zero taxes. But they comprise, at our estimate, only 2% of all those who consider themselves libertarians, and are so considered by others. But if taxes were really slavery, then we would have to conclude that the likes of minarchists and classical liberals such Ayn Rand, Ron Paul, Rand Paul, Robert Nozick, Andrew Napolitano, Charles Murray, Richard Epstein, Milton Friedman, Friedrich Hayek, Ludwig von Mises, all outspoken and famous libertarians, favored slavery, akin to the institution that took place in the U.S. before 1865. This sound like a harsh criticism levelled by a bitter enemy of libertarianism, not something the present authors would want to come within a million miles of asserting.

Every year, the Tax Foundation calculates Tax Freedom Day for the United States. Tax Freedom Day is the first day of the year that individuals work for themselves rather than for government. In other words, if government at all levels (federal, state and local) confiscated 100% of the fruits of your labor starting January 1, and continued to confiscate 100% of the fruits of your labor until it had collected your total tax liability for the year, when is the first day the government would stop confiscating the fruits of your labor? In 2019, the most recent date available as of this writing, that day in the USA would be April 16 (York 2019).

105 days/365 days = 29%

Thus, in 2019, the average American worker was robbed to the tune of 29% of his annual income. If annual federal borrowing were included, which represents future taxes owed, Tax Freedom Day would be May 8, or 22 days later (York 2019).

127 days/365 days = 35%

So, a more accurate estimate would be that the average American worker is relieved of his rightfully owned property to the extent of 35% and is 65% free. If those figures were to be broken down into hours and minutes, the average American worker working an 8-h day would have to work about 2.8 h each day [.35 × 8], or 2 h, 48 min, before being able to keep the fruits of his labor.

But actually, even that estimate is a little too optimistic. Laws and regulations that restrict non-rights-violating activities chip away at individual freedom as well. These "death by a thousand cuts" laws and regulations cannot easily be measured in numerical terms, but they restrict freedom nonetheless. To the extent that you cannot use your body as you see fit because of some law or regulation, someone else has a property interest in your body. It this case, it is the state.

In a democracy, individuals can vote to decide who their legal robber will be, whereas under pre-U.S. Civil War slavery, slaves could not choose who owned them. Another difference between modern tax "slavery" and the former chattel slavery is that plantation slaves who escaped to the north or Canada or some other place became totally free, whereas modern tax "slaves" only have the option of voting with their feet to escape to another tax jurisdiction.[10]

Tax Freedom Day is different every year, depending on the ratio of taxes to income, and it is different in every country. In the UK, Tax Freedom Day in 2021

[10] Well, to be fully inclusive there is always suicide as an escape from the taxman. What about living homeless or in the woods? But even there if the would-be escapee purchases anything, he has to pay sales tax.

Table 7.1 List of selected countries and their Tax Freedom Days

Country	Year	Tax Freedom Day	% Robbery[a] (excluding deficit spending)
USA	1900	January 22	5.9
USA	1920	February 13	12.0
USA	1940	March 7	17.9
USA	1960	April 11	27.7
USA	1980	April 21	30.4
USA	2000	May 1	33.0
USA	2019	April 16	29.0
India	2000	March 14	20
Australia	2019	April 17	29
Switzerland	2015	May 1	33
Uruguay	2010	May 13	39
Brazil	2014	May 31	41
Slovakia	2017	June 5	42
UK	2017	June 12	44
Canada	2019	June 14	45
Greece	2012	June 19	46
Spain	2016	June 30	50
Germany	2015	July 11	52
Belgium	2018	July 17	54
Israel	2013	July 14	54
Norway	2007	July 29	57
France	2018	July 27	57
Austria	2019	August 5	59

Source: Wikipedia 2021

[a]This is only robbery for the anarcho-capitalist libertarian. Consider the calculation for the USA in 1900. This would not be theft at all for any of the minarchist versions of libertarians, since it is roughly compatible with their view of legitimate levels of taxation

was conservatively estimated to be May 31 (Adam Smith Institute 2021). Thus, the Brits are 41% tax "slaves." (Table 7.1)

Tax Freedom Day in the United States went from January 22 in 1900 to April 16 in 2019, during which the percent of taxation (excluding future tax liabilities caused by deficit spending) rose from 5.9% to 29.0%. The percentage of such takings in most other countries is even higher, reaching 57% in Norway and France, and 59% in Austria.

7.3 Fairness Issues

Governments were supposedly formed to protect the life, liberty and property of the individuals living within their jurisdictions. Arguments have been made that individuals have a duty to pay their "fair share" of government expenditures. The problem with any fair share argument is that it is conveniently undefinable (McGee 1999).

Is it ever fair that some people should be forced to pay for the education of other people's children? Or other people's health care? Should some individuals be forced to subsidize the housing costs of others?

> But you might say, if government didn't do all that it's doing we wouldn't have a *just* society. What's *just* has been debated for centuries but let me offer my definition of social justice: I keep what I earn and you keep what you earn. Do you disagree? Well then tell me how much of what I earn *belongs* to you – and why? (Williams 1987, 62).

The anarcho-capitalist libertarian position is that all taxes are violations of property rights and are, therefore, unjust and unfair. Hoppe considers taxation to be an "attack on and punishment of the acquisition and production of property", which reduces wealth formation and the general standard of living (Hoppe 2006, 34). In contrast, for the minarchist, the constitutionalist, the classical liberal libertarians, only those taxes over and above the level justified in their various philosophies would be consider unjust.

7.4 Efficiency and Value Issues

To an anarcho-capitalist, efficiency issues are not entirely irrelevant. The perspective emanating from this quarter is that if libertarian deontology is undertaken, then prosperity will ensue. But rights are the "dog," pragmatic concerns are only the dog's tail. And the former wags the latter, not the other way around. As an epistemological matter, moreover, it is far easier to determine in advance what is, and what is not, a rights violation, than which public policy, of which there are potentially thousands, will lead to human well-being. So, goeth out there and violate no rights, and utilitarianism will also be attained. We will be led by an "invisible hand" (Smith 1776) in that very direction.

The use of force to confiscate assets can never be justified, regardless of the use to which those assets are put. Fully consistent libertarians would fully agree with this position. Since all taxation requires the forcible confiscation of someone's property, it is reasonable to assume that the use to which the tax funds are put is less efficient or has less value than the use to which they were put prior to the confiscation.[11] Otherwise, those assets would have already flowed to those uses voluntarily. Thus, all taxation results in shifting assets from higher value to lower value uses. However, most libertarians would qualify this claim. The minarchists, the constitutionalists, the classical liberals would make exceptions to this general principle. They would aver that when "market failures" occur, it would actually be overall beneficial for the government, *to a very limited degree*, to divert resources from

[11] "I'm from the government, and I'm here to help you" would be considered a sick joke in this quarter.

where the free enterprise system would place them, to armies, courts, police, education, etc.

Eminent domain laws have been used to confiscate assets that are considered to be used less efficiently, and then invested to create higher value for society in general (Main 2007) as demonstrated in *Kelo v. City of New London.*[12] For example, some builder goes to the local government and has property condemned so that he can purchase the property for pennies on the dollar to build an apartment complex or casino or shopping mall. Such property is indeed being shifted from lower use to higher use – in the eyes of these criminals – but hardly in the view of the property owners. If the latter would have been the case, the resources would already have changed ownership in this direction. For example, Kelo would have sold her home to the developers. But, as a matter of fact, she refused to do so, indicating that from her perspective her home was worth more to her than the amount bid for it by those who wanted to convert it to an alternative use.[13]

That issue is irrelevant because force is being used to confiscate assets. The fact that those assets are being confiscated from one individual and redistributed to another makes the confiscation that much worse morally, because the force of government is being subverted to confiscate property rather than to protect it.

7.5 Redistribution

Confiscating one person's property and transferring it to another person is inherently immoral (Jouvenel 1952). Some classical liberals believe that the only kind of confiscations that are permissible are those that are spent for the benefit of the general public, such as supporting the police, the court system, and some kind of national defense. Anarcho-capitalists would not approve even of these uses, since they believe the market and private contributions would raise the funds necessary to pay for these services. They maintain that all functions currently performed by governments should and can be privatized,[14] or should be abolished.

There would be competing fire departments and competing police departments. They would gain consumer support by offering better services at lower prices as in the case of more traditional goods and services. Subscribing to their services would be voluntary, which means that some individuals would decide to not subscribe, and therefore assume the attendant risk. If a nonsubscriber's house were burning down, he could contact one of the competing fire departments and negotiate a price to

[12] *Kelo v. City of New London*, 545 U.S. 469 (2005) (O'Connor, dissenting).

[13] For more on this unsavory episode in jurisprudence, see Block (2006a); Epstein (2005); Kinsella (2005); Somin (2015).

[14] For the case in behalf of privatizing roads, streets and highways, see Block (2009c); for oceans, rivers and lakes, Block and Nelson (2015); for space travel, the Moon and Mars, etc., Nelson and Block (2018).

provide assistance in putting out the fire,[15] or could suffer the consequences of not subscribing to any fire service. No one would be forced to subsidize the benefits of others.

7.6 Are Some Taxes Better Than Others?

All taxes distort the economy because they shift resources from best uses to second or third or tenth best uses. There is no such thing as a neutral tax (Rothbard 2011, 490–493). However, some taxes are better than others, in the sense that they do less damage. Low taxes are to be preferred to high taxes because the degree of property confiscation is less, as is the distortion to the economy. Some libertarian-leaning commentators have taken the position that a flat income tax is to be preferred to a graduated income tax (Hall & Rabushka 1985). A properly structured flat tax would be simpler to compute, would have less of an adverse effect on investment, and would distort the economy less than would a complicated graduated tax system (Blum and Kalven 1953), or so the argument goes. Rothbard (2011, 533–549), has offered a substantive critique of the flat tax, and finds it wanting. Supposedly, a flat tax would eliminate special interests. Rothbard asks whether *all* special interests are bad. He concluded that they are not. For example, if the movie industry (a special interest) lobbied for the repeal of a tax that was imposed against it, that would be a good thing because they would be allowed to keep more of the money they earn.

Another problem with the flat tax is that it is not really flat. Even those who propose such a tax argue for exemptions for certain groups, such as the poor. Many so-called "loopholes" would be closed, which means that certain groups would have to pay more because the current tax law confiscates less of their property than it does from other groups. Tax-free fringe benefits might go by the wayside, which could affect millions of individuals. If interest payments became nondeductible, homeowners would be adversely affected, as would the housing industry.

Fairness is often used to justify the flat tax. Rothbard (2011, 543–545) challenges the unsupported assumption that a flat tax would be fairer than a graduated tax. If a young man and an old man have equal incomes, but the young man is just starting out and has more expenses, and perhaps more medical bills, the old man, who has perhaps accumulated much more wealth, would pay exactly the same tax. Should a sick person pay the same tax as a healthy person if they have the same income? In the final analysis, there is no such thing as a fair tax, because all taxes rely on unjustifiably confiscating property.

The ability to pay principle is morally bankrupt because there should be some relationship between the amount paid and the amount of benefits received. There is

[15] This might well be a much higher price than would have been the case had the homeowner patronized the private fire company. For one thing, it would have constituted a "fire sale" pardon the pun. For another, it would serve as an object lesson for other property owners reluctant to hire fire companies.

no consensus on how to determine ability to pay without massive intrusion into the privacy of all taxpaying individuals, so people who earn more are taxed at a higher rate than people who earn less, as a way to approximate ability to pay (McGee 1998). However, if government is the servant and the people are the masters, then people should receive value for the taxes they are forced to pay. Someone who earns $10X income every year should not be forced to pay 15 times as much as someone who earns $1X per year. The person who earns $10X probably does not receive 15 times as much in benefits as the person who earns just $1X. In fact, it is quite possible that the individual who earns more may actually receive less in net benefits than the individual who earns less. In many cases, the government does more *to* rich people than it does *for* them. They are more likely to be audited. They are excluded from receiving certain benefits. A larger absolute amount of their property is confiscated by income, property and estate taxes.

It has been argued that a consumption tax would be better than one on income. Taxing income has a negative effect on the incentive to create and produce, whereas a consumption tax does not. One may avoid or defer the payment of taxes by producing but not consuming. Imposing an income tax requires individuals to keep records, and the Internal Revenue Service can violate their privacy by examining these records and demanding even more documents, which invades privacy even more. With a consumption tax, there is no need for individuals to keep records of their income, and the IRS would not be looking over their shoulder to make sure that they are not hiding income. Taxes are collected at the point of sale, and it is the seller who is responsible for turning the funds over to the government.

Others argue that an income tax is superior to a consumption tax because a consumption tax weighs heavily against consumer goods. Rothbard (2011, 515–531) critiques the consumption tax and finds it wanting. As a practical matter, a consumption tax would not replace the income tax, but rather would be a supplement to it. Once the political limit of an income tax is reached, government must look elsewhere for additional tax revenue. One place it has found is the consumption tax, which could take several forms, such as the retail sales tax or the value added tax. Rothbard asserts that a value-added tax (VAT) would not only not eliminate the current IRS despotism, but would make it even worse. From the perspective of business, a value-added tax would impose a burdensome record-keeping system. From the personal experience of one of the current authors, it was learned that Turkey at one time imposed more than 10,000 different tax rates, depending on which good or service was being taxed. As a result, there were major definitional disputes regarding which rate should be imposed for any particular good or service. The tax authorities would often argue for a different classification, which naturally had a higher tax rate, while the business owner would insist on an alternative classification, which was taxed at a lower rate. The VAT can be a very complicated tax (van Brederode 2021).

Rothbard considers the retail sales tax to be superior to the VAT because it is simpler, less distortive to the economy, and enormously less despotic and bureaucratic than the VAT. However, he does not advocate it because it necessarily involves the confiscation of property. He considers consumption taxes in general to be a payment for permission to live (Rothbard 2018, 740).

Visible taxes are better than hidden taxes. People should know what they are paying. If taxes were not withheld from paychecks, workers would be able to feel the pain when they were forced to write a check to the government. The fact that they never actually receive a portion of the fruits of their labor makes it easier for governments to confiscate a portion of their wages because they never have to physically surrender that portion of the assets that would otherwise be in their pockets or bank accounts.[16]

Another hidden tax is the corporate income tax. Ultimately, it is individuals who pay the corporate tax. Corporations try to pass along the tax in the form of higher prices to consumers. If they are able to do that, the individuals who purchase the corporation's products or services end up paying the tax. If a corporation is unable to pass the tax along to consumers, it must either reduce dividends, or limit wage increases, and perhaps hire fewer workers. In any event, it is individuals who bear the burden of the corporate income tax. Many of the dividend payments eventually land in workers' pension funds, which do not grow as rapidly because of the corporate income tax. This view is not confined to economists. It has spread to the philosophical literature (Hospers 1971, 323–324).

According to the Tax Foundation (Enache 2021), corporate taxes account for just 3.9% of total tax collections in the United States. It would be very easy to abolish the corporate income tax with minimal loss of revenue. The billions of dollars spent on expensive lawyers and tax accountants would then be free to create wealth and jobs rather than minimize the tax bite taken by government from their corporate employers.

McGee and others (2012a) distributed surveys based on the Crowe (1944) rationales given to pay or not pay taxes. They found that there was less resistance to taxes when the taxpayers received benefits in exchange for their tax payments, or when the taxes were spent on worthy causes, even if those causes did not always benefit the particular taxpayer. Support for taxes was significantly less in cases where the taxpayer did not receive much in the form of benefits, where the government was corrupt or had totalitarian tendencies, or where tax rates were deemed to be too high.

Social Security taxes are bad for a variety of reasons. For one, collecting them requires the confiscation of someone's assets. From a utilitarian perspective, they are a bad investment. If the same funds were placed in private investments, the payoff would be much higher.[17] Also, those who pay into a private retirement fund would accumulate a pool of assets, which they could either spend or pass on to their heirs. The government Social Security program does not offer many desirable features. It is a Ponzi scheme. One group of individuals pays into the system, while

[16] Milton Friedman has made many and important contributions to the free enterprise philosophy. However, he was guilty of inaugurating the withholding system. See Vance (2005) on this tax policy.

[17] Mangu-Ward (2016); Higgs (2007); Friedman (1999).

another group withdraws funds from the system. Actually, Social Security is worse than a private sector Ponzi scheme. In a private sector Ponzi scheme, participation is voluntary, and individuals may cash out any time they want. In a government Social Security system, participation is mandatory, so there is no escape, and they may not choose to stop participating. Rothbard (2018, 697) considers the Social Security system to be "the biggest single racket of all the welfare programs."[18]

Is there a moral duty to refuse to accept Social Security payments if you are eligible to receive them? Libertarians are not in agreement on this point. Some libertarians would refuse to accept Social Security payments even if they qualify because the funds they receive constitute stolen property. Other libertarians would accept the funds, considering the payments to be a partial refund of the excess taxes they have paid in the past.[19]

Estate taxes are also problematic, not only because they confiscate assets, but also because there is no relationship between payments made and benefits received. Estate taxes confiscate the assets of deceased individuals, who are incapable of receiving benefits from government. The people who suffer from estate taxes are the individuals who otherwise would have inherited those assets. Rothbard considers a graduated inheritance tax to be even worse than a graduated income tax. It is a tax on capital, which leads to impoverishment. "Not only should there be no progressive inheritance tax, there should be no inheritance tax at all. An inheritance tax is pure evil, and no valid arguments can be found for it" (Rothbard 2011, 569).

Buchanan (1983) another fair weather free enterpriser not only supports an inheritance tax, but would peg it at 100%.[20] States Rothbard (1973) on this matter:

"Many people are willing to concede the justice and propriety of property rights and the free-market economy, to concede that the farmer should be able to charge whatever his wheat will bring from consumers or the worker to reap whatever others are willing to pay for his services. But they balk at one point: inheritance. If Willie Stargell is ten times as good and 'productive' a ball player as Joe Jack, they are willing to concede the justice of Stargell's earning ten times the amount; but what, they ask, is the justification for someone whose only merit is being born a Rockefeller inheriting far more wealth than someone born a Rothbard? The libertarian answer is to concentrate not on the recipient, the child Rockefeller or the child Rothbard, but to concentrate on the giver, the man who bestows the inheritance. For if Smith and Jones and Stargell have the right to their labor and property and to exchange the titles to this property for the similar property of others, they also have the right to

[18] On Social Security as a Ponzi scheme, see Galles (2013); Goodman (2015); Kotlikoff (2014); Salsman (2011); Sowell (2016).

[19] For the argument in favor of (libertarians and non-statists) taking money from government, even if they have not paid a single penny in taxes, see Block (1972, 2002b, 2004b, 2006b, 2007a, 2008, 2009a, b, c, 2010, 2011a, b, c, d, 2012b, 2016a, b, c, d); Block and Arakaky (2008); Block and Barnett (2008). The argument is that government is a thief, and it is justified to relieve robbers of their ill-gotten gains.

[20] Other supporters of the inheritance tax include Batchelder (2009–2010); Matthews (2014); Prabhakar et al. (2008); White (2008).

give their property to whomever they wish. And, of course, most such gifts consist of the gifts of the property owners to their children—in short, inheritance. If Willie Stargell owns his labor and the money he earns from it, then he has the right to give that money to the baby Stargell."[21]

An example of a tax that according to some is not quite so bad is a gasoline tax, provided the funds are used to maintain streets and highways. One positive aspect of such a tax is that the people who benefit from the use of the roads are the ones who pay the tax. Those who do not use the roads are not forced to pay it. Such taxes have many attributes of user fees. However, gasoline taxes become offensive when some of the proceeds are used for other purposes, such as education, or when the funds are poured into the general fund. However, even in this case there are difficulties. For, if the roads were privatized (Block 2009a, b, c) fees would be far more aligned with use.

A poll or head tax is sometimes considered to be the least bad form of tax (Hoppe 2011b; Rothbard 2018). Under a poll tax, every individual would pay the exact same amount, regardless of income level or economic condition, the thought being that every individual receives equal protection under the law; therefore, it would be unjust to charge some individuals more than others. One problem with a poll tax is that some individuals would not be able to afford it, especially if they had no income or assets. Another problem that results whenever some government attempts to impose a head tax is that many individuals have the mistaken moral belief that some individuals should have a greater amount of property confiscated from them merely because they are able to pay more than other individuals. The libertarian opposition to the poll tax is based on the fact that it involves the confiscation of property.

Perhaps the best tax from a libertarian point of view would be the much reviled and hated head or poll tax. Each taxpayer would be dunned by the exact same amount, with no "loopholes" or exceptions. For example, everyone would "contribute" $100 per year to the government. There would be no upward creep,[22] since poor people, arguendo, would not be able to pay any more than that. Now *this* is a tax that even the most consistent libertarian can get behind, if he were compelled to choose one type of tax.

Should taxes be regressive, proportional, or progressive? The head or poll tax would be about as regressive as can be imagined. Most statists favor progressivity; they believe that not only should the rich pay more absolutely, but also the proportion of their income and wealth that should be vulnerable to the revenooer should increase with greater ability to pay. This would be anathema to the libertarian. Even the proportional or flat tax would be highly problematic to this corner of the

[21] For further support of the Rothbard position in support of the right of inheritance, and in opposition to inheritance taxation, see Block (2011e, 2012a); Rothbard (1973); Tabarrok (2005); Tullock (1971).

[22] When the infamous income tax was introduced in 1913, it was pegged at 1% on incomes above $3000 (which would be about $81,000 today) and a surtax of 6% on incomes over $500,000 (which would be about $13,500,000 today). Understatement of the century, it is quite a bit higher nowadays.

political economic spectrum. To see this, posit not that the tax system is proportional, but that the price system is. That is, the poor man would pay $0.10 for a loaf of bread, middle class folk such as the authors of this volume would be charged $10 for this product, and the Bill Gates's of the world would have to cough up, oh, $100,000 for this sandwich material. If our calculations were correct, everyone would end up with the same amount of goods and services. The egalitarian dream of absolute commercial equality would have been achieved. There would no longer be any financial advantage in working harder or smarter. Brilliant inventors and lazy bums could enjoy exactly the same lifestyle. With a progressive price system, today's billionaires would be even poorer in terms of goods and services than the most impecunious of today.

7.7 Is There a Moral Limit?

Anarcho-capitalists believe that there is no moral justification for taxes because the state is no more than a collection of organized gangsters. Just as there is no moral duty to transfer your assets to a private-sector gangster, there is no duty to transfer your property to a group of gangsters who are elected or appointed or hired to collect them. There is never any moral duty to pay a tax (Hoppe 2011a, b), although many libertarians suggest that paying them anyway is a good idea because failure to pay could result in fines, imprisonment, or even death, depending on the level of resistance offered by the tax evader.

Classical liberals believe there is some duty to pay something, but that the maximum is something far less than 100% of income or assets. For example, when the Foundation for Economic Education was located in Irvington-on-Hudson, New York, its property was exempt from tax because of its nonprofit status. However, it voluntarily paid the local government an amount it thought was equal to the value it received in terms of utility use and police protection.[23]

Is there a moral obligation to pay at least some taxes when the taxpayer receives benefits from government? Surveys that have asked this question found that a majority of individuals believe there is some moral duty to pay taxes when the taxpayer receives benefits (McGee 2012a). However, majority opinion does not determine morality (some would disagree with this statement). Let's say that you are parked at a stop light, and someone walks up to your car and starts washing your windshield. That person has performed a service for you. Are you obligated to pay? Many people would pay, either because of guilt, or compassion, or fear, but there is no moral duty to pay because you have not requested this service.

What if you receive a package in the mail from a company that expects you to pay for the product that is in the package. If you did not order the item, there is no

[23] Author's conversation with Bettina Bien Greaves.

moral duty to pay. What if you want the item and decide to keep it? Is there a moral duty to pay? There is no moral duty to return the item, whether you want it or not.

Martin T. Crowe (1944), a Catholic priest, surveyed 500 years of Christian (mostly Catholic) religious and philosophical literature to determine what scholars had written about the obligation of paying just taxes.[24] He discovered that there are three basic views: there is always a moral obligation to pay taxes, there is never a moral obligation to pay taxes, and there is some obligation to pay taxes, but that the obligation is less than absolute. McGee (2012b) discussed a fourth view, that there is sometimes a moral obligation not to pay taxes. For example, people, Jews and non-Jews alike, living in Nazi Germany not only had no duty to pay taxes to Hitler, but had a moral duty not to pay, if possible. A similar view relates to the just war theory, which holds that there is a moral duty not to pay taxes to a country that is engaged in an unjust war.

The view that there is always a moral duty to pay taxes has several philosophical roots, all of which are flawed. One justification for this view is what might be called "The law is the law" (Cohn 1998, 2012). In other words, one must obey every law, no matter how bad it is, either because disobedience would tear at the fabric of society, or because individuals have chosen to reside in that particular tax jurisdiction, and thus have implicitly consented to obey all the laws of that jurisdiction, or because the ruler has been placed in a position of authority by God, and violating any law would be an offense against God (McGee 2012a). Martin Luther King would not agree with this view. In fact, he has said that one has a moral duty to disobey unjust laws (King 1963). Gandhi, Thoreau, Jefferson, and many others have espoused similar views over the centuries. In fact, anyone who espouses civil disobedience espouses some version of this view. Just because something is law does not mean that obedience is required in order to act morally. Slavery was legal, and even justified in the Bible, yet it is not moral. Killing Jews was legal in Nazi-Germany, yet was not moral.

The view that the ruler has been placed there by God would be dismissed immediately by atheists, and by almost all theists, although both the Christian Bible and the Jewish religious literature put forth this justification for obedience (Cohn 2012; McGee 2012a). This view is still believed by some Muslims, but only in cases where the country is ruled by Sharia law (Jalili 2012).

Paying taxes to fund abortion may be viewed from several perspectives. Both libertarians who support the idea of abortion and those who oppose it are opposed to forcing individuals to pay for other people's abortions because it is forcing some individuals to pay for the benefits of other individuals. Libertarians who oppose abortion also oppose forcing people to pay for abortion because they abhor the practice; forcing someone to pay for something they find morally repugnant is itself morally repugnant.

[24] This phrase, "just taxes" is a logical contradiction for the anarcho-capitalist.

7.8 Taxes in a Libertarian World

How would governments be funded in a libertarian world? Of course, an anarcho-capitalist would be quick to point out that there would be nothing to fund, since there would be no government. All services would be provided by the market or by private contributions.

In contrast, most libertarians would try to privatize as much as possible, thus minimizing the need for taxes, and would choose taxes that have a minimal effect on redistribution. Spending would be limited to the defense of life, liberty and property. Could the income tax be totally eliminated? Yes. The income tax did not exist in the United States prior to 1913.[25] The federal government of the United States was able to function from the 1790s to 1913 without an income tax. It raised funds primarily through tariffs and the sale of western lands. Of course, it could be pointed out that tariffs are a form of tax, and that the federal government's claim to the lands it sold was questionable, but we will save discussion of these points for another day.

A few scholars have outlined plans for the funding of services in a libertarian state. Murray Sabrin (1994) offered a suggestion that would totally eliminate taxes in the United States. Government has grown far beyond its legitimate scope. Its functions must be cut back drastically. Social Security, Medicare, Medicaid, and interest on the national debt would be phased out. All major federal taxes would be eliminated. The gasoline tax would remain for a time, provided the proceeds were restricted to the maintenance of the roads. Of course, in a totally libertarian society, all roads would be privately owned, thus eliminating the need for a gasoline tax. The federal highway system would be sold to private investors.[26] The proceeds from their sale and the sale of other government assets could be used to fund a fully privatized Social Security system. Since taxpayers would no longer be burdened with the income and other taxes, they would be free to spend or invest those funds as they choose, causing a shift away from government and into the more productive private sector. The economy would boom.

Healthcare would be privatized, and individuals would be able to choose their doctor and the level of healthcare they want to pay for. Customized private insurance plans would pop up to serve consumer needs. One group of individuals would no longer be forced to pay for the health benefits received by other individuals. Men would no longer be forced to pay for hysterectomies, women would no longer be forced to pay for prostate cancer surgeries, and no one would be forced to pay for

[25] This is with the exception of the income tax Lincoln instituted during the war between the states, which was repealed in 1872, and the income tax enacted as part of the 1894 Tariff Act, which was declared unconstitutional in *Pollock v. Farmers' Loan & Trust Company*, 157 U.S. 429 (1895), affirmed on rehearing, 158 U.S. 601 (1895).

[26] A libertarian objection to this scheme might be couched as follows. Only the proper owners of resources may sell them. The government is not the legitimate owner of the roads. Therefore, this entity would be prohibited from selling them. Moreover, when you sell something, you typically are paid resources. But, if the government is no more than a criminal gang, it would be illicit to give them any money.

condoms used by others. Those who are unable to pay would be taken as indigent patients or would be provided for by community groups or private charity rather than the confiscation of other people's property. Government intervention in the healthcare market has caused medical costs to skyrocket. A privatized healthcare system would be better able to control healthcare costs.[27]

The property tax could be eliminated. Property taxes in the U.S. generally finance the collection of garbage and support education. Since some individuals would no longer be forced to pay for the education of other people's children, they would be able to use those tax funds to spend or save as they saw fit. Parents would pay for the education of their children and no longer be able to force others to pay for their benefits. Parents who were unable to pay for their children's education could obtain relief through scholarships and private charity. Garbage collection would be privatized.

The defense budget would be cut drastically, since U.S. taxpayers would no longer be forced to pay for the defense of Europe, much of Asia, and Latin America. Entangling alliances would be abolished. There would be no need for NATO and other such organizations that have lived off of American taxpayers' forced contributions for decades.

Sabrin (1994) recommends we suspend the payment of interest on the debt. If there are any proceeds left after selling federal assets and fully funding Social Security, those funds could be used to partially pay down the national debt.[28]

The banking system would have to be radically transformed. Inefficient banks would be allowed to fail rather than being bailed out. The Federal Reserve would no longer prop up failing banks and would itself be abolished.[29] Fiat currency would be replaced by commodity-backed currency, thus eliminating the Fed's ability to inflate the currency (inflation is a tax on money holdings). It is quite possible that the United States could function without a central bank. The Federal Reserve Bank did not exist prior to 1913, so it cannot be said that a national bank must exist, because the United States did quite well without this institution for about 100 years.[30] Just

[27] See on this Block (2003, 2013); Friedman (1962); Goodman and Musgrave (1992); Gratzer (2005); Hamowy (1984); Herbener (1996); Holly (2013); Hoppe (1993b); Johnson et al. (1998); Layden and Block (1996); McGuff and Murphy (2015); McMaken (2019); Murphy (2017); Porter (2006); Tepper (2019); Terrell (2003).

[28] Rothbard (1992) recommends the repudiation of the entire national debt. Does this not violate contractual and property rights of the bond holders? They should not have lent money to an illicit institution in the first place.

[29] For the case in behalf of ending the Fed see Auerbach (2008); Grim (2009); Murphy (2010); North (2012); Paul (2009); Rothbard (1984); Salerno (2012); Sowell (2011).

[30] One mission of the Fed was to protect the value of the dollar. It has atrophied to about 4 cents since its inception. The other mission was to quell the business cycle. But a comparison of the century before and its advent shows that oscillations have increased, not decreased. Since it has done such a great job with these goals it is now taking on two more: global warming and racial and sexual balance.

like there is[31] a separation of church and state, there would be a separation of money and state.

Bernard Curry (1982) published a detailed set of principles for taxation in a libertarian society. He believed that some taxation is necessary to support a government whose sole functions are to protect liberty and property, and to quell fraud and violence. Both taxation and the role of government should be limited. Taxation should not be based on income, but on spending. Those who spend more would pay more tax than those who do not spend. In other words, consumption would be taxed, not income. Governments would raise funds through sales taxes, not income taxes. Companies would be exempt from taxation because they only produce; they do not consume. The products and services that companies produce would be taxed when they are purchased by the end user (consumer).

Others have suggested that lotteries and voluntary contributions could be used to fund governments (McGee 2012a). However, government lotteries could not be set up as monopolies. They would have to compete against private-sector lotteries. Voluntary contributions could flow to government just like voluntary contributions flow to nonprofit organizations. Donors could earmark their donations to be used for certain projects or functions, or they could decide to have their contributions deposited in a general fund. In order to attract donors, governments would have to spend their funds efficiently and wisely, lest they lose contributions. Under the present tax system, "contributors" are forced to donate, so governments do not have to pay a penalty for inefficiency, providing poor services, or corruption. In a privatized system, intelligent contributors would cease to contribute to inefficient, wasteful, or corrupt governments.

Ayn Rand's economic and political philosophy was basically minarchist. She believed that government should exist, but that its authority should be severely circumscribed. She believed that taxation was theft, and that government services should be paid for by voluntary contributions, payment of fees and a government lottery. Those who are relatively rich might voluntarily contribute more, since they have the ability to do so, much like the case of charity, where the rich contribute more than the poor (Binswanger 1986, 493–494; Rand 1964, 116–120). When asked whether it was morally right to refuse to pay taxes, she said yes, that it was morally right, but that this political right is not recognized, and that the penalty for nonpayment would be too high (Mayhew 2005, 7).

Overview of Case Law

United States

Pollock v. Farmers' Loan & Trust Company, 157 U.S. 429 (1895), affirmed on rehearing, 158 U.S. 601 (1895).

Kelo v. City of New London, 545 U.S. 469 (2005) (O'Connor, dissenting).

[31] Well, should be, given that the government has been shutting down churches of late.

References

Adam Smith Institute. 2021. *Tax Freedom Day 2021 is May 31st*. https://www.adamsmith.org/taxfreedomday/

Anderson, Terry, and P.J. Hill. 1979. An American Experiment in Anarcho-Capitalism: The Not So Wild, Wild West. *Journal of Libertarian Studies* 3: 9–29. http://mises.org/journals/jls/3_1/3_1_2.pdf.

Anderson, William L. 1998. *Market Failure?* October 8. http://www.mises.org/story/53

Auerbach, Robert D. 2008. *Deception and Abuse at the Fed: Henry B. Gonzalez Battles Alan Greenspan's Bank*. Austin: University of Texas Press.

Barnett II, William, Walter E. Block, and Michael Saliba. 2005. Perfect Competition: A Case of 'Market-Failure'. *Corporate Ownership & Control* 2 (4): 70–75.

Batchelder, Lily L. 2009–2010. What Should Society Expect from Heirs – The Case for a Comprehensive Inheritance Tax." *Tax Law Review* 63: 1. http://heinonline.org/HOL/LandingPage?handle=hein.journals/taxlr63&div=5&id=&page=

Benson, Bruce L. 1989. Enforcement of Private Property Rights in Primitive Societies: Law Without Government. *The Journal of Libertarian Studies* 9 (1): 1–26. http://mises.org/journals/jls/9_1/9_1_1.pdf.

———. 1990. Customary Law with Private Means of Resolving Disputes and Dispensing Justice: A Description of a Modern System of Law and Order without State Coercion. *The Journal of Libertarian Studies* 9 (2): 25–42. http://mises.org/journals/jls/9_2/9_2_2.pdf.

Binswanger, Harry, ed. 1986. *The Ayn Rand Lexicon: Objectivism from A to Z*. New York: New American Library.

Block, Walter E. 1972. The Polish Ham Question. *The Libertarian Forum* 4 (6–7): 5. http://www.mises.org/journals/lf/1972/1972_06-07.pdf; http://mises.org/daily/4054; http://archive.lewrockwell.com/block/block143.html.

Block, Walter. 1989. The Justification of Taxation in the Public Finance Literature: A Critique. *Journal of Public Finance and Public Choice* 3: 141–158.

———. 1993. Public Finance Texts Cannot Justify Government Taxation: A Critique. *Canadian Public Administration/Administration Publique du Canada* 36 (2): 225–262.

Block, Walter E. 2002a. All Government is Excessive: A Rejoinder to 'In Defense of Excessive Government' by Dwight Lee. *Journal of Libertarian Studies* 16 (3): 35–82. http://www.mises.org/journals/jls/16_3/16_3_3.pdf.

———. 2002b. Accepting Government Subsidies. *Fraser Forum*. February, 27. http://oldfraser.lexi.net/publications/forum/2002/02/section_13.html

———. 2003. Socialized Medicine is the Problem. *Surgical Neurology* 60 (5): 467–468. http://tinyurl.com/ypzmx8.

———. 2004a. Are Alienability and the Apriori of Argument Logically Incompatible? *Dialogue* 1 (1) http://www.uni-svishtov.bg/dialog/2004/256gord6.pdf.

———. 2004b. Radical Libertarianism: Applying Libertarian Principles to Dealing with the Unjust Government, Part I. *Reason Papers* 27: 117–133. http://www.walterblock.com/wp-content/uploads/publications/block_radical-libertarianism-rp.pdf.

———. 2006a. Coase and Kelo: Ominous Parallels and Reply to Lott on Rothbard on Coase. *Whittier Law Review* 27 (4): 997–1022.

———. 2006b. Radical Libertarianism: Applying Libertarian Principles to Dealing with the Unjust Government, Part II. *Reason Papers* 28: 85–109.

———. 2007a. *Ron Paul and Matching Funds*. October 1. http://archive.lewrockwell.com/block/block86.html

———. 2007b. Anarchism and Minarchism; No Rapprochement Possible: Reply to Tibor Machan. *Journal of Libertarian Studies* 21 (1): 91–99.

———. 2008. *Replies to Readers*. September 23. http://archive.lewrockwell.com/block/block108.html (libertarians hypocrites for using public school?)

Block, Walter E. and Chris Arakaky. 2008. *Taking Government Money for Grad School?* May 23. http://archive.lewrockwell.com/block/block100.html
Block, Walter E. and William Barnett II. 2008. Continuums. *Journal Etica e Politica / Ethics & Politics* 1: 151–166 June. http://www2.units.it/~etica/; http://www2.units.it/~etica/2008_1/BLOCKBARNETT.pdf
Block, Walter E. 2009a. Libertarian Punishment Theory: Working For, and Donating To, the State. *Libertarian Papers* 1. http://libertarianpapers.org/2009/17-libertarian-punishment-theory-working-for-and-donating-to-the-state/
———. 2009b. Toward a Libertarian Theory of Guilt and Punishment for the Crime of Statism. In *Property, Freedom and Society: Essays in Honor of Hans-Hermann Hoppe*, ed. Jorg Guido Hulsmann and Stephan Kinsella, 137–148. Auburn: Ludwig von Mises Institute.
———. 2009c. *The Privatization of Roads and Highways: Human and Economic Factors*. Auburn: The Mises Institute.
Block, Walter E. 2010. *You are a rotten kid (rent control and libertarianism)*. February 27. http://archive.lewrockwell.com/block/block150.html
———. 2011a. *It's Ayn Rand Bashing Time, Once Again*. February 18. http://archive.lewrockwell.com/block/block172.html
———. 2011b. *May a Libertarian Take Money From the Government?* March 11. http://archive.lewrockwell.com/block/block175.html; https://www.lewrockwell.com/2011/03/walter-e-block/may-a-libertarian-take-money-from-the-government/
———. 2011c. Toward a Libertarian Theory of Guilt and Punishment for the Crime of Statism. *22 Journal of Libertarian Studies*: 665–675. http://mises.org/journals/jls/22_1/22_1_33.pdf.
———. 2011d. Hoppe, Kinsella and Rothbard II on Immigration: A Critique. *Journal of Libertarian Studies* 22: 593–623. http://mises.org/journals/jls/22_1/22_1_29.pdf.
———. 2011e. Toward a Libertarian Theory of Charitable Donations. *Economics, Management, and Financial Markets* 6 (4): 9–28. http://www.walterblock.com/wp-content/uploads/V.378_Toward-a-libertarian-theory-of-charitable-donations.pdf.
———. 2011f. Governmental Inevitability: Reply to Holcombe. *Journal of Libertarian Studies* 22: 667–688. http://mises.org/journals/jls/22_1/22_1_34.pdf
———. 2011g. Rejoinder to Murphy and Callahan on Hoppe's Argumentation Ethics. *Journal of Libertarian Studies* 22: 631–639. http://mises.org/journals/jls/22_1/22_1_31.pdf.
———. 2012a. James Buchanan on Inheritance: A Critique. *Journal of Entrepreneurship & Public Policy* 1 (2): 159–165.
———. 2012b. *Yes to Ron Paul and Liberty*. Ishi Press.
———. 2013. *Forced Vaccinations*. February 4. http://lewrockwell.com/block/block217.html
Block, Walter E., and Peter Lothian Nelson. 2015. *Water Capitalism: The Case for Privatizing Oceans, Rivers, Lakes, and Aquifers*. New York City: Lexington Books, Rowman and Littlefield.
Block, Walter E. 2016a. *Defining anarchism*. January 1. http://www.targetliberty.com/2016/01/walter-block-on-definition-of-anarchy.html?utm_source=feedburner&utm_medium=email&utm_campaign=Feed%3A+TargetLiberty+%28Target+Liberty%29.
———. 2016b. *On anarchy*. January 3. http://www.targetliberty.com/2016/01/walter-block-responds-on-anarchy.html?utm_source=feedburner&utm_medium=email&utm_campaign=Feed%3A+TargetLiberty+%28Target+Liberty%29; https://news.bitcoin.com/toward-techno-anarchy-blockchain-tech-will-thwart-government-transform-society/; http://www.targetliberty.com/2016/01/should-libertarians-attempt-to.html?utm_source=feedburner&utm_medium=email&utm_campaign=Feed%3A+TargetLiberty+%28Target+Liberty%29
———. 2016c. *Walter Block Responds to Robert Wenzel's Charge That He is Not an Anarcho-Capitalist*. February 1. http://www.targetliberty.com/2016/02/walter-block-responds-to-my-charge-that.html; http://www.targetliberty.com/2016/02/walter-block-responds-to-my-charge-that.html?utm_source=feedburner&utm_medium=email&utm_campaign=Feed%3A+TargetLiberty+%28Target+Liberty%29

———. 2016d. *Is It Compatible With Libertarianism to be a Banker? Yes!* September 29. www.lewrockwell.com/lrc-blog/compatible-libertarianism-banker-yes/

Blum, Walter J. and Harry Kalven, Jr. 1953. *The Uneasy Case for Progressive Taxation.* Chicago/London: University of Chicago Press.

Brederode van, Robert F. ed. 2021. *Virtues and Fallacies of VAT: An Evaluation after 50 Years.* Kluwer Law International.

Buchanan, James M., and Gordon Tullock. 1962. *The Calculus of Consent: Logical Foundations of Constitutional Democracy.* Ann Arbor: University of Michigan.

Buchanan, James. 1983. Rent Seeking, Non compensated Transfers, and Laws of Succession. *Journal of Law and Economics* 26 (1): 71–85.

Callahan, Gene. 2000. *Market Failure Again?* April 4. http://www.mises.org/story/407

Casey, Doug. 2010. *Doug Casey on Anarchy.* March 31. http://www.caseyresearch.com/cwc/doug-casey-anarchy

———. 2018. *Anarchy and Voluntaryism.* February 7. https://www.lewrockwell.com/2018/02/doug-casey/anarchy-and-voluntaryism/

Cohn, Gordon. 1998. The Jewish View on Paying Taxes. *Journal of Accounting, Ethics & Public Policy* 1 (2): 109–120.

———. 2012. The Traditional Jewish View of Paying Taxes. In *The Ethics of Tax Evasion: Perspectives in Theory and Practice*, ed. Robert W. McGee, 149–158. New York: Springer.

Cowen, Tyler, ed. 1988. *The Theory of Market Failure: A Critical Examination.* Fairfax: George Mason University Press.

Crowe, Martin T. 1944. *The Moral Obligation of Paying Just Taxes.* Washington, DC: The Catholic University of America Press.

Curry, Bernard. 1982. *Principles of Taxation of a Libertarian Society.* Glendale: BC Publishing Company.

DiLorenzo, Thomas J. 2010. The Culture of Violence in the American West: Myth versus Reality. *The Independent Review* 15 (2): 227–239. http://www.independent.org/pdf/tir/tir_15_02_4_dilorenzo.pdf.

DiLorenzo, Thomas. 2011. A Note on the Canard of 'Asymmetric Information' as a Source of Market Failure. *Quarterly Journal of Austrian Economics* 14 (2): 249–255. http://mises.org/journals/qjae/pdf/qjae14_2_6.pdf.

Eabrasu, Marian. 2009. A Reply to the Current Critiques Formulated Against Hoppe's Argumentation Ethics. *Libertarian Papers* 1 (1) http://libertarianpapers.org/2009/20-eabrasu-critiques-argumentation-ethics/.

Enache, Cristina. 2021. *Sources of Tax Revenue: U.S. vs. OECD.* The Tax Foundation. February 17. https://taxfoundation.org/publications/sources-of-us-tax-revenue/

Epstein, Richard A. 2003. *Skepticism and Freedom: A Modern Case for Classical Liberalism.* Chicago/London: University of Chicago Press.

Epstein, Richard. 2005. Blind Justices: The scandal of Kelo v. New London. *Wall Street Journal.* July 3. http://www.opinionjournal.com/extra/?id=110006904

Epstein, Richard A. 2014. *The Classical Liberal Constitution: The Uncertain Quest for Limited Government.* Cambridge: Harvard University Press.

Friedman, David. 1989. *The Machinery of Freedom: Guide to a Radical Capitalism.* 2nd ed. La Salle: Open Court. http://www.daviddfriedman.com/Libertarian/Machinery_of_Freedom/MofF_Chapter_41.html

Friedman, Milton. 1962. *Capitalism and Freedom.* Chicago: University of Chicago Press.

Friedman, Milton, and Rose D. Friedman. 1999. *Two Lucky People.* Chicago: University of Chicago Press.

Galles, Gary. 2013. *Social Security: The Most Successful Ponzi Scheme in History.* November 22. https://mises.org/library/social-security-most-successful-ponzi-scheme-history

Goodman, John C., and Gerald L. Musgrave. 1992. *Patient Power: Solving America's Health Care Crisis.* Washington, DC: Cato.

Goodman, John C. 2015. *Why Was Social Security Designed Like A Ponzi Scheme?* August 13. http://www.forbes.com/sites/johngoodman/2015/08/13/why-was-social-security-designed-like-a-ponzi-scheme/#2ae06a10734f
Gordon, David. 1988. Radical & Quasi-Kantian. *Liberty* (November): 46–47. http://www.libertyunbound.com/sites/files/printarchive/Liberty_Magazine_November_1988.pdf.
Gratzer, David. 2005. The Return of HillaryCare: Socialized medicine is still not a good idea. *The Weekly Standard*. May 23. http://www.medicalprogresstoday.com/spotlight/spotlight_indarchive.php?id=778
Gregory, Anthony. 2011. *Abolish the Police*. May 26. http://www.lewrockwell.com/gregory/gregory213.html
Grim, Ryan. 2009. *Priceless: How The Federal Reserve Bought The Economics Profession*. October 23. http://www.huffingtonpost.com/2009/09/07/priceless-how-the-federal_n_278805.html
Guillory, Gil. 2005. *What Are You Calling Failure?* May 5. http://www.mises.org/story/1806
Guillory, Gil, and Patrick Tinsley. 2009. The Role of Subscription-Based Patrol and Restitution in the Future of Liberty. *Libertarian Papers* 1 (12): 12. http://libertarianpapers.org/2009/12-the-role-of-subscription-based-patrol-and-restitution-in-the-future-of-liberty/.
Hall, Robert E., and Alvin Rabushka. 1985. *The Flat Tax*. Stanford: Hoover Institution Press.
Hamowy, Ronald. 1984. *Canadian Medicine: A Study in Restricted Entry*. Vancouver: The Fraser Institute.
Hasnas, John. 1995. The Myth of the Rule of Law. *Wisconsin Law Review* 1995. http://faculty.msb.edu/hasnasj/GTWebSite/MythWeb.htm
Hayek von, Friedrich A. 1944. *The Road To Serfdom*. Chicago: The University of Chicago Press.
Heinrich, David J. 2010. Justice for All Without the State. *The Libertarian Standard*. May 6. http://www.libertarianstandard.com/articles/david-j-heinrich/justice-for-all-without-the-state/
Herbener, Jeffrey. 1996. Socialized Medicine, Take Two. *The Free Market* 14(7). http://www.mises.org/freemarket_detail.asp?control=172&sortorder=articledate
Higgs, Robert. 1995. The Myth of 'Failed' Policies. *The Free Market* 13(6). http://www.mises.org/freemarket_detail.asp?control=239&sortorder=articledate
———. 2007. *Income-Tax Withholding. Foundation for Economic Education*. November 1. https://fee.org/articles/wartime-origins-of-modern-income-tax-withholding/
———. 2009. *Why We Couldn't Abolish Slavery Then and Can't Abolish Government Now*. August 20. http://www.lewrockwell.com/higgs/higgs128.html
———. 2012. *What is the point of my libertarian anarchism?* January 16. http://archive.lewrockwell.com/higgs/higgs180.html
Holly, Mike.2013. *How Government Regulations Made Healthcare So Expensive*. December 17. http://bastiat.mises.org/2013/12/how-government-regulations-made-healthcare-so-expensive/
Hoppe, Hans-Hermann. 1988a. On the Ultimate Justification of the Ethics of Private Property. *Liberty*, September.
———. 1988b. The Justice of Economic Efficiency. *Austrian Economics Newsletter*. Winter.
———. 1988c. From the Economics of Laissez Faire to the Ethics of Libertarianism. In *Man, Economy, and Liberty: Essays in Honor of Murray N. Rothbard*, ed. Walter E. Block and Llewellyn H. Rockwell. Auburn: The Mises Institute.
———. 1988d. Utilitarians and Randians vs Reason. *Liberty* (November): 53–54. http://www.libertyunbound.com/sites/files/printarchive/Liberty_Magazine_November_1988.pdf
———. 1993a. *The Economics and Ethics of Private Property. Studies in Political Economy and Philosophy*, 204–207. Boston: Kluwer Academic Publishers.
———. 1993b. A Four-Step Health-Care Solution. *The Free Market* 11(4). http://www.mises.org/freemarket_detail.asp?control=279
———. 1995. *Economic Science and the Austrian Method*. Auburn: The Ludwig von Mises Institute. http://www.mises.org/esandtam/pes1.asp; http://www.mises.org/esandtam/pfe3.asp; http://mises.org/pdf/esam.pdf.
———, ed. 2003. *The Myth of National Defense: Essays on the Theory and History of Security Production*. Auburn: The Ludwig von Mises Institute.

———. 2006. *The Economics and Ethics of Private Property*. 2nd ed. Auburn: The Mises Institute.
———. 2008. *Reflections on the Origin and the Stability of the State*. June 23. http://www.lewrockwell.com/hoppe/hoppe18.html
———. 2011a. *State or Private Law Society*. April 10. http://www.lewrockwell.com/hoppe/hoppe26.1.html
———. 2011b. Interview with *Philosophie Magazine*, reprinted in Hans-Hermann Hoppe. In *The Great Fiction: Property, Economy, Society, and the Politics of Decline*. Second expanded ed.. 2021, 519–524. Auburn: Mises Institute.
Hospers, John. 1971. *Libertarianism: A Political Philosophy for Tomorrow*. Los Angeles: Nash Publishing.
Huebert, Jacob. 2010. *Libertarianism Today*. Santa Barbara: Praeger.
Jalili, Reza. 2012. The Ethics of Tax Evasion: An Islamic Perspective. In *The Ethics of Tax Evasion: Perspectives in Theory and Practice*, ed. Robert W. McGee, 167–199. New York: Springer.
Johnson, Clint, Walter E. Block, and Thomas Oxner. 1998. Notes on Health Care Financing and Free Markets. *Journal of Accounting, Ethics and Public Policy* 1 (3): 488–502.
Jouvenel, Bertrand de. 1952. *The Ethics of Redistribution*, 1990. Cambridge: Cambridge University Press. Reprinted by The Liberty Fund, Indianapolis.
King, Martin Luther, Jr. 1963. *Letter from Birmingham Jail*. April 16. https://letterfromjail.com/
King, Seth. 2010. *Daily Anarchist Interviews Walter E. Block*. September 9. http://www.lewrockwell.com/block/block165.html
Kinsella, Stephan. 1996. New Rationalist Directions in Libertarian Rights Theory. *Journal of Libertarian Studies* 12 (12): 323–338.
Kinsella, N. Stephan. 2002 [2011]. Defending Argumentation Ethics: Reply to Murphy & Callahan. *Anti-state.com*, September 19 [July 2]. http://www.anti-state.com/article.php?article_id=312
Kinsella, N. Stephan. 2005. *A Libertarian Defense of 'Kelo' and Limited Federal Power*. August 28. http://www.lewrockwell.com/kinsella/kinsella17.html
Kinsella, N. Stephan. 2009. *The Irrelevance of the Impossibility of Anarcho-Libertarianism*. August 20. http://www.stephankinsella.com/2009/08/20/the-irrelevance-of-the-impossibility-of-anarcho-libertarianism/
Kotlikoff, Lawrence. 2014. *America's Ponzi scheme: Why Social Security needs to retire*. April 7. http://www.pbs.org/newshour/making-sense/americas-ponzi-scheme-why-social-security-needs-to-retire/
Layden, William R., and Walter E. Block. 1996. Health Security. *Nomos* 47/48: 38–45.
Libertarianism.org. 2021. *What is a Libertarian*. https://www.libertarianism.org/what-is-a-libertarian
Long, Roderick. 2004. *Libertarian Anarchism: Responses to Ten Objections*. http://www.lewrockwell.com/long/long11.html
MacKenzie, D. W. 2002. *The Market Failure Myth* August 26. http://www.mises.org/fullstory.aspx?control=1035
Main, Carla T. 2007. *Bulldozed: 'Kelo,' Eminent Domain and the American Lust for Land*. New York: Encounter Books.
Mangu-Ward, Katherine. 2016. Milton Friedman Helped Invent Income Tax Withholding. *Reason*. April 18. https://reason.com/2016/04/18/milton-friedman-helped-invent-income-tax/
Matthews, Dan. 2014. Why Isn't Inheritance Tax 100%? *Forbes*, July 24. http://www.forbes.com/sites/danmatthews/2014/07/24/why-isnt-inheritance-tax-100-per-cent/#43124e9d6408
Mayhew, Robert, ed. 2005. *Ayn Rand Answers: The Best of Her Q & A*. New York: New American Library.
McConkey, Michael. 2013. Anarchy, Sovereignty, and the State of Exception: Schmitt's Challenge. *The Independent Review* 17 (3): 415–428. http://www.independent.org/pdf/tir/tir_17_03_05_mcconkey.pdf.
McGee, Robert W. 1998. Is the Ability to Pay Principle Ethically Bankrupt? *Journal of Accounting, Ethics & Public Policy* 1 (3): 503–511.

———. 1999. An Ethical Look at Paying Your 'Fair Share' of Taxes. *Journal of Accounting, Ethics & Public Policy* 2 (2): 318–328.

———. 2004. Property Rights vs. Utilitarianism: Two Views of Ethics. *Reason Papers* 27: 85–112.

———. 2012a. *The Ethics of Tax Evasion: Perspectives in Theory and Practice*. New York: Springer.

———. 2012b. Four Views on the Ethics of Tax Evasion. In *The Ethics of Tax Evasion: Perspectives in Theory and Practice*, ed. Robert W. McGee, 3–33. New York: Springer.

———. 2013. The Body as Property Doctrine. In *Handbook for the Philosophical Foundations of Business Ethics*. vol. 3, Christoph Luetge, ed., 1275–1304. Dordrecht, Heidelberg, New York and London: Springer. Also published in SpringerLink.

McGuff, Doug and Robert P. Murphy. 2015. *The Primal Prescription: Surviving the "Sick Care"* Sinkhole. http://store.mises.org/Primal-Prescription-Surviving-The-Sick-Care-Sinkhole-P11014.aspx

McMaken, Ryan. 2019. *Single-Payer Healthcare Is the Worst Kind of Universal Healthcare.*. May 17. https://mises.org/wire/single-payer-healthcare-worst-kind-universal-healthcare

Meng, Jude Chua Soo. 2002. *Hopp(e)ing Onto New Ground: A Rothbardian Proposal for Thomistic Natural Law as the Basis for Hans-Hermann Hoppe's Praxeological Defense of Private Property.* Working paper, http://www.mises.org/journals/scholar/meng.pdf

Mises von, Ludwig. 1998. *Human Action: A Treatise on Economics*. Auburn: Ludwig von Mises Institute.

Mises Institute. 2021. *History of Austro-Libertarian Thought: 384BC-2020AD*. Auburn: The Mises Institute. https://mises.org/history-of-austro-libertarian-thought?subject=759&person=All.

Molyneux, Stefan. 2008. *The Stateless Society: An Examination of Alternatives*. http://www.mail-archive.com/libertarianenterprise@yahoogroups.com/msg02056.html

Murphy, Robert P. 2005. *But Wouldn't Warlords Take Over? July 7*. http://mises.org/story/1855;. http://mises.org/library/wouldnt-warlords-take-over.

———. 2010. *The Fed: The Chicago School's Achilles Heel*. December 13. http://mises.org/daily/4875

———. 2017. *Did Obamacare Really Save Lives?* June 30. https://mises.org/blog/did-obamacare-really-save-lives

Murray, Charles. 1997. *What It Means To Be A Libertarian*. New York: Broadway Books.

Napolitano, Andrew B. 2011. *Theft by Any Other Name; It Is Dangerous to Be Right When the Government Is Wrong: The Case for Personal Freedom*. Thomas Nelson Inc.

Nelson, Peter Lothian, and Walter E. Block. 2018. *Space capitalism: the case for privatizing space travel and colonization*. Palgrave Macmillan.

North, Gary. 2012. *How to End the Fed, and How Not To*. September 10. http://mises.org/daily/6175/

Nozick, Robert. 1974. *Anarchy, State and Utopia*. New York: Basic Books.

Paul, Ron. 2000. *A Republic, If You Can Keep It*. Lake Jackson: Foundation for Rational Economics and Education.

———. 2008a. *The Revolution: A Manifesto*. New York: Grand Central Publishing.

———. 2008b. *On the Inner Contradictions of Limited Government*. http://www.youtube.com/watch?v=7o4kiWpqoeg&feature=PlayList&p=9645F6A68683F679&playnext=1&playnext_from=PL&index=4; http://libertyupward.com/ron-paul-religious-icon/

———. 2008c. *On the Inner Contradictions of Limited Government*. http://www.youtube.com/watch?v=7o4kiWpqoeg&feature=PlayList&p=9645F6A68683F679&playnext=1&playnext_from=PL&index=4

———. 2009. *End the Fed*. New York: Grand Central Publishing.

Porter, Michael. 2006. *Redefining Health Care: Creating Value-Based Competition on Results*. Harvard Business Review Press. https://www.amazon.com/dp/1591397782/ref=cm_sw_r_cp_dp_T2_GoRuzbVZG2TDD.

Prabhakar, Rajiv, Karen Rowlingson, and Stuart White. 2008. *How to Defend Inheritance Tax*. Fabian ideas, 623. Fabian Society.

Raimondo, Justin. 2000. *An Enemy of the State: The Life of Murray N. Rothbard*. Amherst: Prometheus.
Rand, Ayn. 1964. *The Virtue of Selfishness*. New York: The New American Library.
Rockwell, Lew. 2013. *What Would We Do Without the State?* March 31. http://www.lewrockwell.com/blog/lewrw/archives/134782.html
Rothbard, Murray N. 1973. *For a New Liberty*. New York: Macmillan. http://mises.org/rothbard/newlibertywhole.asp.
———. 1975. Society Without a State. *The Libertarian Forum* 7 (1) http://www.lewrockwell.com/rothbard/rothbard133.html.
———. 1977. Do you hate the state? *The Libertarian Forum* 10 (7). http://www.lewrockwell.com/rothbard/rothbard75.html.
Rothbard, Murray. N. 1978. *For a New Liberty*. Rev. ed. New York: Macmillan.
Rothbard, Murray N. 1984. The Federal Reserve as a Cartelization Device: The Early Years, 1913–1930. In *Money in Crisis: the Federal Reserve, the Economy, and Monetary Reform*, ed. Barry N. Siegel, 89–136. Cambridge, MA: Ballinger Publishing.
———. 1985. *"Airport Congestion: A Case of Market Failure?" The Free Market*. Auburn: The Ludwig von Mises Institute, January. http://www.mises.org/econsense/ch52.asp.
Rothbard, Murray. 1988. Beyond Is and Ought. *Liberty* (November): 44–45. http://mises.org/daily/4629/Beyond-Is-and-Ought; http://www.libertyunbound.com/sites/files/printarchive/Liberty_Magazine_November_1988.pdf.
Rothbard, Murray N. 1992. Repudiating the National Debt. *Chronicles*, June, 49–52. http://mises.org/article.aspx?Id=1423
———. 1998 [1982]. *The Ethics of Liberty*. New York: New York University Press. http://www.mises.org/rothbard/ethics/ethics.asp
Rothbard, Murray. N. 2005. The Ancient Chinese Libertarian Tradition. *Mises Daily Articles*. December 5. Auburn, AL: The Mises Institute.
Rothbard, Murray N. 2009. *Anatomy of the State*. Auburn: The Mises Institute.
———. 2011. *Economic Controversies*. Auburn: The Mises Institute.
———. 2018. *Rothbard A to Z, compiled by Edward W. Fuller, edited by David Gordon*. Auburn: The Mises Institute.
Sabrin, Murray. 1994. *Tax Free 2000: The Rebirth of American Liberty*. Lafayette: Prescott Press.
Salerno, Joseph T. 2012. Fractional Reserves and the Fed: Testimony before the U.S. House Committee on Financial Services, Subcommittee on Monetary Policy (Chairman: Ron Paul). *The Free Market* 30(6): 1–4. http://mises.org/journals/fm/June2012.pdf
Salsman, Richard M. 2011. Social Security is Much Worse Than a Ponzi Scheme – and Here's How to End It. *Forbes* (September 27) http://www.forbes.com/sites/richardsalsman/2011/09/27/social-security-is-much-worse-than-a-ponzi-scheme/#2fa2c532cdc6.
Simpson, Brian. 2005. *Markets Don't Fail*. New York: Lexington Books.
Smith, Adam. 1937 [1776]. *The Wealth of Nations*. New York: Modern Library.
Smith, George F. 2017. *The Patsy and the Culprit*. June 8. https://www.lewrockwell.com/2017/06/george-f-smith/the-patsy-and-the-culprit/
Somin, Ilya. 2015. Lessons From a Little Pink House, 10 Years Later; Since the Kelo decision, 45 states have passed laws reforming eminent domain, with mixed results. *Wall Street Journal* June 21. https://www.wsj.com/articles/lessons-from-a-little-pink-house-10-years-later-1434922686
Sowell, Thomas. 2011. *Fed Up With the Fed?* May 5. https://www.lewrockwell.com/2011/05/thomas-sowell/fed-up-with-the-fed/
———. 2016. *The Collapsing Social Security Pyramid Scheme*. February 8. http://www.wnd.com/2016/02/the-collapsing-social-security-pyramid-scheme/
Spooner, Lysander. 2008a. *Let's Abolish Government*. Auburn: The Ludwig von Mises Institute.
———. 2008b. No Treason: The Constitution of No Authority. In *Let's Abolish Government,* Lysander Spooner, ed. Auburn: The Ludwig von Mises Institute.
Stringham, Edward, ed. 2007. *Anarchy and the Law: The Political Economy of Choice*. Somerset: Transaction Publishers.

Tabarrok, Alex. 2005. *Death Taxes: Theory, History and Ethics*. July 20. https://mises.org/system/tdf/deathtax_4.pdf?file=1&type=document
Tannehill, Morris and Linda Tannehill. [1970] 1984. *The Market for Liberty*. New York: Laissez Faire Books. http://www.lewrockwell.com/orig11/tannehill1.html
Tax Foundation. 2021. https://taxfoundation.org
Tepper, Jonathan. 2019. The Doctor Monopoly is Killing American Patients: How the American Medical Association deliberately created a U.S. physician shortage in order to protect jobs and inflate pay. *The American Conservative*, August 1. https://www.theamericanconservative.com/articles/the-doctor-monopoly-is-killing-american-patients/
Terrell, Timothy D. 2003. Socialized Medicine in America. *The Free Market* 23(11). http://www.mises.org/freemarket_detail.asp?control=458&sortorder=articledate
Tinsley, Patrick. 1998–1999. With Liberty and Justice for All: A Case for Private Police. *Journal of Libertarian Studies* 14 (1): 95–100. http://www.mises.org/journals/jls/14_1/14_1_5.pdf.
Tullock, Gordon. 1971. Inheritance Justified. *The Journal of Law & Economics* 14 (2): 465–474. http://www.jstor.org/stable/724956?seq=1#page_scan_tab_contents.
Van Dun, Frank. 2009. Argumentation Ethics and The Philosophy of Freedom. *Libertarian Papers*, No. 19. http://libertarianpapers.org/2009/19-van-dun-argumentation-ethics/
Vance, Laurence M. 2005. *The Curse of the Withholding Tax*. April, 21. http://mises.org/daily/1797
Wenzel, Robert. 2013. *Robert Ringer's Strawman Anarchist*. February 2. http://archive.lewrockwell.com/wenzel/wenzel211.html
———. 2016. *Has Walter Block Left the World of Anarcho-Capitalist Advocacy?* February 1. http://www.targetliberty.com/2016/02/has-walter-block-left-world-ofanarcho.html?utm_source=feedburner&utm_medium=email&utm_campaign=Feed%3A+TargetLiberty+%28Target+Liberty%29
Westley, Christopher. 2002. *The Myth of Market Failure*. June 14. http://www.mises.org/story/982
White, Stuart. 2008. What (if Anything) is Wrong with Inheritance Tax? *The Political Quarterly* 79(2): 162–171. http://onlinelibrary.wiley.com/doi/10.1111/j.1467-923X.2008.00921.x/full
Wikipedia. 2021. *Tax Freedom Day*. https://en.wikipedia.org/wiki/Tax_Freedom_Day
Williams, Walter. 1987. *All It Takes Is Guts: A Minority View*. Washington, DC: Regnery Books.
Woods, Thomas E. Jr. 2009a. *Krugman Failure, Not Market Failure*. June 19. http://www.lewrockwell.com/woods/woods116.html
———. 2009b. *Response to the 'Market Failure' Drones*. June 10. http://mises.org/story/3503
Woods, Tom. 2014. *Four Things the State Is Not*. July 29. http://www.lewrockwell.com/2014/07/no_author/4-things-the-state-is-not/
York, Erica. 2019. *Tax Freedom Day 2019 Is April 16*. Tax Foundation. https://taxfoundation.org/tax-freedom-day-2019/

Robert W. McGee is a professor at the Broadwell College of Business and Economics, Fayetteville State University, USA. He has earned 23 academic degrees, including 13 doctorates from universities in the United States and four European countries. He is also an attorney and Certified Public Accountant (CPA – retired), has worked or lectured in more than 30 countries, and has published more than 60 books, including five novels, and more than 1000 scholarly papers. Several studies have ranked him #1 in the world for both accounting ethics and business ethics scholarship. He is also a world champion in taekwondo, karate, kung fu and tai chi (both Yang and Sun styles). His career gold medal count is 800+.

Walter E. Block is Harold E. Wirth Endowed Chair and Professor of Economics, College of Business, Loyola University New Orleans, and senior fellow at the Mises Institute. He earned his PhD in economics at Columbia University in 1972. He has taught at Rutgers, SUNY Stony Brook, Baruch CUNY, Holy Cross and the University of Central Arkansas. He is the author of more than 600 refereed articles in professional journals, three dozen books, and thousands of op eds (including the New York Times, the Wall Street Journal and numerous others). He lectures widely on college campuses, delivers seminars around the world and appears regularly on television and radio shows. He is the Schlarbaum Laureate, Mises Institute, 2011; and has won the Loyola University Research Award (2005, 2008) and the Mises Institute's Rothbard Medal of Freedom, 2005; and the Dux Academicus award, Loyola University, 2007. Prof. Block counts among his friends Ron Paul and Murray Rothbard. He was converted to libertarianism by Ayn Rand. Block is old enough to have played chess with Friedrich Hayek and once met Ludwig von Mises, and shaken his hand. Block has never washed that hand since. So, if you shake his hand (it's pretty dirty, but what the heck) you channel Mises.

Chapter 8
Legal Positivism and Tax Law: Kelsen, Is/Ought and Capital/Revenue; Hart, Open Texture and GAARs

John Prebble and Darien Shanske

Abstract Positivism, as a theory of law, is primarily a description of what the law is – or is not. And, speaking roughly, positivism holds that law is to be distinguished from morality by certain formal structures characteristic of law. The formal structure of tax law would seem to make it a useful example for the elucidation of positivism as a descriptive theory. In this chapter, we show, through the work of two leading positivists, Kelsen, and Hart, that matters are not so simple.

Kelsen distinguished between "is" and "ought", for instance in the conditional syllogism that he propounded as the canonical form of the legal norm: "If fact X exists then consequence Y ought to follow". Readers know that his observation is fundamental to a number of Kelsen's insights. Nevertheless, there is a more fundamental question: can a rule that breaches Kelsen's canon and that instead takes the form: "If X ought to be then Y ought to follow", qualify as valid law?

The question seems ridiculous. How could there be a rule that not only omits a conditional factual statement but that comprises "ought" statements on both sides of the syllogism? In principle, such a rule is nonsense; yet such rules serve as foundations of income tax law. All rules that depend on distinguishing capital from revenue are of this kind.

For example, the rule, "An expense that is capital ought not to be deducted in calculating income" observes Kelsen's canonical form only if the question of whether a particular expense is capital or is revenue is a matter of fact. But courts aver that the distinction between capital and revenue is a matter of law. As a result, in respect of the many questions that fall into the capital–revenue divide, we can establish fact X of Kelsen's syllogism only as a fictional construction of the law.

The primary author of the sections on Kelsen was Prebble and the primary author of the sections on Hart was Shanske.

J. Prebble (✉)
Victoria University of Wellington, Wellington, New Zealand
e-mail: john.prebble@vuw.ac.nz

D. Shanske
School of Law, University of California, Davis, CA, USA

R. F. van Brederode (ed.), *Political Philosophy and Taxation*,
https://doi.org/10.1007/978-981-19-1092-0_8

Intuitively appreciating the logical flaw thus revealed, courts fall back on holding that the capital/revenue distinction is a question of degree. But as Kelsen explained, "[A] graduation of an objective value is not possible because a behavior can only conform or not conform with an objectively valid norm, but cannot do so more or less" (Kelsen H, *Pure Theory of Law* (trans: Knight M). University of California Press, 1967, p 21) Nevertheless, tax law breaches Kelsen's canon, replacing fact with fiction when framing many rules.

Tax avoidance often operates by clothing economic substance with contrived, essentially fictional, legal transactions. If a rule involves a fiction in the first place, it is relatively easy to replace that fiction with another in avoiding tax.

Many rules of income tax law, such as the debt/equity distinction, have the capital/revenue divide at their foundation. It is not surprising that such rules are prone to exploitation by tax avoiders: deficient law may be expected to have sub-optimal results at best.

As for Hart and tax law, we investigate the complicated relationship between tax law and positivism through the lens of General Anti-Avoidance Rules, or GAARs. Such anti-avoidance standards, the application of which can lead to the retroactive change of tax results that appear to follow from a strict application of the tax law, are not straightforwardly analyzed under Hart's rubric. We conclude that, at the very least, and perhaps surprisingly, there is a strong argument that GAARs are consistent with the description of law developed by Hart.

Keywords Kelsen · Hart · Legal positivism · Income tax · Revenue · Capital · GAAR

8.1 General Introduction

Positivists as to the nature of law have long emphasized that they approach the law as a descriptive matter, that law is separable from morality or, as Austin put it: "The existence of law is one thing; its merit or demerit is another" (Hart 1957, 596, citing Austin 1954, 184). It has long been understood by positivists (see, for example, Hart 1957, 185), that many areas of the law, such as criminal law, confound this simple distinction because the law that *is* (according to positivists) and the law that many think *ought to be* tend to converge in actual legal systems. Murder is prohibited both by law and by customary morality. For positivists it is particularly important for such cases that the law is distinguished from other normative systems by means of certain formal features. For instance, Austin's explanation was that law takes the form of a command (See Austin, 1954, Lecture 1).

Tax law would seem to represent congenial ground for a positivist. It is hard to argue that, as a matter of morality, or other non-legal system, that I should owe just so much in income taxes. Yet the tax law does make such a precise command and it does so manifesting other formal features, such as Hart's union of primary and secondary rules. Yet, as we explain in this chapter, the connection between tax law and positivism as a descriptive theory is more complex.

8.2 An Introduction to Legal Positivism and Its Meaning for Tax Law

In other chapters of this book, different philosophical positions are argued to have implications for what a tax system should look like: who should pay, how much and for what. As descriptive theories, positivist theories of law have less to say – at least directly – on such questions of distributive justice. That said, the themes sketched in this chapter relate to larger issues of justice in at least two ways. First, if there is something defective about the operation of tax law – or parts of tax law – *as* law, then this suggests possible rule of law issues. Alternatively, if the tax law fails to be law according to a positivist description of law, this might indicate limitations as to the value of positivism as a descriptive theory. Second, and relatedly, there are some aspects of tax law, such as anti-avoidance rules, that have clear rule of law and distributive justice implications. Anti-avoidance rules are particularly important for restraining those with the resources from devising structures that evade the purpose of the tax law. If such anti-avoidance rules are not consistent with the rule of law, that might make it harder for a tax system to advance certain visions of distributive justice.

8.3 Kelsian Analysis Reveals the Confusion of "Is" and "Ought" in Income Tax Law

8.3.1 Introduction

For many jurisdictions, income tax law is the most challenging of legal disciplines. Legislators are forever reforming the law and trying to improve it. Statutes and secondary legislation get forever longer, with no end in sight. Explanations for this complexity and resistance to reform include that governments succumb to using the tax system to promote social or economic objectives (which obscures the policy and structure of tax laws) and that business forms and transactions being infinitely variable, governments must respond with equally complex legislation.

While there is some truth in both these explanations, Prebble (1994a, b, 1995, 1996, 1998) argued that the incoherence of tax law is more basic, in that such incoherence is essential to the nature of the concept of income, and therefore to the nature of income tax law.

This present chapter approaches the same issue from a different direction. It compares certain fundamental rules of income tax law with some of the criteria for judging the quality of law propounded by the philosopher, Hans Kelsen (1881–1973). It finds that income tax law suffers from shortcomings in meeting Kelsen's criteria, shortcomings that go a long way to explaining tax law's incoherence and resistance to reform.

8.3.2 Hans Kelsen (1881–1973)

Kelsen was a legal positivist. He studied law as a social fact, explaining the nature of law and explaining what was and what could not be law, as he saw it. His oeuvre was immense, though his main theses relevant for the purposes of this chapter may be found in three leading works, with the dates of their publication in English: *Pure Theory of Law* (1967), *General Theory of Norms* (1991), and *What is Justice?* (1960) a collection of essays.

As mentioned, Kelsen's objective was to explain law as a fact. Considering that in one way or another law addresses a large fraction of all human endeavour, Kelsen's goal meant that much of his writing takes the form of finely crafted generalizations that describe law or its qualities: generalizations that are often difficult to unpack, but that are very illuminating when the reader succeeds in doing so. This chapter examines one generalization in particular, namely that we, and law, must distinguish "is" and "ought". Kelsen expressed this generalization in a number of ways, such as, "The behavior that is cannot be the behavior that ought to be" (Kelsen 1967, 7). His argument applies Hume's is/ought reasoning (Hume [1739] 2007, 335) to the world of law. Kelsen's point will be examined further, after the following comment on his modus arguendi.

Necessarily, Kelsen used particular examples to illustrate his arguments, but these examples were mainly from basic fields like criminal law and constitutional law. He said very little about income tax law. There is a rare example in *Pure Theory of Law* (1967, 8), where Kelsen distinguishes between a tax official's order to hand over money and the same order delivered by a gangster. At one level, the two orders are remarkably similar. How do we recognize the order of the official as lawful?

The difficulty is that from the subjective perspective of the person at whom the order is directed there is no apparent difference. Both commands are orders that will be backed up with force if necessary. But objectively, the command of the official is a valid norm that is binding by law on the person to whom it is directed.

Kelsen uses this example to illustrate that we cannot derive a norm from a fact. That is, we cannot conclude from the fact that there is an order that is backed by force, or that there are many such orders, that the order is law, or, as Kelsen would put it, that the order is a valid norm.

This example is vivid and useful, but it tells us more about the nature of law in general than it does about income tax law. In fact, the present author has argued elsewhere that income tax law often breaches the principle that we cannot derive a norm from a fact, and that the explanation of some confusing norms of income tax law is that, as far as income tax is concerned, we can, or at least do, derive norms from facts (Prebble and McIntosh 2015). This chapter will address this theme at some length. Meantime, suffice it to say that the author, and others who would use Kelsen's work to analyse income tax law, must rely mainly on his generalizations if we are to shed light on the nature of income tax law. This conclusion is not surprising. It is unlikely to have occurred to Kelsen that there is anything peculiar about tax law.

8.3.3 Pre-Enlightenment Law

The modern world's understanding, with Kelsen, that we cannot derive a norm from a fact is a corollary of our understanding that there are two forms of law, which look similar, but which are quite different: laws of nature and norms of behaviour. The former are falsifiable by scientific study, but the latter are ought statements that it is illogical to suggest might be either true or false. Thus, if one day the sun should rise in the West, we realize that the supposed law that the sun invariably rises in the east is not in fact a law. In contrast, we understand that a law that forbids a crime, say, burglary, remains valid notwithstanding that some who break that law are never caught.

What is now obvious was not always so. Until the Enlightenment, people thought that the two forms of law were one. What did happen ought to happen. It was God's law, for instance, that the sun rose in the east. It did rise in the east, as it circled the Earth, so it should rise in the east, and woe betide heliocentric heretics like Galileo who taught otherwise. This article argues that examination of crucial rules of income tax law through Kelsen's lens reveals that those rules are analytically the same as the rules that the Inquisition enforced against Galileo. Kelsen explained that a "law" that prescribes that something ought to happen which must happen anyway cannot be a norm of behaviour, though it may be a law of nature. He said:

> [T]he possibility of an antagonism between that which is prescribed by a norm that ought to be and that which actually happens must exist; a norm, prescribing that something ought to be, which, as one knows beforehand must happen anyway according to a law of nature, is meaningless–such a norm could not be regarded as valid (Kelsen 1967, 213).

8.3.4 Kelsen's Generalisations and Tax Law

As has been mentioned, the usual explanation for complexity of tax law is that governments distort tax law by using it to promote economic and social purposes. Legislative changes in New Zealand between about 1985 and 1990 demonstrated that although this explanation is correct it is insufficient. During that period, the New Zealand parliament eliminated nearly all tax preferences, creating an income tax system that was, and that remains, nearly as pure as is possible. Nevertheless, New Zealand tax law kept increasing in complexity, and still does so. What is the problem with tax law?

The hypothesis of the present author is that tax law differs in certain essential respects from law in general. These differences may be revealed by judging tax law against theories of law propounded by legal philosophers. Does the law (or alleged law) in question meet the requirements of law as worked out by scholars?

8.3.5 The Capital/Revenue Distinction

This chapter employs the capital/revenue distinction to show how Kelsen's positivist principles reveal flaws in income tax law. (Other areas would afford equally effective demonstrations.) In pursuit of this objective, the chapter measures tax law against the criterion that law must distinguish between "is" and "ought". By way of context, a broad description of capital and revenue (or income) within tax law follows. Rules vary in detail between jurisdictions, but a tax on income is inevitably shaped by at least the following considerations.

For jurisdictions that tax income but not capital gains the capital/revenue distinction determines the limits of income tax law. Other jurisdictions, such as the United Kingdom and Australia, tax capital gains under a separate regime. And some jurisdictions, such as the United States of America, never recognised the distinction and taxed all gains, whether revenue or capital. But in most such jurisdictions the distinction remains almost equally important, because they frequently tax capital gains at a different rate from income.

Not only does the capital/revenue distinction determine whether receipts are assessable, and, if so, at what rate, but it is also fundamental to rules of income tax law that, in calculating profits, taxpayers may subtract (or "deduct", as it is usually put) revenue, or income, expenses but not capital expenses. For example, in calculating profits, manufacturers will start with sales and deduct the expense of wages, raw materials, heat, light, power, property taxes, and so on. They do not, however, deduct the cost of machinery. To do so would distort the result, since the cost of a machine will repay itself over a period.

Some kinds of expense are sometimes capital and sometimes income. For instance, manufacturers' costs of occupying their factories may be rent, which is deductible, or the price of the factory, which is capital and therefore non-deductible. Here, problems can arise. For instance, how should income tax law treat payments pursuant to a rent-to-buy contract where the rent is inflated so that part of it amounts in economic terms to instalments of price, although the payments are still labelled "rent"?

At least when such scenarios are unpacked it is reasonably easy to see what is happening. But in other cases, taxpayers may convert revenue to capital, and vice-versa, with more obscure sleight of hand. Take, for instance, investors who are shareholders in a company that is pregnant with profits. Options to make some or all of the profits available have very different tax consequences. Most obviously, the company may declare a dividend, which will be taxable as income in the hands of the investors in most tax systems. Alternatively, the investors may sell the shares for a price that in their hands is capital, and therefore not taxable. But that price will represent both the underlying value of the share and the accumulated profits. As just explained, these profits would ordinarily be taxable as income if distributed as a dividend, but they are ordinarily not taxable if they are represented in the price received for a share.

This difference is in a sense more enigmatic than the difference in the example of inflating a manufacturer's deductions for rent by employing a rent-to-buy contract. There, we can at least imagine that tax law might deny a deduction for the part of the outgoing that relates to price rather than to rent.[1] But jurisdictions that observe the rule of law struggle to tax as income a price that an investor receives for a company share. One result is schemes whereby shareholders sell shares *cum div* and repurchase them *ex div*, known as "dividend stripping", which have troubled such senior courts as the House of Lords[2] and the Privy Council.[3] Some countries pass specific anti-avoidance rules to frustrate dividend stripping.[4]

8.3.6 Nature of Capital/Revenue Distinction

Distinguishing between capital and revenue poses an impossible problem for legislators and tax authorities. An income tax system must draw the distinction. Income tax cannot treat short-term and long-term transactions in the same manner. Take the cost of a factory as only one of many possible examples. To deduct the total cost of the factory in the year of purchase as one would deduct, for instance, wages for machine operators, would distort the year's results. Workers provide their labour as they are paid, but the manufacturer will have the factory for many years. Most of the value remains at the end of the year for use in future years. It would be illogical to set the whole cost against a single year's sales. But what sort of different treatment might be appropriate? The difficulty is that the distinction between capital and revenue is at bottom a fiction. From an economic perspective, capital and revenue are merely points on a continuum of values that are of essentially the same quality.

Generally, the law does not distinguish between facts that are of the same quality. For instance, as regards criminal liability, there is no difference between a 20-year-old and a 60-year-old. There is a difference only if the material facts are different, for instance if the perpetrator is an infant.

Worse, as demonstrated by the dividend-or-price example of distributing corporate profits, whether a value is capital or revenue can be changed by purely legal manoeuvres that make no difference to the essential economic nature of the sum in question. Essentially, as Prebble (2010, 40) has explained, the capital-revenue distinction is a fiction.

The distinction may be a fiction, but any income tax system must assume that the fiction is essentially true. The result is an assumption that can be operated only by dint of rules that are arbitrary and often artificial.

---

[1] Compare, e.g., Lord Millet in *Peterson v. Commissioner of Inland Revenue* [2006] 3 NZLR 433 (PC).

[2] E.g., *Lupton v. FA and AB Ltd* [1972] AC 634.

[3] E.g., *Newton v. Commissioner of Taxation* [1958] A.C. 450; [1958] 2 All E.R. 759.

[4] E.g., Income and Corporation Tax Act 1988 (UK) Part XVII; Income Tax Act, (Republic of South Africa) s 22B and Sched 8 para 43A; Income Tax Act 2007 (NZ) s GB 1.

A good, though slightly misleading, example of such a rule is the tax year itself. An income tax system must treat short-term transactions differently from long-term transactions; so, we must define the boundary. But the definition can only be arbitrary. Eleven or thirteen months would be equally valid as the year that, *faute de mieux*, every jurisdiction employs. It is true that in choosing the year we are influenced by the seasons, but this is a matter of convenience, not an essential material fact.

The tax year is a good example because it is arbitrary. It is misleading because its function is not to *define* what is capital and what is revenue but to tell us the *consequence* of that defining: if the item is revenue, then it must be fitted into the annual accounts of a particular year. If it is capital, it is not part of those accounts, though most tax systems have added elements that mitigate this consequence. Allowances in respect of depreciation of capital assets are the primary example. Where, then, do we find the rules that tell us what is capital and what is revenue? To put that question another way, what is the source of this law?

8.3.7 Sources of Law

Lawyers, or at least lawyers who are not tax lawyers, might expect that legislation that is as finely granulated as most tax statutes would codify the basic rules that specify what is capital and what is income. But that is not so. Instead, taxpayers and their advisers must extract the rules about capital and income from the cases, just as if the question were one of the common law, such as, for instance, the sufficiency of consideration.[5]

One reason is no doubt the magnitude of the task that would face a drafter who attempted to codify the rules as to what amounts to capital for purposes of income tax law. Covering all fields of trading and investment would be practically impossible. But a more fundamental reason is that income tax law's rules of capital and revenue are, in a sense, defective. The defects can be obscured in the text of judgments, but reducing capital/revenue rules to statutory rules, which must be both concise and applicable generally, would not be possible. Nevertheless, there are rules of tax law, or, at least, statements that plausibly masquerade as rules of tax law. It helps to analyze these rules if we first frame them in what Kelsen propounded as the canonical form of a rule.

[5] All textbooks on the law of contract contain an explanation of sufficiency. See, e.g., M.P. Furmston, *Cheshire, Fifoot, and Furmston's Law of Contract*, Oxford, 17th ed 2017, chapter 4.

8.3.8 Forms of Rules: Kelsen's Paradigm of a Norm[6]

Kelsen explained that the canonical form of a rule of law is a norm that is a syllogism of a minor and a major premise in the form, "If a is, x ought to be." For example, "Theft ought to be punished" (Kelsen 1967, 72),[7] or, in a fiscal context, "If you fail to report income to the tax authorities, you ought to be punished."

In each case, the minor premise states a fact and the major premise explains what ought to happen. Such norms of behaviour are clearly different from rules of the natural world. Among other things, the norms remain valid even though offenders are not apprehended.

Such norms may be more informative if they are more detailed, such as this rule, which is found in most countries' income tax laws: "If you receive a bonus from your employer, you ought to report it as income even though by definition there is no contractual entitlement to the bonus." Norms relating to the capital/revenue distinction might start with: "If you incur a capital expense you ought not to deduct that expense in calculating your assessable income". And on the receipts side, "If you derive a gain that is revenue you ought to report that gain as income" and, vice–versa, "If you derive a gain that is capital, you need not report that gain as income."

If we fit tax law to Kelsen's paradigm in this manner, we see that in each of the examples the minor premise makes a conditional statement of fact. Theft, expenditure, receipt, tax evasion and capital are facts, each connected by ought to another fact, what ought to happen.

It is submitted that this analysis conforms to reality. How do we judge whether an item is capital or revenue? The answer is that this is a matter of business and of economics, of factual reality, not of law. If the owners, or the prospective purchasers, of a manufacturing business want to know the year's profits they want to know total sales less expenses for the year. They are certainly interested to know that a disused factory site was re-zoned for office development and was sold at a handsome profit, but they are well aware that simply adding that profit to the current year's trading figures will distort the results. The business does not expect that kind of windfall every year. Its profit statement must exclude the receipt from the sale of the factory.

If the owners or purchasers of the business want to know the true profit, they ask an accountant to give them the facts. In short, what is excluded as a matter of capital is a factual decision for an accountant, whose object is to take a true and fair view of the business. Thus, the Lord President, Lord Clyde, explained in *Whimster & Co v. Inland Revenue Commissioners*[8]

---

[6] Kelsen 1967, 25 and 194.

[7] Author's elaboration: "If a person dishonestly takes property of another intending permanently to deprive the other of it (in short, "steals") he ought to be punished (often "sanctioned" in Kelsen's writing).

[8] [1926] SC 20, 25 (CS), per the Lord President, Lord Clyde.

> [T]he account of profit and loss to be made up for the purpose of ascertaining that difference must be framed consistently with the ordinary principles of commercial accounting, so far as applicable …

On this view, since the question of whether an item is capital or revenue is a question of fact, rules associated with the exercise of distinguishing between capital and revenue would comply with Kelsen's paradigm. The problem is that for income tax purposes the rules that determine whether an item is capital are defective in that they either treat the issue as a question of law rather than of fact, or are equivocal on the point.

8.3.9 How Are the Rules That Distinguish Capital and Revenue Defective?

We reach the conclusion just stated by testing the rules of capital and revenue according to criteria that Kelsen identified, two of which are primarily relevant. The first has been mentioned: the need to distinguish "is" and "ought," otherwise norm and fact. The second, which works in tandem, is Kelsen's expression of the canonical form of a law, which, as mentioned, may be paraphrased and summarised as: "If fact X exists then consequence Y ought to follow".

This second criterion is not independent of the first. Rather, it is a logical corollary. If an "if, then ought" syllogism is to make sense, the "if" element must be a statement of fact. Let us test this assertion by examples. "If employees take their employers' money without consent then they ought to be punished" is a workable rendition of a law that forbids embezzlement. Contrast this expression with a syllogism where each of the two elements is an ought statement, such as, "If the action of employees taking their employers' money without consent should be sanctioned, then employees who embezzle ought to be punished." This syllogism works as a statement of policy, but not as a legal rule that governs behaviour. This argument needs no further justification. As Kelsen (1967, 7–8) put a closely related point:

> The difference between is and oughtIs and ought cannot be explained further. We are immediately aware of the difference. Nobody can deny that the statement: 'something is'–that is, the statement by which an existent factFacts is described–is fundamentally different from the statement: 'something ought to be'–which is the statement by which a normNorms is described.

And he elaborated (1967, 7–8):

> Nobody can assert that from the statement that something is, follows a statement that something ought to be, or vice versa.

A primary thesis of this chapter is that, when analyzed, the "rules" that distinguish capital and revenue are not true rules at all, because, although they may be framed as norms in the canonical "if, then" form, they in fact contain ought statements in both minor and major premises. In other words, rules that purport to distinguish between capital and revenue breach the elemental separation of "is" and "ought" as Kelsen describes that separation.

The paragraphs that follow try to demonstrate this point in two ways. First, they explain that although logically the minor premise of a syllogism that refers to the distinction between capital and revenue should, as mentioned, be a conditional statement of fact, it frequently, perhaps even always, is an ought statement, sometimes a half-hearted ought statement. Secondly, this chapter offers a number of examples from the broad category of payments made to establish business arrangements or to compensate for the termination of business arrangements. Such payments or receipts commonly give rise to questions of classification as capital or revenue.

8.3.10 The Question of Capital: Law or Fact?

Within the law, it is often necessary to determine whether a statement is a statement of law or of fact. For example, in many common law systems factual questions are for the jury and legal questions for the judge. Also, it is not uncommon that, procedurally, an appeal lies against a determination of law, but a finding of fact is final, or may be the subject of appeal only if the finding is so perverse that a reasonable jury or judge could not have reached it. As a result of such considerations, judges to whom it would never have occurred to wonder whether their statements of law comply with Kelsen's canonical paradigm, in the capital/revenue context often express opinions on whether they are making a statement of fact or expressing a holding of law. Examination of such findings and holdings shows sharp, though often unconscious, contradictions, sometimes even by the same judge within the same judgment.

For two reasons, a statement holding that a particular sum is either capital or revenue should be a statement of fact. The first reason is the one already mentioned, that such a statement is the first element of a rule expressed in the form of an if (fact) then ought (norm) syllogism. The second is that whether a sum is capital or revenue is in any event logically a matter of economics or accounting or business, and thus a question of fact, not of law, as Lord Clyde explained.[9] Putting the matter less precisely than Lord Clyde, Lord Upjohn said in *Regent Oil Co Ltd v. Strick*:[10]

> [The capital/revenue distinction] is a question of fact and degree and above all judicial common sense in all the circumstances of the case.

And Lord Pearce said in *BP Australia Ltd v. Commissioner of Taxation* that the solution is[11]

> not to be found by any rigid test or description ... [but]
>
> has to be derived from many aspects of the whole set of circumstances.

---

[9] Above, text accompanying n.8.

[10] [1966] AC 295, 345. (HL). See further footnote 37 and accompanying text.

[11] [1966] AC 224, 264–265; [1965] 3 WLR 608 (PC).

What is required is[12]

> a commonsense appreciation of all the guiding features [that may turn on] questions of emphasis and degree.

Section 8.3.13 of this subchapter develops this argument further.

8.3.11 Capital/Revenue as a Matter of Law

Lords Clyde, Upjohn, and Pearce are, however, probably in a minority. Possibly because the higher courts are reluctant to contemplate that a finding of capital or revenue might not be appealable, it is more common for judges to hold that the issue of capital or revenue is a matter of law. Considered examples include Megarry J in *Pitt (Inspector of Taxes) v. Castle Hill Warehousing Co. Ltd*[13] and Lord Wilberforce in *Inland Revenue Commissioners v. Carron Company*[14] and *Tucker v. Granada Motorway Services Ltd.*[15]

Almost equally common are judicial statements that unconsciously bet both ways. For instance, in *Regent Oil Co Ltd v. Strick,* Lord Reid first endorsed[16] Lord Clyde's accounting/factual approach in *Whimster & Co v. Inland Revenue Commissioners,*[17] mentioned above, but went on to say[18]

> The question is ultimately a question of law for the court, but it is a question which must be answered in light of all the circumstances which it is reasonable to take into account, and the weight which must be given to a particular circumstance in a particular case must depend rather on common sense than on a strict application of any single legal principle.

In the following passages, Lord Macmillan and Lord Denning adopt essentially factual approaches, but frame them as if they were holdings of law.

Van Den Berghs Ltd. v Clark (Inspector of Taxes), per Lord MacMillan[19]

> While each case is found to turn upon its own facts, and no infallible criterion emerges, nevertheless the decisions are useful as illustrations and as affording indications of the kind of considerations which may relevantly be borne in mind in approaching the problem.

---

12 [1966] AC 224, 264–265; [1965] 3 WLR 608 (PC).

13 [1974] 1 WLR 1624 (Ch D) (Megarry J).

14 [1967] SC 204; [1967] S.L.T. 186 (CS); [1968] SC 47; [1968] SLT 305 (HL).

15 (1979) 53 TC 92. [1979] 1 WLR 683 (HL).

16 [1966] AC 295, at p 312, [1965] 3 All ER 174, 178–9 per Lord Reid (Capital/revenue ultimately a question of law).

17 [1926] SC 20, 25 (CS), per the Lord President, Lord Clyde.

18 [1966] AC 295, at p 312, [1965] 3 All ER 174, 178–9 per Lord Reid (Capital/revenue ultimately a question of law.

19 [1935] AC 431 (HL). Lord Macmillan for the court.

Heather (HM Inspector of Taxes) v P-E Consulting Group Ltd., per Lord Denning MR:[20]

> The question–revenue expenditure or capital expenditure– … assumes that all expenditure can be put correctly into one category or the other: but this is simply not possible … the border … is a blurred and undefined area in which anyone can get lost. Different minds may come to different conclusions with equal propriety. It is like the border between day and night or between red and orange … the only safe rule is to go by precedent. So the thing to do is to search through the cases and see whether the instant problem has come up before. If so, go by it. If not, go by the nearest you can find.

Conventional legal reasoning suggests that if an issue is one where "Different minds may come to different conclusions with equal propriety," it is curious to find that an appellate court that is willing to substitute its judgment for the judgment of the trier of fact.

8.3.12 Examples of Capital or Revenue Questions

Section 8.3.9 of this chapter foreshadowed that the author would try to demonstrate in two ways that rules of income tax law breach the canonical distinction between "is" and "ought". The first is by explaining that although logically the minor premise of a norm that refers to the distinction between capital and revenue should be a factual statement, courts frequently treat the distinction as a matter of law. The paragraphs above address that argument. Those that follow address the second, which is to give examples from decided cases. To enable more instructive comparison, most examples are from cases that relate to payments for entering business arrangements, or to payments of compensation for the termination of business arrangements.

In principle, taxpayers are subject to the same rules, whether they make or receive such payments. The payer will usually argue "revenue", and therefore deductible, while the recipient will usually argue "capital", and therefore not assessable to income tax (though possibly subject to a tax on capital gains).

The examples to be discussed are all classic cases that may be thought of as part of the canon. Even if one could count all the cases that hold for revenue, and all those that hold for capital, the result would be hopelessly invalid as a statistical predictor, but for what it is worth, the present author's impression is that more courts plump for capital than for revenue. A leading example is *Van Den Berghs Ltd v. Clark (Inspector of Taxes),*[21] which involved a cartel in the margarine trade between Van Den Berghs and another company that had 13 years to run. Van Den Berghs agreed to terminate the cartel in return for receiving £450,000 in compensation. Common sense tells us that, however the money was labelled, it was for loss the of

[20] (1973) 48 TC 293, 321, [1973] 1 All ER 8, (CA) per Lord Denning MR.

[21] [1935] AC 431, 19 TC 390 (HL). Lord Macmillan for the court.

13 years' prospective profits that would have been taxable when received. Nevertheless, the House of Lords held that the sum was a non-taxable capital receipt, explaining:[22]

> If the payment had been in respect of a balance of profits due to the appellants by the Dutch Company for the years 1914 to 1927, different considerations might have applied, but it is agreed that it is not to be so regarded. [Unconvincingly][23] [The cartel agreements] provided the means of making profits, but they themselves did not yield profits.

The most charitable thing that can be said about the difference that their Lordships purported to have found is that it was a distinction without a difference. Not surprisingly, a case on materially indistinguishable facts, namely *Anglo-Persian Oil Company Ltd v. Dale (HM Inspector of Taxes),*[24] came to the opposite conclusion. There, Anglo-Persian had appointed Strick, Scott & Co to manage their business for 10 years, extendable for another ten. The contract proving unfavourable, Anglo-Persian paid Strick, Scott a lump sum to be released from the last 14 years. The Court of Appeal held that the sum was deductible as a revenue expense.

Nevertheless, it is unfair to criticise the judges. As judges, they must decide cases that come before them, they must judge according to law, and they must give reasons. They cannot dodge these duties on the basis that the case at bar requires them to decide between two elements of a distinction that does not have a material difference.

One result is that judges seize on reasons that appear plausible but that do not withstand investigation. For instance, one reason given by Lawrence LJ in the *Anglo-Persian* case was that dismissing an agent like Strick, Scott is similar to dismissing a servant, and compensation paid to a dismissed servant is revenue and therefore deductible. But whether Strick, Scott was technically an agent is surely immaterial. The fact is that Strick, Scott controlled the whole of Anglo-Persian's business, more widely and deeply than the company's cartel arrangements affected Van Den Berghs. But if a plausible argument is available, a court faced with an impossible decision can hardly be blamed for grasping it. For the same reason the employer in *Mitchell v. B. W. Noble Ltd*[25] established that a payment to be rid of a life director was deductible as revenue. And yet, in *British Insulated and Helsby Cables Ltd v. Atherton,*[26] a sum to establish the nucleus of an employee pension fund, undoubtedly a personnel matter, was not deductible. Lord Cave LC held that:[27]

> [W]hen an expenditure is made, not only once and for all but with a view to bringing into existence an asset or advantage for the enduring benefit of a trade ... there is very good reason (in the absence of special circumstances leading to an opposite conclusion) for treating such an expenditure as properly attributable not to revenue but to capital.

---

[22] 19 TC 431.

[23] 19 TC 432.

[24] [1932] 1 KB 124, [1931] All ER Rep 725, 47 TLR 487, 16 Tax Cas 253 (CA).

[25] [1927] 1 K.B. 719; 43 T.L.R. 245 (CA).

[26] [1926] AC 431, 442, 10 T.C. 155, 192 (HL).

[27] [1926] AC 431, 442, 10 T.C. 155, 192 (HL) per Lord Cave.

This sort of confident, stipulative, reasoning is persuasive until one considers that it was no doubt for the enduring benefit of the trade of B.W. Noble Ltd. to be rid of a non-performing life director, and it was certainly for the enduring benefit of Anglo-Persian to be rid of Strick, Scott. Yet the payments to achieve these riddances were held to be revenue.

These cases, however, illustrate the point of this chapter. One cannot say that an expense is capital or revenue as a matter of fact without first or contemporaneously categorising the expense as a matter of law. And the relevant law is most uncertain. For instance, arguably, *Mitchell v. B. W. Noble Ltd*[28] is authority for a norm in the form of "If a payment relates to a personnel matter then it is revenue". But *British Insulated and Helsby Cables Ltd v. Atherton*[29] demonstrates that this rule is by no means general. More often than not, payments in respect of restrictive covenants are held to be capital,[30] but that rule is not general, either.[31] And personnel and restrictive covenants are two areas of relative certainty.

8.3.13 Questions of Degree

Forgoing sections of this chapter have argued that Kelsenian analysis reveals at least two problems with rules of income tax law that categorise items as capital or as income. First, the minor premises of such rules are apt to turn out to be statements of law rather than of fact. Secondly, the statements of law in question must clearly be qualified, but how and when?

One answer to this last question is that, contrary to what we expect of rules in other areas of law, rules of capital and revenue operate by degree. A celebrated pair of cases decided one after the other by the House of Lords and the Privy Council, with the same bench, on similar facts, sheds some light. The cases were *BP Australia Ltd v. Commissioner of Taxation*[32] and *Regent Oil Co Ltd v. Strick.*[33] In each case, the issue was whether payments by oil companies to retailers in return for tied forecourt arrangements were revenue or capital. Neither judgment referred to the other, but both mentioned the relevance of questions of degree.

In *BP Australia*, Lord Pearce said that the solution to capital/revenue problems was[34] "not to be found by any rigid test or description [but] has to be derived from

---

[28] [1927] 1 K.B. 719; 43 T.L.R. 245 (CA).

[29] [1926] AC 431, 442, 10 T.C. 155, 192 (HL).

[30] Compare *Higgs (H.M. Inspector of Taxes) v. Olivier* [1952]1 Ch 311, (1952) 33 TC 13 (CA) with *Anglo-Persian Oil Company Ltd v. Dale (HM Inspector of Taxes)* [1932] 1 KB 124, [1931] All ER Rep 725, 47 TLR 487, 16 Tax Cas 253 (CA).

[31] E.g., *Birkdale Service Station Ltd v. Commissioner of Inland Revenue* [2001] 1 NZLR 293 (CA).

[32] [1966] AC 224; [1965] 3 WLR 608 (PC).

[33] [1966] AC 295, at p 312, [1965] 3 All ER 174, 178–179 per Lord Reid (Capital/revenue ultimately a question of law.

[34] [1966] AC 224, 264–265; [1965] 3 WLR 608 (PC).

many aspects of the whole set of circumstances." Cases required[35] "a commonsense appreciation of all the guiding features" and the answer may turn on "questions of emphasis and degree". In *Regent Oil*, as already quoted, Lord Upjohn averred[36] that the capital/revenue distinction "is a question of fact and degree". Lord Reid's remarks in the same case, also already quoted, do not use the word "degree" but are to similar effect.

It is unlikely that Kelsen read these remarks, but from his generalizations we can predict his reaction. He published only a year later (Kelsen 1967, 21 n. 7):

> If a norm prescribes a behavior which is permissible in different degrees, it looks as if the norm could be obeyed in different degrees, that is, more or less. This is a fallacy, Kelsen (1967, 21) had no doubt about such a purported norm. It was invalid. He said:

> [A] graduation of an objective value is not possible because a behavior can only conform or not conform with an objectively valid norm, but cannot do so more or less.

At least in the United Kingdom and Commonwealth, if such a norm is found in a judgment of the House of Lords or the Privy Council no one would pronounce it invalid. But Kelsen's words bring home to us that the norm is essentially worthless, except as window-dressing for a judgment that must draw a distinction where none exists. In income tax law, meaningless window dressing has a long and almost honourable pedigree. For instance, circular reasoning is common. As long ago as 1916, Lord Sumner said in *Usher's Wiltshire Brewery, Limited, v. Bruce*, no doubt with a straight face:[37]

> [A] deduction, ... is to be made or not to be made according as it is or is not, on the facts of the case, a proper debit item to be charged against incomings of the trade.

These words are no more than authority to deduct an expense in calculating income if one has authority to make the deduction. Income tax judgments are full of holdings that are hardly more meaningful. Another capital/revenue example may suffice. In *Inland Revenue Commissioners v Carron Company*[38] Lord Wilberforce echoed an argument made in this chapter by saying that the distinction between capital and revenue is "by nature a commercial decision". But he went on to say that the expenditure in question, which was to acquire a new constitution for the company,

> ... procured indeed an advantage–important and not of a transitory nature–but one essentially of a revenue character in that it enabled the management of the Company's business to be carried on more effectively.

---

[35] [1966] AC 224, 264–265; [1965] 3 WLR 608 (PC).

[36] [1966] AC 295, 345. (HL). Compare *Evans Medical Supplies Ltd* v *Moriarty (HM Inspector of Taxes)* 1957 37 TC 530 (HL), reported *sub nom Moriarty (Inspector of Taxes) v Evans Medical Supplies Ltd* [1957] 3 All ER 718 (HL), per Upjohn J at first instance 37 TC 549 "[The capital/revenue] question is essentially a question of fact".

[37] [1915] AC 468, 6 T.C. 399, 436 per Lord Sumner (HL).

[38] 1967 SC 204, 1967 S.L.T. 186 (CS);1968 SC 47, 1968 SLT 305 (HL), approved *Regent Oil Co Ltd v. Strick* [1966] AC 295, at p 312, [1965] 3 All ER 174, 178-9 per Lord Reid (HL).

How could this test possibly distinguish capital from revenue? With a number of exceptions, such as the purchase of trading stock, virtually all corporate expenditure, except that procured by fraud, enables "the management of the Company's business to be carried on more effectively." Even buying trading stock may enable business to be carried on more effectively if buyers have their wits about them. One would hope that most capital expenditure, such as new machinery, would enable "the management of the Company's business to be carried on more effectively."

8.3.14 Conclusion

When examined closely, income tax law is seen to operate very oddly. This oddity goes a long way to explaining why, despite the best efforts of generations of tax officials, income tax law can only be reformed to a point. It is surprising that tax law, a seemingly highly formal enterprise, is resistant to Kelsen-inspired positivist analysis. Interestingly, as we discuss in connection with Hart, another aspect of tax law, anti-avoidance rules, also resists straightforward analysis from a positivist perspective.

8.4 Hart and Tax Law: The Case of GAARs

8.4.1 Introduction

H.L.A. Hart was the most important Anglo-American legal philosopher of the twentieth century. His work is essential reading for anyone writing about jurisprudence or law and philosophy; he did not, however, write about tax specifically. There are, nevertheless, several ways in which Hart's central contributions to jurisprudence may be relevant to philosophical discussions of taxation. We will canvas a few.

In explaining what separates a legal system from other normative systems, Hart emphasizes that the "union of primary and secondary rules" is at the "centre of a legal system" (Hart 2012, 99). The most important function of the secondary rules, generally known as rules of recognition, is that they pick out which primary rules, the rules that govern behaviour, are properly part of the legal system. One application of Hart's thinking to tax law involves using Hart's insights as to harder to characterize aspects of tax law, particularly international tax (Dean 2011–2012). What is the rule of recognition that governs international tax, if there is one, and which primary rules does it pick out?

Hart is also famous for explaining that law has an "open texture," that there are unavoidably indeterminate areas of the law, though there is much that is determinate as well (Hart 2012, 128). Another application of Hart's thinking is to consider what such open areas consist of in tax law and how they might be addressed (Pasternak & Rico 2008).

A related issue, and our focus, will be on how to analyze General Anti-Avoidance Rules (GAARs). Returning to the famous Hart-Fuller debate, Hart accepts that moral considerations can override traditional rule of law concerns with retroactivity, but his clear preference is for retroactive legislation rather than creative work by judges as to what the law really was in the past (Hart 1957, 619). As tax avoidance is clearly less morally obnoxious than the laws passed by the Nazis, one might wonder how Hart would have considered retroactive legislation or judicial doctrines that take away a tax result that the formal rules in place at the time of transaction would seem to have permitted. In this chapter, we will discuss GAARs, either as general statutes or judge-made doctrines, the existence of which precede the transaction in question that has its desired results changed.[39]

There are many varieties of GAARs and so we will focus on the type with which one of us, Shanske, is most familiar: the economic substance doctrine as part of US tax law.

8.4.2 The Rule of Law and GAARs

In brief, and returning to its original formulation by the U.S. Supreme Court in *Gregory v. Helvering*, "the question for determination is whether what was done, apart from the tax motive, was the thing which the statute intended."[40] In that case, using a tax-free division statute to avoid paying corporate level tax was not what Congress intended. As now formalized in U.S. statutory law, the test has two prongs, objective and subjective: A transaction must change the taxpayer's economic position "in a meaningful way (apart from Federal income tax effects)" and the taxpayer must have "a substantial purpose (apart from Federal income tax effects)" for entering into such transaction.[41]

There are, at least, four ways to consider how Hart's teaching on the rule of law relates to GAARs. First, one might argue that, once codified, GAARs are part of the law and hence pose no particular rule of law concerns. This does not strike us as entirely satisfactory on its own, as the whole point of the statute is to apply a malleable backup standard in cases where other rules followed strictly would seem to imply a different result. Indeed, the codifiers of the economic substance doctrine in the U.S. were so concerned that the codified rules would themselves become subject to gaming, the codification includes the following provision:

> The determination of whether the economic substance doctrine is relevant to a transaction shall be made in the same manner as if this subsection had never been enacted.[42]

[39] For a general discussion of tax legislation with retroactive effect, see Prebble et al. 2012. For a specific discussion/application of US law, see Avi-Yonah et al. (2021).

[40] *Gregory v. Helvering*, 293 U.S. 465, 469 (1935).

[41] IRC Sec. 7701(o)(1).

[42] IRC Sec. 7701(o)(5)(C).

And so, another way to analyze GAARs is to see them as illegitimate as violations of the rule of law. If the core of a GAAR is to trip up the expected tax treatment on the basis of strict following of the published rules, the conflict with rule of law values appears unavoidable. Note that one need not throw one's hand up and declare it open season on tax avoidance if one takes this position. With the right political economy, a Legislature could regularly pass statutes closing abusive loopholes or, in many circumstances, a revenue agency could promulgate appropriate regulations. If the revenue department and the Legislature were fast enough, then, at least in theory, abuse could be kept under control without sacrificing rule of law values. From this perspective, GAARs are essential because the tax laws are overly complex/poorly drafted, the revenue authority is understaffed, or the Legislature is for some reason not able to act expeditiously. None of these would seem to be good enough reasons to sacrifice the rule of law as compared to the moral harms avoided by retroactively rejecting Nazi law.

A third approach accepts that GAARs *do* violate the rule of law but maintains that this alone does not render them illegitimate. There is more to value than just the rule of law and sometimes the rule of law must give way.[43] Again, Hart himself famously argues as much when he advocates a retroactive statute as a means of dealing with Nazi law. His prescription is to be forthright about the retroactivity and the other values being advanced. It is worth observing that Hart is an inclusive legal positivist, which would permit him to accept that even explicitly moral reasons could be incorporated into the law as justification for a GAAR (Hart 2012, 247–48). Note that the rule of law violation does not have to be administered through the courts using a GAAR; there could be retroactive legislation specifically denying certain tax results. Presumably, Hart would have preferred the latter if either is permissible.

Trying to adjudicate which of these last two responses is more "Hartian" would seem to involve weighing the other principles involved. It seems easy to put Nazi law to one side rule of law notwithstanding, but how does preventing the income shifting of large multinational corporations weigh in the balance against the rule of law? This is a hard question that rapidly brings in multiple other factors. For instance, as Morse and Deutsch (2015) argue, it is easier for parliamentary systems to pass remedial legislation than for the U.S. Congress, which suggests that the harm from lack of a GAAR is different depending on the larger structure of the political system.

The harm to the rule of law is also affected by the nature of the tax system in question. Consider a system where the tax law provides ambiguous guidance to most citizens most of the time. There could be a property tax system where the value of all property is re-assessed annually on the basis of eight different complicated formulas, with the highest result the one that is taxed, but with ample room for discretion by individual administrators. Injecting a GAAR into a tax system like that

[43] For a more developed version of this argument see Prebble & Prebble 2010 ("Tax avoidance is a very real evil for society: A breach of the rule of law seems to be a necessary remedy.").

would seem to impose an even greater cost on the rule of law precisely because in that case the GAAR could be said to deprive citizens of the rule of law as to tax altogether. Thus, the clearer the tax system, the less work there is for a GAAR to do and the reduced harm to the rule of law if a GAAR operates at the margins, even important ones.

And this brings us to a fourth approach, which argues that, at least in some cases, the rule of law is *not* violated by GAARs.[44] To see how this could be so, let's consider our actual tax systems, which do, we would argue, in fact, give clear guidance to most taxpayers most of the time. That is, returning to Hart's language, there is a lot more core than penumbra. This is in part because tax codes tend to be written by experts trying to anticipate the most common fact patterns. But tax codes are not just lists of rules for every case. They contain a certain logic. For example, if there is an exchange of property, then the exchange should trigger income under an income tax. If there is an untaxed kind of exchange, then the tax system will distort economic activity because taxpayers will engage in that kind of exchange and the income tax will raise much less revenue. And, if the exchange does not trigger gain because of a non-recognition provision of some kind, then the tax basis in the property should be carried over so that the gain inherent in the property is taxed at some point because, otherwise a deferral provision becomes a forgiveness provision (with attendant behavioral and revenue consequences).

To this point, all this example shows is that a GAAR ought to amount to a minor deviation from the rule of law in tax systems we tend to be familiar with, but arguably this example does more than that. After all, if a tax system in good shape tends to manifest an inner logic,[45] then that inner logic should be what guides the application of a GAAR (or remedial retroactive legislation).[46] In many cases, however well they might follow formal rules, abusive tax shelters spectacularly fail basic income tax logic. For example, one kind of shelter shifts assets from tax-indifferent parties (public transit agencies) to profitable businesses that are not in the infrastructure business (e.g., banks) so that these profitable private businesses can take advantage of the depreciation.[47] Note that such transactions not only flout tax logic, but because they are so devoid of any real world context, they can be deployed ad infinitum until there is no tax liability at all – at least for those who can afford to play the game. These shelters could be legislated against, but at least in the American context the legislation would likely always come far too late.[48] It would thus be consistent with

[44] For a somewhat differently developed version of this argument, see Bogenschneider 2018.

[45] Though subject to the important limitations we discuss as to the income tax in connection with Kelsen.

[46] I use the inner logic advisedly knowing that it echoes Lon Fuller's claim that law generally has an inner morality (Fuller 1969). Note that Hart himself accepts that a legal system must require a kind of procedural minimum; he just denies that that minimum is inconsistent with a generally iniquitous legal regime (Hart 2012, 207).

[47] See *Wells Fargo & Co. v. U.S.*, 641 F.3d 1319 (2011).

[48] See generally Bankman 2000.

the inner logic of the tax law, and hence with the rule of law, not to mention distributive concerns, for these kinds of transactions to be rejected, even retroactively.

Where is any of this in Hart? In his famous discussion of the open texture of law, Hart argues that certain areas of law are governed by standards because "uniform rules cannot be usefully framed by the legislature in advance" (2012, 131). One of Hart's examples of such an area of law relates to utility rate regulation. At first sight, it might seem odd to analogize tax law to rate regulation, but I on analysis it is no stretch to analogize a "fair rate" with "economic substance." Both relate to underlying facts. At least as to a narrow slice of (often artificially) complicated transactions, or of ordinary-looking transactions that are infected by artificial values, a GAAR in effect delineates a standard to be administered by regulators and courts. Thus, GAARs are not a violation of the rule of law, but represent a different kind of rule of law, a standard, for situations that do not lend themselves to rules.[49]

8.4.3 Conclusion

This chapter on positivism and tax law has not sought to establish a normative argument as to tax – at least not directly. Yet positivism attempts to limn the boundaries of what law is and hence normative concerns are always in the background. We have demonstrated that the form of the income tax law seems to be in tension with the form of law articulated by Kelsen, which has implications both for the nature of tax law and for Kelsen's theory. We also turned to Hart to consider the special case of GAARs, which are arguably a moral intervention that is not properly part of law. We argued that GAARs can be viewed as operating within Hart's vision of law, though determining the best reading of Hart or of GAARs generally, is beyond our scope.

Table of Cases

United Kingdom, Australia, and New Zealand

Usher's Wiltshire Brewery, Limited v. Bruce [1915] AC 468, 6 T.C. 399, 436.

Whimster & Co. v. Inland Revenue Commissioners [1926] SC 20, 25 (CS).

British Insulated and Helsby Ltd. v. Atherton [1926] AC 431, 442, 10 T.C. 155, 192 (HL).

Mitchell v. B.W. Noble Ltd. [1927] 1 K.B. 719; 43 T.L.R. 245 (CA).

Anglo-Persian Oil Company Ltd. v. Dale (HM Inspector of Taxes) [1932] 1 KB 124; [1931] All ER Rep 725, 47 TLR 487, 16 Tax Cas 253 (CA).

Van Den Berghs Ltd. v. Clark (Inspector of Taxes) [1935] AC 431 (HL).

[49] To be sure, understanding GAARs as a justified deviation from the rule of law in contrast to a different kind of rule of law is a subtle one.

Higgs (HM Inspector of Taxes) v. Olivier [1952] 1 Ch 311, (1952) 33 TC 13 (CA).
Moriarty (Inspector of Taxes) v. Evans Medical Supplies [1957] All ER 718 (HL).
Newton v. Commissioner of Taxation [1958] A.C. 450; [1958] 2 All E.R. 759.
Regent Oil Co. Ltd. v. Strick [1966] AC 295, 345 (HL).
BP Australia Ltd. v. Commissioner of Taxation [1966] AC 224, 264-265; [1965] 3 WLR 608 (PC).
Inland Revenue Commissioners v. Carron Company [1967] SC 204; [1967] S.L.T. 186 (CS); [1968] SC 47; [1968] SLT 305 (HL).
Lupton v. FA and AB Ltd. [1972] AC 634
Heather (HM Inspector of Taxes) v. P-E Consulting Group Ltd. (1973) 293, 321; [1973] 1 All ER 8.
Pitt (Inspector of Taxes) v. Castle Hill Warehousing Co. Ltd. [1974] 1 WLR 1624 (Ch D) (Megarry J).
Tucker v. Granada Motorway Services Ltd. [1979] 1 WLR 683 (HL).
Birkdale Service Station Ltd. v. Commissioner of Inland Revenue [2001] 1 NZLR 293 (CA).
Peterson v. Commissioner of Inland Revenue [2006] NZLR 433 (PC).
United States *Gregory v. Helvering, 293 U.S. 465, 469 (1935).*
Wells Fargo & Co. v. U.S., 641 F. 3d 1319 (2011)

References

Austin, John. 1954. *The Province of Jurisprudence Determined.* Library of Ideas.

Avi-Yonah, Reuven. 2021. Is New York's Mark-to-Market Act Unconstitutionally Retroactive? *Tax Notes State* 99: 541.

Bankman, Joseph. 2000. The Economic Substance Doctrine. *Southern California Law Review* 74: 1.

Bogenschneider, Bret N. 2018. 5 1/2 Problems with Legal Positivism and Tax Law. *Pepperdine Law Review* 2017: 1.

Dean, Steven A. 2011–2012. Neither Rules nor Standards. *Notre Dame Law Review* 87: 537.

Fuller, Lon. 1969 [1964]. *The Morality of Law*. New Haven: Yale University Press.

Furmston, Michael P. 2017. *Cheshire, Fifoot, and Furmston's Law of Contract.* 17th ed. Oxford: Oxford University Press.

Hart, H.L.A. 1957. Positivism and the Separation of Law and Morals. *Harvard Law Review* 71: 593.

———. 2012 [1961]. *The Concept of Law*. 3rd ed. Oxford: Oxford University Press.

Hume, David. [1739] 2007. *A Treatise of Human Nature*. London: NuVision Publications.

Kelsen, Hans. 1960. *What is Justice?* Berkeley and Los Angeles, CA: University of California Press.

———. 1967. *Pure Theory of Law.* Transl. Max Knight. Berkeley: University of California Press.

———. 1991. *General Theory of Norms.* Transl. Michael Hartney. Oxford: Clarendon Press.

Morse, Susan C., and Robert Deutsch. 2015. Tax Anti-Avoidance Law in Australia and the United States. *International Lawyer* 49: 111.

Pasternak, Menahem, and Christophe Rico. 2008. Tax Interpretation, Planning, and Avoidance: Some Linguistic Analysis. *Akron Tax Journal* 23: 33.

Prebble, John. 1994a. Why is Tax Law Incomprehensible? *British Tax Review*: 380–393.

———. 1994b. Ectopia, Formalism, and Anti-avoidance in Income Tax Law. In *Prescriptive Formality and Normative Rationality in Modern Legal Systems: Festschrift for Robert*

S. Summers, ed. Werner Krawiets, Neil MacCormick, and Georg H. von Wright, 367–383. Berlin: Duncker & Humblot.

———. 1995. Philosophical and Design Problems That Arise from the Ectopic Nature of Income Tax Law and Their Impact on the Taxation of International Trade and Investment. *Chinese Yearbook of International Law and Affairs* 13: 111–139. (Reprinted as "Ectopia, Tax Law, and International Taxation." [1997] *British Tax Rev*. 383).

———. 1996. Can Income Tax Be Simplified? *NZ Journal of Taxation and Policy* 2: 187.

———. 1998. Should Tax Law Be Written from a Principles and Purpose Point of View of a Precise and Detailed Point of View? *British Tax Review* 112.

———. 2010. *Fictions of Income Tax*. Victoria University of Wellington Legal Research Paper No. 29/2011.

Prebble, John, et al. 2012. Legislation with Retrospective Effect, with Particular Reference to Tax. *New Zealand Universities Law Review* 22: 17.

Prebble, John, and Hamish McIntosh. 2015. Predication: The Test for Tax Avoidance in New Zealand from *Newton* to *Ben Nevis*. *VUWLR* 46: 1011–1030.

Prebble, Rebecca, and John Prebble. 2010. Does the Use of General Anti-Avoidance Rules to Combat Tax Avoidance Breach Principles of the Rule of Law? A Comparative Study. *Saint Louis University Law Journal* 55 (1): 21–45.

John Prebble, QC, BA, LLB (Hons) (Auckland); BCL (Oxon); JSD (Cornell); Inner Temple (London); LEANZF, is one of Her Majesty's Counsel and an Emeritus Professor of Law at Victoria University, Wellington. He has written or edited 12 books on tax and business law and has published over 200 articles in scholarly and professional journals. He is a former Trustee of the International Bureau of Fiscal Documentation, Amsterdam, and a member of the Editorial Boards of several scholarly journals. He has held research fellowships or visiting chairs at leading universities in the United Kingdom, Australia, Europe, and the United States. He is a Gastprofessor, Institut für Österreichisches und Internationales Steuerrecht, Wirtschaftsuniversität Wien and an Adjunct Professor of Law, Notre Dame University of Australia, Sydney, NSW. He has served as a member of several government consultative committees on income tax reform.

Professor Prebble's research focuses on fundamental issues of income tax law, such as the capital/revenue divide and form and substance, and on international taxation. He has pioneered the study of jurisprudential perspectives of taxation law, that is, applying the theories of legal philosophers to judicial reasoning in income tax cases.

Darien Shanske holds a J.D. from Stanford Law School, a Ph.D. from UC Berkeley in Rhetoric, an M.A. from McGill University in Philosophy, and a B.A. from Columbia University. He currently serves as Professor of Law at the University of California, Davis, School of Law. Shanske's interests include taxation, particularly state and local taxation, local government law, public finance, and political theory, particularly jurisprudence.

Chapter 9
Egalitarianism and Taxation

Jørgen Pedersen

Abstract Egalitarianism is roughly the idea that people should be more equal than they are in most societies today. Among different versions of egalitarianism, this chapter focuses on social egalitarianism whose ambition is to eliminate relationships of domination and ensure a democratic distribution of power. John Rawls is a key thinker within this tradition, and he has had deep influence on Thomas Piketty's understanding of distributive justice. It is argued that both hold an ideal that justifies a capital ceiling and a capital floor. Taxation is one of the most important measures to realize this ideal, and progressive taxation of income, inheritance and wealth is likely to be included in schemes to implement such an understanding of what a just society is. However, an egalitarian society will need several other measures in addition to taxation to be realized. Thus, the distinction between predistribution and redistribution is explored. Drawing on Murphy and Nagel, the chapter goes on to discuss whether pre-tax income and distribution of the tax burden are relevant in a theory of justice. The chapter concludes with a discussion of the relationship between the state and the individual and whether social egalitarianism is best realized in a property-owning democracy or under liberal socialism.

Keywords Egalitarianism · Taxation · Rawls · Piketty · Property-owning democracy

J. Pedersen (✉)
Department of Business Administration, Western Norway University of Applied Sciences, Bergen, Norway
e-mail: Jorgen.Pedersen@hvl.no; Jorgen.Pedersen@uib.no

R. F. van Brederode (ed.), *Political Philosophy and Taxation*,
https://doi.org/10.1007/978-981-19-1092-0_9

9.1 Introduction

Egalitarians holds that people should be treated as equals in some respect.[1] There are, however, many different ways that people can be treated as equals, and the term is normally taken to mean that people should be more equal when it comes to income and wealth compared to how things are in most societies today (Arneson 2013).[2]

In contemporary political philosophy, two different egalitarian theories stand out.[3] Luck egalitarian theories are developed from the work of Ronald Dworkin who argued that a just egalitarian society should hold people responsible for their choices and compensate them for circumstances outside their control (Dworkin 2000). Developing this idea further, the luck egalitarian version of egalitarianism holds that society "ought to compensate people for undeserved bad luck" (Anderson 1999, 288). Undeserved bad luck includes such factors as being born with poor native endowments or bad parents, suffering from accidents and illness, etc. Thus, the luck egalitarian ideal is normally taken to require regulation of inheritance and other measures required to hold people responsible for their choice for example of how much or how hard they chose to work.

Social (or relational) egalitarian theory draws on John Rawls and holds that egalitarians should not primarily be oriented towards eliminating the influence of luck, but instead fight repression, inherited status hierarchies and class privilege and ensure a democratic distribution of power (Scheffler 2003).[4] According to relational egalitarians, individuals should be considered as free and equal citizens and society should be designed to eliminate relationships of domination. In such a society, large inequalities in wealth and power must be avoided because it will produce hierar-

[1] The chapter has been presented at the comparative political economy seminar at the University of Bergen. Thank you to the participants for comments and criticism. In addition, I would like to thank Dan Halliday, Bjørn Sandvik, Preben Sørheim and Robert van Brederode for valuable feedback on an earlier version of the manuscript.

[2] It should be noted, however, that this definition of egalitarianism is narrow. As Elisabeth Anderson has argued, there are forms of egalitarianisms that has been concerned with other things than distribution of goods. The feminist movement and the LGBT movement are egalitarian, but not primarily concerned with distributive justice (Anderson et al. 2014, 258).

[3] There are other distinctions that are relevant, such as the distinction between intrinsic and instrumental egalitarianism and deontic and telic egalitarianism. The development of these concepts is heavily influenced by Derek Parfit's paper *Equality or Priority* (Parfit 1997), and there is no doubt that the literature following Parfit's paper has improved the understanding of egalitarianism. However, these debates have not been connected to matters of taxation. Therefore, I shall not explore them here. For a useful discussion see Hirose (2015).

[4] The distinction between the two camps should not be drawn too sharp. For recent attempts to defend versions of luck-egalitarianism that are designed to overcome some of the criticism that was levelled at the first generation of luck-egalitarianism, see Tan (2012) and Lippert-Rasmussen (2015). For recent attempts to define and discuss egalitarianism see Hirose (2015), and Moss (2014). Note also that Dworkin is heavily influenced by Rawls, so the pedigree of egalitarian theory is more complex than simply saying that one develops from Rawls and the other from Dworkin.

chies and class privilege and prevent individuals from relating to each other as free and equal citizens (McTernan et al. 2016, 139). Thus, the ideal of social egalitarianism is normally taken to require strict measures to prevent inequality of wealth and income from becoming problematic.[5]

Taxation is a key mechanism for governments to finance public expenditure, to influence individual behavior and to ensure a more equal distribution of income and wealth. Despite this, philosophers have not been much involved in the detailed discussion of the role taxation should play in a just society (Murphy and Nagel 2002, 4; Halliday 2013, 1111; Dietsch 2015, 8). Recently, however, discussions of taxation have become more prominent, and much of this work has been done within the Rawlsian version of egalitarianism. The standout text is Liam Murphy and Thomas Nagel's *The Myth of Ownership* which has been described as broadly Rawlsian (O'Neill and Williamson 2015, 827). I shall therefore primarily focus on this tradition, broadly defined, and sometimes use Dworkin and luck egalitarianism as a contrast to bring out differences within the two different strands of egalitarian thinking.[6]

In *Capital and Ideology*, Thomas Piketty, the French economist who has had tremendous influence on the debate about inequality in recent years, described himself as belonging to the same tradition or school of thought as Rawls (Piketty 2020, 970). Both have strong affinities to a way of thinking that has been influenced by the British economist James Meade. This tradition is called property-owning democracy. Property-owning democracy has received a lot of attention in recent years, and it is characterized primarily through an opposition to concentration of capital.[7] Concentration of capital is to be avoided because it allows those with much capital to dominate and control others. Rawls provides strong justifications for property-owning democracy, and Piketty has a very detailed account of how the ideal can be institutionalized.

Although taxes are key to bringing about egalitarian justice, they are not the only mechanisms necessary. Countries that are normally described as egalitarian employ other measures in combination with the tax system in order to achieve equality. For example, the Nordic countries have strong labor unions pressing for a compressed wage structure. This ensures distribution *prior* to taxation. This type of distribution is often referred to as predistribution. Thus, in the recent literature an important distinction is drawn between pre- and redistribution. One purpose of this chapter is to describe and discuss how egalitarians (should) think about how the tax system can be combined with other measures and mechanisms to achieve egalitarian justice.

The chapter will be organized as follows. Section 9.2 outlines the core ideas of property-owning democracy. Focus is primarily on Rawls and how he defends two

[5] Much of the early discussion between egalitarians was about what it is that is to be distributed if one cares about equality. This "equality of what debate" has consolidated around three main answers on what it is that should be distributed: welfare, resources and capabilities. This debate is important, and in order to have a full theory of justice, it is necessary to clarify 'the what' question. Here, however, I will not enter into this debate. For a useful discussion see Moss (2014, chapter 2).

[6] For discussions of tax policy in the tradition from Dworkin, see Halliday (2016) and Duff (2016).

[7] See O'Neill and Williamson 2012a, Thomas 2017.

principles of justice. I argue that Rawls' distributive ideal requires a capital ceiling and a capital floor. In Sect. 9.3, I present Rawls' view on taxation and connect this to what egalitarians have had to say about the appropriate choice of tax base. I show that Rawls' comments on taxation are rather puzzling and argue that under circumstances like the one we face in many countries today, a Rawlsian would be in favor of progressive taxation of inheritance, wealth, and income. I proceed to present Thomas Piketty's recent proposal for participatory socialism (Sect. 9.4). The distributive ideal that follows entails that there should be no room for billionaires, and that everyone should be granted starting capital at the age of 25. In the next Sect., 9.5, I demonstrate how a combination of Rawls and Piketty provides a robustly justified egalitarian ideal as well as a detailed picture of how this ideal can be put into practice. I go on to elaborate on the distinction between predistribution and redistribution and show that, although this is an important distinction, it is not as straightforward as people may tend to think (Sect. 9.6). In Sect. 9.7, I outline some key claims defended by Murphy and Nagel before I discuss some controversies on taxation within the egalitarian camp (Sect. 9.8). These controversies follow from Murphy and Nagel's work and includes whether distribution of the tax burden is a relevant question about justice, and whether egalitarian justice requires progressive taxation. In the next section (Sect. 9.9), I briefly consider how egalitarians recently have thought about the relationship between the individual and the state. Finally, in Sect. 9.10, I discuss a central question of distributive justice that has been much discussed in the recent literature: which social system is best suited to realize social egalitarian ideas: property-owning democracy or liberal socialism.[8]

9.2 Property-Owning Democracy: Meade and Rawls

The Scottish conservative politician Noel Skelton first employed the term "property-owning democracy" in 1923 (Jackson 2012, 38; Thomas 2017, xxii; Edmundson 2017, 45). Skelton's main objective was to provide an alternative to socialism, which was on the rise and perceived as dangerous. In this context, it was imperative for conservatives to come up with an alternative. Skelton suggested a number of policies to meet the needs of the newly enfranchised working class. Among these policies was measures of profit sharing and mechanisms to include workers in the decision making of firms. However, Skelton's proposals were not egalitarian and did not include any measures to tax wealth (Jackson 2012, 39).

[8] In this chapter I will not discuss global justice and how egalitarians think about justice in an international setting. Globalization is a challenge when it comes to how to tax multinational companies and the wealthiest, but it does not follow that there is no room for the nation state (Saez and Zucman 2019a, 195). As Piketty notes, "governments have considerable freedom to maneuver. They can make progress toward reducing inequality and establishing more just forms of ownership without waiting for international cooperation to be achieved" (Piketty 2020, 991). For an influential political-philosophical discussion of tax competition and tax evasion see Dietsch (2015).

This anti-egalitarian version of property-owning democracy was later to be picked up by Anthony Eden in the 1940s and by Margaret Thatcher in the 1980s. The liberal-conservative strand of property-owning democracy mainly focused on homeownership and did not advance policies to disperse property. Focus was instead on individual responsibility where people should be allowed to own property if they worked hard and experienced success in the market. The strategy was to convert part of the class-conscious proletariat into property owners and thus to prevent them from joining the socialist ranks (Jackson 2012, 47).[9]

Another version of property-owning democracy had developed within the British socialist tradition. The intellectual roots of this tradition can be traced back to Jean-Jacques Rousseau and Thomas Paine. This is the tradition that is most alive today and the version that we shall focus on here. The main characteristic of this egalitarian-republican version of property-owning democracy is to equalize wealth in order to prevent the wealthy from dominating the rest of society. The British economist James Meade (1907–1995) is the key early figure, and his work strongly influenced the philosophical defense Rawls was later to give of property-owning democracy.

Meade's scheme for property-owning democracy must be understood in the context of the debate between capitalism and socialism that emerged after the Second World War. He defended a liberal-socialist synthesis, which was to overcome the type of planned economy associated with Soviet style communism. Meade's version was explicitly focused on achieving a more equal division of private property, and in contrast to the liberal-conservative strand of property-owning democracy, Meade regarded progressive taxation as an appropriate measure to achieve this ideal (Jackson 2012, 43–46). In particular, large inequalities of wealth were seen as problematic because the wealthy would be able to dominate those without property:

> Extreme inequalities in the ownership of property are in my view undesirable quite apart from any inequalities of income which they may imply. A man with much property has great bargaining strength and a great sense of security, independence and freedom; and he enjoys these things not only vis-à-vis his propertyless fellow citizens but also vis-à-vis the public authorities. He can snap his fingers at those on whom he must rely for an income; for he can always live for a time on his capital. The propertyless man must continuously and without interruption acquire his income by working for an employer or by qualifying to receive it from a public authority. An unequal distribution of property means an unequal distribution of power and status even if it is prevented from causing too unequal a distribution of income (Meade 1993, 41).

Thus, one of the distinct features of property-owning democracy is the focus on dispersal of wealth, rather than simply focusing on dispersion of income. Meade had a number of proposals to avoid unequal distribution of property. These included steep taxation of gifts and inheritance, as well as wide dispersal of ownership and control over productive assets. In addition, Meade was also in favor of other egalitarian strategies such as state funded education open for all as well as profit sharing

[9] For a more detailed discussion of how these two versions of property-owning democracy differ and how they grew out of the same roots see Thomas (148–154).

schemes. Applying such policies would make it more likely that even those who were worse off should be able to own property (O'Neill 2012, 79; Ypi 2018, 161–162).

Rawls was inspired by Meade, and his perspective is critical of large concentrations of capital.[10] Rawls' major work *A Theory of Justice* (henceforth *Theory*), was written from the perspective of an American in the 1950s and 1960s. Rawls presented and defended his theory called *justice as fairness*. This was a period of time with a historical high level of taxation with rates of 70–90% on top incomes and inheritances (Piketty 2020, 985). Even from the egalitarian 1970s, Rawls held that the distribution of income and wealth should have been much more egalitarian (O'Neill 2021a, 2) but was sometimes misunderstood to allow substantial inequalities. Rawls continued to refine his theory throughout his lifetime. In his final work, *Justice as Fairness. A Restatement* he is explicit that his distributive ideal is more egalitarian than the contemporary welfare states that existed at his time. This "radicalization" of Rawls can be explained both by the inegalitarian development of the US since Reagan, and the fact that Rawls felt that he had been misunderstood to allow for substantial inequalities when he was in fact a true egalitarian. In the following I will include references from both of the two books mentioned here, but the emphasis will be on *Justice as Fairness* where Rawls defends a distributive ideal that is clearer and more radical compared to what he did in *Theory*.

Rawls' goal in *Theory* was to formulate principles of justice for a society in which individuals are seen as free and equal, and where society is understood as social cooperation to achieve common advantages with justice requiring that such cooperation be conducted on fair (not merely mutually advantageous) terms. To Rawls, these two ideals are fundamental to modern democracies.

The principles of justice are designed to regulate the basic structure of society. These principles shall regulate core economic and legal institutions. The tax system is one example of what belongs to the basic structure of society.

The most important principle is the Liberty Principle. This principle is often ignored and believed to be without importance for the distribution of goods in society. That is unfortunate as it is the Liberty Principle that has the most serious implications for distribution (Daniels 1975, 280; Edmundson 2017, 55–56). The liberty principle reads:

> Each person has the same indefeasible claim to a fully adequate scheme of equal basic liberties, which scheme is compatible with the same scheme of liberties for all.

The Liberty Principle ascribes to each individual an *equal* right to basic liberties, such as liberty of conscience and freedom of association, freedom of speech and liberty of the person, the right to vote and to hold public office, and, crucial to our argument here, the right to influence national elections. Rawls takes the right to equal opportunity to influence the political process seriously and therefore adds that *the fair value* of this right must be secured. This right must not be considered as just a formal right; it demands special protection. Social class and economic inequality

[10] The interpretation of Rawls outlined here is based on Pedersen (2021a).

cannot be allowed to determine how citizens conceived as free and equal should be able to participate in society's political institutions. Those similarly motivated and endowed must not be excluded from office or influence.

Rawls' distinction between formal and fair value of equal political liberties is inspired by Karl Marx. Marx claimed—for example, in *On the Jewish Question*—that liberal capitalist societies ascribed to citizens formal liberties that would necessarily be undermined by the inequalities produced by capitalism. Rawls took Marx's criticism of merely formal liberties very seriously (Rawls 2001, 148–150, 176–179).

The reasoning runs as follows: If everyone really is to be ensured equal opportunity to influence politics, one cannot allow too much inequality. With large inequality, there will always be a danger that the wealthiest use their economic power to achieve political power.[11] Rawls is especially concerned that the very rich would unite on questions having to do with the advancement of their own interests and privileges (Rawls 1999, 198). However, even separately, the best off may achieve power by, for example, threatening to withdraw their investment in a local community if they are not given the conditions they desire. Alternatively, they could give large donations to political parties to ensure their own interests. Rawls thinks one can guard against the last kind of influence by introducing special arrangement such as public financing of political parties, limits on how much individuals can donate to candidates and parties as well as ensuring everyone equal access to the media. These measures are normally referred to as insulation strategies because their purpose is to insulate politics from the influence of money. However, according to Rawls, such interventions are necessary but not sufficient to ensure the fair value of equal opportunity to affect politics. In addition to such special arrangements, one must prevent too great concentration of capital (Rawls 1999, 198).[12]

Furthermore, Rawls defends the principle of fair equality of opportunity. The principle of fair equality of opportunity is similar to the general principle of equality of opportunity. Even though this ideal is well known, the principle is "not altogether clear" (Rawls 2001, 43), and most people would agree that it should not be completely realized. For example, research indicates that parents who read to their children provide their children with several benefits. However, few think that it follows

---

[11] It is important to note that it is not only individuals, but also corporations that can use money to influence politics. Thus, a complete account of the worry that money can influence politics in a problematic way must also take this complication into consideration. Thanks to Dan Halliday for pointing this out.

[12] There are different interpretations of Rawls in the secondary literature when it comes to Rawls' view on these insulation strategies. O'Neill (2012, 82–83) claims that Rawls is in two minds about the insulation strategy. On the one hand O'Neill claims, Rawls holds that these strategies are necessary and sufficient to safeguard the fair value of the political liberties. On the other hand, Rawls formulates himself as if these strategies are necessary, but not sufficient. Thomas (2017, 95) interprets Rawls differently when it comes to the question of necessary and sufficient means to ensure equal opportunity to influence. According to Thomas, Rawls thinks such a set of special arrangements sufficient on their own to ensure political liberties; if they work, the fair value of political liberties does not require additional extensive redistribution as it does on my interpretation.

from this that the state should ban parents from reading to their children because of the inequalities thus created between those who are read to and those who are not.[13]

Rawls, however, has a particular interpretation of this principle. Here, we must make a distinction between *formal* equality of opportunity and Rawls' more demanding notion of *fair* equality of opportunity. Formal equality of opportunity is a well-known principle implemented in public institutions through legislation in many countries. It requires that, for example, a company advertising a position must choose the best qualified applicant for the job. One cannot give the job to someone on the basis of a preference to hire a woman or a man. Such a principle contributes to justice because it ensures that a person's fate is determined by their qualifications, and not by their gender or family background.

Rawls' notion of fair equality of opportunity is more demanding. It requires not only that positions be open to those best qualified, but also that people with comparable innate abilities and motivation have equal prospects of becoming best qualified (Rawls 1999, 63). Fair equality of opportunity also entails that one must correct for disadvantages that are due to social background. In practice, this means that everyone must be ensured equal access to education; that one must establish a right to basic health care for all; and that the state limits the concentration of capital if such concentration impacts fair equality of opportunity (Rawls 2001, 174). We know that in most societies, children born in the middle or upper classes have better opportunities to take longer education and achieve prestigious positions compared to those born in the lower classes. This is the kind of inequality the principle of fair equality of opportunity is supposed to correct. It is therefore a radical principle and would require significant state intervention to be realized.

Rawls' ideal of fair equality of opportunity does not eliminate inequalities that are due to effort and talent. He thinks that people who have the same abilities and motivation should have the same prospects. However, if two people have the same abilities but different motivation, the one who works hard may end up with more than the one who does not. Furthermore, differences in innate abilities will also entail that some end up with more than others. If, for example, Peer and Pål are born with similar family background, but Peer is born with an IQ of 150 and Pål with one of 75, chances are that Peer will be better off than Pål, even if they are ensured fair equality of opportunity. IQ is an important part of one's innate abilities.

Many would therefore think that one *deserves* that which one acquires by virtue of one's talent. Rawls does not agree. He thinks that the talent with which one is born is arbitrary from a moral point of view. Therefore, the principle of fair equality of opportunity cannot be the sole principle to regulate the basic institutions of society. It must be supplemented by the difference principle. To Rawls, people do not deserve the advantages they get from their innate abilities. However, if the work of those better endowed is necessary to maximise the position of the worst off, this difference in endowment is no longer unjust. Those who are talented will then perform their work in a way that benefits those who have not been as lucky in what

[13] For a discussion, see Brighouse and Swift (2014, 124–125).

Rawls calls "the natural lottery", that is, the random allocation of natural endowments (Rawls 1999, 64).

It is important to note how Rawls, with the help of the difference principle, attempts to reach a compromise between two views that have played important roles in questions of just distribution: Adherents of outcome equality have argued in favour of equal material distribution between all members in society. Humans are morally equal, and equality of material goods is the best way of maintaining this moral equality, they claim. Opposed to this view is the view popular among economists: That the wealth in a society will increase if we allow those who produce the most to earn the most. With the difference principle, Rawls tries to bridge these two views. The principle allows inequalities in outcome if and only if it is necessary to provide benefits for the worst off compared to what their situation would be with strict outcome equality.

The difference principle therefore builds in an incentive argument: Differences in income and wealth can improve the prospects of those worst off, for example, by giving talented people the incentives to do work in which their talents can create assets for society, assets which may, in turn, be redistributed. The total size of the pie can be increased, either by talented people working harder, thus raising the total tax income, or by new jobs being created as a result of incentives motivating people to innovate (Cohen 2008, 35). Thus, the difference principle is attractive because it formulates an egalitarian impulse while at the same time being oriented towards efficiency.

The principles of justice are lexically ordered. That means that the first principle (the liberty principle) must be completely satisfied before the next principle can come into force. In other words, one cannot justify violations of the liberty principle by pointing to improvements in economic or social conditions that might be otherwise recommended by the two subordinate principles. The basis of this lexical ordering is that the principles can come into conflict. This may best be illustrated with an example. We could imagine a society that, by limiting the freedom of expression, would become more stable, increase its production, and thereby be able to provide tax exemptions to the worst off (Holtug 2003, 398). Without a lexical ordering of the principles, this would be a possible interpretation. To Rawls, however, this is unacceptable. The liberty principle always has priority.

The lexical ordering also applies within the second principle. The first part must be satisfied before the second can come into effect. Fair equality of opportunity must be satisfied before the difference principle can be applied. However, the principles must be seen in relation to each other, as a unit (Rawls 2001, 46). The difference principle is not the only principle relevant to questions of just distribution—contrary to the impression one might get from reading the discussion that followed the publication of *A Theory of Justice*. The other two principles also affect distribution, as explained above. Starting with the liberty principle, one can mount an argument against economic inequalities that hinder people from participating in politics on a par with others.[14] Large economic inequalities may also make it almost impossible for poor people to be elected to political office or to advance their political views. Moreover, starting with the principle of fair equality of opportunity, one can argue that large economic inequalities in society negatively impacts fair equality of opportunity.

What are the consequences for distribution that follows from these principles? We shall elaborate on this ideal of distribution by looking closer at Rawls' notion of a pure procedural background justice. Rawls writes:

> In a well-ordered society, in which both the equal basic liberties (with their fair value) and fair equality of opportunity are secured, the distribution of income and wealth illustrate what we may call pure background procedural justice. The basic structure is arranged so that when everyone follows the publicly recognized rules of cooperation, and honors the claims the rules specify, the particular distributions of goods that result are acceptable as just (or at least not unjust) whatever these distributions turn out to be (Rawls 2001, 50).

We have pure procedural background justice when the basic institutions of society are arranged so that the liberty principle and the principle of fair equality of opportunity are satisfied. Rawls' point is that, for justice to be established and maintained, one needs continuous state regulation to ensure that people have equal political rights and fair equality of opportunity.[15]

Seen together, the ideal of distribution that follows from *justice as fairness* is a radically egalitarian ideal. The inequality it allows must be kept within strict limits, especially in the case of inequalities of wealth. Rawls writes that the background institutions must:

> work to keep property and wealth evenly enough shared over time to preserve the fair value of the political liberties and fair equality of opportunity over generations. They do this by laws regulating bequests and inheritance of property, and other devices such as taxes, to prevent excessive concentrations of power (Rawls 2001, 51)

For our purpose, this is perhaps the most important insight offered by *justice as fairness*: The ideal requires an upper and lower limit on the concentration of capital. It requires, in other words, what Kevin Vallier has called a capital ceiling and a capital floor (Vallier 2019, 144). The capital ceiling is there to stop the wealthiest from dominating the rest of society, whereas the capital floor is necessary to allow everyone opportunities for education and economic success irrespective of social background.[16]

The specific distributive ideal that follows from the two principles of justice requires society to avoid too large concentration of capital while at the same time ensuring that everyone who participate in social cooperation are secured sufficient

---

[14] This understanding of Rawls is often neglected, but not new. As Daniels puts it, "it is the First Principle, rather than the Second, which carries the egalitarian punch" (Daniels 1975, 280; see Edmundson 2017, 55–56).

[15] Note that the difference principle does not play a decisive role in this interpretation of Rawls. In my opinion, the difference principle has attracted too much attention when it comes to how Rawls' overall position should be interpreted.

[16] For elaboration on the justifications for a wealth ceiling and a wealth floor see White (2020).

capital.[17] This is to secure all citizens the basis for self-respect, and to avoid anyone dominating and controlling anyone else.[18] The basic structure must thus ensure a particular pattern of distribution by continuously correcting the inequalities created by the market. How such a distributive ideal affects the design of a tax system is a topic I will return to in the next section.

Some of Rawls' critics have argued that his ideal is abstract and has little to offer when it comes to levels of inequality (Piketty 2020, 969). Others conclude that justice as fairness does not have a critical sting and is therefore without much practical relevance.[19] The interpretation I have given here shows that this is not the case. The critics, in my view, put too much emphasis on the difference principle.[20] In order to understand Rawls and appreciate his position, it is, as I have argued, necessary to focus on the combined effect of the liberty principle and the principle of fair equality of opportunity. This gives us an ideal that demands a capital ceiling and a capital floor, and this is a radical egalitarian ideal with plenty of critical potential.

Rawls uses the two principles to settle what he calls the main problem of distributive justice: to determine which social system is the most just (Rawls 1999, 242; Freeman 2013, 9). To Rawls, therefore, it is not sufficient to formulate abstract principles of justice. As his thinking matured, he became more and more concerned with specifying which institutional arrangements would best realize the principles. This effort culminated in *Justice as Fairness: A Restatement* (Thomas 2017, xviii). Here, Rawls distinguishes between five ideal types of social system or regimes: Laissez-faire capitalism, state socialism, welfare capitalism, property owning democracy, and liberal socialism (Rawls 2001, 136). All these regime types can be evaluated using the two principles of justice.

Laissez-faire capitalism is not concerned with ensuring fair value of the political liberties or fair equality of opportunity. Market outcomes are seen as just so long as formal equality of opportunity endure. State socialism violates the principle of

---

[17] I am indebted to Alan Thomas (2017) for this point; see also O'Neill and Williamson (2012a, 9).

[18] Beyond this, I will avoid assuming a position on what overall ideal of distribution follows from *Justice as Fairness*. This is a complicated question, not least because Rawls sticks to the lexical ordering of the principles while also claiming that they are a unified whole. Samuel Freeman claims that the difference principle is the most important principle, but also points out that the liberty principle and the principle of fair equality of opportunity affect distribution. From his interpretation, it follows that inequalities due to the difference principle cannot be accepted if they are in conflict with the liberty principle or the principle of fair equality of opportunity. Within the framework of a property-owning democracy, the difference principle and the principle of fair equality of opportunity requires that the worst off are secured opportunities to achieve positions and posts and to control the means of production employed in their work (Freeman 2007, 139–140). Alan Thomas provides an alternative interpretation. Thomas thinks the best interpretations of *justice as fairness* should disregard the lexical priority and consider the principles as a unified whole. Furthermore, the principles must be institutionalized in the proper background context, namely property-owning democracy (Thomas 2017, 95).

[19] Philip Pettit defended this claim in a lecture in Bergen on August 31, 2017. Pettit defends a similar view in Pettit (2012, 123–127).

[20] And, as Fleurbaey argues, this principle has been very influential in normative economics (Fleurbaey 2021).

fundamental rights by its lack of democratic procedures. Most interesting, however, is Rawls' discussion of capitalist welfare states. For a long time, there was a general assumption that Rawls held a comprehensive welfare state to be the institutional arrangement best suited to maintain the two principles. In his later works, however, Rawls points out that this rests on a misunderstanding (Rawls 1999, xiv–xv; 2001, 135 ff.).

The welfare state is seen by many to be a successful solution worth defending. It provides a safety net for those who need health services, ensures a minimum of means to those who have no income, and guarantees everyone the right to education. The Nordic welfare states, which ensure extensive benefits, are celebrated the world over and used as models in countries wanting reforms. But are capitalist welfare states just? Rawls did not think so. Capitalist welfare states allow too much concentration of capital. Moreover, since economic resources are often convertible into political capital, Rawls argues that capitalist welfare states violate the most important principle of justice: to ensure basic liberties for all.

If welfare states are not just, what is the alternative? Rawls argues that both liberal socialism and property-owning democracy can satisfy the principles of justice (Rawls 2001, 138). Liberal socialism is characterized by publicly owned means of production and worker-controlled companies (Rawls 1999, 248). However, Rawls does not thoroughly discuss this kind of regime, and hence it is property owning democracy that has gained the most attention, and which is generally viewed as the kind of regime Rawls is trying to defend.[21]

The most important trait of property-owning democracy is thus that it avoids significant concentration of capital. Therefore, it depends on arrangements that spread capital around, and ensure everybody access to capital.[22]Adherents of property-owning democracy should therefore defend progressive wealth tax and high taxes on capital income and inheritance, coupled with arrangements that allocate capital to everyone.[23]

The problem with capitalist welfare states, as Rawls sees it, is that they allow too much power to those who are best off. In capitalist welfare states, the worst off are treated as a group that has to be compensated for low income or other factors

[21] For discussions of property-owning democracy, see Freeman (2013), and O'Neill and Williamson (2012a, b, c). For a discussion of the history of this ideal, see Jackson (2012). Thomas (2017) argues that Rawls' two principles will be best realized under property-owning democracy whereas Edmundson (2017) gives a recent defense of the claim that Rawls is in favor of liberal socialism. We shall return to this discussion in the final section.

[22] Property owning democracy must therefore keep economic inequalities within strictly limited bonds. As Ben Jackson has shown, some of the early republican thinkers express similar views. Rousseau, for example, maintained that: "Do you, then, want to give the state stability? Bring the extremes as close together as possible; tolerate neither very rich people nor beggars", and he subsequently added the famous sentence which states that no citizen should "be so very rich that he can buy another, and none so poor that he is compelled to sell himself" (Rousseau cited in Jackson 2012, 34).

[23] Rawls' take on taxation is complex, and I shall return to this. Rawls explicitly endorses inheritance taxation but does not discuss wealth taxation.

(Freeman 2013, 22). Rawls claims that the logic of capitalist welfare states entails compensation for the worst-off ex post. The logic of property-owning democracy, in contrast, is to equip free and equal citizens with the resources they need for full participation from the beginning (Rawls 2001, 139–140). In other words, capitalist welfare states merely mitigate social hierarchy, whereas property owning democracy attempts to remove it.

Property owning democracy therefore requires predistribution and not just redistribution. Predistribution requires limiting people's pre-tax income, while redistribution requires more well-known but less radical mechanisms such as tax on income and wealth. Predistribution has been described as reforming the market so that one promotes a more equal distribution of economic power and market outcomes *before* the government collects taxes (Hacker 2011, 35). An example of predistribution would be changing the laws protecting intellectual property rights so that these rights do not last as long as they do today. This would reduce pre-tax inequalities (Scanlon 2018, 102). Wealth tax is an example of redistribution which reduces post-tax inequalities.[24]

Property owning democracy rests on a combination of predistribution and redistribution. The result is not necessarily harsher taxation overall, but a transition from tax mainly on income to tax on wealth and inheritance, where the goal is to avoid concentration of capital (O'Neill and Williamson 2012b, c, 12–13). The goal of both predistribution and redistribution is to ensure the spread of capital. Capital here also means human capital; property owning democracy requires full access to high-quality education for all (Rawls 2001, 160–161; Scanlon 2018, 102).

Justice as fairness is thus a radically egalitarian ideal that demands state intervention to regulate concentration of capital. Capitalist welfare states are not just, since they allow some to control large quantities of capital, which may also give them political power. This way of interpreting Rawls is relatively new. In the first decades after the publication of *Theory*, many thought that Rawls defended the welfare state. More recently, Rawls' criticism of the welfare state and the alternatives he proposes to it have become more central to the debates about his theory.

9.3 Rawls on Taxation

What role should the tax system play to realize Rawls' radical egalitarian ideal? Or to be more specific: what role should income tax, expenditure tax, inheritance tax and wealth tax play in the overall set of institutions designed to realize Rawlsian ideal. The answer to these questions is not straight-forward. Despite the enormous amount of secondary literature on Rawls, there is still much work to be done in

[24] Other mechanisms for predistribution involve the educational system, minimum wage, and worker representation on company boards (Piketty 2020, 528–538). I shall return to the distinction between predistribution and redistribution in section V.

order to establish how Rawlsians should think about taxation (cf. O'Neill and Williamson 2015, 827).

In *Justice as Fairness: A Restatement*, Rawls makes three points to illustrate how it might be possible to use tax measures to ensure background justice. Rawls mentions inheritance tax, taxation of wealth, income tax and tax on consumption. I will present and discuss Rawls' take on taxation and use the opportunity to say something general about how egalitarians think about these taxes. Rawls starts by defending the inheritance tax:

> We borrow from Mill (and others) the idea of regulating bequests and restricting inheritance. To do this an estate itself need not be subject to tax nor need the total given by bequest be limited. Rather the principle of progressive taxation is applied at the receiver's end. Those inheriting and receiving gifts and endowments pay a tax according to the value received and the nature of the receiver. Individuals and corporate bodies of certain kinds (educational institutions and museums say) may be taxed at different rates. The aim is to encourage a wide and far more equal dispersion of real property and productive assets (Rawls 2001, 160–161).

To Rawls, it is necessary to tax inheritance to avoid capital from being concentrated to the detriment of the political liberties and fair equality of opportunity. The suggestion from Mill is that everyone should be entitled to *bequeath*. This follows from Mill's understanding of private property rights. But Mill wanted to limit the amount a person is allowed to *receive* during her lifetime. Thus, the Millian scheme supported by Rawls entails that a person can give away all her money without being taxed, given that what she bequeaths is spread among different receivers.[25] However, if the recipient receives more than the limit allows, she will be taxed at steep rates.

Among egalitarians there seems to be almost unanimous support for inheritance taxation. Piketty supports such a tax, and so does Dworkin and representatives of the luck-egalitarian tradition.[26] Inheritance tax is thus unequivocally supported by Rawls and there is wide consensus among egalitarians that this is a necessary and just tax.

Rawls treatment of wealth tax and income tax is less unequivocal. This can be seen in his short comment on income and wealth taxation. As he puts it:

> The progressive principle of taxation might not be applied to wealth and income for the purposes of raising funds…but solely to prevent accumulations of wealth that are judged to be inimical to background justice, for example to the fair value of the political liberties and to fair equality of opportunity (Rawls 2001, 161).

Recently, Piketty (2020, 9075) and Saez and Zucman (2019b) have defended a progressive wealth tax in order to combat increasing inequality. The quoted paragraph is not explicitly stating that a wealth tax is necessary to combat wealth inequality.

[25] For a discussion of the Mill scheme see Cappelen and Pedersen (2018).

[26] See Dworkin (2000, 346–349), and Halliday (2018, 74–100) and Barry (2020) for discussions of inheritance taxation within the luck egalitarian tradition.

But it lends support to a progressive wealth tax given that inequalities of wealth put the fair value of political liberties and fair equality of opportunity at risk.[27]

Contrary to the inheritance tax, there is no general consensus among egalitarians when it comes to wealth taxation. Among political philosophers, the wealth tax has not attracted anything close to the same attention as the inheritance tax. This is perhaps due to the fact that the wealth tax does not raise problems that are of the same normative interest to philosophers. Normative justifications for wealth tax seem to rely more on one's general take on distributive justice and taxation.[28]

At first sight, from a luck-egalitarian perspective, wealth tax is not a just form of tax. In this, then, the two dominant egalitarian theories disagree. In a Rawlsian perspective, the wealth tax can be justified by the need to protect a democratic practice. As we have seen, this practice requires that the wealth of the very richest is limited. According to the luck egalitarian ideal, one cannot justify putting limits on people's wealth by pointing to the need that we are free and equal citizens in a constitutional democracy. To luck egalitarians, someone's wealth is just if it follows from choice, and unjust if it is due to factors outside their control. In principle, therefore, the luck egalitarian ideal is compatible with very large inequalities in wealth.[29]

Finally, Rawls notes that

> income taxation might be avoided altogether and a proportional expenditure tax adopted instead, that is a tax on consumption at a constant marginal rate. People would be taxed according to how much they use of the goods and services produced, and not according to how much they contribute (an idea that goes back to Hobbes) (Rawls 2001, 161).

Rawls' take on income and consumption taxes has been described as puzzling (Fried 1999; Sugin 2004, 1994; O'Neill and Williamson 2015, 826). Commentators find this puzzling because Rawls seems to support proportional over progressive taxation and tax on consumption over income tax. Both measures are normally considered deficient if the ambition is to employ the tax system to achieve a more equal society. Furthermore, most countries treat income as the largest tax base and as key to redistribution. Let us first focus on the income tax. As Fried (1999, 185) puts it:

> In the context of the overall Rawlsian scheme, the right not to have one's income taxed at a higher marginal rate than one's neighbor's stands as an island of deontological rights swamped by a sea of redistribution.

---

[27] For an attempt to justify a wealth tax by combining Rawls and Piketty see Pedersen (2021a, b, chapter 11).

[28] For a recent influential defence of wealth taxation see Saez and Zucman (2019b)

[29] If someone *chooses* to save, it follows that the part of their wealth that is due to this choice is just, and not something that should be taxed. Nevertheless, one may, as Duff has pointed out, justify a wealth tax based on Dworkin's theory. This may be due to two conditions. First, the rejection of wealth tax presupposes that income and inheritance is taxed prior to being saved. If this is not the case, Dworkin's position may allow taxation of wealth as the second-best solution. Second, wealth tax may be necessary if a society is class-divided and individuals may reasonably be supposed to have insured against ending up among the worst off in that society. In general, however, Dworkin is against wealth tax (Duff 2016, 27–28). For a luck egalitarian critique of the wealth tax, see Rakowski (2000). For a critique of Rakowski based on the argument that the luck-egalitarian position on wealth tax is not as straight forward as it seems, see Fried (2000).

What can explain Rawls' comment here? The first thing to note is that we must distinguish between two different levels of theorizing (O'Neill and Williamson 2015, 826). Ideally, in a property-owning democracy, Rawls assumes that there are mechanisms in place that secure procedural justice. To simplify, this means that there are mechanisms to safeguard the political liberties and to ensure fair equality of opportunity. In other words, *if* there are measures of predistribution to protect the conditions necessary, additional taxation might be proportionate and on consumption. With such a system in place, we can understand what Rawls has in mind when he suggests that we might even avoid the income tax altogether. However, as Rawls notes in *Theory*, if these ideal conditions are not in place, that is, under conditions more similar to the ones we face in most western countries today, even steeply progressive income taxes may be justified (Rawls 1999, 246–247; O'Neill and Williamson 2015, 826–827).

What about the expenditure tax, or the VAT?[30] This tax is normally taken to be regressive: a poor person will have to pay a larger fraction of their income to buy an item compared to a rich person. Piketty and Saez and Zucman's conclusion on the VAT is that it should be avoided altogether due to its regressive effects (Piketty 2020, 1001; Saez and Zucman 2019a, b, 185–187). Murphy and Nagel appear to be with Piketty in this discussion. Thus, there seems to be consensus that the VAT has negative consequences from an egalitarian perspective. However, there has been various attempts to redesign this tax rather than abolishing it.[31]

The upshot of all this is that Rawls' discussion of taxation has limited value. Under less ideal circumstances than those assumed by Rawls, or to be more precise, under conditions in most countries in our present time, Rawls must be understood to be in favour of, or at least not opposed to, strongly progressive taxation of income, wealth, and inheritance. In contexts where there is a level of capital concentration threatening the political liberties and fair equality of opportunity, and where other measures are unavailable, it is necessary to employ tax measures suitable to address these problems. Given what we know about the recent levels of income and wealth inequality, the Rawlsian position should be to endorse progressive taxes on income, wealth and inheritance at least as an intermediate set of measures that might be revised once ideally just conditions can obtain. The political liberties and fair equality of opportunity have absolute priority in the Rawlsian system, and it is hard to see how these ideals can be realized without a tax system with the three taxes we discuss here playing a crucial role.

However, it is important to see that these tax measures are instruments. If there are other instruments available, they must be considered. It is not essential what mechanisms one employs in order to safeguard the political liberties and fair

[30] The value added tax (VAT)is the European equivalent to a consumption tax. See Saez and Zucman (2019a, 185–187) for a short history of the tax and a brief explanation of why they are against it.

[31] See Halliday 2015 for a discussion on Murphy and Nagel on consumption taxes and for an attempt to show how consumption taxes can be redesigned to overcome the standard egalitarian objection to it.

equality of opportunity. What is essential is that they are secured, one way or the other. Sugin has put this point accurately:

> Rawls uses the tax system as a means of achieving distributive justice, rather than as a requirement of justice itself – the features of the tax system are not constitutional essentials (Sugin 2004, 1997).

Constitutional essentials, for Rawls, are those rights and liberties that the constitution must safeguard. Securing the two principles of justice is thus a constitutional essential, whereas what mechanisms employed to guarantee them are not.

In my view, Piketty, and the other commentators we have discussed here are correct to say that Rawls should have been more detailed in his treatment of taxation. However, this raises other issues in political philosophy. The first issue is that political philosophers differ when it comes to how detailed they should be in laying out the mechanisms necessary to achieve justice. Second, it touches upon questions that have to do with the right division of labor between philosophers and economists (and other social scientists). I cannot provide a discussion of these issues here. In the following section, I shall suggest that Piketty's proposal for a participatory socialism provides the institutional mechanisms necessary to realize Rawlsian ideals.

9.4 Piketty's Participatory Socialism

Piketty wrote *Capital and Ideology* 50 years after Rawls' *A Theory of Justice*.[32] The book was written from the perspective of a French economist who had spent much of his early academic years in the US. *Capital and Ideology* builds and expands upon *Piketty's Capital in the Twenty-first Century*. In the latter, Piketty draws on extremely rich empirical data sets to demonstrate that in the major western economies, inequality in both income and wealth has increased substantially since the 1980s. He argued that the tendency of increasing inequality would continue unless radical measures were taken. Focusing on the U.S., Piketty warned against "a drift toward oligarchy" (Piketty 2014, 514) to make it clear that the existence of democracy was threatened by the increasing gap between rich and poor.[33]

Piketty follows Meade and Rawls on the importance of avoiding concentration of capital, and he includes a number of the proposals Meade and Rawls are in favor of. But his alternative proposal is more detailed and is, as far as I can tell, the most elaborate proposal on how the ambitions of property-owning democracy can be reached. It is important to note at the outset, however, that the precise figures presented by Piketty are meant as illustrations and point of departure for debate. Piketty is not looking to close the debate, but to open it. He is committed to deliberative

---

[32] This and the following section are based on Pedersen (2021b).

[33] Piketty's warning against a drift to oligarchy was focused on the U.S., but he also demonstrated that European countries normally regarded as social democratic had failed to contain the increasing inequality.

democracy, and the proposal presented is an invitation to an open debate on these issues (Piketty 2020, 968; O'Neill 2021b).[34]

The scheme for participatory socialism can be reconstructed to be based on four pillars:[35]

1. A redistributive tax system
2. A combination of a universal capital endowment, universal basic income, and an ambitious welfare state[36]
3. Workers on the boards of companies
4. Educational justice

If these measures are institutionalized, it will contribute to a rethinking of private property rights. The scheme will ensure that private property will circulate instead of being gradually concentrated on fewer hands (Piketty 2020, 976). With such a system in place, all citizens will have a real opportunity to participate in economic life and in democratic decision making. In this way, capitalism can be transcended, and a *new* form of socialism can be realized.

The tax system proposed by Piketty includes progressive taxation of income, inheritance and wealth. Piketty suggests that the income tax shall be calculated based on the average income in the economy. If you make ten times the average, you will pay 60–70% income tax. If you make hundred times the average, the tax may be as high as 80–90%.[37] Piketty argues that such a level of taxation existed in the U.S. and the UK between 1930 and 1980, and this was a period with strong economic growth (Piketty 2020, 985).

Inheritances should be taxed with 70–80% or even more for the highest transactions. However, it is important to note that despite these high rates, the proposal is that most people will pay a much lower rate. If you inherit 100.000 Euro, you will have to pay 5% tax, that is 5000 Euros (Piketty 2020, 988). Only the very high transfers are to be taxed with 70% or more.

The progressive wealth tax is the cornerstone of the tax scheme, and thus the most important measure to achieve circulation of capital. Piketty holds that from a historical perspective, high income taxes and high inheritance taxation is insufficient to stop the process of growing concentration of capital. Progressive income tax is insufficient because the very rich will often have a taxable income that is much

[34] For further discussion of this democratic element of Piketty's approach see O'Neill (2021b).

[35] The following presentation is primarily based on chapter 17 in *Capital and Ideology*. Note that I will limit myself to the institutional measures that can be undertaken by the nation state. Piketty includes a discussion of global justice with reference to tax competition and tax havens. I will not discuss questions of global justice here.

[36] The term "circulation of capital" might not be precise. After all, capital could circulate even if it there are very few people amongst which it circulates. What Piketty has in mind is probably that capital must both be deconcentrated and that it must circulate. In the following I will use the term circulation of capital in this way.

[37] Piketty shows that the *marginal rates* on the highest income was between 70% and 90% historically (Piketty 2020, 1004), whereas his own tax scheme refers to *effective rates* (Piketty 2020, 982).

lower than their actual income (Piketty 2020, 976). And the progressive inheritance tax is insufficient as a measure to tax newly created wealth (Piketty 2020, 978).

The proposal of how to design the wealth tax must be seen in light of the galloping increase of wealth inequality seen in recent years. Piketty demonstrates that the largest fortunes have increased with 6–8% annually since the 1980s (Piketty 2020, 988). The following is a good illustration of how the tax is to be designed:

> The tax rate is 0.1 percent for wealth below the national average, rising gradually to 1 percent at twice the national average, 10 percent at one hundred times the national average, 60 percent at 1,000 times the national average… and 90 percent at 10,000 times the national average (which would be 2 billion euros) (Piketty 2020, 987).

According to Piketty, such a tax of 90% on the largest fortunes will reduce the billionaires share of national wealth and bring it below the level of 1950–1980. Thus, such a tax would contribute substantially to solving the crises of inequality facing many countries today.

A proposal for a wealth tax of 90% is of course extremely controversial, and these high rates attract most of the attention and create headlines. Piketty makes it clear that under normal circumstances, where there is not a crisis of inequality, these kinds of rates would not be needed. Rates of 10–20% would be able to reduce even the highest fortunes during a few years, and that would be sufficient (Piketty 2020, 988). Furthermore, Piketty claims that his proposal will reduce the wealth tax for 80–90% of those who pay the tax, while the highest rates will only hit the few extremely wealthy individuals and families.

I cannot provide a thorough discussion of the various tax mechanisms Piketty suggests here. However, since the wealth tax has a prominent place in Piketty's scheme and in the recent debate, I shall briefly touch upon some of the most important points. The first thing to note is that a wealth tax with the rates suggested by Piketty will induce rich people to move abroad with their wealth in order to avoid tax.[38] There are two kinds of replies to this. First, the British philosopher Brian Barry has argued that one should rather increase the restrictions on those who are tax refugees (Barry 2005, 192–193). Barry holds that tax refugees should only be allowed to come to their country of origin under special conditions, such as in the event of serious illness or death in their close family. After all, tax refugees have chosen to emigrate to avoid having to pay tax and, therefore, limiting their opportunity to spend time in their country of origin does not constitute a wrong.[39]

[38] For an example of this objection against wealth tax see Smith (2020), for a brief response see Saez and Zucman (2020).

[39] Whether such a change actually will stop people from becoming tax refugees depends on how important it is for them to be able to spend time in the given country. More knowledge is needed here about how potential tax refugees think. Moreover, a suggestion like this presupposes that one can distinguish between ordinary people and tax refugees so that the arrangement does not impact ordinary persons who live abroad, and who have not moved to avoid paying taxes. Barry also argues that tax refugees should not be given the same opportunity to donate money to political parties, own newspapers, etc. (Barry 2005, 193)

Another policy option is to introduce an exit tax. It involves a 40% tax on net worth if you decide to expatriate for tax reasons (Saez and Zucman 2019a, b, 27; Piketty 2020, 571, 994). Piketty provides the following precise argument for why such a tax is just:

> The justification for an exit tax is that there is no natural right to enrich oneself by taking advantage of a country's legal and educational systems, and so on, and then extracting the wealth without returning part of it to the community (Piketty 2020, 994).

A combination of Barry's proposal and the exit tax shows that the threat of losing large amount of capital due to tax refugees should not be exaggerated. Of course, it will depend on the rates imposed, and the most aggressive rates suggested by Piketty might be just, but still have negative consequences if only implemented in one single country.[40]

Let me now return to the overall scheme. The combined effect of the proposal is to make the tax system much more progressive than it is (in all countries) today. An illustration of this is that Piketty's proposed tax system does not include a VAT as this is a regressive tax (Piketty 2020, 1001). In addition, the tax scheme includes a progressive tax on carbon emissions. Such a tax, Piketty argues, will have to be designed in order not to hit the worst off. If this is not the case, there is a danger of unrest, as it has been exemplified by the yellow vests in France (Piketty 2020, 1004–1006). Overall, the reshaping into a more progressive tax system will make it more realistic for more people to acquire property, and that is of course an important ambition for everyone supporting a property-owning democracy (Piketty 2020, 987). We shall return to this.

The proposed tax system is supposed to finance a capital endowment for all, a universal basic income, welfare services, education, and pensions. Let us look first at the capital endowment. The basic idea is that everyone is to receive a lump sum when turning 25. This sum is to be financed through the wealth tax and the inheritance tax. Piketty estimates 120,000 Euro as a possible amount. The point is that everybody, and not only a few privileged people, are to receive something like an inheritance at the beginning of their grown-up life (Piketty 2020, 983). Such "public inheritance for all" will allow *everyone* a kind of startup capital as opposed to private inheritance today, which is distributed to a select group of heirs to the wealthy when in their fifties and sixties.[41]

---

[40] There are other arguments against the wealth tax that I cannot discuss here. Some argue for example, that the wealth tax is double taxation, others hold that such a tax is hard to implement due to valuation issues. Furthermore, in the US, some will simply say that the wealth tax is unconstitutional and, therefore, not something to be considered. The argument about double taxation is problematic because no tax system can rely only on income taxation, the fact that the wealth tax has been part of the Norwegian system for hundred years shows that valuation problems can be overcome (see Pedersen 2021a, b, chapter 11), and finally, as Saez and Zucman (2019a, b, 22) have argued, the constitutionality of the wealth tax depends "on the make-up of the supreme court".

[41] In his proposal for a capital endowment Piketty draws on Thomas Paine and Anthony Atkinson. In contrast to Atkinson, Pikety includes both a wealth tax and an inheritance tax as ways to finance the endowment, and this allows him to envisage a much larger sum compared to Atkinson whose proposal is based on funding by an inheritance tax only.

Traditionally, supporters of unconditional grants have defended either a one-time endowment or a basic income in the form of regular repeated cash instalments. Piketty's proposal is radical partly because it includes both (Piketty 2020, 984). In addition to a one-time endowment, citizens shall be guaranteed a universal basic income of 60% of average post tax income, but this sum will be reduced gradually if the basic income is replaced by other kinds of income (Piketty 2020, 1001).[42] It is important to note, that the basic income scheme comes in addition to, and not as a supplement for, an ambitious welfare state (Piketty 2020, 1004).

Both reforms are justified with reference to the extreme inequality of wealth that exists in every country around the world. The bottom 50% in all countries own only 5–10% of total wealth, with their share decreasing since the 1980s (Piketty 2020, 979), and they only receive 5–10% of the total amount of inheritance (Piketty 2020, 983). According to Piketty, this injustice against the worst off justifies a rethinking of how the basic institutions of society are arranged.

Another key element in this rethinking is co-management on the boards of companies. Piketty refers to Germany and the Nordic countries where this kind of arrangements exist for a long period of time. In Germany, half of the seats in the boards are reserved for the workers. Piketty claims that this model has been a large success and can explain why the country has succeeded in being productive without producing vast inequality. Involving the workers in the boards of the companies is claimed to be an important antidote to shortsighted owner interests (Piketty 2020, 972–973). Piketty discusses several different proposals to expand on this and achieve more social ownership. An important justification for co-management is that companies that are run by a one-share-one-vote logic misses out on broad discussions that can improve the company. Thus, in short, on Piketty's view, co-management increases the influence of the workers and limits the influence of investors, and the claim is that this is good for the productivity of the company.

Piketty emphasizes that educational justice is of crucial importance to a just society. Figures from France show that on average, a 20-year-old will receive approximately 120,000 Euro through investment in education (Piketty 2020, 1008). How much each individual receive varies substantially. Those who leave the educational system at an early age receive somewhere between 65,000 and 70,000 Euro. Those who are educated the most, receive somewhere between 200 and 300 thousand Euro. It is often the case that those who spend most time in the educational system (and therefore benefit most of educational subsidies) are also the ones who receive most of the inheritance transfers. Piketty claims the uneven spending breaches a norm that all should have an equal right to an equal amount for educational purposes. One way to get closer to such a norm would be to compensate those who spend the least time in the educational system by granting them a right to free education later in life. Another suggestion is to compensate the same individuals by increasing their endowment at the age of 25. An even more important suggestion

[42] In this sense, the basic income scheme defended by Piketty is not unconditional.

would be to have early measures to equalize differences between young people with different social backgrounds.[43]

A final important point is that Piketty holds that some fundamental elements of distributive justice must be protected by the constitution. The main argument for this is that many of the constitutions that exist today were written in a time when property owners were given a disproportionate level of respect and protection. If capital is to circulate instead of concentrate, Piketty holds that it will be necessary in many countries to implement constitutional change. One important move would be to constitutionally enshrine what Piketty refers to as fiscal justice. This will make it impossible for the extremely rich to pay a lower share in taxes compared to other groups in society (Piketty 2020, 995–996).

The progressive wealth tax and the progressive inheritance tax is to finance the endowment for all, while the progressive income tax is to finance the universal basic income and the welfare state. The following table sums up Piketty's proposal for participatory socialism (Piketty 2020, 982) (Table 9.1).

Let us now turn to why it has been necessary to propose an alternative set of institutions which are supposed to transcend capitalism. According to Piketty, the current capitalist system is based on permanent private ownership. The tendency in this system is towards increasing concentration of capital. Participatory socialism, as envisaged by Piketty, is instead designed for temporary private ownership. A just society cannot accept the trend towards stronger concentration of capital, it is necessary to institutionalize mechanisms to ensure the circulation of capital.

Table 9.1 Circulation of property and progressive taxation

Progressive property tax (financing the capital endowment to each young adult)			Progressive income tax (financing the basic income scheme and the social and ecological state)	
Multiple of average wealth	Annual property tax (effective rate)	Inheritance tax (effective rate)	Multiple of average income	Effective tax rates (including social taxes and carbon tax)
0.5	0.1%	5%	0.5	10%
2	1%	20%	2	40%
5	2%	50%	5	50%
10	5%	60%	10	60%
100	10%	70%	100	70%
1,000	60%	80%	1,000	80%
10,000	90%	90%	10,000	90%

Source: Thomas Piketty: *Capital and Ideology*, 982
Explanation: The tax system assumes that if an individual has 10 times more wealth than the national average, the individual must pay a wealth tax of 5%. If an individual makes 10 times the national average income, she must pay 60% tax

[43] For the discussion of educational justice, see Piketty (2020, 1007–1016).

The proposed wealth tax is designed to establish a capital roof. Simplified, we might say that no one shall be allowed to become a billionaire. As Piketty puts it in an interview:

> No, there won't be billionaires anymore. How can we justify that their existence is necessary for the common good? Contrary to what is often said, their enrichment was obtained thanks to these common goods, which are public knowledge, the infrastructures, the laboratories of research (Piketty quoted in Frank 2019).

In addition to the capital roof, it will also be necessary to establish a capital floor which ensures everyone access to capital to allow all to participate in economic and political life.[44] This is ensured through the endowment for all and the basic income scheme. Even the bottom 50% will be given the opportunity to start a business. With such mechanisms in place, permanent ownership is replaced by temporary ownership. Participatory socialism in other words, allows everyone "to participate as fully as possible in the various forms of social, cultural, economic, civic and political life" (Piketty 2020, 967–968). This enables a *new* form of socialism not to be confused with those forms of socialism that have been brought about throughout history. Participatory socialism is also a radical alternative to social democracy, which, on Piketty's account has failed to solve the problems for the twenty-first-century (Piketty 2020, 970).[45]

9.5 Combining Rawls and Piketty

As a number of commentators have suggested, there are good reasons for egalitarians to combine Rawls and Piketty.[46] In this section I will outline how such a combination provides an egalitarian ideal that is strongly justified (in lack of a better term), and at the same time detailed when it comes to the measures necessary to realize the ideal. I will start by looking at the criticism Piketty directs against Rawls.

Piketty has discussed Rawls in *Capital in the 21st Century* and in *Capital and Ideology*. In the latter work, Piketty claims that the "principal limitation of the Rawlsian approach is that it remains fairly abstract and says nothing precise about the levels of equality and fiscal progressivity the principles imply" (Piketty 2020,

[44] Note that a general floor provided through a cash endowment will also be able to secure everyone the opportunity for participation.

[45] See chapter 11: *Social Democratic Societies: Incomplete Equality* for a detailed analysis of what the social democratic societies have succeeded and failed to achieve. In short, Piketty claims they failed to go far enough in co-management, that they did not bring about educational justice, and that the social democratic countries failed to bring about distributive justice through taxation due to the massive tax competition between countries.

[46] For example, Kevin Vallier suggests that "introducing Piketty's work into a Rawlsian framework strengthens Rawls' critique of the welfare state and his case for property-owning democracy" (Vallier 2019, 142), and Martin O'Neill holds that "Piketty's substantive normative view is in its specifics a remarkably Rawlsian one" (O'Neill 2017, 355).

969). I believe that the interpretation I have outlined here dampens the critique of Rawls' theory being too abstract. The theory defends a capital ceiling and a capital roof, and it should not be expected from a philosopher to answer questions of exactly how to determine where the ceiling and roof should be set.

Piketty is, however correct in his assertion that Rawls should have been more detailed and should have discussed questions of taxation in more depth. Rawls himself acknowledges that his take on taxation is "illustrative and highly tentative" (Rawls 2001, 136). This may be explained from the perspective of a division of labor where the philosopher is concerned with justifying principles of justice and the economist is focused on the modalities of a progressive tax system to counter the level of inequality in a given society.

In general, such a division of labor can be justified. However, as we have seen, Rawls' position on taxation has led to misunderstandings and his view has been described as puzzling.

Does Rawls have anything to offer when it comes to how Piketty's proposal on participatory socialism is justified? In my view, the answer is yes. In the introduction to the chapter on participatory socialism, Piketty discusses what a just society is. The answer is that a just society

> is one that allows all of its members access to the widest possible range of fundamental goods. Fundamental goods include education, health, the right to vote, and more generally to participate as fully as possible in the various forms of social, cultural, economic, civic, and political life. A just society organizes socioeconomic relations, property rights and the distribution of income and wealth in such a way as to allow the least advantaged members to enjoy the highest possible life conditions (Piketty 2020, 967–968).

Piketty goes on to argue that absolute equality is not just if people have different ambitions and make different choices. But the ideal implies that everyone, and not only the privileged few, must be allowed to participate on equal terms, also in the political processes. Thus, the ideal of participatory socialism contains the Rawlsian point that inequalities must be limited due to the political liberties. However, the formulation given is so abstract that this insight might be lost. Drawing on the Rawlsian apparatus—as Piketty suggests—can therefore help to explicate what actually follows from the definition of a just society as proposed by Piketty.

The abstract formulation is of course not necessarily problematic. A division of labor with each discipline specializing in different aspects needed in a full-blown theory of justice is not a problem. What it does show, however, is the necessity to combine insights from both Rawls and Piketty in order to arrive at a well-grounded and institutionally anchored blueprint for a just society. Rawls provides insight when it comes to justification, Piketty on institutional design.

Let me clarify this point by looking at Piketty's claim that capital should circulate and not be concentrated. Why should we establish a system where capital circulates? Piketty's reply is that we must ensure that capital circulates in order to allow everyone the capacity to participate on equal terms. But what, more concrete, does that mean? The Rawlsian reply is that a just society must avoid concentration of capital to ensure that the extremely rich are not given the opportunity for more political power than others, and to ensure fair equality of opportunity. In order to achieve that, it is necessary to establish a capital ceiling and a capital floor. Only if society limits how much capital the richest can control will it be possible to ensure everyone's equal opportunity to influence the political process. And only if everyone is ensured *some* access to capital will it be possible for all to develop their talent and ability in a way that is good for the individual and for the community.

These are powerful justifications for the circulation of capital. They can be rooted in even more fundamental ideals. Securing everyone equal access to political influence is an important part of the idea of all being free and equal, and this idea is fundamental to liberal constitutional democracy. This holds true as well for the fundamental idea of ensuring fair equality of opportunity for all. We understand ourselves as free and equal citizens and to uphold this understanding, fair equality of opportunity is crucial. As free and equal citizens we cooperate and through this cooperation we produce much more than we would produce individually. Thus, to Rawls, the question of distributive justice is how we shall distribute a social product; that is a product that we produce together.

The two fundamental Rawlsian ideas that all should be considered free and equal, and that society should be understood as social cooperation in order to achieve common advantages is safeguarded by the two principles. The two ideas express a kind of solidarity and a sense of community that can only be realized in an egalitarian society. This gives expression to a critique of capitalism developed by Rawls, and probably shared by Piketty. Both are extremely concerned with how the major institutions of society (such as the tax system) are arranged. In a society with just institutions, there are reasons to believe that people can relate to each other in a different way than under capitalism. Under capitalism, people act in the market based on an idea of maximizing benefits for themselves. In a society with just institutions, people will be less inclined to demand extra pay in order to do their very best. Just institutions will, in other words, change how people relate to each other. The tax system is key to a just system of institutions. Let me illustrate with an example.

Piketty has argued that, when the tax level in the U.S. was 80% for the top incomes, those with highest income did not have very strong incentives to negotiate for even higher pay; much of their salary (including any raise) would disappear in tax anyway. When the taxes were heavily reduced after Reagan in the 1980s, this changed, and top managers with high salaries had increased incentives to push for even higher wages (Piketty 2014, 335, 512). In the same way, one could imagine that, if the background structure keeps inequalities within strictly defined boundaries where those who earn and own the most are only allowed to earn and own *some* more, but not much more than others, the incentives will also change. Demanding much more than others will not get you very much more, and so people will change their demands. In time, one may hope that people also change their way of thinking by living under institutions that promote egalitarian relations. If that were to happen, we would have an example of institutions shaping people's way of thinking and acting.[47]

Thus, behind the focus on institutions, there is a perception that a different society is possible, a society more characterized by solidarity and a sense of community. In this egalitarian society, people relate to each other based on the understanding that they are part of a cooperative enterprise, and not based on pure selfishness. The combination of Rawls and Piketty, in other words, enables us to understand how an egalitarian ethos can be established and maintained through just institutions.[48] Rawls' justification for the two principles of justice provides a good answer to *why* circulation of capital is more just compared to concentration of capital, whereas Piketty's institutional scheme provides an interesting suggestion as to *how* the ideal can be realized.

A second issue were a combination of Rawls and Piketty is powerful is the following: A possible objection to the scheme outlined by Piketty is that it violates property rights. Deontological theories with roots in John Locke have claimed that individuals own themselves and have strong demands on what they modify through their own labour. Deontologists claim that fundamental rights are pre-political, and that the legitimacy of the political system depends on whether the system honors these rights. Deontological theories often support the belief that individuals have rightful claims to something that can be said to be their own, and that the state must provide special justification if it is to levy taxes (Murphy and Nagel 2002, 42). I believe this objection can be answered by combining Rawls and Piketty.

Rawls provides a more limited defence of property rights (compared to the Lockean deontologists). To Rawls, it is crucial that everybody has a "right to hold personal property" (Rawls 1999, 53). This right is essential because it guarantees "a sufficient material basis for personal independence and a sense of self-respect" (Rawls 2001, 114). The possibility of having the opportunity to own one's own home may be seen as a fundamental right. However, the right to own or control the means of production and natural resources cannot be accorded a fundamental status. In Rawls' view, property rights also do not imply the right to bequeath one's assets (Rawls 1996, 298).

On this basis, we may distinguish between a thick and a thin theory of property rights (Persky 2010; see also Brennan and Tomasi 2012). A thick theory of property rights, like the deontological one mentioned above, provides a strong defence of the institution of private property. It does not give full freedom to do as one may please

[47] As Rawls notes, "the social system shapes the wants and aspirations that its citizens come to have. It determines in part the sort of persons they want to be as well as the sort of person they are" (Rawls 1999, 229). We shall return to the question of social system in the final section.

[48] Rawls has been criticized for being exclusively focused on the institutional. G.A. Cohen argued that Rawls' focus on the basic structure made him ignore the importance of how people relate to each other (Cohen 2008). According to Cohen, a just society requires both just institutions and individuals who relate to each other in an egalitarian way. In my view, Cohen is right to insist that a just society must be based both on just institutions and on how people relate to each other. But this view is shared by Rawls. This argument is indebted to Thomas (2017). For a more detailed exposition, see Pedersen (2021a, b, chapter 4).

with one's property, for, as Nozick points out, I am not free to place my knife in your chest (Nozick 1974, 171). What the strong defence of property rights does establish, is that the state cannot put limits on property. Concentration of capital is not seen as something bad. The thin theory of property rights is in line with Rawls' general view of distributive justice, and in my view provides sufficient protection of private property. The thin theory maintains that individuals have an inviolable right to private property, but not to owning natural resources and the means of production. Rawls therefore provides a limited defence of property rights, something that is in line with his view on the negative consequences of a high degree of capital concentration.[49]

Piketty questions the thick theory of property rights through a discussion of how assets are created. It is wrong, according to this line of thinking, to hold that a large amount of wealth is solely created by the individual herself and therefore something that she can claim an exclusive propery right over:

> The idea that strictly private property exists and that certain people have an inviolable natural right to it cannot withstand analysis. The accumulation of wealth is always the fruit of a social process, which depends, among other things, on public infrastructures (such as legal, fiscal and educational systems), the social division of labor, and the knowledge accumulated by humanity over centuries. Under such conditions, it is perfectly logical that people who have accumulated large amounts of wealth should return a fraction of it to the community every year: ownership thus becomes temporary rather than permanent (Piketty 2020, 990).

Permanent ownership relies on a thick theory of private property. This implies that the owners of capital, often the owners of corporations, can decide whom they want to hire and at what wage (Piketty 2020, 971). Furthermore, it gives them the full right to bequeath property and thus to transfer wealth from one generation to another. Inheritance tax and income taxes are mechanisms that limit permanent ownership and the idea of a thick property right. Historically, these measures have been employed. However, according to Piketty, they are necessary, but not sufficient. Therefore, it is necessary to introduce measures for power-sharing in firms and a progressive wealth tax in combination with the other mechanisms we mentioned above to be able to realize the idea of temporary private ownership.

Another issue that allows us to see the strength of a combination of Rawls and Piketty regards the justification of constitutional limits on inequality. Piketty shows that history is full of examples of judges finding progressive taxation to be unconstitutional. One example is Germany where it was decided that it was not allowed according to the constitution to tax more than 50%. Piketty's point is that when history displays such examples, it makes no sense to dismiss the opposite view, that is to have a constitution to secure that inequality is kept in check, or that the tax system cannot be regressive (Piketty 2020, 995–100).

Rawlsian ideas offer a deeper justification to constitutional guarantees against inequality. Imagine the conservative critic claiming that it is wrong to introduce

---

[49] For a recent critique of Rawls' idea of private property, see von Platz (2020). For a defense of Rawls, see Thomas (2020).

constitutional measures against inequality because the level of inequality a society should allow must be decided by ordinary democratic decisions. The Rawlsian reply is that a fundamental idea of a constitutional democracy is that all citizens are free and equal and must be granted equal opportunity to influence democratic decisions. If limiting inequality is a precondition for a well-functioning democratic practice it precludes prioritizing freedom to such an extent that it undermines democracy. Taking the fundamental ideal of citizens as free and equal seriously requires that everyone must be granted the same opportunity to influence political decision-making. If isolation strategies are not a sufficient measure, as I have argued above, the idea of free and equal citizens requires constitutional limits to prevent large inequalities.

Overall, the combination of Rawls and Piketty gives a strong justification for an egalitarian organization of society and that such a society must be ensured by the constitution. It should be added that in both cases the framework established by Rawls and Piketty is in need of interpretation and development. For example, neither of the two conducts, as a far as I can see, a sufficient discussion of whether isolation strategies can succeed in isolating the political processes from the influence of money.[50] Nevertheless, the combination of Rawls and Piketty provides an extremely rich resource for egalitarians.[51]

9.6 Pre- and Redistribution

Piketty's scheme provides, as we have seen, a combination of taxes and other measures in order to establish a more just society. To realize a well-functioning egalitarian society, taxation is not enough. Recently, the distinction between predistribution and rediistribution has received a lot of attention. The distinction has been emphasised to illustrate that the egalitarian needs to focus on a broad set of mechanisms. As Piketty puts it, 'it is at least as essential to look at 'predistribution' policies (which affect primary inequality) as at 'redistribution' policies (which reduce inequality of disposable income for a given level of primary inequality)' (Piketty 2020, 529). Predistribution affects the primary inequalities, or inequalities prior to taxation. However, as we will see, the distinction between predistribution and redistribution is not straight-forward and we have to be careful in applying it.

Predistribution can be seen as analogous to preventative strategies in public health , where one seeks to limit people's smoking and consumption of unhealthy food, so that fewer people will need treatment for COPD or obesity (Gregg 2012).

[50] Rawls is not clear on this crucial issue, and his opinion seems to have changed over time (O'Neill 2012, 81–82). Piketty holds that there is surprisingly little coordination and learning between countries when it comes to how politics can be isolated from the influence of money. See Piketty (2020, 1017–1024) for his treatment of this.

[51] For a more nuanced recent discussion of the relationship between Rawls and Piketty, see O'Neill (2021b).

Similarly, it is necessary to fight pretax inequalities because large inequalities are bad for society , and because there are limits to how much one can reduce inequality with the help of tax mechanisms. As Joseph Stiglitz puts it: 'If we succeed in making market incomes more equal, there is less burden on redistribution' (Stiglitz 2019 quoted by O'Neill 2020b, 65).

Now, what counts as examples of predistribution? Active measures to increase the bargaining power of wage earners has been highlighted as the best way of ensuring income equalization, and reduce what Piketty calls 'primary inequality'. Research from the OECD shows that this kind of measure efficiently equalizes income, while not being detrimental to growth (O'Neill and Williamson 2012b, 5; OECD 2012). The IMF has also recently shown that a decreasing degree of unionisation is strongly correlated with a rise in the highest incomes (Dabla-Norris et al. 2015, 21). Thus, measures to strengthen unions are very important to limit primary inequality.[52]

Another important example is the regulation of minimum wages. A relatively high minimum wage will reduce income inequality (prior to taxation). In the US the minimum wage has been reduced substantially since 1980, and this has significantly diminished the bargaining power of the working class. As Piketty (2020, 531) argues,

> many works have shown that the drop in the minimum wage in the United States contributed strongly to the declining position of low-wage workers since the 1980s in a general climate of decreased worker bargaining power.

With reduced bargaining power, the relative share going to workers is reduced, and income inequalities will increase.

Thus, both a minimum wage and strong union bargaining power can ensure a compressed wage-structure. Different countries rely on different mechanisms. The Nordic countries have, as we have seen, a tradition for wage bargaining, whereas countries such as the UK, Germany and France have tended to rely more on minimum wage (in recent years) (Piketty 2020, 532). Thus, if we want to understand the very high income inequalities in he U.S., we can explain it as a result of three factors: it can be explained as a result of lower taxes, weaker unions and lower minimum wages. The two latter mechanisms are crucial to reduce primary inequality, whereas taxation helps to reduce post tax inequalities.

Other examples of predistribution includes the legal framework for intellectual property (Scanlon 2018, 102). If patents or intellectual property rights held by corporations would have a shorter lifespan than they have today, it would reduce inequality.[53] Widespread use of land value taxation is another example of predistribution (Kerr 2016). This is the taxation of limited natural resources that belong to

---

[52] It should be noted, as Martin O'Neill (2020a, 74–75) has emphasized, that predistributive policies are not necessarily progressive. If a conservative government for example weakens the bargaining power of unions and makes it easier for employers to sack employees, this would reduce the power of labor v. employer, and most likely decompress the pay structure prior to taxation. Such policies would be predistributive in the sense that they would affect distribution of income prior to taxation, but not in a sense that would help an egalitarian agenda.

[53] For an overview of different proposals for predistributive policies see O'Neill (2020a, 65).

the community. Norway's oil policy is an example of a natural resource that has been subject to land value taxation. Instead of selling of the continental shelf, the state issues licences to companies and remains in control of the oil and levies an extra tax on the revenue.[54] Thus, land value taxation ads an additional tax on these resources and will consequently yield more income to the state and reduce the profit going to the companies exploiting the resources.[55]

It is, however, important to see that the distinction between predistribution and redistribution is a complex one. Tax measures can have predistributional effect even though they appear to belong on the redistributional side. And measures that are primarily seen as predistributive can have redistributional effects. Ahlquist (2017) has argued that strong unions contribute to both predistribution and redistribution. Predistribution because strong unions increase worker salaries and reduces executive salaries prior to taxation. Redistribution because union work gives people a form of political experience. Many are drawn into political work, and then often on the left, and a stronger left will normally result in more redistributive taxes.

This example demonstrates, as Martin O'Neill (2020a) have recently shown, that it is difficult to distinguish between predistributive and redistributive *policies*. This is because traditional redistributional measures such as top rate income taxes can have a predistributional effect. As we have seen, very high top tax rates can change how people think. With such measures in place, highly paid workers will be less focused on bargaining for higher salaries.[56] Thus, a classical redistributive policy produces predistributive effects. Because of this difficulty of distinguishing between the two forms of distribution, O'Neill argues in favor of reconstructing the notion of predistribution. Instead of understanding it as different types of policies, it should be understood as different types of aims or effects of policies.

Following O'Neill, we can thus distinguish between predistributive and redistributive policy aims. Some policy aims will be to reduce inequalities prior to taxation. Other policy aims will be to reduce post tax income. Drawing the distinction in this way allows us to recognize that high marginal taxes can have both redistributive and predistributive effects, and this broadens our understanding of how taxation work.

[54] In the Norwegian context there is an ongoing debate of whether the successful recipe of land value taxation on the oil industry can be extended to other natural resources such as wind/hydropower and aquaculture (Brigham and Moses 2021).

[55] The call for predistribution has also reached the realm of practical politics. It was employed for example by Elizabeth Warren in the 2020 US election campaign (O'Neill 2020a, b, 66).

[56] O'Neill calls this the Piketty-Saez-Stancheva effect: "When top marginal rates of income taxation are very high, with a comparatively large gap between gross and net pay at the top end of the distribution, highly paid workers will be less likely to focus on the extrinsic financial rewards of their positions, and focus more on the intrinsic rewards of prestige and authority in large organizations" (O'Neill 2020a, b, 83).

9.7 Murphy and Nagel on Distributive Justice and Taxation

The Myth of Ownership (2002) is, as noted in the introduction, the most important book on taxation written from a political philosophical perspective.[57] The book can be seen as Rawlsian in one sense although it rejects some of Rawls' concrete proposals on taxation: as O'Neill and Williamson put it:

> Although Murphy and Nagel's approach is fully Rawlsian in its structure and assumptions, they strongly dismiss a number of the particular views that Rawls is tempted to endorse: e.g. fairness-based arguments for favoring consumption as the tax base, and the preference for proportional rather than progressive taxes in funding public services (O'Neill and Williamson 2015, 827).

Thus, Murphy and Nagel plainly dismiss those of Rawls' proposals that we have described as puzzling, but they endorse the deeper idea that what we are to distribute is a social product, and the idea that the tax system is one mechanism among many that needs to be considered in a theory of justice.[58]

One of the reasons for the importance of *The Myth of Ownership* is that it challenges some ideas held by many people that are of particular importance to taxation. I cannot do justice to all the themes discussed in the book but will simply focus on three related issues. The idea of *pre-tax income* as it is understood in what Murphy and Nagel calls *everyday libertarianism*, and the claim that discussions on the justice of taxation policy should not be *myopic*. I shall present these themes here, and in the next section I will highlight an example that demonstrates how these concepts can be used to understand different egalitarian positions regarding tax justice.

What, then, is pre-tax income, and what role does pre-tax income play in a theory of just distribution? Your paycheck states how much you earn before taxes. Does that mean that pre-tax income is an actual thing? Murphy and Nagel deny that it is. They think pre-tax income is a myth. How can they claim that, given that pre-tax income is listed on everyone's paycheck?[59]

The basic claim is as follows: Pre-tax income may exist as a concept in accounting, but that does not mean that it should be ascribed normative value (Murphy and Nagel 2002, 36). That is, pre-tax income cannot be used to figure out how much it is just to pay in tax. Or, to put it differently: The concept of pre-tax income should not be given a significant role in determining what constitutes just taxation. The importance of pre-tax income is closely connected to everyday libertarianism.

Everyday libertarianism is a light-version of the theory of justice from which it derives. It is a view that has significant political influence, in particular on matters of tax justice.

The core of everyday libertarianism can be reconstructed through five steps:

---

[57] This section draws on Pedersen 2021a, chapter 8.

[58] For a brief statement on how the approach taken by Murphy and Nagel can be seen as broadly Rawlsian, see O'Neill and Orr (2018).

[59] This way of framing the question is inspired by Zelenak (2003).

1. We have a tendency to think that what we have earned belongs to us. Our net income is ours, in an original sense (even though value added tax is a limitation on this).
2. Therefore, politicians can trick people into thinking that increased taxes involve taking something that is rightfully theirs.
3. From this, it is but a short jump to the corresponding idea that tax cuts return to us "our own money".
4. Thus, the idea that the taxes we pay really belong to us.
5. Finally, this leads to the thought that we have a rightful claim to our pre-tax income (Murphy and Nagel 2002, 35).

Even though few people think that all taxation is bad because it takes away "my money", many think that the state, through taxation, take something that actually belongs to them. Here, the idea of pre-tax income plays an important role.

Murphy and Nagel hold that pre-tax income is a myth, and that everyday libertarianism is fundamentally confused. Pre-tax income is income in the absence of tax. But in the absence of tax, there is no state, and in the absence of a state, there is no market (in the modern sense).[60] In the absence of a market, there is no income. Therefore, pre-tax income is a myth (Murphy and Nagel 2002, 32). However, pre-tax income is not an innocent myth. It perverts many people's understandings of what is just, and is tied, in particular, to everyday libertarianism.

The problem with everyday libertarianism is that in part it rests on a logical fallacy, and that in part the assumption about the justness of market outcomes is wrong. First to the logical fallacy: libertarianism states that people have rights to their pre-tax income. However, since there can be no market (in the modern sense) without a state, and since there can be no state without taxes, it is "logically impossible that people should have any kind of entitlement to all their pre-tax income" (Murphy and Nagel 2002, 32). Without a legal/judicial system—which must be financed by taxes—it is hard to imagine a well-functioning market economy.

Specifically, without a legal/judicial system, it is hard to imagine the existence of the kinds of institutions that are indispensable for a modern market economy: money, banks, corporations, stock exchanges, and so on. Without a legal/judicial system, meaning, in practice, a state, it is, put briefly, impossible to have an income. From this it follows that one cannot evaluate the justness of a given tax on the basis of pre-tax income.

Second, consider the claim that market outcomes are just. By market outcomes, we here mean the outcomes of an unregulated market. There are mainly two arguments that are used to justify the claim that the outcomes of an unregulated market are just. The first is that market outcomes are just because they give people what

[60] Murphy and Nagel do not themselves employ the distinction between simple and modern markets. However, because it is likely that there may have existed forms of barter between individuals independently of any state, I think this clarification is necessary. That said, the fact that there may historically have been state-independent markets does not affect the normative question with which we are here concerned. It does not justify any claim that we have a right to our pre-tax income.

they deserve. I cannot discuss this in dept here, but simply note that market outcomes are affected by arbitrary factors such as genetic and social luck, and hence cannot be deserved. The second argument—which is the argument of the libertarian—is that market outcomes are just because they give people what they are entitled to. This argument builds on the view that voluntary transactions are just. But, as G.A. Cohen has argued, voluntary transactions can affect third parties who have no say in the transaction (Cohen 1995, 26–27). Thus, voluntariness is not a sufficient condition for justice, and this is an important argument against the view that the outcomes of an unregulated market are just.[61]

These theoretical considerations about market outcomes can also be supported by common sense. Just think about how arbitrary the distribution provided by the market may be. If a real estate broker earns 10 times more than a medical doctor trying to cure Alzheimer's disease, one may point to supply and demand as a justification. However, there are no good reasons to assume that what follows from supply and demand is just. Or, to use an example that frequently crops up in debates on just wages, one may think it unjust that certain business executives earn more than the prime minister (the "executive" of the whole country). It is difficult to see what good reasons there are for saying that people have a rightful claim to whatever the market gives them. Market outcomes rest on a whole range of arbitrary factors, and hence are not just. Therefore, discussion of just taxation must be freed from everyday libertarianism, which implicitly presupposes that the distribution created by the market is just, and hence that all departures from this distribution must be justified (Murphy and Nagel 2002, 36).

To Murphy and Nagel, the state is a precondition for any market in the modern sense. There are no markets, and there can be no markets that are not framed and regulated by a state-sanctioned set of rules. Therefore, the "logical order of priority between taxes and property rights is the reverse of what assumed by libertarianism" (Murphy and Nagel 2002, 33). Pre-tax income, is, as we have already seen, a fictitious entity that is morally irrelevant (Murphy and Nagel 2002, 99).

Let me try to clarify. Discussing justice in taxation is a complex matter. People work and produce goods and services and then the state comes in and demands a part of it. If people do not comply, the state will use its machinery to force them to comply. From this perspective, it is no surprise that many people are hostile to taxation. What Murphy and Nagel ask us to consider is whether this picture is correct. If people instead were to consider how much of what they do in their daily life has been made possible because of taxation, the hostility might change: when I go to work, the roads and pavements I walk on, the fact that the colleagues I work with are healthy and able to work, and the fact that they are educated is all made possible through taxation (Barry and Halliday: podcast). Without all of this, I would not be able to produce much, and my own and my fellow citizens' well-being would be reduced. Instead of the hostility towards the state that is characteristic of everyday

[61] I cannot provide a full discussion of these two arguments here. For discussion, see Olsaretti (2004), and for a brief statement, see Murphy (2019, 8).

libertarianism, the state should be seen as what enables us to have an income, and more generally, for individuals to have a prosperous life.

We can therefore distinguish between the following ways of framing questions about justice in taxation: The libertarian asks: "How much of what is mine should be taken from me to support public services or to be given to others?" The egalitarian asks: "How should the tax system divide the social product between the private control of individuals and goverment control, and what factors should it cause or permit to determine who ends up with what?" (Murphy and Nagel 2002, 175–176).

Now consider how discussions of tax justice are often myopic: It is often the case that taxes are discussed without mentioning how the proceeds are used. In contrast to this, Murphy and Nagel hold that one cannot discuss just taxation without taking into consideration the distribution of the services of the state. The question of whether a given tax is just or not cannot be separated from how the state uses the income generated by this tax. "It seems clear", write Murphy and Nagel, "that a tax burden that is matched by an equivalent transfer is not, in the relevant sense, a burden at all" (Murphy and Nagel 2002, 14). Taxes therefore cannot be evaluated in isolation—that is without taking into consideration the services provided in return by the state—when we are concerned with evaluating whether they are just. What matters from the perspective of justice is whether the services of the state and the state's collection of taxes are just when seen under one. This point is similarly put by Piketty: "Taxation is neither good nor bad in itself. Everything depends on how taxes are collected and what they are used for" (Piketty 2014, 481).

If we are not to discuss tax based on pre-tax income, and also cannot discuss tax without including the services provided by the state, what then should we discuss? What we should discuss is what people are left with after taxation including state transfers and services, and whether this is just. Murphy and Nagel therefore think that we must leave behind the narrow discussion of what constitutes just tax, and replace this with a comprehensive perspective on justice: 'Our main message throughout this book has been that societal fairness, rather than tax fairness, should be the value that guides tax policy' (Murphy and Nagel 2002, 173). If we discuss what people should be left with after tax, we have entered the general debate about justice, and it is more important to tackle this debate than to continue the debate on false premises.

9.8 Controversies Within the Egalitarian Camp

In this section, I will include discussions where egalitarians express differences when it comes to taxation. This includes the related issues of progressivity and the distribution of tax burdens. In debates about these issues there seems to be different approaches taken by egalitarian philosophers and egalitarian economists. Recently, Saez and Zucman's book *The Triumph of Injustice* demonstrated that the American tax system is flat or even regressive. Their research showed that the extremely rich pay a lower percentage of their income compared to everybody else (Saez and

Zucman 2019a, xi, 14). Is this, in itself, an instance of injustice? Saez and Zucman argue that it is, and this might intuitively resonate with how most people think. However, when confronted with the framework from *The Myth of Ownership*, the picture becomes more complex.

To see this, suppose that you have a tax system that is regressive, but to compensate for this you introduce cash grants and a number of other public policies to the benefit of low-income groups. The net effect is that the welfare of the low-income group is better than any alterative system. Is the overall system still unjust simply because of the regressive tax system? If we follow the line of reasoning taken by Murphy and Nagel, concluding with a yes to this question would be an example of myopia as introduced in the previous section. It would be, in other words, to conclude that the system is unjust without considering the totality of the issue. To conclude that the American tax system is unjust we need to study not just the progressivity of the tax system, but also the services provided by the state and the various measures employed to regulate what Piketty called "primary inequality". Only in this way will it be possible to conclude whether the American system as a whole is just.

Saez and Zucman's approach is motivated partially by how central institutions like the IMF and the World Bank act when it comes to tax policy. These institutions, according to the authors, insist that it does not matter how progressive the tax system is: "how taxes are levied is irrelevant, collecting revenue is what matters" (Saez and Zucman 2019a, 177). In practice, revenue has been collected using value added taxes, and progressive income taxes, inheritance taxes and wealth taxes has been reduced. The effect is that the tax system is regressive. Saez and Zucman contend that even though this way of generating revenue is not without merit, it comes with a large cost. It comes with a cost because it undermines an idea of societal development where burdens are shared in an equitable way:

> Development is not primarily a matter of mechanically collecting taxes to fund spending, no matter how useful this spending may be. Development is about building trust in institutions, including, most importantly, governments. When governments take more from the poor than from the wealthy, sustained trust becomes impossible (Saez and Zucman 2019a, 177–178).

According to Saez and Zucman, when governments collect a larger share from the poor than they do from the wealthy, there is an imminent danger of tax revolts like the one we have seen with the yellow vest movement in France (Saez and Zucman 2019a, 178). As a consequence of their approach, they formulate their critique as saying that the U.S. is unjust because it has a flat or regressive tax system.

What is at stake here? Is it wrong to conclude that a regressive tax system is unjust? In principle, Murphy and Nagel are correct to insist that questions regarding justice in America must involve a holistic perspective and take societal justice into account. This implies that when justice in America is the topic, it is necessary to go beyond the tax system and look at the public policies outside the tax system itself. In practice, it is likely that Saez and Zucman presupposes that the policies in the U.S. are insufficient to counter the inegalitarian tendency in the tax system. They should have made this point explicitly, but their criticism of the IMF and the World Bank is likely to be valid even though they have not examined all the public policies employed in combination with the tax system. This should remind egalitarians to be careful when claims about justice in a country are introduced. Simply put; justice is different from tax justice.

Now consider how Murphy and Nagel's framework applies to the notion of a fair distribution of the tax burden. We have seen that the authors argue that pre-tax income is of no moral importance. The problem with the idea of a fair distribution of the tax burden is that it presupposes that it makes sense to start out with pre-tax income and move from there to what is a fair distribution. But if pre-tax income is "morally arbitrary" (Murphy and Nagel 2002, 30), it cannot be used as a baseline to determine what a fair distribution of the tax burden consists of. If we say that Tom the carpenter's tax burden is unjustly too high, we normally mean that he pays to much measured against his pre-tax income. But if pre-tax income is a myth, it makes no sense to dismiss Tom's tax burdens as unjust. This enforces the conclusion that we have to give up talking about tax justice and move to societal justice instead.

To Murphy, the approach taken by Saez and Zucman is an example of an analysis that makes a mistake both when it comes to being myopic and in its talk about unjust burdens:

> Justice in taxation is not a matter of some fair distribution of tax burdens as measured against pretax income. It is about how well or badly the tax system, together with the other elements of the economic and welfare system secures just results... Even if Saez and Zucman are right that we now have a flat effective tax rate, that is not necessarily a sign of unfairness or injustice. Such a tax scheme, coupled with very significant tax grants, could in principle be part of an overall just approach. The distribution of tax burdens is important only insofar as it is informative for policy makers thinking about how taxes can play their part in overall social policy aimed at making our society more just (Murphy 2019, 4).

According to this logic, it would be wrong to talk about Tom the carpenter as someone who suffers from injustice because he pays a larger share of tax compared to the rich owner of the company he works for. To make such all things considered claims about whether there is injustice we must disregard Tom's tax burden and compare his overall welfare level with the overall welfare level enjoyed by his boss.[62]

This demonstrates that there might be a conflict between the holistic perspective required to make claims about justice, and the more limited claims that address tax justice. For practical political purposes it might be extremely difficult to engage the public in the holistic debate about societal fairness. This point has been recognized by Sugin. In her discussion of Murphy and Nagel she argues that

> On the one hand, their insistence that pre-tax market outcomes provide individuals with no presumptive ownership claims lowers the bar for arguments in favor of taxation of all kinds. Without such presumption in the way, we only need to make arguments about the desirability of a tax according to whatever theory we believe most persuasive, whether it be Rawlsian, utilitarian, or even religious. But at the same time, the demands of their analysis

[62] Martin O'Neill (2020b) has argued in a similar way that Saez and Zucman's focus is to narrow on tax issues.

> to treat the tax system as one component in a larger, integrated scheme of distributive justice subordinates the tax system and weakens its institutional role…The irony of Murphy and Nagel's argument is that in their concern for distributive justice, they possibly discount the one real-world tool that is regularly employed toward achieving it (Sugin 2004, 2014).

Tax fairness and tax burden are topics the public can identify with. If we cannot speak about tax burdens, the practical political consequence could be that it would be even harder to achieve social justice.

If this claim is correct, it enforces the point made earlier; that we have to discuss the role of political philosophy and how it should relate to matters of practical-political concerns. To simplify, we must ask whether political philosophers should figure out what justice is, or whether political philosophers should instead focus on how to bring about justice in a feasible way. I cannot, however, address this complex issue in this chapter.[63]

9.9 Social Egalitarianism, Taxation, the State, and the Individual

According to the broadly Rawlsian perspective we have studied here –a perspective that encompasses Piketty and Murphy & Nagel—distributive justice concerns the just distribution of a collectively manufactured product. Recall that for Rawls "the idea of society as a fair system of cooperation over time from one generation to the next" is "the most fundamental idea" of justice as fairness (Rawls 2001, 5). At this point it makes sense to revisit this fundamental idea.

The way Rawls sees it, questions of justice arise from the conflicts of interests in a society with moderate scarcity of goods. In such a situation, people will realize that cooperation pays, because through cooperating it is possible to produce more than individuals could do on their own. By dividing different tasks between them, so that some become specialists in producing one kind of good, and others become specialists in producing another good, the total amounts of goods in society increase. At the same time, this perspective on society makes it clear that people are dependent on each other, both when it comes to people in the same generation, and when it comes to the productions and innovations of previous generations. Through division of labor, and by using natural resources and infrastructure generated over centuries the net sum of what is produced in society is dramatically increased. This cooperation yields a *social product*, and it is how we are to distribute this product that is the correct question to ask when discussing distributive justice.

According to this understanding of society, the state cannot be seen as a hindrance, but rather as a precondition for a well-functioning economy. Through taxation and other measures, the state coordinates and ensures a framework for a modern

[63] For an excellent discussion of the different roles political philosophers can play, see Stemplowska and Swift (2012).

market and allows individuals the opportunity to have an income. Cooperation yields a social product to be divided by the cooperative members of society. Taxation coordinated by the state will play a key role in the distribution of this social product. Thus, the egalitarian theories we have examined here share the opinion that regulations by the state are necessary to allow a society where individuals are allowed to flourish.

Still, we should ask what more the state should be expected to do, and what role the state should play in facilitating individual flourishing. One major difference between egalitarians and their conservative or libertarian critics is that the former holds that a big state is necessary to avoid some individuals (the rich) to control and dominate the rest of society. The conservative or libertarian critics tend to be more afraid of the domination of the state over its subjects. Their fear is that the state will dominate the individuals in a way that undermines individual freedom (Thomas 2020, 115). Since the 1980s, and in various ways, progressive politicians have followed their conservative or libertarian counterparts and distanced themselves from the state as a proper tool for solving the main challenges of our time. Bill Clinton's "the era of big government is over" (1996) epitomized this shift. Increasingly, the market was seen as the preferred problem solver and business, not politics became the place to be for people who wanted to change the world (Giridharadas 2019, 18–20). Instead of being seen as the instrumental force for a good society, as Murphy and Nagel argue, the state has been portrayed as inefficient and old fashioned.

Against this background we should ask whether a well-functioning democratic society requires a big state, a state that provides health care, education and childcare? Should the state play a key role regarding work and industrial policy by directing investment and other kinds of macroeconomic planning? Answering these questions will help to address what relationship egalitarians would support when it comes to the relationship that should exist between citizen and state, and in answering what role taxation should play in this relationship.

In a recent attempt to address these questions, several prominent social egalitarians have defended the need for a big state. Social egalitarians should, they argue, resist the conservative claim that what a just society requires is a big society and a small state. This, they claim, is the wrong way to go. Instead

> the answer of how to create a just society is to have a *big state*: a state that ensures none are dominated, marginalized or oppressed, and one that expresses respect for its citizens by providing them with high-quality benefits, goods and services on a footing of equality (McTernan et al. 138–139, emphasis in the original).

To social egalitarians, it is crucial that no member of society must be dominated by others and to ensure that all relate to each other as equals. This requires, as we have seen, that there are limits to how much wealth the richest people can control. However, it also requires that markets be shaped by the state. Public services are a way of shaping the market, and it is important to see how the goods and services provided by a robust welfare state play a crucial role in such market-shaping. When the state provides universal access to health care services, it simultaneously provides employees with a condition necessary to meet employers on an equal footing.

To see this, consider an example introduced by Martin O'Neill. Imagine first an employer in a country where health care services are organized through private insurances. In this system the employees' health care services are tied to their employment status, and the employer functions as a gatekeeper with the opportunity to decide what access employees will have to better health insurance plans. In this scenario, the workers are dominated by the employer in the sense that they do not feel free to criticize working conditions in their workplace. Their destiny is, in a sense, in the hands of the employer. If they were to lose their job, they would find themselves without provision of health care services, and thus to be in a very difficult situation. In a different system, with tax funded public provision of good health care services, the employee's situation is different. The cost of losing their job is much lower, and thus they are not as afraid of criticizing conditions at their workplace, and not as afraid of losing their jobs. In short, the employees' bargaining power is much better in a system with a welfare state supplying universal health care and other services (O'Neill 2020a, b, 76–77).

The social egalitarian ideal of equality where no one is dominated by others requires public services to allow employees to bargain with employers on equal terms. If employees are secured public provision of health services and a number of other goods, they can enter the negotiations with their employers with a confidence they would not have in a society with a weak state. As O'Neill puts it:

> The tax funded provision of public services is not of interest to progressives or egalitarians *only* because it is directly a way of benefiting everyone at a cost that falls disproportionally on those who have more, but *also* because of second-round effects that the provision of public services can have in terms of the structure and distribution of power in economic relationship within that society. The public provision of services such as health care, education and childcare, or even provision of goods such as transportation and public parks, creates the background conditions against which different groups and different sectional interests fight their corner and negotiate their economic relationships (O'Neill 2020a, b, 77, emphasis in the original).

Thus, it is crucial to have a state that can facilitate relations of non-dominance. This requires provisions of a number of public goods to allow employees to negotiate from a position of security and confidence.[64]

We can now turn to our second question. What role should the egalitarian state play when it comes to work and industrial policy? This question is increasingly discussed with reference to the various crises the world has experienced recently. The inequality crisis, global warming and most recently Covid 19 have made it necessary to rethink what role the state should occupy in solving the most pressing problems of our time.

Many (egalitarian) commentators have turned to history for guidance in times of crises. To combat climate change, growing unemployment and the increasing gap between the rich and the poor, the argument is that an updated version of Franklin

---

[64] We could be facing a shift towards a bigger state in practical politics as well. As Robert Reich has argued, President Clinton's claim that "The era of big government is over" is currently being challenged by President Biden (Reich 2021).

D. Roosevelt's New Deal is called for (Guinan and O'Neill 2020; Sachs et al. 2020; Mazzucato et al. 2021). Roosevelt's radical reforms were designed to solve the crisis in the interwar period through massive public investments to build infrastructure, create jobs and increase the net income of the worst off. In 2021 this comes in the form of various calls for *Green* New Deals. I shall highlight two proposals to face the current crisis by calling for a more active state.

In a recent proposal for a new industrial strategy for Norway, Mariana Mazzucato and her cowriters (Mazzacuto et al. 2021, 9–10) presented a plan for how Norway can take the economy through a green transformation. Norway is a rich oil producing country with the world's largest sovereign wealth fund. The expected lowered demand for petroleum will reduce revenue and reduce demand for the technological expertise Norway has in the petroleum industry. To face this challenge, the suggestion is to turn Norway into a green giant where the sovereign wealth fund is employed and where the technological expertise shifts from petroleum to renewable energy production. The proposal contains the following factors:

- A green industrial investment bank.
- A Norwegian bank for sustainable international cooperation.
- A mission-oriented policy for state-owned enterprise.[65]
- To take Equinor (the largest oil company) off the stock market and make it a mission-oriented state-owned company.
- Establish a green industrial state holding company.

The purpose of the proposal is to allow "the state take on an active role in investing and coordinating the shift from a fossil-driven to a green engine in the Norwegian economy" (Mazzucato et al. 2021, 9). Through and active state, policymakers will have the opportunity to determine the direction of growth and to ensure industrial innovation to create new green jobs in a changing market. Such a state-led process also involves an alteration of how to distribute the profits "As the state contributes capital and workers contribute labour to the innovation process, such stakeholders should also participate in sharing the rewards" (Mazzucato et al. 2021, 20).

The second proposal develops the idea of a state holding company. Discussing how it is possible to rebuild the economy in the UK after Covid 19, Joe Guinan and Martin O'Neill warn against increasing inequality as many small or medium enterprises are likely to struggle and could be overtaken by larger firms. To ensure a recovery for everyone and not only for big firms, the suggestion is to look to FDR's proposal of a Reconstruction Finance Corporation. A state holding company should support small and medium enterprises to get through the crisis, and

> later, where appropriate, this holding company could relaunch many of these rescued businesses under conditions of worker or community ownership or mission-driven social

[65] President Kennedy's moonshot is seen as key example of a mission-oriented policy. It is argued that to enable the green transition, it is necessary to learn from previous examples and to see that for the green shift, "The role of the state is key… since it is the only institution with the power to shape markets and direct economic activity in socially desirable directions" (Mazzucato et al. 2021, 19).

enterprises. In this way, the holding company could become an important instrument in a green transition, building community wealth by supporting local economic activity (Guinan and O'Neill 2020).

Thus, it is claimed that a public holding company could reduce the negative economic effects of the Covid crisis, assist the green transition and reduce inequality.

What these two proposals have in common is a call for a more active state in order to solve the various crises currently facing every country on the planet. To return to the social egalitarian justification for such a state, it is crucial that measures are taken to avoid marginalization and domination of vulnerable individuals. Thus, the state can be seen as crucial in times of crisis where it is necessary to create new stable jobs and through other measures make sure that the burden of the crisis is not put on the shoulders of those who are worst off:

> A big state managing structural change… and providing its citizens opportunities to escape unemployment, marginal employment and precariousness, would be one that takes its responsibility for their life time prospects seriously. It would not do so by regarding them as passive victims dependent on continuous assistance, but would express respect by actively providing them with secure opportunities to make something out of their lives and to live as active economic agents under conditions of greater social equality (McTernan et al. 2016, 142).

Thus, we might say that according to the social egalitarian ideal, the big state coexists with strong and independent individuals. Or, to put it even stronger, *only* the big state allows for *everyone* to be strong and independent individuals.[66] I shall not discuss this further here but move to discuss a closely related question I have postponed from earlier sections: the choice of social system.

9.10 The Choice of Social System

In this final section we shall return to the question of what social system is best suited to realize justice. This question is the main problem of distributive justice according to Rawls (Rawls 1999, 242; 2001, 135–136; Freeman 2013, 9). Our focus on egalitarianism and taxation points towards this question. As we have seen, the various tax schemes and other mechanisms suggested by Rawls and Piketty are designed to transcend the currently existing social system. In other words, investigating the debate on the choice of social system is to investigate what the ultimate

[66] An interesting objection put to me by Robert van Brederode is how individuals can be independent when they rely on the state to create opportunities for them. I cannot discuss this in depth here, but one way to respond is that the state must be assumed to be a well-functioning state that is democratically controlled by the individuals. If this is the case, the state should be seen as part of the individual and therefore not something that will dominate them or make them dependent on the state in a problematic way. Although this idea will seem naïve in some contexts, the high level of trust that individuals have towards governments in the Scandinavian countries shows that it is possible to have a big state without jeopardizing individual freedom.

goal of the tax system and the other distributive mechanisms have. I shall therefore conclude with a brief discussion of what social system should follow from Rawls and Piketty's approach and focus particularly on the question of what makes a social system stable. This question of stability should be seen in the context of Piketty's warning against a drift to oligarchy. I will first examine the most important discussions among Rawlsians, and subsequently situate Piketty's proposal for participatory socialism within this debate.

As we have seen, Rawls regards liberal socialism and property-owning democracy as the two social systems able to realize his two principles of justice. Both systems are liberal constitutional democratic alternatives to capitalism. Both guarantee the fair value of the political liberties, and both regime types will provide everyone with educational opportunities, disperse wealth and guarantee the right to hold personal private property (Edmundson 2017, 133–134).

The fact that Rawls wrote more about property-owning democracy compared to liberal socialism does not mean that the question about what would best realize justice is settled for him. On the contrary, Rawls emphasized that the choice between these two regime types must be based on contextual knowledge of a particular society's "historical circumstances" as well as its "traditions of political thoughts and practice" (Rawls 2001, 139). Thus, Rawls leaves it open what kind of regime would best realize his two principles.

Two of the most prominent participants in the debate on social systems, Alan Thomas and William A. Edmundson agree that Rawls' agnosticism when it comes to the choice of a social system is wrong. However, they disagree when it comes to what social system best realizes justice as fairness. Thomas (2017) defends property-owning democracy whereas Edmundson (2017) defends liberal socialism.

Thomas maintains that to ensure that the two principles are fulfilled it is necessary of institutional arrangements "to guarantee universal access to capital to all citizens and to put in place mechanisms for its wide dispersal on an ongoing basis" (Thomas 2017, 135). Furthermore, to avoid a drift to oligarchy it is necessary for these mechanisms to be constitutionalized. Defenders of property-owning democracy thus allow private ownership of the means of production but demand that measures to disperse capital must be safeguarded by the constitution to avoid capital interests from gradually taking control of politics.

On Edmundson's account, liberal socialism is better equipped to secure stability and avoid a drift to oligarchy. According to Edmundson, what makes socialism distinct is public ownership over the means of production. He defines the major means of production to be

> those areas that most citizens, most of the time, must have access to in order to be productive, cooperative members of society, and are therefore likely to be unfair to allot to any private person or entity as a source of rent (Edmundson 2017, 42).

Important examples most liberal socialists would agree on would include the financial sector and major industries. Alternatively, a more nuanced view would include banking, insurance, railroads and energy companies, as well as real estate and a number of other factors as belonging to the major means of production. According to Edmundson, Rawls' position on liberal socialism is that the *major* means of production must be publicly owned under such a scheme. Small-scale production would not have to be publicly owned (Edmundson 2017, 39–40).

Defenders of liberal socialism agree with property-owning democrats that there will always be a danger of a drift to oligarchy if you do not constitutionalize measures to disperse capital. However, they defend liberal socialism as the best way to secure Rawlsian justice, arguing that it is necessary to have "constitutionally entrenched joint ownership of the major means of production" (Edmundson 2017, 152; see also Holt 2017). The argument has to do with stability. For a constitutional regime to be stable, it is necessary that it takes divisive issues off the agenda as much as possible. Edmundson calls this the reconciliation requirement. Liberal socialism does better than property-owning democracy because it takes one such issue, namely the issue of public ownership of the major means of production off the agenda. Property-owning democracy risks instability because it leaves the question of ownership of the means of production to majoritarian decision. Hence, the reconciliation requirement appears to favor liberal socialism (Edmundson 2017, 143).[67]

Piketty employs the term participatory socialism to describe his own position but adds that the substance of his proposal is more important than the label employed to describe it (Piketty 2020, 970). Is his defense of a particular version of socialism able to illuminate the debate? The first step in answering that question is to ask another question. Is Piketty a socialist? If socialism is defined as Edmundson suggests, then clearly, the answer is no. Piketty does not suggest that the state must own the major means of production. Instead, his version of socialism is defined through circulation of capital.[68] We should therefor ask whether it makes sense to define socialism exclusively with reference to who owns the means of production. The answer is no. Socialism is a multifaceted tradition with a long history with divergent answers to what its core idea(s) consists of. Socialism is also often defined as a system realizing democracy at the workplace. Defined in this way, socialism replaces a system where decisions are made by the employer (capitalism), with a system where decisions are made democratically by the employees (socialism). Piketty does not argue in favor of full democracy at the workplace. But his proposal suggests a way to democratize the workplace to give employees increased influence on their own lives and to reduce inequality. Thus, if we use this definition of socialism, it makes more sense to argue that Piketty is a socialist (cf. O'Neill 2021a).

The discussion between defenders of property-owning democracy and liberal socialism raises interesting philosophical questions but does not have to be framed as an either-or question (cf. Thomas 2017, 216). As Jackson and O'Neill have argued, Meade was in favor of a hybrid egalitarian strategy which combined elements from the capitalist welfare state with that of property-owning democracy and liberal socialism. Such a hybrid strategy would include increased joint ownership as

[67] Note that Edmundson's argument is more complex than the simplified version I have presented here.

[68] One interesting question following from Piketty's position is whether circulation of capital is sufficient to abolish economic class hierarchy.

well as comprehensive welfare state measures combined with wide dispersal of private property (Jackson 2012, 46; O'Neill 2021a).[69] If such a hybrid strategy also includes a strict isolation strategy, there is no decisive evidence to conclude that such a society would necessarily drift to oligarchy. Piketty has demonstrated that existing versions of social democracy have an inbuilt tendency for growing inequalities. However, a property-owning democracy or a hybrid egalitarian society like the one envisaged by Meade has never existed. Whether such a society can be stable cannot be precluded.

References

Ahlquist, John S. 2017. Labor Unions, Political Representation, and Economic Inequality. *Annual Review of Political Science* 20: 409–432.

Anderson, Elizabeth. 1999. What Is the Point of Equality? *Ethics* 109 (2): 287–337.

Anderson, Elizabeth, Ben Jackson, and Anne Phillips. 2014. A World Turned Upside Down: Social Hierarchies and a New History of Egalitarianism. *Juncture* 20 (4): 258–267.

Arneson, Richard J.2013. Egalitarianism. In *The Stanford Encyclopedia of Philosophy* (Summer 2013 Edition), ed. Edward N. Zalta. http://plato.stanford.edu/archives/sum2013/entries/egalitarianism/.

Barry, Brian. 2005. *Why Social Justice Matters*. Cambridge: Polity Press.

Barry, Nicholas. 2020. Luck Egalitarianism and Inherited Wealth. *Law, Ethics and Philosophy* 8: 42–57.

Barry, Christian, and Dan Halliday. (podcast) Equality. In *Dialogues*, a series of podcasts on ethics.

Brennan, Jason, and John Tomasi. 2012. Classical Liberalism. In *The Oxford Handbook of Political Philosophy*, ed. David Estlund. Oxford: Oxford University Press.

Brigham, Anne Margrethe, and Jonathan W. Moses. 2021. Den nye oljen. *Norsk statsvitenskapelig tidsskrift* 37 (1): 4–25.

Brighouse, Harry, and Adam Swift. 2014. *Family Values*. Princeton: Princeton University Press.

Cappelen, Cornelius, and Jørgen Pedersen. 2018. Just Wealth Transfer Taxation: Defending John Stuart Mill's Scheme. *Politics, Philosophy & Economics* 17 (3): 317–335.

Cohen, G.A. 1995. *Self Ownership, Freedom and Equality*. Cambridge: Cambridge University Press.

———. 2008. *Rescuing Justice and Inequality*. Cambridge, MA: Harvard University Press.

Dabla-Norris, Era, et al. 2015. *Causes and Consequences of Income Inequality: A Global Perspective*, IMF SDN 15/13. Ottawa: International Monetary Fund.

Daniels, Norman. 1975. Equal Liberty and the Unequal Worth of Liberty. In *Reading Rawls. Critical Studies of a Theory of Justice*, ed. Norman Daniels. Oxford: Blackwell.

Dietsch, Peter. 2015. *Catching Capital. The Ethics of International Tax Competition*. New York: Oxford University Press.

Duff, David G. 2016. Tax Policy and the Virtuous Sovereign: Dworkinian Equality and Redistributive Taxation. Downloaded from: http://commons.allard.ubc.ca/cgi/viewcontent.cgi?article=1120&context=fac_pubs.

Dworkin, Ronald. 2000. *Sovereign Virtue. The Theory and Practice of Equality*. Cambridge, MA: Harvard University Press.

Edmundson, William A. 2017. *John Rawls: Reticent Socialist*. Cambridge: Cambridge Winners University Press.

[69] However, as Jackson has argued, Meade's own view was closer to Rawls' understanding of liberal socialism than to property-owning democracy (Jackson 2012, 46).

Fleurbaey, Marc. 2021. Economics and Economic Justice. *The Stanford Encyclopedia of Philosophy* (Summer 2021 Edition), ed. Edward N. Zalta. Available at: https://plato.stanford.edu/archives/sum2021/entries/economic-justice/.

Frank, Robert. 2019. Billionaires hurt economic growth and should be taxed out of existence, says bestselling French economist. *CNBC*, 12.09.2019. Downloaded from: Billionaires should be taxed out of existence, says Thomas Piketty (cnbc.com).

Freeman, Samuel. 2007. *Rawls*. London: Routledge.

———. 2013. Property-Owning Democracy and the Difference Principle. *Analyse & Kritik* 1: 9–36.

Fried, Barbara H. 1999. The Puzzling Case for Proportionate Taxation. *Chapman Law Review* 2: 157–195.

———. 2000. Compared to what: Taxing Brute Luck and Other Second-Best Problems. *Tax Law Review* 53 (3): 377–396.

Giridharadas, Anand. 2019. *Winners Take All: The Elite Charade of Changing the World*. London: Penguin Books.

Gregg, Paul. 2012. Predistribution Opens up a New Set of Policy Tools But Also a Key Constraint. *Policy Network*, 25 September.

Guinan, Joe, and Martin O'Neill. 2020. Only Bold State Intervention Will Save Us from a Future Owned by Corporate Giants. *The Guardian*. 06.07.2020. Downloaded from: https://www.theguardian.com/commentisfree/2020/jul/06/state-intervention-amazon-recovery-covid-19.

Hacker, Jacob S. 2011. The Institutional Foundations of Middle-Class Democracy. *Policy Network*, 06.05.2011.

Halliday, Daniel. 2013. Justice and Taxation. *Philosophy Compass* 8 (12): 1111–1122.

———. 2015. Egalitarianism and Consumption Tax. In *Philosophical Explorations of Justice and Taxation*, ed. Helmut P. Gaisbauer et al. Cham: Springer.

———. 2016. Inheritance and Hypothetical Insurance. In *The Legacy of Ronald Dworkin*, ed. W. Waluchow and S. Sciaraffa. New York: Oxford University Press.

———. 2018. *The Inheritance of Wealth. Justice, Equality and the Right to Bequeath*. Oxford: Oxford University Press.

Hirose, Iwao. 2015. *Egalitarianism*. London: Routledge.

Holt, Justin P. 2017. The Requirements of Justice and Liberal Socialism. *Analyse & Kritik* 39: 171–194.

Holtug, Nils. 2003. Politisk Filosofi. In *Engelsk og Amerikansk filosofi*, ed. Poul Lübcke. København: Politikens Forlag.

Jackson, Ben. 2012. Property-Owning Democracy: A Short History. In *Property-Owning Democracy. Rawls and Beyond*, ed. Martin O'Neill and Thad Williamson. Malden: Blackwell Publishing.

Kerr, Gavin. 2016. Predistribution, Property-Owning Democracy and Land Value Taxation. *Politics, Philosophy & Economics* 15 (1): 67–91.

Lippert-Rasmussen, Kasper. 2015. Luck Egalitarianism Versus Relational Egalitarians: On the Prospects of a Pluralist Account of Egalitarian Justice. *Canadian Journal of Philosophy* 45 (2): 220–241.

Mazzucato, Mariana, Rainer Kattel, Jonas Algers, and Olga Mikheeva. 2021. *The Green Giant: New Industrial Strategy for Norway*. UCL Institute for Innovation and Public Purpose. IIPP policy report (PR21/01). Downloaded from: Microsoft Word - TheGreenGiant_Final_19 Jan.docx (ucl.ac.uk).

McTernan, Emily, Martin O'Neill, Christian Schemmel, and Fabian Schuppert. 2016. If You Care About Social Equality, You Want a Big State: Home, Work, Care and Social Egalitarianism. *Juncture* 23 (2): 138–144.

Meade, James E. 1993. *Liberty, Equality and Efficiency*. New York: New York University Press.

Moss, Jeremy. 2014. *Reassessing Egalitarianism*. London: Palgrave Macmillan.

Murphy, Liam. 2019. How Not to Argue for Tax Justice. *Boston Review*, 30.10.2019. http://bostonreview.net/class-inequality/liam-murphy-how-not-argue-tax-justice.

Murphy, Liam, and Thomas Nagel. 2002. *The Myth of Ownership: Taxes and Justice*. Oxford: Oxford University Press.
Nozick, Robert. 1974. *Anarchy, State and Utopia*. Malden: Blackwell Publishing.
O'Neill, Martin. 2012. Free (and Fair) Markets Without Capitalism: Political Values, Principles of Justice, and Property-Owning Democracy. In *Property-Owning Democracy. Rawls and Beyond*, ed. Martin O'Neill and Thad Williamson. Malden: Blackwell Publishing.
———. 2017. Survey Article: Philosophy and Public Policy After Piketty. *The Journal of Political Philosophy* 25 (3): 343–375.
———. 2020a. Power, Predistribution and Social Justice. *Philosophy* 95 (1): 63–91.
———. 2020b. Forum Response: Taxing the Superrich. *Boston Review*, 09.04.2020. Downloaded from: http://bostonreview.net/forum/taxing-superrich/martin-o%E2%80%99neill-economic-justice-requires-more-wealth-tax.
———. 2021a. *Social Justice and Economic Systems: On Rawls, Democratic Socialism, and Alternatives to Capitalism*. Repository Copy. White Rose Research Online URL for this paper: http://eprints.whiterose.ac.uk/165444/.
———. 2021b. Justice, Power and Participatory Socialism: On Piketty's Capital and Ideology. *Analyse & Kritik* 43 (1): 89–124.
O'Neill, Martin, and Shepley Orr. 2018. Introduction. In *Taxation: Philosophical Perspectives*, ed. Martin O'Neill and Shepley Orr. Oxford: Oxford University Press.
O'Neill, Martin, and Thad Williamson, eds. 2012a. *Property-Owning Democracy. Rawls and Beyond*. Malden: Blackwell Publishing.
———. 2012b. Philosophical Foundations for Good Capitalism? Labour's Business Agenda, John Rawls and Property-Owning Democracy. *Renewal. A Journal of Social Democracy* 20 (1): 20–32.
———. 2012c. The Promise of Pre-Distribution. *Policy Network*: 1–7. Available at: http://www.policy-network.net/pno_detail.aspx?ID=4262&title=The-Promise-of-Pre-distribution.
———. 2015. Taxation. In *The Cambridge Rawls Lexicon*, ed. Jon Mandle and David A. Reidy. Cambridge: Cambridge University Press.
OECD. 2012. *Going for Growth*. Available at: http://www.oecd.org/eco/public-finance/49421421.pdf.
Olsaretti, Serena. 2004. *Liberty, Desert and the Market*. Cambridge: Cambridge University Press.
Parfit, Derek. 1997. Equality and Priority. *Ratio* 10: 202–221.
Pedersen, Jørgen. 2021a. *Distributive Justice and Taxation*. London: Routledge.
———. 2021b. Thomas Piketty, Eierskapsdemokrati og Deltagende Sosialisme. *Agora. Journal for Metafysisk Spekulasjon* 1 (2): 116–146.
Persky, Joseph. 2010. Rawls's Thin (Millian) Defense of Private Property. *Utilitas* 22 (2): 134–147.
Pettit, Philip. 2012. *On the Peoples Terms: A Republican Theory and Model of Democracy*. Cambridge: Cambridge University Press.
Piketty, Thomas. 2014. *Capital in the Twenty-First Century*. Cambridge, MA: The Belknap Press of Harvard University Press.
———. 2020. *Capital and Ideology*. Cambridge, MA: The Belknap Press of Harvard University Press.
Rakowski, Eric. 2000. Can Wealth Taxes Be Justified? *Tax Law Review* 53: 263–375.
Rawls, John. 1996. *Political Liberalism*. New York: Columbia University Press.
———. 1999. *A Theory of Justice*. Cambridge, MA: The Belknap Press of Harvard University Press.
———. 2001. *Justice as Fairness. A Restatement*. Cambridge. MA: The Belknap Press of Harvard University Press.
Reich, Robert. 2021. Bidenomics Beats Reaganomics and I Should Know, I Saw Clintonomics Fail. *The Guardian*, 14.03.2021. Downloaded from: https://www.theguardian.com/commentisfree/2021/mar/14/joe-biden-coronavirus-covid-stimulus-trump-tax-cuts-welfare-reagan-clinton.
Sachs, Jeffrey D., Guido Schmidt-Traub, Christian Kroll, Guillaume Lafortune, Grayson Fuller, and Finn Woelm, eds. 2020. *The Sustainable Development Goals and COVID-19*, Sustainable Development Report 2020. Cambridge: Cambridge University Press.

Saez, Emmanuel, and Gabriel Zucman. 2019a. *The Triumph of Injustice. How the Rich Dodge Taxes and How to Make Them Pay*. New York: W.W Norton & Company.
———. 2019b. Progressive Wealth Taxation. *Brooking Papers on Economic Activity*. https://www.brookings.edu/wp-content/uploads/2019/09/Saez-Zucman_conference-draft.pdf.
———. 2020. Taxing the Superrich. Forum Final Response. *Boston Review*, 09.04.2020. Downloaded from: http://bostonreview.net/forum/taxing-superrich/emmanuel-saez-gabriel-zucman-wealth-tax-can-work%E2%80%94and-its-one-essential-tool.
Scanlon, Thomas. 2018. *Why Does Inequality Matter?* Oxford: Oxford University Press.
Scheffler, Samuel. 2003. What Is Egalitarianism. *Philosophy & Public Affairs* 31 (1): 5–39.
Smith, Karl. 2020. Forum Response: Taxing the Superrich. A Wealth Tax Will Hurt the Economy by Encouraging the Wealthy to Leave the United States and by Bringing in Less Tax Revenue Over Time. *Boston Review*, 09.04.2020. Downloaded from: http://bostonreview.net/forum/taxing-superrich/karl-smith-wealth-tax-will-hurt-economy-not-help.
Stemplowska, Sofia, and Adam Swift. 2012. Ideal and Nonideal Theory. In *Oxford Handbook of Political Philosophy*, ed. David Estlund. Oxford: Oxford University Press.
Stiglitz, Joseph E. 2019. *People, Power and Profits: Progressive Capitalism for an Age of Discontent*. London: Allen Lane.
Sugin, Linda. 2004. Theories of Distributive Justice and Limitations on Taxation: What Rawls Demands from Tax Systems. *Fordham Law Review* 72 (5): 1991–2014.
Tan, Kok-Chor. 2012. *Justice, Luck and Institutions. The Site, Ground and Scope of Equality*. New York: Oxford University Press.
Thomas, Alan. 2017. *Republic of Equals. Predistribution and Property-Owning Democracy*. New York: Oxford University Press.
———. 2020. Rawls on Economic Liberty and the Choice of Systems of Social Cooperation. In *John Rawls. Debating the Major Questions*, ed. Jon Mandle and Sarah Roberts-Cady. New York: Oxford University Press.
Vallier, Kevin. 2019. Rawls, Piketty and the Critique of Welfare-State Capitalism. *The Journal of Politics* 81 (1): 142–152.
von Platz, Jeppe. 2020. Rawls' Underestimation of the Importance of Economic Agency and Economic Rights. In *John Rawls. Debating the Major Questions*, ed. Jon Mandle and Sarah Roberts-Cady. New York: Oxford University Press.
White, Stuart. 2020. We Need a Wealth Floor, Not Just a Wealth Ceiling. *Boston Review*, 09.04.2020. Downloaded from: http://bostonreview.net/forum/taxing-superrich/stuart-white-we-need-wealth-floor-not-just-wealth-ceiling.
Ypi, Lea. 2018. The Politics of Reticent Socialism. *Catalyst* 2 (3): 156–175.
Zelenak, Lawrence. 2003. The Myth of Pretax Income. *Michigan Law Review* 101: 2261–2274.

Jørgen Pedersen is a political philosopher and a professor at Western Norway University of Applied Sciences in Bergen, Norway. His last book is *Distributive Justice and Taxation* (Routledge 2021). He has also written several articles on inheritance taxation and is presently working on a book on global justice. He is currently teaching distributive justice, corporate social responsibility and sustainable development.

Chapter 10
Tax's Power: Feminism, Tax, and the Making of Society

Tessa Davis

Abstract Telling a story of feminism and tax means telling a story the end of which is unknown and in which the players may be unaware of their roles. Many essential feminist thinkers wrote little, if at all, of tax. To the casual observer, the relevance of feminism to tax may not be clear. Tax is the law of dollars and cents driven by the revenue demands of the government and shaped by the wisdom of economic theory. This is, of course, a caricature—elements of truth but missing detail and nuance. Tax, no matter how much it may be shaped by economics, is not a science. It is not simply dollars and cents. Tax is political. And feminism knows the political.

Students of tax policy learn that the primary goal of any tax system is to raise revenue and that the metrics by which we evaluate the soundness of the regime as a whole, or its parts in isolation, are simplicity, efficiency, and fairness. This picture is incomplete. Studying tax through the lens of feminism clarifies just how incomplete the conventional understanding has been. Neither feminist thinkers nor their ideas have been regularly brought to the table in the discussions that shaped this system, but not for lack of relevance. Consider the essential questions for any tax system: a government must decide what to tax (a base), to what extent (a rate), to what ends (revenue, regulation, social policy), and from whom. Feminist thought has insights for each. And feminism has made inroads into tax scholarship. The choice and breadth of the tax base has been a focus of feminist tax scholarship, seen in debates over such issues as the taxation of unpaid domestic labor and the tax treatment of caregiving expenses. Progressivity has been the focus of feminist inquiry for many reasons, not the least of which is the secondary-earner bias that results from the interaction of our progressive rate structure with the choice of a taxable unit. And in its continued debates over the nature of equality, feminism is an essential player in the questions of rights and harms, community and belonging,

Thank you to Jennifer Bird-Pollan for her mentorship, Isabela Blanes, for her excellent research assistance, and Jon Huggett for his support.

T. Davis (✉)
University of South Carolina School of Law, Columbia, SC, USA
e-mail: davistes@law.sc.edu

R. F. van Brederode (ed.), *Political Philosophy and Taxation*,
https://doi.org/10.1007/978-981-19-1092-0_10

discrimination and remedy that shape our understanding of what society can and should do for individuals.

This chapter explores both feminist tax scholarship and the lessons for tax that follow from feminist thinkers who wrote little, if at all, of tax. Taking a closer look at feminism and taxation reveals how necessary feminism is if we are to have a robust discussion of tax law and policy. Feminism is not monolithic, so the prescriptions of feminism for tax are not always consistent. But bringing the two together sharpens our understanding of both, highlighting the unifying threads of different veins of feminist thought and pushing us to think critically of tax's capacity to shape society. Tax is a conversation, not an equation. And feminism is an essential voice at the table.

Keywords Feminism · Tax · Tax policy · Taxation · Feminist theory · Equality · Gender bias · Secondary-earner bias · Patriarchy

10.1 Taxation and Belonging—Early Feminist Thought and the Tax Nexus

As first wave feminists pushed for governments (and their citizenry) to recognize women's rights, they demanded formal recognition of the intrinsic equality of women and men with a particular eye to securing the same legal and political rights. For early feminist thinkers, the right to vote loomed large as an essential steppingstone toward the goal of equality. As they crafted their arguments, such feminists were well aware of the strong thread in American political thought that held there should be a close nexus between the benefits and burdens of citizenship (Bartlett 2012; Williamson 2017; Mehrotra 2013). It should not be surprising, then, that taxation was sometimes woven into arguments for the vote. A prominent example of suffragists appealing to this entrenched dichotomy is found in Elizabeth Cady Stanton's 1848 address at Seneca Falls[1] (Wellman 2010). Therein, Stanton bemoaned the injustice of taxing women to support institutions the entry to which they were denied:

> When woman instead of being taxed to endow colleges where she is forbidden to enter, instead of forming societies to educate young men shall first educate herself, when she shall be just to herself before she is generous to others—improving the talents God has given her and leaving her neighbour to do the same for himself we shall not then hear so much of this [man's] boasted greatness (Gordon 1997).

Suffragists like Stanton demanded no less than that which was an essential element of the founding myth of our nation: no taxation without representation

[1] Seneca Falls is the site of the first women's rights convention in the United States and holds an important place in women's and feminist history not only because of the renown of its organizers and attendees but for the role it played in galvanizing the movement (Wellman 2010).

(Kessler-Harris 2001; Tutt 2010)—"[W]e [ ] assemble to protest against a form of government existing without the consent of the governed, to declare our right to be free as man is free—to be represented in the government which we are taxed to support" (Gordon 1997). The nation could not, in their view, maintain its ideals as it denied to women the benefits of citizenship while placing its burdens on their shoulders.

Such a close connection between taxation and the rights and responsibilities of citizenship is a common thread in tax (see, *Cook v. Tait* 1924).[2] The power of the connection derives from the work it does both to define the taxable community and to determine the appropriate relative contributions from individuals. Before ability to pay became the preferred principle for allocating the responsibility to pay tax, benefit theory dominated with its deceptively complex assertion that individuals should pay tax corresponding to the extent they benefit from the presence and operation of government. This strong nexus between benefits and burdens has often made taxation, specifically taxpayer status, a powerful claim in the fight for equality and civil rights. Paying taxes gives one purchase on community membership and a ground for grievance when one is denied the benefits accorded others. It is unsurprising, given the rhetorical heft of the benefit/burden frame, that reformers often deploy status as a taxpayer as a means of making demands for fundamental political rights (Davis 2017; Mason 2016; Walsh 2018). But a transactional view of rights and responsibilities, of benefits and burdens, can be a double-edged sword. If taxpayer status is necessary to claim a right to vote, for example, then voting rights can

[2] In *Cook v. Tait,* the Court considered the reach of the U.S.'s taxing power. "The contention was rejected that a citizen's property without the limits of the United States derives no benefit from the United States. The contention, it was said, came from the confusion of thought in 'mistaking the scope and extent of the sovereign power of the United States as a nation and its relations to its citizens and their relation to it.' And that power in its scope and extent, it was decided, is based on the presumption that government by its very nature benefits the citizen and his property wherever found, and that opposition to it holds on to citizenship while it 'belittles and destroys its advantages and blessings by denying the possession by government of an essential power required to make citizenship completely beneficial.' In other words, the principle was declared that the government, by its very nature, benefits the citizen and his property wherever found, and therefore has the power to make the benefit complete. Or, to express it another way, the basis of the power to tax was not and cannot be made dependent upon the situs of the property in all cases, it being in or out of the United States, nor was not and cannot be made dependent upon the domicile of the citizen, that being in or out of the United States, but upon his relation as citizen to the United States and the relation of the latter to him as citizen. The consequence of the relations is that the native citizen who is taxed may have domicile, and the property from which his income is derived may have situs, in a foreign country and the tax be legal-the government having power to impose the tax" (*Cook v. Tait* 1924, 56).

be denied to those who do not pay taxes.[3] And even if taxpayer status helps a marginalized group gain formal equality, substantive equality may not follow. As incomplete and tenuous as taxpayer status arguments were and remain, they resonate throughout history, arising in current debates over, for example, the taxation of corporations and immigration. For feminists, as for others, the argument was a tactical move on the path toward equality.

10.2 What Equality Demands—Bringing Wollstonecraft and Mill to Tax

Foundational feminist writings speak little, if at all, of tax and taxation. Nevertheless, the seeds of later feminist work that focused more specifically on taxation may be found in the oft-cited early writings of both Mary Wollstonecraft[4] and John Stuart Mill.[5] Both authors were most focused on establishing the fundamental equality of women with men. They challenged mainstream assumptions of inherent differences between women and men in capacity or aptitude—finding the origins of any observed differences in legal, social, and cultural constraints. But their ideas hint at specific policies that may support the pursuit of equity.

In her foundational *A Vindication of the Rights of Woman*, Mary Wollstonecraft argues that the economic, cultural, and legal restraints on women squelch their

[3] This sentiment seems to underlie then Presidential candidate Mitt Romney's now infamous statements regarding the 47% of Americans who do not pay taxes. "Well, there are 47 percent of the people who will vote for the president no matter what. There are 47 percent who are with him, who are dependent upon government, who believe that they are victims, who believe that government has a responsibility to care for them, who believe that they are entitled to health care, to food, to housing, to you-name-it. That that's an entitlement and government should give it to them. And they will vote for this president no matter what. I mean, the president starts off with 48, 49 … I mean, he starts off with a huge number. These are people who pay no income tax; 47 percent of Americans pay no income tax. So our message of low taxes doesn't connect. He'll be out there talking about tax cuts for the rich. I mean, that's what they sell every four years. And so my job is not to worry about those people. I'll never convince them they should take personal responsibility and care for their lives. What I have to do is convince the 5 to 10 percent in the center, that are independents, that are thoughtful, that look at voting one way or the other depending upon, in some cases, emotion, whether they like the guy or not, what he looks like" (Editorial 2012). Mr. Romney's statement was deeply misleading, as it failed to acknowledge the taxes other than the income taxes, such as federal employment taxes and state and local taxes, that individuals pay regardless of their income tax liability. But it is also illuminating in the connection that Mr. Romney seems to make between the worth or validity of one's vote and their taxpayer status.

[4] A well-known and highly influential British feminist, Mary Wollstonecraft's most famous work, *A Vindication on the Rights of Women*, is an essential feminist text (Wollstonecraft 2019). For a biography of Wollstonecraft (Lorch 1990). This chapter explores two parts of *Vindication*: "Of the Pernicious Effects Which Arise from the Unnatural Distinctions Established in Society" and "On National Education" (Wollstonecraft 2019).

[5] Though not necessarily first introduced as a feminist John Stuart Mill's many impactful works include his feminist text *On the Subjection of Women* (Capaldi 2004).

potential as human beings and citizens. Confined by the strictures of society to dependency on men, women's intellects and potential are squandered (though she admits the rationality of women's focus in light of the constraints faced), on pleasing men[6] (Wollstonecraft 2019). And the loss is profound not just for individual women so limited, but for society:

> How many women thus waste life away the prey of discontent, who might have practised as physicians, regulated a farm, managed a shop, and stood erect, supported by their own industry ... Would men but generously snap our chains, and be content with rational fellowship instead of slavish obedience, they would find us more observant daughters, more affectionate sisters, more faithful wives, more reasonable mothers-in a word, better citizens (Wollstonecraft 2019, 265).[7]

Expanding women's civil, political, and economic rights would benefit the entire nation, not just the women who sought equality. Rather than a zero-sum proposition, the liberation of women from their legal, political, and cultural strictures would inure to the benefit of men as much as women. If it is not immediately clear what this vision of equality demands of law broadly, it is because the discussion is still ongoing. There are threads in Wollstonecraft's writing woven into more contemporary feminist thought and there are hints of how we might reconcile a modern tax system[8] with her views on women's rights and equality, particularly in her writings on education and accumulated wealth.

Virtue (Wollstonecraft 2019, 255)[9]—of both men and women—is a key element of Wollstonecraft's writings. The concept, sometimes gendered, shapes her arguments on the need to curtail the accumulation of wealth and to provide for education for both boys and girls. And it is this suspicion of wealth and support for education

---

[6] This thread runs through much contemporary feminist thought, not the least of which is Catherine MacKinnon's influential work on power, gender, sex, and the law (MacKinnon 1989).

[7] "We should then love them with true affection, because we should learn to respect ourselves; and the peace of mind of a worthy man would not be interrupted by the idle vanity of his wife, nor his babes sent to nestle in a strange bosom, having never found a home in their mother's" (Wollstonecraft 2019, 265).

[8] When focused on specific reforms, this chapter is grounded in the U.S.'s income tax regime though the principles explored could be applied to other tax systems.

[9] Wollstonecraft saw it the duty of government to act as the better angel of human nature—to create structures and systems that would point them toward virtue. "The preposterous distinctions of rank, which render civilization a curse, by dividing the world between voluptuous tyrants, and cunning envious dependents, corrupt, almost equally, every class of people, because respectability is not attached to the discharge of the relative duties of life, but to the station, and when the duties are not fulfilled, the affections cannot gain sufficient strength to fortify the virtue of which they are the natural reward. Still there are some loop-holes out of which a man may creep, and dare to think and act for himself; but for a woman it is an herculean task, because she has difficulties peculiar to her sex to overcome, which require almost super-human powers. A truly benevolent legislator always endeavours to make it the interest of each individual to be virtuous; and thus private virtue becoming the cement of public happiness, an orderly whole is consolidated by the tendency of all the parts towards a common centre. But, the private or public virtue of women is very problematical; for Rousseau, and a numerous list of male writers, insist that she should all her life, be subjected to a severe restraint, that of propriety" (Wollstonecraft 2019, 255).

that can be brought to tax as suggesting an appetite for redistribution. Consider first her writings on wealth: Wollstonecraft decries the "destructive" force of wealth and privilege and (Wollstonecraft 2019, 253)[10] the "preposterous" nature of status that severs esteem from worth. However destructive wealth may be to both men and women, it is women, in her view, who are most harmed (Wollstonecraft 2019, 256).[11] Because a woman's only means of attaining security and esteem is derivative—because society prevents her from crafting a life of her own—women are left more "debased and cramped" (Wollstonecraft 2019, 253) as they are forced to grasp for another's wealth and privilege; left to men to "guide their tottering steps aright" (Wollstonecraft 2019, 256). The imagery in the last statement is deliberate: that of a woman walking unsteadily in heels donned as part of a broader effort to make herself "alluring" so as to gain the affection and attendant support of a man. Society gives women no greater option than this and the result, for Wollstonecraft, is the degradation of all, a degradation only exacerbated by entrenched wealth and privilege.

Would Wollstonecraft support a progressive tax system? A wealth tax? An inheritance or an estate tax? Her critical view of accumulated wealth and privilege suggests it is certainly possible. Each can serve to break up accumulated wealth. Or perhaps Wollstonecraft would support taxing gifts as income to recipients, or the repeal of stepped-up basis to tax appreciated assets. The technical moves tax could make toward achieving the goal are many, but the goal seems clear, clearer still when paired with her writings on education.

Wollstonecraft's ideas on education lend further support to reading her open to a redistributive tax system. If wealth is a corrupting force, education is corrective one. Wollstonecraft was a strong advocate of educating girls and boys alongside one another (Wollstonecraft 2019, 255)[12] in schools funded by the government and open to all:

---

[10] "Destructive, however, as riches and inherited honours are to the human character, women are more debased and cramped, if possible by them, than men, because men may still, in some degree, unfold their faculties by becoming soldiers and statesmen" (Wollstonecraft 2019, 253).

[11] "Women are in common with men, rendered weak and luxurious by the relaxing pleasures which wealth procures; but added to this, they are made slaves to their persons, and must render them alluring, that man may lend them his reason to guide their tottering steps aright" (Wollstonecraft 2019, 256).

[12] Education, for Wollstonecraft, played an important role in socializing children. "If marriage be the cement of society, mankind should all be educated after the same model, or the intercourse of the sexes will never deserve the name of fellowship, nor will women ever fulfil the peculiar duties of their sex, till they become enlightened citizens, till they become free, by being enabled to earn their own subsistence, independent of men; in the same manner, I mean, to prevent misconstruction, as one man is independent of another. Nay, marriage will never be held sacred till women by being brought up with men, are prepared to be their companions, rather than their mistresses; for the mean doublings of cunning will ever render them contemptible, whilst oppression renders them timid. So convinced am I of this truth, that I will venture to predict, that virtue will never prevail in society till the virtues of both sexes are founded on reason; and, till the affection common to both are allowed to gain their due strength by the discharge of mutual duties" (Wollstonecraft 2019, 255).

> Let an enlightened nation then try what effect reason would have to bring them [women] back to nature, and their duty; and allowing them to share the advantages of education and government with man, see whether they will become better, as they grow wiser and become free. They cannot be injured by the experiment; for it is not in the power of man to render them more insignificant than they are at present. To render this practicable, day schools for particular ages should be established by government, in which boys and girls might be educated together. The school for the younger children, from five to nine years of age, ought to be absolutely free and open to all classes (Wollstonecraft 2019, 298).

"Free and open" schools to develop boys and girls as individuals and citizens. In this commitment she expressly rejects a model in which schools are dependent upon parents for their funding—citing how such a model incentivizes such schools to take on more students than they can effectively teach and the potential control over instruction such dependency gives parents (Wollstonecraft 2019, 290).[13] Taxes being a ready means of funding free, public education, Wollstonecraft's conviction that such a system is essential is an additional data point suggesting her likely embrace of a redistributive tax system. But there is a different frame for the question of how Wollstonecraft's work comes to bear on tax. Tax needs a mooring. Rates do not set themselves. There is no natural law of income. So, the better frame for the question is: if we find Wollstonecraft's core observations compelling—that women are fundamentally equal to and deserving of the same rights as men and that the whole of society suffers from their subjugation—what system of taxation best supports the realization of equality? In this frame, feminism guides the ends and tax becomes a means of achieving them. Feminism sets the goals that tax must pursue.

Prolific and influential, John Stuart Mill's writings come to bear on tax and political economy in many still-debated ways. He stands with Wollstonecraft as an early proponent of women's rights in his *On The Subjection of Women* (Mill 2000), and in it are views on property ownership that can inform tax law and policy. Just as later feminist thinkers would build upon Wollstonecraft's foundation, so too would they expand upon and broaden the reach of Mill's challenge to naturalized gender inequality (Mill 2000, 22).[14] Society, not nature, in Mill's view, is to blame for women's subjugation and appeals to "natural" capacity or other essentialist arguments are nothing more than self-serving rationalizations—"was there ever any domination which did not appear natural to those who possessed it?" (Mill 2000, 22). Of particular note for tax, however, are Mill's views on property ownership:

> [A] woman's inheritance or gains ought to be as much her own after marriage as before. The rule is simple: whatever would be the husband's or wife's if they were not married, should be under their exclusive control during marriage ... Some people are sentimentally shocked at the idea of a separate interest in money matters as inconsistent with the ideal fusion of two lives into one. For my own part, I am one of the strongest supporters of community of

[13] "This train of reasoning brings me back to a subject, on which I mean to dwell, the necessity of establishing proper day-schools. But these should be national establishments, for whilst schoolmasters are dependent on the caprice of parents, little exertion can be expected from them, more than is necessary to please ignorant people" (Wollstonecraft 2019, 290).

[14] "But was there ever any domination which did not appear natural to those who possessed it?" (Mill 2000, 22).

> goods, when resulting from an entire unity of feeling of the owners. But I have no relish for a community of goods resting on the doctrine, that what is mine is yours but what is yours is not mine; and I should prefer to decline entering into such a compact with any one, though I were myself the person to profit by it (Mill 2000, 83–84).

Though the equality Mill argues for was a long way off, the idea is one that later feminists would take up to challenge the married filing jointly status of the income tax system (Kornhauser 1993, 1996). Of course, neither Mill nor Wollstonecraft were writing in a time when either the United Kingdom or the still young United States had adopted anything resembling a modern income tax. Their writings are unsurprisingly quite different than the technocratic literature that now dominates tax law and policy. But their key arguments, while not providing uncontestable policy prescriptions, provide a foundation from which tax can depart. And later feminists would expand upon these ideas, using them to shape both feminism and tax.

Reflecting upon how early feminist activists and thinkers intersect with tax reveals a particular way of interacting with the tax system. For suffragists, taxpayer status was both evidence of injustice—in so far as women were asked to be taxpayers while denied the benefits of full citizenship—and grounds for claiming full community membership. The tax system is tacitly accepted—not itself the focus of reform or critique. Wollstonecraft and Mill's works stand to tax in a different, more prescriptive posture. Where tax, for suffragists, was one of a laundry list of injustices, taxpayer status provided an argument in support of their larger political agenda—not essential to the movement but convenient. Suffragists took the tax system that was and used it toward activist ends. Wollstonecraft and Mill's works speak to what could be: A tax system may be in tension with or in support of the societal change both envision. But it is their broader visions that set the goals and guardrails within which tax should exist as part of the legal system. In both frames, tax is somewhat secondary, a tool in pursuit of other ends. This next part explores feminism as a tool of critique where tax is the focus.

10.3 Ends Meet Means: Feminist Tax Scholarship

Within the United States, second wave feminism developed and expanded its intellectual reach as the country came to rely more heavily upon the income tax as a key source of federal revenue. Yet at a time when feminism was pushing for equality, the intersection of tax—an increasingly impactful site for the protection or neglect of economic equality—and feminism remained largely undertheorized (Abreu and Greenstein 2018). This should not be wholly surprising. Tax has long been a male-dominated field and remains so. More specifically, it is a white male dominated area of practice and scholarship (Abreu and Greenstein 2018; Schenk 2012). Focusing just on the legal academy, one finds that tax is both more white and more male than is the legal academic field taken as a whole (Schenk 2012). Scholars have opined as to why this may be the case and the harms caused by that the lack of diversity (Abreu and Greenstein 2018). One clear harm is that tax scholarship has lagged behind the (already slow) shift of legal academia toward recognizing and engaging with non-white male views. Feminist tax scholarship did not begin to make inroads until the 1980s and even then, such work was in short supply. So, for a time, as feminist thought developed tax was on a separate path.

While tax seemed to exist outside the revolution, feminist theory flourished. Second wave feminists clarified the multitude of ways in which formal power—legal, political, and economic forces—and more difficult to situate informal forces—social norms, assumptions, and expectations—reflected and reproduced gender inequality. In *The Second Sex*, Simone de Beauvoir offered her nuanced and incisive account of how society genders bodies, making woman as it makes her both other and inferior (Beauvoir 2010). Kate Millett, in *Sexual Politics* (2016), synthesized the ways in which patriarchy winds its way through all aspects of life, dissolving any clear line between public and private, the personal and the political. Bell Hooks (1981) identified the bias of much feminist work itself that focused largely on experiences of heterosexual, middle and upper middle class white women. When feminism came to tax, it came as a well-developed tool for challenging the orthodoxy.

Feminist tax scholars drew upon three key insights of feminist thought. The first is that even the most seemingly mundane of legal categories and doctrines can reflect and reify gender division and bias. The second is that law is often an agent of gendered power. The third is that legal theory and reform often fail to account for the ways in which gender intersects with other aspects of identity such as class, sexuality, and ability. These insights may be more strongly associated with one or the other of the necessarily imperfect groupings of feminist thinkers—difference feminists, dominance feminists, cultural feminists, liberal feminists, radical feminists, and so on (Baier 1987; Becker et al. 1994; Fineman 2005; Hampton 2005; Menkel-Meadow 1992; Rhode 1991; Sunstein 1988). But exploring the relevance of these insights for tax does not require drawing or redrawing lines between different camps within feminist thought. Indeed, feminist tax scholars drew from different areas as they worked to shift the entrenched ways of thinking within the discipline. This part highlights two key areas of focus within feminist tax scholarship to explore how feminism has been applied as tool of critique within tax.

Much feminist scholarship in tax has focused on one or both of the following issues: individual versus joint filing and the tax treatment of caregiving (Abramovitz and Morgen 2006; Alstott 1996; Davis 1988; Kornhauser 1996, 1997, 2002; McCaffery 1993, 2007). To some extent it is unsurprising that these issues were the initial focus of feminist tax scholarship, as both are connected to the deeply intertwined concepts of the family and gendered labor that were early areas of analysis and critique by feminist legal scholars. Take the tax treatment of caregiving costs first. There are at least two questions to consider at the intersection of caregiving and tax. The first is whether and how caregiving costs are connected to the definition of income itself. The second is the extent to which caregiving is a public concern; an issue which will be taken up in the concluding part. Because our income tax system endeavors to tax one's net rather than gross income, the law must provide for a means of reducing your gross income by the costs of producing that income. The key statutory authority on deductible business expenses is §162 which reads (in pertinent part): "there shall be allowed as a deduction all the ordinary and necessary expenses paid or incurred during the taxable year in carrying on any trade or business" (26 U.S.C. § 162(a)). Each element of the rule has been further fleshed out over time but the requirement that a cost incurred be ordinary is the doctrinal hook for feminist insight and critique.

"Ordinary" in the context of the statute means commonplace within the community—something another similarly-situated person *would* do if faced with the same facts (*Welch v. Helvering* 1933). There is, of course, nothing inherently gendered in the language of the statute nor in the court's opinion in *Welch v. Helvering*, an early case interpreting the statute that remains a touchstone. In that opinion, Justice Cardozo opines on the means of sorting ordinary (and deductible) from extraordinary (and nondeductible): "[h]ere, indeed, as so often in other branches of the law, the decisive distinctions are those of degree and not of kind. One struggles in vain for any verbal formula that will supply a ready touchstone. The standard set up by the statute is not a rule of law; it is rather a way of life. Life in all its fullness must supply the answer to the riddle" (*Welch v. Helvering* 1933). Herein, the feminist insight that seemingly neutral language and law can reflect and reify gendered views and bias looms large. "Life in all its fullness" connects the interpretation of a statute—the very definition of a concept—to life experience. And one need only look to a Board of Tax Appeals decision from 6 years later to see the feminist critique of such "neutral" standards play out in doctrine.

In *Smith v. Commissioner*, the Board interpreted the application of §162 to childcare costs. Its decision endures and childcare remains classified as a personal, nondeductible expense. In that decision, the Board wrote:

> We are not prepared to say that the care of children, like similar aspects of family and household life, is other than a personal concern. The wife's services as custodian of the home and protector of its children *are ordinarily rendered without monetary compensation.* There results no taxable income from the performance of this service and the correlative expenditure is personal and not susceptible of deduction (*Rosa E. Burkhart*, 11 B.T.A. 275). Here *the wife has chosen to employ others to discharge her domestic function and the services she performs are rendered outside the home*. They are a source of actual income and taxable as such. But that does not deprive the same work performed by others of its personal character nor furnish a reason why its cost should be treated as an offset in the guise of a deductible item.[15]
>
> We are not unmindful that, as petitioners suggest, certain disbursements normally personal may become deductible by reason of their intimate connection with an occupation carried on for profit. In this category fall entertainment, *Blackmer v. Commissioner*, 70 Fed.(2d) 255 (C.C.A., 2d Cir.), and traveling expenses, *Joseph W. Powell*, 34 B.T.A. 655; affd., 94 Fed. (2d) 483 (C.C.A., 1st Cir.), and the cost of an actor's wardrobe, *Charles Hutchison*, 13 B.T.A. 1187. The line is not always an easy one to draw nor the test simple to apply. But we think its principle is clear. It may for practical purposes be said to constitute a distinction between those activities which, *as a matter of common acceptance and universal experi-*

[15] It is worth noting the inconsistency here. That the imputed income domestic labor generates goes untaxed in fact strengthens the argument for deductibility by those, like the Smiths, who pay someone outside the family for the same work.

> *ence*, are 'ordinary' or usual as the direct accompaniment of business pursuits, on the one hand; and those which, though they may in some *indirect and tenuous degree* relate to the circumstances of a profitable occupation, are nevertheless personal in their nature, of a character applicable to human beings generally, and which exist on that plane regardless of the occupation though not necessarily of the station in life, of the individuals concerned (See *Welch v. Helvering*, 290 U.S. 111).
>
> In the latter category, we think, fall payments made to servants or others occupied in looking to the personal wants of their employers (*David Sonenblick*, 4 B.T.A. 986). And we include in this group nursemaids retained to care for infant children (*Smith v. Commissioner* 1939).

A cornucopia of gendered assumptions, the brief opinion is a near textbook example of the type of "logical" conclusion that feminist theory challenged. To the Board, the wife was expected to provide childcare; she was the "custodian" of the home. Caregiving was a woman's "domestic function." The "common acceptance" and "universal experience" that the Board used as it applied *Welch* and §162 to the Smiths' decisions were androcentric-shaped by the male decisionmakers' experiences. These men's experiences were treated as universal meaning "[l]ife in all its fullness," in practice, excluded half the population. Operating with an understanding of gender roles as part of the natural order of society, the Board sees Mrs. Smith as shirking duties that were properly hers. It is unsurprising, then, that the Board views the childcare costs incurred as falling outside the ordinary standard of *Welch*. A man with a wife at home to care for the house and the children has no need to pay for childcare, meals, or housekeeping. If a man did incur such costs, they would hardly be ordinary or directly related to his employment. Why pay for services that you could have for free? Even more aberrant would be the two-earner couple. So, when the Board considered the Smiths' costs, they viewed them through a lens of gendered expectations for behavior and household organization and through that lens the couple was different. They were extraordinary. Life, in all its gendered fullness, prescribed the answer.

Related to but distinct from the proper tax treatment of caregiving is the question of how to define the taxable unit. The United States allows married couples to file a joint return, treating the married couple as one unit rather than two individuals. Still a site of debate and criticism, individual versus joint filing was an early point of focus of feminist tax scholarship. A brief explanation of the impact of joint filing is necessary to understand the feminist arguments on the issue.

While the number of brackets and the rates themselves have fluctuated over the years (sometimes significantly), the United States has long used a progressive system of taxation of income. Assume a simplified three bracket rate schedule where the first $20,000 of income is taxed at 10%, the next $20,000 at 20%, and everything over $40,000 is taxed at 30%. If an individual earns $30,000 of taxable income, she'll pay $2000 of tax on the first $20,000 (20k taxed at 10%) and another $2000 on the last $10,000 (10k at 20%) for a total $4000 of tax. Now assume that same individual marries someone who has an income of $15,000 (tax of $1500). Should the couple's income be pooled together or should they continue to be treated as individuals and taxed on their own income? If taxed as separate individuals using the rate schedule above, the couple's total tax liability would be unchanged by marriage. But under a system of joint filing where their income is pooled, their liability could change. If the couple pools their income and the rate schedule is the same for unmarried and married individuals, the couple's tax liability will increase from $5500 to $7500 ($20,000 at 10% + $20,000 at 20% + $5000 at 30%). The pooling of their income results in losing one application of the 10% rate and their total income bumps them into the highest rate bracket, creating what is known as a marriage penalty. The marriage penalty can be erased by creating a different rate schedule for married couples who file jointly that doubles the amount of income a couple can earn before moving up to the next rate bracket. Doing so, however, creates the potential for some couples, particularly those with a sole breadwinner or a significant disparity in earnings, to find marriage reduces their tax liability, creating what is known as a marriage bonus. Though it has often been the focus of tweaks that shift the distribution and/or the amount of marriage penalties and bonuses, the U.S. system of joint filing has long permitted income pooling paired with different progressive rate schedules for married and unmarried individuals, and the bonuses and penalties have followed. So too has feminist focus on the regime.

Bound up within income pooling and marriage bonuses and penalties is the secondary-earner bias. Because the breadwinner's income uses up the lower brackets, the lower earning spouse's income layers on top of the breadwinner's. Using the brackets above, if the breadwinner's income places the couple in the 20% bracket, the lower earning spouse's first dollar of earned income is taxed at 20% rather than 10%. So, the first dollars of the lower earning spouse's income are worth less than those of the higher earning spouse. That tax cost may be compounded by the other costs the couple may incur because both spouses engage in market work, such as childcare, house cleaning, and other services. If the second earner's income is understood to be discretionary, the couple may decide her income is not worth the cost, opting instead for the lower earning spouse to forego market work and provide caregiving and household services for the family. Stated differently, tax may create a bias against two-earner couples that pushes some out of the labor market.

Feminist tax scholars used feminist thought to challenge this regime. In doing so, they took on an issue as seemingly mundane as the choice of a taxable unit and revealed its potential connection to gender, patriarchy, and power. Feminist thought offers an array of insights in this space. The first insight is that the secondary-earner bias is not neutral as to gender. Women, more often than men, are understood as the secondary earner, so more women than men may be pushed out of the workforce. The second insight is that the income pooling that is an assumed basis for joint filing may be just that—an assumption. A thru line from Mill, if partners do not share property equally, any financial benefits of joint filing may not inure to the woman and may weaken her control over money and property (Kornhauser 1993). To the extent tax shapes behavior, it may incentivize patriarchal familial structures. Though the secondary-earner bias literature offered such critiques, it is itself the subject of important criticism. Scholars such as Dorothy Brown highlighted how the literature fails to account for class and race in its picture of marriage and familial options and structure (Brown 1997, 2021; Harris 1990).[16] Scholars such as Pat Cain (1990) drew attention to the heteronormativity of the discussions in this space and within tax policy broadly. Taken together, these scholars used veins of feminist thought to challenge the very notion that tax was neutral, apolitical, just dollars and cents.

Feminist thought shifted our understanding of a tax question as foundational as the taxable unit. The question then becomes how to move forward. Using feminism as a tool of critique—to show the deeply socially embedded nature of tax—becomes generative. Tax is a tool to someone's ends—the question is whether it will be a feminist one or not. Once over the hurdle of arguing about whether tax is gendered, however, the difficult work still lays ahead. Joint filing and the tax treatment of caregiving activities are two of the most prominent, albeit fairly discrete, issues over which there is far from universal agreement on the best solutions (and indeed, whether there is even a problem). How the path to equality flows through tax is not always clear. There is, nevertheless, a unifying thread through the diversity of approaches and reforms within feminist tax scholarship: the potential for tax to be a tool for bolstering women's economic security. Subsidies for childcare (McCormack 2019, 2020a, b) and proposals to tax the imputed income created by domestic work (Staudt 1996), calls to abolish the joint return (Brown 1997; Kornhauser 1993, 104, 109) and some to preserve it (Philipps 2011), all aim to increase women's control over and amount of after-tax income. But knowing that tax *can* be used to advance feminist goals is not the same as knowing *how* it should be crafted to do so. The last part returns to the work of leading contemporary feminist scholars on their own terms to better understand how their ideas have already influenced tax and how they may continue to do so.

10.4 Many Paths to Equality

Feminist tax scholarship has and will continue to influence tax law and policy. Understanding how scholars have brought feminism to tax—to craft specific reforms, to highlight deep failings, to upset the orthodoxy—is an essential part of telling the story of feminism and tax. This section returns to the theory itself before it was applied to tax. Drawing upon the work of representative feminist scholars in three impactful areas of feminist thought—intersectional feminism, difference feminism, and dominance feminism—this section considers the questions left to be answered and how the relationship between feminism and tax illuminates both.

---

[16] Professor Brown's work is in conversation with that of Professor Crenshaw (discussed in this chapter) and Professor Angela P. Harris that identified and explored the failings of feminist legal scholarship such as its tendency to essentialize.

10.4.1 Intersectional Feminism

In her pathbreaking work critiquing legal theory and doctrine on discrimination, Kimberlé Williams Crenshaw introduced the concept of intersectionality—"the unique compoundedness of discrimination" (Crenshaw 1989, 150) against persons who occupy many marginalized identities. Intersectionality challenged the conventional understanding of gender and race discrimination as wholly separate, either/or forces. Instead, Crenshaw argues, the discrimination a Black woman experiences may be the product of the combined influence of gender and race discrimination that is distinct from the racial discrimination a Black man experiences and the gender discrimination other women experience:

> It seems that I have to say that Black women are the same and harmed by being treated differently, or that they are different and harmed by being treated the same. But I cannot say both. This apparent contradiction is but another manifestation of the conceptual limitations of the single-issue analyses that intersectionality challenges. The point is that Black women can experience discrimination in any number of ways and that the contradiction arises from our assumptions that their claims of exclusion must be unidirectional. Consider an analogy to traffic in an intersection, coming and going in all four directions. Discrimination, like traffic through an intersection, may flow in one direction, and it may flow in another. If an accident happens in an intersection, it can be caused by cars traveling from any number of directions and, sometimes, from all of them. Similarly, if a Black woman is harmed because she is in the intersection, her injury could result from sex discrimination or race discrimination (Crenshaw 1989, 149).

That the concept of intersectionality has entered the political lexicon and been built upon and expanded within academic and activist communities, is a testament to power of Crenshaw's critique.[17] Though she was not the first to criticize the feminist movement for being largely focused on the experiences of white, middle- and upper-class women, Crenshaw's precision and her pairing the critique with that of laws that were purportedly aimed at addressing both racial and gender discrimination, revolutionized thought on discrimination.

Because tax impacts the bottom line, the operating assumption has often been that its focus should be on a particular type of difference: socio-economic class. That more men than women benefit from the capital gains preference is not a gender issue for the Code but the product of tax mapping onto a world in which men just happen to hold more wealth than women[18] (Kornhauser 2011). That more white families benefit from the home mortgage interest deduction is not an instance of racism in the Code, but instead the result of economic inequality (Brown 2021). Fix economic inequality or property ownership disparities and the Code will be fixed (or so the thinking goes). Implicit in this view are two ideas: (1) that tax is exclusively about money and class, and (2) that class and other aspects of identity are

[17] The term has been taken beyond Crenshaw's original argument by both friendly and unfriendly audiences (Coaston 2019).

[18] A version of this argument is within the statement of Republican Senator Mike Crapo ahead of the April 2021 Senate Finance Committee hearing on racial and gender inequality in the Code (Full Committee Hearing 2021).

separate. Crenshaw's work—and its extensions to discrimination on the basis of ability, sexuality, and other aspects of identity—pushes back on such binary thinking.[19] The Code does not impact persons along a single axis. Crenshaw's work undergirded critiques of feminist tax scholarship on the joint return. It makes clear that a feminist tax system cannot treat "women" as a uniform, cohesive group but instead must acknowledge heterogeneity, their different experiences and opportunities shaped by all aspects of their identity of which gender is only an element.

Reformers and policymakers could read intersectional feminism to support an array of specific provisions—technocratic solutions to complex problems. At a more foundational level, however, intersectional feminism calls into question the validity of conventional metrics for assessing the fairness of the tax system: horizontal and vertical equity. Both concepts rely upon income as a means of sorting individuals. But a holistic understanding of how tax impacts a person cannot be garnered from an income figure. A white woman's poverty is not the same as a black woman's, whose experience is, in turn, different than that of a trans woman's or that of a woman with disabilities. Tax may be a particularly useful tool for addressing economic security but policymakers, intersectional feminism counsels, must move beyond binaries in designing and drafting law or risk unintended consequences or ineffective policy.

10.4.2 Difference Feminism and Autonomy

Other veins of feminism wrestle less with differences among women than differences between women and men. Much feminist legal theory has been written on the nature, relevance, and best response to differences between the genders. An essential work in difference feminism, Carol Gilligan's *In A Different Voice*, described the differences in moral reasoning she observed in interviews with male and female study participants. Women, Gilligan argued, operate with a more relational ethic of care—"rest[ing] on the premise of nonviolence—that no one should be hurt" (Gilligan 1982, 174) —while men do so with an ethic of justice—"proceed[ing] from the premise of equality—that everyone should be treated the same" (Gilligan 1982, 174). At its core, the tension between the two approaches is experienced as one of conflict between responsibility for others and an understanding of liberty and equality that is individualistic:

[19] "[Previously discussed cases] are doctrinal manifestations of a common political and theoretical approach to discrimination which operates to marginalize Black women. Unable to grasp the importance of Black women's intersectional experiences, not only courts, but feminist and civil rights thinkers as well have treated Black women in ways that deny both the unique compoundedness of their situation and the centrality of their experiences to the larger classes of women and Blacks. Black women are regarded either as too much like women or Blacks and the compounded nature of their experience is absorbed into the collective experiences of either group or as too different, in which case Black women's Blackness or femaleness sometimes has placed their needs and perspectives at the margin of the feminist and Black liberationist agendas" (Crenshaw 1989, 150).

> Thus in the transition from adolescence to adulthood, the dilemma itself is the same for both sexes, a conflict between integrity and care. But approached from different perspectives, this dilemma generates the recognition of opposite truths. These different perspectives are reflected in two different moral ideologies, since separation is justified by an ethic of rights while attachment is supported by an ethic of care.
>
> The morality of rights is predicated on equality and centered on the understanding of fairness, while the ethic of responsibility relies on the concept of equity, the recognition of differences in need. While the ethic of rights is a manifestation of equal respect, balancing the claims of other and self, the ethic of responsibility rests on an understanding that gives rise to compassion and care (Gilligan 1982, 164–65).

Balancing a perceived conflict between individual and collective interest is a core tension in tax and if Gilligan is right, a tension that men and women navigate differently.

Combining Gilligan's observations with feminist legal scholar Martha Fineman's work on autonomy yields insights for tax. Fineman describes the dominance of what Gilligan termed the ethic of justice in American law and policy: "Equality [in America] is manifested in mere formal or legal guarantees of sameness of treatment for individuals. Inherent in sameness of treatment is the absence of the affirmative governmental measures designed to raise the unequal to a more equal position" (Fineman 2004, 10). This formal equality approach turns upon an assumption of a very particular notion—a "myth"—of autonomy[20] that Fineman identifies as being entrenched in American thought; autonomy as "the absence of economic dependence on outsiders, particularly on the government" (Fineman 2004, 9). In Fineman's view, this notion of autonomy is a significant hurdle to substantive equality because it denigrates social support as it encourages looking away from systemic barriers to access and opportunity (Fineman 2004, 9).[21] If Gilligan is right that an ethic of care is gendered—"In the gendered universe of patriarchy, care is a *feminine* ethic, not a universal one. Caring is what good women do, and the people who care are doing women's work" (Gilligan 2020)—and if Fineman's theories on autonomy and subsidy are right—as political rhetoric and decades of policies aimed at privatizing dependency suggest they are—then core tax policy debates emerge as deeply gendered. And, it follows, a tax system informed by difference feminism, would build upon existing features and change others of our current system.

[20] Gilligan understands an ethic of care as consistent with a lived experience that highlight connectedness: "Since the reality of connection is experienced by women as given rather than as freely contracted, they arrive at an understanding of life that reflects the limits of autonomy and control. As a result, women's development delineates the path not only to a less violent life but also to a maturity realized through interdependence and taking care" (Gilligan 1982, 172).

[21] "I argue that this sense of autonomy is on a collision course with another important aspiration in the American constellation of political ideals—the promise of equality of opportunity and access to societal goods and services. It is so because it posits that state delivery of subsidy creates dependency and evidences a loss of autonomy in the recipient, notwithstanding that for the poor and many of the struggling middle class, some infusion of economic and other resources is essential if they are to be able to take advantage of the access and opportunity that society provides formally" (Fineman 2004, 9).

Taken together, Gilligan and Fineman's work puts another thumb (or a whole hand) on the scale of progressive taxation. The parallels of the tension Gilligan describes between the ethic of care and of justice to arguments in tax is striking. Gilligan writes that "[t]he moral imperative that emerges repeatedly in interviews with women is an injunction to care, a responsibility to discern and alleviate the "real and recognizable trouble" of this world" (Gilligan 1982, 100). Proponents of progressive taxation track this view, emphasizing the responsibility one has to her fellow citizens. Men, Gilligan writes, instead experience "the moral imperative … as an injunction to respect the rights of others and thus to protect from interference the rights to life and self-fulfillment" (Gilligan 1982, 100). Opponents of progressive taxation articulate a similar view, bemoaning the excessive burdens placed on those higher up the income ladder. But in isolation, Gilligan's observations do not point to any necessary resolution. One could argue that the ethic of justice should dominate, or the ethic of care, or some compromise of the two. Folding in Fineman's work on autonomy points toward feminist thought requiring an ethic of care not because it is feminine but because it is true to lived experience.

Because the power to tax gives the state some claim to the property of those subject to its jurisdiction, tax is often construed as a taking, a burden. It is a short jump, for many, to argue that tax can take too much such that it impedes on an individual's ability to pursue his desires, that it makes him too responsible for others. But as Fineman so aptly argues,

> We all live subsidized lives. Sometimes the benefits we receive are public and financial, such as in governmental direct transfer programs to certain individuals like farmers or sugar growers. Public subsidies can also be indirect, such as the benefits given in tax policy. Private economic subsidy systems work in the forms of foundations, religions and charities. But a subsidy can also be non-monetary, such as the subsidy provided by the uncompensated labor of others in caring for us and our dependency needs. It seems clear that all of us receive one or the other or both types of subsidy throughout our lives (Fineman 2000, 23).

To paraphrase the title of Fineman's book, autonomy is a myth. The choice is not between a tax system that respects the ethic of justice read as separation, meritocracy, and robust individual rights to property and one that respects an ethic of care read as collective responsibility. It is not a choice between autonomy and subsidy; a competition between taxpayers and taxeaters. If all of us live subsidized lives, then redistribution of resources is always occurring. The question then is not *should* our tax system reallocate resources but *how* it should do so. An ethic of care would suggest a system that tracks need, asking more of individuals whose needs are met so as to be able to satisfy those in need.[22] In brief: progressivity.

[22] Fineman's work on autonomy seems consistent with the work on progressivity of philosophers Murphy and Nagel in *The Myth of Ownership* (2002). The text made a splash in the tax world, in part, for its argument that the common pre-tax/after-tax frame for analyzing tax burdens is fundamentally flawed. The flaw, in their view, stems from the weak moral claim an individual has to call every penny of her pre-tax income her own. Though the law may give her a *legal right* to the income, there is only a weak (if any) *moral right* because at least some amount of any individual's income stems from the fact that she lives and works within a functioning society (Fineman 2004). See (Kornhauser 1987)

Feminist work on difference and autonomy also suggests the need to change the tax treatment of caregiving. At a minimum, Fineman's work makes clear that caregiving should be understood as a collective responsibility. Under current law, caregiving costs are treated as taxable consumption, so deductions or credits that reduce tax liability to account for caregiving expenses are construed as tax expenditures. A shift in view in accordance with Gilligan, Fineman, and like-minded feminist thinkers would turn that frame on its head. If we all are the beneficiaries of caregiving activities and if we recognize the essential social reproduction function of such work, caregiving cannot be cordoned off as private and consumptive. Caregiving is, instead, productive and communal. Tax could respond with targeted reforms such as making caregiving costs deductible (overruling *Smith v. Commissioner*) or dramatic expansion of existing provisions like the child tax credit (Fact Sheet 2021). Or the tax system could simply be the source of revenue to allow for direct spending programs. The ends that this vein of feminism prescribes—a world where caregiving is a communal and robustly publicly-supported activity—may be clearer than the means by which they should be achieved. And considering the best means raises a point of tension with another important vein of feminist thought: dominance feminism.

10.4.3 Dominance Feminism

Gilligan does not naturalize difference by attributing the differences[23] she observed to a particular cause such as biology.[24] She recognized that the differences in moral reasoning she observed were rooted in socialization. In later writings reflecting on *In a Different Voice,* Gilligan closely connected the feminization of the ethic of care to patriarchy:

> Within a patriarchal framework, care is a feminine ethic. Within a democratic framework, care is a human ethic. A feminist ethic of care is a different voice within a patriarchal culture because it joins reason with emotion, mind with body, self with relationships, men with women, resisting the divisions that maintain a patriarchal order. To borrow the anthropologist Clifford Geertz's distinction between thin and thick interpretations of cultures—or rather the psychologist Niobe Way's use of these terms to contrast cultural stereotypes or clichés with an analysis of the culture itself—a feminist ethic of care rests on a thick rather than thin understanding of democracy. A thin interpretation of democracy homogenizes

[23] Feminists differ in their sense of the cause of such difference. Gilligan herself was not so much making an essentialist claim but an observation that the different ways of thinking about moral judgment tracked gender lines. See also (MacKinnon 1987, 39).

[24] "The different voice I describe is characterized not by gender but theme. Its association with women is an empirical observation, and it is primarily through women's voices that I trace its development. []. No claims are made about the origins of the differences described or their distribution in a wider population, across cultures, or through time. Clearly, these differences arise in a social context where factors of social status and power combine with reproductive biology to shape the experience of males and females and the relations between the sexes" (Gilligan 1982, 2).

differences in the name of equality, whereas thick democracy rests on the premise that different voices are integral to the vitality of a democratic society (Gilligan 2020).

This view is consistent with intersectional feminist theory. But in the view of dominance feminists—another impactful vein of feminist thought—Gilligan does not go far enough. And the distinctions between the two veins raise questions of how and the extent to which tax can advance feminist goals.

Dominance feminism sees gender difference through the lens of power. Catherine MacKinnon, an essential dominance feminism scholar writes: "Gender is an inequality of power, a social status based on who is permitted to do what to whom. Only derivatively is it a difference... Inequality comes first; differences come after" (MacKinnon 1987, 8). Gender difference is, then, a construct that justifies power disparities and social and economic inequality. MacKinnon's critique of difference feminism is that as it places value on that which is understood as feminine—a radical act in itself—it accepts the legitimacy of difference. Responding specifically to Gilligan, MacKinnon writes:

> [S]he achieves for moral reasoning what the special protection rule achieves in law: the affirmative rather than the negative valuation of that which has accurately distinguished women from men, by making it seem as though those attributes, with their consequences, really are somehow ours, rather than what male supremacy has attributed to us for its own use. For women to affirm difference, when difference means dominance, as it does with gender, means to affirm the qualities and characteristics of powerlessness. [...]
>
> Women value care because men have valued us according to the care we give them, and we could probably use some. Women think in relational terms because our existence is defined in relation to men. [...]
>
> So long as these issues are framed this way, demands for equality will always appear to be asking to have it both ways: the same when we are the same, different when we are different (MacKinnon 1987, 38–39).

For MacKinnon, difference is the wrong frame because what differences exist are the product of and reify women's subordination. To build systems that turn upon gender difference is to maintain the existing patriarchal power structure. Further, when paired with the liberal preference for formal equality, any laws or policies that turn on difference can be critiqued as unfair advantage, special preference, and so on, making difference a tenuous foundation for reform.[25]

---

[25] "Tolerance of systematic inequality has been liberalism's solution to the famous obsession with the 'slippery slope' that its penchant for abstraction creates. As liberals see this problem they invented, the trouble with doing anything about anything is that if you do something for somebody, you might have to do everything for everybody. It follows that nothing gets does for anybody... Every time something is considered that would benefit a 'discrete and insular minority' United States v. Carolene Products Co., 304 US 144, 153 n. 4 (1938), we hear that it cannot be done for anyone because it would have to be done for everyone. Never why it should or shouldn't be done for all. Or that it *won't* be 'while this court sits.' Panhandle Oil Company v. Knox, 277 US 218, 223 (1928) ("the power to tax is not the power to destroy while this Court sits" (Holmes, J., dissenting). And never that no minority is more discrete and insular than the one that runs this country, and everything is done for them—and only for them" (MacKinnon 1987, 14–15 n 36).

MacKinnon's critique comes to bear on tax in two ways. The first is essentially a strategic note. MacKinnon's insight on how difference and formal equality interact rings especially true in tax. There is a voluminous literature that attempts to define tax expenditures and what exactly counts as a loophole (Field 2018) and an equally voluminous literature made up of scholars and policymakers making their case for a given provision to be adopted, reformed, or repealed. Targeted provisions can be decried as special treatment by whomever feels excluded. Consider, for example, proposals to tax women at lower rates to account for the wage gap and women's labor supply decisions. Setting aside the constitutional questions[26] that such an approach might raise, such a targeted provision would likely face significant political headwinds, decried as law that creates difference or inequity rather than an attempt to resolve persistent, historic inequity.

The second point that emerges from bringing MacKinnon's work to tax is thornier than the first. Return to the joint return considered in the preceding part. One critique of the joint return was that the filing structure may not simply *reflect* gendered assumptions but rather that it may *create* and *perpetuate* them. Stated differently, that tax can influence social norms as complex as family structure and organization. MacKinnon's understanding of gender as power suggests that we should pause when considering provisions that are designed around how women "typically" act because such provisions—e.g., provisions regarding caregiving, a re-envisioned women's trade or business deduction, etc.—risk bolstering assumptions of what is and is not a woman's work, space, and nature. In brief, that in a move to "valorize" (MacKinnon 1987, 39) women's experiences and seeming preferences, we further entrench the patriarchy (MacKinnon 1987).

10.5 Money, Power, and the Path Forward

That feminism is not monolithic should be understood as a boon rather than a bane for tax. Too often tax operates in binaries—it is about raising revenue *or* social policy; a cost is business *or* personal. And feminism itself can fall into such either/or thinking. Feminist philosopher Martha Nussbaum argues that some feminist debates turn upon whether the one sees women's sexual oppression or economic oppression as primary. Writing of feminist thought on international development, Nussbaum (2000, 290/1) observes:

> For one group, let's call it group S, the essence of feminism is a critique of sexual domination, and the essence of change is changing socially constructed gender roles. For the other group, let's call it group T, the essence of feminism is a critique of women's economic dependency, and the most desirable change is to give women more economic options. Members of S are likely to focus on domestic violence, sexual abuse of all sorts, sexual

[26] The tax case, *Moritz v. Commissioner*, made famous by the recent biopic on Justice Ruth Bader Ginsburg entitled "On the Basis of Sex" involved an individual challenging the constitutionality of the disallowance of a deduction that aimed to provide relief for caregiving expenses. For an accessible write-up of the case, see Lipman 2019.

> harassment, and prostitution as the major ills, and they are likely to criticize a project as insufficiently feminist if its focus is purely economic and doesn't involve a major component of consciousness raising.... But in fact the split lies deep: the two groups have different intuitions about the root cause of women's subordination. Members of S typically think that subordination is all about wanting a submissive sexual outlet, and that economic aspects of subordination are posterior. Members of T think that women's subordination is all about men wanting to control income and property and to have willing domestic servants –and that the sexual aspects of women's subordination are posterior.

She goes on to add that "in many respects the entire dispute seems peculiar. Why should we have to say that the subordination of women is about just one thing? Clearly, it has aspects that are sexual and aspects that are economic. Both of these are socially shaped, and each reinforces the other. Men have seen women as their sexual property, and they have also seen them as their economic servants" (Nussbaum 2000, 293). These threads run through the works examined in this chapter, starting with Wollstonecraft's critique of women's economic dependency and through to MacKinnon's focus on power and its connection to gender and sex. And, as intersectional feminist thought makes clear, the multi-faceted nature of women's oppression is not simply sexual or economic. That oppression functions and is experienced differently by women based upon their race, class, ability, sexuality, and expression of their gender identity. If tax endeavors to be responsive to feminism, it must be in conversation with feminist thought as a whole rather than simply a given subset. Doing so requires tax recognize its dual-nature and shift its thinking.

Tax feels as though it is at an inflection point. Growing awareness of income inequality and persistent discrimination have led to increased interest in the policies that have brought us to the current moment, and the reforms that could help move us beyond such discrimination and inequality (Crawford and Infanti 2017). In April 2021, the United States Senate Finance Committee held a hearing on the nexus between the tax code and discrimination: "Combatting Inequality: The Tax Code and Racial, Ethnic, and Gender Disparaties" (Full Committee Hearing 2021). In his opening statement, Finance Committee Chairman Ron Wyden (D-Oregon) spoke to the need for the hearing and for legislation:

> Inequality isn't just about race, it's also about gender. Women business owners, particularly women of color, are underrepresented, undercapitalized and underappreciated. The share of business revenues that go to women-owned businesses hasn't budged in 20 years. It's stuck at 4 percent. Along with Senator Cortez Masto and Senator Hassan, Senator Cardin and I are introducing the PROGRESS Act that will help to increase that figure. Our bill is all about promoting investment in women- and minority owned businesses and helping them grow and hire more workers.
>
> The fact is, the tax code isn't strictly about government funding. Congress decided long ago to use the tax code to tackle major economic and social challenges. The words Black or White or Asian or Latino or Native American don't have to appear anywhere in the code for tax laws to affect those groups differently. Too often, those differences are adding to inequality (Press Release 2021).

That this hearing occurred feels like progress. That Congress is interested in how the purportedly gender (and race) neutral language of the Code may in fact not be so neutral—that it may instead exacerbate inequality—suggests that some of the key insights of feminist thinkers have gone mainstream. But difficult work remains. Feminist thought does not clearly translate into a prescription of specific tax provisions. And areas of debate among feminist thought may lead tax to different conclusions. There is no single iteration of a feminist tax code. But a way forward can be found in acting upon shared insights across feminist thought and in remaining in conversation where there is conflict.

Feminism makes clear that neutrality in tax is a myth. The choice for tax has never been between a neutral and a gendered Code. Tax law overlays upon an ableist world where cisgender heterosexual male has been the standard, the norm by which the rest of us are judged as conforming or aberrant. Tax, then, must recognize that gender does not arise in the Code merely when it intersects with "women's issues" such as family and caregiving. Gender runs through the Code as courts define the trade or business deduction using "life in all its fullness" as a guide. The Code is gendered—the choice for tax is the extent to which it will passively reflect, actively reify, or work to rectify such inequity.

Feminism makes clear that the division between economic and social policy is, at minimum, porous, if not nonexistent. Tax is both economic and social because the economic is social. This insight flows into a third: that while social and economic power are deeply intertwined, they are not coterminous. As feminism focuses on ends, tax looms large as a potentially impactful means of achieving those ends (Nussbaum 2004, 15). Tax provisions that aim to put more money in women's pockets and to support their control over their property can serve as essential steps towards advancing the goal of gender equality.[27] But those same provisions will not impact all women in the same way. Nor will they remedy all power imbalances between men and women. Society is not static, nor are women's challenges; so, any

[27] Nussbaum discusses her view on the role of tax in advancing women's rights, advancing a capabilities approach that recognizes that economic independence, achieved through developing human capacities, places women in a better bargaining position such that their social power may increase: "As we think this way, the capabilities approach, together with a bargaining approach, helps us to make sense of what we find. We begin with the idea that both employment-related capabilities and sex-related capabilities (such as bodily integrity, emotional health, and the capacity for sexual expression) are fundamental human capabilities that should not be abridged. The bargaining approach then helps us to think about the many ways in which the two capabilities complement one another. Women who wish to avoid sexual brutality or exploitation in marriage, and to pursue sexual autonomy, can do so far more easily if they are in a strong bargaining position; and access to employment, credit, and land rights are important sources of strength for their bargaining position" (Nussbaum 2000, 293). She elaborates on this point in a 2004 lecture, stating that: "Moreover, a focus on capabilities, although closely allied with the human rights approach, adds an important clarification to the idea of human rights: for it informs us that our goal is not merely 'negative liberty' or absence of interfering state action—one very common understanding of the notion of rights—but, instead, the full ability of people to be and to choose these very important things. Thus, all capabilities have an economic aspect: even the freedom of speech requires education, adequate nutrition, etc.… 'In the domestic case, we can easily say quite a lot about which institutions bear the burden of supporting the capabilities of the nation's citizens: the structure of institutions laid out in the nation's constitution, together with the set of entitlements prescribed in the constitution itself. This structure will include legislature, courts, administration and at least some administrative agencies, laws defining the institution of the family and allocating privileges to its members, the system of taxation and welfare, the overall structure of the economic system, the criminal justice system, etc.'" (Nussbaum 2004). Tax, in this view, is ultimately a technocratic means to an end.

one-size-fits-all reforms risk aiding some women while marginalizing others. A feminist tax code is one that is in conversation with all feminist thought, nimble and open to experimentation to ensure it supports the equality of all.

Overview of Case Law

United States

Cook v. Tait 265 U.S. 47 (1924).
David Sonenblick, 4 B.T.A. 986 (1926)
Panhandle Oil Company v. Knox, 277 US 218, 223 (1928).
Rosa E. Burkhart, 11 B.T.A. 275 (1928)
Charles Hutchison, 13 B.T.A. 1187 (1928)
Welch v. Helvering 290 U.S. 111 (1933).
Blackmer v. Commissioner, 70 Fed.(2d) 255 (C.C.A., 2d Cir.) (1934)
United States v. Carolene Products Co., 304 US 144, 153 n. 4 (1938)
Smith v. Commissioner. 1939. 40 B.T.A. 1038, 1039, *aff'd*, 113 F.2d 114 (2d Cir. 1940).
Joseph W. Powell, 34 B.T.A. 655; affd., 94 Fed. (2d) 483 (C.C.A., 1st Cir.) (1945)
Moritz v. Commissioner 469 F. 2d 466 (1972)

References

Abramovitz, Mimi, and Sandra Morgen. 2006. *Taxes Are a Woman's Issue: Reframing the Debate*. New York: Feminist Press at the City University of New York.
Abreu, Alice G., and Richard K. Greenstein. 2018. Rebranding Tax/Increasing Diversity. *Denver Law Review* 96 (1): 1–50.
Alstott, Anne L. 1996. Tax Policy and Feminism: Competing Goals and Institutional Choices. *Columbia Law Review* 96 (8): 2001–2082.
Baier, Annette C. 1987. The Need for More Than Justice. *Canadian Journal of Philosophy* 17: 41–56.
Bartlett, Bruce. 2012. *The Benefit and the Burden: Tax Reform-Why We Need It and What It Will Take*. New York: Simon & Schuster.
Beauvoir de, Simone. 2010. *The Second Sex*. Trans. Constance Borde and Sheila Malovany-Chevallier. New York: Alfred A. Knopf.
Becker, Mary, Cynthia Grant Bowman, and Morrison Torrey. 1994. *Cases and Materials on Feminist Jurisprudence: Taking Women Seriously*. St. Paul: West Publishing Co.
Brown, Dorothy A. 1997. Race, Class, and Gender Essentialism in Tax Literature: The Joint Return. *Washington & Lee Law Review* 54 (4): 1469–1514.
———. 2021. *The Whiteness of Wealth*. Crown: Penguin Random House.
Cain, Patricia A. 1990. Feminism and the Limits of Equality. *Georgia Law Review* 24 (4): 705–732.
Capaldi, Nicholas. 2004. *John Stuart Mill: A Biography*. Cambridge: Cambridge University Press.
Coaston, Jane. 2019. The Intersectionality Wars. *Vox*, May 28. https://www.vox.com/the-highlight/2019/5/20/18542843/intersectionality-conservatism-law-race-gender-discrimination.
Crawford, Bridget J., and Anthony C. Infanti, eds. 2017. *Feminist Judgments—Rewritten Tax Opinions*, Feminist Judgments Series: Rewritten Judicial Opinions. Cambridge: Cambridge University Press.

Crenshaw, Kimberlé. 1989. Demarginalizing the Intersection of Race and Sex: A Black Feminist Critique of Antidiscrimination Doctrine, Feminist Theory and Antiracist Politics. *University of Chicago Legal Forum* 1: 139–167.

Davis, Laura Ann. 1988. A Feminist Justification for the Adoption of an Individual Filing System. *Southern California Law Review* 62 (1): 197–252.

Davis, Tessa. 2017. The Tax-Immigration Nexus. *Denver Law Review* 94 (2): 195–254.

Editorial. 2012. Romney's Speech from Mother Jones Video. *The New York Times*, September 19. https://www.nytimes.com/2012/09/19/us/politics/mitt-romneys-speech-from-mother-jones-video.html.

Fact Sheet: "The American Families Plan." 2021. *The White House Briefing Room*, April 28. https://www.whitehouse.gov/briefing-room/statements-releases/2021/04/28/fact-sheet-the-american-families-plan/.

Field, Heather M. 2018. A Taxonomy for Tax Loopholes. *Houston Law Review* 55 (3): 545–608.

Fineman, Martha Albertson. 2000. Cracking the Foundational Myths: Independence, Autonomy, and Self-Sufficiency. *American University Journal of Gender, Social Policy and the Law* 8 (1): 13–29.

———. 2004. *The Autonomy Myth: A Theory of Dependency*. New York: New Press.

———. 2005. Feminist Legal Theory. *American University Journal of Gender, Social Policy and the Law* 13 (1): 13–24.

Full Committee Hearing. 2021. *Combating Inequality: The Tax Code and Racial, Ethnic, and Gender Disparities*. Filmed Virtually April 20, 2021 at the United States Senate, Washington, D.C. Video. https://www.finance.senate.gov/hearings/combatting-inequality-the-tax-code-and-racial-ethnic-and-gender-disparities.

Gilligan, Carol. 1982. *In a Different Voice: Psychological Theory and Women's Development*. Cambridge, MA: Harvard University Press.

———. 2020. Looking Back to Look Forward: Revisiting *In a Different Voice*. *The Center for Hellenic Studies, Harvard*. https://chs.harvard.edu/classics9-carol-gilligan-looking-back-to-look-forward-revisiting-in-a-different-voice/.

Gordon, Ann D. (ed.). 1997. Address by Elizabeth Cady Stanton on Woman's Rights, September 1848. In *Selected Papers of Elizabeth Cady Stanton and Susan B. Anthony, vol. 1, In the School of Anti-Slavery, 1840 to 1866*. New Brunswick: Rutgers. https://susanb.org/wp-content/uploads/2018/12/Elizabeth-Cady-Stanton-Sept.-1848.pdf.

Hampton, Jean. 2005. Feminist Contractarianism. In *Feminist Theory: A Philosophical Anthology*, ed. Ann Cudd and Robin Andreasen, 280–301. Malden: Blackwell.

Harris, Angela P. 1990. Race and Essentialism in Feminism Legal Theory. *Stanford Law Review* 42 (3): 581–616.

Hooks, Bell. 1981. *Ain't i a Woman: Black Women and Feminism*. New York: Routledge.

Kessler-Harris, Alice. 2001. *In Pursuit of Equity: Women, Men, and the Quest for Economic Citizenship in 20th Century America*. New York: Oxford University Press.

Kornhauser, Marjorie E. 1987. The Rhetoric of the Anti-progressive Income Tax Movement: A Typical Male Reaction. *Michigan Law Review* 86: 465–523.

———. 1993. Love, Money, and the IRS: Family, Income-Sharing, and the Joint Income Tax Return. *Hastings Law Journal* 45 (1): 63–112.

———. 1996. Theory Versus Reality: The Partnership Model of Marriage in Family and Income Tax Law. *Temple Law Review* 69 (4): 1413–1450.

———. 1997. What Do Women Want: Feminism and the Progressive Income Tax. *The American University Law Review* 47 (1): 151–164.

———. 2002. A Legislator Named Sue: Re-imagining the Income Tax. *Journal of Gender, Race and Justice* 5 (2): 289–326.

———. 2011. Gender and Capital Gains Taxation. In *Challenging Gender Inequality in Tax Policy Making: Comparative Perspectives*, ed. Kim Brooks, Asa Gunnarson, Lisa Philipps, and Maria Wersig, 275–291. Portland: Hart Publishing.

Lipman, Francine J. 2019. Pro Bono Matters in 'On the Basis of Sex'. *Tax Notes* 164 (7): 1037.

Lorch, Jennifer. 1990. *Mary Wollstonecraft: The Making of a Radical Feminist*. Oxford: Berg Publishers, Ltd.

MacKinnon, Catherine A. 1987. *Feminism Unmodified: Discourses on Life and Law*. Cambridge, MA: Harvard University Press.

———. 1989. *Toward a Feminist Theory of the State*. Cambridge, MA: Harvard University Press.

Mason, Ruth. 2016. Citizenship Taxation. *Southern California Law Review* 89 (2): 169–240.

McCaffery, Edward J. 1993. Taxation and the Family: A Fresh Look at Behavioral Gender Biases in the Code. *University of California Los Angeles Law Review* 40 (4): 983–1060.

———. 2007. *Taxing Women*. University of Chicago Press.

McCormack, Shannon Weeks. 2019. America's (D)evolving Childcare Tax Laws. *Georgia Law Review* 53 (3): 1093–1168.

———. 2020a. Taxing Parents: Welfarist Theories. *Brigham Young University Law Review* 46 (1): 85–146.

———. 2020b. Caregivers and Tax Reform: Before and After Snapshots. *Virginia Tax Review* 40 (1): 53–92.

Mehrotra, Ajay K. 2013. *Making the Modern American Fiscal State: Law, Politics, and the Rise of Progressive Taxation, 1877–1929*. New York: Cambridge University Press.

Menkel-Meadow, Carrie. 1992. Mainstreaming Feminist Legal Theory. *Pacific Law Journal* 23 (4): 1493–1542.

Mill, John Stuart. 2000. *Subjection of Women*. London: Electric Book Co. http://ebookcentral.proquest.com/lib/southcarolina/detail.action?docID=3008446.

Millett, Kate. 2016. *Sexual Politics*. New York: Columbia University Press.

Murphy, Liam B., and Thomas Nagel. 2002. *The Myth of Ownership: Taxes and Justice*. Oxford: Oxford University Press.

Nussbaum, Martha C. 2000. *Women and Human Development: The Capabilities Approach*. Cambridge, MA: Cambridge University Press.

———. 2004. Beyond the Social Contract: Capabilities and Global Justice. An Olaf Palme Lecture, Delivered in Oxford on 19 June 2003. *Oxford Development Studies* 32 (1): 3–18.

Philipps, Lisa. 2011. Income Splitting and Gender Equality: The Case for Incentivizing Intra-Household Wealth Transfers. In *Challenging Gender Inequality in Tax Policy Making: Comparative Perspectives*, ed. Kim Brooks, Asa Gunnarson, Lisa Philipps, and Maria Wersig, 236–254. Portland: Hart Publishing.

Press Release. 2021. Wyden Statement at Finance Committee Hearing on Inequality in the U.S. Tax Code. *United States Senate Committee on Finance*, April 20. https://www.finance.senate.gov/imo/media/doc/042021%20Wyden%20Statement%20at%20Finance%20Committee%20Hearing%20on%20Inequality%20in%20the%20U.S.%20Tax%20Code.pdf.

Rhode, Deborah L. 1991. *Justice and Gender: Sex Discrimination and the Law*. New York: Harvard University Press.

Schenk, Deborah H. 2012. Reflections on Women in Tax Law Academia. *Georgetown Journal of Gender and Law* 13 (1): 47–58.

Staudt, Nancy C. 1996. Taxing Housework. *Georgetown Law Journal* 84 (5): 1571–1648.

Sunstein, Cass R. 1988. Feminism and Legal Theory. *Harvard Law Review* 101 (4): 826–848.

Tutt, Juliana. 2010. 'No Taxation Without Representation' in the American Woman Suffrage Movement. *Stanford Law Review* 62 (5): 1473–1512.

Walsh, Camille. 2018. *Racial Taxation: Schools, Segregation, and Taxpayer Citizenship, 1869–1973*. Chapel Hill: University of North Carolina Press.

Wellman, Judith. 2010. *The Road to Seneca Falls: Elizabeth Cady Stanton and the First Woman's Rights Convention*. University of Illinois Press.

Williamson, Vanessa S. 2017. *Read My Lips: Why Americans Are Proud to Pay Taxes*. Princeton University Press.

Wollstonecraft, Mary. 2019. *The Feminist Papers: A Vindication of the Rights of Women*. Layton: Gibbs Smith.

Tessa Davis is an Associate Professor of Law at the University of South Carolina School of Law specializing in taxation and tax policy. Professor Davis focuses her research on how tax law reflects and shapes social phenomena, often exploring tax and the intersection of other areas of law such as family law and immigration. Her scholarship has appeared in respected journals, including the *George Mason Law Review, Denver Law Review*, *Kentucky Law Journal*, the *Virginia Journal of Social Policy & the Law*, the *Florida State University Law Review*, and the *Cardozo Journal of Law & Gender.* Prior to joining the faculty at the University of South Carolina, Davis was a Visiting Assistant Professor at Tulane University Law School. Davis earned an LLM in Taxation in 2012 from New York University School of Law and received her JD from Florida State University College of Law, where she graduated Order of the Coif. Davis graduated from Davidson College with a BA in Anthropology and received an MSc in Social Anthropology from the London School of Economics.

Chapter 11
A Summary Proposal for Democratized Taxation

Robert F. van Brederode

Abstract This chapter (The author is grateful to Jane Frecknall-Hughes for her comments on an earlier version of this chapter.) is a comment on the current state of governmental organization and, in particular, decision- and rulemaking. It is critical of the trend towards concentration, of legislative delegation, and of majoritarianism, which are all inherently undemocratic and an obstacle to the exercise of true citizenship. A solution is proposed in reorganizing political society by decentralization and privatization of government functions, allowing individual citizens to attend to most of their interests through private, voluntary allegiances with others. This would remove or at least vastly reduce the need for regulation by the unelected administrative state, counter illiberal tendencies to forms of absolutism, and restore efficient governance as political fragmentation would disappear. As a first step, the proposal is to allow taxpayers to determine government expenditure. Allocating budgetary authority to taxpayers would enhance public involvement in the decision-making process, reduce dominance, improve the democratic legitimacy of tax law in terms of consent of the governed, reduce wasteful spending and the influence of special interest and lobby groups, improve democratic equality by empowering minority views, and infuse a needed grass-roots element in the political decision-making model.

Keywords Tribute · Feudalism · Sovereign state · Nation state · Absolutism · Democracy · Decentralization · Taxation · Voluntary allegiances

R. F. van Brederode (✉)
BrederodeTax, LLC, Fuquay-Varina, NC, USA

Global Humanistic University, Sint Willibrordus, Curacao

R. F. van Brederode (ed.), *Political Philosophy and Taxation*,
https://doi.org/10.1007/978-981-19-1092-0_11

11.1 The Birth of Taxation and the Birth of the Nation State

Taxation does not have an unblemished birth history. Taxes were often the result of conquest and looting, modified into annual tributes to be paid out by the defeated nation or tribe to the victorious one. Stephens (1979) describes how the Hittites dominated neighboring peoples based on their military might and developed a sophisticated system of dominance to ensure timely and recurring payment of tribute from the subjugated tribe or state. This form of taxation was also applied by other conquering nations, for example, the Macedonians under Alexander the Great, the Scythians, the Egyptians, the Mesopotamians, the Romans, and the Mongols under Genghis Khan all extracted tribute from conquered and subdued territories. One may counter that these tributes do not completely fulfill modern definitions of taxation, but I hesitate in applying modern concepts to ancient societies. These tributes certainly share some characteristics with the modern concept of taxes in that they were compulsory, coerced by the power of the levying authority, and they might partly be used for public purposes. Absent was a legal basis and the tribute was mostly used for the private purposes of the dominant tribe, although tribute might partly function as payment for military protection. In any event, these tributes served to extract value from a society and transmit it upstream to the dominant external rulers or class. Taxation may have its origin in morally disputable subjection and extraction, but this does not mean by extension that modern taxation – regardless that elements of subjection and extraction are still present – must lack sufficient justification.

After the conquest of England William of Normandy confiscated all land, the primary capital asset in an agricultural society, essentially concentrating the accumulated wealth of all of England into himself, then divided it among his barons under the obligation to provide services or scutage,[1] what some today might call rent. I agree with Seto (2016, 4) that there exists no real difference between a ruler who leaves existing property rights in place and levies a tax, and a ruler who asserts (through force) control over property and extracts rent. Feudalism was not a single but a multiple system, respectively for the nobility, the church, peasantry, cities, and between these groups. Concentrating on nobility, personal relationships were the foundation of the political structure. These relationships were non-exclusive: a lord could have multiple vassals, each of whom could have vassals of his own. A single person could have multiple titles of various levels of the hierarchy, signifying different vassalage. Although feudalism indicates a hierarchical form of social organization of lords and vassals with the monarch at the top of the pyramid, hierarchy was weak owing to the non-exclusive character of the relationships and the concurrent

[1] "Scutage arose originally as a feudal due (servitia debita) owed to the king in respect of grants of land (fees) made to tenants-in-chief. As a condition of occupying land and receiving rents from it, tenants were obliged to provide a number of knights to fight on the king's behalf when called upon to do so. By the reigns of Richard and John, it was common for scutage to be commuted to a sum of money, a fine in lieu of military service, often referred to as an aid on the knight's fee" (Frecknall-Hughes and Oats 2007, 86–87).

difference in vassalage (see, generally, Spruyt 1994, Ch. 3). Feudalism should not be understood as a political society but rather as a web of personal allegiances. Relationships were personal, based on private contracts, establishing reciprocal rights and obligations, including property rights (Snape 2017, 10).

The sovereign state developed in Europe out of feudalism during the High Middle Ages (1000–1350 CE) in rivalry for dominance with other systems of government, such as city-states (Italy) and city leagues (e.g., the Hanseatic League), a process that was completed with the Peace of Westphalia of 1648. The exploration of the reasons explaining why the nation state became the dominant form of socio-political organization, is beyond the scope of this chapter.[2] Important, however, is the observation that social organization has had multiple models of operation indicating that the current, dominant model of the sovereign nation state is not inevitable. Social contract theory functions as the justification or legitimation of the nation state because it creates the illusion that we have chosen the nation state as our model of organization and are thus bound by it. This strengthens the status quo and slows down social and political organizational change. Bentham, as explained in Chap. 3, already postulated this objection to social contract theory where he characterized the social contract as a way of subordinating the people to the state (king) and, consequently, to laws not of their own making.

11.2 The Administrative State

The nation state has become the administrative state with a multitude of governmental agencies carrying responsibility for the execution of sectoral policies. Through the democratic process, ideally, government is accountable to its citizens; and through that same process, again ideally, the citizens have control over the functioning and output of the government. However, particularly since the mid-twentieth century, we can notice a delegation and sometimes appropriation of legislative authority from the state in both the upward direction, i.e., to the federal or supranational level, and in the downward direction to a myriad of agencies.

The governmental organization of the United States (U.S.), for example, is based on a balance of powers not only between the three branches of government, following Montesquieu's *Trias Politica* ([1748] 1989),[3] but also between the federal

[2] Spruyt (1994, Ch. 8) gives several explanations, including that the nation state had the most Darwinian strength compared to the competition, i.e., it was more efficient and effective in mobilizing society's resources. Tilly (1992) points to military innovation in pre-modern Europe and the associated high cost as a constituent element in the development of the nation state, because it required the development of centralized bureaucracies to organize and manage the necessary extraction from society in the form of taxation and conscription.

[3] However, the U.S. Constitution does not prescribe a strict separation of powers under which the legislative branch creates laws, the executive branch executes these laws and the judiciary branch adjudicate disputes and preserves fidelity to the laws and Constitution. Rather, the federal government is a system of 'separated institutions sharing power' (Neustadt 1990, 29).

government and the states. Over time, the federal government has become the dominant force in the nation, taking responsibilities far beyond those received through constitutional attribution. In turn, the federal government has created a large number of agencies[4] not only to exercise executive power but also delegated legislative authority, agencies with which individual citizens have no or little affinity and over which they have no democratic control. The delegation of legislative powers to government agencies exacerbates Bentham's subordination argument mentioned before. The dominance of bureaucratic rulemaking is irreconcilable with the concept of citizenship, individual autonomy, and democracy. The absence of accountability and democratic control resulting from the legislative delegation undermines the legitimacy of the nation state and by extension of the taxes that are levied in its support.

The European Union (EU) may not have so many agencies as the U.S., but lacks structural democratic substance, often referred to as the EU's democratic deficit. The European Parliament is the only institution that is directly elected (since 1979) by the EU citizens.[5] Although its power and influence has grown over time,[6] it still lacks the most important right of initiative, i.e., the right to propose legislation. In the EU, initiating laws (i.e., Directives and Regulations) is exclusively the prerogative of the European Commission, which is in essence the executive branch of the EU.[7] The President of the Commission is proposed by the European Council[8] and confirmed by the European Parliament by majority vote. The other Commissioners are elected by the Council after consultation with the national governments,[9] i.e., the executive branch of the Member States, with the national parliaments and the

[4]According to the *Administrative Conference of the United States* "[T]here is no authoritative list of government agencies. For example, FOIA.gov … lists 78 independent executive departments as units that comply with the Freedom of Information Act requirements imposed on every federal agency. This appears to be on the conservative end of the range of possible agency definitions. The *United States Government Manual* lists 96 independent executive units and 220 components of the executive departments. An even more inclusive listing comes from USA.gov., which lists 137 independent agencies and 268 units in the Cabinet" (Lewis and Selin 2013, 14–15).

[5]Nationals of the Member States are automatically also citizens of the EU ex art. 20 Treaty on the Functioning of the European Union (TFEU), Official Journal (O.J.) 26 October 2012 C326/47.

[6]The European Parliament (EP) has seen its competences grow significantly from its start as an advisory role under the European Coal and Steel Treaty to a genuine co-legislator with the European Council and now holds both budgetary powers and decision-making powers (Hix and Høyland, 2013, 172), changing the Commission-Council tandem into a triumvirate. An important reason for the strengthening of the influence of the EP was the move to streamline decision-making in the Council from unanimity to qualified majority vote, which essentially removed veto rights from individual Member States, who now could be outvoted (Devuyst 2008, 303).

[7]Art. 17(2) of the Treaty of the European Union (TEU), OJ 2012 C326/13. The rationale for attributing the right of initiative to the Commission was that the Commission represents the Union as a whole and law-making would, thus, arise out of the general interest rather than out of the interests of individual Member States (Russack 2019).

[8]For this purpose, the Council is composed of the Heads of Governments (i.e., Prime Ministers and sometimes Presidents).

[9]Art. 17(7) of the TEU.

European parliament exercising little to no influence.[10] The European Parliament does have the right to accept, reject or amend legislative proposals initiated by the Commission on equal footing with the European Council of Ministers, which consists of the Member State portfolio holders responsible for the subject matter covered under proposed legislation (e.g., tax Directives fall under the purview of the Council of Ministers of Finance). Nevertheless, the European Parliament, notwithstanding its growth in influence, remains the weakest member of the European triumvirate.

As in the U.S., we notice a trend towards increasing legislative concentration in Brussels to the detriment of the sovereignty both *de facto* and *de iure* of the Member States (Vos and Decock 2003, 2). The majority of legislation (estimated as close to 70%) passing national parliaments is related to the implementation of EU policy and legislation (Mueller 2000, 219, cited by Vos and Decock 2003, 2). The loss of national parliamentary influence is insufficiently compensated at the level of the European Parliament.

Society is the aggregate of all people and institutions that are instrumental to its constitution. Society and the state are not synonymous. The state is a tool created by or, alternatively, grown out of society to realize certain objectives for the benefit of all. However, the state (and its administrative corpus) often develops its own goals, separate from and sometimes even contrary to the interest of society. In many instances we can observe a state and administrative apparatus that has become dominant in society's affairs and puts its desires and interests above those of society itself and becomes in effect the tail that wags the dog.

The state operates as a legal person and, as such, it has been separated from society and elevated to a status of independence[11] notwithstanding that it was created to be a tool of and, thus, as an institution to be part of and act in servitude to society. In many countries we can observe a dominant state, to a considerable extent free from societal control, characterized by a massive, always expanding bureaucracy, intervening in, and controlling every aspect of peoples' lives. To demonstrate the size of the regulatory oversight of society, we take a look at the output of the U.S. federal government. The U.S. legal code is the codification by subject matter of the general and permanent laws of the U.S. It is divided by broad subjects into 51 titles but does not include regulatory provisions (or case law). In 1982 the Justice Department undertook an attempt to establish the number of laws on a specific subject matter, criminal law, and over a period of 2 years it compiled over 3000 criminal offenses from among 50 titles and 23,000 pages of federal law.[12] The dominance of the unelected administrative state over elected Congress, which is constitutionally

[10]The EU citizens are only indirectly represented in the nomination of Commissioners through the election of their national governments.

[11]This observation was also made by Karl Marx who wanted to end the autonomisation of the state from civil society, see Chap. 5 of this volume.

[12]As to the question how many criminal laws there were, Ronald Gainer, the leader of the research project said in a Wall Street Journal article "[y]ou will have died and [been] resurrected three times," and still not have an answer to this question (Fields and Emshwiller 2011).

charged with law-making, appears from the number of laws made in a Congressional year versus the number of administrative regulations issued. For every law passed by Congress in 2020, under the Trump Administration, the bureaucracy issued 19 rules, for a total of 178 laws and 3353 rules. In 2016, under the Obama Administration, administrative rules and regulations numbered 3853 and 214 laws were passed (Crews 2021). Since 1976, when the *Federal Register* started itemizing them, 201,838 rules have been issued (Crews 2019). The ratio of administrative rules to Congressional laws varies significantly from year to year and averages 27:1 over the last decade as shown in Table 11.1.

The costs and economic effects of regulatory compliance are not budgeted or disclosed as is the case with federal spending. It is relatively easy and preferred by policy makers to impose regulatory costs on the private sector owing to the lack of transparency and accountability (Crews 2019, 17). These costs are considerable, though. Crews (2019, 19ff) estimates the regulatory compliance costs for the year 2018 at USD1.9 trillion or 9 percent of GDP, slightly more than the combined revenue raised from corporate and personal income taxes (USD1.88 trillion) and exceeding the economic output of many of the world's leading economies, larger than Canada's and just behind Italy's (Crews 2019, 27). Regulatory compliance cost is a hidden tax, equivalent to USD14,615 per U.S. household for 2017 and equivalent to 24 percent of the medium pretax income (Crews 2019, 28).

Democratic control is absent where representative office becomes a life-long holding; politics a career instead of service to one's fellow citizens; elected officials identify with the same bureaucracy they are supposed to supervise and direct; law-making through delegation a norm instead of an exception; elections meaningless owing to their dependence on large financial donations affording the very wealthy unequal influence on the outcome of future political decision-making, and due to an electorate that is uninformed, underinformed, or misinformed because of the lack of ideological diversity at educational institutions and the media. When the state

Table 11.1 Agency rule making vs. Public laws

Year	Public laws	Agency rules	Ratio
2010	217	3573	16
2011	81	3807	47
2012	127	3708	29
2013	72	3659	51
2014	224	3554	16
2015	114	3410	30
2016	214	3853	18
2017	97	3281	34
2018	313	3368	11
2019	105	2964	28
2020	178	3353	19
Average	158	3503	27

Source: Crews (2021)

dominates society, unhindered by meaningful democratic oversight, and engaged predominantly in serving its self-interest as an institution rather than the greater common good, the question of legitimacy arises under John Duns' requirement of service leadership and consent of the governed (see Chap. 1). Back in the fourteenth century, Ibn Khaldūn ([1377] 2015) made two observations that are still relevant today: first, that empires fail and are lost when a narcissistic state keeps raising taxes to fund ever-growing expenditures to the point where the levies suffocate the economy; and second that social cohesion disappears when political factions divide constituents in an effort to achieve self-serving political objectives and to consolidate power.

11.3 Opposing Future Forms of Government

In addition to its internal legitimacy struggles, the nation state in its current form is unsustainable in the longer term as a consequence of the increasing globalization of trade, business, and scientific discovery, the mobility of capital and labor, as well as the global scale of security, health, and environmental issues. None of these fit well within the power and control structures of a conglomerate of independent nation states. I see two opposing future developments, as outlined below.

11.3.1 The Centralized, Autocratic State

The nation state may develop into an autocratic state with increasingly centralized power and a top-down approach to policy making, dominated by a large, permanent bureaucracy exercising the majority of executive and legislative authority, and funded by a tax system, primarily instrumental in nature, designed to realize revenue maximization and to strengthen or coerce compliance with government policies at the expense of principle and fairness. In many countries we have witnessed the contours of the autocratic state in their Draconian responses to the Covid-19 pandemic. These autocratic states may then seek to address global challenges through consultation and cooperation with other autocratic states, but will have difficulty in succeeding if they are unable to engage meaningfully the input and cooperation of all other global actors involved in trade, health, security, etc. The trend may move towards top-down, globalized decision-making under a supra-national umbrella, such as the United Nations (UN), with input effectively only from the most influential states and institutions such as the World Bank, the International Monetary Fund (IMF), the World Trade Organisation (WTO), and the Organization of Economic Coordination and Development (OECD), which are all bureaucracies completely exempt from any form of democratic oversight although indirectly funded by taxes paid by the citizens affected by their policies.

11.3.2 Cooperative Networks

Alternatively, and preferably in the long term (given the dynamics of the globalized world and the need for democratic accountability), multiple networks of cooperation may be developed to take on global problems between changing alliances of states, businesses, non-governmental organizations (NGOs), and local communities, in conjunction with a reversal at the national level of the current trend of centralization towards community decision-making. I am not pleading for a return to the feudal system, but an adaptation for today's society of private relationships as the main constituent of our political organization is an attractive idea in my mind, on which I will elaborate a bit in the remainder of this chapter.

11.4 Majoritarianism and Its Consequences for Political Equality and the Legitimacy of Taxation

As stated in the introductory chapter of this book, freedom and equality require a balance. That balance, in my mind, must be based on a broad consensus in society. Were economic equality to be imposed on society by the state through machinations of a miniscule majority temporarily dominating political decision making, such an act would not only be detrimental to our freedom, but the equality thus imposed would be a paradox as what would be gained in economic equality would be lost in political equality. From a Rawlsian perspective, we cannot address the one without simultaneously addressing the other. Political equality requires participation of all in policy-making processes, but also implies voluntary interactions; and subjection to the state is essentially not voluntary but coerced (Huemer 2013, 35), requiring meaningful and effective democratic, i.e., grass-roots, influence on policy outcomes.

Majority democracy violates the principle of equality as it is based on coercion of the minority. Rather, political equality demands that we respect minority views and find ways to guarantee sufficient autonomy to those who prefer a different solution.

It is imperative to analyze accurately the current character of the Western model of the nation state, which creates inequality of decision-making by concentrating that process at the central, i.e., state, or federal level. Through that process of concentration, it also sustains "wider patterns of inequality" (Bailey 2009, 37), contradicting the propagated agency of the state in keeping the wealthy and powerful members of society in check. Many constituents perceive the state, or government more generally, as a public policy monopolist acting through an invisible and often unaccountable, budget-maximizing bureaucracy, which issues by far most of the rules and regulations binding the citizens. Contemporary political philosophers often do not question the justification of the 'modern' state as they are preoccupied with the modifications of the institute of the state. It is important to take a step back and examine the state's justifications and claims over territory, people, and property,[13] including the right to tax.

These observations have consequences for taxation. If a government loses its legitimacy to the extent that it prioritizes its institutional interests above the interests of the people it is held to serve, then, equally, taxes levied to fund the self-interest of the state lose their moral standing and legitimacy. Taxes imposed by majoritarian power play, circumventing political compromise, to fund controversial policies and programs, cannot morally bind the minority to comply, because the input of the minority has effectively been ignored during the decision-making process. Although, practically, it is impossible to give weight to every sliver of dissent, in the aggregate compromise and consensus are required for a society to function adequately.

Majority rule is based on the premise that legislative action must reflect the preferences of the current majority. To be acceptable, given the reality of shifting majorities, it must also be possible to alter choices made by prior majorities. Unconstrained majoritarianism may lead to tyranny in the form of confiscatory taxation of the minority, for instance. Brennan and Buchanan (1980, 202) argue that the protection of the individual requires the imposition on majority rule of additional constitutional constraints. Universal consent is the most far reaching in that respect but is also unrealistic and impractical (Schön 2020, 267). Instead of majority rule, for tax law, a constitutional unanimity requirement could be introduced, but where majority rule may lead to majority tyranny, unanimity may create minority tyranny (Shapiro 1999, 237). Supermajority requirements, especially for tax legislation, would be a more viable option. Modern democratic states offer some degree of protection against excesses of majoritarianism in the plurality of political parties that prevents any single party from reaching majority status. Instead, the political parties are often pressured by their pluralism to engage in the process of forming a ruling coalition which requires political compromise and moderation of policy positions. In the U.S., which *de facto* employs a two-party system, the possibility of majoritarian overreach is tempered by the bi-cameral nature of the legislature in combination with biennial elections of part of the legislators, and the veto power of the President as head of the executive branch. A trifecta where the president's party also controls both chambers of Congress does occur but generally only for a brief period of 2 years.[14]

However, as Pildes (2021) observes, democracy faces a great challenge, both in Western Europe and in the U.S. because of a decline in effective government caused by political fragmentation.[15] In the U.S, the two main political parties are increasingly

[13] A good and accessible effort to formulate a normative theory of the state is made by Morris (1998).

[14] Since the advent of the modern party system in 1857, a unified government, i.e., when the President's party also controls both chambers of Congress, has occurred 48 times, 23 times under Democratic control and 25 under Republican control. Source: U.S. House of Representatives, https://history.house.gov/Institution/Presidents-Coinciding/Party-Government/. Accessed November 12, 2021.

[15] Pildes (2021, 1) mentions as an example that in the ten most polarized Congressional terms about 10.6 significant laws were enacted, while in the ten least polarized terms the number went up to 16, a 60% increase.

internally divided and are increasingly unable to work together, paralyzing the political process (Pildes 2021, 11). In Europe, political fragmentation has taken the form of the emergence and proliferation of many new political fringe parties, both on the left and right, significantly reducing the voting share of the traditional main parties and forcing new coalition governments after very long formation negotiations, which often do not last long due to the underlying ideological differences, forcing new elections (Pildes 2021, 6–10).[16]

Majority rule opens the door for the misuse of power to the detriment of the interests of others. Democratic non-domination requires an on-going equality in the decision-making process. Equality is a principle of democratic governance traceable back to John Locke who referred to the "equal right that every man has to his natural freedom, without being subjected to the will or authority of any other man" (Locke [1689] 2008, Ch. 6, sec. 54). In the realm of policy making, law making, and government action the decision-making process is an exercise of power, from which follows the need to moderate excessive influence by one faction (including special interest groups) over the outcome of that process to prevent harm to the interests of other participants, which is the art of managing power relations (Shapiro 2016, 33). Tax policy has a direct impact on the allocation of economic resources and has, therefore, a determining influence (positive or negative) on the welfare of each individual citizen. The marketplace is a moderating influence on private sector output because supply and demand are interdependent, and the price of individual goods and services is determined by the dynamics of the push and pull between these two forces. No rational producer would keep a product in the market without adequate demand at a price level sufficient to at least cover the cost of production.[17] If a producer has an idea for a new product or service, it can evaluate through marketing research the existence and level of demand at the preferred price prior to launching the product. The public sector is devoid of the marketplace dynamics to determine the needs of the public for specific government services. New services and programs are initiated on the basis of the lobbying activities of special interest groups and the perceptions of lawmakers. Governments create their own demand and set the price arbitrarily, by (a) establishing a monopoly, such as for utility services or liquor sales; (b) mandating services, such as licenses, for fixed user fees; or (c) introducing new programs funded by taxes on the general public, i.e., paid for by others than the beneficiaries. Governments can unilaterally increase the price of their services by raising taxes and fees, because demand is artificially made to be (almost) non-elastic. It is practically quite difficult for policymakers to assess the degree of the usefulness and quality of their services relative to the costs owing to the absence of a marketplace with competition and a demand response. If a private

[16] Pildes (2021) gives examples of Austria, Belgium, Denmark, France, Germany, the Netherlands, Spain, Sweden, and the UK.

[17] An exception applies for so-called loss leaders, i.e., a pricing strategy where a product or services is sold below its market cost for the purpose of triggering demand for other products or services that do generate sufficient profit to absorb the initial loss.

enterprise fails, the owners will shut it down as they will not continue to throw their own good money to bad money. However, a failing government enterprise or program will be expanded as the result of the availability of taxpayer funding, i.e., other people's money (cf. Friedman 1993, 8–9).

11.5 Political Decentralization and Privatization Through Voluntary Alliances

Contemplating reversing the trend towards centralization and globalization seems to be the logical consequence of the above analysis. The fundamental idea is to bring decision making back to the level where it matters most. Democratizing decision making requires a reversal of the top-down model and empowerment of those most affected by the outcome of the decision-making process. This could take place in different forms and at different levels of decision making. The further a governmental body is removed from the citizens, the less influence it should have on decisions that are immediately relevant to those citizens. As a consequence, federal or supranational governments or institutions would only have limited, and preferably enumerated, and clearly delineated powers. Within federal and similar structures, subnational states would be allowed to make alliances to serve shared special purposes. State A could have an alliance for one particular purpose with states B, G, K, O and P; and for another purpose, with states C, D, L and R; etc. Legislation to serve such purposes would be binding only on the participating states and exclude other states within the federal or similar structure. A first step in that direction is the so-called enhanced cooperation mechanism accepted in the EU that allows at least nine Member States to introduce secondary EU law which is only binding among these Member States. From an internal market perspective, enhanced cooperation laws are unique as they lie somewhere between unilateral Member State laws and uniform EU law. The law creates harmonization and coordination between the participating Member States but may introduce trade obstacles in relation to non-participating Member States. Such a system introduces much needed flexibility into a complex multi-state governmental system that allows serving policy goals that are not relevant to all Member States. Values which may not be able to justify a single Member State's trade obstacles may outweigh pure internal market needs if an entire group of Member States finds these values worthy of protection (see Heber 2021). The EU cooperation mechanism should be an inspiration for other supranational and federal systems to create flexible cooperative subdivisions within their union. Subnational cooperation could mitigate tension between opposing state interests by allowing all interests to be served, albeit only within a group of states that share the same interest, and would preclude the dilemma of choosing winners and losers among conflicting policies due to the need to reach a national solution. In other words, it prevents the negative result of majoritarianism in a federal or similar environment and, thus, promotes long-term cohesion of the federal or similar union.

In turn, state involvement would also be pushed down to provincial (county) and municipal levels. Most importantly, citizens would create their own contractual allegiances, free from the interference of any level of government, to accommodate the plurality of their interests at the local level, each interest being served by a different allegiance. Not only is government not needed for this purpose, but government would be counter-productive because it would implement a single solution for all, whereas private contractual allegiances allow for choice from a multitude of solutions. Most decisions would be made at the interpersonal level between people with shared vision and values. This could be referred to as the privatization of government. It is reminiscent of feudal contractual relationships in that they are personal and create reciprocal rights and obligations (Snape 2017, 11), but differ in that they are aimed at realizing a communitarian purpose. Another similarity with feudalism is that such contractual allegiances are not political but personal in nature. Only those decisions that cannot be made on individual and group levels would be elevated to municipal, provincial (county) level and beyond to state and federal level, applying the subsidiarity principle. This could be referred to as the decentralization of government. Decentralization and privatization of government combines positive aspects of feudalism with individual autonomy and Nisbetian communitarianism. It would also minimize the regulatory power of the administrative state, since most of the rules and regulations currently in force would become redundant as they cover issues no longer regulated by government but instead dealt with through private contracts. Moreover, it would restore agency and self-determination to both society and individual citizens. Political fragmentation and the resulting ineffective government would be avoided because people would manage their own affairs through private alliances, small and larger, with others.

Political decentralization and privatization would also lead to a reduced tax burden as governments at all levels would be much less involved in regulating people's lives. Instead, many government functions would be replaced by private contractual arrangements and paid for privately.[18] The total costs of 'managing' society mainly through private alliances would be less than those generated by the complex welfare state, because, obviously, the deadweight cost associated with bureaucracies intermediating in the performance of services would be avoided. Where role, size and, thus, cost of government are significantly reduced, the opportunity would arise to re-evaluate fundamentally the tax system and make a principled decision on what, whom and how to tax. Since government would require less funding, there would be no reason to maintain all the different taxes applied today at reduced rates, but a choice could be made to rationalize the tax system and select the most efficient taxes to fund national and local governments. Such an evaluation should include whether to abolish corporate and/or personal income taxation, which are inefficient, unavoidably complex, and inherently intrusive of privacy violating the principle of liberty. Moreover, corporate income tax triggers exceptionally high transactional costs relative to revenue owing to its complexity which is exacerbated by the global

[18] Cf. Chaps. 2 and 7, respectively for similar libertarian and Anti-Federalist views

footprint of many corporations. Eliminating the corporate income tax would also remove the coercive chains of undemocratic, unaccountable institutions and cartels, such as the OECD,[19] from global businesses and smaller low-tax jurisdictions and restore the latter's fiscal sovereignty. Abolishing income taxes may be possible because, potentially, a combination of direct user fees and a general consumption tax would be sufficient to fund all levels of government.[20] However, it is beyond the purpose of this short chapter to present a complete evaluation of what is desirable and feasible in terms of tax reform enabled by reduced cost of government due to the process of privatization of government functions.

The problem of democratic legitimacy of taxation goes beyond the mere imposition of taxes - including type of taxes, tax rates and other intrinsic modalities - and includes the expenditure side of government. The presupposition is that government output is always beneficial to society, aimed at society's common well-being, and non-controversial in nature, which is likely to be true when government output is limited to road construction, common defense, police, etc.[21] However, particularly since the emergence of the welfare state in the middle of the last century, government is involved in almost every aspect of its citizens' lives and the economy, increasing the risk of discontent with some of the state's output financed through taxes, such as certain social policies, wasteful spending, e.g., to fund administrative agencies that show no beneficial output, or to subsidize activities of organizations that do not contribute to the common good (van Brederode 2020b, 3). Decentralization and privatization of decision-making as proposed earlier would remove many of these objections as government output would be limited to non-controversial services. The influence of special interests and wasteful spending would be substantially eliminated as most of the expenditure would be made voluntarily as a result of the participation in private allegiances. Governments from local to federal level would be more efficient because they could each concentrate on a much smaller but streamlined portfolio of tasks and responsibilities. Fragmented interests would no longer have to compete for attention from the centralized government, but instead these interests would be served by their constituents through the forging of private allegiances. However, that is not where we stand now.

---

[19] The anti-tax competition argument used by the OECD to force other countries through blacklisting etc. to accept the OECD's norms of adequate taxation (such as a minimum tax rate) and forced information exchange is unconvincing. As sovereign nations, low-tax countries have rights equal to those of high-tax nations in autonomously designing their tax regimes. In essence, the OECD approach constitutes a form of price fixing for government services and, therewith, the OECD is, essentially, behaving like a cartel, trying to protect the extensive portfolio of government services provided by its member states, the large bureaucracies needed to manage, and the high taxes required to fund these services (van Brederode 2020a, 341–342).

[20] Abolishing income taxes would remove the need to report income, costs, deductibles, including private matters as health care cost and mortgages. Tax evasion and avoidance through complex offshore constructions would be unnecessary. Base Erosion and Profit Shifting (BEPS), the Foreign Account Tax Compliance Act (FATCA), Common Reporting Standard (CRS), and other reporting requirements could be eliminated as they would no longer serve a purpose.

[21] Cf. for similar views expressed by the Anti-Federalists, Chap. 2.

11.6 A First Step: Democratized Taxation

Under the current form of government, i.e., the welfare state, democratic legitimacy of taxation could be significantly improved, and in consequence voluntary compliance, if taxpayers were allowed to direct how their taxes should be spent beyond what is needed for the basic function of the state. That is the proposal I am making, and it aligns to a certain extent with the earmarking idea expressed both by libertarians (see Chap. 7) and by contemporary Marxists, such as Krätke (see Chap. 5). The proposal is summary in character in that the following only provides an outline of the idea, and finer details need to be developed to operationalize the proposal into an implementable design. At the same time, the proposal is ambitious in terms of scope and ultimate objective. In effect, giving taxpayers a direct voice on the spending side of their contribution, would bring some degree of market dynamics into the process of determining government output which, as posited earlier, is currently dearly missed in the present government decision-making model. Owing to lack of funding, this could reduce wasteful spending and subsidization of special interests. It would also remove resistance to the use of taxes for the funding of controversial activities, such as, for example, abortions, because those who object would no longer be required to co-fund these activities. If a taxpayer is assessed to pay $1000 and $500 is needed to fund basic government functions, she can allocate $500 in any way she likes to an enumerated list of programs: for example, she could allocate $40 to education, $20 for more defense, $10 to support the arts, $80 to protect wildlife, $100 to protect the environment, $150 for infrastructure projects, $50 to prison reform, $30 for running the National Parks, and $20 to adoption services. Such choices will have to be made prior to the start of the tax year to allow the government to adjudicate correctly the funds it receives during the year. Under-funding would be prevented as part of the tax revenue would be reserved to cover the cost of the basic elements of government's primary functions. Over-funding of particular governmental activity is feasible and a mechanism for fund reallocation would need to be developed that renders justice to the preferences of the taxpayers (but that is beyond the scope of this summary proposal). The budgetary authority of the legislature would essentially be reduced to half the expected tax revenue for a year; and in addition, the legislature would have exclusive competency to compile the list of budget choices, which should be recompiled not annually but every 4 years to satisfy legal certainty requirements. The budget choices are categorical, and the legislature would retain its discretion to allocate funds within each category.

In my view, partly allocating budgetary authority to taxpayers would enhance public involvement in the decision-making process, reduce dominance, improve the democratic legitimacy of tax law in terms of consent of the governed, reduce wasteful spending and the influence of special interest and lobby groups, improve democratic equality by empowering minority views, and infuse a needed grass-roots element in the political decision-making model. Democratized taxation could be a first step towards decentralized and privatized government which truly embodies Lincoln's ideal of a "government of the people, by the people, for the people".[22]

References

Bailey, David J. 2009. *The Political Economy of European Social Democracy: A Critical Realist Approach*. London: Routledge.

Brennan, Geoffrey, and James M. Buchanan. 1980. *The Power to Tax: Analytical Foundations of a Fiscal Constitution*. Cambridge: Cambridge University Press.

Crews, Clyde W., Jr. 2019. *The Thousand Commandments: An Annual Snapshot of the Federal Regulatory State*. Washington, DC: Competitive Enterprise Institute.

Crews, Clyde W. Jr. 2021. The 2021 "Unconstitutionality Index": 19 Federal Rules and Regulations for Every Law Congress Passes. *Forbes* (February 2, 2021). Available at The 2021 "Unconstitutionality Index": 19 Federal Rules And Regulations For Every Law Congress Passes (forbes.com). Accessed 15 Nov 2021.

Devuyst, Youri. 2008. The European Union's Institutional Balance After the Treaty of Lisbon: 'Community Method' and 'Democratic Deficit' Reassessed. *Georgetown Journal of International Law* 39 (2): 247–326.

Fields, Gary, and John R. Emshwiller. 2011. *Many Failed Efforts to Count Nation's Federal Criminal Laws*. New York: Wall Street Journal (July 23, 2011). Available at https://online.wsj.com/article/SB10001424052702304319804576389601079728920.html. Accessed 15 Nov 2021.

Frecknall-Hughes, Jane, and Lynne Oats. 2007. King John's Innovations: Extortion, Resistance, and the Establishment of the Principle of Taxation by Consent. *Accounting Historians Journal* 34 (2): 75–107.

Friedman, Milton. 1993. *Why Government is the Problem*, Essays in Public Policy, No. 39. Stanford: Hoover Institute.

Heber, Caroline. 2021. *Enhanced Cooperation and European Tax Law*. Oxford: Oxford University Press.

Hix, Simon, and Bjørn Høyland. 2013. Empowerment of the European Parliament. *Annual Review of Political Science* 16 (1): 171–189.

Huemer, Michael. 2013. *The Problem of Political Authority: An Examination of the Right to Coerce and the Duty to Obey*. New York: Palgrave Macmillan.

Ibn Khaldūn. [1377] 2015. *The Muqaddimah: An Introduction to History*. Trans. Franz Rosenthal. Princeton: Princeton University Press.

Lewis, David E., and Jennifer L. Selin. 2013. *Sourcebook of United States Executive Agencies*. Washington, DC: Administrative Conference of the United States. Available at https://www.acus.gov/sites/default/files/documents/Sourcebook%202012%20FINAL_May%202013.pdf. Accessed 14 Nov 2021.

Lincoln, Abraham. *The Gettysburg Address*, November 19, 1863. Available at http://www.abrahamlincolnonline.org/lincoln/speeches/gettysburg.htm. Accessed 14 Nov 2021.

Locke, John. [1689] 2008. *Two Treatises of Government*, ed. P. Laslett [1689]. Cambridge: Cambridge University Press.

Montesquieu. [1748] 1989. *The Spirit of the Laws (L'Esprit des Lois)*. Trans. and Ed. Anne M. Cohler, Basia C. Miller, and Harold F. Stone. Cambridge: Cambridge University Press.

Morris, Christopher W. 1998. *An Essay on the Modern State*. Cambridge: Cambridge University Press.

[22] Abraham Lincoln, *The Gettysburg Address*, November 19, 1863.

Müller, Wolfgang C. 2000. Austria. In *The National Co-ordination of EU Policy: The Domestic Level*, ed. Hussein Kassim, Guy Peters, and Vincent Wright, 201–218. Oxford: Oxford University Press.

Neustadt, Richard E. [1960] 1990. *Presidential Power and the Modern Presidents: The Politics of Leadership from Roosevelt to Reagan*. New York: Free Press.

Pildes, Richard H. 2021. *Political Fragmentation in Democracies of the West*. Available at: https://ssrn.com/abstract=3935012. Accessed 2 Nov 2021.

Russack, Sophia. 2019. EU Parliamentary Democracy: How Representative? In *Representative Democracy in the EU: Recovering Legitimacy*, ed. Steven Blockmans and Sophia Russack, 45–63. London: Rowman & Littlefield Int., Ltd.

Schön, Wolfgang. 2020. Taxation and Democracy. *Tax Law Review* 72: 235–303.

Seto, Theodore P. 2016. *A Forced Labor Theory of Property and Taxation*, Legal Studies Paper No. 2016-04. Los Angeles: Loyola Law School. Available at https://ssrn.com/abstract 2727378. Also published in *Philosophical Foundations of Tax Law*. 2017. Monica Bhandari (ed.). 193–216. Oxford: Oxford University Press.

Shapiro, Ian. 1999. *Democratic Justice*. New Haven: Yale University Press.

———. 2016. *Politics Against Domination*. Harvard: Harvard University Press.

Snape, John. 2017. The 'Sinews of the State': Historical Justifications for Taxes and Tax Laws. In *Philosophical Foundations of Tax Law*, ed. Monica Bhandari, 9–33. Oxford: Oxford University Press.

Spruyt, Hendrik. 1994. *The Sovereign State and Its Competitors*. Princeton: Princeton University Press.

Stephens, W. Richard, Jr. 1979. The Rise of the Hittite Empire: A Comparison of Theories on the Origins of the State. *Mid-American Review of Sociology* 4 (1): 39–55.

Tilly, Charles. [1990] 1992. *Coercion, Capital, and European States, AD 990-1992*. Cambridge, MA: Wiley-Blackwell.

van Brederode, Robert F. 2020a. Countermeasures to Tax Fraud, Evasion and Avoidance: A Critical review. In *Ethics and Taxation*, ed. Robert F. van Brederode, 323–358. Singapore: Springer Nature.

———. 2020b. Introduction: Why Ethics Matter in Taxation. In *Ethics and Taxation*, ed. Robert F. van Brederode, 1–19. Singapore: Springer Nature.

Vos, Hendrik, and Jeroen Decock. 2003. *Democratic Legitimacy in the EU: The Role of National Parliaments*. Available at http://aei.pitt.edu/473/1/parliaments.htm. Accessed 17 Nov 2021.

Robert F. van Brederode (LL.M., Utrecht University, 1985; PhD Tax law, Amsterdam University, 1993) is University Professor at the Global Humanistic University, Curaçao, name partner of a niche tax consultancy firm, and an independent legal scholar. He is a former Big 4 partner, practicing in Europe and the U.S., and former in-house tax counsel to a Fortune 100 company. Previously, he served as assistant professor at Maastricht University, School of Law, professor of tax law at the Erasmus University, School of Economics, and adjunct professor at New York University, School of Law, Graduate Tax Program. His research area is public law and tax law both from a legal and economic perspective with concentration on International Tax and Global Indirect Taxes and particular interest for comparative studies, tax law interpretation, tax policy, and normative aspects of taxation. Robert published dozens of journal articles and 10 books on tax topics. His most recent books are *Virtues and Fallacies of VAT: An Evaluation after 50 Years* (Kluwer Law International, 2021), *Ethics and Taxation* (Springer, 2020), and both with Richard Krever *Legal Interpretation of Tax Law* (Kluwer Law International, 2nd ed., 2017) and *VAT and Financial Services: Comparative Law and Economic Perspectives* (Springer, 2017).

Name Index

R. F. van Brederode (ed.), *Political Philosophy and Taxation*,
https://doi.org/10.1007/978-981-19-1092-0

Subject Index

R. F. van Brederode (ed.), *Political Philosophy and Taxation*, https://doi.org/10.1007/978-981-19-1092-0

C

MIX
Papier aus verantwortungsvollen Quellen
Paper from responsible sources
FSC® C105338

If you have any concerns about our products, you can contact us on
ProductSafety@springernature.com

In case Publisher is established outside the EU, the EU authorized representative is:
Springer Nature Customer Service Center GmbH
Europaplatz 3, 69115 Heidelberg, Germany

Printed by Libri Plureos GmbH
in Hamburg, Germany